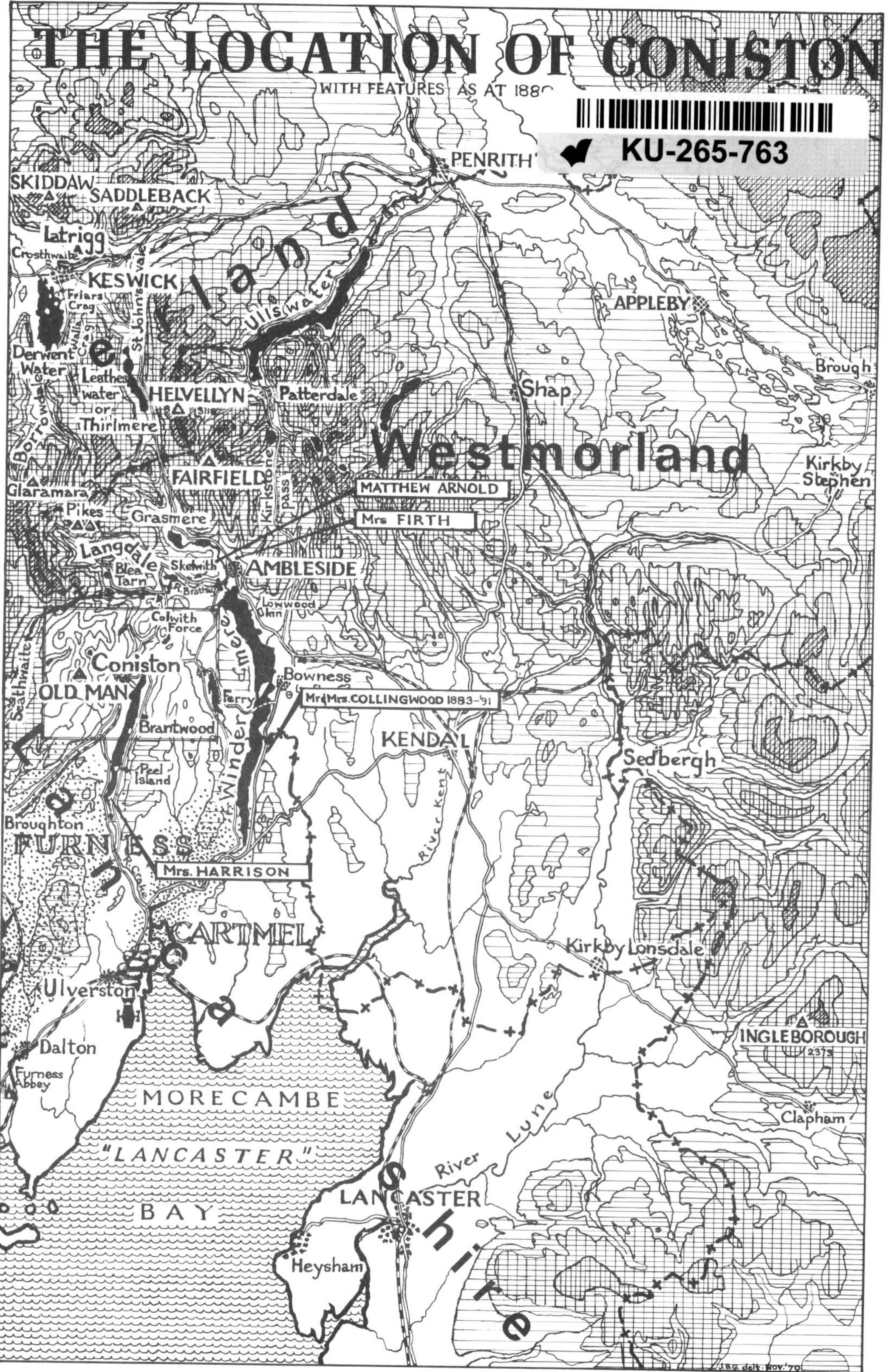
THE LOCATION OF CONISTON
WITH FEATURES AS AT 188
PENRITH
SKIDDAW
SADDLEBACK
Latrigg
Crosthwaite
KESWICK
Friars Crag
Walla Crag
St John's Vale
Derwent Water
Leathes water or Thirlmere
HELVELLYN
Patterdale
Ullswater
APPLEBY
Brough
Shap
Westmorland
Kirkby Stephen
Borrowdale
Glaramara
Pikes
FAIRFIELD
Grasmere
Kirkstone pass
MATTHEW ARNOLD
Mrs FIRTH
Langdale
Blea Tarn
Skelwith
AMBLESIDE
R. Brathay
Lowwood Inn
Colwith Force
Coniston
OLD MAN
Seathwaite
Windermere
Bowness
Ferry
Mr & Mrs. COLLINGWOOD 1883–'91
Brantwood
KENDAL
Sedbergh
Peel Island
Broughton
FURNESS
Mrs. HARRISON
River Kent
Crake
CARTMEL
Kirkby Lonsdale
Ulverston
INGLEBOROUGH
2373
Dalton
Furness Abbey
MORECAMBE
"LANCASTER"
BAY
Clapham
River Lune
LANCASTER
Heysham
Lancashire
J.B.G. delt. Nov. '70

The Brantwood Diary of John Ruskin

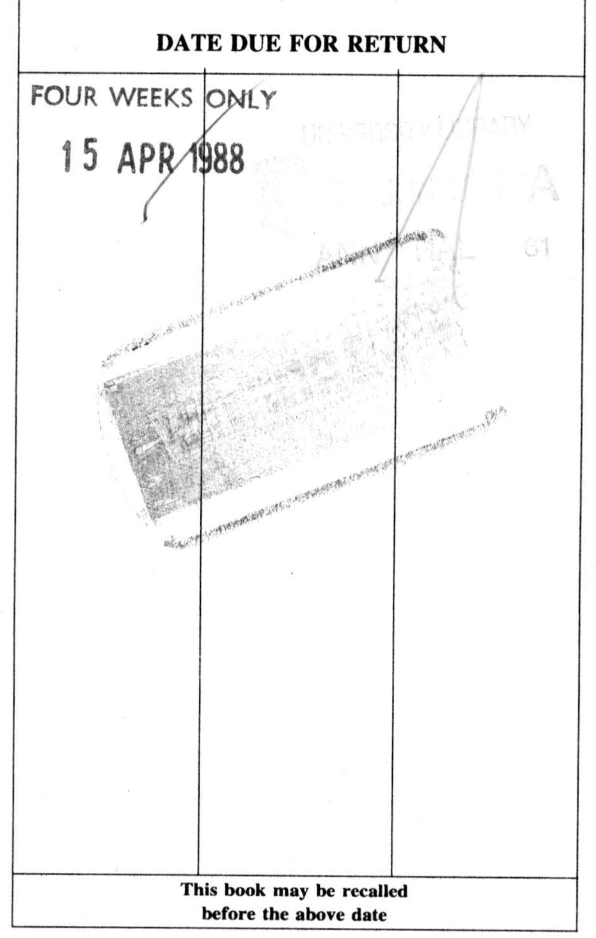

THE BRANTWOOD DIARY OF

John Ruskin

TOGETHER WITH SELECTED
RELATED LETTERS AND SKETCHES
OF PERSONS MENTIONED

EDITED AND ANNOTATED BY
Helen Gill Viljoen

Yale University Press, New Haven and London

1971

Published with assistance from the Louis Stern Memorial Fund.

Library of Congress catalog card number: 72–99844
International standard book number: 0–300–01227–6

Designed by John O. C. McCrillis,
set in Baskerville type,
and printed in the United States of America by
The Colonial Press, Inc., Clinton, Massachusetts

Distributed in Great Britain, Europe, and Africa by Yale University Press, Ltd., London; in Canada by McGill-Queen's University Press, Montreal; in Mexico by Centro Interamericano de Libros Académicos, Mexico City; in Central and South America by Kaiman & Polon, Inc., New York City; in Australasia by Australia and New Zealand Book Co., Pty., Ltd., Artarmon, New South Wales; in India by UBS Publishers' Distributors Pvt., Ltd., Delhi; in Japan by John Weatherhill, Inc., Tokyo.

In Memory of F. J. Sharp

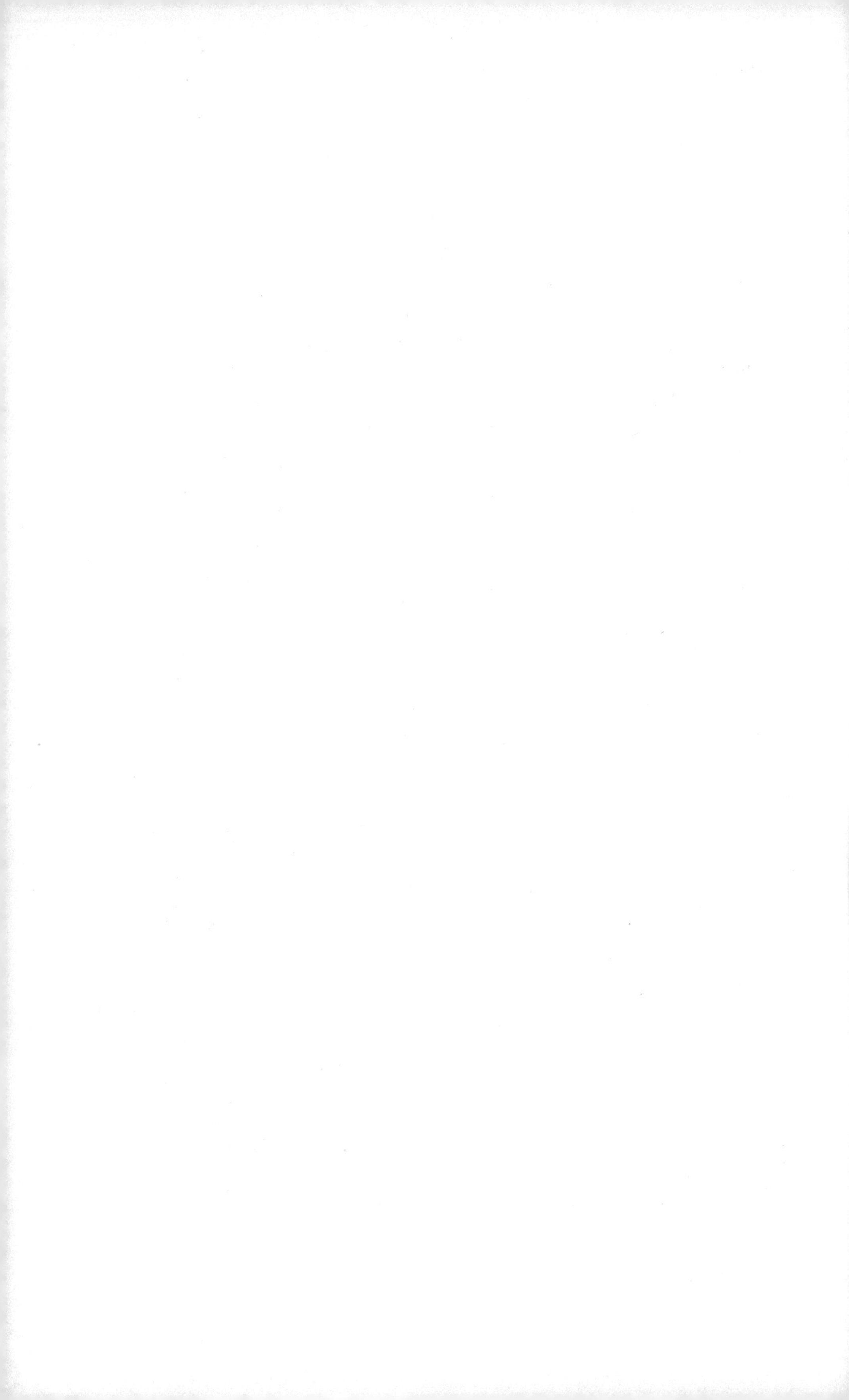

Preface

Basically an edition of Ruskin's Brantwood Diary, this book has been prepared as a Memorial to Mr. F. J. Sharp, who, just before his death in 1957 (aged 77), expressed the wish that I be given his collection of Ruskiniana—which I received as a most precious gift from his heir, Mrs. Martha Holmes. Among the manuscripts in his collection Mr. Sharp had felt special concern over this volume of the Diaries, which contains the record of Ruskin's life at Brantwood from 1876 into 1881 and during 1883. Partly because many of the entries for these years are directly relevant to Ruskin's long struggle against insanity (several entries of 1878 having been written while he was succumbing to his first mental collapse), Mr. Sharp was unwilling to have the material in this manuscript included in the three-volume Oxford University Press edition of the Diaries, which was then being prepared by W. H. Whitehouse and Joan Evans. Helped by other documents in Mr. Sharp's collection—especially by the letters now represented in this volume—I have attempted to edit the material so that the story of Ruskin's life at Brantwood and of his health, work, and pleasures which is implicit in the entries will become imaginatively comprehensible—or "real"—through a book which, I trust, can be considered an appropriate expression of my gratitude to Mrs. Holmes and to Mr. Sharp.

Within the canon of Ruskin's writing, the Diaries are exceptional in having been written not for others but for himself—a fact which has essentially determined my editorial treatment of the entries in this Brantwood Diary as annual units. Long troubled by illnesses or by "symptoms," which doubtless were largely psychosomatic, and also realistically aware, for many years, that he was threatened by insanity, Ruskin made it a point watchfully to keep track of his health (psychological as well as physical) through his jottings. (In this respect, thinking of the Diaries—in contrast to some of his letters—like Scott, he could have said: "Nay, Willie, only see that the doors are fast. I would fain keep all the cry as well as all the wool to ourselves.") Analogously, in later years (after he had become haunted by the presence of the "plague-cloud") he tried to keep a daily record of the weather through his entries. Otherwise, unless he had reason to launch into passages of description, he seldom wrote more than succinct notes which henceforth would adequately help him to remember and to date what he had been thinking, whom he had been seeing, and what he had been doing—year by year, from day to day.

This being the nature of the Diaries, to most readers (even to those who have a more or less specialized knowledge of Ruskin) the mere text of the entries cannot be particularly meaningful, however useful it may be in providing factual details. Characteristically, these entries, *en masse,* can be likened to little more than a great heap of bare bones—bones which need to be clothed with flesh and blood. Ruskin, to be sure, could animate them readily enough through the memories evoked by his notations—for example, "Diddie came" (June 9, 1876), "call[ed] on the Marshalls" (June 13, 1876), "Miss Thackeray and M[r.] L. Stephen to tea" (July 9, 1876), or any one of the innumerable variants thereof. To bring such notations to life, insofar as one is able to realize what they signified in reality, is a chief function of the Background Sketches (enabling us, for instance, to become reasonably well acquainted with "Diddie" as a most interesting personality) and of the footnotes which underflow the text.

A different approach to problems related to the nature of the Diaries is represented by the Introductions to the annual units. With or without footnotes, the entries within any one group are not likely to coalesce so that their ultimate import becomes clear. In this respect it is as though the reader cannot perceive the scene as a whole because he must give his immediate attention to the trees, one by one. Furthermore, the significance of a unit as a whole or of individual entries is sometimes contingent upon what has happened in the past and/or what will happen in the future—for example, the entries of July 1883 in which Ruskin baldly notes the presence of Mr. and Mrs. La Touche. Each annual Introduction is therefore designed to provide an orienting comment upon Ruskin's health, work, and contacts with friends (often natives of Coniston), as revealed through relevant entries, and to supply any information related to the past or future which helps to determine the real meaning of what he writes.

In addition, there are the Letters—this section being primarily designed to cast further light upon events and people mentioned in the Brantwood Diary, although it can also seem particularly appropriate to include these letters in a book conceived as a memorial to Mr. Sharp. In his collection, as the chief source of this section, there is a wealth of unpublished letters, many of them written by Ruskin (herein represented by some of his letters to the Simons and to Francesca Alexander, among others) and many more which friends addressed to Ruskin and to Mrs. Severn. Here, for example, we have letters written by Miss Beever which can leave the reader feeling that he now knows her as a friend who has infinite charm. In a different category there are the letters written to Dr. Simon, in which Mrs. Severn and the local Dr. Parsons reported daily developments as they cared for Ruskin while he was ill. More incidentally, through a few lines sent by the clergyman Dr. Chapman, we are reminded that Ruskin could be counted on to behave like a good citizen within his community. But chiefly, through many another letter, we catch a glimpse, as though at first hand, of people whom Ruskin valued as friends and of their personal feelings for him.

Other unpublished letters, usually quoted through no more than brief excerpts, have supplied a good deal of information that becomes functional both in the annual Introductions and in the Notes. For permission to publish such material I am greatly indebted to the administrators (directors, governors, trustees) of the following: The Coniston Museum; the Feinberg Collection; the Libraries of the Baillie's Institution, Columbia University, Yale University; the Houghton Library of Harvard University; the Ruskin Galleries, Bembridge School; the Berg Collection and the G. N. Montague Collection in the New York Public Library; and the Pierpont Morgan Library.

Relatedly, I wish to express regret that at certain points it becomes desirable to quote passages from my transcriptions of unpublished letters which at present cannot be located in manuscript. Specifically, at Brantwood I transcribed letters from Ruskin to Mrs. La Touche and to Lady Mount-Temple which have never, to my knowledge, been heard of since the Sotheby sales of 1930–31. (For these transcriptions, see Letters XXVIII, Section 3 and Letters XXX, Section 1.) Next, in 1950, through the kindness of the late Mr. Charles E. Boesen, I made transcriptions of letters from Ruskin to Henry and Emily Swan, subsequently to learn that there is no record which would enable me to discover the present owner of these manuscripts, whom I have otherwise vainly attempted to locate. Nor have I been able to locate the letters of Ruskin to Dr. John Brown, preserved through transcription in the Yale University Library.

As yet another item, there are Supplementary Notes to the final entries made in the 1878 unit of this Diary, just before Ruskin suffered his first mental breakdown (his atypical Matlock delirium of July 10–20, 1871, presumably having been an effect of the high fever caused by acute inflammation of the bowels, as diagnosed by Dr. Acland and his consultants). Within these 1878 entries Ruskin gave no more than a series of free associations which, on the surface, can sound like little more than the writing of a man who already had become insane. Here, therefore, the key question is what, from phrase to phrase (sometimes even from word to word), these apparently disconnected jottings signified to him. To provide an answer, insofar as possible, is the function of the Supplementary Notes to 1878. The analysis, interestingly enough, serves to show, first, how an emotional underflow caused one thought to give rise to the next, as expressed through the stream of associations represented by these entries; second, how his abiding grief over the loss of Rose La Touche, with subordinate memories of his father and mother, had become psychologically dominant just before he completely lost rational control.

For unique help related to local people and places named in this Diary I am deeply grateful, as well as infinitely indebted to, my dear friends the late Mrs. Oscar Gnosspelius and her daughter Janet, the Liverpool architect who, for some years, has been working on churches in the Lake District. As a daughter of Ruskin's friend and biographer, W. G. Collingwood, Mrs. Gnosspelius provided her memories of the Brantwood entourage and of local people whom she knew either personally or by their immediate reputation. Through freely flowing letters most generously written in response to my own stream of questions, she has given much information which would not have been otherwise available. A selection from all that she has contributed has been incorporated in the Background Sketches and occasionally in footnotes. Miss Gnosspelius continued to help me with, if possible, increasing generosity. As someone who has spent most of her life in Coniston, she provided further information about local folk—such as Libby Newby, Mrs. Sly, and the Wilkinsons. But, above all, thanks to her knowledge of the district and to her training as an architect, she contributed the maps which are published herein. Map A provides a survey of the places within the general region of Coniston to which Ruskin refers in this Diary. Map B shows landmarks within the more immediate neighborhood—particularly tarns and peaks upon which Ruskin bestows special names, as when he calls The Bell "St. George's Crag" and Wetherlam "Agnello"; it also locates places of interest—such as churches and the homes of friends who lived near the shore of Lake Coniston. All in all, thanks to the contributions thus made by Mrs. and Miss Gnosspelius, I sometimes can feel that "A Book of Coniston" might be an appropriate subtitle for this Brantwood Diary.

It is also a pleasure to acknowledge my indebtedness to Miss Vera J. Ledger, as my research assistant, and to Mr. James S. Dearden, Curator of the Ruskin Galleries, Bembridge School. I shall always most appreciatively remember Miss Ledger's persistence and professional skill, combined with imaginative resourcefulness, as she investigated, for example, the James Burden trial and the Dalbeattie Exhibition, and provided many dates through locating records of birth, marriage, and death. With deep appreciation I also thank Mr. Dearden for having made it possible to explain, editorially, the Brantwood Diary references to material in books and manuscripts of which he is now the custodian and for having frequently provided miscellaneous help. To Mr. Wayland W. Schmitt, editor of the Yale University Press, I am indebted for creatively helpful ideas about the organization of the editorial apparatus. I am also indebted, most gratefully, to Dr. Gotthard Booth for having deepened my understanding of Ruskin's more particularly personal problems as a human being, while enabling me to pursue my overall work as a Ruskinian.

As other friends, personal and professional, who have helped me through their specialized knowledge, I wish to thank, warmly, Herbert Cahoon, the late Miss Mary Kenway, Raymond Newhouse, Mrs. Richard A. Parsons, Mrs. Merle Spiegel, Miss Margaret A. Webb, Drs. Robert H. Ball, Joseph H. Brewer, Van A. Burd, Daniel J. Donno, Konrad Gries, Emory Holloway, Samuel Lieberman, George B. Parks, John D. Rosenberg, Esther K. Shelden (Mrs. James F. Becktold), Rose Wolfson, and Marianne Zerner.

Less personally, albeit in fellowship, I wish to acknowledge my indebtedness to those who during recent years have been widening the base for greater comprehension of Ruskin by making more and more conveniently available the wealth of knowledge to be gained from the multitudinous and lamentably scattered Ruskin manuscripts. For such help I am particularly indebted to Lady Sheila Birkenhead for having included in *Illustrious Friends* (1965) many passages from Arthur Severn's *Memoir of John Ruskin* and from Ruskin's unpublished correspondence; to John Bradley for his assemblage of Ruskin's *Letters to Lord and Lady Mount-Temple* (1964); to Van A. Burd for his generously and informatively annotated edition of *The Winnington Letters* (1969); to James S. Dearden for Arthur Severn's *Memoir of John Ruskin,* as published fully in *The Professor* (1967); to Joan Evans for the text of the main body of Ruskin's *Diaries* (1956–59); to the late Derrick Leon for material related to the La Touches in *Ruskin. The Great Victorian* (1949); to Mary Lutyens for selections from The Bowerswell Papers in *Effie in Venice* (1965) and in *Millais and the Ruskins* (1967); to Margaret Spence for the letters in *Dearest Mama Talbot* (1966); to Rayner Unwin for Ruskin's letters to Kathleeen Olander in *The Gulf of Years* (1953).

Contents

List of Illustrations

(following page 206)

Maps

(by Miss Janet Gnosspelius)

A Note on the Text

The Diary entries from 1876 into 1881 and during 1883 were made in a bound volume (6 by 13 inches) with the word *LEDGER* stamped in gold upon its spine. The volume begins with twelve alphabetized pages on which Ruskin wrote the addresses of friends. The rest of the volume consists of 263 pages, numbered so that the same numeral is stamped upon the left-hand and the right-hand pages, which face one another. The first entry (May 7, 1876) appears on the right-hand page 1, and the following right-hand pages, through page 242, contain entries for 1876 through April 8, 1881. The first entry for 1883 appears on the left-hand page 1, and the 1883 entries (followed by one entry for 1884) are continued on the left-hand pages through page 244, excepting pages 105–211, which had already been used for a translation of Books I and II of Plato's *Laws.* Pages 245–63 were used for an index to the volume as a whole.

Presenting the Diary, I have provided a faithful rendition of the text, except for the regularization of Ruskin's spelling of "today" (inconsistently, in script, "to day" and "today") and for the substitution of the word "yesterday" for Ruskin's frequent use of "Y." Otherwise I have retained his characteristic spelling of words such as "did'nt" and have made no changes when he failed to capitalize the first word of a sentence or to use a period. Passages from the Diary which have been published by Cook and Wedderburn are indicated by angular brackets. In connection with my editorial commentary, I can but express personal regret that reigning "scholarly" practice has made it impossible to indicate whether or not I have quoted a sentence in whole or in part, apropos of its beginning and/or end.

Part One

The Brantwood Diary

1876–1884

1876

After a winter spent mainly at Oxford, Ruskin reached his home on May 6, 1876, accompanied by the Severns. On August 1, leaving them to enjoy Brantwood until October, he himself set forth for a long stay in Venice.

The interest of his almost daily entries during this period lies, initially, in his references to his health and in his record of phenomena connected with the weather. These primarily concerned him while he was making his own index to the Diary as a whole, seeking especially to trace possible symptoms of the approach of the mental illness which first overcame him in 1878, and gathering data which would be used in his lecture of 1884, *The Storm-Cloud of the Nineteenth Century*. There he quoted the only passages which have been published from this section of the Diary, except three words from his entry of May 10. He began the record in "a fit of quite terrible languor" and depression, on the more immediate causes of which his June *Fors Clavigera* casts light. In about a fortnight he was once more in "good heart" and was enjoying (though sometimes without "feeling") not only the sights of sunset and of dawn but also the effects of sun and mist and rain upon the pastoral mountainland about his lake, or the "divine beauty of thyme and rose" in the twilight, or the "sunshine on the cocks." Often little more than shorthand notes, these entries served him adequately as "reminders."

Rather less apparent is the interest of the underflow—to him, the overflow—of work. Only once does he refer to the incessant duty of producing the "next" *Fors,* though during this period he wrote the issues of June, July, and August as part of his routine. By the last week of each month the manuscript usually was ready to send off to his publisher, George Allen, at which point, in May, he felt "crushed under business" (May 23). In June he dispatched what he calls "the central Fors" (June 27)—"central" in that it contained an exposition of the nature of St. George's

Guild, which was at present central to all his writing and more serious activities. As "Master" of the Guild, he was now occupied (apart from *Fors*) by two main projects—the editing of a series of books to be called the *Bibliotheca Pastorum,* or "Shepherd's Library," and the classifying of a group of minerals, selected from his own collection, to be given to the museum he was founding near Sheffield. The "Shepherd's Library" was to contain books that would be helpful in his "schools": the home of any one of his "Companions," or of those who were like-minded, could of course, like a picture gallery (or "Academy"), be thought of as a school. His gift of minerals he saw as the beginning of the collection of pictures, books, and minerals eventually assembled in what he conceived as a school for the workingmen of Sheffield—namely, the Museum of the Guild, or Companions, of St. George.

The Diary entries of this period show him constantly endeavoring to serve these interests through purposefully coordinated work. "Collingwood" calls to give him "pleasant news of our Xenophon" (June 29), and in July *The Economist of Xenophon* appeared as the first number of the *Bibliotheca Pastorum.* Carlyle's niece having told him that she could not translate the dialect in her copy of Gotthelf's *Ulric,* a novel of Swiss peasant life which he had hoped to make the second volume of the series, he notes (June 20) that he has gone to Ambleside to see Mrs. Firth, the Companion who ultimately provided the translation. A week later (June 27) he records that he has started work on the edition of Sir Philip Sidney's *Psalter* issued, in 1877, as *Rock Honeycomb,* the second volume in the "Shepherd's Library," and within three weeks (July 10) its Preface was under way. To edit Sidney's version of the Psalms was doubtless a less imaginatively demanding task than it would have been to write the *Life of Moses,* which he had conceived as yet another volume in the series, though he notes (May 16) that he had "finish[ed] the first study" for this *Life.* By mid-July his thought was also being given to the pending issues of *Deucalion* (July 17) in which he would present his classification of the minerals soon to be displayed in the one room of the house in Walkley (about two miles from Sheffield) which, for the present, would suffice the need of his Museum. When Leslie Stephen came to tea, the apparent disparateness of such work induced Ruskin ironically to jest "that he was correcting eight sets of proofs at once" (Leslie Stephen, *Some Early Impressions* [London, 1924], p. 182).

Meanwhile, through calls and callers, there was still other business connected with the Guild. Visiting Mrs. Firth, he elicited a communication which he could use in *Fors* (*Works, 28,* 709–10); and after another Companion, Miss Annie Somerscales of Hull, had called (July 5), she would write a letter, no less apt for *Fors,* about her pupils whose homes were in the riverboats (*Works, 28,* 770–71). From the Isle of Wight came Mr. Rydings (May 20), in whose home there was no piece of cloth which had not been woven either by his wife or by her mother, some of it from flax grown in their own garden, and he had sheets which he had used for almost thirty years, as yet without a sign of wear. Soon a river in the Isle of Man would be propelling a waterwheel which worked the machinery of "St. George's Woolen Mill" as women once more earned a living at their spinning wheels instead of in the mines.

Before Ruskin left for Venice, he went to Wales to see the fisher-folk at Barmouth, who lived in the eight cottages which had been given to the Guild as St. George's first "Estate." "It is no business of mine to think about possibilities," he had remarked in the July *Fors*; "—any day, any moment, may raise up someone to take the carrying forward of the plan [of the Guild] out of my hands, or furnish me with larger means of prosecuting it; meanwhile, neither hastening nor slackening, I shall go on doing what I can, with the people, few or many, who are ready to help me" (*Works, 28,* 656).

Yet, together with Ruskin's work, there was a good deal of diversion as he called on neighbors and, in turn, entertained them and other friends. Now one and now another would join him when it was time to take a walk or to clear the channel of the stream or trim the branches of the wraithlike trees upon the "Brant" (or steep) wooded slope behind his house. Tired, after the six-o'clock dinner he would take a nap, returning to read aloud until about 10:30 (Scott, Miss Edgeworth, Richardson), to enjoy the singing of a guest, or to display his minerals or some other treasure which he planned to send to a museum.

For his immediate family he had Mrs. Severn—his Cousin Joan

(now 30 years old)—and, more or less as adjuncts, her husband, the landscape artist Arthur Severn, and their first three children: Lily, a three-year-old, with "young Arthur," two, and Agnew, six months. When Joan married Arthur, Ruskin had given them the lease on the Herne Hill home of his boyhood, which remained their permanent address until 1889, when, because of Ruskin's health, they settled at Brantwood. In and out and round about there were the younger friends—at this time the 20-year-old Laurence Hilliard ("Lolly" or "Laurie"), who served as the Brantwood secretary, and Sara D. Anderson ("Dido" or "Diddie"), who, as a houseguest (June 8–July 16), had come to help edit Sidney's *Psalter* by copying the Psalms Ruskin wished to annotate. More fleetingly came those who are sometimes referred to by no more than provocative first names. One also sees his friendly contacts with his neighbors—Major Harrison who lived across the Lake (May 20) or the Victor Marshalls of Monk Coniston (June 13 and 30)—and with the villagers and country folk, from whose point of view he could seem " 'terble humble-minded . . . he tret poor and rich alike, it wadn't a mattered a pin whedder it was a lord or a sarvin' man, if he could hev deun owt for ever he wad a deun it' " (H. D. Rawnsley, *Ruskin and the English Lakes* [Glasgow, 1902], p. 71). Curiously, during the whole summer there is no record of his having visited his only intimate friend among them all—Miss Susan Beever of The Thwaite, now 69 years old, though on one afternoon she comes to tea (July 6) and, on the day before he leaves (July 30), she calls. From Charles Eliot Norton there came emissaries to be entertained, such as Professors Gurney (July 28) and C. H. Moore (*Works, 37,* 204) of Harvard. Less congruously, Norton's friend Leslie Stephen appears upon the scene, living in a cottage with his sister-in-law, Anne Thackeray. Hence, against a background of meetings of the Metaphysical Society in London and of Stephen's sympathy with Rationalists, Evolutionists, and Alpine Climbers such as Tyndall, he too was made appropriately welcome.

Before long, from Wales, Ruskin was writing Norton: "I left, on Monday, my pleasant Brantwood, and Miss Thackeray, and Leslie Stephen, and my Joanie, and all, to begin the movement

Venice-wards" (*Works*, *37*, 204; letter of August 2, 1876). At Brantwood he also had left, in this unit of the Diary, his account of weeks meaningful in relaxation and work—succinctly yet richly recorded if one but reads his notes with an awareness of only a small part of all that he could trust his memory to supply.

May 7th Sunday. 7, morning. Begin new diary: after seeing Helvellyn and my terrace field in divine sunshine and peace. Lake calm since morning, now breeze from north.

May 8th Monday. Yesterday exquisite afternoon. I up by tarn cascades, by Hunt's subject,[1] and down dingle home. Today also divinely calm and clear. I most strangely languid, after being late in going to bed—fire staying in all night.

May 9 Tuesday. Yesterday one of the divinest days of intense and cloudless light and blue I ever saw, showing that all smoke and human disturbance of the air is comparatively powerless when the air itself is pure. I out of doors all day, lying about on the grass, but terribly languid and am so again this morning

May 10. Wednesday. Still fine! though yesterday and today colder and a little hazy with the evil wind from N[orth], but very beautiful–and at present cloudless—only I with a fit of ⟨quite terrible languor⟩[2]—joylessness and stomach deadness and discomfort on me, such as I have never quite had to this degree— I dragged one leg after the other on the moor yesterday afternoon and did'nt care for a single sight or thing. My Father's Birthday!

May 11 Thursday. Yesterday quite lovely again, picnic with Joan[3] at Colwith forcc,—lovely drive home

1. The scene depicted in *Summer Days with Me,* to which Ruskin had introduced the watercolor landscapist Alfred William Hunt (1830–96) while Hunt was his guest in June 1873. (For the letter Hunt sent Ruskin after this visit, see Letters, xxv; see also Map B.)

2. Previously published (E. T. Cook and Alexander Wedderburn, eds., *The Works of John Ruskin, 28* [Library ed., 39 vols. London, 1900–12], xxxiv), as marked by angle brackets. Henceforth this use of angle brackets will be considered self-explanatory.

3. Mrs. Arthur Severn (1846–1924), née Joan Agnew.

through divine light by the old Waterhead.[4] I steadily depressed and languid through all! This morning cloudy; but softly and kindly so—a few gaps of blue.

May 12 Friday More or less fine all day, yesterday and lake beautifully calm, with soft cloud above, today shepherds beginning to complain of drought. no rain for a fortnight

I a little better, but very low, still.

May 13 Saturday. Exquisitely clear, with purple dawn, but cold. I a little better. Yesterday working on bank to get down to rocks forenoon and afternoon.

May 14 Sunday. I have seldom passed so depressed or useless a week: [5] But am supremely thankful for the good weather and light, showing me what can be. Wind now gone to the south, and sky gray.

May 15 Still desperately sad, all yesterday though pleasant work on my rocks—but no old delight in lovely things—only the better knowledge of them, and to my sorrow, of myself. A little rain and scudding cloud, of the bad kind—spoiling sunset. today, soft but impure.[6] I a little better, only oppressed by flying days.

May 16th Tuesday. Almost sleepless night with quaint

4. Probably the site of the Waterhead Inn at the head of the lake, which, Miss Gnosspelius states, "was pulled down ca. 1848 when the Marshalls of that day built the Waterhead Hotel." See Map B.

5. He began, forthwith, the June issue of *Fors Clavigera,* dated "14th May."

6. In the "Letter" of *Fors Clavigera* now under way, Ruskin remarked: "my hands are cold this morning, after the horror, and wonder, and puzzlement of my total Sun-less day." He then reaffirmed his conviction "that you cannot love the real sun, that is to say physical light and colour, rightly, unless you love the spiritual sun, that is to say, justice and truth, rightly." Concluding, he announced his belief that, as though to complement corruptions in humanity, "the powers of Nature" had become "depressed or perverted, together with the Spirit of Man; and therefore that conditions of storm and of physical darkness, such as never were before in Christian times, are developing themselves, in connection also with forms of loathsome insanity, multiplying through the whole genesis of modern brains" (*Works, 28,* 614–15).

dream of keeping everybody waiting while I was packing, and finding a superb cinnabar with native mercury, a foot long of rich red and silver dew, left without any cover in the bottom of a cupboard Rain on the hills this morning at last. I deciphering life of St Bernard[7] after bringing on above nightmare by eating too much of Susie's asparagus,[8] and proceed to finish the first study for the life of Moses.[9]

Lithospermum[10] (Borage)
Deep blue, like gentian in Miss Beevers garden coming thus [two diagrammatic sketches] clear out of its green calyx, the tube passing from the upper blue through purple to white at base, B. The tube hairy & texture coarse, throughout.

May 17 Wednesday. Still fine though for the last four days impure again, but with formed clouds and pretty effects of rays. I a little better getting into my rock work heartily.

May 18 Quite lovely all yesterday, with exquisite blue constant here,—a little dark with haze over Helvellyn I out all day nearly, unable to work indoors, and am better this morning, which is also fine, but gathering I think to rain.

May 20th Saturday. Unbroken fine weather. Supremely

7. Probably St. Bernard of La Fontaine and Citeau (1091–1153), who founded the Cisterian Abbey of Clairvaux; possibly St. Bernard of Annecy (d. 1081), who founded the Benedictine Monastery, with its Hospice, on the Pass of the Great St. Bernard. Ruskin's imaginative preoccupation with St. Bernard of La Fontaine, in whose activities he could find an image for his own concern with social reform, had been foreshadowed by references in *Fors Clavigera* to this Saint of the Valley (*Works, 28,* 112, 541).

8. For Susan Beever and her garden, see Background Sketches (henceforth designated B.S.) and Letters, IV.

9. One of the volumes which were to represent "standard" theology in the *Bibliothea Pastorum* (*Works, 28,* 500).

10. Written on the left-hand page opposite the entry for May 16, 1876.

beautiful all Thursday, crystalline clear,—with crimson sunset. Yesterday hazy—but beautiful in evening walking to Major Harrisons with Mr Rydings[11]—calm as heaven Today, calm, but close haze.

May 17th [sic] Wednesday. (Nonsense: I am thinking of Orchis's, I mean.)

May 21st Sunday. Entirely divine day again yesterday. I terribly tired with little work, but got an orchis drawn[12]

Porphyria veris.[13]
With pinguicula[14] in the marshy bit under wild oaks on moor, frequent and I suppose, in the marshiest bits—at all events, very locally in my low meadow

---

May 22 Monday. Rain at last, but very quiet and soft—hardly felt here, dark on the Old Man. Since morning however the clouds have been natural in their old white wreaths—now it is getting Manchestery.

Yesterday the first steady wind from south, but got a good piece of wood & rock work done

May 23 Tuesday. Yesterday quite heavenly purple hills with golden lights, in old way, and wreathed grey cloud in evening glorious.

Today, darker and a little corrupted again. I crushed under business.

11. For Major Harrison and Mr. Rydings, see B.S.

12. Presumably the 1876 "Meadow Orchis" or "Purple Wreathe-wort," reproduced in an 1879 issue of *Proserpina* (*Works, 25,* Pl. XXIII. "Ink drawing, washed with neutral tint; to my own mind one of the best I ever made" (*Works, 21,* 286).

13. This entry appears on the left-hand page, opposite the entries dated May 17 and 21. In the June *Fors* Ruskin remarked: "I've been two whole days at work on the purple marsh orchis alone, which my botanical readers will please observe is in St. George's schools to be called 'Porphyria veris,' 'Spring Purplet' " (*Works, 28,* 630).

14. The "Bog-Violet, or, more familiarly, Butterwort" (*Works, 25,* 425).

May 24 Wednesday Yesterday the loveliest purples in hills, and true fleecy reposing and changing clouds, with [most] exquisitely clear blue sky at end of lake that I have yet seen here, since I was a child, or at all for five years

It cleared too, beautifully, in evening but is raining now. Overslept myself.

May 25 *Τῶν ἀιωνιών ἀυτôυ καὶ ακηράτων ἀγαθων ποιôυσα κληρονομον.*

Greek Psalter, 158; line 17, page ~~111~~ 112 of Broadlands book[15]

idiot that I am! and was, never to be able to put a reference right[16]

May 26 Friday. Hesitating half rain half mist on hills and the same for the last three days, with pretty gleams of sky, sometimes.

After a week of despondence in the finest weather I have had for years, I am now in good heart again in the grey!

May 27 Saturday. Yesterday lovely in variable skies—a glorious golden sunset over noble couchant grey lion clouds on the Vecchio.[17]—Out most of the day. Saw Mr Bowness[18] make a chopper.

Today lovely fleecy clouds and rainbow.

May 28 Sunday. Yesterday a fair and warm day, ending

15. The "Broadlands book" is Volume 20 of *The Diaries of John Ruskin* (ed. Joan Evans and John Howard Whitehouse [3 vols. Oxford, 1956–59]), which contains entries from May 11, 1875, to May 7, 1876. "The Psalter in question," Mr. James S. Dearden explains, "is a MS. dated 1396, which is now in the Coniston Museum." On the left-hand page of the "Broadlands book" Ruskin made transcriptions from the Psalter. The relevant line on page 112, Mr. Dearden continues, "is part of a prayer to a 'Super-holy Goddess' and, in context, reads: '. . . [making me worthy] of the joy of those on the right hand, coming down to meet me in this fearful judgment, making me as an inheritor of his eternal and unblemished blessings."

16. He had had to transpose one word in the quotation, to insert line 17, and to correct the number of the page.

17. Ruskin's name for the Old Man.

18. Thomas Bowness (1846–1920), a Coniston blacksmith, whose name—"T. Bowness"—is clearly inscribed on Ruskin's billhook for cutting coppice (now in the Coniston Museum).

in perfect evening of the old sacred type, with utterly quiet clouds and blue hills—dark clear —and new moon stooping to them through translucent grey twilight. Walked up and down on road under house, listening to Coniston band across the lake, thinking of my poor father, and what he would have given for such an hour.[19]

Today, beautifully clear, sharp wind from Vecchio, with fleecy cloud capping him, & showing his form.

May 29 Monday. Yesterday much broken, fierce gusts from Vecchio & evil clouds, yet not all evil. Now, grand cumuli, on Agnello, and blue,—but not pure.

May 30 Tuesday. Now all gusty & broken with minglings of bad wind, yet no rain. Yesterday flying kite, and playing with Lily,[20] on dry grass!

May 31 Wednesday— It settled, as it seemed to rain yesterday but clears, with wind this morning: all the streams dry on this side the lake.

June 1. Alas,—only three weeks more of lengthening days

But they are long enough, and lovely. Yesterday up Wetherlam with Louise,[21] better able than I expected, but a little stiff and tired this morning At 4, the dawn on lake, crimson passing into tenderest russet against green, with shafts of cloud shot by breezes from the shore over the absolute dream of the calm water, quite ineffably beautiful. I cold to it all! more interested in my writing If I got drawing again instead, it would be different.

19. John James Ruskin (1785–1864) had keenly relished music of this type, as becomes recurrently apparent from Ruskin's letters to his father. For a description of the present performance, see *Works, 31,* 105.

20. Possibly his cat, but, alternately, Lily Severn (1873–1920).

21. Probably Louise Virenda Blandy (see B.S.). The Wetherlam was a mountain about two miles northeast of the Vecchio.

June 2. Friday. Yesterday entirely perfect—calm, warm. hills inlaid like green jasper in sapphire and finally, dispersed gold in divine jewellery through gray and blue, in radiant sunset. They to Colwith and Skelwith—enjoying it. I idle pretty nearly all day, but none the better this morning having overate as well as overidled.

June 3. Saturday. Utter black fog in the old way—over all things. Yesterday hot & hazy. I much out of sorts,—called on Mr Howells,[22] and enjoyed Heart of Midlothian in evening.

June 4. Sunday Yesterday terrific storm of wind with rain, the poor birds blown on their nests into fluff and rocked me as if at sea, but I hope all safe, yet. An idle day for me, nearly, it proving very dark.

June 5 Monday. Tremendous rain most of night kept me awake, but after church I had a lovely walk by gusty lake on shallow shore—long waves like sea on sand, and all the trees in the green joy of first spring fulness—chestnut blossom and hawthorn fresh.

June 6 Tuesday. Fine again, though unsettled but on the whole natural and very blessed. I sitting up too late at night; and a little rheumatic and not up to work, and my work up to and overhead of *me*.

June 7. Wednesday. Exquisite yesterday in afternoon took early tea at Study window—the narrow sides of it showing divinest lake—meadow and sheep in afternoon light

Thundrous rain this morning, but natural, with cumuli in blue to south—

June 8 Thursday. Slightly raining, but with natural mist on the hills. Yesterday up to tarn with Louise, but gray and not nice

22. The Reverend George Howells (1827–90), resident minister of the Baptist Chapel of Coniston from 1865 to 1886. Ruskin often made him his almoner.

I cant get one of these new pens to write This is an old one—a little better—it is a modern plague this woolly point of pens.

June 9. Friday. Yesterday calling on nice friends of Dr Brown,[23] and Diddie[24] came. On the whole, fine —but unsatisfactory. today misty.

June 10. Saturday. Yesterday partly fine, but fearful *wind on lake,* frightening, and even *somewhat endangering Doanie*[25] *& Diddie* Lovely twilight afterwards at ten oclock to ¼ past. Dreamed a double dream, of carrying a hammer & pickaxe up a hill, to a rail station where I found a great packet sent to me, which I tore open and found valuable specimens of paper, MSS, &c—then left it open on the ground, walked dreamily down the hill without either hammer or pickaxe, and then told the whole, *as* a dream, to somebody, I forget whom,—saying "the dream was so vivid that just now, wide awake, I started, thinking I had really left that parcel open and its contents lying about, at the r[ai]l[wa]y station.["]

June 12 Monday. Yesterday an entirely divine day with blue like opal, and white, fixed precious clouds, like background of deeply glowing Italian picture— Langdale Pikes relieved against two sickles of white cloud dovetailing into an S with larger mass above to finish.[26] Diddie enjoying her walk, and helping me to chase a lamb (whose distress she first saw) over the tarn bridge back to its mother

Clouded over as we returned faster than I

23. Dr. John Brown (1810–82), physician of Edinburgh and author of *Rab and His Friends*—a treasured friend who had been in correspondence with Ruskin for 30 years (see Letters, v).

24. The diminutive of "Dido," a pet name for Sara Martha Anderson (see B.S. and Letters, II).

25. Joan, Mrs. Arthur Severn

26. On the opposite page a pen and ink sketch illustrates the *S* formation of this cloud.

ever saw. Now, a sweet soft white morning rain —diffused.

June 13 Tuesday. No getting things done in this house. Lost all yesterday calling on Marshalls[27] in morning. Fine afternoon, throwing down stones in the wood with Diddie and Maggie[28] Exquisitest purple I *ever* saw on hills, in afternoon, and arch of rosy cloud all over old man and opalescent green-blue and rose over blue Helvellyn, divine, but my evening spoiled by finding the poor chaffinch's nest in ruins, and nestlings dying. A hawk, I fancy, pouncing on the mother;—not able to return for the brood. Lolly[29] came

June 14 Wednesday. Exquisite fine woven sunset—and lovely morning. Change suddenly to evil temper at ½ past 6.

The Melly's[30] yesterday to tea. Lolly came.

June 15 Thursday. Black cloud and rain, very bad—and sorrowful to me because nice American[31] has only one day. Yesterday in the morning and nearly all day, lovely.

June 16 Friday. Fine again yesterday with quite glorious and wonderful sunset—over blue soft wreathed cloud, exquisite— lurid blue, writhing on the hill summit under pure emerald with scarlet bars Today, though it is partly fine the bad wind is on again from the south

June 17. Saturday Another exquisite sunset a little digging—a little letter-seeking rather than answering—a great deal of nothing—brings me to

27. For the Victor Marshalls, see B.S. and Letters, XXIX.

28. Unidentified.

29. Laurence Hilliard (see B.S. and Letters, XXII).

30. For Mrs. Ellen Melly and her family, see B.S.

31. Probably Norton's friend, John W. Field (see *Works, 37*, 204; letter of August 2, 1876, to C. E. Norton). During this period, however, Professor Charles H. Moore, traveling with his wife and daughter, also called (ibid).

another day But the blessed fine weather is not wasted on me.

June 18th Sunday. It came wild, all day yesterday however, but natural wind and rain upsetting Lollie and blowing away his boat to the other side of the lake Grey, but well formed and natural cloud now on green wet hills

June 19th Monday. Yesterday a lovely breezy afternoon—clear sunshine—and sweet twilight Today misty half rain. I had dull headache all yesterday but am well now. (Q[uestion] too many shrimps on Friday)

June 20 Yesterday to Ambleside, Mrs Firth,[32] with Lollie and Diddie & Joan. Foul mist coming back Clear again today Bad Toothache, going

June 21 Perfectly fine, after the most terrific thundrous heat Yesterday at ten, morning—to 12. Clearing to evening. There was no night. exquisite *bright* twilight over Helvellyn at midnight. Not grey twilight, soft, or languid; but keen twilight, like an arrested glow of sheet-lightning.

June 22 ⟨Thunderstorm—pitch-dark, with no blackness, —but deep, high, filthiness of lurid—yet not sublimely lurid smoke-cloud—dense manufacturing mist—fearful squalls of shivering wind—making Arfie's[33] sail quiver like a man in a fever fit,—all about four afternoon—but only two or three claps of thunder and feeble, though near, flashes. I never saw such a dirty, weak, foul storm. It cleared suddenly after raining all afternoon at ½ past 8 to 9, into pure natural weather—low rainclouds on quite clear green, wet hills.⟩[34] And today it is sweet and clear. Arfie

32. Mrs. Julia Firth (see B.S.).

33. Arthur Severn, Sr. (1842–1931), who was on the lake as Ruskin watched from his study window.

34. Published (with minor changes) in *Works, 34,* 36–37.

& Lollie and the two boats on lake in worst time. Susie in Lodge[35]

June 23. Friday. Soft rain with natural cloud after lovely afternoon, very warm—but midges quite horrible in evening on lake, Arthur says. Diddie and Lolly cutting trees with me in the wood by the great rose-bush

June 24 Saturday. Yesterday pouring rain. all day in house. Played chess all afternoon and am headachy this morning. Lovely success with my stream in the new rock channel.[36]

Aurora red in evening—amber green twilight under the clouds it coloured over lake—most marvellous and beautiful

June 25 Sunday. ⟨Yesterday an entirely glorious sunset—unmatched in beauty since that at Abbeville[37]—deep scarlet and purest rose, on purple gray—in bars and stationary plumy sweeping filaments, like "*using up the brush,*" (above, in upper sky) said Joanie; remaining in glory—every moment best—changing from one good into another—(but only in colour or light—form steady) for half an hour, full—and the clouds afterwards fading into the grey against amber twilight, stationary in the same form for about two hours, at least,⟩—the loveliest bit of intense light like a Tintoret dash of brush (free?), behind the hills (A, opposite, but why *curved.*)[38] ⟨The dark-

35. Probably the Lodge ("a miniature Brantwood, turret and all") which Ruskin had built for the family of Frederick Crawley (d. 1898, aged 69), who had become his valet in 1852. Toward the end of 1875 Mrs. Crawley had died in an insane asylum, leaving her husband with three children, whereupon Ruskin had arranged to have Crawley become Caretaker of the Oxford Drawing School. The Brantwood Lodge was consequently left empty (Baxter had not as yet joined the staff) and could have been made available to Miss Beever.

36. For a description of how Ruskin landscaped his domain during the 1870s, see W. G. Collingwood, *Ruskin Relics* (London, 1903), pp. 35–36.

37. On October 1, 1868 (*Diaries,* p. 658).

38. A pen sketch on the opposite page (entitled "A") shows two crescents of light as curved lines that sweep through the otherwise horizontal lines, or "bars," of the sky.

ening rose tint remained till ½ past 10, the grand time being at nine

The day had been fine,⟩ but midgy, ⟨*exquisite* green light on afternoon hills.⟩[39]

June 26 Monday. ⟨Yesterday in entirely perfect summer light, up old man. Lancaster bay all clear,—Ingleborough and the great Pennine fault as on a map. Divine beauty of thyme and rose.—Then twilight—of clearest warm amber, far into night—of pale amber, all night long, hills dark clear against it⟩ Now quite exquisite sun, and calm lake.* [40] In the Coniston Hall [41] meadow, at sunset Rose cloud & new moon on left—blue trenchant Robson[42] Yewdale crags—afterglow of pure light over Brantwood—the air balm—and no midges!

*⟨and so it continued only growing more intense in blue and sunlight all day. After breakfast, I came in from the spring under strawberry bed to say I had never seen anything like it, so pure or intense, in Italy, and so it went glowing on, cloudless with soft North wind, all day.⟩ conf. entry 16th July ⟨the sunset almost too bright *through* the blind for me to read Humboldt [43] at tea by—finally new moon like a lime-light—reflected on breeze-traces, across

39. Published (with minor changes) in *Works, 34,* 35–36.

40. In the MS asterisks indicate that the paragraph which follows should be read as a continuation of these remarks.

41. "Just opposite Brantwood, across the lake, is the old Coniston Hall, built in the fifteenth century as the home of the Flemings of Coniston, but nearly two hundred years ago abandoned and left to ruin." Here, according to tradition, Sir Philip Sidney had lived with his sister, the Countess of Pembroke. "Early in the nineteenth century the ruins were fitted up as a farm" (Collingwood, *Ruskin Relics,* p. 23).

42. George Fennel Robson (1790–1833), of the Old Water-Colour Society, who dwelt on "the clear repose of the northern twilight" (*Works, 33,* 384).

43. In *The Laws of Fésole,* Part I (1877), he would give a long quotation from Alexander von Humboldt's *Personal Narrative of Travels to the Equinoctial Regions of America during the Years 1799–1804* (*Works, 15,* 393–94).

dark calm of reflected hills.)[44] (Lolly and I here: the rest at Ambleside).

June 27 Tuesday. Perfectly fine, but misty. Got off central Fors,[45] yesterday. today begin work for Psalter, thoroughly (Sir Philip Sidney)

June 28 Wednesday. Yesterday misty and sunny, but over-hot—beautifully fine in afternoon—but on the whole tainted. Today, after gleam of promise of enchanting rise of white mists, at 6 oclock, blue glinting through, the weather changed temper in five minutes, in the old way—got first foul,—now it looks like natural rain, which I hope. Yesterday in afternoon drawing birch trunk

June 29 Thursday. Absolute calm, with soft cumulus cloud. At ½ past 3, divinest level unaccountable breeze mists—and rose-purple dawn cloud on green sky Yesterday very fine all day but a little dulled in evening. Diddie & Lollie at tea —Collingwood called, & told me pleasant news of our Xenophon.[46]

June 30 Oh me,—the last day of June! All yesterday beautiful and cool—no midges. I fatigued & fretful—because Angie Acland[47] could'nt understand me! (and now myself going off again on same tack of thought![)] The Marshalls with Miss Herschel[48] at dinner, all nice. Today soft

44. Published (with minor changes) in *Works, 34,* 36, the last sentence being misdated "16th July."

45. The *Fors* of July 1876 was devoted to elaboratively recapitulating the purposes and methods of St. George's Guild, the qualifications and duties of the Companions, and the prerogatives of the Master. Here, too, in 16 aphorisms, he gave "the substance" of what he had tried to teach in *Fors Clavigera* about the basic principles of national conduct and individual education.

46. For W. G. Collingwood and "our Xenophon," see B.S.; see also Letters, x.
basic principles of national conduct and individual education.

48. Unidentified. One naturally wonders whether she may have been a daughter of the astronomer Sir John Herschel, whom Ruskin, as an Oxford undergraduate, had met at Dr. Buckland's table and with whom he subsequently had some correspondence.

clouds on soft hills—all sweet & calling me to see.

1st July. Finished the month happily with a day of play with Kathleen Gordon.[49]

July 2nd Sunday. Wet all yesterday softly and naturally —but gloomy today. At work on Sidney

July 3. Monday. Yesterday beautifully fine. This morning divine calm on fields and lake, but the clouds and sunshine a little foul Yesterday at church— Miss Beevers. cutting woods in sunny afternoon—pleased to find I had really gained strength Boys at boats in evening very funny.

July 4th Boys at chess in evening very naughty. Diddie at coffee in morning very charming. — Weather broken—rapid changes of old character but much beauty in morning light today.

July 5 Lovely afternoon Collingwood with evangelical Mr Edwards,[50] and Miss Somerscales with her brother and sister[51]— afterwards nice work at rock and walk with Diddie. "Great expectations" about a two sailed boat vanishing into air, & sweet sunset

July 6th Yesterday Susie at tea, and nice time afterwards —reading the last bits of Old Mortality. Lovely twilight, and sweet morning.

July 7th Friday — Lovely morning yesterday heat-cloud with exquisite calm in afternoon. Diddie sailing the boat for the boys to draw— Hard at work on magnetic iron and usury.[52] — called on Miss Thackeray.[53]

July 8th Saturday. Yesterday a wonderful day, digging

49. For Kathleen Gordon, see B.S.

50. Unidentified.

51. For these guests, see Miss Annie Somserscales, B.S.; see also Letters, XXXVIII.

52. The August issue of *Fors* was devoted to an attack upon "Usury." Preparing to write this essay, Ruskin had analyzed "the terms 'Increase' and 'Usury' throughout the Old and New Testaments" by collating the terms in the English version of the Bible and the Greek (*Works, 28,* 672).

53. For this call, see Anne Isabelle Thackeray, B.S.

harbour with Kathleen,—having visits from Mr Fowler[54] & Miss Somerscales— nice talk with Diddie in evening Soft rain & silver cloud all day. Now, more gray, but still lovely

July 9. Sunday. Hard at work on Psalms and Minerals, all forenoon. Cutting wood. — Miss Thackeray & Mr L. Stephen at tea.[55] Weather broken—but divine blue yesterday, and much more beauty than I had time to look at

July 10 Monday. Wrote preface for Sidney and heard St Peter's speech read in II lesson—in church debate in Acts with new light on it.[56] Chopped wood and finished Old Mortality, everybody sorry But the novel is more hurriedly done and ill held than most.

July 12 Wednesday. Yesterday chiefly on useless letters but did fine bit of Usury. — in wood with Diddie—and pleasant quiet evening Today, exquisite couched grey cloud and quite divinely wonderful (grey-clear) reflections–dimmed with breeze-grey

July 13 Thursday. — Yesterday chiefly Kathleen at Rock promontory and Miss Thackeray— Then the magnificent, entirely marvellous sky—of which—I can't write this morning—which has been entirely heavenly in sweet cloud Calm lake, and sunshine. I too busy thoughted to see anything! too woful—this constant work

July 14. Friday Yesterday delicious warm afternoon

54. John Edwards Fowler (see B.S.).

55. For Anne Thackeray Ritchie's description of the evening, see her *Records of Tennyson, Ruskin, Browning* (New York, 1892), pp. 68–77. For Leslie Stephen as Ruskin's guest, see B.S.

56. For St. Peter's speech, see Acts 2:14–36, inclusive of the verses (quoted from Joel): "and your young men shall see visions, and your old men shall dream dreams . . . And I will shew wonders in the heaven above, and signs in the earth beneath; blood and fire, and vapour of smoke: The sun shall be turned into darkness, and the moon into blood."

working in wood with M[a]ggie and Diddie sweeping the rocks for me. exquisite twilight in evening. All white mist, now

July 15 Saturday. Entirely divine clear sunshine and cool, pure air, and the lake a mirror. Roses and white rhododendron all in bloom—& dew on fresh mown lawn—but Diddie going away, which makes it all very woful.

July 16th[57] Sunday. Yesterday another of the supreme cloudless Italian days—blue calm unmatchable in peace and azure light,—the second of which I am inclined to say, I never saw its like,[58] but fearfully hot in afternoon, and now dead calm with most oppressive dim heat— Sweet sprinkled white clouds in sky.

July 17th Monday. Woke at dawn—¼ to 4—in the most exquisite panorama of blue and acicular—infinitely sharp and fine shafts of scarlet cloud, behind purple hills— one lovely thing after another,—only seen to be forgotten–unspeakable—my head all the time in Deucalion and my business[59]—and the beauty useless to me, but in being there assuredly, FREE OF CURSE, as in my youth Yesterday a lovely evening. *Sandro Botticelli roses* against twilight

July 18th Tuesday. Weather still quite celestial *I never saw anything like the blue yesterday,*—not with too great heat Quiet misty clouds and calm lake today.

57. Like the entries for June 22, 25, and 26, those for July 16, 17, and 18 are marked marginally, in MS, by a line ruled in black ink, as though they, too, contained material to be published in *The Storm-Cloud.*

58. See entry for June 25, 1876.

59. He was now selecting and classifying minerals for the Museum of St. George's Guild. "I am working hard at the catalogue of its mineral collection," he announced in the *Fors* of August 1876; "and the forthcoming number of *Deucalion* will give account of its proposed arrangement" (*Works, 28,* 677). This proposed arrangement was duly discussed in Parts III and IV of *Deucalion,* issued in November and December, 1876 (*Works, 26,* 197–218).

July 19 Wednesday. to Hawick. 20th Thursday to shepherds on Cheviot with Dr Brown[60] and in afternoon up Rubislaw[61] in the divinest crystal clearness of sky and far folded hills, and silver quiet cloud I ever saw.

21st Friday. Jedburgh. 22nd Saturday back here, much depressed by all I had seen (Compare entry at page 20.[)] [62]

July 23 Sunday. And weary this morning though all lovely still, beautiful haycocks on Major Harrison's field

July 24 Monday. Down in my lovely little study with bright sunshine on haycocks— all lovely yesterday to evening—no midges—nor mist—nor anything but divine old ways of Nature Poor Joanie ill—cold & headache, drawback enough. At tea at Miss Thackerays.

July 25 Tuesday. Yesterday lovely again: building harbour tower with Kathleen, very happy— Mrs. Marshall and her elder sister calling in the evening, (afternoon) I eating strawberries, & little meat, bilious— *have dream at night in spite of pleasant day, too disagreeable to be written,* and am not well up to my work now.

July 26 Wednesday. Yesterday nice afternoon call from Miss Thackeray and 'Pinkie' [63]— Today at last, rain—to refreshment of all things poor Joanie with bad cold, keeps me sad.

July 27 Thursday. Rain, yesterday quite refreshing with endless variety of bronze and brick red, and amber clouds at sunset, beautiful in texture

60. Dr. John Brown of Edinburgh.

61. Having written *Ruberslaw,* he changed the word to read "Rubislaw." The Rubers Law is a minor peak in the northern foothills of the Cheviots, the range of "hills" between Northumberland and Roxburghshire whose watershed forms the border between England and Scotland.

62. See entry for July 21, 1877, where the spelling, "Rubislaw," is repeated.

63. Laura Stephen, Miss Thackeray's six-year-old niece.

though coarse in colour. Today fine, but with impure clouds of the bad kind [64]

July 28 Friday. Oh me, my sweet last week two thirds gone. Yesterday drawing with Kathleen in afternoon—nice American and wife, Mr & Mrs Gurney[65] in evening

July 29 Saturday Rain in broken showers, yesterday and today, can't fill the streams, all the moss so dry. I wander about wistfully, sorry I'm going. What fearful loss the ruin of Switzerland is to me; and now with the old memories I cant bear going away anywhere

July 30th Sunday. Yesterday Miss Thackeray at lunch then Kathleen—then Susie— I hope they all liked coming. Kathleen criticising my drawing as it went on deliciously[66] Today windy & wet. Yesterday breezy but drawable in. I very woful at going away.

Namely—to Dolgelly.[67]

See 1st August, beginning in Venice book. (i.e. diary of journey to and residence in Venice, 1876,7 [)]

Here ends Diary for 1876.

64. On the left-hand page, opposite this entry, he itemizes a deposit "Sent today to Union Bank."

65. For Professor E. W. Gurney's account of these hours, see B.S.

66. For Ruskin's comment on this sentence (made on the opposite page), see entry of January 25, 1883.

67. Dolgelly, Wales, is a few miles from Barmouth, where, for the first time, Ruskin saw the eight cottages of the cliff-side property given to St. George's Guild by Mrs. T. G. Talbot (1824–1916) in December 1874.

1877

Home on July 17 after an absence of almost 11 months, the last of which had been spent with the Severns at Herne Hill, Ruskin turned to the Brantwood Diary on July 21 and used it for the daily record until he left for Oxford on November 5. The special interest of this unit lies in what the entries indicate about his health, his work, and his relationships with human beings during the three months of what he could misleadingly call "rest" after eight months of veritably exhausting work in Venice.

His habitual concern about his health now became attached to a dual theme: dimness in sight and giddiness in head. Off and on, since his student days at Oxford, he had worried about his "eyes," which to the end would serve him well. Less explicitly but recurrently, for at least fourteen years he had had premonitions that, if he did not watch himself, he might become insane. Now, in August, he ventured once more to articulate this dread: he told one correspondent that he had "neither time nor, at present, power" to analyze why they differed in opinion, "being nearly as ill, I fancy, as you are, though without pain, but with threatening, if I over-think myself, of worse than headache" (*Works, 29*, 591; letter to T. C. Horsfall, August 24, 1877). In about six months, despite his watching, with related efforts to control his lot, the "worse than head-ache" had materialized. At times the very handwriting in this section of the Diary "shows that Ruskin consciously faced the possibility that he was threatened by insanity," according to Dr. Rose Wolfson, a clinical psychologist and specialist in graphology.

It is possible that while he was in Venice he had had his first definitely demented episode, which may have been, to some degree, permanently deleterious in its effect. During the Christmas season (he recounts in the *Fors Clavigera* of February 1877), as a "handmaiden" of St. Ursula, or even as St. Ursula herself, his lost Rose La Touche (who had died in May 1875) had sent him "signs," directing him in conduct and in thought. These strange experiences were first recorded in his Venetian Diary of 1876–77 (see *Diaries,* pp. 920–26) and were then described more fully and coherently in a series of as yet unpublished letters to Mrs. Severn (in the F. J. Sharp Collection) which he called *The Christmas Story.* In all, the evidence clearly shows that for about a fortnight, even if this episode falls short of the psychotic, he had penetrated dangerously far into the twilight zone through which sanity merges into the deranged.

In retrospect, he himself was left convinced that, largely through the mystic agency of "Fors," or "chance," he had had direct communication with some World of the Supernal in which the spirits of the departed veritably "live" and from which they can guide those whom they still love. More and more, however, the knowledge which he believed that he had gained through an immediacy of insight had receded into merely a remembrance. Nevertheless, because of these experiences his faith in personal immortality (which he had lost about fifteen years before the death of Rose) had been restored. And although his mind's eye truly had grown "dim" in sight as the "visionary gleam" had faded before the returning light of a more common day, he still sometimes could hope that Rose (or, now alternately, St. Ursula) had not forgotten him. "That the eyes of man are of his soul" (*Works, 22,* 513) was one of the themes to be stressed in his pending series of lectures at Oxford, where "for the first time," he would tell Miss Beever, "I have been able to speak to them boldly of immortal life" (*Works, 37,* 231; letter of December 2, 1877).

Fatigue, he thought, had caused this trouble with his eyes and head, the fact being that in Venice he *had* "overworked" as he gathered his material for *St. Mark's Rest.* But additionally, since leaving Brantwood on July 31, 1876, he had published 11 issues of *Fors Clavigera,* 10 of which had been composed while he was on the wing. In September he had written "Thirty Years Since" to publish as an extra chapter in Part IV of *Deucalion* (issued in December 1876). Doubtless helped by notes made in earlier years, he had written and published (March 1877) his *Guide to the Principal Pictures in the Academy at Venice.* He also had completed *Mornings in Florence* (Part VI, "The Shepherd's [Giotto's]

Tower") and had seen through press Sir Philip Sidney's *Psalter,* as *Rock Honeycomb* (both issued in July). In writing *St. Mark's Rest,* as his main interest, he had been interrupted by the call to prepare, with difficulty, the Letter to be used as the Preface to Count Zorzi's pamphlet of protest against the pending *Restoration of the Basilica of St. Mark's* (1877). Nevertheless, *St. Mark's Rest* was well under way: its first three chapters had appeared in April as Part I, and chapters 4–7 would be issued in October as Part II. While in mere quantity his achievement can seem astounding, in quality this part of his work has been perhaps, to date, much too conventionally appraised.

On his return to Brantwood there must have seemed to be two major needs: his commitment to the monthly *Fors* and the completion of *St. Mark's Rest.* But there was also Part I of *The Laws of Fésole* (September 1877) to be readied for the students in his Oxford Drawing School, and on October 1 he was to lecture at Kendal on problems illustrated by local geology. Incidentally he would issue several "Public Letters," a second edition of the *Ethics of the Dust,* and, for private circulation, a "Catalogue of Silicious Minerals for St. George's Museum, Sheffield." Finally, there was a course of lectures to be delivered in November and December, when he would return to Oxford to resume his duties as the Slade Professor, after a year's leave of absence. Toward the end of September he told George Allen: "I'm perfectly overwhelmed under the quantity of things which must be kept in my mind, now, going like a juggler's balls in the air—a touch first to one, then another. . . . The mass of work I shall (*D.V.*) bring out this autumn will astonish people, I think, who know what work costs" (*Works, 37,* 227). In the October *Fors,* under "Affairs of the Master," he reported: "Too many for him: and it is quite certain he can't continue to ride so many horses at once, or keep so many balls in the air. All that he thinks it needful, in this *Fors,* to say, is that, whatever he may cease to hope of doing, he will not fail from St. George's work, as long as he has strength for any work at all" (*Works, 29,* 248).

Hence his dedication to this type of work is once more shown through little more than a succession of names which appear in the Diary. First Mr. Walker and then Mr. Rydings are welcomed as accountants for the Guild, to be followed by the public-spirited Robert Somervell, who handled the Guild's legal affairs. Then a day is given to Mr. Horsfall, who would found a museum for workingmen in Manchester; and Henry Swan, Curator of the Museum at Sheffield, intrusively appears with his wife, evidently to discuss the gifted Sheffield grinder, Benjamin Creswick—to whom, as a sculptor, Ruskin soon gave a sitting. From Venice, at the beginning of the year, he had written a Companion (Katherine Bradley): "my real pleasure as far as any is left me now in this [world], is . . . in being useful, above all in teaching or comforting people who can be easily taught—or greatly comforted" (Sturge Moore, T. and D. C., eds., *Works and Days: From the Journal of Michael Field* [London, 1933], p. 152; letter of February 21, 1877). By spring: "But I must not think of what I have lost or may regain: my only duty at present is to keep myself in active work and thought for the present needs of people round me" (ibid., p. 153; letter of April 4, 1877).

Throughout the summer he would also entertain his more personal friends—from within the neighborhood, the Marshalls and Miss Beever, and, more transiently, the four Bennett sisters who had settled for a season near Miss Beever, if not within The Thwaite itself, to become prospective Companions of St. George. From further afield came Leslie Stephen, to be duly welcomed by a call (August 9) which he perhaps did not return; Lazarus Fletcher (September 8), whose friendship, as Keeper of Minerals at the British Museum, would be commemorated through Ruskin's gift to the Museum of the Colenso Diamond and the Edwardes Ruby; Aubrey de Vere (September 16), who hoped increasingly that Ruskin might join him in the Catholic faith; William Mallock (September 20), who had recently, and skillfully, depicted Ruskin in *The New Republic*; James Reddie Anderson, or "Jamie" (September 20), of Balliol, who had led the Hincksey Diggers and whose knowledge of Carpaccio would be highlighted by his writing chapter 11 for *St. Mark's Rest*. "Jamie's" cousin, Sara Anderson ("Diddie"), had reached Brantwood in July, to remain as an assistant until sometime in September; and Alexander Wedderburn had returned in early August, evidently (by providing secretarial services) to replace the absent Laurence

Hilliard. Mrs. Severn's nieces, Martha and Marion Gale, had arrived in mid-August to enjoy some weeks of play—once, as "the children," playing audibly "in the passages" until midnight (August 22), probably with "Diddie" and "Alic." Joan, could she resist the mirth, would have been in bed, since she was in distress which culminated, some weeks hence, in a miscarriage (October 8), with Ruskin setting forth, shortly after 5 A.M., to meet the doctor, after agonizing hours of anxiety.

By then he had been able to send Norton reassuring words about himself. True, he had "not yet been able to finish the notes on Venice got this winter! everything falling through—and back—and so many things that I could do, if I had only time—calling to me to do them before I die, if it may be. But I never really overwork—in fact I *cannot*—when I am tired I *can* neither draw nor think—and am simply forced to go out of doors and dig—or prune—at least—cut down or away the brittle—not *logs* perhaps, but stems—good for nothing but faggots—." (Unpublished letter of October 3, 1877; Harvard University Library. (Too readily, the Severns had had a laugh when they learned that he had told Norton, in an earlier letter, that *he* was feeling like a "brittle log."

Often, through this period, one finds him setting forth, usually with one or more of the "young people," to study the mystery of mountain tarns or crags or of the Yewdale Beck, with its dark pool, as it flowed through the valley to its delta in Lake Coniston. In the Diary he notes no more than the bare fact of having taken this walk or made that climb. Compositely, however, these outings led to "The Yewdale and Its Streamlets"—first delivered at Kendal and then published in *Deucalion* (1879) as part of his attack upon the folly and pretentiousness of those who saw in "modern" science the highway which would lead to human happiness, together with man's full comprehension of his own world in relation to the universal past and the present. The relation of his personal past to his present, as reflected by changes in his understanding of the life of man and the nature of God, was a subject which would engross his attention after he reached Oxford to review his own work through those lectures of the first term, *Readings in "Modern Painters,"* which he would call "this course of lectures on myself" (*Works, 22,* 511).

July 20th—(No. 21st. Saturday.[)] [1]

A year, today since I climbed Rubbislaw [sic]—and found the grass so slippery and myself so nervous.[2] I was stronger, I think, this year at Gondo,[3] but ⟨feel very much *overworked,* now, in head and eyes.⟩[4] A wet morning, very dark, and *sleep only from 12 to 4,*—make it worse.

July 22 Sunday. Perpetual wet, and midges in evening, and confusion worse confounded in all work. Better a little today, opening my old Henry Milner at page 108, first part, where I have marked it.[5]

July 23 Monday. Pouring rain— Mr. Walker[6] of Union Bank to tea—gave me curious

1. In the upper margin Ruskin comments: "1877 Diary. Begins abruptly, on return from Venice See warning symptoms in Head and eyes, and lost sleep."

2. Indexing this volume, he entered under *N*: "Nervousness, my own, on Rubislaw about eyes and blood to head twice, same page, a year after!"

3. Returning from Venice, he had noted on June 7, 1877: "A little better in heart, though my eyes dim and tired in walking up from Gondo" (*Diaries,* p. 958).

4. The italics in this entry, like most of those used elsewhere, represent underlinings evidently made in later years when Ruskin was indexing this volume. The words enclosed in angle brackets, both here and in subsequent entries for 1877, were published when Cook and Wedderburn characterized Ruskin's health and interests during this period (see *Works, 25,* xxi–ii).

5. On page 108 of the 1823–27 edition (London) of Mrs. Sherwood's *The History of Henry Milner,* Mr. Dalban tells the gardener, Mr. Baring, that in his opinion "there is no flower on earth in all respects equal to the moss rose." The gardener is "much of the same opinion. . . . Take the rose for colouring, scent, and beauty of shape, I doubt whether it has its equal in the world." In the following paragraph: " 'You know, Mr. Baring,' said Mr. Dalben, 'that our blessed Saviour compares himself in Solomon's Song to the Rose: "I am the rose of Sharon," he says. Methinks I have ever loved the rose since I learnt that it has afforded a similitude to the perfections of the Saviour.' " One or both of these passages might well have been marked in Ruskin's "old Henry Milner."

6. William Walker of the Union Bank, London, served the Guild as an "honorary" accountant, cosigning with Mr. Rydings the statements of Guild finances published in *Fors Clavigera.*

insights. I ⟨still anxious *about* sense of blood going to head,⟩—and something like tremour which I can't understand —Saw it first at Domo d'Ossola, as if it had come suddenly—above left thigh.[7] But all my work pleasant if I had'nt too much.

July 24 Tuesday. Got letter enclosing wonderful ones of my Father's, and introducing three—I hope nice—girls, whom I must go and see today.* But I *can't get my head and eyes* right at all—and am fretted

* 1883—Bennetts—Rose drowned since, Florence dying[8]

July 25 Wednesday. Yesterday over to Coniston after rowing Joanie to Waterhead in grand sea waves,[9]—to call on Florence Bennett and her sisters Then up to the rough side of Yewdale crag—feeling a moment on it as the child of old time —the thrill of the free mountain turf. Then round by the stream and called on Mr. Bowness.[10] Walked home with Joanie and Lily.

July 26 Thursday. Got Fors finished well and

7. Indexing the volume, Ruskin noted under *I*: "Illness—beginning of vexing symptoms at Domo d'Ossola in 1877." Spending a week in Domo d'Ossola as he returned from Venice, he had noted on May 31: "bilious gloom concentrated by failure of eyes and a strained or relaxed sinew of the thigh, giving me unconquerable anxiety" (*Diaries*, p. 956).

8. For the Bennetts, see B.S.

9. When the wind was right, it was his habit to row, driven by the waves, to the northern end of Lake Coniston, where he would leave his boat, walking back to Brantwood.

10. "The principal flank of Yewdale is formed by a steep range of crag, thrown out from the greater mass of Wetherlam, and known as Yewdale Crag [or Crags]" (*Works, 26,* 254; see also Map B.) The smithy of John Bowness was on the bank of Yewdale Beck.

St. Jerome[11] on foot—and recovered a little about eyes. Yesterday — I neednt always write Y. now,—understanding that every day tells *what story it can* of the day before

Diddie came in the afternoon, which is *a very nice story*.[12]

Today, for the first time, quite calm mirror-smooth lake with soft & pure cloud mantling about, till now 7, when it is beginning to get impure and wrong.

July 27 Sweet–showery, dark and light on hills —would be lovely if I had mind to look at it, but head full of Carpaccio.[13]

Florence Bennett and her sisters—very amusing yesterday and Turner's came down safe— My little bedroom, all bright again.[14]

July 28 Saturday. — My head so full of Carpaccio that I could write a volume on him —and can scarcely get a sentence done in the continual letterwork, and yet that needful and now doing much good.

11. One section of "The Shrine of the Slaves," issued in December 1877, as a Supplement to *St. Mark's Rest* (Parts I and II), interprets Carpaccio's three "visions" of St. Jerome—leading the lion into the monastery, lying in death, and working in his study.

12. In MS a straight line connects the wordplay, as italicized.

13. Because of "The Shrine of the Slaves," written as "a guide to the principal pictures by Victor Carpaccio."

14. At least five new Turners had come from Herne Hill, where they had been awaiting his return from Venice, and another was expected. In June part of the Collection of R. A. J. Munro ("of Novar") had come up for sale at Christie's: "there were four which I've been looking after for thirty years—and I would have bought them with my last guinea," he had explained to Mr. Walker (*Works, 37,* 223; letter of June 9, 1877). His own collection had been depleted by his gifts of 1861 to Oxford and Cambridge Universities, by sales made in 1869, and, of late, by "loans" to his Drawing School at Oxford. "I think the getting these new Turners will be of great importance to me," he had told Mrs. Severn. "It will set me *on* Turner again, and I think I shall now give a course of lectures on him at Oxford (*Works, 25,* xix; letter of June 10, 1877).

Play in hayfield yesterday, but rain steady again today. poor Mr. Usher[15] will have a bad bargain of his field.

July 29. Sunday. Close rain and hot midgy air—and over-eating, spoiled afternoon. Volunteers arrived, red specks moving between gaps in hedges, to the tents, white like flock of sheep. The mischief it all means! in spite of good intent except as a wholesome play! Yet, if it led to the forming [of] a national force indeed! [16]

Today gleams of sun—and much lovely—if I could look.

July 30 Monday. Yesterday calling on Miss Beevers and young Miss Bennetts, greatly tired by the many problems which the curious girls gave to me—in themselves and their ways. A scramble by the stream above Bowness's[17]—the rocks all dripping and thickets drenched, refreshed me Still raining, perpetual Scotch mist on the Vecchio, and I awake since four, and eyes dark

July 31. Tuesday. I see last year I went away, and in a month more, was well-nigh Venice — And August only now between me and the short days. May—'June—July' —the two summer months between Domo [d'Ossola] and this,—gone like a flash.

15. George Usher (see B.S.).

16. The Volunteers (red-coated, like all British soldiers before the Boer War) were local organizations of soldiers with regular jobs, who "volunteered" to train part time. With the Militia, they constituted the infantry reserves of the small regular army until 1907, when the "reserves" were reorganized as the Territorial Army (information supplied by Miss Gnosspelius).

17. Presumably John Bowness (1818–1881), whose son Thomas made Ruskin's billhook

Yesterday at stream below Cowards[18] in the wood, with Diddie, Arfie and Joanie. Walked round by the Marshalls slate quarry, examining its endless cleavages—home by Waterhead & Miss Rigby[e]'s.[19]

1st August. Wednesday.
Bright at last—after another day of perpetual warm drizzle, and midges. Dreamed that Emily's[20] two children were going to live with me, or I with them, and that I felt it was all that was needed to keep the end of my life in peace, and, when I said so, the elder girl —(I think I fancied they were both girls,)—knelt down and prayed at the far end of the room, and I seeing her, did the like; and then poor old Ann[21] got up out of her bed (it was morning in a bedroom)—saying something about "her opinion of the weather"!!

Lay awake from five to six, planning a Fors on slavery, to begin with Patmore's letter, showing how we thought the lower classes murderers and left them so. — Then of neglected children, my wild swinging gate one at Verona. Of slaves looked after the school at Cowley—(School of infanzia—& orna-

18. Edward Coward (d. 1881, aged 77) and his son Richard, of Far-End House, were the craftsmen to whom Ruskin turned when he wished to have toys constructed, after his own design, for some child.

19. Miss Harriette Rigbye (d. 1894, aged 82) lived at Thwaite Cottage, a small house close below The Thwaite, home of her intimate friends the Beevers, beside whom she is buried in the Coniston Churchyard. See also Letters, xxxv.

20. Mrs. Bernard Ward, née Emily La Touche (see B.S.).

21. Anne Strachan (d. 1871, aged 77), Ruskin's nurse until around 1831 and then for about forty years (serving Ruskin's mother) a Lady's Maid—the occupation stated on her death certificate. This certificate also indicates that Ruskin was mistaken when in effect he said that Anne had died when she was seventy-two (*Works, 27,* 518).

ment at Verona.) Separation of Brother & sister—"stole a boat—&c—" [22]

August 2nd. Thursday. Bright and calm, though with forming clouds,—but, looking at my drawing of Wetherlam,[23] am more hopeless than usual—feeling something now permanently injured in my power of sight. Chiefly—it is a form of fatigue however and is most at early morning before I am well awake.

Yesterday sauntering about at camp, and waterhead, and giving Rose Bennett a drawing lesson— Heard some things of the Spiritual Powers that were good for me

August 3. Friday—a day more than I thought counting tomorrow Sunday. — Yesterday terribly hard worked—getting diagrams right for Fesole[24]—at camp in afternoon—and talk with Rose Bennett. —Today pouring wild rain: but I am better in heart a little.

August 4th Saturday. Loveliest crimson-tawny dawn on Vecchio and calm lake in loveliest films of breeze. I lying awake planning trine groups for Fésole,[25]—MORE HAPPY THAN FOR MANY A DAY, in having proof of an Adversary, having heard yesterday from Rose Bennett *the first entirely clear and perfect account of the vision of an evil spirit that has ever been given*

22. This "Fors on Slavery" was not written, although Ruskin included the Coventry Patmore letter in the August issue (*Works, 29,* 177), and in the September issue spoke of it from the point of view here noted (*Works, 29,* 194).

23. See p. 13 n. 21.

24. Part I of *The Laws of Fésole* (its Preface dated "Brantwood, 31st July, 1877") was issued in September. Chapter 3, "First Exercise in Right Lines," contains several diagrams.

25. Doubtless the various groupings of circles used to illustrate Chapter 5, "Of Elementary Forms."

to me,—sealing all my own experience of the grotesque truth of mediaeval theology—and then much of the purgatory of Dante explained afterwards—and a happy evening— Fireworks to finish very beautiful against dark hills—after ⟨a quite exquisite Italian sky to south with divinest jewels of white cirri—and a long riband like a renaissance angels sash—or Botticelli Madonnas, flying up high to the zenith⟩ I never saw quite the match of it.

August 5th. Sunday. Overeating, and Joanie making me anxious by getting neuralgia with sitting in the rain—and a dream of *quarrelling* with, or at least—*steadily resisting my mother,* about a letter which she wanted me to write again differently—altogether waked me at ½ past three, and now a dark morning with soft rain on calm lake, finds me ⟨dim-eyed and confused with *mixture of music, Yewdale streams and St Marks mosaic,* buzzing in my head with *free trade* and *Venice fruit law,*[26] all the morning⟩

August 6th. Monday. Much wearied by stupidity of girl visitors and alarmed about *dizziness in head and eyes,* but slept well, and ⟨feel up to work this morning, on any single thing but not on two dozen.⟩

August 7th. Tuesday. Terribly hot, dark, moist, thundrous cloud, ending in mere Manchester blackness, yet I had a marvellous

26. Part II of *St. Mark's Rest* would be issued in October 1877, and on October 1 Ruskin was to lecture on the streams of Yewdale. The effect on English children of the laissez-faire economy, as reflected in the high price of fruit, would be discussed in the October *Fors Clavigera,* and Plato on education had plunged him into considering the role of different kinds of music in man's development (the central theme of the November *Fors Clavigera*).

walk through Yewdale and up the glen to the first fall out of Tilberthwaite among the stones of the divine stream

Now, lake dead calm but fog on hills half way down. See entry for June 22nd [18]76, et seq.

August 8th Wednesday. Worked through constant rain, yesterday and did nothing—but lose all appetite,—till 8 in evening when Wedderburn[27] came. Slept well—but woke at 4, useful thoughts however arranging themselves

Rain again, today gaps of blue sky behind house going away Black Vecchio extending his sway.

August 9. Thursday. Terrific Thunder, yesterday in going across to call on Miss Beever and Mr Leslie Steven [*sic*]. Utter veil of rain now—steady blackness or wet always, just like our old times. I better though, for which I am very thankful

August 10. in gloomiest day, yesterday to call on nice old couple, Mr and Mrs Barratt[28]—but I very ill and made worse by effort to make myself pleasant.

Thoroughly unwell this morning also and must mind what I am about.

August 11th. The most divine beauty of mist and pure clear hill above with calm lake, out of my window—on all sides this morning at ½ past six—but *I wretchedly cold and thankless, misusing or losing all.* Very wonderful to myself. ⟨The perfectness and brightness, and delicacy—and infinite quantity to be looked at and hayfield in front of house, all Etruscan

27. Alexander ("Alec," "Alic," "Alick") Wedderburn (see B.S.).
28. For the Barratts, see B.S.

—worked with bosses seven to eight hundred cocks at least—spotting it in zones to the waters edge⟩

Yesterday a strangely successful day—with delightful afternoon— Began with solitary breakfast—History of Tyre[29]—and sheep's foot[30]—ended with digging and well making with Diddie & Alick

August 12th. Sunday. Slept well, yet feel more than commonly giddy & stupid after great plague yesterday with preface to elements of drawing,[31] and everything falling behind Lovely morning, but always clouding towards seven. — View now from turret window quite inconceivably lovely, with the new hay & green mown fields

August 15th. Wednesday. I have had two complete holidays in lovely sunshine on Yewdale crag,—three virtually—finding out waterfall and climbing to top, and bringing down basalt pillar,[32] half way, on Sunday afternoon. Then, Monday scramble with Diddie and Alic, and Alic brings down basalt altogether—and yesterday by myself, studying Anagallis & sundew,[33] Diddie rowing me over the

29. Probably the unfinished "history of Tyre" posthumously published under the heading "Tyre: Study on Ezekiel" (*Works, 24,* 447–50). "The Burden of Tyre" had already appeared as chapter 1 of *St. Mark's Rest.*

30. Two wash drawings of a sheep's foot were published (July 1878) as Plate VI in *The Laws of Fésole.* (The originals are now in the F. J. Sharp Collection.)

31. In subsequent entries he refers to *The Laws of Fésole* as his "elements of drawing."

32. He was studying the basaltic structure of Yewdale Crag for his Kendal lecture (see *Works, 26,* 254).

33. On his Monday climb he had found, "in perfect beauty," some "full-opened flowers" of the Anagallis tenella (bog Pimpernel), with some "stars of sundew" (*Works, 25,* xli–ii, where the "Aug. 14th" notebook entry of 1877 is misdated "1876"; see also *Works, 25,* 543–44, for a passage on the Anagallis tenella intended for *Proserpina*).

lake. Better while I am on the holiday, but *still giddy-pated this morning.*

August 17th. Friday. Joe Tylor,[34] and Miss Wedderburn[35] and Miss Wakefield [36] nearly occupied all day—and confused thoughts and gluttony the rest.— A little bit of chapter on pith reviewed, and a pleasant letter answered to Venice—R[awdon] B[rown],[37] and thistle sent to Allen,[38] filled the day

August 18 Saturday. Pouring, with yellow fog, but had delicious walk up Yewdale stream with Diddie and Alic and felt stronger than for some time But totally discouraged about all powers and plans

August 19 Sunday. Bad night—and *eyes dim* this morning,—steady rain hindering all exercise and midges intolerable. Marion and Martha Gale[39] come.

August 20th. Monday. Pouring rain always, and I terribly languid—*eyes certainly failing as never before,* and all things now done by me merely with view of summing up my work to its end. Summing up what is worthless—instead of beginning what is worth—seems to be the old man's lot

August 21. Tuesday Rain and thunder and darkness,—yesterday calm lake with cease-

34. Presumably Joseph John Tylor (1851–1901), an engineer and Egyptologist—son of Ruskin's good friend Alfred Tylor

35. Alexander Wedderburn's only sister, Marion Hester, who in 1881 married Captain Stephen Blythe Moore.

36. Augusta Mary Wakefield (see B.S.).

37. For Rawdon Brown, see B.S. and Letters, VI.

38. The next number of *Proserpina,* illustrated by one of Ruskin's thistles, appeared in 1882, with the drawing suggestively entitled "States of Adversity" (*Works, 25,* Pl. 17). The discussion of pith in *Proserpina* was not published until 1885 (*Works, 25,* 486–95).

39. For the Gale sisters, see B.S.

less gloom and rarely ceasing rain, all day long.

Work at cascade[40] and on Fors, and reading Nigel,[41] filled the day.

August 22. A quite frightful fit of depression brought on by my curator and his wife[42] coming when they shouldn't—and by thoughts about *good* vulgar and impertinent people very painful and troublesome The children playing till 12 oclock in the passages[43]

August 23 Thursday. The first really fine and divine morning I have had for a month—and I think my eyes are better, but I am not at all satisfied about either them, or my head.

August 24 Friday. Had quiet good day, yesterday and reading of Humboldt in sunshine but bad nightmarish night—clearly from wrong eating. Must absolutely stop this.

40. A "deep and steep watercourse" which fell in a "succession of cascades" bounded one side of his woodland garden. He would "sometimes humorously complain of the trouble it cost him to keep the beck clear of stones" (Collingwood, *Ruskin Relics,* p. 36).

41. In the November *Fors Clavigera* he would quote at length from Scott's Introduction to the *Fortunes of Nigel,* copying the passage "from the dear old manuscript" which he had taken "reverently" from his own bookcase (*Works, 29,* 263–64).

42. In January 1876, Henry Swan (d. 1889, aged 64) had become Curator of the Museum of St. George, which he had aroused Ruskin's interest in founding, as a school for workingmen of Sheffield. As plans for this Museum began to form, Ruskin had asked Swan, who was already a resident of Walkley: "Can you get with any Sheffield help, a room with good light, anywhere accessible to the men who would be likely to come to it? If so, I will send you books and begin with minerals of considerable variety and interest, with short notes on each specimen, and others of less value, of the same kinds which the men may handle and examine at their ease" (unpublished letter of 12 July, 1875; present whereabouts unknown). Now, as Curator, Swan was living rent-free, with an annual stipend, in a small house near Sheffield which Ruskin had bought, one room of which constituted the Museum.

43. Doubtless Sara Anderson, the Gales, and Alexander Wedderburn.

August 25 Saturday. Yesterday the most exquisite broad rainbow filling up half the valley above Coniston, bringing back to me that great question of the breadth and narrowness of rainbows never yet at all settled in my mind. — But until one has seen a bow of this broad kind, in low curvature covering a great space of country or cloud, one has not properly seen rainbow at all.

Mr Rydings broke up the day and Fors must suffer.

August 26. Sunday. Rain again—yesterday fine in morning, thundrous and dark in afternoon. Pleasant visit from Somervell,[44] and play among the young people Joan, Diddie, Martha and Marion all in conclave against Alic—seated in the passage opposite my door. Got on a little with Plato and Fesole, & felt stronger.

August 27 Monday. Very tired and blind this morning, but probably all my own fault for continually eating what I should not. The air however really relaxing, and a thunderous darkness nearly continual very melancholy.

Great pleasure in reading Nigel in the evening, to the young people

August 28th. I might nearly print Rain with a stamp, it was tremendous at my window last night

Got some good Athens work done with Alic, and some Plato really worked out,[45] but no exercise, yet slept well from 11 to 6.

44. Robert Somervell (see B.S.).

45. Ruskin correlated his work on Plato's *Laws* with study of Athenian history; see, for example, the passage quoted from Müller's *Dorians* in the the October *Fors Clavigera* (*Works, 29,* 221–22).

August 29. Wednesday. Got scarcely anything done yesterday but a fine time with all the children washing my rock—a pretty scene—and finishing fortunes of Nigel, which all much enjoyed. Sunshine on the hill masses, fitful, with heavy, but impure clouds.

August 30th. Thursday. Pouring rain, which however happens to be convenient to me. Yesterday very delicious on the lake, Diddie and Martha rowing me. Took the Lippi angels[46] to Susie, and had tea with the children, to the great satisfaction of Baby, the best child dancer I ever saw.[47]

August 31. Friday. Actually a month since the walk to pool in Yewdale with Joanie and Arfie —and nothing done! [48]

Today, the most glorious rainbows I ever saw, for intensity—staying each about ¼ of a minute—with grey lake all foamed into white like seagulls, seen through them and the fields becoming radiant violet and moss-gold orange,— the dark place, or space between the double rainbows, the glowing mingling of the red with it, and the opalescent luminousness of the innermost violet,— exquisite in beauty, all clearer than I ever saw them.

September 1st Saturday. Yesterday up Yewdale Crag by the waterfall with Diddie, Marion & Martha—and found myself pretty active still,—and found a new mass of basalt

46. C. F. Murray's copy of "Children and Their Guardian Angels," from Filippo Lippi's *Coronation of the Virgin,* to be sent to the Sheffield Museum in November.

47. Probably Lily Severn had remained "Baby" after the arrival of her brothers Arthur (1874–1949) and Agnew (1875–1929).

48. Namely, to prepare his Kendal lecture, "The Yewdale and its Streamlets," for delivery on October 1

which I must find the junction of with the slates. Bright today though flickering and I curiously well, after eating everything that I should'nt at dinner. Eyes not, though.

September 2nd Sunday. Everybody got the completest wetting in hail and thundershower I up to junction of basalt & slate—but all one torrent. Now—low gray mist and much colder.

September 3rd Monday. Up late—though after some useful thinking of 'Liberal' education[49] which I've not had the like of for long having been too despondent to think of anything since I left Venice Settled gray sky, very gloomy. Yesterday wrote letters, and dug at rocks,—thinking of my mothers birthday last year at Domo d'Ossola, when I walked in the evening up the winding road among the chapels till I came to the top of the quarry

September 4th. Tuesday. Grand walk yesterday beside the steep waterfall up to the tarn[50] on the Vecchio—and down by slate quarries examining the transition to slate. *I wonder if I could make a model of the Vecchio!*

Today, after *lovely serene sunset*—one of the ineffable white, levelled mist and *purple mornings—unspeakable in beauty—* I quite cold to it all but this because my mind is on other things.

Inflammation of eyes making me anxious but sight very clear today.

49. As though commemorating his mother's birthday (September 2), he made ideals and methods in education the central interest in the next two issues of *Fors Clavigera.*

50. Probably Low Water.

For next Fors, at least something of the practical results of *Brother* going to law with *brother*.[51]

September 5. Wednesday. Yesterday up the Vecchio after lunch, calling first on Miss Beever & Mrs Allen[52]—up by the steep waterfall and tarn,[53] then round by the north side and up and back along the ridge. On the top at 6—down at lake shore at ¼ past seven, losing ten minutes by taking wrong horse path and having to recover across stones, over here at harbour two minutes under the hour and half from top, and I less fatigued than ever before, and less stiff this morning,—scarcely at all— Very curious—I suppose I have really been living happier and more strengthening life with St Ursula's help.[54]

Today—marvellous purple dawn over perfectly green fields, with a red rainbow—only the red band possible in the red light—feeblest orange, and *no* violet whatever,—the orange scarcely dimmed by the χλωρος[55] of the green

September 6 Thursday. Yesterday merely writing letters— got some useful one's done—and just a spray of ivy in afternoon's work, and some Renan[56] read. Abbot much enjoyed in reading to children in the eve-

51. This subject was not discussed.

52. Presumably Mrs. George Allen (the sister of Ruskin's former valet, "George" Hobbs) who, before her marriage in 1856, had been the servant "Hannah" of Ruskin's mother. The Allens sometimes stayed in Coniston while on a vacation.

53. Levers Water? (see Map B)

54. In effect, the help of Rose La Touche.

55. Greenness.

56. Ernest Renan (1823–92). In 1872 Ruskin had been reading *St. Paul* (1869) as one volume in *The Origins of Christianity*.

September 15 Saturday. Yesterday got a little bit of lecture ["Yewdale and Its Streamlets"] done, and some Anagallis and saw help given to Sheffield Mr Creswick Fri-[day] the 14th the fiercest day of rain I ever had here—and streams highest in flood. Again all last night. Today, clear & calm and very lovely—

September 16th Sunday — Aubrey de Vere[66] at dinner ⟨ever so nice⟩—and exquisite morning now. I in better heart than for many a day. Kendal lecture taking good shape too—at last.—

September 17th [sic] — No—not yet—only 16th— continued to say there's a bird singing and *perfect sun on the hills.* Richters seasons[67] I think have chiefly helped me

September 17th Monday. — And when the month turns —how it seems to collapse to its end. — Up the Vecchio from the great Tarn,[68] yesterday—but curiously tired—and very languid this morning,—*which is as clear as crystal.* — Must get Fors off.

September 18th. Tuesday. I see I was terribly interrupted last week, and shall not be much better this. But five days ought to do a good lecture—and the rest diagrams.[69] *A heavenly morning—sweetest sun on my central peak* above the tarn[70]—the lake all calm enchantment.*

* The Eaglet.

66. Aubrey de Vere (see B.S).

67. The designs of Ludwig Richter (1803–84) in *The Lord's Prayer, Sunday,* and *The Seasons* "represent all that is simplest, purest, and happiest in human life, all that is most strengthening and comforting in nature and in religion," he would state in an Oxford lecture of 1883 (*Works, 33,* 285).

68. Probably Levers Water.

69. See the four diagrams (three in color) in *Works, 26,* Pl. 15.

70. Levers Water.

September 19th. A nice mess of diary,[71] this Wednesday morning, and my brains in a mess, too —no exercise yesterday and perpetual whirl of things to be thought of. *Divine misty morning, showing folded hills by their edges and calm lake below*

September 20th. Thursday. ENTIRELY CONFUSED IN HEAD after sleeping ill— a lovely morning— and I full of thoughts—as the spongy moss of streams—but all getting choked into bog. Yesterday Mallock[72] & Jamie[73]

September 22 Saturday quite bright, but I very languid after sick and threatening stomach attack in Yewdale, brought on by rowing hard after lunch and then getting a chill— Ate no dinner, and am languid now.

September 24. Monday. Yesterday a quite divine day, climbing on Yewdale Crag,—after being at quiet church and staying sacrament with Joanie—Mr Chapman[74] assuring the congregation that he told them his own conviction, in saying positively that Noah's deluge was universal

---

M[OSAIC LAW] Begin Mosaic Law again, today. Strangely—I open my diary at the very page, of the Ark, Moses' not Noahs! page 51, Broadlands, 22nd Oct[ober, 18]75, where the quoted XIII of Wisdom fits exactly my todays Fors.[75]

71. He had misdated the two preceding entries.

72. W. H. Mallock (see B.S.).

73. J. R. Anderson (see B.S.).

74. The Reverend Charles Chapman, Vicar of Coniston from 1870 until his death in 1905. See also Letters, VIII.

75. In the "Broadlands" Diary he had made notes on the Mosaic Law as he prepared to write his proposed *Life of Moses*. These notes, Mr. Dearden states, are scattered through the Diary from December 5, 1875, until April 30, 1876. The

M. Revise, then begin, with M[osaic Law] 1 here as in the former book, when I can.

1. Copy Broadlands p[age] 51, A–B [76]

Then

Egressus est post hec vir de domo Levi: et accepit uxorem stirpis sue, que concepit et peperit filium, et videns eum elegantem abscondit tribus mensibus.[77]

September 25. Tuesday. Pitch dark with grey fog and I can't see my blue lines[78] after yesterday the clearest, exquisitest day of warm sun and north wind—spent with Herdson[79] and Baxter[80] on the basalt crags after tiring myself to death with the new Fors.

A quite terrific dream in its extreme & prolonged sadness, a walk in waste country with feeling that I was never to work any more—and my mother in some strange way, now forgotten, though distinct when I woke, suffering with me,—was I believe wholly the *result of brain exhaustion with a little cold*—having

---

entry for October 22, 1875, on page 51 of this MS, contains a reference to the "Wisdom of Solomon XIII.I" (see *Diaries,* p. 867). In the October *Fors* of 1877, as he quotes at length from Plato's *Laws,* he notes: "Compare the Wisdom of Solomon, xiii.1–9," quoting these verses (see *Works, 29,* 227–29 and 229n.).

76. In the "Broadlands" Diary the entry for October 22, 1875, contains: "A. First article of St. G[eorge's] Creed. Believe in Almighty, i.e., in a Law. . . . ¶B. John Mill Liberty—nobody to be guided" (*Diaries,* pp. 566–67).

77. "And there went a man of the house of Levi, and took to wife a daughter of Levi. And the woman conceived, and bare a son: and when she saw him that he was a goodly child, she hid him three months" (Exod. 2:1–2).

78. The "Ledger" used for this Diary is marked by faint blue lines.

79. As coachman and head gardener, Dawson Herdson (d. 1899, aged 63) served his "beloved master" at Brantwood for 28 years.

80. By August 1876, traveling with Ruskin to Italy, Peter Baxter (d. 1918, age 73) had replaced Frederick Crawley as Ruskin's valet. Baxter cared for Ruskin to the last and then remained with the Severns as a "Steward." By 1886 he had a wife and four children in the Brantwood Lodge.

had to talk at dinner to Mr Geldart[81]—*and Joanies choking herself with her coffee*—all intensified by my having *taken an egg at tea on Sunday* and mixed with wine

September 26. Wednesday. A little better. Bright

M[OSAIC LAW] 2 His ark, fiscella [a little osier basket], was really a coracle [a boat of waterproofed basketwork]—a fruit-basket of rushes, such as Virgil weaves in the 10th Eclogue, singing,[82]—covered within and without with—what!

1. Oxford Lecture. Repeat from new elements,—all art—praise of greatness, by a great soul— To see that—to know ones self little— To *be* little, is the pleasure being modest—to be as a child. —Make everybody big— Frogs nothing to it—but also—the plague of Egypt—frogs and lice— Manchester & Thirlmere.

Frogs must live— Lice must live
Fools must live—[blank space]—ma foi
—je n'en vois pas la necessité

But, the Art schools training to make everybody clever! and to live by their cleverness

Froudes—You put it—Professor on your card.[83]

81. Probably the Reverend Edmund Geldart (1844–85), who was the minister of the Hope Street Unitarian Chapel in Liverpool from 1873–77. He then settled in Croydon, as pastor of the Free Christian Church until a year or two before his death.

82. "The verse was that I ow'd my suff'ring friend. / This while I sung, my sorrows I deceiv'd. / The bending Osiers into baskets weav'd" (trans. Dryden, 11.101–03).

83. A distinctly different plan was followed in the first Oxford lecture of the autumn series, delivered on November 6. He did, however, quietly make the point

September 27 Thursday. — Up sounding Goatwater seeing sheep on Dhu crag—in quite terrific places,[84]—and a twilight as I came down in the quiet air wholly supreme Then divine autumn twilight.

M[OSAIC LAW] 3 Kate[85] tells me she used constantly when a child, to make 'butterbaskets' as pretty as could be, of the bulrush.

If I am to go on with this, begin with first law, page 74 [presumably of Broadlands Diary]

September 28. Friday. Worse and worse falling behind giving up first one thing then another. Mr Tylor[86] came last night—*and our worst fog weather* spoils his view this morning

September 29. Saturday — Worse and worse. Fog,—confusion and discomfiture reigning everywhere. Fog now half hiding hills in dismallest steady way. Miss Herschel & Miss Marshall at lunch—nice, both.

September 30th. Sunday. — Overate myself—again like

that the health of Art consists in the humility of the artist" (*Works, 22,* 509; from "Readings in 'Modern Painters' ").

84. The Reverend F. A. Malleson (d. 1897, aged 78) recalls having walked up the Old Man with Ruskin "to view a group of remarkable rocks by the desolate, storm-beaten crags of Goat's Water, that saddest and loneliest of mountain tarns, which lies in the deep hollow between the mountain and its opening buttress, the Dow Crags"; he then speaks of "the bleak desolation, the terrible sublimity of the mountain tarn barriered in by its stupendous crags, amongst which lay those singular-looking, weather-beaten, and lightning-riven rocks which were the more immediate object of our visit." (See F. A. Malleson's "Essays and Comments," in his edition of John Ruskin, *The Lord's Prayer and the Church* [London, 1880], p. 51; see also Map B.)

Dow Crag, alternately Crags, is a corruption of the older, alternative form, "Dhu Crag" (Miss Gnosspelius comments)—*dhu* being the Gaelic word for *black,* "and these crabs are black enough."

85. Kate Mary Smith (see Mrs. R. T. Raven, B.S.).

86. Presumably Ruskin's devoted friend, the distinguished geologist Alfred Tylor (1824–84), of Carshalton.

an idiot, & villain—and had a bad night —one piece of its grotesque nightmare being that Joanie was playing at *chess with me—and forked me on* FIVE *pieces at once, and triumphed in it contemptuously* What a lesson, of the subtle power of evil.

October 4th. Thursday. Back in peace, after a dismal time of *illness and failure at Kendal.*[87] Kind people always and wonderful girls, the Wakefields—partly saddening me in envy of their father.

October 5th. Friday. *Poor Joanie fell ill before breakfast,* yesterday and my day was very woeful, and my days are too likely to be so, with her's, for a while[88]

October 6 Saturday. I have often felt more languid in power for work, but I think, never so languid in liking for it, as I do this morning, though after a sound sleep—and Joanie—thank God—better all yesterday a ⟨priceless relief⟩ to me.

October 8th Monday. — Yesterday a day of deep lessons to me— At ½ past three waked by Joanie's wailing,— then two hours of bitter grief and anxiety—ending with weary dark walk to meet the doctor—then—in another half hour—Joanie free

87. His lecture, delivered on October 1 at the Literary and Scientific Institute of Kendal (with the Wakefields in attendance), had nevertheless been a success, and he himself evidently thought well of it: on December 8 he redelivered it at Eton, "which ended my year's work satisfactorily and serviceably" (*Diaries,* p. 968); by July 1878 it was published in Part V of *Deucalion.*

88. On October 7, addressing George Allen (1832–1907), he explained: "Mrs. Severn got a fright, about two months ago, which left her permanently ailing,—and she over-fatigued herself last week, bringing on premature labour. The instant danger, thank God, is over, and the doctor says there will be no ultimate harm as far as he can judge. It has been good for *me* in making me feel what a comfort and blessing I had [sic] in her. She always behaves beautifully in illnesses" (unpublished letter; Columbia University Library).

of pain and thenceforward better into her gay self at end of day,—all matter of ⟨profoundest emotion to me.⟩ Today though after thankfully sweet sleep, much exhausted.

October 9th. Quite celestial frosty morning with the usual magic of level mist and breeze, gray white flakes of spiritual lake under amber hills. Indescribable—to me how useless, now that I can't paint nor care to see, the heavier cares of the world taking all that pleasure out of me

October 10th Wednesday Dark, with small rain I rheumatic—disconsolate, scornful of myself—more uncomfortable than ever yet —in fading interest in all things, but ⟨Joanie going on well, which is everything to me.⟩

October 11th. No, 12th it must be. Friday—utterly ashamed of slackness in work and thought, and thankfulness for Joanie's comfort and cure. Terrific storm yesterday with hail and wild rainbow this morning.

October 13 Saturday. Past seven—and dreadfully dark—crashing rain and frantic wind—*and the leaves rattling for entrance at the door, dead.* — Oh me, the Devil has his regular part in Heaven and Earth, as well as his usurped one.

October 14th Sunday. Very thankful for change between last Sunday morning and this. But the morning dreadfully dark, and the sense of gathering winter woful.

October 15th Monday. I never wrote diary with so little care or satisfaction, feeling how the useless mass accumulates—but must note this most terrific morning of rain with frantic N. W wind I have ever seen —dashing rain on my window simply in pailfuls, while the lake is covered with clouds of white down rising into columns and swirls, like thick white smoke, —and the *whole air bellowing like a bull.*

October 16th Tuesday. — Quite cold, and snow on Vecchio—russet fern and woods below, warm sunrise—bleak north wind. Chopping wood with Downes[89] very pleasantly, yesterday and Saturday and getting on.

October 17th Wednesday. Had fine chopping and burning in woods in lovely though cold afternoon. Arthur coming up to his first experiment playing on Harmonica. Also began model of old Man in the morning Bright today, with snow on top of him. Began Apocalypse again in my old 4° [quarto] new Test[ament].

October 19th Friday. *Miserable dark fog, and I cant see blue lines* Lost diary yesterday doing photographs but got some order into them. SKY. Susie. Oct[ober] 17th "How lovely the sky last night, it looked as if all the swan's down in the world had been shaken out into it and some of the clouds were *trimmed* with it round their edges["]

October 20th Saturday. Pouring steadily yesterday all day. Worked at letters with a will To-day, quite languid and stupid after dream of walking through deep boggy meadow, leaping ditch, and not being able to get up the other side

October 21. Sunday. Black—black—black—soot and

89. David Downs, alternately Downs (see B.S.).

rain mixed—and my own mind—in some ways like it. But got much in order and out of hand, yesterday. Can't possibly see to write. ½ past 7.

October 22 Monday. Wild rain—perpetual mist—flooded harbour—exquisite cascades—early dinner—idle afternoon—(yet put minerals in order)—and have more satisfaction in my cabinet than for the last two years—chiefly by clearing out.

October 23 Tuesday. Got lovely new silver and felspar last night—and an exquisite lesson in all ways *out of my old G[ree]k Testament, in 1st verse of II Apocalypse—read as spoken to myself.*[90]

— Such quaint dreams of beautiful old marketplaces and interesting houses going to be pulled down—and a nice one of Diddie. And the morning hitherto bright though misty.

October 25th. Thursday, I believe—shall be very glad if it's Wednesday—but got reading Apocalypse and forgot diary—finding out correspondence of *attribute with* MESSAGE in II Apoc[alypse]

(This must be done in a separate book—or in Fors.[)][91]

October 28th Sunday. Diary being given up a woful sign, and ½ seven for coffee—instead of seven—no morning bath— yet gaining

90. In the December *Fors Clavigera,* having presented "the charge" given to each of the angels of the Seven Churches in the Apocalypse, Ruskin begins his commentary: "Let us now read the charges in their detail, that we may understand them as they are given to ourselves" (*Works, 29,* 300.) The first charge in "II Apocalypse—read as spoken to myself" begins: "Unto the angel of the church of Ephesus write; These things saith he that holdeth the seven stars in his right hand, who walketh in the midst of the seven golden candlesticks; I know thy works, and thy labour, and thy patience, and how thou canst not bear them which are evil" (Rev. 2:1–2).

91. See the December *Fors Clavigera* (*Works, 29,* 298–300).

lately much in health & spirit and my work good, though little Terrible sleepless night however yesterday with many thoughts,—a lovely letter from Diddie beginning them— Ending in a wonderful dream of an old French gentleman of the high noblesse

October 29th. Monday. Half sleepless night again—and entirely disgusting dream, about men using flesh and bones, *hands of children especially,* for fuel—being out of wood and coals. I took a piece to put on someones fire, and found it the side of an animals face, with the jaw and teeth in it.

October 30th. Tuesday. — Got a good deal in nice order, yesterday—and my last Fors well begun. Slept better and there is some light in sky, but the evil wind is in it again *and I am numb and useless.*

October 31st. Wednesday — Pestered with the entirely accursed idiot, Peter Bayne,[92]—to loss of a day. Desperate gale

(I forget what this was, some book or letter of his.)[93]

The horriblest mad gale at night—keeping me awake— but down this morning to write my chalcedony article,[94] in some peace and sunlight

November 1st Thursday Slept well, and have had a lovely time reading Timothy '—rebuke with all authority—let no man de-

92. For Peter Bayne, see B.S.

93. This parenthesis, written at the bottom of the page, was evidently added in later years.

94. Possibly the "Chalcedony" section in his unfinished *Grammar of Silica* (*Works, 26,* 535–37).

spise thee[']—&c. and see my way all clear at Oxford at once[95]

November 2. Friday. My diary for this summer ends with much thanksgiving: yesterday All saints having been a day of singular good to me— pleasantest woodwork—pleasantest stone-work in Deucalion connected with it—successful paper from Winsor and Newton[96]—finish of Bewick 1st vol[ume][97]—and—best of all—in morning reading—of the IInd Titus verse[s] 11 to 15,[98] most precious in the Greek. — All this given me on the Ogni Santi[99]—and power of making Susie and Joanie very happy,—may well end diary in thankful peace.

November 4th Sunday. I stayed after all and did some

95. Here Ruskin quotes St. Paul's words to Titus, rather than to Timothy. Timothy was told: "These things command and teach. Let no man despise thy youth; but be thou an example of the believers. . . . Neglect not the gift that is in thee. . . . Take heed unto thyself, and unto the doctrine . . . for in doing this thou shalt both save thyself, and them that hear thee" (I Tim. 4:11–16). The theme developed in the pending Oxford lectures was the need to resist the "two parties [who] would divide this great university, of which the one would look with scorn upon Nature, and the other upon her Maker" (*Works, 22,* 512), and to embrace the ancient Christian faith, now "openly said" to be "a foolish dream" (*Works, 22,* 535). This thesis would be discursively supported by the explication of how his own thought had developed so that, in doctrine, what he now taught was in harmony with what he had maintained in his youth, especially in *Modern Painters, II.*

96. Viz. he liked the drawing paper supplied by the firm of Winsor and Newton.

97. His first edition of Thomas Bewick's *History of British Birds,* in two volumes (1797 and 1804), was given to St. George's Museum, Sheffield, with its first volume, on land birds, heavily annotated.

98. "For the grace of God that bringeth salvation hath appeared to all men, Teaching us that, denying ungodliness and worldly lusts, we should live soberly, righteously, and godly, in this present world; Looking for that blessed hope, and glorious appearing of the great God and our Saviour Jesus Christ; Who gave himself for us, that he might redeem us from all iniquity, and purify unto himself a peculiar people, zealous of good works. These things speak, and exhort, and rebuke with all authority. Let no man despise thee" (Tit. 2:11–15).

99. All Saints' Day, November 1.

finishing to Deucalion and trust to have yet this quiet day among precious stones and hills

1878

This section of the Diary begins with Ruskin's return to Brantwood after a notably successful course of Oxford lectures (*Readings in "Modern Painters"*: November 6—December 1), followed by three weeks of relaxation at Herne Hill, with a lecture at Eton and a visit at the Hilliards' home in Cowley. Then he returned to Oxford for the week of Christmas, followed by a weekend at Windsor Castle with Prince Leopold, after which he spent several days with the Gladstones at Hawarden. The final entry, of February 22, is followed by a blank page headed: "February. — to April — the Dream." The next page contains a brief record of various expenditures that marked the interim of April 23—July 1. For the remaining months of this year there is no more than a scattering of entries in two other manuscripts (see *Diaries,* pp. 976–77), supplemented by the "bit of diary in my first vol. of Bacon" noted in his entry for August 22 (*Diaries,* p. 976; see also Miscellaneous Entries, pp. 353–54).

Returning to Brantwood with Laurence Hilliard as his companion, he had two immediate objectives: the completion of Part II of *The Laws of Fésole*—"virtually done" before he left for Oxford, he had told George Allen (*Works, 37,* 227)—and of the Catalogue *Notes* for his Turner drawings to be exhibited, during March, in the Galleries of the Fine Art Society, London. Incidentally he was concerned because he had not yet issued, with a Preface, the notes on Carpaccio which James Reddie Anderson had prepared for his use. And there was always, to be sure, the "next" issue of *Fors* to get ready for George Allen.

When he picked up this work, he had no premonition that five weeks hence he would succumb to his first attack of insanity: "Back, after two months' and ten days' as good work as I've ever done," he had remarked in the last entry in the volume of the *Diaries* used while he was away (January 16, 1878; p. 975). "I and my work in more order than for some time" was his first comment as he turned to the volume used for the record of his life at Brantwood (January 17). Then, on February 8: "I ought to be very thankful to be down at 7 in the morning . . . in good active health, ready either for writing or for woodchopping, on my 59th birthday and with so much in my hands to do for everybody." Some years later, rereading his account of the walks taken on January 31 and February 1, he remarked that these entries were "very solemn warning not to over-rate appearances of strength—Only 21. days then before my mind totally failed" (see March 3, 1883).

Knowing that he needed "rest," he at first had refrained from putting pressure on himself. Nevertheless, by January 25 he could note: "got Fesole with 4 plates off yesterday," and "26th January, 1878" became the date of his Preface to J. R. Anderson's "The Place of Dragons" (chapter 11 of *St. Mark's Rest*). On February 1 he was writing his Preface to W. H. Harrison's *Notes and Reminiscences,* in response to Mrs. Harrison's request. By February 15 he was rounding out "The Snow Manger," to be issued in March as "Letter 87" of *Fors,* with the publisher announcing, as of February 26: "Professor Ruskin, who is at present lying dangerously ill—from prostration, caused by overwork—will not, until further notice, be able to issue 'Fors,' his medical advisors having ordered absolute rest for some time" (*Works, 29,* xxx).

Meanwhile, he had been arranging the 120 Turners scheduled for exhibition by March 1, upon the first 70 of which he had provided a substantial commentary: 13 editions (1,000 copies each) of these *Notes on Turner* appeared during 1878. The first edition, dated in manuscript "February 21, 1878" (*Works, 13,* 471), contained remarks (beginning with Drawing No. 85) which were evidently written on or after February 15 and reveal a slackening of intellectual control, with loss of critical acumen, as he penned forth a flow of freely associated ideas (see *Works, 13,* 399–401). Having reached the editor, in manuscript, by February 27, this Catalogue appeared with the following statement (retained through six editions): "In consequence of Mr. Ruskin's sudden and dangerous illness the latter portion of these Notes is presented in an incomplete state, and the Epilogue remains unwritten" (*Works, 13,* 394).

Here and there in the Diary, on and after February 9 one

catches a glimpse of the gathering cloud, as when (on the 10th) he notes a "depression of my total me—body and soul,—not in any great sadness, but in a mean, small—withered way." During his stay at Hawarden (January 11–14), while winning the love of Mary Gladstone through his suavity and wit (he could be masterful in his quiet use of irony), someone whose words were anonymously published—perhaps the Rt. Hon. George Wyndham—observed that though his "talk at dinner was altogether delightful," there was nevertheless "an utter hopelessness; a real, pure despair beneath the sunlight of his smile, and ringing through all he said. Why it does not wholly paralyze him I cannot make out" ("Extracts from an Old Journal," included in Ruskin's *Letters to M*[*ary*] *G*[*ladstone*] *&* *H*[*elen*] *G*[*ladstone*] [London and New York, 1903], p. 4). And despite his brave birthday-entry in the Diary, he had written "Jamie" on February 8: "Your letter does me most solemn kindness today. ¶I never needed it more, having got, somehow—into a stony and cold—or worse—muddy and poisoned—state of mind, which won't quit hold of me just now. All I can do is to hold on through foul or fair, but I am very thankful for your letter" (unpublished letter to J. R. Anderson; Baillie's Institution Library). By the 11th: "*I stop writing* [in the Diary], *and get dreaming, and the light gains—and the day, and it has, how much to do if it can*—AND A GREAT DEAL THAT IT MUST—EVEN IF IT CAN[']T!" At dawn, on the 12th, he was concluding his Introduction to the *Notes on Turner*:

> Morning breaks as I write, along those Coniston Fells, and the level mists, motionless, and grey beneath the rose of the moorlands, veil the lower woods, and the sleeping village, and the long lawns by the lake-shore.
>
> Oh, that some one had but told me, in my youth, when all my heart seemed to be set on these colours and clouds, that appear for a little while and then vanish away, how little my love for them would serve me, when the silence of the lawn and wood in the dews of the morning should be completed; and all my thoughts should be of those whom, by neither, I was to meet more! (*Works, 13,* 409–10)

"Down in dreamy scatterment & bewilderment—" was noted in his Diary on the morning of that day.

More and more, through the entries, one perceives "the Dream" closing in, although the pages filled with an increasingly uncontrolled flow of associated ideas (his profound agitation being frequently revealed, even to a lay reader, by the script) do not begin before his entry of the 17th. Yet by the 15th—as he himself wrote, for immediate publication—at "half-past seven morning" he was completing the March issue of *Fors,* "being in a dream state, and not knowing well what I [am] doing" (*Works, 29,* 374). Even so, Miss Susan Beever—ten days hence—would receive news of his illness with amazement: "*Never* did I see him so happy or so cheerful as on Sunday week [February 17]— Never did I so enjoy his conversation," she answered the announcement. "Almost his last words as he went away, were, 'I'm coming again very soon'—" (unpublished letter to Mrs. Severn, February 26, 1878; F. J. Sharp Collection. See also Miss Beever's letter to Ruskin, of February 23; Letters, IV).

What is signified by the entries from around February 15 through the 22d may be at least somewhat more clearly comprehended through such knowledge as can be gained about what he suffered during the weeks of delirium. As he would tell presumably Dr. George Harley (who became his physician in 1880), during that "Good Friday" night of February 22, he became "powerfully impressed" by the idea that he was about to be seized by the Devil, feeling also "convinced that the only way to meet him was to remain awake waiting for him all through the night, and combat him in a naked condition." He therefore took off his clothes, to spend the hours marching back and forth, in his nakedness, on the alert against his prospective opponent. At dawn, "wondering at the non-appearance of [the] expected visitor," he went to the window "to make sure that the feeble blue light really was the heralding of the grey dawn"—and as he reached out his hand "towards the window, a large black cat sprang forth from behind the mirror!" So "here at last" was "the foul fiend," to be seized and flung with "all my might and main against the floor. . . . ¶A dull thud—nothing more. . . . I had triumphed! Then, worn out with bodily fatigue, with walking and waiting and watching, my mind racked with ecstacy and anguish, my body benumbed with the bitter cold of a freezing February night, I threw myself upon the bed, all unconscious." There, in the morning, he was found, in prostration, bereft of reason (*Works, 38,* 172; "Mr. Ruskin's Illness Described by Himself, *British Medical Journal,* 1900").

Ever seeking to comprehend his own feelings and behavior and thereby to prevent the recurrence of such "mania," he would remark, in 1883: "Well—the first thing to be noted . . . is that in the first [illness] there was the great definite Vision of the contention with the Devil, and all the terror and horror of Hell—& physical death" (see February 2, 1883). More immediately, writing George Richmond, he observed: "The dream itself, though full of *merest* fantasy and madness in many respects, was on the WHOLE a sifting examination of me, by myself, on all the dark sides and in all the dark places; coupled with some passages of proud conceit enough; and other of great beauty and bright jest" (*Works, 37,* 246–47; letter of May 31, 1878). More specifically, this first illness was "one continued vision to me of my selfishnesses, prides, insolences, failures, written down day by day, it seemed to me, with reversed interpretation of all I had fondly thought done for others, as the mere foaming out of my own vanity" (*Works, 37,* 244; letter to the Reverend J. P. Faunthorpe, April 17, 1878). All three of the attacks which he had suffered before 1883 had taught him, he said, "the lessons . . . of contention between good and evil!" (see February 2, 1883).

For ten days it was uncertain whether, physically, he would survive, a chief danger being his refusal to take food (see letters from Dr. Parsons to Dr. Simon; Letters, XXXII). Mrs. Severn was summoned: "The only gleam of light is, that he should know you!" Miss Beever remarked in her letter of February 26. But such recognition as this did not continue. By the 26th Dr. Simon had also arrived, and he was to remain in attendance until March 11, with a return for ten days on April 18. "Last Thursday night [February 28] we gave up all hope," Mrs. Severn would write Norton, "—then he slept, and seemed better" (unpublished letter of March 3; Harvard University Library). "It seems as if the turning point was between twelve and one o'clock on Thursday night," George Richmond would observe (responding to a letter from Arthur Severn), "when Mr. Simon gave him the milk

&c. for at three you gave him the brandy 'and he said a word or two in his old way.' This is delightful and wonderfully encouraging" (unpublished letter of March 2, 1878; F. J. Sharp Collection). "The worst has now passed," Dr. Simon would write Norton on March 4. "There is not at present any immediate anxiety as regards the body; and the mind is, I think, gradually getting again into something like shape. What may be the degree of eventual recovery I cannot yet judge; but even at the best a long time must pass before there can be any return to such free life as would test his powers of safe self-management, and it would at present be mere dreaminess to speculate whether he will ever again hold his pen or pencil for any end of use or enjoyment" (unpublished passage in letter of March 4, 1878; Harvard University Library).

For a month this anxiety about his restoration to sanity remained almost unrelieved. On March 10 Dr. Acland, en route to Oxford after some days at Brantwood, was telling the Gladstones:

> I write to you, I own, simply or in large part as a relief to pent-up feelings which either did not exist or had no expression while I was with him. For now his mind is utterly gone. He cannot be rightly said to know anyone. He *raves,* in the same clear voice and exquisite inflection of tone, the most unmeaning words—modulating them now with sweet tenderness, now with fierceness like a chained eagle—short disconnected sentences, no one meaning anything, but beautiful to listen to for the mere sound, like the dashing of Niagara. It did not move me, though he would alternately strike at me and tenderly clasp my hands—once only giving almost certain sign of knowledge. To my question, "Did you expect to see me by your bed?" he answered in the most pathetic tone: "Yes, I expected you would come," and then no more light any more.
>
> . . . The hours spent with him seem to have added a new and solemn act to the whole drama of life; and though I looked on almost stolidly at the time and quite unmoved, I look back with a certain holy, strange awe at the mystery of a human soul displayed on earth; the deep, pathetic mystery of every human life.

> . . . I shall be back presently, God willing, at my daily work; may it be better done and more wisely and holily—and if I find I can yet help Ruskin, I shall go back again. (Mary G. Drew, *Catherine Gladstone* [London, 1919], pp. 161–63)

Ten days later, Mrs. Severn was writing Norton: "It is sometimes quite heart-breaking to see him as he is, rarely conscious—and then only for a minute at most" (unpublished letter of March 20, 1878; Harvard University Library). Now too, Mrs. Simon sent word: "He seems more *quiet,* and has ceased a way he had of *continually* clapping his hands—he still speaks beside the mark, but no longer repeats over and over again senseless formulae as he did at first; and John [Dr. Simon] thinks that all is as well as we could expect after such catastrophe" (unpublished letter to C. E. Norton, March 20, 1878; Harvard University Library). By the end of the month Mrs. Severn would confess: "a horrible dread still takes possession of me lest (this quite entre-nous) with returning bodily strength—his precious mind should not quite recover— his intervals of consciousness are always more or less, after a few minutes, so mixed up with delusions —and the sorrow and anxiety about him are sometimes quite heart-breaking— ¶He has a fair amount of food, and natural sleep—we only give chloral, when it seems a necessity" (unpublished letter to C. E. Norton, March 20, 1878; Harvard University Library).

The daily letters through which Mrs. Severn reported his condition to Dr. and Mrs. Simon after Dr. Simon's return to London are also a source of information about his delusions during the last half of March, when he believed that "the Queen" (presumably one aspect of his mother) wished to have him poisoned, decapitated, or shot and that treacherously his own "Doanie" (Joan) was serving as her agent. (See M. Spence, ed., *Dearest Mama Talbot* [London, 1966], p. 80; letter of March 14, 1878; and Sheila Birkenhead, *Illustrious Friends* [New York, 1965], pp. 262–67, for excerpts from this letter and others of the period.) After the death of his mother, "Doanie" had revealingly become the "Di Ma" ("Dear Mama") of the daily letter which, all through his life, he had been expected to write to his father and, after his father's death, more voluntarily to his mother, whenever he traveled. Now, petting and feeding him in his helplessness as though he were veritably her child, Mrs. Severn was uncomprehendingly bewildered to find that he responded to her maternity sometimes with reviling reproach and sometimes, most tenderly, with love. For example, she had just had "a good cry," she told Dr. Simon: "—it is so difficult *not to mind* when he speaks in a calm deliberate voice accusing me of the most dreadful things! saying he *knows* I am the cause of all this—& through *me* he has been poisoned—& he is lying dead in his coffin, as he holds my hand—& that I only *think* he is living—& that I have set everybody against him—& that I have killed him to get his house & property—it breaks my heart! & I implore him not to say such things—then he says, 'why cry now? its [sic] too late, too late'!" (Spence, p. 86; letter of March 27, 1878).

Subsequently, within the Diary, from time to time Ruskin would record his own fragmentary memories of what had happened while he "dreamed." Apparently forgetting that at one point he himself had been the target of cannon balls fired by the Queen, he wrote: "The notion of guns . . . was quite constant, through a part of the dream. (1878) I was shot, myself, twenty times over, and was attendant on a desperate artillery man who fired batteries of ball and grape into opera-houses and shot whole audiences dead at a discharge. I have greatly forgotten the long and complex tortures of this fancy" (see February 5, 1883).

He also would remember how, while he was ill, his dear friend Georgiana Jones had become a living presence as she played the role of "a continually protecting and—sometimes disagreeably Advising Matron' " (*Works, 37,* 247; letter to George Richmond, May 31, 1878). Ultimately, however, he would not let himself forget

> the great contest between the Devil and—Georgie! (who represented throughout the adverse queenly or even archangelic power,) for the Kingdom of the world. I dreamed that every seven thousand years it had to be run for in a chariot race—and that the Devil won always, because he knew some way of overlapping at the end of the last round, and counted the turns so that he always must win. This is the part that has

> got dim to me; but I thought that the secret had somehow become known to Georgie and that she raced him, and won. (See January 21, 1880)

John Ruskin, however, she could not help—first because she did not trust him when he said that he wanted "to get out of some enclosure or under some bar," and this "mistake brought on the misery—more and more—and it went on afterwards by her coming to disentangle me from some net, and my being forced to get entangled again—till she thought I was doing it on purpose, and left me indignantly and despairingly" (see January 30, 1880).

Less beneficently, the mother who had so memorably trained her child to accept her evangelical beliefs was probably adumbrated through the Bishops who aroused intense resentment after it was realized that in their teaching of the Bible they were false. Retrospectively, Ruskin believed that he himself had been victimized by such teaching. From his later point of view it had undermined the value of books (conspicuously, *Modern Painters, II*) which had incorporated his inevitable acceptance of what his own Mother-Bishop had taught. Next, this type of teaching agonizingly had helped to cost him Rose La Touche—obviously (and infuriatingly while, subtly, perhaps also appealingly?) in her religious beliefs a replica of his mother. Within "the dream," he would recall, as "the more or less ruling idea . . . two Bishops had been sent—after digging a hole for them—to the center of the earth," and "these Bishops had agreed . . . to bring up a false report in favour of Scripture," whereafter "the British mob having discovered this false report, was minded to lynch" them. They "thereupon secreted themselves somewhere—and became byewords of iniquity to be extinguished—so that the cry 'Bishop him'—became synonymous with that of Damn him, or Hang him—in the popular mind, and this went on till the very birds took up the cry—and sang 'Bishop him' at the dawn of morning at my window" (see January 15, 1880).

Much of the action within this episode, he continues,

> passed at the top, though more at the bottom of this episcopal pit— One most tormenting scene at its mouth—a deep funnel, was the election of a new Bishop by some kind of ballot at

> the bottom of it . . . I recollect only the emotions of a thrilling and passionate contest about it, in which two amiable women were chiefly eager and that they and I, and the right side people, were in some way cheated, and saw with astonishment and terror—(for some awful fate was at issue on the election—) an hypocrite & false Bishop ascend from the funnel and display himself at the top with bland assurance to the acceptant people as the elected one. (See January 16, 1880)

So far as is now known, he made only one direct reference to his father while he was ill: toward the end of March (as Mrs. Severn told Dr. Simon), he requested one of his attendants to hand him a drawing by Samuel Prout. When the man hesitated, Ruskin said: " '*that* one hanging beside my dear Father's portrait' —adding 'you know my father is in heaven, where I soon shall be!' " (Spence, *Dearest Mama Talbot,* p. 86; letter of March 27, 1878).

Self-reproachfully, after his recovery he would state: "the chief final result of that long Dream was a terrible impression of my failure in duty to my father, and of the pain I had caused him, and my best friends" (*Works, 37,* 246; letter to George Richmond, May 31, 1878). In the same vein, evidently when Dr. Simon was facing the loss of *his* father, Ruskin wrote:

> My dearest brother John.
> Jane [Mrs. Simon] tells me that the dark time when the great Honouring is to be no more possible but in memory, is coming to you—as it came—and remains for me—every day darker, since you first comforted me through the sudden stress of it [in 1864]—how little then I knew what its long weight would be. — But I have a thousand things to reproach and shame myself for, and mourn for in the pain they gave my father, with a grief far worse than shame—while you have only well done duty to him, and his unhindered and untormented pride in you, for the after-glow of your twilight time. (See letter of December 6, 1879; Letters, XXXVII)

In John James Ruskin he in reality had had an excessively demanding, as well as also, in some ways, a devotedly indulgent

Father, whose inner need for *self*-respect had been fed with unfailing bounty not only by the worship of his wife but also by the genius of "my Son." Yet this gifted son had always been treated as though he remained but a child who had increasingly become what might aptly be called this father's Beloved Fool. Ruskin had consequently been left hungering for the ultimate respect for his personal dignity, knowledge, and good judgment which he believed (rightly) that his Father did not grant. Eloquently enough, in 1873—having traveled to Oxford for a series of lectures, with Prince Leopold as a companion, he had commemorated his Father's birthday: "If he could have known that yesterday his son should have come down to Oxford—one of its most honoured teachers, and with one of the Princes of England. That his portrait would be over my door—and a Titian beside it" (Diary entry for May 9, 1873; see Miscellaneous Entries, p. 352). Until the death of John James he had spent his days in the performance of Filial Duty—forever meeting (as but one typically exasperating example) that Due Date which, regardless of his own need or desire and always primarily for the sake of the Father, had habitually been set for his *return* to Denmark Hill. Writing Henry Acland shortly after John James' death, he had succinctly expressed one of his deepest convictions: "But you never have had—nor with all your medical experience have you ever, probably, seen—the loss of a father who would have sacrificed his life for his son, and yet forced his son to sacrifice his life to him, and to sacrifice it in vain" (*Works, 36,* 471; letter of March 9, 1864). Therefore, if the ultimate "result of that long Dream" was to impress him with his failure in Duty to his Father, the profound resentment which he had harbored against John James—naturally with its counterpart of love—might readily have become a well-spring of the conflict between Hate and Love, or Evil and Good, as throughout the Dream his better self struggled, so helplessly, against the Fiend.

At one point his friend Dr. Henry Acland (by whose family Ruskin, always chirping, was called "Cricket") became an actor on the stage set by his delirium. Both as a devotedly admiring and protective friend and as a doctor wise in admonition, Sir Henry Acland (Regius Professor of Medicine, at Oxford) might appropriately have appeared, within the Dream, as an alternate for

John James Ruskin. "I . . . was entirely unconscious of Henry Acland's living presence at the time when I was most concerned with him in the Dream," Ruskin would tell George Richmond (*Works, 37,* 247; letter of May 31, 1878), having already informed Acland: "You had a large part in the play yourself, as an *entirely tiresome Incredulous* person! and it greatly puzzles me to find any clue to this persistent course of imagination" (*Works, 25,* xxviii; letter of May 1, 1878). Appropriately, too, while he was ill both Dr. Simon and Dr. Parsons became targets for his animosity.

That he had found his actual father a most tiresomely incredulous person he would indicate (citing chapter and verse) as soon as he had sufficiently recovered from his illness to complete the Epilogue to the *Notes* on his Turner drawings—dating this unit "10th May, 1878 / *Being my Father's birthday.*" Four days later he received Turner's *Pass of the Splügen* as a gift from the many who would thus express their joy over his recovery. All but spontaneously, £1,000 had been contributed with which to purchase the drawing. Hence, in the Epilogue, he gave a vividly detailed account of how, as a young man, he had lost this Turner because the Merchant-Father "was travelling for orders, and I had no authority to do anything." Instantly he had seen the *Splügen Pass* to be what in his opinion it remained—"the noblest Alpine drawing Turner had ever till then made." Available for only 80 guineas, it was bought by Munro of Novar, whereafter John James grumblingly but indulgently consoled his foolish and extravagant child by supervising their acquisition of a second choice. Next, for another 80 guineas, he was coaxed into buying a *Lucerne* for which, in later years, Ruskin found himself willing to accept a cheque for £1,000 (*Works, 13,* 480–81). ". . . humiliation,—resisted necessarily by a dangerous and lonely pride," was "the enduring calamity" under which he toiled, he would state when he was again able to address the readers of *Fors*: "and if any one ask me faithfully" what had caused the " 'wounds' of which that fire in the flesh came," he could "faithfully give the answer of Zechariah's silenced messenger, 'Those with which I was wounded in the house of my friends' " (*Works, 29,* 386; Letter 88, March 1880).

As his friend and physician, Dr. Simon was confident that

overwork had been the cause of collapse. Writing Norton, he remarked: "You know, without my telling it, all that has brought this dreadful disaster on him,—the utterly spendthrift way in which (with imagination less and less controlled by judgment) he has for these last years been at work with a dozen different irons in the fire—each enough to engage one average man's mind. And his emotions all the while as hard-worked as his intellect—they always blowing the bellows for its furnace. As I see what he has done, I wonder that he has not broken down long ago" (*Letters of John Ruskin to Charles Eliot Norton* [2 vols. Boston and New York, 1904], *2*, 146–47; letter of March 4, 1878). Against this diagnosis Ruskin (resuming *Fors*) would protest: "The doctors said that I went mad, this time two years ago, from overwork. I had not been working more than usual, and what was usual with me had become easy" (*Works, 29,* 386). More immediately, to Norton: "The doctors say it was overwork and worry, which is partly true and partly not. *Mere* overwork and worry might soon have ended me, but it would not have driven me crazy" (*Works, 37,* 252; letter of July 23, 1878)

He himself would reveal considerable insight as he attempted to determine *the* "cause." Sometimes, addressing those who were not close friends, he might casually refer to "that overwork illness" (*Works, 37,* 343; letter to F. J. Ellis, March 22, 1881). He was more likely, however, to ascribe variant causes, these being more closely interrelated than intercontradictory as he shifted in stress. Generalizing, he would eventually assert: "in every case these illnesses were brought on not by overwork, as many have supposed, but by acute mental suffering or misfortune" (*Works, 38,* 173; "Mr. Ruskin's Illness Described by Himself").

His explanations ranged from the highly personal to the relatively selfless. By June, in the *Notes* to his own "Handiwork," he remarked: "it is not the work, but the sorrowful interruptions of it, that overthrew me; and . . . [friends who suppose overwork to have been the cause of my recent illness] will now do me more grace by leaving me in quiet, to use in some consummation of purpose the materials collected during the last forty years, than by the most affectionate solicitude which requires me to answer letters, and divert my mind from the things it has hold of" (*Works,*

13, 502). But why should he have felt thus compulsively "required" to respond—as though he were still that Son to whom the long daily letter to a solicitous Father had been, for so many years, an interruptively distracting *must?* Factually speaking, the number of his surviving letters (thousands of which remain to be published) in union with their average length, is phenomenal.

Less personally, as he explained in 1880, "the illness which all but killed me two years ago, was not brought on by overwork, but by grief at the course of public affairs in England, and of affairs, public and private alike, in Venice [during his visit of 1876–77]; the distress of many an old and deeply regarded friend there among the humbler classes of the city being as necessary a consequence of the modern system of centralization, as the destruction of her ancient and religious buildings" (*Works, 24,* 412; from *Circular Respecting Memorial Studies of St. Mark's . . .*). Analogously, with reference to his work of around 1881: "I don't *anger* my soul nor vex my *own* heart, I relieve it, by all violent language. . . . ¶I *live* in chronic fury only softened by keeping wholly out of the reach of newspapers or men, and only to be at all relieved in its bad fits by studied expression" (*Works, 37,* 371; letter to the Reverend J. P. Faunthorpe, July 20, 1881). This type of "fury," less and less "studied" in expression, was what he had vented most freely in *Fors,* from the start. Hence he was referring to the very nature of *Fors Clavigera* rather than to "work," or labor in itself, when, in 1883, he rebuffed a correspondent who had suggested that he publish a book of extracts from *Fors*: "No indeed, you do not—nor ever did worry me: but if you remember that in these three years you have been waiting, I have been three times frantically mad for three months [sic] each time, you may forgive my not having turned,—when I got better, again to the work that drove me wild" (unpublished letter to Susanna A. Miller, July 18, 1883; Yale University Library).

Recognizing a connection between emotion and health, Ruskin had remarked in 1875, wisely enough: "But the emotions of indignation, grief, controversial anxiety and vanity, or hopeless, and therefore uncontending, scorn, are all of them as deadly to the body as poisonous air or polluted water; and when I reflect how much of the active part of my past life has been spent in these states,—I begin to ask myself, with somewhat pressing arithmetic, how much time is likely to be left me, at the age of fifty-six, to complete the various designs for which, until past fifty, I was merely gathering materials" (*Works, 26,* 95–96; Introduction to *Deucalion*).

More poignantly, as a "cause," there was the retreat into his personal past—signalized not least by his last words in the Introduction to the *Notes on [His] Drawings by Turner,* written as day dawned on February 12, with "all [his] thoughts" turning to those whom he would never "meet more!" (*Works, 13,* 410). Doubtless his thoughts had become particularly channeled toward the past through his recent course of lectures—the partly extemporized *Readings in "Modern Painters."* Prompting him to *re*-view his life and work, the series would inevitably have reactivated his memory both of old griefs, resentments, and discouragements (see, for example, the notes for "Lecture VI," in *Works, 22,* 523) and of old joys and companions. Still more intimately, such memories would have been evoked as he prepared the *Notes* on his Turner drawings, every one of which carried for him emotionally, to some degree, some special charge. These *Notes,* culminating in his exaggerative tribute to the Father *"who—though . . . he sometimes would not give me this, or that,—yet gave me not only all these drawings, but Brantwood—and all else"* (*Works, 13,* 485), were under way within a few days after his return to Brantwood (see January 20, 1878). Emerging from a second attack of the "delirium," he would tell Dr. Brown, of Edinburgh: "But *both* these illnesses [of 1878 and 1881] have been part of one and the same system of constant thought, far out of sight to the people about me, and, of course, getting more and more separated from me as *they* go on in the ways of the modern world, and I go back to live with my Father and my Mother and my Nurse, and one more,—all waiting for me in the Land of Leal" (*Works, 37,* 348; letter of March 29, 1881).

That grief over his loss of Rose La Touche as the "one more" was the precipitating cause of his collapse is indicated by statements which he made after his recovery and by references to her which pervade the final phase of his entries (February 14 ff.) in this unit of the Diary. In these entries, however, she is not often explicitly named, even though he may be recording a memory so specific as that of "the hymn said in my arms" (February 15). Nevertheless, she is recurrently present in the guise of one of her many counterparts—among others, for example, St. Ursula, St. Catherine of Bologna, Ruth, Joan of Arc, Proserpina, and "little Ophelia—who bewept to her grave did go" (February 17). Or she may be betokened by his references to some plant such as the fleur-de-lis or vervain, or to some print in which the rose is depicted, such as Richter's *Love Is Stronger than Death.*

He himself, writing Norton in retrospect, would half jest: "I went crazy about St. Ursula and the other saints,—chiefly young-lady saints. . . . But the doctors know nothing either of St. Ursula or St. Kate [i.e. St. Catherine of Bologna], or St. Lachesis —and not much of anything worth knowing" (*Works, 37,* 252; letter of July 23, 1878; for St. Lachesis, see ibid., *20,* 246: "by noble enchantment," she raised the island of Rhodes out of the sea for Apollo, "after he had been left without inheritance"—Rhodes being the birthplace of Athena, as Wisdom). In the same vein: "And, the fact is, these illnesses of mine have not been from overwork at all, but from over-excitement in particular directions of work. . . . The first time, it was a long piece of thought about St. Ursula" (*Works, 37,* 355; letter to C. E. Norton, April 26, 1881). Or, specifically, albeit too hopefully, when he assured Mrs. Severn that she need not "fear my ever over-exciting or tormenting myself again. And think what exciting work—what killing sorrow—I had [apropos of Rose], in 1872—1874—1875—and that, all after 1865–1866 of such bright hope [that she would become his wife]! . . . Think of it all, it was *those* things that made me ill—never my work" (*Works, 37,* 422; letter of November 28, 1882). Demented on the morning of the 21st, he announced, addressing their mutual friend George MacDonald: "We've got married—after all after all" (Derrick Leon, *Ruskin the Great Victorian* [London, 1949], p. 510).

Retrospectively, he would also discuss the manifestations of "Fors" as the "Chance" through which he believed that some supernal power provided personal guidance (often noted while he was making these entries) and that the spirit of Rose might communicate with him. As he explained, addressing Dr. John Brown of Edinburgh:

> The curious part about [any approach of the illness] is that there are always entirely separate conditions of accessory coincidence, which had increased the excitement, as for instance, when I perfectly well knew I was in some danger last September, and was most carefully watching myself, this illness always being primarily founded on too much thinking about my dead Rose,—suddenly one evening a letter came from a friend of long ago enclosing a drawing by R[ose] of a palm blossom, which of course made me think of all sorts of things, and in these dangerous times, my books always open, perhaps ten times during the day, at passages which strike back into the line of thought, no matter how apparently foreign to it the book may have been,—Punch, or Dante is all the same, they are sure to open like Sortes. Whereas, at present, and in times when I am fairly tranquil and safe, they never play me such tricks. (Unpublished letter of December 28, 1881; Yale University Library)

Interflowingly, there is the current of parental memories, expressed directly only after he has chanced to see his mother's watch "in the case I used to be so fond of," and when, through Susan Beever's prayer, he receives "my mother's part of the message," after which he spends some time pacing to and fro, in a favorite field, "thinking of my Father" (see February 17), finally to note, in the last words written on February 22, the time as told "by my Father's watch." But there are also references to the Edgeworthian morality and evangelical theology inculcated by his mother (see February 14)—whose "law," as thus impressed on him through interminable hours of religious indocrination, he had definitely forsaken and sometimes even mocked; and already, by February 17, the Devil is threatening to seize his soul. The two main motifs (marked, in progress, by eddying references to related characters and events) become harmoniously integrated through the transformations always wrought within the realm of "dream"—as when, for example, the major theme of Rose is fused with the parental theme by means of the Hamlet imagery, wherein Rose becomes transformed into Ophelia as he himself becomes identified with Hamlet and Laertes in their struggle with one another and against a King and Queen by whom a Son was initially betrayed.

Through the Diary entries made during the week that preceded his collapse, one finds him progressively approaching insanity as a rationally controlled daily account of his activities and thought is replaced by an increasingly full record, from day to day, of freely associated ideas which were evoked through the immediate process of writing. Nevertheless, these entries signify a stream of thought which flowed on the level of conscious knowledge while he was writing and which thus differs from the thought inaccessibly buried within his many accounts of what he had dreamed during hours of sleep or from the ideas which, somewhat more meaningfully, he would mistake for reality while he was insane. Because of this difference, the information which he himself presumably would have provided to explain each of these onflowing references becomes enlightening insofar as it can be supplied: hence the Supplementary Notes appended to this group on entries. If read with even a partial understanding of what the freely associated words and phrases signified, consciously, to him, these entries no longer sound like the mere ravings of a madman. Having reread them after his restoration to health, he obviously exaggerated when he asserted that the state of mind which they reveal was "entirely healthy." Apart from this conclusion, however, he could reasonably maintain, when he was able to resume the monthly publication of *Fors Clavigera*:

> For a physician's estimate of [the illness], I can only refer [friends and readers] to my physicians. But there are some conditions of it which I know better than they could: namely, first, the precise and sharp distinction between the state of morbid inflammation of brain which gave rise to false visions . . . and the not morbid, however dangerous, states of more or less excited temper, and too much quickened thought, which gradually led up to the illness, accelerating in action during the eight or ten days preceding the actual giving way of the brain . . . and yet, up to the transitional moment of

> the first hallucination, entirely healthy, and in the full sense of the word "sane." (*Works, 29,* 381–83; Fors Letter of March 1880)

Viewed as a manifestation of repressed emotion, this record of Ruskin's flight-of-thought can become absorbing in its eloquence and pathos, even while it becomes colored by the elements of pity and terror as one perceives the imminent defeat of his long effort to maintain an intellectual control over all by which he had been tormented, dating back and back into his earliest years of life. It is also revelatory that, as the subconscious gains ascendance, we should be companioned not by the ugly and the gross but, rather, by the beauty and the purity evoked by almost every reference he makes.

Having spent the last six days of February and the whole of March in madness, he surprised them all by making a remarkable recovery during the first week of April. On April 26, after ten days spent at Brantwood, Dr. Simon could tell Norton: "The convalescence has been more rapid than I expected—more like convalescence from severe fever-delirium than convalescence from mania; but it is not on that account the less satisfactory" (unpublished letter; Harvard University Library). For himself, making a Diary entry on June 18, Ruskin noted briefly: "On the 7th of April, this year, I got first down into my study, after illness such as I never thought to know. Joanie brought me through it" (*Diaries,* p. 976). For others, resuming *Fors Clavigera* to celebrate his birthday (February 8) in 1880, he would state, in his introductory discussion of this illness, that it was "Dr. Parsons of Hawkshead" who, never losing hope, "really carried me through" because only Dr. Parsons apprehended "that there *were* any mental wounds to be healed" (*Works, 29,* 382).

January 16. Wednesday, begins diary for spring, this year

January 17. Thursday Morning entirely divine and I and my work in more order than for some time Lolly in happy aid. Lake in sweetest variableness.

January 18. Friday. — Wet mist—and not much spirit in me,—lovely letter from Miss Gladstone[1]—and good letters from others mostly,—*must* be answered—and then I hope to get to my feathers.[2]

January 19th Saturday I don't like this not getting up till eight at all and it seems to put me out even with appetite. *Eyes very dim too* this morning Sky grey & cheerless table in litter after all my work at tidying, *brains in litter too.*

January 20. Sunday. Still letter writing only, and a bit of exhibition catalogue—great scramble to get up once more at 7,—but feel the better for it. Blank wretched fog these two days and rain now

January 21. Monday Yesterday walked from church up Tilberthwaite—and up ravine to the plain of bog under Weatherlam longing so much to get to work upon *things—cut all that bog out for peat, and have a lake instead*[3] Then to Thwaite and long talk with Susie

Then rowed home in bitter wind and dark. For a month after shortest day it is still very dismal, now at 7 still as black as pitch

January 22 Entirely overslept myself, Kate calling me at seven!—after windy night and restless sleep, till 3. Well, now, but eyes more dim than usual—

1. Mary Gladstone (see B.S. and Letters, xv).

2. Presumably illustrations for *The Laws of Fésole,* to be issued in July 1878 (see *Works, 15,* 406–11 and Pl. V).

3. Ruskin entered "Of Bog cultivation" in the index under *Projects.* "—It ought to be a long one—this article of Index!"

can't read Smiths Dic[tionary][4] even with spectacles by the candlelight, yet without them, see my blue lines here!—

Fine, at last after one unbroken black drench of storm all yesterday. Read vow of Nazarite[5]—all ceremony—no vow, very puzzling.

January 23. Wednesday. Up in time, wildest shrieking wind all night making me restless— Yesterday rain all afternoon—and only a little index[6] and letters done—but I am getting rest.

January 24 Thursday. Awake since 1/4 to 3 with *the most hellish—frantic, terrific* wind I've ever listened to, the climax of two days and nights perpetual black with sleet—one gleam of watery sunset for *five seconds, or perhaps—six 1/2—on the russet woods as Loll and I were chopping* The weather will neither let me see by day nor sleep by night Kate called me at 7.

Now to p[age] 155[7]

January 25 Friday. Shivery & languid, with snow all over the place,—but got Fesole with 4 plates off yesterday and good indexing done, and lot of nice wood chopped, but I think the cold wind was too much for me.

GALATIANS, 5th, finally shows in reference to circumcision that all the talk about 'the law' means only Jewish ceremonies, not the moral law at all—which is what St Paul calls the Spirit, developing *this* law from the 14th of Chapter 5, to the end.

This morning I write the following letter to Cardinal Manning.[8]

4. William Smith's *Dictionary of the Bible.*

5. Numbers 6—discussed in his first draft of the March *Fors,* dated "22nd Jan., 1878" (see *Works, 29,* 596).

6. Probably the annotated listing of his drawings for the exhibition *Catalogue.*

7. A reference added in later years (see entry for August 13, 1879, with its description of the "most terrific and horrible thunderstorm . . . I ever remember").

8. For Cardinal Manning, see B.S.

⟨My dear Lord Cardinal

It was a great joy to me to receive your letter, in all but that it told me you had been ill. There are few people now left for me in the world whose illness troubles me; yours does, both for my own heart's sake, and in its anxiety for the good of the Christian Church—(when does one get over that wicked foolishness of anxiety?)—which can ill spare you, it seems to me.

Yes,—that Oxford lecture in common with all I have written since 1875, means, what you desire it should; and that in the ultimate degree implied in what I am well assured you remember my once saying to you, that "no educated man could be a Christian, without also being a Catholic"—and yet, your Eminence's interpretation of that last word would be—is—so much other, (and so much narrower!) than mine, that I fear you are a long way yet from being able to rejoice over your 'piece which was lost.'

For, while my own hardness of heart, and folly, and sin do so hinder and blind me that I know not where I am nor what I do, and utterly forbid my speaking with any confidence of the higher truths of Christianity,—so far as I imagine myself to know these, or dare to speak of them, it seems to me that your Catholic Hierarchy is—to the Christian Church it governs, now, precisely what the Hierarchy of Caiaphas was to the Jewish Church, and that you are as a priestly order, leading it to its ruin,—desirous, at heart, the main body of you, only of your own power or prevalence in doctrine, and regardless, wholly, of the infinite multitude of your flock, who are perishing because you do not separate yourselves heroically from the rich, and powerful, and wicked, of this world; but entangle yourselves in their schemes, comply with their desires, and share with them in the spoils of the poor.

So that I believe the existing Hierarchies of Christianity must perish,—and the King Himself—in some way we dream not of, come to possess His people in peace.

Let me thank your Eminence once more from my heart for your kindness in thinking of me and pray you to believe me

Your Eminence's
Faithful & grateful serv^t. J R. (Full-signed [)])⟩[9]

January 26. Saturday

Above letter, beautifully written by Lolly, not a bad before-breakfast piece of work yesterday — Bitter cold & drifting snow all day—then thaw now bright moon and stars and *by my feeling frost, I take to the close fireside instead of my long table.*[10]

1883 — (An epoch in my life. I never went back to the long table.[)]

Read yesterday Mr Brassey on slavery[11]—conf Warwick rascals, for whose liberty the best connection with the earth would be that it should open and swallow them.

G. 2 GALATIANS, Above, p. 50.[12] The whole [of chapter 5 is] a pleading for the guidance of the Spirit against formal law, and for deliverance 'from this present world'

4. and that deliverance to be from the lusts of

9. Published in *Works, 37,* 240–41; transcribed into the Diary by Laurence Hilliard.

10. See *Works, 23,* Pl. B, for "Ruskin's Study at Brantwood," showing in the foreground the "long table" henceforth to be used for summer work and, near the fireplace, the small octagonal table to be used during the winter.

11. See Thomas Brassey, *On Work and Wages* (London, 1872), ed. Sir Arthur Helps. For letters to Ruskin from Sir Arthur, see Letters, XXI.

12. That is, see entry for January 25, in which he begins the commentary on Galatians 5. (Here and in the following entry he indicates marginally the number of his comment rather than of a chapter in Galatians.)

the Flesh, enslavers of all men. Then,—after Warwickshire slavery,—quote Brassey on the 'hospitality' to sailors and Scott on that of Scotchmen[13]

January 27. Sunday. Yesterday very lovely with bright snow & calm lake,—but got all grey at sunset, and is now pitch black, and raw cold. But got some good feather and Bewick[14] work done, and Froude[15] in evening

G 3. The morality of the whole then is to forbid totally

1. All lasciviousness,—V. 19, 21
2 Idolatry and witchcraft
3 Variance. Wrath. Strife
4 Seditions. Heresies
5 Envyings. Emulation
6 Hatred. Murder.
7 Drunkenness Revelling[16]

January 28. Monday. Yesterday utterly black and wet all day—thaw on the edge of frost, snow not lying, but sticking, about in the nastiest way

Got room well in order and lot of letters done

G. 4. The 6th Galatians terribly confused between "bear ye one another's burdens" and "every man shall bear his own burden." [17] There is no really making it out, the writing is utterly bad and unintelligible, but the fourth verse tenable,

13. Presumably ideas for an issue of *Fors Clavigera* which would not be written because of his pending illness.

14. He was probably at work on his drawing of the plumage of a peacock, to be used in *The Laws of Fésole*. "The execution of the plumage" in Thomas Bewick's *History of British Birds,* he had said, was "the most masterly thing ever yet done in wood-cutting" (*Works, 15,* 223).

15. In the *Fors* of March 1878 Ruskin directs readers to "the ninth chapter of Froude's *History of England,*" from which he quotes at length (*Works, 29,* 373–74).

16. "Now the works of the flesh are manifest, which are these; Adultery, fornication, uncleanness, lasciviousness, Idolatry, witchcraft, hatred, variance, emulations, wrath, strife, seditions, heresies, Envyings, murders, drunkenness, revellings, and such like" (Gal. 5:19–21).

17. Vv. 2 and 5.

anyhow—"let every man prove his own work"

And I think the meaning is that the blame of each others faults, we are to bear with them, as partly guilty of them, and to desire no praise in being better than they: but to prove our own work well to ourselves and win our *own* praise honestly.

January 29 Tuesday. Ive got a little rheumatism in right shoulder which fidgets me but am gaining strength and heart with my rest, very steddily (that first d is a, of course!) Lovely pure snow all over Helvellyn. Yesterday—went along road to see it—poor Dr Parsons[18] hunting for me in the wood

Slept all night sound came down at 7,—a gleam of light outside

G. 5. The sum of Galatians then is in the full history of St Pauls own conversion—of his quarrel with Peter;—and of the troublesome Jewish teachers with him;—then the too difficult passages about faith, and the full morality of the Spirit

E 1. Then Ephesians begin with what I never noticed before—the great chapter of praise to God the *Father*. Putting in capital H. always for the Him which refers to the Father, down to the hope of His calling, v. 18, the chapter becomes a totally changed thing[19]

January 30. Wednesday. Lovely dawn—rose & violet on snow—and quite clear and sweet day yesterday & good work on missals. —I sleep wonderfully well at present—though with disorderly and discreditable [dreams]—not tormenting but more or less dirty, degrading confused and useless

18. Dr. George Parsons (1849–1933) of Hawkshead, Ambleside, to whose insight as a physician Ruskin believed himself to have been particularly indebted (see *Works, 29,* 382, and Letters, XXXII).

19. In MS the following comment appears on the left-hand page: "Dec. 14th, 1880 I re-read and carry on the opposite entry [on Eph. 1]. Correct the holy & saints,—either must be one or other, v[erses] 1 and 4. Dispensation! to economy! v[erse] 10"

Suppose I try a little fasting! The older I grow, the less I like it.

E. 2 Then I have a quite new light on Ephes[ians] 2, 11 to end, today—the 'enmity' (v. 16) and throughout being that of Jew and Gentile not at all of God and Man! as one used to read carelessly

January 31. Thursday ⟨Yesterday had the divinest walk in snow since Saleve times[20]—hard and dry and rippled like the lake in its long wreaths beneath the grey rock ridges and their green mantlings of moss—and sunshine warm as summer—and air motionless lake a mirror

Found the exquisite farm under hill opposite me—nothing ever like it I think—then pleasant chat with Susie & row home—chess with Lol, his first victory.

Then—a most strange nightmare of overturning a great Sarcophagus down a hill in some ornamental Tuileries-like gardens, and sneaking away for fear of being caught—nobody else in the gardens for a mile—and then getting into an ugly town and not being able to support conversation properly! and always wondering when the police would come after me. Finishing off with being left by an express train without courage to get into the carriage, every one going faster and faster past me— Like these days of January,—but kind & grateful goodbye to them. They[']ve been good to me⟩[21]

February 1. Friday Yesterday up Vecchio in the snow, with quite cloudless sunshine all day,—only Whitehaven and Lancashire lost in smoke. Ive talked so much of it that I can't write— It was so still on the top that Loll sate on a stone and

20. August 1862 to June 1863, when he was living in Mornex, on the slope of Mont Salève.

21. Published in *Works, 25,* xxiv.

made a lovely drawing of icicles Slept entirely sound from 11 to 6 only with quaint dream of having to strip myself among a company of fashionable people, and they saying I was pretty well if I had'nt such a small navel, and my arguing that all pretty statues had small navels, and then *αιλη*[22] came and told me there was some stain or dirt on my shoulder. Ah me, if there was none any where else!

E[pistles] 3 E. may stand now for Epistles, for they must be taken together

Galatians, giving the spirit of Christ as against the law.

Ephesians The great hymn to the Father in Christ

Philippians, personal, rejoicing

Colossians, the sum and enforcement of Eph[esians] and Gal[atians].

Then Thessalonians are entirely comfort in the Resurrection

February 2. Saturday. — Down all right, after waking at ½ past 4, and sleeping again through a long St Gothard dream—mixed of sugary ice—where I was a little girl frightened at a sorcerer for a while, and running away along a hoarfrosty road, and then was with my father on the great Scheideck and could'nt see the Eiger for storm, till it came out apparently just overhead, and then down St Gothard somewhere, among horrible new hotels and railway lines, and had to take my mother into a table d'hote, very uncomfortable, and many other things *all so mixed and broken as I never had dream yet.* I had fair exercise too—chopping in quiet grey day and digging among the icicled ground

February 3. Sunday. Down after sound sleep, but with little

22. Mrs. Cowper-Temple (who in 1880 became Lady Mount-Temple), 1822–1901 (see Letters, xxx).

spirit—always oppressed with something that must be done for somebody, and at present, in spite of Bible study, getting more cold and dead than I've been for long. Sunday as much a dread to me as when I was a child

February 4. Monday. Late up getting room in order after two eggs at tea—and nothing worse at night than a dream of some head of a college dining with me, of my wearing a white surplice—which dropped under the table after dinner and got mixed up with my napkin, and of my just recollecting after the head of a college had departed that I had'nt given him any wine.

Slept well till ¼ to six, and feel up to work, generally. Yesterday got the great root out of the rock; and shaped a new chopping trunk under the holly mound

February 5. Tuesday. Late down. I think the eggs came into play the second day,—but there was bad fish at dinner, peasoup and pheasant—any how I had a horrid dream of being on a slope of crumbling earth above a chasm a thousand feet deep, with no way of moving visible but to fall—and woke with taste in mouth,—and all wrong. Now, the grey light coming, and I feel well enough but stupid for writing.

E 4, and St Paul little good to me, note however first his terrific interpretation of liberty = crucifixion, Gal[atians] V. 13,—24;[23] but in Ephesians, which is altogether exulting and rejoicing the figure is of resurrection and quickening from death, not crucifixion, but sitting in heavenly places. conf [Ephesians] II. 1—3, 6, 20,[24]

23. "For, brethren, ye have been called unto liberty; only use not liberty for an occasion to the flesh, but by love serve one another. . . . And they that are Christ's have crucified the flesh with the affections and lusts" (Gal. 5:13, 24).

24. "And you hath he quickened, who were dead in trespasses and sins; Wherein in time past ye walked according to the course of this world, according to the prince of the power of the air, the spirit that now worketh in the children of

and then all holy life is *renewal* IV. 23, 24[25]

February 6. Wednesday. Very languid and heavy this morning—damp fog outside, and damper fog in my own heart and head. — Chiefly from self indulgence and various victory of devil lately, I fancy. Yeterday called on Miss Melly and her mother —more pleased with both than I have been yet.

February 7. Thursday. Steady fog these three days and Lollie getting miserable and I in a curious state of dreaming all night long it seemed to me—one of sitting sketching at a door where an old woman wanted to get in and she asking timidly at the other side of the lane how to pass—and I getting up and putting all aside to let her pass, and quite spoiling my sketch afterwards,—could'nt put in some burnt sienna iron balcony rods—and another of being up and out for a long walk in early morning and seeing London in golden sunrise—but all vague—broken—meaningless

Next W. H. H. is 12.[26]

February 8. Friday I ought to be very ⟨thankful to be down at 7 in the morning or only 5 minutes later in good active health, ready either for writing or woodchopping, on my 59th birthday and with so much in my hands to do for everybody⟩[27]

---

disobedience: Among whom also we all had our conversation in times past in the lusts of our flesh, fulfilling the desires of the flesh and of the mind; and were by nature the children of wrath, even as others. . . . And [God, having quickened us together with Christ] hath raised us up together, and made us sit together in heavenly places in Christ Jesus. . . . And [ye therefore] are built upon the foundation of the apostles and prophets, Jesus Christ himself being the chief corner stone" (Eph. 2:1–3, 6, 20).

25. "And be renewed in the spirit of your mind; And that ye put on the new man, which after God is created in righteousness and true holiness" (Eph. 4:23–24).

26. Presumably he had finished 11 pages of his essay on William Henry Harrison (1808–74), "My First Editor." Undertaken in response to a request from Mrs. Harrison, this essay is dated February 1, 1878, to be issued in the *Dublin University Magazine* (April 1878) as a Preface to the serial publication of Harrison's *Notes and Reminiscenses.*

27. Published in *Works, 25,* xxiv.

February 9th Saturday. I think I never saw a more dismal 9th Feb. or had a stupider—not woful, but good-for-nothingly dismal walk round from Susie's, yesterday. Indeed the Waterhead with its outcast shore of straw, was wretched enough and I, was ⟨only *not* wretched, from being *weary with wretchedness* in thinking of old days, *so selfish—yet so happy—now I am kind, & sorrowful*⟩[28]

February 10th Sunday. Perpetual fog, and depression of my total me—body and soul,—not in any great sadness, but in a mean, small—withered way. Got room in order last night, and am up in fair trim, in the foggy morning. Lovely *letter from Jamie helped me, about the saints.*

Next W. H. H. 15

February 11th. Monday. Bright, pale marvellous calm on lake and hills, and I—for me, bright and calm—with loveliest loving letters coming to me ⟨*I stop writing, and get dreaming, and the light gains —and the day, and it has, how much—to do if it can*—AND A GREAT DEAL THAT IT MUST—EVEN IF IT CANT!⟩[29]

It was quite lovely all day, and I was out chopping in sunshine at 11

February 12 Tuesday.—⟨A day gained! Ive been thinking it was 13th. Down in dreamy scatterment & bewilderment—the horror of this Turk war—and shame of my own selfishness and faithlessness—heavily weighing on me. Yet I slept well and dreamed that αιλη wrote to me about R[ose]⟩[30]

February 13th. Wednesday. Overate and drank myself and had one of the old horrible bilious serpent dreams, —note also I had had much disgust and anger

28. Published ibid., xxv.

29. Published ibid.

30. Published ibid. The end of his Introduction to the *Notes* on his Turner drawings, for the March exhibition, is dated February 12.

and sitting "in cathedra pestilentiae" [31] all day. Lay awake, fighting thoughts, some time too, did some Fors—of a Spiritual nature!—which Ive got to write now.[32]

[February 14th][33] ST VALENTINE — and Ive had the Madonna for a Valentine! — Fors gave me her from the Beata Vigri—the first thing I set eyes on—and all her beauty in the Moon dawned on me as I looked— With another omen—the (for the present,) loss being left at Hawarden of my St C. Missal, which I take to mean—first rebuke, generally and second—that I must give up selfish thoughts—even of Heaven—

A lovely bit about Miss Edgeworth's morality and Pilgrims progress divinity

February 15. Friday. My Valentine has been on my chimney piece, with Solomon and the Queen of Sheba,—giving me no end of practical teaching about the uses of pictures, and the—police news—and my lecture—and Miss Edgeworth's Ormond, and the mystery of Morality— Above all—Carlyles lovely moral sense,—and the hymn said in

31. In *Rock Honeycomb* he had explained: "This throne of pride," which makes a man unkind, impatient, or intolerant, "is, in the Vulgate, called the throne of *Pestilence*" (*Works, 31,* 120; "Beatus qui . . . in cathedra pestilentiæ non sedit," Psa. 1:1). In the *Fors* which was now in progress, having pointed out the pettiness and vulgarity of Harriet Martineau "in her conceit," he observed: "I am getting into that Cathedra Pestilentiæ ['seat of the scornful'] again!" (*Works, 29,* 365).

32. Probably paragraphs 12–14 of the March *Fors,* developing the thesis: "If the Word of Christ be true, the facts of the physical universe are *not* steadfast. They are steadfast only for the infidel. . . . they ARE changed by human fancies, and by human follies (much more by human wisdom),— . . . the laws of the universe . . . WILL relax in the presence of human weakness, and DO give way under the pressure of human passion and force" (*Works, 29,* 370–71).

33. Thoughts of Rose La Touche (1848–75), followed by memories of his mother's teaching, are now recorded as he is threatened by the loss of rational control. See Supplementary Notes, p. 105.

An analogous flow of free associations, which invite a similar study, is to be found in Ruskin's entries for September 22–October 1, 1881 (*Diaries,* pp. 999–1005), although at this time he escaped the pending collapse until March 1882 (his third breakdown).

my arms. ⟨I *must* get to work,—or I shall get utterly—into dreamland.⟩[34]

February 16. Saturday. — Such a bewilderment as Santa Vigri sent me yesterday! and horrible fog, and all the devils doing their best against her! I never had such a day of good work[35]—of hard fighting, of need for prudence—patience—for — And what else!—should I expect? — because Ive never practised patience or prudence before—little wicked lamb that I've been—and now setting—sticking—taking—myself up for a knight!

Did I think I was to sit in that stall—yet not to watch my arms!

February 17. — Sunday. Stopped upstairs behind Kate to pray, a little—after "seeing my way" [36] at last at ½ past three this morning—with beata Vigris help—and Ophelias.— Let in—that out— Departed, never more

✠

The devil put a verse into my head just now — "let us not be desirous of *vain* glory." I am NOT oh Devil. I want useful Glory. — "provoking one another" — Oh Devil—cunning

34. Published in *Works, 25,* xxv. Read as a whole, the entry indicates how the copy of Carpaccio's *Solomon and Sheba* activated thoughts of the picture by Veronese which had precipitated the crisis of 1858 in Ruskin's thought about religion and morality, giving rise to questions recently answered, in Venice, through the help of St. Ursula as the counterpart, within his "vision," of Rose La Touche. Throughout this entry thoughts of Rose and of his mother (at one in their religious faith) continue to be interfused (see Supplementary Notes, p. 107).

35. On February 15 he had completed the March *Fors* (*Works, 29,* 374), after which he had resumed work on his Catalogue for the Turner Exhibition (*Works, 13,* 399). The last section of the March *Fors* is notably expressive, through its freely flowing associative technique, of the "dream state" in which he undertook to explicate certain proverbs of Solomon—significantly inclusive of the verses: "My son, hear the instruction of thy father, and forsake not the law of thy mother: For they shall be an ornament of grace unto thy head, and chains about thy neck" (Prov. 1:8–9).

36. He had seen his way into "giving up all [his] Turners for the Tredegar people" (see entry for February 21).

Devil—do you think I want to provoke Beata Vigri and little Ophelia then—? [37]

I will—pro—voke—Somebody else, God willing "to day" and to purpose.[38]

And Bishop Laertes,—you had as lief take your fingers from my throat— The Devil will not take my soul, yet a while— Also—look you —and also looking other [things may be at YOUR throat before long.] [39] (Thou pray'st not well—even by your own account and the Devil will not answer you therefore[)] and least said is soonest mended—for—if up when the scuffle comes—the foils should be Sheffield whettles— it is dangerous work—Laertes—'very'—as Mr Jingle said,[40] even the public press & Mr Jingle will advise you of that.

Public press Mr Jingle, in then! and St George of England both

Advise you of that.

"Forty thousand brothers" Yes, and sisters too, and I have a few—in Heaven—besides little Ophelia—who bewept to her grave did go, larded all with sweet flowers.

Walking about the room, and thinking—after writing the opposite page[41] I pick up little Lily's "nice little nest with birds in it" and put

37. Now identified with Ophelia, Rose La Touche apparently can still evoke thoughts to be denounced as having been instigated by the Devil (see Supplementary Notes, p. 107).

38. In the MS an arrow directs the reader to the writing which fills the opposite (left-hand) page, whereon the loosely governed script in itself sufficiently reveals the receding intellectual control.

39. In MS the bracketed words are deleted by a straight line.

40. The voluble and inconsecutive "stroller," Mr. Alfred Jingle, of *Pickwick Papers,* whose remarks are tagged "very." Here, between lines and down the margin, Ruskin scrawled, reiteratively: "Dangerous work—Very—Laertes—very Dangerous work, Laertes, very—."

41. In MS the handwriting becomes far more controlled as he returns to the right-hand page, and the script remains relatively unagitated until he reaches the second half of the entry for February 22.

it away in my drawer of precious things, with Wisies violets.[42]

Putting it into the drawer I come on my mothers watch in the case I used to be so fond of. What o clock is it?

Six minutes to 12—and a few seconds over—as far as I can see with my magnifying glass—my old eyes wont. — Oh yes the second-hand— — (Second! life) twenty one seconds. — Time — Twice and a half time or so. I[']m wasting it—Devil puts me in mind of Iachimo—Imogene dear—& the mole cinq spotted—[43] we'll beat him, wont we?

Course of the day. Write letters till ½ past 11—get them all finished—rise and see the sun on snowdrops— Then gather, the one beside me, from cluster on lawn nearest the house—finding a perfect fence of them all round the front wall of the house—along it, I mean. Then go out and cut down the useless chopping blocks, in the sweet calm sun. Find rose tree with its fruit, and leave tree to support it. Come in to lunch after going round by fishpond. Kate rang the bell for dinner I called down to her, I wished she could ring it for the Tre-garden-people, too, (meaning Tredegar)[44] She did not quite hear—said—shall I ring it at the back door Sir. "Yes Kate by all means.["] So she went and rang it loud towards the south.

I, laughing, as I laughed at Jamies St Je-

42. Probably he placed a "drawing" given him by little Lily Severn with some portrayal of violets once given him by Emily La Touche, as "Wisie."

43. He has now envisaged the scene in which Iachimo observes the breast of the sleeping Imogene, with its "mole cinque-spotted, like the crimson drops / I' th' bottom of a cowslip . . ." (*Cymbeline,* II.2).

44. Within a week he had received a letter, quoted as part of the finale of the March *Fors,* in which a clergyman, the brother of a Coniston friend, described the desperate destitution of the ironworkers in Tredegar, Monmouthshire (see *Works, 29,* 378–79). By now, in this old mining town, the ironworks were almost at a standstill because of foreign competition.

rome,[45] said grace. Then—dinner lunch— Pea-soup, broiled—(fried) herrings. Loll tells me statistics of herrings (—7 times as much food as people want?)

I finish a letter or two— He then Lollie rows me over the lake to the Thwaite. Wind with us. — Susie at the Thwaite gives me a birthday book to write in for her I write, having taken my pen in my breast pocket[46] and Monks[47] letter on purpose.

Susie repeats to me her prayer for the Jews.[48]

I perceive this to be my mother's part of the message.

I return, walking by the Waterhead. There I pause and am puzzled by storm in the grey air and evil clouds. I look at the water awhile, can't make it out. Go on at last, doubting not to understand afterwards.

As I passed Jacksons,[49] thought I would call on him. Called and made him and his wife happier.

Arrived at home a little after six. Felt I was too soon—didn't want to come in. Went in—found tea was'nt till 7,—went out again—up to little garden in the twilight across the bridge,

45. For J. R. Anderson's belief, which Ruskin endorsed, that Carpaccio's *St. Jerome in His Study* is intended to represent the joyous life of St. Jerome in Heaven, see *St. Mark's Rest,* with Ruskin's tempered comment: "I was myself brought entirely to pause of happy wonder when first my friend showed me the lessons hidden in these pictures" (*Works, 24,* 356).

46. Evidently in honor of Miss Beever's birthday, he was equipped with the silver pen with which Sir Walter Scott had written the Waverley novels. Scott had given this pen to Maria Edgeworth; Maria Edgeworth's niece, Mrs. Arthur Gray Butler of Oxford, had loaned it to Ruskin.

47. Henry Wentworth Monk (see B.S.).

48. Repeating her prayer (whatever it may have been), Susan Beever doubtless remembered that Ruskin's prayer for "all Jews, Turks, infidels and heretics" was that God would make them "honest." "But I pray that prayer for myself as well as others" (*Works, 27,* 547; from *Fors Clavigera,* June 1873).

49. Lachial Jackson, who lived at How Head (see Map B), served as the "Outdoors Steward" of Brantwood, where he cultivated memorable rhubarb.

down to terrace of great garden— To and fro there a little. Down to the gate and up again—after standing at the gate, (wishing gate) and saying the Lords prayer— Went up then into my field—to and fro there, thinking of my Father.

Down into the road. Saw light of moonrise. Walked to end of lower field—& back to Lodge

Called on Baxter. Found him reading the Bible by a little lamp Sent him to call his wife. Took Bible to lamp. Found it at Matthew XI, first verse.[50] Went home, ordered honey for tea Heard Pallmall Gazette read and marked it. Played a game of Chess with Lollie. — As it ended, exactly at the last move, Mr Gould [51] came in. A young man had preached—not Mr Howells. I asked him what the text was.

"Who is this that cometh up out of the Wilderness, leaning upon her beloved." [52]

✠

And now, ten, I must finish my letters.

February 18 Monday, writing with my own pen now, but much more than—the world could contain, to say with it.

— Must get to plain business— Kate tells me about northern and southern bread, to begin with.[53] I lay awake after writing till 12—till 3,

50. "And it came to pass, when Jesus had made an end of commanding his twelve disciples, he departed thence to teach and to preach in their cities."

51. David Gould (d. 1916) of Ambleside was an assistant now engaged in coloring engravings and photographs of details from Carpaccio.

52. S. of Sol. 8:5.

53. Kate doubtless was explaining why "northern" and "southern" bread differed in lightness and in whiteness, the degree of difference (Miss Gnosspelius explains) being determined by the amount of gluten left in the meal after the milling process. In a highly self-respecting "southern" household, such as that of Ruskin's mother, a Kate would probably have used the most highly refined, pure white flour of corn (or wheat) when she baked bread, whereas now, even at Brantwood, she might well have been using the coarser, darker. less expensive "household" flour ground in

I fancy—meditating in night watches, but fell asleep at last, my snowdrop[54] and the Jerusalem by Turner—Pool,[55] and Monks letter on chimney piece first things I saw in the morning Now, rainy sweet clouds on the fells and blue above,—six minutes past seven by my Father's watch.

February 19th.[56] Tuesday. — Woke at ½ past 4, and all the calling of names came into my head—and the Swans by sweet St Mary's lake, — and I said—Good God—in exclamation at the float double — seeing *my* bit, anyhow—of Solomon and Sheba and Miss Melly's cygnets[57]—and now—this with Sir Walters pen again I must put it all down as fast as I can— First though—thanking for my two (Fors anda R[ose]) texts, 'today'—and Now—Usury, & the pigs head and why I changed— Today if Ye will hear his voice— Oh me— And the seal on Chalcedony—and the Kettle and Geysers and boiling over and not boiling— I got all that too—besides the names, this morning and had all but forgotten it till the seal brought it back

Finally, St Pauls own text to me 'today'—

---

local mills—at Broughton, perhaps, or Kendal. Differences in the quality of flour would particularly have interested Ruskin, with his proposal that a "pound of bread" be adopted as a standard of currency (*Works, 29,* 579).

54. For Ruskin the snowdrop, in its "abundance and brightness," had become the emblem of humility, especially in the Christian faith; it "is the Amaryllid, the field-lily of the Christian; literally the 'clothed grass of the field'" (*Works, 21,* 116–17)—"which to day is and to morrow is cast into the oven" (Matt. 6:30).

55. Presumably *Jerusalem: The Pool of Bethesda,* made for *Finden's Bible* to illustrate John 5:1–9 (describing the halt and blind gathered around the Pool of Healing).

56. At this point the chain of references becomes predominantly a series of free associations rather than a rationally controlled development of thought. For the meaning of his remarks, with their emotional implications and interrelatedness, see Supplementary Notes.

57. Mrs. Andre Melly, who now lived at Lanehead with her daughter, was something of a farmer, keeping fowls and the like—hence Ruskin's reference to her daughter's "cygnets."

reading my bit of Galatians that all things may be done decently and in order—is Gal[atians] III, 28 Yes—St Paul—yes,—but—you *are* a little hasty and confused sometimes you know—you don't mean we shan't know which is which? (for I should'nt like THAT at all—I[']m sure —) I[']m an Englishman,—and you're a Jew you know,—still—an't you now? ——

Evening. In my study, with St Ursula in front of me, the token snowdrops—violets, maidenhair fern and fleur-de-lys, sent me by Susie from Wisie—and Joan of France— On my right hand, these; then, Dantes font stone—the Angel of the Law just behind— I find, yesterday, I made a mistake—and the message was not from St Paul but from the ἀγαπητος, and is,—his last message.

John III, 14
Amen.

February 20*th.* Wednesday. Down a little late— Wisies violets and Jeannes fleur-de-lys, (dark fleur-de-lys)—kept me awake nearly all night—teaching me.

First—the meaning of the bit of "blasphemy" I had to take out of the first volume. Then—of Turner's last two pictures—which no mortal could understand—(Exile & Rock limpet, I did —but [1] Moses and [2] the Visit beat *me*, till now—"tonight," I mean.) Then Worums and my first necromancy!

Then—messages one after another crowding in—so fast—so innumerably— Titania—and Bottom the Weaver and the Kier at Thirlmere ("Remarkable passages in Shakespeare" lying on my toilet table) — Horace St Mary's hall, — Polly* put the kettle on *(The little beauty from Cheshire must go with Polly)—Flo—Flo

—Flo— Telegraph Post. — Talk about Astrology and Horace.

"When itie pigs have muffins hot."

Ever so much more—which I must not stop now to remember—but try the Spirits whether they be of God, with patience.

"Soft. No Haste."
"The Jew shall have all"
"Justice"

Dreadfully tired—but trying to do everything decently and in order I wrote as opposite, and then read my bit of Galatians, which Fors gave me—as Ive dated it.

February 21. The 20th — 2 X 10— I shall have a good deal to do with decimals, I fancy in keeping the accounts in my house—at New-bridge.

Up, like Sir Charles Grandison.

Stayed up a little though after dressing deliberately—as on the 17th— I read the entry at p[age] 63 and forgot *how* I saw my way! — but certainly in one thing—to giving up all my Turners for the Tredegar people, — leaving my nets.

Last night—went to sleep after looking over the Furs Haus Fruhling— getting "I am the Resurrection," and the flight of angels, and the Mi-Himmel. Lolly gave me (from another number,) the "time of Roses" saying—it would be difficult to get *you* round *that* corner.

I wasn't so happy in thought as I expected to be, — got for text in daybook, Enter ye in— R[ose] of course—did'nt say that—it was said to both of us. R[ose] very quiet—saying nothing it seemed to me I fell asleep—woke at 3— Understood by thinking—that even in the Heavenly love—when the first time is—and thoughts meet thoughts Tobias prayer is still true.

Lay awake I fancy till about 5 thinking of messages. Then fell asleep and dreamed of a beautiful restoration of a cathedral gate. Woke at six exactly,—got up,—was going to dress without fire—but got taught that that would be ascetic—not happy. Bathed nicely, and got dressed in nice time but only just. Rain clouds on hills blue sky breaking.

February 22nd. Fors text kept open by Pallmall,—no—I kept it open—(the Bible) all night long at II Timothy 3, with the Pallmall Gazette in it and on my dressing table—with it—my box-bible with the Cardinal binding;—my present from Jamie, and Susie's Shakespeare.

On my little dressing table—by my head, Richters Love is stronger than death.

— With all I've left there.

— And on my chimney piece, Turners Jerusalem—and Blake's Ruth. Left there also

Now,—opening by Fors, I get John III.3 and read on to—wrought in God,—but hastily, knowing it by heart leaning a little selfishly on "How can a man be born when he is old?"

— Too much to write. — I don't think I shall forget—the chief message to myself as a painter, coming after a Sculptor.

• Delphi first. Then Ægina •
• Behind Carpaccio •

February 22. [continued] *Good* Friday

Recollected all about message from Rosie to me as I was drawing on the scaffolding in St Georges Chapel— My saying I would serve her to the death—

Tonight—(last night)—lying awake—came—Ada with the Golden Hair.

1 —Can the Devil *speak truth* (confer letter to Francie about her little feet.)

and 2 If that thou beest a devil &c. connected with, (Made wanton— &c. the night with her)

To Burne-Jones. — Oh, my Black Prince— and they take you for one of the firm of Brown —&c.— See Brown, &c. away on Lago Maggiore—

Tintoret—⟨Sempre si fa il Mare Maggiore⟩

To Connie— Oh Connie—did'nt we quarrel among the Alpine Roses, and make it up again by the moonlight.

— And was'nt I naughty sometimes!—and do you recollect bidding me go *before* you, at Verona? Ask Rosie to make your back better *She* knows something about backs.

— To Madge. Oh, Madge—so do *you* don't you, but why do you ever play with darling old Vulgar Baxter —see opposite

darling old vulgar Baxter—(and our American cousin—)—: Baxter did so spoil that loveliest part of yours—Madge,—when you made somebody so jealous, and had to go away again —you naughty lamb of a Madge.

To Joseph Severn— Keats—Endymion— quenched in the Chaste beams— yes—oh yes— Proserpina mine. I have not looked back, nor took my hand from the Jason plough.

And when Gold and Gems adorn the plough! Oh—you dear Blake—and so mad too—

Do you know what Titians good for *now* you stupid thing?

I did'nt know where to go on—but don't think I should stop. — And Andrea Gritti— then? quite unholy is he, you stupid? And Dandolo then, I suppose? and the Blind Guide that had celestial light? Yes—and you barefoot Scotch lassies—Diddie and all of you you dears — —if only you *would* go barefoot a bit, in the streets So pretty—so pretty.

Naked foot,
That shines like snow—and falls on earth—
or gold—as mute.

Oh—dear doge Selvo, I want to know the shape of your cap, terribly. I dont know which is best—yours—or Gritti's. — Tell me all about it—Raphael dear—from the angle then and pleas[e] angel of the lagoons from the Paradise —tell me what my own sweet Tintoret meant by those— Yes

"Send for the lady to the Sagittary."

⟨And praise be to thee—oh God. We praise thee Oh God, we acknowledge thee to be the Lord.⟩

Finished, and my letter from 'Piero' my Venetian gondolier put it in, here, and all. I am going to lock up with the Horses of St Marks. ¼ to one (20 minutes [)] by my Father's watch—22nd February 1878*

*I couldn't find the key and then remembered I had not thanked the dear Greek Princess—nor Athena of the Dew—and Athena κεραμιτς

February, — to April — the Dream[58]
[heading of a blank page]

April 23 Sent Mrs Talbot's cheque of date Feb[ruary] 6th for 100 pounds, to Union bank, in part payment of my disbursement of 132 pounds for Mr

58. The page headed by this entry is left eloquently blank. They had found him demented on the morning of February 23. In February 1880, when he resumed his work upon *Fors Clavigera,* he would say that he had looked back "in my diary for the place where it had broken off before my illness" and had found it "full of notes for next intended Fors" (unpublished passage written as part of the first draft of Letter 88, issued in March 1880; F. J. Sharp Collection).

	Small's picture for the Sheffield Museum. Returned for endorsement sent again on 1st			
May 1st	Allen's,	31	10	
	for drawings of my own[59]			
May 1st	Mrs Browne	100	0	0
May 1st	Mr Kingsley	3	0	0
May 15th	Susie			
	from Frondes. 8. 11. 6	9	12	6
	Her own Sub[n]. 1 1			
June 11th	By Post Order to Oxford	5	0	0
	Louisa Stephens, for her sister			
June 11th	by post-order to Coniston		10	
	J. T. Rowlands			
July 1st	Memoranda of cash in petty cash drawer			
	Ada Hartnell	5		
	Margaret Cox	5		
	Miss Colenso	2	8	
		12	8	0

59. Opposite each entry, on the left-hand page, Ruskin notes that each sum was a "G[uild]" expenditure, except the May 1 payment to George Allen, which was charged to "R[uskin]." The picture referred to in the entry for April 23 is William Small's water-color *The Shipwreck,* "a replica of an oil-picture which was exhibited in Royal Academy of 1876" (*Works, 30,* 249). Mrs. G. T. Talbot was the Companion of St. George who, in 1874, had given to the Guild "eight cottages, on freehold land, at Barmouth" (ibid.). The other names in this group of entries either have been annotated elsewhere (see Index) or are those of friends of St. George's Guild who remain unidentified.

[February 14]

Beata Vigri. Vigri was the family name of the only woman painter ever canonized—St. Catherine of Bologna (1413–63). "I have just had help from the Beata Vigri at Venice, who sent me her own picture and St. Catherine's, yesterday, for a Valentine," Ruskin remarks in the March *Fors* (*Works, 29,* 374). He had evidently received from Mrs. Henry Goodwin the copy she had made of Caterina Vigri's *St. Ursula*: "St. Ursula with four saints; the nun, Caterina Vigri, who painted the picture, at her feet" (*Works, 30,* 356).

The Gladstones would remember how, in January, showing them three of his St. Ursula (signifying Rose La Touche) drawings from Carpaccio, he had told them "of her loveliness and radiant purity and holiness; and how she died ere she should wed the rude English king who wooed her" (*Letters to M. G. & H. G.*, p. 19). Long ago he also had told the George MacDonalds that, in character, Rose La Touche was "so like St. Catherine of Bologna" (Greville MacDonald, *Reminiscences of a Specialist* [London, 1950], p. 110)—a remark he would repeat in a letter to Mary Gladstone. The likeness of Rose and of this St. Catherine, as personalities, was in fact striking; see, for example, "Caterina Dei Vigri, The Nun," in Laura M. Ragg, *The Women Artists of Bologna* (London, 1907).

St. C. Missal. "Ruskin used the word 'missal' loosely to describe almost any medieval liturgical manuscript," Mr. Dearden comments, in a letter to the editor. "This 'missal' was evidently a 15th century Book of Hours which Ruskin had given Rose La Touche and which, after her death, was presumably returned to him with his letters to her and with two other MSS she had received from him as gifts. Although its present whereabouts is not known, in an unpublished letter of 20 March, 1888 (at Bembridge) Ruskin told Mrs. Severn that he had been to the village of Lyminge, near Sandgate, 'to present Rosie's St C. missal [sic] to the shrine of Queen Bertha' as 'a thank offering not to Bertha herself—but to

St Ethelburga of Lyminge.' In this letter he speaks of the 'interpolated letters St C in the calendar of the manuscript—a reference which positively identifies the 'St C. missal' with the 'missal of the fifteenth century, dear to me because of some writing in its calendar by a friend' (*Works, 28,* lxviii). The 'St C.'—signifying John Ruskin as St. Chrysostom (the 'Golden-mouthed'), alternately St. Crumpet—may have been written in the calendar for 8 February (Ruskin's birthday). This 'St C. missal' is listed as No. 63 in my Catalogue of Ruskin's illuminated manuscripts (The Bibliographical Society, 1966)." It is shown in Alexander Macdonald's 1881 drawing of Ruskin's study: "the smaller book is my most valued of all, which has my St C initials written in its calendar—not by me" (Spence, *Dearest Mama Talbot,* p. 109; see also *Works, 23,* xxviii, Pl. B).

Miss Edgeworth's morality. Directing her son's education during early years, Margaret Ruskin (1781–1871) had manifestly followed the precepts of Maria Edgeworth, especially as these had been presented in *Practical Education.* In the Epilogue to the *Notes on [his own] Drawings by Turner,* Ruskin had included a "lovely bit" of irony. Recounting how, in 1842, he had lost Turner's *Splügen Pass* to Munro of Novar because of "filial piety," he had written, in first draft: "And so, you see, everything went right, and according to Miss Edgeworth's notions of the way in which beautiful behaviour and filial piety is rewarded" (*Works, 13,* 481n.). As he had stated in the *Ethics of the Dust,* "Her good characters never are brought into the deadly trial of goodness,—the doing right, and suffering for it, quite finally. And that is life, as God arranges it" (*Works, 18,* 300).

The "Pilgrim's progress divinity" is, of course, a reference to "the religion . . . of John Bunyan, and of my mother, which I was first taught" (*Works, 37,* 216; letter to C. E. Norton, 1877).

[February 15]

Uses of pictures. Apparently Mrs. Goodwin's copy of Caterina Vigri's *St. Ursula* (his "Valentine") had been accompanied by her copy of Carpaccio's *Solomon and the Queen of Sheba* (a picture now usually ascribed to Carpaccio's master, Bastiani). In *St. Mark's Rest* (1877) Ruskin had used the *Solomon and Sheba* to epitomize (as though autobiographically) the young Carpaccio's "faculty of vision"—that is, his "singular power . . . of seeing things in vision as if they were real," and his industriously cultivated habit "of spiritualizing, or reading like a vision, whatever he saw with eyes either of the body or mind" (*Works, 24,* 363).

Police news. Probably a reference to the sentence quoted from the *Evening News* and used as a theme in "The Snow Manger" *Fors* he was now writing: "The mother got impatient, thrust the child into the snow, and hurried on—not looking back" (*Works, 29,* 367).

My lecture. The "Oxford Lecture," published in the *Nineteenth Century* of January 1878 (*Works, 22,* 529–38), revealed changes in Ruskin's religious thought that had enabled him to reconcile his present beliefs with articles of faith which he had held while writing *Modern Painters, I-IV* and had forsworne in 1858 (according to the oversimplified account of the change to be given in *Praeterita*) while he was studying, in Turin, Veronese's *Solomon and the Queen of Sheba* (*Works, 35,* 495–96).

Ormond. In the *Fors* now in progress, he speaks of the "true insight into the proper way of managing Irish people" (the La Touches were preeminently "Irish") given in *Ormond* (*Works, 29,* 363), in which, as a responsible landlord, Sir Herbert Annaly improves the lives and characters of the peasants on his estate (see *Ormond,* chap. 23).

Carlyle's moral sense. In *Val D'Arno* Ruskin had quoted a passage from Carlyle on the mystery of the "Moral Sense" which connects Man with his Maker (*Works, 23,* 131–32). In his personal relationship with Ruskin, Carlyle had revealed this "Moral Sense," particularly, by stressing the importance of Ruskin's performing, with tranquillity, his filial "duty," as Ruskin recounts in *Praeterita* (*Works, 35,* 540–41).

The hymn said in my arms. Rose "was out of her mind in the end," he would explain; "one evening in London she was raving violently till far into the night; they could not quiet her. At last they let me into her room. She was sitting up in bed; I got her to lie back on her pillow, and lay her head in my arms, as I knelt beside it. ¶They left us, and she asked me if she should say a hymn. And I said yes, and she said, 'Jesus, lover of my soul,' to the end, and then fell back tired and went to sleep. And I left her" (L. G. Swett, *John Ruskin's Letters to Francesca and Memoirs of the Alexanders* [Boston, 1931], p. 118; letter of 1886).

[February 17]

Ophelias. In Ophelia, "the true lost wife of Hamlet" (*Works, 17,* 258n.), Ruskin also had a counterpart of Rose, as the victim of parental folly and of personal shortcomings, because of which she had failed her lover and had herself gone mad. (Rose might well have said to her own father: "but, as you did command, / I did repel his letters and denied / His access to me.") In *Hamlet,* Ruskin had observed, "all the bitter catastrophe" occurs "because [Ophelia] fails Hamlet at the critical moment, and is not, and cannot in her nature be, a guide to him when he needs her most" (*Works, 18,* 114; from *Sesame and Lilies*).

Departed, never more. From the song of Ophelia: "To-morrow is Saint Valentine's day, / All in the morning betime, / And I a maid at your window, / To be your Valentine: / Then up he rose, and donn'd his clothes, / And dupp'd the chamber-door; / Let in the maid, that out a maid / Never departed more" (IV.5). While succumbing to his next attack of mental illness, he again would cite the last two lines (see *Diaries,* p. 1000; September 22, 1881).

Provoking one another. In context: "And they that are Christ's have crucified the flesh with the affections and lusts. If we live in the Spirit, let us also walk in the Spirit. Let us not be desirous of vain glory, provoking one another, envying one another" (Gal. 5:24–26). The first of these verses may have been signalized by his having drawn the Greek Cross (of St. George) in repudiation of the "lusts" connoted by Ophelia's song. It was as though each of his first three attacks of delirium was designed to teach him that "If ye live after the flesh, ye shall die," he remarked in later years (see entry for February 2, 1883).

Bishop Laertes. The epithet "Bishop" probably connotes the hortatory strain in Laertes' farewell to Ophelia, as he admonishes her to "Be wary" of any love which Hamlet may profess. Ophelia herself urges Laertes not to resemble "some ungracious pastors" (I.3). (For the false Bishops within "The Dream," see entry for January 15, 1880.)

The Devil will not take my soul. Struggling against Hamlet within Ophelia's grave, Laertes exclaims: "The devil take thy soul!" (V.1).

Look you. In context, this "look you" would seem to echo Hamlet's remark after he has first seen his Father's ghost: "for mine own poor part, / *Look you,* I'll go pray" (I.5). Nevertheless, these words may carry a multiple freight inasmuch as when Hamlet again sees his Father's ghost, he exclaims: *"Look you,* how pale he glares! / . . . / Why, *look you* there! *Look* how it steals away; / My father, in his habit as he liv'd; / *Look!"* (III.4). Hamlet also tells his mother: *"look you* now, what follows. / Here is your husband; like a mildew'd ear, / Blasting his wholesome brother. Have you eyes?" (III.4). Suggestively, too, addressing Hamlet's mother, Polonius urges: "He will come straight. *Look you* lay home to him; / Tell him his pranks have been too broad to bear with . . ." (III.4).

Thou pray'st not well. To Laertes' exclamation, "The devil take thy soul," Hamlet responds: "Thou pray'st not well. / I prithee, take thy fingers from my throat . . . / Away thy hand!" (V.1).

Least said is soonest mended. The proverb stems from *Don Quixote.*

Forty thousand brothers. "I lov'd Ophelia: forty thousand brothers / Could not, with all their quantity of love, / Make up my sum" (V.1).

Sweet flowers. From Ophelia's song: "Larded with sweet flowers; / Which bewept to the grave did go / With true-love showers" (IV.5).

[February 19]

Calling of names. Probably a reference to Dante's sight of Semitamis, Cleopatra, Helen, Achilles, Paris, Tristan, "and beside / A thousand more he show'd me, and by name / Pointed them out, whom love bereav'd of life" (*Divine Comedy,* VI.5.66–68). The analogous listing of names in the *Aeneid,* Book VI, and the *Odyssey,* Book XI, seems less relevant to Ruskin's underlying stream of thought.

Float double. "The swan on still St. Mary's Lake / Float double, swan and shadow" (Wordsworth, *Yarrow Unvisited,* ll. 43–44).

Pigs head. Recently Ruskin's friend Henry Willett had sent him a copy of John Blaxton's *The English Usurer: Or Usury Condemned* (1634), in which there was a bookplate with "a pig's head for a crest." Ruskin had responded: "It's mine too! and has the double meaning of being *pigsticker* in general and yet having a certain quantity of piggishness for grubbing up ground myself. Where *did* you find it?" (*Works, 37,* 237; letter of January 8, 1878). As he explains in *Praeterita,* his father had chosen the boar as the Ruskin family crest (*Works, 35,* 390–91).

Voice. ". . . it is said, To day if ye will hear his voice, harden not your hearts" (Heb. 4:7). For his own seal, Ruskin explains, he had adopted the motto " 'To-day,' tacitly underlined to myself with the warning, 'The night cometh, when no man can work' " (*Works, 35,* 391; from *Praeterita*).

Chalcedony. Ruskin's "seal with the motto 'To-day' [was] cut in the apex of a big specimen of chalcedony" (W. G. Collingwood, *The Life and Works of Ruskin* [2 vols. Cambridge, Eng., 1893], *2,* 49). Ruskin himself had been addressed as "you dear Chalcedony" by Susan Beever (see below, letter of April 18 [1874], Letters, IV).

Boiling over and not boiling. In the *Punch* of February 16, 1878, the weekly feature, PUNCH'S ESSENCE OF PARLIAMENT, was illustrated by a cartoon entitled "Boiling Over," in which a Kettle is emitting "geysers" of steam that form themselves into the heads of two political figures. After prolonged debate, a motion to provide £6,000,000 to strengthen the armed forces has been defeated. "And now the collision between the Government's demand of Six Millions and the Opposition's Amendment is over, *Punch* begs to move his Amendment, the substitution of coolness for heat, argument for recrimination, common effort for a common end" (*Punch, 74,* 62).

In order. "Let all things be done decently and in order" (I. Cor. 14:40).

Gal. III, 28. "There is neither Jew nor Greek, there is neither bond nor free, there is neither male nor female: for ye are all one in Christ Jesus."

Fleur-de-lys. The "fleur-de-lys" is the dark purple iris, symbolizing the rule of "spiritual thought and law" (*Works, 23,* 146). This iris is also specifically the flower of "Cora-Persephone" (*Works, 21,* 107–08)—namely, of Rose La Touche. (Spelling *Proserpina* to himself, he once said, he always omitted the first *P* and the second *r,* leaving *Rose*pina [unpublished letter to Dr. John Brown, May 5, 1874; Yale University Library].)

Joan of France. The betrayed Joan of Arc, type of "all stainless maids" (*Works, 28,* 357), could also function readily as a symbol for Rose La Touche.

Dante's font stone. In 1873 Ruskin had acquired "three marble figures . . . chiselled by Nicolo Pisano" (*Works, 23,* xxviii) which came from the font in the Baptistry at Florence that Dante had broken "to save a child from drowning" (*Works, 22,* 343).

Angel of the Law. Probably a reference to C. F. Murray's watercolor study of St. Michael—a patron saint of St. George's Guild in its "warfare against evil" (*Works, 27,* 482n.). Lecturing at Oxford in 1874, Ruskin had compared the old Etruscan race to "a St. Michael putting on his armour, the riveted and rigid steel of inviolable law" (*Works, 23,* 228; from *The Schools of Florence*); in a *Fors* of 1876 he had referred to the Guild as "this present body of believers in God and His law now called together in the name of St. Michael and St. George" (*Works, 28,* 514). C. F. Murray's copy of the St. Michael in Botticelli's *Madonna de S. Barnaba* was among the pictures which Ruskin would give to the Museum of St. George (see *Works, 30,* 192; see also *Works, 33,* 273, for his special admiration for the Botticelli portrayal of St. Michael). Although Murray's copy is undated, Ruskin was encouraging him to make it in 1876 (see *Works, 37,* 196).

John III, 14. "But I trust I shall shortly see thee, and we shall speak face to face. Peace be to thee. Our friends salute thee. Greet the friends by name." (See also entry for January 3, 1880.) Among the disciples, St. John the Apostle was the "Beloved," or αγαπατος —a word which Rose had used as salutation in at least one letter to her "John" (see *Diaries,* p. 782; March 29, 1874).

[February 20]

Teaching me. On the opposite page he adds: "Susie's, beside Wisies bouquet— I put the bouquet there, but still did not notice the book there 'by chance' Frondes agrestes to purpose."

The overguiding "Fors," in other words, had arranged not only that Miss Beever's iris (fleur-de-lis), as the flower of Joan of Arc (Rose), should be placed beside those violets of Emily La Touche but also that Miss Beever's *Frondes Agrestes* (her 1875 book of "Selections from *Modern Painters*") should be included in the group. The presence of this book would have been "to purpose" because it also could serve as a token of the overwatching spirit of Rose. One reaches this conclusion by realizing (1) that the *Fawn* had become, to Ruskin, a deeply moving symbol for Rose La Touche and (2) that "Horace says [the trees] shed their leaves in honour of the Faun— 'Spargit agrestes tibi silva *frondes*' " (*Works, 17,* xlviii; letter of 1861, my italics)—this line being implicit in the title of Miss Beever's book.

First volume. Presumably a reference to some passage deleted from *Modern Painters, I* when Ruskin was revising the text for the "New Edition" of *Modern Painters* issued, as a whole, in 1873. He himself defined *blasphemy* as "the bearing of *false* witness *against* one's neighbour" (*Works, 34,* 366).

Exile & Rock limpet. Namely, *Napoleon* or *War: The Exile and the Rock Limpet,* an oil painting which Turner had exhibited in 1842. Standing before the sunset on the shore of St. Helena, Napoleon addresses a rock limpet: "Ah, thy tent-formed shell is like / A soldier's nightly bivouac, alone / Amidst a sea of blood —— / —— But *you* can join your comrades." In *Modern Painters, IV*

Ruskin noted that Turner habitually uses "his most deeply *crimsoned* sunset skies" to indicate "the association of any subject with circumstances of death, especially the death of multitudes" (*Works, 6,* 381). What the picture could say to him more personally, he indicated when he wrote Kate Greenaway: "I am in an extremely apathetic state after 14 lectures, and you must think of me as—well, I should think the likest thing to me was a limpet. —Did you ever see Turner's Napoleon and the rock limpet? (How much of the man's soul that fancy meant.) — But Kate and the Rock Limpet's rather like it. All your fire and force—helpless above my insensitive tent on the stone!" (unpublished letter of December 9 [1884]; Pierpont Morgan Library).

[1] *Moses and* [2] *the Visit.* Fully entitled (1) *Light and Colour (Goethe's Theory) — The Morning after the Deluge — Moses Writing the Book of Genesis,* followed by six lines from the *Fallacies of Hope* and exhibited in 1843; (2) *The Visit to the Tomb,* followed by a line from the *Fallacies of Hope* and exhibited in 1850 as one of the four pictures in the Aeneas-Dido series. These two paintings, to be sure, cannot be accurately designated "Turner's last two pictures." So far as is known, Ruskin made no supplementary references to them.

My first necromancy. Presumably a reference to what (in my opinion) there is good reason to believe may have happened in actuality—the burning of a large number of reputedly pornographic Turner sketches, by Ruskin and Ralph Nicholson Worum (1812–77), Keeper of the National Gallery, while Ruskin was arranging the Turner Bequest in 1857–58.

Thirlmere. He was intensely distressed because "the little lake of Thirlmere," fed by the stream of his symbolic St. John's Vale, was about to be (as Puck would say) "translated" into a large rectangular reservoir, thence to be drained into the "water-closets" of Manchester (*Works, 29,* 162; from *Fors,* July 1877)—among cities conspicuously the iron-fingered and thus, in pending parable, of *Cotton* (vs. the Shakesperian *Bottom*) the *Mechanic* "Weaver." (For the contrast between the weaving and reweaving of the silken web of a bird's feather—like a tapestry fashioned by Penelope—and the "sewing" of Manchester, "with Thirlmere to fill your boilers," see *Works, 15,* 399–401; from *The Laws of Fésole.*)

"Remarkable passages in Shakespeare." Miss Beever's book of selections, associatively connected with "Horace" (as the next key-word) because of her analogous "Selections" from *Modern Painters—Frondes Agrestes.*

St Mary's Hall. Probably a reference to the help which he had recently received from "the Principal of St. Mary's Hall . . . (Madonna help, surely)" (*Diaries,* p. 974; January 9, 1878).

Polly put the kettle on. Presumably a reference to Polly Bell—"a dear girl but *such* a bad cook" (see B.S.).

The little beauty from Cheshire. Probably someone whom he had met through Blanche Atkinson, of The Gables, Rock Ferry, Cheshire; perhaps the friend whom he had met, as her companion, during August, 1875 (see *Diaries,* p. 856; August 14). In MS the words set off (editorially) by the parenthesis appear on the page opposite those in the remainder of this paragraph and are attached to the name "Polly" by an asterisk.

Flo—Flo—Flo. Doubtless some association with Flora Shaw, author of *Castle Blair.* In the March *Fors* he remarked: "there is a quite lovely little book just come out about Irish children, *Castle Blair,*—(which . . . I have strong personal, though stronger impersonal, reasons for recommending, the writer being a very dear friend; and some Irish children [Rose and 'Wisie'], for many and many a year, much more than that)" (*Works, 29,* 362). For Ruskin's friendship with Flora Shaw, see B.S.

Telegraph Post. Probably a reference to some item, relevant to his present flow of thought, which he had marked, as was his custom (often for use in *Fors Clavigera*), in a current issue of the paper.

Astrology and Horace. All who knew "the traditions of Chaldean astrology [recognize] that its warnings were distinct,—its promises deceitful," he would state in *The Storm-Cloud of the Nineteenth Century.* "Horace thus warns Leuconoe against reading the Babylonian numbers to learn the time of her death [*Odes*

1.11: "Tu ne quaesieris"],—he does not imply their promise of previous happiness" (*Works, 34,* 45).

When itie pigs have muffins hot. From one of his "pig-wiggian" rhymes of self-reproach—originally in a letter of 1867, addressed to "Joanie": "When little pigs have muffins hot, / And take three quarters for their lot, / Then, little pigs—had better not" (*Works, 35;* from *Praeterita*).

Try the Spirits. "Beloved, believe not every spirit, but try the spirits whether they are of God" (I John 4:1). Analogously, Hamlet addresses his Father's ghost: "Be thou a spirit of health or goblin damn'd," and Horatio warns against the "form, / Which might deprive your sovereignty of reason / And draw you into madness" (I.4).

Justice. "Soft! / The Jew shall have all Justice. Soft! no haste" (*Merchant of Venice,* IV.1). The arrangement of the words suggests that there may be, in echo, Hamlet's "Soft you now! / The fair Ophelia!" (III.1).

Decently and in order. I Cor. 14:40.

As I've dated it. The "bit of Galatians" is not dated in the Diary, in which the final paragraph of this entry appears on the left-hand page, "opposite" the words "Soft. No Haste. . . . Justice."

[February 21]

My house—at New-bridge. Probably a reference to some philantrophic proposal which Ruskin had made in response to the letter describing the sufferings of the Tredegar colliers and ironworkers. Products of the Tredegar ironworks were sent to nearby Newbridge-on-Usk for transportation to Newport, by river. As "Fors" would have it, the Harristown address of Rose La Touche had been "*Newbridge,* Ireland."

Up, like Sir Charles Grandison. Namely, ready to behave vivaciously and cheerfully, with self-command, sympathetic insight, and unfailing wisdom as the friend and benefactor of all within his sphere—he himself, like Sir Charles, to be unostentatiously and unmoralistically the model of a "Good Man" in his courage, prudence, tolerance, kindness, unobtrusive piety, and absolute integrity, together with all the other virtues which Samuel Richardson has portrayed in his characterization of a Christian Gentleman. When Ruskin was a boy, his father had introduced him to this Model for Behavior by reading *Sir Charles Grandison* aloud, through excerpts, during the evenings at Herne Hill. When he was 22, having read the Clementina episode, he noted in his Diary: "at present I feel disposed to place this work above all other works of fiction I know. It is very, very grand, and has, I think, a greater practical effect on me for good than anything I ever read in my life" (Diary entry for November 18, 1841, first published in *Praeterita*; see *Works, 35,* 308, and *Diaries,* p. 220). By December he would be reading this novel aloud to the family and guests, "until bedtime," Constance Hilliard would tell Norton (unpublished letter of December 18, 1878; Harvard University Library).

Entry at p. 63. See first sentence of the entry (on p. 63 of the MS) for February 17.

Leaving my nets. That is, to become a Fisher of Men, among the destitute: "And [Jesus] saith unto [Simon called Peter, and Andrew his brother], Follow me, and I will make you fishers of men. And they straightway left their nets, and followed him" (Matt. 4:18–20).

During the day he would complete the Notes for his Catalogue of the pending Exhibition, in which the last item—No. 120. *Mont Blanc*—is followed by the date-line: "Brantwood / February 21, 1878."

Fürs Haus Frühling. As issued, *Fürs Haus* consists of a series of four folders which contain loose sheets of drawings and woodcuts, almost all by Ludwig Richter, accompanied by passages of verse—one number being devoted to each of the four seasons. One sheet contains the Table of Contents for each of the four "numbers." "October, 1858" appears on another sheet, which seems to give the introduction to the series, printed by "Breitkopf und Hartel" of Leipzig, with the publisher designated "Dresden / Vering von J. Heinrich Richter." (From a description supplied by Miss Gnosspelius, who has at her disposal a set of the unbound illustrations. *Fürs Haus, Frühling* is now available in Volume I of Richter's *Werke.*)

"I am the Resurrection." In the Spring number, "I am the Resurrection" is entitled *Ich weiss das mein Erloser lebt.* A seated angel, facing a mother and three children, points to the standing figure of Christ. This drawing is accompanied by the lines from Agaber: "Christ is arisen, / From all the Martyrdom: / We should rejoice, / Christ will be our comfort."

The flight of angels. The illustration entitled *Frühlings Einzug* shows a mountainous landscape above which angels are in flight and is accompanied by six lines from Bocci: "Awake, awake, you valleys, you meadow, field, and forest! / Awake, awake to light, you night-encompassed seed, / Spring out in thousand stalks! The time of May is near. / Awake, awake, you sleepers, to deeds from your repose! / A messenger of God calls it to you, the spring shouts it to you."

The Mi-Himmel. Mi Himmel (the title is unhyphenated in the original) shows a young man seated beside a girl within an open shed upon the roof of which an infant angel sits piping, and illustrates four lines from Hebel: "The spring waves into the valley, and the little brook flows / And the bird flies from one region to another in the world, as I should like to ride. / When I sit in my little inn, in my gay little room, / This little room is my world, and this, may God forgive me, is my Heaven!"

The "time of Roses." As the second design in the Summer number of *Fürs Haus, Rosenzeit* shows a lady seated on a bench beneath two trees as she gazes at roses held within her hands, and illustrates four lines from Goethe: "She picked roses in her lap, / And she is winding a little wreath most skilfully, / With light buds and leaves in it: / For whom should this be the little crown?"

Text in daybook. Rose had given him a book which contained two biblical texts for each day—one verse in English and one in Greek. (For this "daybook," see Rayner Unwin, ed., *The Gulf of Years. Letters from John Ruskin to Kathleen Olander* [London, 1953], p. 65.)

Enter ye in. "Enter ye in at the strait gate: for wide is the gate, and broad is the way, that leadeth to destruction, and many there be which go in thereat: Because strait is the gate, and narrow is the way, which leadeth unto life, and few there be that find it" (Matt. 7:13–14).

In the heavenly love. Seeking to comfort Ruskin after the death of Rose La Touche, George MacDonald had written: "It may be she haunts you now with ministrations. Anyhow the living God does. Richter says it is only in God that two souls meet. I am sure this is true" (*Leon, Ruskin,* pp. 500–01).

Tobias prayer. On his wedding night Tobias prayed, with Sara, that God "have pity on us," for "It is not good that man should be alone" (Tobit 8:4, 6).

[February 22]

II Timothy 3. With St. Paul's behest that "in the last days" the Thessalonians remain steadfast to the doctrine in which they had been bred: "For men shall be lovers of their own selves, covetous, boasters, proud, blasphemers, disobedient to parents. . . . But continue thou in the things which thou hast learned and hast been assured of, knowing of whom thou hast learned them; And that from a child thou hast known the holy scriptures, which are able to make thee wise unto salvation through faith which is in Christ Jesus" (II Tim. 3:1–15).

My box-bible . . . and Susie's Shakespeare. That is, Miss Beever's *Remarkable Passages in Shakespeare* lay on the table with J. R. Anderson's gift. This was "probably a Bible which had once been used by a Cardinal, with his arms stamped on the binding," Mr. Dearden comments. "Presumably it would have been a large Bible, since the average carved wood box formerly used to protect the Bible as a valuable family possession measures about 9 x 26 inches. There seems to be no record of the Bible to which Ruskin was referring."

Love is stronger than death. As the fourteenth drawing in the Summer number of *Fürs Haus, Liebe ist stärker als Tod* shows a maiden crowned with roses as the skeleton-like figure of Death kneels behind her, about to cut the stalk of a rose bush with the sickle in his right hand. It illustrates four stanzas (anonymous) which read, in part: "There is a Harvester called Death, / He has power from God, most high, / Today he waves the knife, / Already it cuts much better; / Soon he will cut into it. / We can only endure. / Be careful, beautiful little flower! / . . . [The precious narcissi, the hyacinths, and Turkish lilies will be swept away, falling beneath his sickle by uncounted thousands. He will wipe out the roses and lilies, and will not spare the crowns of emperors.] / Be careful, beautiful little flower. / Withstand! Death, come here, I do not fear you, / Withstand, come here at one stride. / Even if I am hurt, / I shall be transplanted, / Into the heavenly Garden, / For which we all wait. / Rejoice, beautiful little flower."

With all I've left there. An echo from the Book of Ruth, the "handmaiden" who had "left [her] father and [her] mother, and the land of [her] nativity" (Ruth 2:11). Even so, "Rosie must come out from her country and kindred for me, like Ruth or Rebekah —or she is not worthy of the love I bear her," Ruskin had told Lady Mount-Temple (J. L. Bradley, ed., *The Letters of John Ruskin to Lord and Lady Mount-Temple* [Columbus, Ohio, 1964], p. 114; March 26 [1867]).

Turners Jerusalem—and Blake's Ruth. For Turner's *Jerusalem* ("The Pool of Healing"), see above, entry for February 18. Blake's *Ruth Parting from Naomi* was the original watercolor (13¾ x 12½), used in Blake's *Illustrations of the Bible.* In this drawing, Ruth is "a tall slender figure, with long yellow hair" (comment on Pl. IX, *Burlington Fine Arts Club Catalogue. Blake Centenary Exhibition*). Rose La Touche, etherially slender, with deeply grey-blue eyes and flaxen hair, was "tall and brightly fair," as Ruskin would tell a friend of later years (*Works, 35,* lxxv).

I get John III. 3 and read on. "Jesus answered and said unto him, Verily, verily, I say unto thee, Except a man be born again, he cannot see the kingdom of God. Nicodemus saith unto him, How can a man be born when he is old? can he enter the second time into his mother's womb, and be born? Jesus answered . . . That which is born of the flesh is flesh; and that which is born of the Spirit is spirit. . . . For every one that doeth evil hateth the light. . . . But he that doeth truth cometh to the light, that his deeds may be manifest, that they are wrought in God" (John 3:3–21).

Myself as a painter, coming after a Sculptor. ". . . whenever and however we bring a shapeless thing into shape, we do so under the laws of the one great art of Sculpture," Ruskin had said in a lecture of 1870, "Of the Division of Arts." Analogously, he had said that "Painting" signifies *"every mode of disposing colours in a permanent relation on, or in, a solid substance"* (*Works, 20,* 201; from *Aratra Pentilici*). As a writer, he himself indubitably had many a "mode of disposing colours."

Delphi first. Then Aegina. / Behind Carpaccio. Against the background of Ruskin's published work, this group of words presumably means, in brief, that the highly visionary and individualistic "Gothic" (or as we might be inclined to say, "Romantic"—and probably "Ruskinian") genius of a Carpaccio stems from a "Greek" (or "Classically" disciplined) youth during which (1) the self-control and love of Truth epitomized by *Delphi* and (2) the obedience to Eternal Law epitomized by *Aegina* were inculcated in a man or, alternately, in a nation.

First, according to Ruskin's *Delphic* symbolism, the individual or nation must gain control over brute appetites or impulses, and learn to love and speak the Truth. At this point in a man's development, Apollo has killed the Python, or "worm of corruption" (*Works, 19,* 363; from *Queen of the Air,* 1869), and "the contest of life with clay"—in other words, the war of the gods with the "mud-begotten" giants (*Works, 20,* 269; from *Aratra Pentelici,* 1870)—has been won. But though the "Delphic Power is Truth"—"Falsehood in the moral world being what corruption is in the physical" (*Works, 31,* 13 and n.; from Preface to *The Economist of Xenophon,* 1876)—"yet the oracle is from the breath of the earth" (*Works, 19,* 364; from *Queen of the Air*), and its voice may be deceptive (see *Works, 24,* 203; *34,* 45–46).

Next, as epitomized by *Aegina,* man-made Laws of Justice are established for society. Aegina was the island of Aeacus ("Lord of Justice"), "where Eternal Law, Saviour of men . . . is obeyed with more than human truth" (*Works, 20,* 382; from "The Tortoise of

Aegina"). Although the justice established by Aeacus during his reign over the industrious and commercial Myrmidons (or "Ant-people") was related "chiefly to property" (*Works, 27,* 409; from *Fors,* November 1872), Ruskin speaks of the tortoise as "the type of Aegina" and makes the tortoiseshell (in the lyre of Hermes or Orpheus) a symbol of "the measured Harmony and spheric Order of Life" (*Works, 20,* 389; from "The Tortoise of Aegina").

Then, in the history of nations (or of individuals), there comes the second great phase of human development—in England signalized by Chaucer, in Venice by Carpaccio. The man (or people) having been "knit in Draconian strength" through Spartan training, the "day of Manifestation" comes, as though "sword-leaved lilies" had branched "into buds . . . rich in hope" (*Works, 31,* 21–22; from Preface to *The Economist of Xenophon*). Ruskin himself had found Carpaccio's art placed, literally, beside that of Aegina, in 1876, when two of Carpaccio's pictures of St. Ursula which he especially wished to study had been taken to a room in which "there were a series of casts from the Aegean marbles;" thus, he said, he had been able to observe, at his right hand and his left, "the best pre-Praxitelite Classic art, and the best Pre-Raphaelite Gothic art" (*Works, 33,* 315; from *The Art of England,* 1883). His central essay on Carpaccio, with whom he had obviously in many ways identified himself, had recently been published (in December 1877) as "The Shrine of the Slaves," in due time chapter 10 of *St. Mark's Rest.*

Message from Rosie to me as I was drawing . . . in St. Georges Chapel. This memory dates from the spring of 1870 when, in the Church of San Giorgio de' Schiavoni, Venice, Ruskin had made his copy of the "Red Parrot" nibbling at a spray of vervain in the foreground of Carpaccio's *Baptism of the Sultan,* in St. George's Chapel. In self-symbolism, he calls Carpaccio's "Parrot" *Porphyrio,* "St. George's bird"—"the bird of chastity" (*Works, 21,* 135; *24,* 230; see also *24,* Pl. LXII—another one of the Ruskinian "Self-Portraits"). Although seven years later he would say that he had made this watercolor (10¼″ x 7½″) in 1872 (*Works, 24,* 341), he had displayed it at an Oxford lecture of February 1871, at the same time speaking (as though no more than literally) of the "absurdity" of hanging "Venetian pictures above the line of sight" (*Works, 22,* 54).

This watercolor was intimately associated with Ruskin's thoughts of Rose. He reiteratively states that the vervain (Latin, *verbena*) is a plant sacred to St. Ursula, without indicating that in Latin the *verbena* is also known as the *Ros marina*—namely, as Ophelia's "*Rose*mary, that's for remembrance." In the spring of 1870 Rose had once more "come back" to him (Leon, *Ruskin,* p. 481), although what "message" she may have sent him at this time is not known. Subsequently, however, while copying the vervain in Carpaccio's *Dream of St. Ursula,* he believed that Rose (who had died seven months before) had communicated with him through sending him, on Christmas Day of 1876, "a dried sprig of . . . the sacred vervain, by the hands of [a] friend" (*Works, 29,* 31; from *Fors Clavigera,* February 1877).

I would serve her to the death. When George MacDonald had remarked, "It may be she haunts you now with ministrations" (Leon, *Ruskin,* p. 500), Ruskin had responded: "I can take . . . for myself [the verse from Novalis] . . . 'My faith to thee I break not / If all should faithless be, / That gratitude forsake not / The world eternally. / For my sake Death did sting thee / With anguish keen and sore, / Therefore with joy I bring thee / This heart forever more' " (MacDonald, *Reminiscences of a Specialist,* p. 122).

Ada with the Golden Hair. Probably Adela ("Ada") Dundas; possibly Ada Hartnell. *Ada Hartnell* (d. 1893, aged 61), niece of the portrait painter Nathaniel Hartnell, was an Original Companion of St. George and one of the contributors to the Gift of the *Splügen Pass.* (See also her letter of April 13, 1878, to Mrs. Severn; Letters, xx.) For *Ada Dundas,* see B.S. Expressing gratitude "for much kindness from Mr. Ruskin during past years," her sister Anne would contribute to the Gift of the *Splügen Pass* (letter to the Rt. Hon. Cowper-Temple, April 19, 1878; F. J. Sharp Collection).

Can the Devil speak truth. Banquo's query (*Macbeth* I.4).

Letter to Francie. Frances Graham (see B.S.).

If that thou beest a devil &c. Othello to Iago: "If that thou be'st a devil, I cannot kill thee" (V.2).

The night with her. Iago: ". . . he hath made wanton the night with her, and she is sport for Jove" (II.3).

Burne-Jones. — Oh, my Black Prince. In *The Three Colours of Pre-Raphaelitism,* written shortly after his recovery from this illness, Ruskin called Edward Burne-Jones (1833–98) "the greatest master whom that school has yet produced" (*Works, 34,* 148; published in the November 1878 *Nineteenth Century*). In the *Fors* of July 1877 his contrast between the "incompleteness" in the work of Burne-Jones (one result of a "consummately powerful imagination") and in that of Whistler (the result of "Cockney impudence") had led to Whistler's pending suit for libel (*Works, 29,* 160).

His epithet, the "Black Prince," doubtless connotes primarily the cap plumed with three ostrich feathers, alike the crest of Theseus, of St. George and his Knights, and of the Prince of Wales—the "Black Prince" Edward (son of Edward III) having received this crest from John the Blind, King of Bohemia, who had been slain at Crécy. The ostrich feather, Ruskin had explained, means "order and rule . . . long and loose though the filaments seemed, no wind could entangle or make them disorderly. 'So this plume betokeneth such an one as nothing can disturb his mind or disquiet his spirits, but he is ever one and the same.' Do you see how one thing bears out and fulfils another, in these thoughts and symbols of the despised people of old time?" (*Works, 27,* 512–13; from *Fors Clavigera,* April 1873).

"That's my dear brother, Ned," he would say just before Burne-Jones' death, having paused, as he was going up to bed, to gaze at the photograph of a portrait painted by his godson, Philip Burne-Jones (*Works, 35,* xliii; see also Letters, VII).

One of the firm of Brown. Presumably a reference to the undiscriminating type of "talk" in which the work of Burne-Jones and of Ford Madox Brown (1821–93) could be called, at once, "Pre-Raphaelite." Personally, in Ford Madox Brown, Burne-Jones had found a close and most kind friend. But as Ruskin had advised Miss Heaton: "Do not buy any Madox Brown at present.

Do you not see that his name never occurs in my books— do you think that would be so if I *could* praise him, seeing that he is an entirely worthy fellow? But pictures are pictures, and things that ar'n't ar'n't" (*Works, 36,* 406; letter of 1862).

Away on Lago Maggiore. The name "Brown" seems to have evoked its color image so that his thought of the Pre-Raphaelites as those who had dared to paint trees *green* instead of "brown" ("Where do you put your brown tree?"; *Works, 3,* 45n.), suggested the Lago Maggiore—possibly through some association with his early Turner watercolor the *Arona,* alternately entitled *Lago Maggiore.* Discussing this picture shortly after he had recovered from his present illness, Ruskin noted that here there were no flowers and that the trees were "black or brown against the sky!" (*Works, 13,* 519). To him personally the "divine" lake signified the last stage of the journey—and thus the "approach"—to Milan, Verona, and Venice (see *Works, 13,* 210; *35,* 320).

Sempre . . . Maggiore. Published *Works, 25,* xxv. In *Modern Painters, II* (1846) Ruskin had first quoted Tintoret's observation: "E faticoso lo studio della pittura, a sempre si fa il mare maggiore" ("The study of painting is laborious, and the sea always gets larger"); so "said he, who of all men was least likely to have left us discouraging report of anything that majesty of intellect could grasp, or continuity of labour overcome" (*Works, 4,* 27). ". . . in their wakening as well as their warning sense . . . those great words of the aged Tintoret: / SEMPRE SI FA IL MARE MAGGIORE" had appeared, printed in capitals, as the last line of Lecture II in *The Two Paths* (*Works, 16,* 318).

To Connie. For Constance Hilliard, see B.S. and Letters, XXII. Ruskin is now recalling some incident of 1866, when, as a girl of 14, Connie was one of his traveling companions on the Continent.

To Madge. Mrs. W. H. Kendal, or "Madge" Robertson (see B.S. and Letters, XXVI—two notes which are typical of those from Mrs. Kendal to Mrs. Severn, in the F. J. Sharp Collection).

See opposite. Having filled the right-hand page, he decided to continue the entry on the lower part of the left-hand page.

Darling old vulgar Baxter. In a letter of 1886 to the *Pall Mall Gazette* Ruskin would refer to Peter Baxter (who had joined the Brantwood staff, as his valet, in 1876) as "my Irish servant, to whom I owe my life many times over, for the care he has taken of me in most dangerous illnesses" (*Works, 34,* 592); and, writing Mrs. Severn, Mrs. Alexander (mother of Francesca) would remark: "What a mercy Baxter is so faithful and so intelligent" (unpublished letter of August 25, 1887; F. J. Sharp Collection). About "our American cousin" nothing specific is known.

To Joseph Severn. As Arthur Severn's father and Keats' friend, Joseph Severn (1793–1879) now rounds out Ruskin's salute to those who had shown themselves to be distinctly mortal (he himself at one with them, by implication, in his relationship with Connie). In the Joseph Severn peroration in *Praeterita,* he deftly indicates what he had always felt to be the relative triviality of this man who "caught the hearts of all in the golden net of his good will and good understanding, as if life were but for him the rippling chant of his favourite song [from Mozart],—'Gente, e qui l'uccellatore' " (*Works, 35,* 278). At the start he had found Joseph Severn "cleverish, and droll, but rather what I should call a cockney, though he has lived twenty years in Rome" (*Diaries,* p. 123; December 12, 1840); and in mid-course, speaking of an opera singer, he had written for his father's eye: "there came in a little man in a brass-buttoned coat, with the most good-humoured English-farmer-like look conceivable—but how he ever got himself to look like an opera hero I understand not. Everybody is fond of him, saying he is one of the most good-natured of men, and I should think they were right. He put me more in mind of Mr. Severn than anybody I can recollect" (*Works, 36,* 136; letter of 1852).

Keats. Ruskin's admiration for Keats (naturally associated with Joseph Severn) had been rather slow in developing, Shelley having won him in his youth. But by 1860: "Keats, (as is his way) puts nearly all that may be said of the pine into one verse. . . . I have come to that pass of admiration for him now, that I dare not read him, so discontented he makes me with my own work" (*Works, 7,*

107n.; from *Modern Painters, V*). And at Oxford, in 1884: "Read as much Keats as possible, and no Shelley" (*Works, 33,* 525).

Endymion. From *Endymion* he repeatedly had used the line, "A thing of beauty . . . ," but at this point the whole theme of the love of a mortal man for an Immortal Virgin is becoming central to the flow of his associations. Endymion loved Artemis. As the Goddess of the Moon who watches over "shy and modest youths," Artemis has as her symbol the "Bear," and sometimes, A. S. Murray notes, young girls are "called 'bears,' in allusion to their patron goddess" (*Manual of Mythology* [New York, 1873], p. 122). In his *Lectures on Art* (1870) Ruskin, in a somewhat different vein of symbolism, had shown Artemis as the Moon of Morning, "singing to her lyre" and walking with a *fawn*—one symbol of his Rose (see *Works, 20,* 147, Fig. 2). Thus this Goddess of the Moon, with her fawn and, more immediately, with her symbol of the bear, is but an alternate for St. Ursula, whose very name means "Bear" and whom Ruskin calls reiteratively "Little bear" (see *Works, 28,* 741; *29,* 36; *33,* 507). And who is St. Ursula, or "Little Bear," if not Rose herself?

Quenched in the Chaste beams. In context: "I saw . . . / Flying between the cold moon and the earth, / Cupid all arm'd: a certain aim he took / At a fair vestal throned by the west, / And loos'd his love-shaft smartly from his bow, / As it should pierce a hundred thousand hearts; / But I might see young Cupid's fiery shaft / *Quench'd in the chaste beams of the watery moon,* / And the imperial voteress passed on, / In maiden meditation, fancy-free" (*Midsummer Night's Dream,* II.1).

So, sometimes, it could seem—although at other times, in the pansy (Shakespeare's "Love-in-idleness") he could see Rose as the "little western flower, / Before milk-white, now purple with love's wound" (ibid.).

I have not looked back. Within the region of Proserpina, the man who memorably "looked back" was Orpheus at his Eurydice, having lost his patience. Contrastingly, Ruskin believed that he himself had patiently pressed forward (doubtless, to some degree, in honor of his vow "to serve her to the death"), with his hand upon the "Jason plough."

The Jason plough. In 1870, lecturing at Oxford, Ruskin had called "the ploughing of Jason," in the *Fourth Pythian Ode* of Pindar, "this great mythical expression of the conquest of the earth-clay and brute-force by vital human energy" (*Works, 20,* 328–29; from *Aratra Pentelici*). Next, he had developed the image of the plough as a tool of the sculptor or of the engraver and, by implication, of all others who "inscribe." "Here," he had concluded, "at the Ford of the Oxen of Jason [meaning, in part, at the Oxford of John Ruskin], are other furrows to be driven than these in the marble of Pentelicus. The fruitfullest, or the fatallest, of all ploughing is that by the thoughts of your youth, on the white field of its Imagination" (*Works, 20,* 329–30).

At still another level, discussing Burne-Jones' *The Two Wives of Jason,* he had remarked: "the name of Jason means the healer" —the Jason of Burne-Jones' picture being shown as married to Hypsipyle, symbolizing "patience and protective gentleness," and to Medea, symbolizing the Wisdom which is "dark and inexorable" in punishment if it is forsaken (*Works, 19,* 208; from *Modern Art*). In the early 1870s, when Rose was gravely ill, he had placed this picture in an alcove of his Drawing School at Oxford, with his own study of Luini's *St. Catherine* (as another personality evocative of Rose) and with Burne-Jones' *Love Leading Alcestis* [*back from the Grave*]. (See *Works, 19,* 207–08, Pls. VI and VII, for reproductions of Burne-Jones' pictures.)

Adorn the plough. "When Gold & Gems adorn the Plow / To Peaceful Arts shall Envy Bow" (Blake, *Auguries of Innocence,* ll. 101–02).

You stupid thing. In *A Descriptive Catalogue* and in *Public Address* Blake had condemned the work of Titian, together with that of Correggio, Rubens, and Rembrandt, while upholding that of Raphael, Dürer, and Michelangelo. These attacks upon Titian had been published in Alexander Gilchrist's *Life of Blake* (1863), which Ruskin knew. In the *Cestus of Aglaia* (1865) he had quoted from the *Public Address* the words italicized in the following statement: "*The unorganized blots and blurs of Rubens and Titian are not art* [my italics], nor can their method ever express ideas or imaginations, any more than Pope's metaphysical jargon of rhyming. . . . ¶I do not condemn Rubens, Rembrandt, or Titian, because they did not understand drawing, but because they did not understand colouring; how long shall I be forced to beat this into men's ears?" (Alexander Gilchrist, *The Life of William Blake* [2 vols. London and New York, 1907], *2,* 148.) Again, in *A Descriptive Catalogue*: "The eye that can prefer the Colouring of Titian and Rubens to that of Michael Angelo and Rafael, ought to be modest and to doubt its own powers. . . . Till we get rid of Titian and Correggio, Rubens and Rembrandt, we never shall equal Rafael and Albert Dürer, Michael Angelo, and Julio Romano" (William Blake, *Poetry and Prose,* ed. Geoffry Keynes [London, 1927], pp. 592–93).

Don't think I should stop. Having filled the lower part of the left-hand page, he might have gone on to the top of that page instead of to the new right-hand page, which was here begun.

Andrea Gritti. Doge Andrea Gritti, a portrait now ascribed to Vincenzo Catena rather than to Titian, was the fragment of a picture otherwise destroyed by fire. Having acquired it shortly after his father's death for £1,000, Ruskin told Rawdon Brown: "It is my notion of Titian's work, and that is all I care about. I bought it of the Dean of Bristol, after it was exhibited at the British Institute, where it looked well, and I've been trying to get it ever since—and have got it at last. . . . [Although fearfully damaged], it is Vecelli's, I'll aver" (*Works, 24,* 184n.; letter of September 2, 1864). At a lecture of 1867 he displayed it, with his copy of the Luini *St. Catherine,* requesting his audience to stand before these pictures and ask themselves whether "men and women such as they [Titian and Luini] represent were trained in a vicious or degraded element, and whether the painters who could understand them and rejoice in making their nobleness eternal, saw them with eyes warped by evil, or painted them with hands enfeebled by guilt" (*Works, 19,* 248).

Dandolo. Ruskin names the Doge Enrico Dandolo (reigned 1193–1205) with David, Leonidas, Cœur de Lion, and St. Louis (among others) as exemplifying the king who was typically the "first soldier" of a nation during the initial, or "military period," of its development (*Works, 19,* 391–92; from *Queen of the Air*)—a "first period" which in Venice "includes . . . her noblest achievements" and "the names of all her hero princes" (*Works, 9,* 20; from *The Stones of Venice*). Dandolo, in his old age and despite his blindness (he is the "blind old Dandolo" of *Childe Harold*), led the army of the Fourth Crusade in its final seige of Constantinople, sending to Venice, as trophies from the Hippodrome, the Bronze Horses of St. Mark's.

Blind Guide that had celestial light. Presumably Milton, with thought of Milton's lamentation of his blindness, concluded by his prayer: "So much the rather thou Celestial light / Shine inward, and the mind through all her powers / Irradiate, there plant eyes . . . / that I may see and tell / Of things invisible to mortal sight" (*Paradise Lost,* III.ll.51–55).

You dears. By now, together with "Diddie" (Sara Anderson), Scotland had given him, especially, his "Francie" and Joan.

So pretty. In September, he would spend "a whole afternoon in Edinburgh Canongate watching barefoot little dances [sic]" (*Works, 34,* 152n.; letter to Frances Graham, November 2, 1878); and in *Praeterita* he would describe the "faultless foot" of "Joanie" when she danced: "faultless in freedom . . . level, and at ease; small, *almost* to a fault, and in its swiftest steps rising and falling with the gentleness which only Byron has found words for — / 'Naked foot, / That shines like snow—and falls on earth as mute' " (*Works, 35,* 559).

Falls on earth—or gold—as mute. The Corsair, 2, par. 12, ll.13–14. The "or gold" may have been inserted in memory of the angels shown by Fra Angelico.

Dear doge Selvo. Doge Domenico Selvo had entered St. Mark's Cathedral bare-foot to receive his scepter, and, when he was deposed in 1096, was "permitted . . . to become a monk" instead of being blinded—the customary punishment for leaders deposed because, as "guides," they had failed to "see" (*Works, 24,* 268–72; from *St. Mark's Rest*). In the last installment of *St. Mark's Rest*

(October 1877) Ruskin had told the story of Doge Selvo, whom he had transformed into a most appealing and distinctly Ruskinian personality. As though in allegory, this Doge had had "David's piety . . . and Solomon's love of fine things," and he had sought his power in "the justice and the joy of human deeds . . . by principle and passion equally" (*Works, 24,* 274). Moreover, he had married a fabulous "Greek maid" (ibid.)—a "princess" whose influence is revealed in the Byzantine chiseling on the Pillars of Jean d'Arc and in the eleventh-century mosaics of St. Mark's (*Works, 14,* 427; from *Notes on Drawings by Prout,* 1879–80; for a nebulous identification of this "Greek maid"—naturally, Rose La Touche—see his reference to "the dear Greek Princess" in the last paragraph of this entry). Furthermore, upon the first church which had been built in Venice (St. James of the Rialto), beneath a Cross of St. George, there had been inscribed, during the reign of Doge Selvo (or so, upon occasion, Ruskin was persuaded to believe), the words which Ruskin personally had discovered and deciphered in 1877: "Around this temple, let the merchant's law be just—his weights true, and his agreements guileless" (*Works, 29,* 99; from *Fors Clavigera,* April 1877; see also *Works, 29,* 268–69).

I want to know the shape of your cap. Presumably because this knowledge would help him to date mosaics to be described in the next installment of *St. Mark's Rest* (delayed until July 1879). For example, conjecturally dating a mosaic which shows a Doge with "Priests, Clergy, People" (see *Works, 24,* Pl. LIX), he notes that the "Doge wears, not the contracted shell-like cap, but the imperial crown. [The] priests and clergy are alike mitred—not with the cloven, but simple, cap, like the conical helmet of a knight" (ibid., 295).

Tell me . . . Raphael dear—from the angle. This appeal is made to Raphael, "the angel of the Lord" (Tobit 12:22), whom God sent in answer to the prayer of the blind Tobit and who, as though a servant, had gone forth to help Tobit's son Tobias, with his dog. Thus, Ruskin had explained, "the angel of all beautiful life" had appeared, "hidden in simplicity of human duty, taking a servant's place for hire, to lead [Tobit's] son in all right and happy ways of life" (*Works, 29,* 35; from *Fors,* February 1877). In the Ducal Palace the Angel Raphael is shown "above the Vine angle [of Noah]," with a "diminutive figure of Tobias [following] at his feet" (*Works, 10,* 363–64; from *The Stones of Venice*; see also Pl. XVII, facing p. 302).

Angel of the lagoons from the Paradise. Because it is conjoined with his appeal to the Angel Raphael, this plea is presumably addressed to the "Angel of the Sea," to whom he calls attention in his description of Tinoret's *Paradise*: "In front, nearer, flies Raphael; and under him is the four-square group of the Evangelists. . . . Far down, under these, central in the lowest part of the picture, rises the Angel of the Sea, praying for Venice; for Tintoret conceives his Paradise as existing now, not as in the future" (*Works, 22,* 106; from *The Relation between Michael Angelo and Tintoret,* 1872). It can seem a pity that this invocation to the "angel of the lagoons" (or "Sea"?) should have ended with the inconclusive *"those."* Yet even so, his reference to Desdemona and Othello, as the next association, would seem to follow naturally from the belief of his "sweet Tintoret" that man *should* know, upon this earth, his Paradise.

Send for the lady. Also in Venice, Othello would have Desdemona bear witness in his behalf: "I do beseech you, / Send for the lady to the Sagittary / And let her speak of me before her father." They may take Othello's office and his life if they find him "foul in her report" (Act I.3). The lady in this guise is manifestly but another image for Rose La Touche. Believing accusations made by "Effie" (Mrs. J. E. Millais) in letters addressed to Mrs. La Touche during 1868 and 1870, Mr. La Touche had relentlessly opposed his daughter's wish to marry Ruskin, who, for his part, could have felt confident that, before her father, he would not have been "foul in her report."

We acknowledge thee to be the Lord. From the *Te Deum* (published in *Works, 25,* xxv).

My letter from 'Piero.' "Piero" had served Ruskin during the months of 1876–77 which he had spent in Venice. Deciding to use this letter as a place-mark, he may have considered its "chance" arrival, from Venice, as yet another "sign."

The Horses of St Marks. The bronze horses of St. Mark's, proudly standing in their harness, had been one of his self-symbols at least since 1871, when, during his illness at Matlock, they had become the subject of the dream described in *Ariadne Florentina.* In that dream the Fisherman, calling him on into water which he feared might be beyond his depth, presently had stopped to show him "the bronze horses of St. Mark's and said, 'See, the horses are putting on their harness' " (*Works, 22,* 446).

The dear Greek Princess. She is the "Greek maid"—also designated "a Greek princess" in his *Notes on Prout*—who became the legendary wife of the Doge Selvo who finally became a monk. For, like other men at their best, Doge Selvo had had his "flaw" and had "married" her. "Liking pretty things, how could he help liking pretty ladies?" (*Works, 24,* 274; from *St. Mark's Rest*). With her excessive otherworldliness, this fabulous lady is inescapably reminiscent of Rose La Touche. She "came with new and strange light on Venetian eyes, and left wild fame of herself: how, every morning, she sent her handmaidens to gather the dew for her to wash with, waters of earth not being pure enough. So through lapse of fifteen hundred years, descended into her Greek heart that worship in the Temple of the Dew" (ibid; see also, below, *"Athena 'of the Dew' "*). She is reported to have been extravagantly fastidious when she ate, as well as lavish in her use of perfumes: "All thy garments smell of myrrh, aloes, and cassia, out of the ivory palaces whereby thou hast made me glad" (ibid., p. 275). Yet she had enabled those who worked, within her reign, to interpret "to her people's hearts, and [make] legible to their eyes, the law of Christianity in its eternal harmony with the laws of the Jew and of the Greek" (ibid., pp. 275–76). Factually, it was crucially through Rose, whose "reign" had not ended with her death in 1875, that Ruskin, by 1877, had attained a religious faith which could harmoniously embrace the insight, with the "law," of Christian, Jew, and Greek.

Athena of the Dew—and "of the Earth." Athena, Ruskin states, "is, physically, the air; morally, the breathing of the divine spirit of wisdom" (*Works, 18,* 348; from *The Ethics of the Dust*). As *Athena of the Dew,* she expressed "the spirit of life" which is represented by "the diffused dew, or dew of heaven," which falls brightly, gently, life-givingly, upon the green pastures (*Works, 19,* 334–35; from *The Queen of the Air*). As *Athena "of the Earth"* (*Keramitis*) she is Queen-Mother of the human Soul or Spirit in its "fire of the heart," its moral passion, its Wisdom of Conduct. It is she who cultivates the capabilities with which an individual has been originally endowed—strengthening them, or maiming, as she fashions a personality, decisively, for evil or for good (ibid., pp. 351–54). She is, in short, "the power which shaped you into your shape, and by which you love, and hate, when you have received that shape" (ibid., p. 351).

It thus would seem as though he had concluded by offering up his thanks to the Mother who, during his childhood, had been so memorably the shaper of his clay, this Mother having also been a First Priestess of the "Dew of Heaven."

1879

On January 13, 1879, the "Diary begins again" (Ruskin's opening words), its entries to be made the first business of each day through September 16, with only here and there a lapse in regularity, except for a week (March 27–April 4), when he was called to London in connection with a trial for forgery. On December 18 the entries were resumed after he had been absent from Brantwood for three months, during which, presumably, he kept no record of his daily activities. Through the main body of entries (January–September) it becomes evident that the year 1879 began as a continuation of a period of progressive recovery.

His very readiness to resume making entries in the Diary indicates that by mid-January he had already regained much of the ground which had been lost. After more than five weeks of "delirium," he had finally, on April 2, 1878, understood Mrs. Severn when she told him about a letter from Norton (noted by Mrs. Severn in a letter of April 3, 1878, to C. E. Norton; all letters cited in this paragraph are unpublished and are in the Harvard University Library). On the 7th, after "two days of perfect consciousness," he took the memorable first trip down to his study, with Mrs. Severn harboring "every hope of his perfect recovery, thank God": "his precious brain [is] as clear, and strong apparently as ever—with memory of the past unfailing—," even though "at times he is very much depressed—awakening to a conviction of all past errors in his life,—I mean the 'little foxes' we have all been sorry about—" (Mrs. Severn to Norton, April 6, 1878). Three days later she could state that they saw "no further reason for anxiety": he had been "*out* in the sunshine," and there was "no evidence of any failure in brain, only he is now more wise—and means to give up all work and worry about things. . . . *great care,* and rest are all we want for him" (Mrs. Severn to Norton, April 9, 1878). Thereafter they watched his daily progress with "thankfulness and joy." Even though he "consider[s] himself a wreck—and usually calls himself a 'rag'—or 'withered leaf,' " he was "every day . . . better thank God—and now actually reads to us in the evenings of Sydney Smith—and lets me play and sing" (Mrs. Severn to Norton, April 16, 1878). As already noted, to Dr. Simon it could seem "more like convalescence from severe fever-delirium than convalescence from mania" (see Introduction to 1878, p. 79).

He himself would recall those weeks of April as an interval during which he had looked upon "The Dream" as a stern punishment for all that he had been made, repentantly, to recognize as having been the selfishness and vanity in which he had indulged himself, back and back through the years, particularly in his dealings with his Father. Toward the middle of May he was addressing Mrs. Cowper-Temple as a "Darling Grannie" to whom he wrote as though he were a child who had been severely punished (see Letters, xxx, sect. 1, May 12, 1878).

By then, more objectively, he had told Dr. Acland that during the early weeks of convalescence marked by "bodily weakness," he had "passed through a threatening phase of humility," but that he was now beginning "to take heart of—I can't call it grace, I suppose, but of impudence again, and, as usual, begin to quarrel with my doctors first. I fancy poor John Simon went away yesterday thinking me worse than ever!" (*Works, 25,* xxvii; letter of May 1, 1878). Dr. Simon presumably had said that as yet he must not do any work. During May he nonetheless had prepared the 60 "Notes on My Own Drawings and Engravings" made to illustrate Turner, for June publication in the ninth and revised edition of the Catalogue of *Notes* on his Turner Drawings, these illustrative drawings having by then been sent to London as a supplementary display. To be sure, as he remarked in the Preface (dated "June 5, 1878") to the *Notes* on his own "Handiwork," he was "shaken and stunned by this present illness,—it has left me not a little frightened, and extremely dull." Moreover, "recovery from such illness . . . must be very slow at best: and cannot be complete, at the completest. Without abandoning any of my former aims, I must not for many a day—if ever—resume my former activities; and though I have now gone so long in literary harness that the pole and collar rather support, than encumber me, I shall venture to write in future, only what costs me little pains" (*Works, 13,* 487–88). ". . . the doctors are all quite unable to make me out," he had told one correspondent by mid-May. "My work is to *me* Air and Water, and they might just as well tell a . . . sick swallow to catch no flies, as me not to catch what's in the air of passing fancy" (*Works, 25,* xxxix; to E. P. Barrow, May 14, 1878).

Even so, he knew that he must be content with relatively unexciting work, such as preparing *The Laws of Fésole* as a substitute for his old *Elements of Drawing* or resuming the geology and mineralogy of *Deucalion* or, more happily, the botany of *Proserpina,* wherein the products of "fancy" could be unobtrusively embodied—as when he personalized (often allegorically) his characterization of flowers. As he would tell Dr. Harley: "I have sometimes wondered whether the peculiar habit of some persons who are forever striving to find a resemblance, or fancy they do, between what they see and something quite different, which they ought not to be thinking about at all, if they would only rightly understand what they are looking at, can be a variation in a mild form of this disease, or whether it is merely the natural perversity of their foolish dispositions" (*Works, 38,* 173; "Mr. Ruskin's Illness Described by Himself").

He recognized at least many of the dangers, and was not inclined to overestimate either his strength or his stability. To do his morning stint of Plato was, in June, impossible (see *Diaries,* p. 976; June 29, 1878), and in early July he was telling Mary Gladstone: "I am in a wonderfully sad marsh and pool of thought myself since my illness" (*Works, 37,* 255; letter of July 4, 1878). Toward the end of August, he was still wondering whether he would ever again "be able to draw at all. I am not, yet; that is to say, it tires me more than anything, when it's the least difficult" (*Works, 37,* 257; letter to Mary Gladstone, August 19, 1878). Meanwhile, the need to restrict himself to "quiet work" by which he would not be excited had become a theme in his letters, recurrently to be stressed until the end of the year. Nevertheless, having gone to London in July because his teeth needed care, he had ventured to give his thought once more to Turner, in order to assemble "a magnificent collection of 251 sketches and drawings," together with several sketchbooks, which had been kept in the basement of the National Gallery and which the trustees had now agreed to send, on permanent loan, to his Oxford Drawing School (*Works, 13,* liii and 560–68). Returning to Brantwood after another sight of beloved scenes in Scotland, he noted: "Again in my study," having "had twenty days' work on Turners in the National gallery, and twenty days' rest in the hills, and ought now to be able for quiet routine" (*Diaries,* pp. 976–77; August 22, 1878).

On August 4 Dr. Simon had sent Norton a description of the case, from his personal as well as professional point of view:

> ⟨In bodily health he appears to be as well as needs be, and in mind he shows no such fault as would strike casual observers⟩: but I suspect that he is more irritable than formerly, and that he is conscious of readier mental fatigue. ⟨He appears to be fairly cautious against dangers of re-upset:—perhaps not so abstinent as I should wish him to be from use of pen and ink, but, for him, self-restraining; and he professes to be on guard against over-colloquism.⟩ I hear, however, to my regret that he is now at work in *London* (whither he had come with Dentistic requirements) on Turner drawings . . . and I fear that this, which probably includes a great deal of both talking [with the National Gallery Trustees] and writing [as he listed the sketches for the Catalogue soon to be issued], may over excite him. In his financial affairs he is, I believe, resolute not to change his old course: he will, I believe, entirely exhaust his remaining few thousand pounds of cash, and will next, from time to time, part with Turners and other chattels while they last; what *then,* God knows. And the difficulty of dealing with him in these matters does not now consist only in the old wilfullness and the inaccessibility to what you and I would consider "common-sense" appeals, but is of course seriously increased by his state of health, and by our consciousness that we are here on very doubtful ground between the sanity and insanity of his mind, and are likely, by over-pressure, to provoke him injuriously. Altogether the position is, I think, sad; and I have little hope of his being secure against very dark sequels. He gives up his

Oxford Professorship, but I suppose may retain his rooms. (Letter of August 4, 1878; Harvard University Library. For the published passages, as marked by angle brackets, see *Letters of John Ruskin to Charles Eliot Norton, 2,* 147.)

Fortunately, this prognosis was unduly dark. For however foolishly headstrong his conduct may have seemed to a guardian-friend, Ruskin remained capable of managing his affairs financially so that the wealth represented by the Brantwood Turners, minerals, illuminated manuscripts, and the like could be passed on to the Severns, together with more orthodox investments—all of which would be dissipated by the ostensibly more "sensible" Severns within about thirty years. For the present he himself preferred overtly to remain the Beloved Fool whose good judgment did not warrant paternalistic respect.

Returning from London, he had shown his own peculiar brand of common sense when he told his Sheffield curator, Henry Swan:

> My health will not admit of my making any more experiments, or allowing myself to be at all involved in the plans and hopes of the British workman in his present state of semi-knowledge and diluted morals. St. George's work, so far as I myself see the bearings of it, shall go on decisively in such lands as we now own, on which it is St. George's opinion that we may advisably grow fruit and corn. . . . ¶And I shall therefore put my full force at present on the carrying out, so far as Abbeydale will go, the principles explained in the Fors of January, 1877. ¶For the money already spent or lost, I shall not trouble the recipients of it. St. George was perfectly willing to let them try their hand at his expense, but declines letting them try again. The plan, they must remember, was originally none of his, and he will not be further troubled with it. (Unpublished letter of August 29 [1878?], present whereabouts unknown; for the Abbeydale experiment, see David Downs, B.S.)

In due time he would be gratified to hear that the authorities at Oxford preferred not to accept his proferred resignation even though he could not lecture as their Slade Professor (see entry for January 30, 1879). More immediately, he had been exasperated

—and not for the first time—by Henry Swan, through a letter which indicated that Swan himself was "still far from well" as he consulted Ruskin about "the towel" and, no less, proposed that some section of the public be granted access to the Brantwood Turners. First expressing sympathy for Swan's state of health, Ruskin replied:

> Please understand, however, now, once for all, that *I* am far from well too, and that, with all the same feelings to my friends I've ever had, I *must* be LET ALONE [the very handwriting shows his anger] just now, and that nobody is on any pretext whatever to trouble me with needless business concerning bath towels or any other thing. ¶And as for seeing the pictures! I should have an excursion train daily from Liverpool, Leeds, Manchester and Birmingham if I let *them* be seen, for the asking! They CAN'T be seen (under ten years' work for the sight of them), put them out of your head, and out of everybody else's you hear talk of them. And if you could but think a little whenever you feel inclined to do, or allow anything to be done, that concerns me that you are knocking at the door of a sick chamber, and had better be sure, first, that you heard the bell—all will go much more smoothly in future. If anybody's feelings are hurt about the towel, I can't help it, for I haven't read your letter, and can't. And I only send this to stop you from sending people to see the pictures! ¶Now for necessary business. . . . (Unpublished letter of September 20, 1878; present whereabouts unknown)

Within a week, the door had opened to permit him to enjoy some visiting: first in Dunira, Perthshire, as the guest of William Graham, M. P. for Glasgow—intimate friend and patron of Burne-Jones and father of Ruskin's "darling Francie," who was also there to welcome him. In Mr. Graham's home he saw the early pictures of Millais, Rossetti, and Burne-Jones, which caused him to write "The Three Colours of Pre-Raphaelitism" for "my Oxford pupils"—to be published in the November and December *Nineteenth Century*—"in the way of autumn lecturing" (*Works, 34,* 147). Next he spent five days with the Gladstones, in

Hawarden, even though he knew (he had found the heart to jest) that Mary Gladstone would be "very *bad*" for him, since he "must *not* be—what the things and people I like always make me—in the least crazy again, if I can help it" (*Works, 37,* 261; letter of October 2, 1878). "Mr. Ruskin came; health better, and no diminution of charm," Gladstone noted in his Diary on October 12; and, on the 14th: "Mr. Ruskin developed his political opinions. . . . All in his charming and benevolent manner" (Preface to *Letters to M.G. and H.G.*, pp. v–vi).

As the year ended, he could feel himself to be reasonably secure, provided that in his work he did not dwell upon the subjects in which he was most deeply interested—which limited him, as he had told Carlyle, to "a very trifling form of thought and direction of work" (*Works, 37,* 249; letter of June 23, 1878). In November it had seemed obvious that he should not be subjected to the strain which would have been entailed by his appearing as a witness to defend himself against Whistler's suit for damages because of "libel"—Ruskin's friends having, by subscription, met the costs (see Letters, XXIV) after Whistler had been compensated by the farthing to be worn thereafter on his watch-fob. During December, as a guest at Brantwood, Constance Hilliard would be saddened as she watched: "He is aged by this illness," she told Norton, "more irritable, poor dear, and more sad; though he draws and works hard every morning, chops for an hour in the wood till dinner, rests a good deal in the afternoon, and reads 'Sir Charles Grandison' or listens to music until bedtime" (unpublished letter of December 18, 1878; Harvard University Library). Yet as the year drew to its close, he could send his old friend Rawdon Brown assurance that, relatively speaking, all was well, so that Rawdon Brown in turn told Norton: "My last letter from Ruskin, dated 17th Dec[embe]r, was satisfactory, for he wrote, 'I keep fairly well, but cannot recover my energy in early rising, and though I think I can draw and write nearly as well as ever on subjects that do not excite me, I fear I am past all emotional and historical work' " (unpublished letter of January 16, 1879; Harvard University Library).

Thus the central interest of the 1879 unit becomes the story told, between the lines, of a continuing return to health. The year begins with Ruskin's recognition of the need still to avoid, with patience, all work that was intellectually demanding, imaginatively stimulating, emotionally exciting. "I've not forgotten St. Ursula [connoting his work on Carpaccio, as the theme of the last chapter of his as yet unfinished *St. Mark's Rest*]," he told Norton, in January, "—but my recovery has been slow, and *emotional* work especially dangerous" (unpublished letter of January 13, 1879; Harvard University Library). Again, in March, writing to James Reddie Anderson about *St. Mark's Rest*: "But I must mind and not lose my wits again—and so am keeping, almost rigidly, to feathers & stones, *yet;* but I shall want to see you before you go [to Venice]—yes—very solemnly. . . . ¶I'm quite well: but weak, since the illness, always,—the doctors said I must be, for a year or two" (unpublished letter of March 13, 1879; Baillie's Institution Library). Or again, to Carlyle, explaining why he had not already called during a week he was spending at Herne Hill: "I am fairly well and can do much, yet—if I keep myself quiet;—but if I read papers, or try to talk, I get excited and weary very soon, so that my days are passed either in my wood or my library, and I dare not come up to London. The lawyers forced me just now" (*Works, 37,* 278; letter of March 28, 1879). Nevertheless, by then only four months had passed since "the lawyers" had refrained from pressing him to appear at the Whistler trial, nor had he found it pleasant to travel to London to testify against a former Companion of St. George who, in the name of "Ruskin," had forged two checks (see entries for Jan. 19 and for April 5, 1879).

As to his writing, Part III of *Fésole* having been issued during October 1878, he notes in the early entries for 1879 that he has begun the "final revise" of Part IV (see entry of January 14), to be issued in March 1879. "Counting, less than most men, what future days may bring or deny to me," he had begun the last sentence of those *Laws,* "I am thankful to be permitted, in the beginning of a New Year of which I once little thought to see the light, to repeat, with all the force of which my mind is yet capable, the lesson I have endeavoured to teach through my past life, that this fair Tree Igdrasil of Human Art can only flourish when its dew is Affection; its air, Devotion; the rock of its roots, Patience; and its sunshine, God" (*Works, 15,* 484–85). Watching himself, he would be able to tell one correspondent, before long, that he was "most solemnly thankful" still to be "permitted [to help others], with unblighted mind" (*Works, 37,* 284; letter to F. W. Pullen, May 22).

Now, too, he had the satisfaction of rounding out his work on the first volumes of *Proserpina* and of *Deucalion.* By the end of January the index for *Proserpina* was under way (see entries for January 28–30) and by February 6 the second volume is said, perhaps too hopefully, to have been begun (see repetition of this statement in entry of July 16). On March 10 he notes: "having finished 1st vol[ume] of Proserp[ina] yesterday,—hope to set to work on finish of 1st vol[ume] Deucalion, 'to day.' " By May 28 the last chapter of *Deucalion, I* (issued in October 1879) had been finished; during June he could send off the index to this volume (see *Works, 37,* 297: this letter to Susan Beever can be dated June 1879 through internal evidence), and before the end of the year George Allen had issued separate title pages and Tables of Content for the use of those who wished to have the separate parts of *Proserpina* and *Deucalion* bound up in volume form.

By the last half of March he was venturing to complete his description of the mosaics in the Baptistry of St. Mark's—his hand, at one point, trembling "with the excitement of the thoughts I have to deal with" (entry of March 17); by July 3,000 copies of Part III of *St. Mark's Rest* had been made available as one of the little red "guide-books" which he himself could read with satisfaction: "mosaics from St. Marks, good" (entry of July 12). During March he had also prepared the "Traveller's Edition" of *The Stones of Venice* so incidentally that in the Diary there is no specific reference to his performance of this task.

Meanwhile, personal associations had doubtless helped to arouse his interest in getting under way, by the beginning of February, another book which did not make too serious demands upon his energy—the compressed version of Sir Herbert Edwardes' *A Year on the Punjab Frontier,* 1848–1849, to be issued (1885) as the fourth volume of his *Bibliotheca Pastorum: A Knight's Faith* (see entries for January 14, 16, 20, February 3).

Sir Herbert had married Emma Sidney, whom Ruskin had known since boyhood, and in whom his mother, until her death, had found a faithful friend. His work upon *A Knight's Faith* could therefore be, in some sort, an act of love which now and then would also bring the widowed "Emma" to Brantwood as one of the relatively few visitors during 1879 (see entries for June 19, July 10, August 5).

Affectionately, too, he gave his time to selecting, dating, and otherwise preparing the drawings to be sent to Charles Eliot Norton for an autumn exhibition of his own work, to be displayed first in Boston and then, during December, in New York. About to ship the first installment (before the end of August, 106 "sketches" had been sent), he explained that he had chosen some which he thought Norton would find "useful" and "others which I believe you may take some pleasure in, partly in friendship, partly in knowledge of the places" (*Works, 37*, 275–76; letter of February 27, 1879). Having discovered, by February, that he was, after all, again "able to draw," he undertook to copy, with improvements, his original sketch of the "North-West Porch of St. Mark's" (*Works, 10*, Pl. D), and finally sent Norton half a dozen other drawings to exemplify the qualities of his present work. As the year began, he had told Liddell: "I am happy in the bright frosty days to find that my own hand and eyes can still do what I ask of them: and I am asking a little more than anybody yet has seen of their doing" (*Works, 37*, 270; letter of January 4, 1879). And though references to his "drawing" or "painting' recur rather regularly in the entries of this year, they do not begin to suggest the pleasure he must have found in the success of this part of his work.

As yet another sign of progressive recovery, his ability to sustain a critical exactitude of thought was marked by his decision to make the translation of Plato's *Laws* which occupies more than 100 of the left-hand pages of this Diary, headed by the note: "Translation begun 4th June [1879]." During the preceding months he had "opened" Plato now and then, but far more often he had turned to Horace, who had regained his interest so distinctly that on March 7 he was planning "the form in which to gather my work on him," having already tentatively decided on a title for that work (see entry for March 7). But after he had recovered intellectual energy, his old habit of turning to the *Laws* for morning reading as a help during periods of stress could reassert itself. As long ago as 1866 (when he was particularly tormented in his relationship with Rose La Touche), he had noted: "To-day began Plato's *Laws* again at breakfast and felt a little brighter" (*Diaries*, p. 596; August 5). Notably, however, during the months of 1876–77 which he had spent in Venice, Ruskin had found such study of some passage in the *Laws* to be therapeutic when his investigation of the pictures of Carpaccio or the mosaics of St. Mark's had left him "jaded" or "discouraged" or "confused in thought." With energies depleted, he had recorded, for example: "Plato begun again, a great calmant, before all"; "Must do my Plato. I'm never well without that" (*Diaries*, pp. 942, 951; March 13 and May 11, 1877). The "Venetian" Diary itself (Vol. *xxi* of the Bembridge MSS) became so filled with his comments on the *Laws* that he wrote "PLATO" on its spine and now calls it the "Plato book" (see entry for July 9), even though this Brantwood Diary contains his sustained translation of the *Laws*, Books I and II.

Repeatedly in *Fors Clavigera*, as well as in other works issued after 1876, he had published in his own translation passages that ranged widely through the "Books" of the *Laws*—even though (or *if*?) he had never completely read Book XII before 1879! (See entry for August 15.) Jowett's translation he considered "a disgrace to Oxford" (*Works*, *37*, 292; letter to C. E. Norton, July 9, 1879); and in 1876, having done his "bit of the *Laws* of Plato to build the day on," he had announced his plan to "do one myself, as I've intended these [roughly speaking] fifteen years" (*Works*, *37*, 210; letter to C. E. Norton, October 5). Hence he now presumably began to translate systematically for eventual publication. After three months, having marked his pace, he calculated that it would take him about three years to complete the whole (see entry of September 1). And he did, in actuality, work on from week to week until he could write that Book II was "Finished, April 20, 1880."

In further token of recovery he undertook to write his letters on *The Lord's Prayer and the Church*, addressed to the friendly

Reverend Malleson, Vicar of Broughton-in-Furness, who would publish them, with an Epilogue by Ruskin, as an almost 400-page book that went through two editions in 1880, to be reissued in 1883. As Malleson explains, "Last June [1879] . . . I proposed to Mr. Ruskin to come to address the members of a Northern Clerical Society, a body of some seventy or eighty clergy," for whom he himself was Honorary Secretary (Ruskin, *The Lord's Prayer and the Church, Letters to the Clergy*, p. 52). In what became the first of these *Letters* Ruskin had replied: "My health—or want of it—now utterly forbids my engagement in any duty involving excitement or acute intellectual effort; but I think, before the first Tuesday in August, I might be able to write one or two letters to yourself" (*Works, 34,* 191; letter of June 20). Ten letters followed, the last one dated September 14, 1879, to be read to the Furness Clerical Society, as Ruskin became what one admirer called "a direct teacher of religion" (*Lord's Prayer,* p. 149). Having defined a "clergyman," Ruskin proceeded to explain what he believed the teaching of a clergyman *should* be—in essence, a teaching which would be based upon the articles of the Lord's Prayer as universally acceptable, regardless of one's "religion" or creed. In the contemporaneously published Part III of *St. Mark's Rest* he mocked what had once been "my own pert little Protestant mind," proclaiming himself by now to be speaking "only as an Arab, or an Indian,—with faint hope of ever seeing the ghost of Laughing Water. A marvellous thing, nevertheless, I repeat,—this Protestant mind!" (*Works, 24,* 277–78). Changing tone, he would say in the 1880 Epilogue: "it was precisely as an arch-pagan that I ventured to request a more intelligible and more unanimous account of the Christian Gospel from its preachers" (*Works, 34,* 216).

Before the end of the year, with Ruskin's permission, Malleson had had these letters printed for private circulation, next giving them to the *Contemporary Review* for December publication. Had he included all the responses they evoked, he would next have been able to publish a much longer book than was the one he edited in 1880. As editor, Malleson remarked: "I do not remember that so bold an attack, and yet so friendly, has ever before been made upon our weak points in modern times; and I may justly claim for Mr. Ruskin's letters a calm, self-searching, and, if need be, a self-condemning and self-sacrificing, examination" (*Lord's Prayer*, p. 108). As for Ruskin, having seen the letters in pamphlet form, he could remark: "I am thankful to see that the letters read clearly and easily, and contain all that it was in my mind to get said" (*Works, 34,* 237; letter of October 17, 1879).

Early in August he had faced his former self (of precisely thirty years ago) by receiving from George Allen a copy of the *Seven Lamps of Architecture* to be readied for a new edition. His first response was one of admiration for the "discipline of style," together with the "extreme and quite unaffected *modesty*"—both "so different from my present manner" (*Works, 8,* xlvii; letter to George Allen, August 1, 1879). Yet by the middle of the month: "I've made myself quite sick and ill in trying to revise 7 L.— The utterly useless twaddle of it—the shallow piety and sonorous talk are very loathesome to me; and I can't go on with it just now. The actual teaching of it is all right, and some bits are good—but it is all Fool's Paradise. I can't be plagued with it more just now" (ibid.; letter of August 15, 1879).

Never, so far, had he left himself to be secure, although "still mending . . . and able to do more work than I ever expected to do again," as he had recently remarked (*Works, 37,* 293; letter to E. D. Girdlestone, July 21, 1879). True, in the Diary entry of June 27 he had found it possible to state: "as well as I ever was in my life—head—legs—mouth, and eyes—the latter of course older, but good of their age—and the first—I hope, older and better of its age" (see also entry for July 18). Or, more somberly, as he had told Dr. John Brown: "The taking away from me of all feverish hope, and the ceasing of all feverish effort, leaves me to enjoy, at least without grave drawback or disturbance, the Veronica blue, instead of the Forget-me-not." (*Works, 37,* 288; letter of June 22, 1879. For St. Veronica as "the seal of an extreme sorrow," see *Works, 25,* 449; from *Proserpina*.) Nonetheless, he was convinced that he never again would see the Alps (*Works, 26,* xlv; letter to W. G. Collingwood, July 25), and he had warned Malleson against making a public announcement of his pending *Letters to the Clergy*: "I am not able to count on my powers of mind for an hour" (*Works, 34,* 193; letter of July 6, 1879). On the next day, in his Diary: "much tired last night . . . must take care, the tiredness showing itself in slight giddiness" (see entry for July 7, 1879). By the end of July he was telling Mary Gladstone that in the autumn he could not come to Hawarden: "in my present state of illness, nearly every word anybody says, if I care for them, either grieves or astonishes me to a degree which puts me off my sleep, and off my work, and off my meat. I am obliged to work at botany and mineralogy, and to put cotton in my ears. . . . ¶ I'm rather going *down* the hill than up just now, it's so slippery; but I haven't turned—only slipped backwards" (*Works*, *37*, 294; letter of July 28, 1879). Within the Diary, on August 4, he made the entry above which he subsequently wrote the word "Insanity."

The Diary itself becomes eloquent enough in signalizing stress through its references to the "diabolic" darkness which characterized the summer of 1879 because of the presence of what would now be called "smog." Locally, blast furnaces at Barrow and Millom were the chief source of the soot which polluted the air, dimming the sun and often changing the color of the sky above Coniston and even the color of the hills; near Whitehaven—at Harrington and Cleator—others were in operation during the 1870s and 80s (see "Iron Works," Map A). "Since Ruskin felt as he did about 'Iron Works,' " Miss Gnosspelius comments, "it is a pity that Brantwood should have been so ringed with them and that the 70s and 80s was a notably booming period for these particular blastfurnaces—the earliest of which had been built as recently as 1854." Toward the beginning of 1879 Ruskin realistically noted in his Diary: "A quite black, deadly curtain over the sky— . . . not fog, but 1000 feet thick of smoke-cloud" (entry for February 15).

Before long, however, the presence of this cloud ("foul"—"filthy"—"impure"—"unnatural") became a reality upon which a convalescent could project the type of personal distress that had found expression during the "delirium" of 1878, when Ruskin had struggled against the Devil and had blamed himself for having been unkind to his Father. Now, by midsummer, the "foul" and "fiendish" weather could signify to him the triumph of a

Devil who, within the darkened heaven, had replaced a Father of Love. Addressing Miss Beever, he asked: "Did you see the white cloud that stayed quiet for three hours this morning over the Old Man's summit? It was one of the few remains of the heaven one used to see—the heaven one had a Father in, not a raging enemy" (*Works, 37*, 297; letter [of August? 1879]). Next he began "to think that the sky's anger is all against *me*" (see entry for August 3). Emma Darwin recalls how, when he saw her parents during August (see entries for August 8, 21, 26), he "spoke to them of the new and baleful kind of cloud which had appeared in the heavens, and his distressed look showed that his brain was becoming clouded" (Henrietta Litchfield, ed., *Emma Darwin, a Century of Family Letters, 1792–1896,* 2 [2 vols. London, 1915], 238). By September, having gained a better balance, he could again realistically record: "All the Lancashire view utterly lost in black smoke. . . . Evidently no more breath of pure air to be drawn in England" (see entry for September 5), after which he generalized: "Anything so vile or monstrous as the weather of the whole year since April, I had not thought the Devil strong enough to make out of the elements" (see entry for September 7).

The following months were marked by a resurgence of his strength. "I am keeping very well, and doing good work," he could assure Mrs. Swan by the middle of September (unpublished letter of September 14, 1879; present whereabouts unknown). In November, assembling his *Notes on Samuel Prout and William Hunt* (promised to the Fine Art Society for a pending exhibition), he told George Baker that he was "at this moment more overworked than I have ventured to permit myself to be since my illness; but I find myself gradually getting stronger and hope not to fail to St. George or you" (*Works, 30*, 303–04; letter of "November"). Toward the end of September, serving St. George and the Guild, he had spent ten days in Sheffield, after which he went to Herne Hill to live with the Severns, except for a fortnight spent at Canterbury with the Gales and a week spent at Broadlands with the Cowper-Temples. While in London he gave sittings to Boehm for a bust and to Herkomer for a watercolor portrait, both of which sufficiently reveal the folly of those who assert that

Ruskin's illness of 1878 had left him, hopelessly, an "old man." Pleased with the portrait, he remarked: "I've been quite a prisoner to Mr. Herkomer—who has, however, made a perfectly beautiful drawing of me—the first that has ever given what good may be gleaned out of the clods of my face" (*Works, 37,* 303; letter to Sara Anderson, December 1, 1879).

January 13. Monday
⟨Diary begins again. Ten oclock, and I but just up,—or just down—having discovered, as I finished arranging books upstairs a new poet, Bloomfield.[1] — A day to date the new beginnings from.⟩[2] Bright sky breaking through mist over fresh-snow.

January 14. Yesterday. Two first sheets of 4th Fesole,[3] for final revise. Painted in background of heath drawing up to edges. Drained ½ foot of water off fishpond and got warm sliding on the wet ice. Pulse beating a little harder than I liked in aft[ernoo]n. Read Edwardes,[4] and a game of chess betw[ee]n La B[ourdonnais] and McDonnell.[5]

January 15. Wednesday. Yesterday dark and wet, indoors all day. Corrected last sheet of 4th Fesole, drew its two woodcuts, wrote important letters.

January 16 Thursday. Yesterday Mr Riley[6] and Mr Salt[7] at lunch. Nearly finished 4th Fesole. Read Edwardes passage on Indus, and got some good business work done.

January 17. Friday. Yesterday painted some rock, rightly; saw Mr Riley again—worked in wood, and saw the purest and loveliest sunset I ever remember here with rayed shade as opp[osite, in sketch] softening the hither shore, the lake more than

1. Robert Bloomfield (see B.S.).

2. Published in *Works,* 25, 131n.

3. The concluding part of *The Laws of Fésole,* issued March 1879.

4. *A Year on the Punjab Frontier,* by Sir Herbert Edwardes. For Sir Herbert and Lady Edwardes, see B.S.; for a letter from Lady Edwardes to Ruskin, see Letters, XII.

5. Four of the famous games between Louis Charles Mahé de la Bourdonnais (1795–1840) and Alexander McDonnell (1798–1835) were included in Henry E. Bird's *Chess Masterpieces,* which was among the books in Ruskin's library.

6. William Harrison Riley (see B.S.).

7. Henry Stephens Salt (see B.S.).

½ frozen, giving strangest broken reflections in dead calm and the mist above it taking the rays. The sky clear, but with some intense golden clouds in bars, which made me think seriously of the possibility of Bottic[ell]i jewellery for landscape Today the lake *quite* frozen over, and rosy dawn—first in sky making hills below green, then on hills

January 18. Saturday. Yesterday the lake frozen an inch thick clear over, in morning Darkness and thaw at five oclock. Today Snow, deep and thick— Thaw and no more— I think beginning to incline to frost again, (two oclock)

January 19. Sunday. Yesterday out for two hours breaking way again out of harbour for the boat, full of snow—a real bit of arctic work, and pulled branches down hill in the deep snow and fall from trees, till I was warm. I ought to be much thankful. Otherwise—day worrying, discovery of forgery[8] and unintelligible accounts.

January 20. Monday. Yesterday half frost again down in boat through ice with children. Painted rock background to heath— much discouraged—but good thoughts of maps for Edwardes Punjab,[9] reading Plutarchs Alexander.

Today, frost again divine light on hills, but I [had] bad night, (taking eggs at tea,) about a horse breaking its back and fish needing salt water &c.

January 21 Tuesday. Yesterday in bright sunshine sliding on the lake— Might have crossed;—several boys did from the Tyson pier. Out all afternoon, I,—in lovely crisp snow, chopping wood Today, by the feel of my hands most bitter, and sky darker.

8. See James Burden, B.S.

9. For the maps, see *A Knight's Faith,* in *Works, 31,* Pls. V, VI, IX, and Fig. 3. In *A Year on the Punjah Frontier,* Edwardes refers to the campaigning of Alexander the Great in the region of the Indus (*Works, 31,* 392).

January 22 Wednesday. Crossed the lake on its marble surface, with Joanie and the children, in bright sunshine, this morning at eleven. painted ling[10] successfully— Sun still bright though a little overcast. Infinite business to be seen to of Sheffield and Oxford. — too much for me

January 23. Thursday. Perfectly cloudless. Branching frost —lovely as can be on window pane— Lake a sheet of marble and hills in folded lace-veils of snow— Lake a sheet, I say—except in one great pool that will not close, though the rest has borne these four days— it runs from near the point at the Hall down as far as Torver[11]— about a 4th of the lakes breadth—as if there was a current there.

My hands, and head—seem all well—yet depression on me, can't see why. Stomach, I suppose

January 24 Friday. Still frost but grey sky. I extraordinarily languid and heartless in my work—after curious long dream about quarrelling with four ladies about their worldly ways, and getting one of them to repent and walk away with me, whom I treated with strawberries—in winter, and cream!

January 27 Monday. After the most solemn resolutions always to do this the first thing, here Ive missed two days!

Yesterday Sunday the 25th [sic] the most perfect frosty day I ever remember, absolutely cloudless from dawn to eve—absolutely calm, the snow like marble dust, and the great tarn[12]

10. Doubtless *"Blosssoming—and Striken in Days": Common Heath or Ling,* to be issued with Part VII of *Proserpina* (*Works, 25,* Pl. IX), presumably as self-portraiture.

11. A small village not far from Coniston Hall, the Hall being across the lake, almost directly opposite Brantwood. See Map B.

12. Levers Water. "A notably solitary scene," Miss Gnosspelius comments, "particularly as you stand by Levers Water."

above the mines the most silent scene I ever stood a living thing in.

January 28 Tuesday. Sliding on lake with ease, to see for best view of house, but snow seems to hurt my eyes more today. Yesterday bitter cold but did good wood work, and this morning index for Proserpina[13] nicely—finishing 4th Fesole, also, yesterday

January 29 [14] Wednesday. Yesterday sliding on fishpond and lake, pleasantly,—work in wood pulling trees in snow on edge of thaw. Icicles now all massed together in blocks half a foot thick—the cascades mere incrustation. Bad beginning of night, (after good work on index, and writing important letter to Lady Edwardes[)]—but got to sleep at last, and did some good index work planning names of leaves over my coffee and reading tenth epistle of Horace.[15]

January 30th. Thursday. Yesterday nearly thaw, but got nice sliding on fishpond Baxter polishing up slides; and got 1st vol[ume] Proserp[ina] index nearly done. Also advice from Oxford that they will have me stay Professor on any terms, which is honourable for *me*, and I hope will turn out well for *them*.[16]

13. Part VI of *Proserpina*, published in April 1879, completed the first volume and included three indices to the whole: I. "Descriptive Nomenclature"; II. "To the Plants . . . English Names"; III. "To the Plants . . . Greek Names."

14. On the page opposite this entry, under the heading "MODERN FICTION," Ruskin noted: "'The fugitives saw an enormous elephant cross the clearing surrounded by ten tigers, some clinging to its back and other's keeping alongside.' Strahan's magazine for 'the young of all ages' June 1879 p. 3328."

15. Addressing his friend Aristius Fuscus, Horace expatiated upon the pleasures and peace of living in the country, not ruled by avarice.

16. Toward the end of 1878 Ruskin had formally resigned the Slade Professorship because, he averred, the Whistler trial had convinced him that he could not "hold a Chair from which I have no power of expressing judgment without being taxed for it by British Law" (Works, *29*, xxv; letter to Dean H. G. Liddell, November 28, 1878). As Slade Professor, he was succeeded by Sir William Blake Richmond (1842–1921), a son of his old friend, George Richmond (1809–96). In 1883 Sir William resigned the chair for Ruskin's reappointment. For George Richmond as Ruskin's friend, see also Letters, XXXIV.

Today, frost still; but not sharp, and hills cloudy. I in better heart for work than for many days back, both yesterday and today.

Got also, yesterday my old Blois[17] on loan, to my great content, D.G

February 1 Saturday. Missed a day again Heaven keep my wits — how is it I can't do such a thing as this regularly

Yesterday over the lake sliding to call on Susie; back down the middle of it to promontory of hall; and so straight across back. Very stiff when I got home. Today still frost, but dark,—hope to get over to call on Kate.

February 2. Sunday. Four inches of snow over all things—lake a true Lac Blanc, we only want the Mont.

Yesterday across it sliding with Joan to call on Kate.

Today, my lettered plate arrives. Et Appellavit,[18]—the beginning I hope of much to many.

February 3. Lovely light though not quite pure, on snowy hills and *wavy* lake, the waves sealed on it by wind with thaw after heavy snow. Very wonderful—making it all look like a photograph. I myself in good heart—though after a bad night with

17. Turner's *Château de Blois* (for *The Rivers of France*) was among the watercolors which Ruskin had given to Oxford.

18. He had, in other words, received the plate of his drawing of the two globes to be used as an illustration in Part IV of *The Laws of Fésole* (see *Works, 15*, Pl. X), issued in March 1879, this plate being lettered: *"APPELLAVITQUE LUCEM DIEM, ET TENEBRAS NOCTEM"* ("And God called [named] the light Day, and the darkness he called Night": Gen. 1:5). Moreover, as "Fors" would have it, this plate had arrived on February 2, the day which Rose La Touche had "named," in 1866, as the Day when she would tell him, three years later, whether or not she would become his wife. "To-morrow, Lady-Day," Ruskin had just written Mary Gladstone, "it will be thirteen years since she bade me 'wait' three, and I'm tired of waiting" (*Works, 37*, 273; letter of February 1, 1879). Therefore in the entry, the *Et Appellavit* can (as Miss Grosspelius initially suggested) be aptly translated: "And *she* named [it]." Having in fact initially "named" this Day, had Rose, in spirit, now appropriately arranged that his *APPELLAVITQUE* plate should have been received upon this *Et Appellavit* "Today"? Such use of double entendre would be highly characteristic of Ruskin's writing, with its constant play on words and multiplicity of meaning.

nasty bilious dreams, and headache in morning. But all brushed away now. Begin work for Herbert's book

February 4. Tuesday. Yesterday thaw, set in after a winters frost,—but I got a good afternoons woodwork, some of it in sweet sunshine. Woke at 4, today, and had disturbed restless dreams, and am now languid, but hope to get dull work off my hands, and so double elasticity tomorrow.

February 5 Wednesday. Snow as fine as salt steadily powdering everything again—frost yesterday and had some good sliding again on fishpond. Lake one wide and washy incongruity of thick and thin—soft and hard, slippery and sloppy

I very languid all day,—stomach of course. Roasted chestnuts and pudding raisins. Joanie numbers my drawers, and I can begin catalogue[19] to purpose.

February 6. Thursday. — Thawing storm all night—after lovely snow all day, now grey waste everywhere. Let me see that I don't thaw away into waste myself, now the Spring's come again for me, once more! Snowdrops on my table, and I begin Proserpina II vol[ume], with Amaryllis,[20] —with my room in fairly good order, and mind and body fairly in tune, D.G. though ill, yesterday.

February 7th. Friday. Steady rain all night; steady and swift thaw of much snow—the stream at the door a torrent, larger than I've yet seen;—the air all fog, and my mind about the same. Threatening toothache at intervals to cheer me, and make me thankful when it goes away again. So begins the last day of my 59th year. Read Johnsons life of Dryden— what a paltry blackguard and hollow

19. Probably of his minerals

20. No discussion of the amaryllis was included in the unfinished second volume of *Proserpina* (published, in parts, 1882 and 1883).

fool the fellow was! At least my early education made me understand the value of truth, the beauty of nature—and the nobleness of obedience and forgiveness—all ideas as foreign to Dryden's mind as snow to a negros.

February 8 Saturday. A pretty gleam of sunshine began the morning; and Joan and Lily came in to brighten it— Foggy now, but I fairly well, and much disposed, beginning my 61st year, to wonder why I can still say "who forgiveth all, and healeth all." [21] Read the two texts given me in Rosie's book for the 21st Feb[ruary], last year,[22]—very noteworthy.

And hope to get some good Rose-work[23] done in course of day. Study in *perfect* order, for once.

February 9. Sunday. Pitch dark rain and fog I can scarcely see to write a letter much less to correct press,—perhaps better left till Monday,—end of first vol[ume] Fésole.

Everything went well, yesterday the most cheerful birthday Ive had for years Did nice bit of botany, and had I suppose, last walk *on* lake in bright sunshine Ice still perfectly safe. Coniston band came and made the evening merry. They kept it up with Miss Bell [24] and the maids till 12 oclock!

February 10. Monday. Languid in my Lily-work[25] yesterday but kept room in perfect order and find it today ⟨like a Carpaccio background to St. Jerome.⟩[26] A sweet white horizontal cloud on lake like Turner's in my old Lucerne but fog above.

21. "Bless the Lord, O my soul . . . Who forgiveth all thine iniquities; who healeth all thy diseases" (Psa. 103:1–3).

22. Matt. 7:13–14 (see 1878, Supplementary Note, p. 116).

23. Namely, work for "P*ros*erpina," with its hidden *Rose*.

24. Presumably either Polly or Libby (Libbie) Bell, daughters of William Bell (see B.S.).

25. That is, amaryllis.

26. Published in *Works, 33,* xxiii (misdated 1880).

February 11 Tuesday Just IX of C.[27] Joanie an hour away, in rosy light, with trail of bright pure steam after her. I very well, broken sunshine on clear hills reflected in the literally 'glassy' lake, still unbroken

Should be very thankful for all things

February 12 Wednesday. A good day yesterday on heath painting and Amaryllis, with wood clearing. Today a quite divine dawn—rosy above grey mist, and hard frost again Conist[on] Hall dark on blue, wonderful

February 13 Thursday. Yesterday rowed round the south border of the ice, all crashing whispering, and even tinkling like musical glasses, when the waves large or low—rose at it and under it from the south. I never heard a sound like it before —most literally of 'breakers'. — The connected ice, cracked through and through like chain mail, undulated exactly like a thin film, far back from the broken edge, a most singular instance of the real 'ductility' of its possible form, even on so small a scale.

Thinking this morning of Nelsons real watchword at Trafalgar, I may note that 'England' had no right to expect more than a certain number of men to do their duty, out of the mass whom she had selected by the pressgang and educated by the cat: but that the Captain *had* the right to expect all to do their duty, whom he had animated by his example as their comrade, and convinced of his skill as their leader.

Foggy and calm. I fairly well, but not lively.

[February 14] St Valentine. Friday

Down at 5 minutes to 9 with my rooms, drawing room and study both in the perfectest order I've ever got into, and—though the night was

27. That is, "Just nine o'clock."

dreamy,—not painfully, of travelling in snow, and once of having business near the lambent fire of a forge, I come down in good heart for Amaryllis work.

A note difference—in my own early blundering work, between mystery and mess.

B. For Museum Fors, picture of war, state finally the literal fact in Righteousness He doth make war.[28] Flanders Forester hanging thieves in his dining hall, so Glasgow bankers, if one were but able[29]

Yesterday wet all day. Gave Mr Gould a drawing lesson.[30]

February 15 Saturday. A quite black, deadly curtain over sky —in the old way—not fog, but 1000 feet thick of smoke-cloud, nothing to be seen or done. Yesterday raining nearly all day:—it is very trying after the bright frosts.

Slept well—only dreaming of a quarrel with Usher for building a new yard & blocking a stream.

February 16. Sunday. Fog, but not black over calm lake. Ice all gone I down to my work in hope to make it worthy of the new spring granted me, though *abased sorrowfully myself.*

28. Rev. 19:11. The next issue of *Fors* (March 1880) contains no discussion of war, although it ends with a section on "the proposed enlargement of our museum at Sheffield" (*Works, 29,* 396–97).

29. In "The Master's Report" dated February 12, 1879, and read at the March 1879 meeting, at Birmingham, of the Guild of St. George, Ruskin refers to the failure, on October 2, 1878, of the City of Glasgow Bank, involving an estimated loss of £8,000,000. "The managers and directors were convicted of uttering false balance sheets, and sentenced to various terms of imprisonment" (*Works, 30,* 15n.).

In *Les Genealogies et Anciennes Descentes des Forestiers et Comtes de Flandres . . . par Corneille Martin . . .* (Antwerp, 1598) he had found stories and pictures "of the first 'foresters' (rulers of woods and waves) in Flanders, where the waves once needed, and received, much ruling." The issue of *Fors Clavigera* in which these "Flanders Foresters" are discussed is illustrated by an engraving of "Robert, Count of Flanders, called 'The Son of St. George' " (*Works, 27,* 297–98; May 1872).

30. Opposite the entry for February 11 he had noted: "Mr. [David] Gould [of Ambleside] to lunch. Thursday.'

Note of colour for Fésole,—I have never yet said briefly enough that when colour is refused in continence from it, it is well, or *may* be well. But if refused in pride, as if form were nobler it is always ill!

I would really have Ilaria[31] in marble, rather than a Vandyke portrait of her. But not in pride.

February 17 Monday. Wet and discomforting but yesterday good in woodwork lilies, and music, my wrist recovering.

Lex Domini *immaculata,* Ps[alm] 19 Annunciation Missal, p. 42, [line?] 2[32]

February 18 Tuesday. Sharp frost again with small snow falling!—winter beginning again. Yesterday little done, but lesson to Mr Gould, I hope useful, and today at breakfast—reading of Arctic voyages,[33] and taught what men can endure—and will—for play—and vanity.

February 19 Wednesday Sharp frost—and three inches of snow—with heavy fall continuing Read the sledge journey of the crew of the Germania in Arctic Voyages:[34] more saddened and humili-

31. The recumbent figure on Quercia's *Tomb of Ilaria di Caretto,* in Lucca, which in 1845 "became at once, and has ever since remained, my ideal of Christian sculpture. It is, I will venture to say, after these forty years of further study, the most beautiful extant marble-work of the middle ages" (*Works, 4,* 347; Epilogue of 1883 to *Modern Painters, II*).

32. Psa. 19:7: "The law of the Lord is perfect, converting the soul," *Lex Domini Immaculata* being the usual heading for this Psalm. None of Ruskin's MSS is known, formally, as the "Annunciation Missal," Mr. Dearden states.

33. The translation (published in 1874) of Captain Karl Koldeway's *The German Arctic Expedition of 1869–70, and Narrative of the "Hansa" in the Ice.*

34. In June 1869 the *Germania,* a steam vessel, had left Bremen, accompanied by the schooner *Hansa,* equipped for an attempt to reach the North Pole by a passage off the eastern coast of Greenland. The *Hansa* having been caught within heavy ice, and crushed, Captain Koldeway of the *Germania* realized that he could not reach the pole. Hence he established winter quarters on the shore as a base from which the crew (after spring had brought daylight) made one long and four short trips by sledge, mapping out about 150 miles of the coastal region. For Captain Koldeway's story of the long "sledge journey," see his *German Arctic Expedition* (London, 1874), Part II, chap. 10.

ated than mended by it but I hope a little mended too and disposed to be thankful for my mercies

February 20 Thursday. Martha and Tottie[35] arriving happily, cheered the evening, yesterday but fog today with frost in morning, and feeling of cold coming on, depress me today, with foolish letters from everybody.

February 21 Friday. Heavy snow again, always thawing as it falls, perpetual cold and mess, but a good deal of wholesome light, and lovely sun on hills yesterday in afternoon teatime I with bad cold and disconsolate about getting nothing done.

February 23. Sunday. In all day—with heavy cold yet missing my diary— I can't keep up with my letters even! Plato! alas—opened for a glance only

Today—lake frozen all over at Seven morning!

February 25 Tuesday. Lake frozen again—dazzling day of frost, and I with a cold since Wednesday never ceasing, and today one convulsion of sneeze all day long, a thing to date from—the Cold of 1879, as the Hot, or Craziness of 78!

February 27. Thursday. Yesterday a quite divine day of frost, the loveliest clouds on the hills—or behind them —we've had this winter: but letters and work unendurably fatiguing and vexatious.

February 28th. Friday. Seriously, as I thought ill last night, much better this morning. Read my diary up, or down to Good Friday [February 22] last year, with great wonder and I trust, some understanding: and ⟨more in my heart than I can write, except that I got two oracles from Horace during the night. 'Fortem memento' I remembered naturally enough⟩—down to Moriture Delli. ⟨But "Mors et fugacem persequitur virum" being opened at—decided me to go to London

35. Claudia Gale (see B.S.).

tomorrow.)[36] Afterward 'Desine Pervicax' for the "vixen violet" given me for help in Botany.[37]

March 1. Up at 1/4 past six, off at 7, drove to Hawkshead, walked back by tarns,[38] in divine frost,—but eyes weak with long cold. Walked home thinking so deeply all the way that I don't remember climbing the hill past Waterhead. Brain much overworked. Afterwards, broke ice across lake for Martha and Tottie and studied first snowdrops A happy day of rest, though weak

Notable, that on first March I was *on* the ice of the tarns in perfect safety.

March 2. Sunday. Up to 1/4 past 6, and down now to my Coffee and Plato. *Heavy-headed, after cold and diarrhoea and quite unbounded irritation from lawyers*[39] Yesterday—my last fight with the ice I fancy— pulling back across lake after landing Martha & Tottie, I found that ice 1/3 of an inch thick let the oars swing back and forward

36. Published (with inaccuracies in transcription and unindicated omissions) in *Works, 33,* xxv–vi. The first "oracle" came from *Ode* 2.3, 1–4: "Remember when Life's Path is steep, to keep an even mind, and likewise, in prosperity, a spirit restrained from over-weening joy, Delius, seeing thou art doomed to die [whether you live always sad, or . . . take delight in holidays]." The second was the message from *Ode* 3.2.14—in context: " 'Tis sweet and glorious to die for fatherland. Yet death o'ertakes not less the runaway, nor spares the limbs and coward backs of faint-hearted youths" (Loeb Classics translation).

The meaning of this entry Ruskin explained by writing C. E. Norton: "I am better, though I was uncomfortably ill last night, and being summoned to London to give evidence on a charge of forgery, variously painful to me, was considering whether I would go or not— I greatly trust in the Sortes Horatianae, as well as Virgilian, at least, for me,—and opening my Horace in the morning at 'Mors et fugacem,' determined at once to go: and have been much more comfortable in mind and body ever since" (*Works, 37,* 276; letter of February 28, 1879).

37. In the end he did not use this help ("Cease, wanton one") from *Ode* 3.3.70, no "vixen" being included in his 1881 discussion of the species of the violet, in *Proserpina* (*Works, 25,* 400–13).

38. Tarn Hows. "*Tarn Hows* and *The Tarns,*" Miss Gnosspelius comments, "were and are alternate names in use on maps and picture postcards for the same place, which Ruskin sometimes refers to as *Mr. Marshall's Tarn(s).*"

39. Doubtless because of the forgery

on it with all their weight, and when broken with a blow, nearly broke the blades with the strain if they caught in it coming up; besides cutting the edges all to shavings. Heaped drift ice at shore lovely. Note A and ω. (Ω) P[lato] VIII. 112[40]

I open my Plato, by Fors, not where I was really stopped, but at the stop before, of the fragmentary study at page 463, where I get the glorious ὐοκοῦν ὦ εἑνε, page 464, VIII to begin again with[41]—and—going to my R[ose] book for March 2nd I find a sheet of writing paper left in at it!—i e. at the last February and 1st & 2nd March place.[42]

March 3. Down rightly to my work. I wonder I wonder I

40. In other words, "Note Alpha and Omega—or the Beginning and the End—on page 112 of Volume VIII in Bekker's 1826 edition of Plato." (See *Works, 29,* 227n., for Ruskin's explanation of his references to Plato. In the Diaries he usually employs the same method.)

Ruskin's annotated copy of Volume 8 in the Bekker edition, containing the *Laws,* is now at Bembridge School. "At the head of page 112," Mr. Dearden states, "Ruskin has noted: 'The great Beginning and End. The always following δικη . . . τιμωρός, noble.' At the foot of the page he has written: 'If I could bring my own work to an end, as I began!' "

The relevant passage, as translated by R. G. Bury, is as follows: "O men, that God who, as old tradition tells, holdeth the beginning, the end, and the centre of all things that exist, completeth his circuit by nature's ordinance in straight, unswerving course. With him followeth Justice, as avenger of them that fall short of the divine law" (Plato, *Laws, 1* [Loeb Classical Library ed., 2 vols. London and New York, 1926], 293).

41. In Plato's *Laws,* Bk. X (Vol. 8, p. 464, in Bekker edition [11 vols. London, 1826], Mr. Dearden states), this phrase, "Surely, oh Stranger," launches the query: "it seems easy . . . to assert with truth that gods exist?" (Bury translation, in Loeb edition, *2,* 301).

In the Diary the page opposite this entry for March 2 is headed: "PLATO. αληθευω," and contains the following translation of "[page] 464. [line] 2 / J[owett] 395": "Does it not then seem to you easy to say, with truth in our hearts and mouths at once, that there are Gods. / Or better, perhaps / May we not hold then, oh stranger, that is easy &c. / ἀληθευω, not merely saying the truth, but meaning it? Or, as Jowett interprets, and as the sequel partly implies 'to say with demonstration?' "

42. Elsewhere Ruskin does not specify the texts. (For Rose's "day book" see February 21, 1878, Supplementary Note, p. 116.)

had not usually more signs on this day.[43] I was past signalling last year in it

Read today, by Fors or my Father's choice—my entry for the 14th, last February, when I took St Ursula for the Madonna.

Much that follows very instructive.

Today dark,—tops of hills grey. Yesterday my grand walk round Waterhead to be written for Deucalion.[44]

March 4. Joanie's birthday has brought me in the afternoon, after very hard work on Deucalion and letters,—and an almost sleepless night before, the most healthy sense of happiness I've had for years.

Just going to finish day, to her health.

March 5 Wednesday. Dark weather and sleepless night on the 3rd have kept me two days in bed to breakfast—today—it is just nine, and I've only done a little bit of Horace, and got down, but comfortable, and tooth which was threatening, relieved.

March 6. Thursday. Down in right time, but after lying awake since 5. Red light but rainy and impure on clouded hills. Planned as I dressed, brief epilogue to Jamie's St George[45]

March 7 Friday. Nones of March: and Ste Felecitas[46] I believe, but can't make out missals.

Lay in bed to obey Joanie, who came back, yesterday D.G. well and very happy. ⟨In reading

43. The anniversary of his father's death.

44. See *Works, 26,* 363–65.

45. Namely, *St. Mark's Rest,* chapter 11, in which J. R. Anderson analyzes similarities between the myth of Perseus and of St. George. This chapter was first issued in April 1879, with its two-sentence Epilogue dated "6th March, 1879": "The Editor had hope of publishing this book a full year ago. He now in humility, yet not in uncertainty, can sum the causes of its delay, both with respect to his friend and to himself, in the words of St. Paul, *καὶ ἐνέκογεν ηνας ὁ Σατνας* [and Satan hindered us]" (*Works, 24,* 400).

46. March 6 is the "day" of St. Felecites of Carthage, martyred in the year 203, during the reign of Severus.

Horace at breakfast—planned the form in which to gather my work on him, to be called either Mella Matini or Exacta Vulturni—but I think the first.—)[47]

March 8 Saturday. — Cold still hanging on me, but a wonderful gush of plans and thoughts again.

Spiculae of ice, 8th March 1879,[48] on open lake,—some a foot long, about 1/4 of an inch wide and quarter inch deep, an average 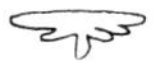 section thus, the keel of serrate rounded points like a prawns horn—pointed towards point of spicula— I think, when perfect the spiculae were thus [diagrammatic sketch] in centre—thinned like a xl [viz. crystal] of carb[onate] lime and going off at each side in opposite direction[49]

March 9 Sunday. Yesterday Frost so sharp that lake froze into spiculae connecting a film on surface about 1/15 of inch thick.[50] Today, diabolical cloud.

March 10. Monday. Very bright—though not quite pure sky, and I up after a thoroughly good piece of work on Horace,—with much in mind, and find my drawings progressing satisfactorily,[51] and, having finished 1st vol[ume] of Proserp-

47. Published in *Works, 33,* xxiii. The first title, "Honey from Matinus," was suggested by the passage: "I, after the way and manner of the Matinian bee, that gathers thyme laboriously around full many a grove and the banks of well-watered Tibur, I, a humble bard, fashion my verses with incessant toil" (*Ode* 2.11.27–30; in Loeb Classics translation). A "fragment" of MS headed "MELLA MATINI. BEGUN, NONES OF MARCH, 1879," indicates that he may have planned to quote passages from Horace followed by a verse translation and by notes explicating Horace's meaning as expressed through his own version (see *Works, 34,* 694).

48. This paragraph appears on the page opposite the brief entry for March 8 and follows an aphorism headed "St. G[eorge's] G[uild]": "There is a wonderful difference between the support which companions can give each other in standing shoulder to shoulder after once they can stand firm apart. But not while they are reeling to and fro and at their wits' end."

49. These observations were reworked for publication in *Deucalion,* where the diagrammatic sketch in the Diary appears as the winged ice-crystal shown in *Works, 26,* 358, Fig. 43.

50. Described in *Deucalion* (see *Works, 26,* 347–49).

51. Namely, the drawings to be sent to C. E. Norton (1827–1908) for exhibition.

[ina] yesterday,—hope to set to work on finish of 1st vol[ume] Deucalion 'today'

This day Sunday, last year I was prayed for in the churches of St Andrews. See Ada Dundas's[52] letter, in R[ose]'s box

March 11 Tuesday. Quite glorious calm, on golden brown grass, and dead fern, or frost-browned mountains in full sunshine under blue sky I very well, and cheerful after pleasant sleep, but with too much in my mind after Horace at breakfast. Got nice beginning of last Deucalion done yesterday. Today—must be on the hills I think

March 12 Wednesday. Chopping and sweeping yesterday in afternoon, with Martha and Tottie;—a pleasant time: and good night's sleep, and much nice in my letters, and more in my mind, if I could only get it written!—or literally—drawn —out Today, violent wind and rain—must find out the breadth of a lake-roller if possible.

March 13 Thursday. Down in perfectly blessed and bright morning—⟨jealous of every golden minute of golden day.⟩[53] Yesterday—making the path up under 'precipice-rock'—I must find some less grand name—with Martha helping nicely in pulling down wood. As I look up the pale blue sky and mountains flooded with light pale amber or dead leaf colour with the bloom of a sunburnt greenage—won't let me write more.

March 14. Friday. Yesterday went out, and found Yew-trunk by lake shore! and got the most wonderful lessons about frost I ever had yet in my life. — Called on Susie in afternoon, and had talk about Jamies letter, telling me of Pervinca and Atlas,[54] which also came Yesterday a wholly

52. For Adela Dundas, see B.S.

53. Published (inaccurately) in *Works, 33,* xxv.

54. "My darling Jamie," he had written J. R. Anderson, "Of all you've done and found for me, this of Atlas and Pervinca are the most precious bits: and coming

blessed day— Today, Snow an inch thick again everywhere—and frost—till just now—9, when it begins to thaw. Good bit of Horace done.

March 15 Sat[ur]day. Wisie's birthday. A perfectly dismal and diabolic cloud on hills—after snow all night, now thawing wretchedly. I depressed enough,—but knowing my battle now better than when it beat me last year—D.G.

March 17. Monday.[55] Yesterday very dismal, working on St Marks mosaics,[56] but I think something will come of it today. Ive got my pretty drawing beside me,[57]—but my hand trembles with the excitement of the thoughts I have to deal with Must do a little geology first to cool me down.

March 18th. Tuesday. White dense mist over nearly pure sheet of snow— Falling heavily yesterday all day long,—quite deep in afternoon though slowly thawing. Kept in all day but did grand work on St Marks, and found out the Cornice derivation from Holy Sepulchre! [58]

March 19. Wednesday. Yesterday Rain all day and I giddy with work on St Marks: but it will come right D.V.

Today sweet morning mist—and opening blue at last.

---

at this moment,—like your journey over the hills last year—supernatural" (unpublished letter of March 13, 1879; Ballie's Institution Library). At the top of this letter Anderson wrote: (1) "'Atlas' refers to the figure [seated beneath 'Astronomy' in the Simone Memmi fresco] in the Spanish Chapel, so called, but denied to be Atlas by the critics though Vasari named it so. I had found that Atlas was right, as is now, I believe recognized." (2) "Per-vinca, the Martyr's crown of periwinkle, quasi from per vincere. I forget where I found the derivation."

55. The page opposite this entry is headed "DELIVER US," followed by the reference: "See notes on Lord's Prayer Venice [18]76 diary page 58." In other words, see the final paragraph for December 31, 1876 (*Diaries,* p. 926; identified, from the MS, by Mr. Dearden).

56. Included in chapter 8 of *St. Mark's Rest,* published July 1879.

57. Probably C. Fairfax Murray's study of "Priests, Clergy, People, Doge" (see *Works, 24,* 295–96, and Pl. LIX).

58. The acanthus leaves on a Byzantine capital of St. Mark's, he explains, "are only the amplification of the cornice over the arches of the Holy Sepulchre at Jerusalem" (*Works, 24,* 288).

March 20 Wednesday. — no! Thursday—alas— I've just been rowed by Herdson into Joanna's bay,[59] through ice right across lake in long flakes—$\frac{1}{8}$ of inch thick and so well knit that his oar in one place slipped on it instead of going through! while yesterday at 12 oclock—I could'nt stand to chop wood, for the heat of sun! And yet today, there's no frost in the ground! see opposite*

* [Opposite] ICE. Mere hoar frost, not penetrating or lifting the ground in the least! while the lake ice lay in lovely plumes seven and eight feet long in the sweep, and with angular ridges of arborescence on surface as sharp as Ive seen this year, and more lovely in curvature!

March 21. Friday. Exquisitely bright day and I well—but tired with thinking over life of Carlo Zeno and all its sadness.[60]

March 22 Saturday. The beginning of the half year of precious days — D.V. I[']ll make something of it, though overtired just now with this vile lawyers work.

March 23 Sunday. Little enough done, yesterday yet always something. Precious map of lagoons found, and Venetian History fairly begun again[61] Rowed over lake with Lolly, Martha & Tottie to see my new boat,[62] and worked well on rocks in wood.

59. "Presumably the bay just to the south of the Brantwood Harbour," Miss Gnosspelius comments. "This bay can be seen in the photograph published in W. G. Collingwood's *Ruskin Relics,* p. 17—to the left of the girls who are sitting upon the Harbour wall."

60. In *The Stones of Venice* he had spoken of the choice of the debatably honorable Morosini as the Doge of Venice in preference to Carlo Zeno—one of "her noblest and wisest children," from whose death, in 1418, he had dated "the commencement of the Fall of Venice" (*Works, 9,* 21).

61. Doubtless for his pending discussion of "the twelfth-century divinity of the mosaics of St. Mark's" (*Works, 9,* 21).

62. The "Jumping Jenny," designed by Laurence Hilliard and constructed by William Bell, of Haws Bank, in his boathouse across across the lake—to be launched, with ceremony, on April 13 (Easter Sunday). See J. S. Dearden, *The Professor, Arthur Severn's Memoir of John Ruskin* (London, 1967), pp. 103–05.

March 24 Monday. Yesterday Jamie came over, with his collie Yarrow, and we had a nice time

Today, North wind and bitter frost! Waterfall under the Tarns[63] all ice and dusty snow over all Middle Pike

March 25 Tuesday. Icicles on wall and chalcedony in ground—East wind and snow!

March 26. Wednesday. Bitter blight—and semifrost. Yesterday to Seathwaite Rayne,[64] in bitterest wind I've felt for ages

March 27 Th. 28 Fri. 29. 30. 1. 2. 3. 4.

April 5th Saturday. The past week very miserable in London,[65] and now quite tired and good for nothing but thankful to be as well as I am

April 6th Sunday. Preparing, as I best can, for tomorrow, the anniversary of my coming down to my study after the dream.

Putting my room in order,—and my mind, a little.

April 7th Monday The anniversary of restoration from worst illness. I am down to my Plato and larch-bud[s],[66] in peace, only tormented that I cannot do a hundred things besides. D.G.

April 8th. Tuesday. Black evil weather greatly oppressing me, and much sense of fatigue and sadness. Dreamed of being at family prayers with R[ose] (my father and mother on the other side of me, and they talked together during the prayers till someone stopped them—or at least prayed them to stop)[67] and being at church service where the sermon was about monuments of men who had suffered persecution.

63. Unidentified.

64. The home of Mrs. Julia Firth, of Ambleside.

65. Because of the James Burden trial for forgery.

66. Presumably the watercolor (7" x 5"), *Larch buds,* enlarged; first exhibited in 1907 by the Fine Art Society (see *Works, 38,* 261).

67. In MS the clauses which are parenthetically enclosed were added, as though a footnote, at the bottom of the page.

Then getting into carriage to go home—and the door and traces were decorated with satin ribands of rose colour, trailing on the miry ground.

Now to work out Larch buds.

April 10. Thursday. a fine business Ive had, too, of my larch buds,—black weather just when I wanted the whitest possible. Did good bit of Horace at breakfast. see opp[osite] *

* [Opposite] ⟨Horace's definition of a gentleman Est animus tibi: sunt mores, et lingua, fidesque Ive learned this today, quite one of the most exhaustive verses in the world.⟩[68]

April 12 Saturday of the Descent.

I have not felt so well and strong for many a day, nor found so many precious things, in Chapman's Homer, and Horace—and even modern foolish books. North Norway, &c[69]— Yesterday out before breakfast at work and nice afternoon in wood working with Mattie and Tottie.

April 13th. Easter-day.

I have been working happily on the Coniferae, noting Loudons account of destruction of Braemar forests,[70] and planning letter to Sir T[homas] Acland.[71]

April 14th Easter Monday. Intensely bright rosy dawn— I

68. Epistles 1.1.57 ("You [Maecenas] have sense, you have morals, eloquence and honour"). Published in *Works, 33,* xxiiin. For Ruskin's interpretation of this "verse," see ibid, p. 306.

69. Georg L. Hartwig's *The Polar World: A Popular Description of Man and Nature in the Arctic and Antarctic Regions of the Globe* (London, 1874). In the *Fors* of September 1881 he would quote from Hartwig's chapter on Norway (*Works, 29,* 406).

70. J. C. Loudon, *Aboretum et Fructicetum Britannicum* (8 vols. 1838). For the *Coniferae,* see Vol. 4, chap. 113; for the "slaughter" of forests in Scotland during modern times, see pp. 2164–69.

71. Sir Thomas Dyke Acland (1809–98), elder brother of Sir Henry, had served with William Cowper-Temple (1811–88) as a trustee of the Fund of the Guild of St. George until June 1877, when both men had resigned.

too much asleep to see it. now that I'm awake all's clouded, but I've plenty to do, & some strength to do it. Nice letter from Dora Thomas,[72] answered first of all.

April 16th. Wednesday. Intensely depressed yesterday. — this morning Mattie and Tottie put me in heart by being themselves out of it. The airs warm too—for the first time!

April 20. Sunday. Three days out before breakfast in sweet sunshine—may perhaps have done me good, but my third finger chilled white this morning after my bath.

Working on larch buds and Deucalion—and Arctic regions.

April 22. Tuesday. Yesterday a good day on Deucalion—feather,[73] and diggings—bright sunset—and primroses at last coming out—everywhere.

Joanie, on Saturday, completed the planting of my lovely little garden of Hyacinth and Anemone, under my 'precipice' rock—and I improved—yesterday, the chant for Tu ne quaesieris,[74] and like it. Today, at work on Iceland[75] and shall do a bit of Plato.

Lake perfectly sweet and calm

72. In the Christmas *Fors* of 1883, she would be listed among the Companions of St. George (*Works, 29,* 477). Under the name Dora H. Thomas, Mr. Dearden states, only an address, "The Hydro, Llandudno," is given in the "new Register" (in Bembridge MS *xxiii*) of those who joined the Guild in 1882.

73. Presumably the *Study of Magnified Pheasant's Feather,* dated 1879, to be sent to C. E. Norton for the autumn exhibition (see *Works, 13,* 588; *38,* 363).

74. One of the two *Odes* of Horace for which Ruskin wrote music, entitling this *Ode* (1.11) "The winter's wave" (*Works, 34,* 691). "Ask not, Leuconoë (we cannot know), what end the gods have set for me, for thee. . . . How much better to endure whatever comes, whether Jupiter allots us added winters or whether this is last, which now wears the Tuscan Sea upon the barrier of the cliffs! Show wisdom. Strain clear the wine; and since life is brief, cut short far-reaching hopes! Even while we speak, envious Time has sped. Reap the harvest of today, putting as little trust as may be in the morrow!" (Loeb Classics translation).

75. Probably encompassing Hartwig's chapters on Iceland, in *The Polar World,* to be used through quotations in chapter 3, "The Dabchicks," of *Love's Meine* (see *Works, 25,* 120–21).

April 23. Wednesday.—Yesterday began drawing rock at the diggings—but today dark and wet,—and general disappointment of garden plans. Yesterday found wonderful rock too above the Thwaite

April 24. Thursday. Not a good night—dreams having some of the old crazy nature in them:—and grey day—with dim eyes, but clear head enough. Begin chapter on crystallization for Deucalion[76]

April 25 Friday. Yesterday Lady Edwardes came—and our new maid—and the primroses are coming at a great rate—and my crystal work is getting on—wrote 5 pages yesterday. Dark weather though, always misty.

April 26 Saturday Still wet,—fearful darkness yesterday at evening— Devils weather entirely the last three weeks.

April 28. Monday. I have seldom felt better or more cheerful than yesterday at Deucalion and other work— finished feather, and planned new glacier business! [77] Today, a little giddy with reading l'ouvrière,[78] at breakfast.

April 29. Tuesday. Slept well and got on with l'ouvrière, but overwhelmed with new thoughts about rocks and ice

April 30. Wednesday. — Slept well, after nice evening, reading Anne of Geierstein to lady Edwardes. — Resolute today for a day of business.

May 1st. Bright sunrise on snow—at ½ past four! snow

76. Chap. 3 of Vol. 2, issued May 1879.

77. Defending James D. Forbes' theory about the flow of glaciers, together with Forbes' honor as a scientist against the charge of plagiarism, Ruskin had been attacking Tyndall's "Regelation Theory," recurrently, since 1873. This attack was resumed in the chapter of *Deucalion* to be issued as "Part VI" in October 1879 (see *Works, 26,* 280–87).

78. By Jules Simon, Paris, 1861. In the *Fors* of March 1880 Ruskin would publish his translation of Simon's descriptions of the slums of Elbeuf, Rouen, and Lille (see *Works, 29,* 391–94).

still deep & low down on Dow Crag, and nearly down to tarn[79] on central peak.[80]
Began day with Primula Farinosa[81] and Centunculus vincimus.[82]

Yesterday Nice evening. Mrs Marshall at reading, quietly.

May 3.[83] Saturday. Perfectly bright and calm but I languid—greatly put out and pulled down by the destruction of all the oxalis at a sweep by a frost, yesterday in morning, which gave me another 1/10 of inch of ice to study from the lake by pierside!

In absolutely cloudless morning I found the moss, No 3.—on the promontory above Fir Isle, and was happy there. Ought to be today for it is cloudless, and I have grand glacier experiment to make

May 4. Sunday. The precious days of the year flying—with little disgusts and worries that spoil them like dead flies. Much enjoyment, however, in glacier study, and mining among the rocks. Today intensely calm and cloudless—not clear—but the mist lovely.

May 7th. — No—not quite so bad—6th. Tuesday — On Sunday walked up to highest knoll of mid crags —(I must give it a name.)* — had tea with Kate—at night—violent feeling of cold and general weakness,—better gradually yesterday though doing little and hope to get to rights today Intensely clear sunshine with North breeze.

79. Levers Water.

80. The Eaglet.

81. The Birdseye Primrose—of all the "constant flowers" of the Alps, Ruskin notes in *Proserpina,* the "most abundant" (*Works, 25,* 410n.).

82. A species of chaffweed; not discussed in *Proserpina.*

83. On the left-hand page of the MS, headed "ICE," he notes: "Fatal frost of 2nd May, see opp[osite entry for 3rd May]."

* St Georges Crag, now[84]

May 8th. Thursday. Much better in health and heart, for staying in all day yesterday and putting rooms in order. Bitter cold—with rain, mostly, — more difficult to be out in, than the hardest frost.

May 12. Monday. Many nice things came to me on my Fathers birthday [May 10], but a sleepless night made yesterday almost useless. today after good sleep, up at five, and now—at ½ nine, I'm tired.

May 13 Tuesday. — Still cold and treacherous though periwinkle and primrose now in finished beauty —but my spring spoiled, as usual, by inevitable worries.

May 15. Thursday. Quite frightful North wind—blighting and boisterous at once— impossible to go out and yesterday unsafe to stand a moment. I am more shut up than in January! Five months now of winter—since the shortest day. Now, the sky growing black, and the wind so searching that I can't arrange my drawers near the window!

May 20th. Tuesday. All sorts of worry with C[onstance] O[ldham],[85] who went away, at last on Saturday, and my head giddy since, with reaction.

May 28th Wednesday. A whole week unrecorded—no Plato done—nor much else,—but the chapter on cleavage for Deucalion,[86] and a good deal of practical cleavage in cutting out the lawn-tennis ground. Head more giddy than I like, still.

June 1st. Sunday. Yesterday up Yewdale crag, defining cleavages. Got them all clear in mind this morn-

84. Known, otherwise, as The Bell.

85. Ruskin's goddaughter, Emma Constance Oldham (1852–1924), daughter of the surgeon James Oldham (1817–81) of Haywards Heath and a niece of his boyhood friend Edmund Oldfield, Assistant Keeper of Antiquities at the British Museum. As a schoolgirl at Winnington, she became "May" in *Ethics of the Dust* (1865) and, by 1884, a Companion of St. George. See Letters, XXXI.

86. The last chapter of Vol. *1* ("Schisma Montium"), to be issued in October 1879.

ing in bed. Walked or rowed from two to seven, but had no tea and was tired.

June 2 Whit Monday. Yesterday to Peel Island and saw hyacinths with Joanie & Ethel.[87] Today, apple-blossoms in rain lovely, but I headachy and wrong.

June 4 Whit-Wednesday,—if there be such a day—becomes black-Wednesday by Joanie's going to London— Yesterday—a lovely walk to slate-cave quarry and up Warder's crag, with Arthur, Lollie and Ethel.

June 5 [88] Thursday. I don't know when I've felt more wretched or good for nothing than yesterday, in calling on Creswick[89] and Susie—or in painting —or anything. All stomach I fancy—but it seems to me the mere being worsted at chess puts stomach out of order! Today a little better.

June 6. Friday. Woke at 10 minutes to 3 but slept again. — Out of heart generally without being really low—and enjoying, in moderation, much. Yesterday nice time in wood with Ethel and Downs. Clay experiment again—of much interest.

June 7. Saturday. Yesterday with Ethel and Lollie to tea-picnic under the highest tarn waterfall,[90]— naming the mine rocks on our way up, Lion, Tiger, and Eagle's peak. I think I shall call the one between it and Weatherlam [sic] the Bracelet.[91] Next we want names for the waterfalls.

Grey today, and I stupid & dull.

June 8 Sunday. Floating mists in my eyes worse than I've yet known them but it must be expected.

Grey and thunderous, and if I mistake not—

87. The 20-year-old Ethel Hilliard (see B.S.) was spending June at Brantwood.

88. In MS this page is headed: "DEPRESSION / CHESS, very curious—5th."

89. The Sheffield ironworker who had modeled the bust of Ruskin in 1877 evidently was now living in the neighborhood (see below, passim).

90. Levers Water.

91. See Map B, with the Rocks and Peak named by JR identified by Miss Gnosspelius.

snow on the upper hills, but I must wait till they clear.

Yesterday dripping all day, and I not out.

June 9. Monday. Yesterday dripping but soft rain—Spring over, all the weeds out, and primroses choked and straggly. Pink & strawberry time coming, however. Today, black and diabolical —in the usual short unaccountable, useless fits.

June 10. Tuesday. Yesterday thundrous, but pleasant dripping work in wood, found lovely large pinguiculas, and drew violet leaves[92] nicely without spectacles.

More pleasure in work than for long, and tried to be better in mind, but can't get right again.

June 11 Wednesday. Yesterday out and out the most glorious afternoon I ever saw here— the woods all in green more precious than gold, and the lake and sky like beds of Forget me not—the higher hills dark clear against the crystal.

At woodwork, with Ethel, very happy, but curiously, stomach wrong this morning, and mouth sore.

June 12 Thursday. Violent face ache keeps me awake all night. How thankful I may be to have nothing worse to keep me awake; and to be pretty bright, though still in pain after a couple of hours sleep in the morning.

Yesterday at village school, and making various plans for it

June 13 Friday. Better, but sadly pulled down— all shivery and cramped last night and feeling as I used to do when I was ill in childhood

Down however to my Plato in the usual time.

June 14 Saturday. Better, but still far from comfortable,

92. One of the drawings sent to C. E. Norton for the exhibition (*Works, 13,* 587); see "VIOLA CANINA / Fast Sketch, to show grouping of Leaves" (*Works, 25,* Pl. XXV).

and weather thundrous & damp. I get little done but pic[ture]s framed for parish school—perhaps as useful work as Ive ever done.

June 15th. Sunday. An entirely sad note from Joanie about her sister[93] puts me blackly off my work, my own cold still bad in dreams and discomfort,—and the day grey. I may be thankful its no worse, if I get Joanie back safe, all will be well. (A cricket answers cheerfully from the hearth.)

June 16. Monday. Still languid and sore and vaut-rien. Hawthorns coming out, remind me of June 1855, and illness at Tunbridge wells. I've done something though, in these 25 years, and may do yet, in next ten!

June 17th. Tuesday. Face-ache, and Joanies sorrow, keep me vaut-rien, but perhaps though I may not know it, resting, after a fashion. The bit of Plato is nearly all I get done. Wet today but with sweet broken clouds, and singing of birds.

June 18 Wednesday. Still very poorly and out of all order, and don't well know what to do, nothing pleasing me or doing me any good just now, and cheek continuing sore

Mantle cloud on Old Man, wonderful. see sketch.[94]

June 19. Thursday. And so the sorrowful turn of daytime comes round again! Well I'm only 60, not 61, yet! and better today,—by Heaven's help,—and a bird singing cheerfully to me—if only I do not any more 'sin my mercies'

93. Mrs. Severn's sister, Mrs. William Milroy (née Mary Barbara Agnew), died in Kirkcudbright on June 15, 1879, aged 36, after two years of suffering from enlargement of the liver. In 1884, commemoratively, Ruskin arranged a gift of minerals for the Museum of Kirkcudbright (*Works, 26,* 458). In later years, Mrs. Gnosspelius recalls, "her daughter Katie was a constant visitor at Brantwood."

94. Possibly the undated watercolor *Fixed Cloud on the Old Man* (*Works, 38,* 246).

Lady Edwardes and Miss Irwin,[95] yesterday in wood with Ettie—at work, *we* young ones,—finishing with bonfire and festive meeting of all the family!

June 20 Friday. Wonderfully good day yesterd[ay] on Bunnoo[96] and violets: and a bit even of cloud study done! Today wet—but soft and sun-gleamy, and work promising.

June 21 Promise of Joanie coming home, will make the longest day longer till she comes.

Very low, all afternoon yesterday— at Monk Coniston quite mute and stupid Cut a lot of wood anyhow, and am better today. Hawthorns utterly divine everywhere. Note order of spring flowers broadly thus— Oxalis, Primrose, Violet, Hyacinth, White Clarissa, Veronica, Hawthorn. One may trust to the succession of these up to the longest day, and then comes rose and pink time. I missed my crab-blossoms this year altogether.

June 22 Sunday. Joanie home safe, D.G.

Fierce thunderstorm last night,—no—I mean afternoon—worse than the Old Man usually lets over here. Rainbow this morning—rather scarlet and lake than orange and violet.

June 23 Monday. A quite singularly bad night and headache in morning, yet I come down in better heart for putting things in order: and not stupider in head than usual. Scott—as I have just re-read—feeling himself fast going to pieces at 54,[97] —and here at 61, I am just thinking of pulling myself better together! D.G

95. Lady Edwardes may have been staying with Miss Irvin of Langdale, whose mother, with a gift for embroidery, became connected with the work of Miss Twelves in "The Ruskin Linen Industry" at Keswick.

96. For Sir Herbert Edwardes' expedition against the wild tribes of Bunnoo, see *A Knight's Faith,* Chaps. 1–8 (1885).

97. Lockhart quotes a passage from Scott's *Diary* which had led Ruskin to state, in 1873, that Scott's "seven years of death" began in 1825 (*Works, 27,* 584–85).

June 24 Tuesday. A dull evening in smoke of foulest thundercloud outside—and pensiveness indoors. Today, as bad, outside, but room and mind in fair order. (I use that word fair—too often thus for 'middling'—a bad habit.— Consider the origin of this sense—*fairly* balanced—)

June 25 Wednesday. A 'fair' day's work done yesterday on Jonathan Otley[98] & St Marks. Arthur left early this morning for his friend Mr Russell[']s [99] — perpetual showers and intermediate midges make wood troublesome

June 27 Friday. Yesterday a horribly bad day of wet—wind—and wet-windy indecision whether I would go to Wastwater[1] or not Decided not, and am down to work this morning, D.G.—(the morning inactivity excepted before seven)—as well as I ever was in my life—head—legs—mouth, and eyes—the latter of course older, but good of their age—and the first—I hope, older and better of its age. The legs carry me still uphill—and the mouth has still teeth enough in it to get on with.

June 28 Saturday. Yesterday a good day—of ceaseless rain—and getting in order. Did a good bit of—sapias—vina liques down to receses—from quae nunc, all at a sitting.[2] Wonder much if any real good in it. Today, beginning to review work done on Scotts life as a whole.[3] Black weather

98. In the October 1879 issue of *Deucalion* Ruskin gave a brief account of "the modest life and intelligent labour of a most true pioneer in geological science" (*Works, 26,* 293–94)—the Keswick guide Jonathan Otley (d. 1857, aged 90).

99. Probably Mr. Odo Russell (1829–84), who had been Resident Secretary in Rome (1858–70), where Arthur Severn would first have known him as a friend of his father, Joseph Severn.

1. A lake in Cumberland, about 30 miles from Brantwood (see Map A).

2. He was still composing music for Horace's *Tu ne quaesieris:* "Sapias vina liques," etc.

3. Through rereading Lockhart's *Life,* he had "got back to Scott again," he had recently told Dr. John Brown, and would have "sad things to say . . . concerning the waste and the cutting short of his days, by the double sin of writing for money and for mob" (*Works, 37,* 281; letter of May 11, 1879).

incessant. D.G. I can see better than last summer. I am sure of this.

June 29 Sunday. Of eyes, see variously inconsistent entries for the 8th, 10th and 27th. The last on the whole right and D G. to be adhered to.

Yesterday dribbled away a lot of time—but got some good Bunnoo done, and practice in chords,—see above [June 28] sapias — &c. Alas, si sapias! — what a si!

By the way—how came the sweet land dove il si suona[4] to sound it? Qu[estion]. Latin forms of assent? [5]

June 30. Monday. Finer a little. I very languid yesterday and with no appetite but got some good ordering done in bookcase, and MSS more comfortable than ever before. Finished [detail?] reading of Scott, and began for breakfast work—Plutarch—old fool — Napoleon's fall might well follow the study of him.[6]

June 31 [sic] [7] [July 1] Tuesday. Pouring; but got room (bedroom) into order, and Downs up to see it, to his extreme satisfaction. Also study bookcases re-arranged—packets of Fors looked over, and a lot of work done with good pleasure in doing. Sound sleep till seven.

[July 2] Wednesday As wild a night June went out with as ever I waked in—the house shook frightfully with one gust, but D.G. I did not wake

4. Dante, *The Inferno,* XXXIII. 11.79–80.

5. In other words, how came the sweet land, Italy, "where they say [sound] *si,*" to sound it? Is the Italian "yes" derived from Latin forms of assent? The answer would be "yes," the Romans having said *sic est* (thus it is), which became shortened into *sic,* whence the Italian *si.*

6. In *A Knight's Faith,* having referred to Napoleon's defeat at Waterloo, he observes that in one trait of "military character" Frederick the Great, Wellington, and Napoleon are alike: they "*hate their enemies,*" whereas "the missionary soldier," Sir Herbert Edwardes, in his Bunnoo campaigne, was "the absolute reverse" (*Works, 31,* 480–81). Unmitigated hatred of the enemy is a characteristic which Plutarch stressed as basic to the victories of Alexander.

7. In MS the three following entries are also misdated.

long, and in a dark and plunging day, am down in good heart to work—with all my rooms and books and drawings in better order than they've been for years.

[July 3] Thursday. ⟨Room in *perfect* order, and I wonderfully well. — Joanie home quite well, and children happy, D.G. and sun on fells—and a cranberry blossom in my saucer ready to be drawn. Yesterday in breezy afternoon, found them on the hill, all sparkling like little rubies.⟩[8]

[July 4] Friday. I believe Im a day wrong somewhere! — I leave gap to put right (Not too far to look— I see I've given June 31 days!) Next page goes right. Pouring steadily—whatever the day is it's a wet one—but I slept well and am down to work in good heart, after reading Don Quixote at breakfast— How admirable it is as a translation the type of prose translation, of the most difficult kind.

Drenching, a better word than pouring for this days rain; it dashes on the window as if out of a garden engine and soaks in at all joints

July 5 Saturday. Drenching rain again—but I've had a good night D.G. in spite of salmon—cucumber, and all manner of imprudences— one has no business to thank God for delivering one from that sort of evil,—and yet what evil is to be feared—but one's own? — Room in order—and cranberry and purple convolvulus on its two tables. Get my days dated right see above— at the 3rd, and so to Plato

July 6. Sunday—Dark without rain, after a day of incessant shower. I a great deal too much indoors, but got nice music done, and slept fairly well— though dreams oppressive—but vague and immemorable.

July 7 Monday. — Indoors all day again and much

8. Published in *Works, 33,* xxii.

tired last night, yet well enough now—but must take care, the tiredness showing itself in slight giddiness. But I had really been at work nearly all day, and long on music which is very confusing if not fatiguing

July 8 Tuesday. Drenching rain again Yesterday sunny and breezy in afternoon,—at Creswick's and Susie's—but sadly dead & listless of all things in evening,—can't understand it Fairly well, now.

July 9. Wednesday. Pouring, this morning and still cloudy—but a bit of pure rainbow showed me the inner red in its pure heath colour, and the outer in its pure brick-colour—while the violet is so narrow within the heath that I should almost rather call the belt—sardine-green, blue and heath, than use the word violet at all—Yellow occurs but for a moment. Moonlight,—see Plato book, p[age] 129.[9]

July 10 Thursday. Miss Wakefield and Miss Sillar[10] with lady Edwardes and the Marshalls at dinner, yesterday— this morning, for once pretty— sun on grass and smiling on waves, and joy in the flowers,—even the struck down foxgloves beginning to rise. Topics, for Broughton.[11] Setting hand to the plough—and taking up cross. — The Grace of Christ—the Love of God—his mercy is over all his works:—[12]

9. "Plato" is written on the spine of Bembridge MS *xxi*, which consequently is here referred to as the *Plato book*. Mr. Dearden states that page 129 of MS *xxi* contains the entry for June 26, 1877: ". . . such a moon, full, returning . . . for tenderness, depth, and glorious melancholy of eternal light, as I never saw in Venice nor Italy" (*Diaries*, p. 963).

10. Probably a sister of R. G. and W. C. Sillar, who wrote pamphlets against "Usury" and whose letters had frequently appeared in *Fors Clavigera.*

11. That is, topics relevant to the *Letters to the Clergy*, four of which had already been sent to the Reverend F. J. Malleson, Vicar of Broughton-in-Furness.

12. Notes for "LETTER V," dated "10th July," in which Ruskin began his clause by clause analysis of the Lord's Prayer. Of the "topics" listed in the Diary, only the last two are developed in the Letter (see *Works, 34,* 196–97).

July 11. Friday. A little sun and sweet sky let me see the blue-bells first out in garden, and walk to meet the poney—and gather strawberries for tea in my own garden, in a highly delectable manner! Today grey again! and I fear going to be wet.

Found out all about larch bud, finally this morning.

And for Broughton—of Hallowed be thy name. This is the name whereby he shall be called—with the will of God—even *your* sanctification—hallowing—while we let the usurer and whore-monger—open their lips in the worship of God. Blasphemy—1. Timothy. 1

"I will be sanctified" in—&c. (Vocation wherewith ye are called).[13]

July 12. Saturday. Perpetual darkness—and yesterday the old diabolic trembling blight Conf. above the lovely July of 76! Yesterday a lot of letters written nicely and mosaics from St. Marks, good.

July 13 Sunday. Yesterday utterly dismal all day long, and I fearfully languid— plashing rain—darkness—Joanie away. — Read Scribe's Mansardo des artistes — nonsense, but refreshing.[14] Its Camille worth noting as the ideal (one of) of French young girls

July 14th. Monday. Down fairly well to work with pretty Fluelen[15] opposite and many powers and hopes yet—D.G. yet in walking up to farm last night to call on Agnes,[16] I felt more despondent and

13. "Topics" for "LETTER VI," dated "12th July," on the meaning of "Hallowed be thy name." Again, he ignored some of the points noted in the Diary, for the sake of developing "while we let the usurer and whore-monger—open their lips in the worship of God" (*Works, 34,* 198–99).

14. "Knowing" French "pretty well," he had wasted "a great deal of time," he would confess, over the novels of Dumas, Gaboriau, and Eugène Scribe (*Works, 34,* 585).

15. Probably the Turner watercolor *Fluelen: Lake Constance,* which was usually in Ruskin's bedroom.

16. Agnes Stalker (see B.S.).

weak—and wanting to be at Dijon or Geneva, than for many a day. Stomach—I believe! mainly. Must see to it, for that discontents one everywhere.

July 15 Tuesday. Awake from 5 to 7, with serviceable thought, yet finding time long! vainly trying to compare the ease of body and mind with hours last year of restless fever & terror. But the time was heavy still and the pictures and green mountains—nothing to me. Note Topffer of persons content at Alessandria! [17] Bright now, with soft clouds on Eagle's peak. — (I think 'Eaglet' will be better for it.) Yesterday fine, much woodwork & digging (began root work)

July 16. Wednesday. Yesterday a good day. Violet, and therewith II. vol[ume] Proserp[ina] begun. Not a good night, yet thoughts enough in my mind now—of Miltons and Shakesp[eare']s violets and primroses.

July 17. Thursday. Yesterday candles at dinner, in the blackest evening the devil has yet brought on us,—utterly hellish, and the worse for its dead quiet—no thunder or any natural character of storm Still the black *shaking,* when that comes, with cold, is worst of all.— there was some beauty in the lake reflections calm and the misty, unconcealed hills, for the black clouds were above them—a mile thick I suppose—yet broken into jagged black and brown. Got some good botany, digging and drawing done, early in day. Today, all grey, but whiter.

July 18th Friday. A misty—more or less wet morning—fire pleasant—in modest flicker and flutter of low voice— Q[uestion] how to describe the low sound of fire, with the time and breaking of a crackle—yet muffled? I down to my Plato with

17. A caricature by the Swiss schoolmaster and artist Rodolfe Töpffer (1799–1846).

room in perfect order, and myself in as perfect health, take it all in all as ever I was in my life—D.G.—in the most solemn sense.

July 19 Saturday. A morning of blackest and foulest fog—London November, with crashing rain at intervals, much discomposes me— also—being kept awake last night—and waking early this morning, but I had a fine day of digging yesterday and painted my first cranberry blossom[18]

The blackness continues, quite hellish, as I work—and, curiously, the sound of railway twice louder than usual in the stillness of it.

July 20 Sunday. Pouring—or cloud-dripping pestiferously among mixed midges, all yesterday—and all this morning—I waking at 3, and now feverish—yet up to work well enough, and did useful thing[s] all the wet afternoon.

July 21. Monday. So—one month towards winter—Strange that I *can't* get a proper system of index for notes.[19] See of spring flowers June 21, of Rainbow 22nd, of eyes—29 of rain 3rd July, and yesterday just such another day,—not quite so drenching in weight but steady—nearly filling the wheelbarrow in the night and day, and when I got out in after evening—after dinner, the rain running down through the gate into field as I never saw it before.

July 22. Tuesday. Drenching again all night wild dirty clouds—and cold wind, now. Got a nice bit of cranberry painted yesterday and parcel off to Norton, not much besides, except some good digging.

July 23 Wednesday. Reading Lowell's Cathedral[20] and

18. Displayed in March 1880, when Ruskin lectured at the London Institution (*Works, 26,* 331).

19. Presumably a reference to his work on the complicated index for *Proserpina.*

20. Addressing C. E. Norton in a letter of 1870, James Russell Lowell had discussed criticism of *The Cathedral,* not wholly favorable, which he had received from Ruskin (see *Works, 30,* xli–ii).

watching lovely mists—but dawdled the morning away somehow, terribly—not down till 1/4 to 9! Yesterday nice walk with Goodwin[21] up to Goats water—but a little feverish at night after it—and one or two very loathsome dreams in a small way, from disordered stomach— then one very delightful one of finding a lovely drawing! of my own! of all things the absurdest to dream —yet certainly I have been busy on my own drawings lately, and to them

July 24 Thursday: — an Edgeworthian probability[22] about it. Broken off entry, yesterday and Plato and all, by a glorious day, which I could do nothing but saunter in, all the morning. — then drove Goodwin through Tilberthwaite in afternoon Conf. for Broughton, here, July 10th & 11th, and Plato VII [sic]. 521, — insisting on *καθαρσια* for clergy themselves.[23] One of the most utterly hellish black fogs, after pretty white mist tempting me up in morning the first time these two months—and now I can scarcely see to write! Dead quiet—and like Fenchurch St[reet Station] in November[24]

July 25 Friday. A wretched night—kept awake at first by indignation at Geikie and Ramsay,[25]—and then

21. The watercolorist Albert Goodwin (1845–1932) was staying in the neighborhood, Ruskin having been his friend and patron since 1871.

22. That is to say, *probable* only in an ideal world.

23. Letters V and VI on "The Lord's Prayer and the Church" are dated "10th" and "11th July." In Letter VI he cites, from Exodus 20:7: "*οὐ γὰρ νὴ καθαρ'6η κύριος* (*Works, 34,* 198). In Letter VIII, dated "9th August," he would urge the need of *καθαρόια* (purification or sanctification) for the clergy themselves (*Works, 34,* 203).

The Plato reference is to the concluding sentences to Book X of the *Laws,* to be found on page 521 of Volume 8 (rather than Volume 7) of the Bekker edition. In Ruskin's copy, Mr. Dearden states, the words *οὐ καθαρὸς ὤν θύων* are underlined in pencil, with the date "25th June, 1879" noted at the foot of the page. In the upper margin Ruskin wrote: "[Line] 13. The tremendous "*ου καθαρος*" 14. *τ̓ό δε παιδειον νη.* Question for Broughton." (In other words, is this, or is this not, a childish offense?)

24. This station on the London Underground Railway was a byword for filth.

25. The geologists Sir Archibald Geikie (1835–1924) and Sir Andrew C. Ramsay

dreaming—the quaintest dream I ever had from disturbed stomach merely—that I was going with Connie Hilliard and various other people to hear some great trial—and we had to scramble to get into court—and then the court was nearly empty and we were ordered to walk to our seats over tables of green baize, and to take our shoes off before doing it—and mine were fine dress boots with my black dress trousers strapped down and I could'nt get the straps unbuttoned, and then the Lord Chief Justice came and talked to me through a window, and complimented me on the attention aroused by the passages in Fors relating to Continental Agriculture, but I forget now what passages they were! and rather think there are none such in the book!

And with this there were mixed afterwards some of the ordinary more or less disgusting things which I have usually in disordered dream, but all connected, rational—and not at all impossible in real life. Rain again this morning—Kitten in bed kept me late—and alls wrong.

July 26 Saturday. A strangely pleasant series of dreams, towards morning (after waking at 3 oclock)—and after taking pease—cucumber, and generally whatever I should'nt, at dinner and tea)—one chiefly, of painting a charming picture, on commission—with the commander of it sitting by and being amazed at the dexterity with which it was done, but all with more of waking thought than should have been. Drenching rain and darkness since ½ past six, now drawing off in couchant mist.

July 27 Sunday. Sound sleep, but woke tired—or at least, ungathered together Now that I think of it, the sleep was not wholly sound, but there was a

---

(1814–91) had endorsed theories about mountain structure and, more particularly, about the flow of glaciers, against which Ruskin had been at war.

painful dream of some one's being very ill—and my not asking how he was in the morning—though I cared really very much but was thinking of other things Also of going to see people—and stay, with a large party of friends—the day before we were expected, and having beds made up in the garrets

Bright sun on hills at last, but impure—nothing as it should be in me, or outside me.

July 28 Monday. Drenching rain; but the first really natural rain Ive seen this summer! with the old soft white cloud, ragged-edged floating down almost to the chimneys of Coniston hall! — Unnatural yet, in the brown darkness before such opening, and returning now, nine oclock—the cloud fusing at the same time into a heavy horizontal mass, with no torn edges.

Very bad night again. I must look to my eating, perhaps also to my drinking—tea & sherry! (I don't mean mixed!—if anybody ever reads this—but too much of both.[)] Got comfort yesterday however—and a great one, in Oslers life of Tintoret The Paradise at 70! [26]

(Always also, in these vile days the railroad noise is twice as loud and *will* be heard—utterly vexing and disturbing me.[)]

July 31 Thursday — So ends the summer of 18–7–9. I can't even date a page of its year I see, rightly[27]—so 'astonied' have I been, these three days back by the stupefaction of all around me,—clouds and waters—Langdale mists and Rydal marsh,

26. "This masterpiece was begun in the year 1588, when Tintoretto was seventy years old" (William Roscoe Osler, *Tintoretto* [London, 1879], p. 3). In 1875 Ruskin had told Emma Oldfield "that he had only 14 years left to work in, and that he must do so diligently; for no man's work was worth anything after he was seventy" (E. A. Horsman, ed., *The Diary of Alfred Domett* [London and New York, 1953], p. 160).

27. Two pages in the MS have been headed: "July 1849."

and the coldness or conceit of human creatures. Read a bit of Val 'd Arno this morning—and wonder more and more at my own vileness in not obeying more hopefully my own true precept.[28] —

August 1. Friday. A little sunshine, but yesterday the closest, wretchedest day of sultry cloud I ever saw or felt. Sadly overwrought too with plaguing letters from fools,—and today, spiritless enough.

August 2 Saturday. Woke terribly languid—stomach chiefly. I have been so grieved by the successive ruin of all the flowers— Oxalis first, by frost— wild roses by rain and wind, and now all my pinks and dark roses rotten in the bud that the obstinacy or dulness of people about me hurts me more than ever—and I've done so much less of Proserpina than I hoped, that its quite awful to think of the years being now narrowing to end.

For Oxalis, see 3rd May, and confer 8th, 13th, and 15th.

I went to take my Fathers Bible[29] to read the end of Habakkuk[30] in it—but opened, instead, at II. Esdras v. 9,[31] and then read all from the 1st verse to the 36th!!! [32] and then was sent on by Fors to my own verse, which I had forgotten

28. Presumably, "If you resolve to do right, you will soon do so wisely; but resolve only to do wisely, and you will never to right" (*Works, 23,* 38n.; from *Val D'Arno*).

29. A Bible "inscribed 'Margaret Ruskin to her husband, John James Ruskin, 1850,'" Oxford, 1846 (*Works, 34,* 702). Cook and Wedderburn add that this Bible was "much marked and annotated" by Ruskin during "later" years.

30. Habakkuk's prayer (chap. 3) that God "in wrath remember mercy" as He destroys the unrighteous: "their rejoicing was as to devour the poor secretly."

31. "And salt waters shall be found in the sweet, and all friends shall destroy one another; then shall wit hide itself, and understanding withdraw itself into his secret chamber."

32. Foretelling the increase of iniquity and of despair, the Angel of the Lord explains that Esdras cannot hope to understand why God afflicts those whom He loves.

(with its precious context.) VIII. 49! [33] D.G. for this and sweet calm on lake—and clouds quiet on the sides of the sunny hills. I down also at 7, in right time!

August 3 Saturday. [sic] Pitch dark again—after a fairly fine, but impure sunny day yesterday,—and I myself so cast down that I begin to think the sky's anger is all against *me*. It is of the very worst fiendish sort, all the leaves quivering and shuddering, the lake dirty brown—the sky and hills dirty gray. Wind due North, where it ought to be crystal-clear. An angry and lurid coppercoloured sunset, yesterday foretold it. lake one glare of new-penny.

August 4 [34] Monday. I've written Saturday yesterday—but dont like scratching out. I do think my diaries better as I get old. If only my Father could have his letters dated, too!

Drenching drizzle, and black fog Could'nt see to shave at ½ past six, but down to my work in good heart. Mr Gatty[35] came yesterday and did a good morning's work on tennis-ground.

I copy an old sentence, too true to be lost, written on a scrap. — Many and many a century —(race, better,) before now, has rushed to its insane death—it and its rattling hallowness of fantasy together,—but at least in every former age, the living head and body led,—the tormenting fury followed,—but with us, head body and limbs are paralyzed,—and instead of the dog

33. "In that thou hast humbled thyself, as it becometh thee, and hast not judged thyself worthy to be much glorified among the righteous." In context: because thou hast not walked in pride, "the tree of life is planted," and "in the end is shewed the treasure of immortality."

34. In the top margin of the page given to this entry, Ruskin has written: "Insanity."

35. Charles Tendal Gatty (d. 1928, aged 76), Curator of the Liverpool Free Public Museum. "I had a most charming week with Mr. Ruskin," Mr. Gatty told a friend. "I learnt in those few days more than many hours' reading and solitary work could give me. He has great ideas about Museums" (*Works*, *37*, 293n.).

dragging the kettle, the kettle drags the dog.

August 5. Tuesday. Down in really good time to work—in good heart—& stronger will than lately. Yesterday lady Edwardes and Mrs Havelock[36] took up the afternoon. — Nice music in evening heard Australian boatmans song—how Vocal rows the mindless Gondolier.

Next to the Metaphysicians, how curious that the worst nonsense extant should have been written by the Musicians.

Of cloud meaning see Venice diary [page] 83 [37]

August 6 Wednesday. Flying days, of course and always rain. — down in time today, but no appetite for my little breakfast—I fancy want of fresh air,—but feel well enough, and find myself able for talk or anything else

August 7. Thursday. The calamity and wonder of the rain increases as in the days of Noah. — Out only for half an hour yesterday after dinner, quite exhausted in the evening, & unable to enjoy Diddie, Alic, Lollie, and Charles— (Gatty.) altogether—the fatigue showing most in chagrin at a bad move in chess! and a pain in bone of brow, to the touch, as if bruised, of which note following See—

Extract of letter from Mr Macdon[al]d.[38] "We live with some very nice people at a small cottage farm. They have cows and fowls, so there is

36. Probably the widow of Major-General Henry Havelock (1795–1857), who had died after his capture of Lucknow.

37. On February 28, 1877, Ruskin had entered on page 83 of his "Venice diary" (Bembridge MS *xxi*): "Truly, the workers are nourished by the Rich, as the Sea is by the Clouds. Spectacular Creatures—very beautiful—but if Clouds without Water?" (*Diaries*, p. 940; p. 83 of the MS contains entries for February 28, March 1 and 2, Mr. Dearden states).

38. Doubtless Alexander MacDonald (d. 1921, aged 82), who in 1871 had been appointed Master of the Ruskin Drawing School at Oxford and who became Deputy Keeper of the University in 1883. He had two daughters and a son—probably "the children" who appear in the following extract from the letter.

plenty of butter and eggs. The bread we eat is made of the corn grown in their own field ground in a small mill driven by a brook at the bottom of the garden where the children like to watch its grinding, and is baked at home. We are about half a mile from the sea, and Cadgwith fishing village, wonderfully clean."

August 8 Friday. A little sun enabled me yesterday to call on Sir C[harles] Darwin,[39] and to climb up by cascades, and I've slept well—yet feel jaded this morning more than usual. Sun bright, but impure, on the grass and roses.

I never thought till this moment because of a letter I've got to answer, of the curious lesson respecting Davids sin. Nathan does not accuse him of adultery, but of robbing the poor. He took the poor man's lamb. I *have* thought before, however, of the 'No Pity,' of David himself.[40]

August 9. Saturday A lovely morning at 5, peaceful and pure, made me feel how much I was losing every day, in having neither dawn nor sunset—and now that I am down to my work, it is all clouded over and foul again— Read Malachi (see last Saturdays entry)[41] instead of Habakkuk, and came on the wonderful verse for clergy[42]

39. For this visit, see Charles Darwin, B.S.

40. See II Sam. 11 and 12:1–7, the story of David's taking the wife of Uriah the Hittite, followed by Nathan's parable of the rich man who took the poor man's one ewe lamb. Then David said: "the man that hath done this thing shall surely die. . . . And Nathan said to David, Thou art the man."

41. In the entry for August 2 see the account of "the successive ruin of all the flowers." God's message, through Malachi, is that He has laid waste the land because of His displeasure with the offerings of the Israelites and with the treacherousness of their priests, and that He will again "smite the earth with a curse" unless His people heed the law of Moses and the words of the prophet Elijah, whom He will send to them to turn "the heart of the fathers to the children, and the heart of the children to their fathers" (Mal. 4:6).

42. "Letter VIII" to "the Clergy," dated "9th August," begins by calling attention to "the second chapter of Malachi"—God's threat to the priests unless they preach the law with truth and knowledge instead of treacherously and hypocriti-

August 10 Sunday. At *last*—after two months of steady foulness, a *pure* day and the mountains all in sacred light over perfect calm of lake. Light wonderfully warm and deep in tone

I was kept awake by cat, half the night—and could hardly get up to 7. coffee—but did—and am fairly well

August 11 Monday. Yesterday very languid all day and beaten by bud of milkwort.[43] —Slept well—and am myself again—what a nuisance it is one must sleep. ⟨Studied dew on sweet William yesterday morning, the divine crimson lighted by the fire of each minute lens. — I never noticed this before!—blind bat.⟩[44]

August 12 Tuesday. I get nothing done but my Plato just now, and that is falling behind—wretched day with Tom Richmond[45] coming and disgusting me, and riotous evening—spoiling what might have been the sweetest summer day we've had yet,—but mist also covering the sun, just when the hayfield with Joan and the children was at its best heavy mist today also—and in general about half a day in a fortnight only of natural or kind weather—and the rest, the devil's.

August 13 Wednesday ⟨The most terrific and horrible thunderstorm this morning I ever remember It waked me at six, or a little before—then rolling incessantly, like railway luggage trains—quite ghastly in its mockery of them—the air one loathsome mass of sultry and foul fog like smoke —scarcely raining at all,—increasing to heavier

---

cally. From this chapter Ruskin quotes verse 17: "Ye have wearied the Lord with your words; yet ye say, Wherein have we wearied Him? When ye say, Every one that doeth evil is good in the sight of the Lord, and He delighteth in them; or, Where is the God of judgment?" (*Works, 34,* 202, where "words" reads "works").

43. To be discussed in *Proserpina, II,* chap. 4, "Giulietta"; published in 1882.

44. Published (with minor changes), in *Works, 33,* xxii, where it is misdated "1880."

45. The Reverend Thomas Knyvett Richmond (d. 1916, aged 67), oldest son of George Richmond, and now Vicar of Crosthwaite, Keswick.

rolling with flashes quivering vaguely through all the air—and at last to terrific double streams of reddish violet fire, not forked or zigzag but rippled rivulets—two at the same instant some 20 to 30 degrees apart—and lasting on the eye at least half a second—with grand artillery-peals following; not rattling crashes, or irregular cracklings, but delivered volleys,⟩ all the worst of it over towards Seathwaite. ⟨It lasted an hour, then past off—clearing a little—without rain to speak of—not a glimpse of blue—and now ½ past seven seems settling down into Manchester devil's darkness.

¼ to Eight,—morning Thunder returned — all the air collapsed into one black fog, the hills invisible—and scarcely the opposite shore—heavy rain in short fits—and frequent—though less formidable flashes, and shorter thunder

While I have written this sentence it [the cloud] has again dissolved itself, like a nasty solution in a bottle, with miraculous and unnatural rapidity and the hills are in sight again—a double forked flash, rippled I mean, like the others, starts into its frightful ladder of light between me and Wetherlam, as I raise my eyes. All black above—a ragged spray cloud on the Eaglet.

½ past eight— Three times light, and three times dark since I last wrote—the darkness seeming each time as it settles more loathsome, at last stopping my Plato in mere blindness. One lurid gleam of white cumulus in upper lead-blue sky, seen for half a minute through the sulphurous chimney-pot-vomit of blackguardly cloud beneath—where its rags were thinnest.⟩[46]

46. Published (with minor changes), in *Works, 34*, 37–38 (*The Storm-Cloud of the Nineteenth Century*, 1884). Seathwaite is a little village in the next valley to the west, about five miles from Coniston over the fells (see Map A).

August 14 Thursday. An unspeakably horrible day of blackness and heat quite crushed me yesterday with distrust of Nature, and God—and all things. Today, sweet clouds and what would have been lovely in calm lake and green hayfield, if I could have seen it—but I'm too much blackened in heart to care for anything by the utter loss of the summer—and I believe now, it is settling down to bad again.

August 15th Friday. One lovely day, and now all black again to hellishness, and going in and out every quarter of an hour. I sadly tired yesterday after doing nothing— Watched the sun set clear, for once, lying on the slope of my field, gathering Brunella blossom; and hearing the voices of the children among the haycocks, soft in the last rays Read by Fors order, today for the first time the Sight of the Sun, Nomoi. 12. 597.[47]

August 16. Saturday. Yesterday dark all day in the saddest manner— today, faint sun and pale blue sky through subdued fog. Slept well—and down to work in fair temper, rather helped by a fit of fury at the d-d impudence of Seymour Haden[48]— (½ past 8. — All sky as black as—again!)

47. In Volume 8 of the Bekker edition, Mr. Dearden states, Ruskin has written at the head of page 597 (*Laws*, Bk. XII), "The Sight of the Sun," and at the foot of the page, "Read first 15th August 1879." He is referring to the passage in which Plato expresses his hope that if "the State we are founding in Crete . . . develop according to plan . . . it . . . will be numbered among the well-ordered States and countries upon which the Sun and all the other gods look down" (Loeb translation, 2, p. 505).

On the first page of Book XII of the *Laws* in his Bekker edition, Ruskin has written (Mr. Dearden continues): "Begun August 3, 1879. To think that till then I had never read this noble law of Theft! Last book read in a month and seven days, gives me good hope." At the end of Book XII he noted: "Sept[.] 4, 1879." Reading these comments, however, one should realize that in the *Fors Clavigera* of October 1877 he had included his own translation of a long passage from Book XII (see *Works*, *29*, 227–28).

48. Sir Francis Seymour Haden (or Hayden, 1818–1910), founder and President of the Royal Society of Painter-Etchers. Ruskin had probably received a copy of the 4th edition of *About Etching*, in which Haden had been highly patronizing as

August 17 Sunday. ⟨Raining in foul drizzle slow and steady —sky pitch dark and I just get a little light by sitting in the bow window, diabolic cloud over everything—⟩ and I more tired and sad than ever since my illness—⟨looking over my [kitchen] garden yesterday, one miserable mass of weeds gone to seed—the roses in the other garden, putrefied into brown sponges, feeling like dead snails—and the halfripe strawberries all rotten at the stalks.⟩[49]

Read for the first time in Plato, the Parliament of the Dawn, which much refreshed me.*

*(Parliament meeting at daybreak—blockhead not to put reference). 1883[50]

August 18. Monday. Good day, yesterday, on Labiatae[51]—must finish, D.V. in these three next days, and then for Norton only— Late down today—waking at three, a bad habit lately got into—and things irritating me more and more in the folly of talkers and writers— Philosophy of Waverley Novels!! [52] &c. &c. &c.—and after puzzling for an hour over the basrelief of the oratory at Lucca, with name Bidanius on cauldron—find Parkers idiotic inscription on the back—even *he* doing his work so slovenly.[53] Diabolic grey clouds closing in from *North,* wind on lake from south.

---

he used Ruskin to exemplify "DOGMATISM IN ART," while contradicting Ruskin's evaluation of various artists and ignoring his study of Turner.

49. Published in *Works, 34,* 38 (*The Storm-Cloud of the Nineteenth Century*).

50. The reference is to the description, in Book XII of the *Laws,* of the synod, composed of "young men and old, which is obliged to meet every day between dawn and sunrise" for "conference and discourse [which] shall deal always with the subject of the laws and of their own State" (Loeb translation, p. 509).

51. Flowers with "lip-like corollas," illustrated by his drawings of the *Menthae* (probably now begun) as discussed in *Proserpina, II* (1885), chaps. 5 and 6.

52. To be dismissed, rather scornfully, in *Fiction, Fair and Foul,* August 1880 (see *Works, 34,* 347).

53. The distinguished archeologist J. H. Parker (1806–84), Keeper of the Ashmolean Museum, whom Ruskin had known as the founder of the Architectural Society when he himself was an undergraduate. At Brantwood he had some of Parker's architectural photographs for reference.

August 19. Tuesday. Down in proper time and the lake quiet and pretty, but thick white fog and general dampness everywhere. Mushrooms having it all their own way, and of course all the nastiest of them the merriest.

8 oclock. All settling down to close rain!—the hay lying out rotting these four days—and the pretty farmhouse among the trees, on Torver road, struck by the flash of lightning I saw the day before yesterday. — Close small rain now! and black smoke cloud.

August 20 Wednesday. Black-leaded evening—rain all night—black-charcoaled morning— Hay yellow-rotten—fungi in full force—and I tired—last night—more than for ages, but I did more in the morning,—and ate gooseberries in the afternoon, and am a goose.

August 21. Thursday. Small thick rain—grey devils cloud fast from the south, nothing else to be looked for— it is as if it would rain and gloom for ever. Planned numbering of pages for Plato trans[lation] and am fresh for work in spite of late hours last night with the two Mr Darwins.[54]

August 22 Friday Such drenching rain and sulphurous cloud as in the last half hour, I have not seen for long. Now cleared again—for a moment and air full of midges,—all too horrible to be believed, if not seen.

August 23 Saturday. Fierce gale and black cloud all yesterday left me terribly tired and depressed, but slept well and a little sun refreshes me now, and the work done is good though little.

August 24. Sunday. Yesterday at last fine and I got walk to hill farm between Yewdale and the narrow glen

54. Presumably Charles Darwin and one of his sons. The addresses of William Erasmus Darwin (1839–1914), who had contributed to the costs of the Whistler Trial, and of Sir George Howard Darwin (1845–1912), who was doing distinguished work as a geophysicist, are recorded in the first section of the Diary.

we have yet no name for, (while Lilias[55] painted the white rose cottage,)—and fell asleep in the sunshine on the hayfield then down and across brook to the heathy rocks under Raven crag and never saw anything more divine than it all was, or more pure—but I feeling old and half dead. Am not, though, yet, D.G.

August 25. Monday A grand walk, yesterday up Raven crag, with Diddie, Lily and Lollie, tired me more than I liked, but leaves me I think, fresher today. The day, for the most part of the walk, lovely. —then grey fish clouds came up. Crashing rain in night and now broken sunshine—but tolerably pure, with heavy white clouds, moving fast.

August 26 Tuesday. — Clattering rain, like hail and wild wind—the like all yesterday—Mr Darwin coming round to see me in carriage, lake impassable — But my Sunday walk did me much good, and I am down in good heart to work—after reading of Schiller's fumy and rockety sputter of a life, brandy-heated and out at 46.[56] How precious I ought to think the days granted me now with all the foregone experience—and present calm, and fair health and limbs and eyes, yet.

August 27. Wednesday. Fireworks and general fuss, with no tea, last night leave me headachy this morning—in dimness of close small rain out side. — Weather beyond everything I conceived possi-

55. Lilias Trotter, whose work was represented in Ruskin's Oxford Drawing School by a number of pocket-book sketches of Norwegian life. In *The Art of England* he speaks of having met her in Venice in 1876, when he had given her a few lessons, having been impressed by the talent expressed through her drawings. Thereafter she became dear as a friend (45 of his letters to her, it is said, are being prepared for publication). In 1886, sending the Duchess of Albany one of her sketches, he called her "one of my best of pupils" (*Works, 37,* 554).

56. A comment apparently evoked by Hjalmar H. Boyesen's *Goethe and Schiller: Their Lives and Works* (1879).

ble of wrong-doing by natural forces. (Must'nt spoil this lovely drawing pen!)

August 28. Thursday. Pouring—as from a watercart all yesterday till sunset then a piece of fair clear sky,—closing in rain again, last night and today.

But did good work yesterday and am fairly fresh now, finding my old Alpine preface to Sesame which I must reprint quickly.[57] And the book itself—can't be better!

August 29 Friday. Yesterday kept awake by fearful wind—gusts of frantic up and down and round about rage,—discomfortable feeling, also—but slept at last—only weak and listless now, though with pleasant work on labiatae, and St Marks finishing fast.

August 30 Saturday. A little dirty sunlight about,—and I well on the whole sleeping soundly, and enjoying botany—but all so slow—so slow.

Reading Ordericus Vitalis[58]— Alas, that good people should be brainless—but how happy for them to be fools in that kind.

August 31 Sunday. Yesterday up to the Lamb's bridge and found Anagallis tenella all in her nests,—more in fulness of blossom than ever, but oppressed and shut under the rain. At least forty blossoms on the moss cushion by the cascade. Found one precious little bit of thyme, and a sundew in flower—and rowed home against wind and water; feeling wrists very weak, however.

September 1. Monday The sad words to write ¼ of a year now given to Plato—a book and a bit only done, but this would do the whole in three years, if I

57. Namely, the Preface to the second edition, of 1865. This Preface, however, was not reprinted when *Sesame and Lilies* was reissued in 1882.

58. *The Ecclesiastical History of England and Normandy* by Ordericus Vitalis (1075–1143?), trans. Thomas Guizot, with notes and introduction (4 vols. London, 1853–56).

keep clear of distractions Froude's vile paper in this month's 19 century[59] like to have become one, but a walk by the lake shore in the morning sun leaves me quieter—and prouder.

September 2 Tuesday. Yesterday very lovely all day, got the hay in finally: lying on a dry slope, a fortnight's washing seems to do it no harm! Today grim and squally, but with bits of blue—and white clouds delicately and sharply streaked with black, very rare.

Thought of ἀφεσις ἀμαρτιων[60]—that the 12th to the 19th century was as a starved wolf to a fat lapdog—that clergymen had better define the difference between 'pardoning' and 'absolving' —before [punning?] both words into same sentence, and before asking any body "unfeignedly["] to believe his holy Gospel had better determine between themselves what the holy Gospel is. And also, that people who announce their resolve to lead a new life every Sunday at ¼ to eleven, will most likely be still leading their old one at twelve.[61]

September 3 Wednesday. I did not forget the birthday,[62] yesterday but every year leaves me more lost to myself and to my memories—a gleaner in reaped—or ravaged fields. Storm—today—and yesterday and always, now, a gleam of blue sky beyond sometimes.

September 4.[63] Thursday. A lovely calm morning but air chilly

59. "A Cagliostro of the Second Century" (an account of the charlatinism of Alexander of Abonotichus).

60. "Be it known unto you therefore, men and brethren, that through this man is preached unto you the *forgiveness of sins*" (Acts 13:38).

61. Thoughts for "Letter X" to "the Clergy," dated "3rd September," explicating the article "Forgive us our sins . . ."

62. Namely, his mother's birthday, September 2.

63. In the upper margin of this page he notes: "For Deucalion, see Timaeus, §35."

and all sense of summer gone. I never passed a year before without *one* summers day. But I am thankful to have passed it at all, and to be as well as I am.

September 5 Friday. A beautiful day yesterday enabled me to walk quietly up to the Eaglet the first time I have been there since my illness, and then round to the Old man, and down the grassy side of him home—out from eleven to seven with a little call at Creswicks, and not a bit over-tired. D.G.

All the Lancashire view utterly lost in black smoke, and the outlines of the Scawfell mass but seen, and no more—through the smoke of White Haven. Evidently no more a breath of pure air to be drawn in England.

September 6. Saturday. Steady black again and thick fog, and midges all day long— it is more like Acheron than Coniston—and I feel like waiting for Charon instead of Joe.[64]

September 7. Sunday. Just the same. Anything so vile or monstrous as the weather of the whole year since April, I had not thought the Devil strong enough to make out of the elements. Lake—hills and sky—today—one black slate.

September 8 Monday. Yesterday Black all day, and this morning wild sooty drift of rain mixed with gleams of sun. Strange dreams, of being at a meeting of a scientific society, where everything went politely—but it ended in gloomy dyspeptic terrors and waked me wondering always more and more what is the real use and meaning of dreams

September 9 Tuesday. Fearful black rain this morning till eight—then clearing to broken clouds and blue; but still very doubtful, dismal and impure. Yet

64. Probably Joe Wilkinson, his servant.

I do good work through it all, and got on with oak leaf,[65] yesterday.

September 10 Wednesday. Sunshine, but through impure air, with smoky cloud, the spirit of evil in all things, —except my good pupils and loving friends, who are very angelic indeed, and more and more wonderful every day.

September 11. Thursday. Yesterday one of the horriblest black-Beelzebub afternoons I ever dug in— today little better: but green fields visible over the lake instead of fog.

Working well on oak leaves however.

September 12 Drove over yesterday with Diddie to Ambleside —found Mrs. Firth gone to Silver-somewhere— and walked home here in rain all the way, and against wind up all the hills and really was not a bit tired, so I could do a little Yorkshire travelling still

Today a little sunshine and some purity and quietness in air. (A delicious new pen to write some Prout[66] with!)

September 13. Saturday. Still a little sunny and a few stars last night. Diddie went away at ½ past 10 yesterday and the house feels very disconsolate.

September 14. Sunday—A bad, feverish beginning of night— after over-excited day— over to draw at Thwaite early—and then visitors—but all would be good for me, if only I managed my*self* well. A lovely morning at last:—early mists on lake at dawn, and all manner of blessed things about me, if I can use them well.

September 15 Monday. The day clouded yesterday at ½ past 4, with at first the divinest emerald broken lights

65. Two watercolor studies of *Oak Leaves*, dated 1879, were sent to Norton for the exhibition. One of them was subsequently given to the Sheffield Museum (see *Works, 14*, Pl. XXII).

66. His *Notes on Prout and Hunt* were first issued as a catalogue for the Loan Collection of Drawings exhibited in London during the winter of 1879–80.

on Coniston— Then sulphurous yellow-brown fumigation closing up all. Today universal grey again.

Yesterday came Mr. Smart[67] from Glasgow much encouraging me about St. George.

September 16. Tuesday. All over grey, as usual—all day yesterday too. Read Help's pretty bit on St George in 'Brevia'—to be compared with Mr. Emerson in Fors XXVI [68]

Painted oak leaf for Susie, yesterday. Alic went away, to my discomfort.[69]

December 18 Thursday Back here on the 16th having been three months away—a fortnight at Canterbury, ten days at Sheffield, a week at Broadlands and the rest, London. Then two days and nights here, unbroken fog,—as in London also—and the lake edge covered with black scum, deposit from Manchester.

December 19 Friday. Yesterday cleared up into divine quiet sunshine,—lovely sunset. Worked all day in the wood, D.G

December 20 Saturday. ¼ to 9, and the sun but just up. I could not properly see to write till now. Frost, with heavy impure clouds on hills. But yesterday quite lovely all day long, calm and golden.

67. William Smart (1853–1915), of the University of Glasgow; author of *A Disciple of Plato. A Critical Study of John Ruskin* (1883).

68. In Letter 26 of *Fors Clavigera* (February 1873) Ruskin had defended St. George against Emerson (see *Works*, 27, 476–78). In *Brevia, Short Essays and Aphorisms* (London, 1871), Helps (1813–75) maintains that St. George has been "largely calumniated": "It will always be a good joke against the English, that they have chosen a contractor for their patron saint; for St. George made his fortune by getting a contract to supply the army with bacon. But this does not imply the extent of vice and wickedness with which poor St. George is universally credited. Gibbon has no words too bad for him. Now let me take down Gibbon, and show you what may be said on the other side. . . . [an analysis of Gibbon's use of weasel words]. This is the way in which men's characters are ruined by insinuation, and this is the way in which great historians sometimes write" (pp. 11–12).

69. At this point he himself left Brantwood: on September 20, writing Ethel Hilliard from Herne Hill, he speaks of having attended *Pinafore* "last night" (unpublished letter: Pierpont Morgan Library).

Only the sun himself seemed to me without the power and effulgence he used to have, and theres always more mist than is natural. Helvellyn scarce visible at sunset,—though a lovely effect of rosy mist on the Old Man. [sketch] the near hills first pronounced against it—then fading into its mass, or it into theirs.

December 22 Monday. Yesterday one of the grey, searching miserable days, that always make me feel exhaustedly ill Today broad russet light on hills, and mostly blue sky but the clouds impure and moving fast.

December 24.[70] Tuesday. Yesterday busy with Bishop letter[71] and various disorderly work,—wet and dark day —at Creswicks and Mr Bells[72] in afternoon.

CHRISTMAS Wednesday. All of us fairly well thank God, and I writing comfortably without spectacles and things prospering in my hand. The first thing I do is to find Luca's Nativity and the first letter I write will be to order it from Florence.[73]

December 26. Thursday. Yesterday at Magic lantern at Monk Coniston; and nice evening with Joanie and Mattie only, but great feeling of general cold and relaxed throat and weakness today and indeed—ever since I left London more sense of declining vital power than Ive ever been conscious of, except on some afternoons at Oxford —which I too easily forget. I hope now, as then

70. For the mistake in date, see entry for December 27.

71. Namely, his "Rejoinder" to the letter he had received from the Reverend James Fraser (1818–85), Bishop of Manchester, in "Reply" to the question published in *Fors Clavigera*: in the Bishop's opinion, was "usury a work of the Lord?" (*Works, 29*, 244; for *Usury: A Reply and a Rejoinder*, see *Works, 34*, 401–25).

72. For William Bell, see B.S.

73. Charles Fairfax Murray (1849–1919) had sent him, from Florence, a photograph of Luca della Robbia's *Madonna and Child*, the faience which, within six weeks, would be hung above his study mantlepiece. He now commissioned Murray to obtain it "for about 180 pounds . . . however—you will do the best you can, and I will remit cheque forthwith" (unpublished letter of "Christmas Day, [18]79"; Pierpont Morgan Library).

it is only temporary illness––coinciding with exhaustion Got a good bit of letter done for Fors,[74] however, yesterday.

December 27 Saturday — All wrong in names of days since the 24th and seem to have lost one. Nowadays— I mostly lose all.

December 28 Sunday. The tiredness pronounces itself as definite cold: which is a relief—with stomach so far wrong as to give just a disagreeable tone to dreams, for instance last night I was at a pleasant musical entertainment, with nicely dressed ladies, which was interrupted by consternation of some managing person who pointed out that small drops of oil were falling from the ceiling. Woke hot and uncomfortable for a while. How strange—that I never dream of what's most in my waking mind. I had been working at serpents all the evening[75]—if I had not, in all probability I should have dreamed of some in my old way— but, having my mind entirely occupied with them I never dreamed of so much as a tail end.

December 29 Monday. Terrific cold and general depression— but was able to read last night,[76]— only woke with the most burning and tearing pain in my throat I ever felt. Took some water and an ipecac lozenge[77] and it gradually got better— more stomachic than anything else I believe,

74. Written as a reply to a letter which he had received from a member of the Guild; published in the September 1880 issue of *Fors Clavigera*, Letter 89 (see *Works*, *29*, 403–05).

75. He was probably reading Patrick Russell's *An Account of Indian Serpents*, which he had asked the bookseller Bernard Quaritch (1819–99) to send him because of the lecture "Living Waves," to be delivered at the Royal Institution during March (see Charlotte Quaritch Wrentmore, ed., *Letters of John Ruskin to Bernard Quaritch*, 1867–1888 [London, 1938], p. 21).

76. Presumably, to read aloud to the usual audience.

77. One of the standard old-fashioned remedies. (In *Clarissa Harlowe*, one recalls, Lovelace takes "ipecacuanha" as an emetic when he wishes to arouse Clarissa's pity: "This ipecacuanha is a most disagreeable medicine," Lovelace writes Belford on May 2. "Two hours it held me.")

but I feel as if I never should be fit for anything again.

December 30 Tuesday. Cold better, but still grievous and all my good old morning work now lost— Evenings more cheerful therefore,—but I never meant my day to get so displaced.

Fearful black storm of wind and rain, from 8 to ½ past nine now breaking up, shows the Old man all snow down to the moorland, but thawing fast.

December 31. Wednesday. A bad night after painful day—in fear—very great for poor Lolly—and recognized infectious illness of children at Lodge;—but comforted by message from Lolly in evening—(of—I mean—not 'from')—yet I am fairly well and up to work, through the darkness of the fourth day of miserable storm— one really has only about the seventh day now of any useable light or endurable air.

1880

As a continuation of the entries made during December 1879, this unit of the Diary contains the record of Ruskin's life at Brantwood from January 1 through August 7, except for February 1–17, when he spent a week in Sheffield, and for March 15–April 1, when he went to London to deliver his lecture on snakes, *Living Waves.* Leaving Brantwood on August 10, he spent ten days at Herne Hill before going to France with Ethel and Laurence Hilliard and their mother—his pet "Connie" having recently become a bride. On October 3 he was back in England to spend a week with the Gales in Canterbury, where Mrs. Severn joined them for the christening of her Violet Susanna, born on August 28 and named in honor of Miss Beever. On October 11 he left for Amiens, accompanied by Arthur Severn and three of the Gale "children." By November 5 he was back in England to meet an engagement to lecture at Eton on the 6th, and on December 1 he reached Brantwood, where he made his entries for December 6–10 in the Diary that contained the record of his travels (Bembridge MS *xxi;* see *Diaries,* p. 996). Then, on December 14, he began to use once more the Brantwood Diary, in which he continued to make the daily record through the early weeks of 1881.

The first part of 1880, he soon discovered, was marked by a discrepancy between the strength which was yet at his disposal and his desire to meet the demands of his work as a servant of God. Believing in the mystical guidance provided by "Fors," on the first morning of this New Year he found himself "directed" to a passage in Titus 2, where he read: "These things speak, and exhort, and rebuke with all authority. Let no man despise thee." Then, on the morning of the birthday of Rose, he was given the verse: "We know that we have passed from death unto life" (see entry for January 3); and on the evening of "her" day there came the only sunset, out of "a whole winter," which was memorably beautiful (see entries for January 4 and 11). Nevertheless, since his return to Brantwood his "vital energy" had declined (see entry for December 26, 1879), and despite the "sudden call . . . for action" and the "clear guiding," he found himself "jaded" and "dead" (see entries for January 2 and 4). By April 9 he remarked: "But I am utterly down—and must take warning never in future to use my strength as soon as I get it."

First, as an immediate response to the "call," on New Year's Day he had begun to write another Letter for *Fors Clavigera,* in which he referred to "the teaching of *Fors*" as his "main work" (*Works, 29,* 385–86). The early days of February were therefore "overwhelmed" by his "doing" this "new Fors . . . twice over," with the "inevitable fatigues and confusions" (February 18). Issued in March as an effectively organized communication, this "Letter 88" was dated "Brantwood, 8th February, 1880"—the anniversary of his birth.

Immediately, too, he felt pressed to answer the letter upon "Usury" through which, from his viewpoint, the Lord had at last delivered into his hands the Bishop of Manchester (see entry for December 24, 1879). Otherwise known as the Reverend James Fraser, this Bishop was important as the "Pastor" or "the Overseer of the greatest Mercantile City in England" (*Works, 29,* 591; letter to T. C. Horsfall, August 25, 1877), from which the smoke helped to defile the skies of Coniston. In a *Fors* of 1875 Ruskin had first addressed Dr. Fraser by asking: "Who *are* the true Israelites? . . . perhaps, the Bishop of Manchester will take up the challenge, having lately spoken wisely—in generalities—concerning Fraud. Who are the true Israelites, my Lord of Manchester, on your Exchange?" (*Works, 28,* 243). This challenge made, the Bishop's silence had become, in *Fors,* a taunting theme. But now, having sent his response, the Bishop also had said that Ruskin might publish his letter for the sake of making a "Rejoinder." The "challenge" had come to his attention for the first time, Dr. Fraser professed, when he saw a reference to it in the "Letters to the Clergy" while reading the *Contemporary Review* of December. Hence, finally, he had explained why, in his opinion, "Usury"—which Ruskin defined as the taking of "any money paid, or other advantage given, for the loan of anything which is restored to its possessor uninjured and undiminished" (*Works, 34,* 408)—was compatible with the teachings of the Bible and the will of God.

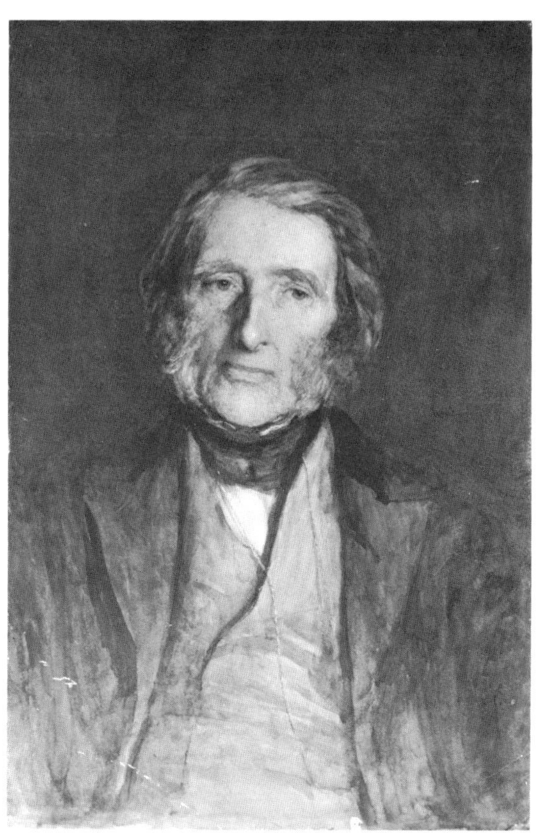

Ruskin in 1879

Portrait by H. Von Herkomer (1849–1914). Courtesy National Portrait Gallery.

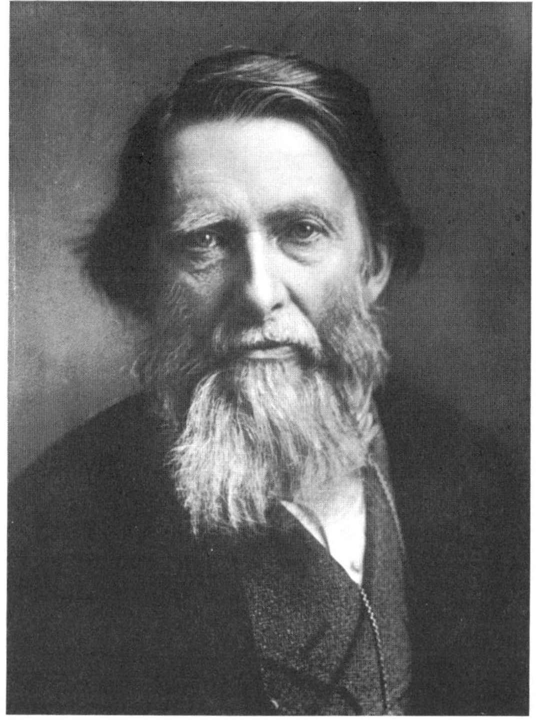

Ruskin in 1882

Photograph by Messrs. Elliott and Fry. Courtesy Ruskin Galleries, Bembridge School.

The Brantwood Diary

right-hand page: Conclusion of last entry written before Ruskin's collapse, February 22, 1878. See text, pp. 101–02.

left-hand page: Entry of April 5, 1883, with Ruskin's remarks concerning the facing page. See text, pp. 313–14, 102.

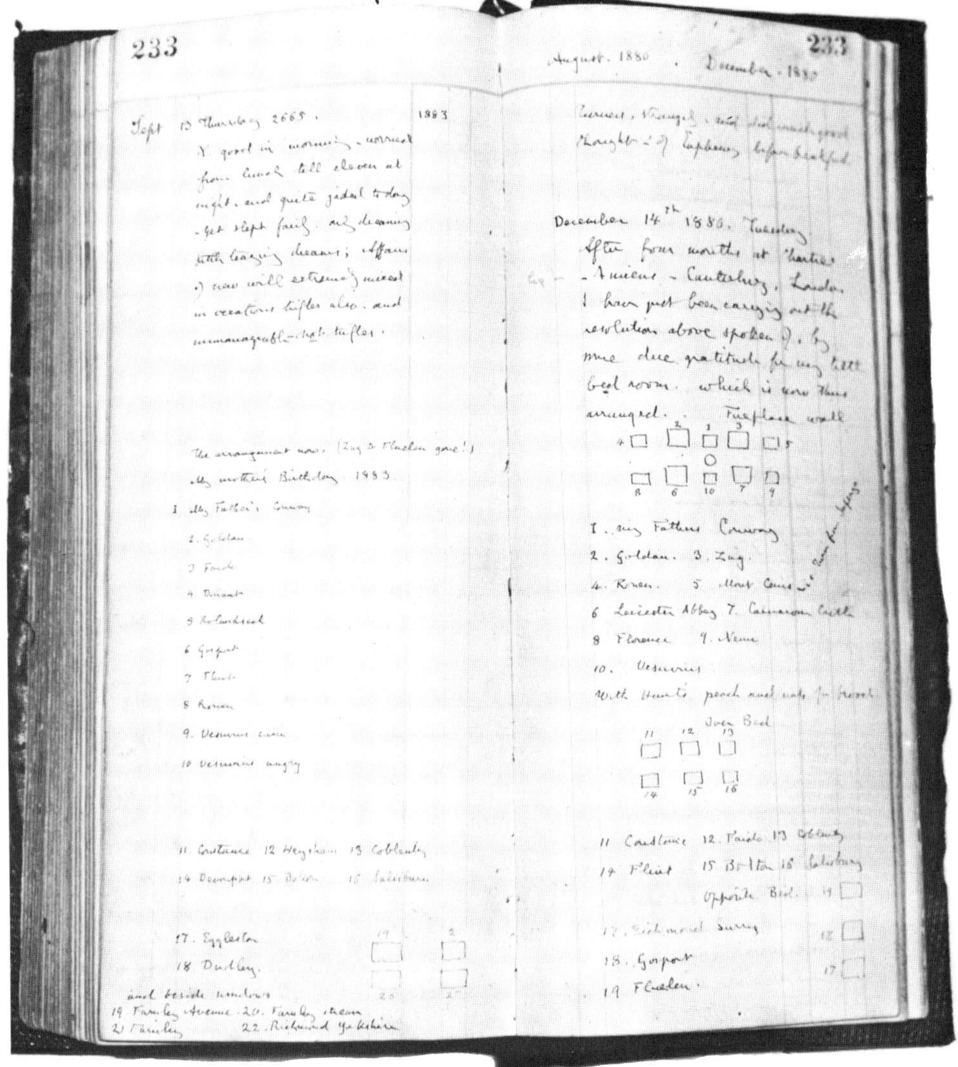

The Brantwood Diary

right-hand page: Entries of August 8, 1880 (conclusion), and December 14, 1880, showing Ruskin's arrangement of the paintings in his bedroom. See text, pp. 249–51.

left-hand page: Entries of September 13, 1883, and "My mother's Birthday" [September 2], 1883, with Ruskin's remarks concerning the new arrangement of the paintings. See text, pp. 336, 333.

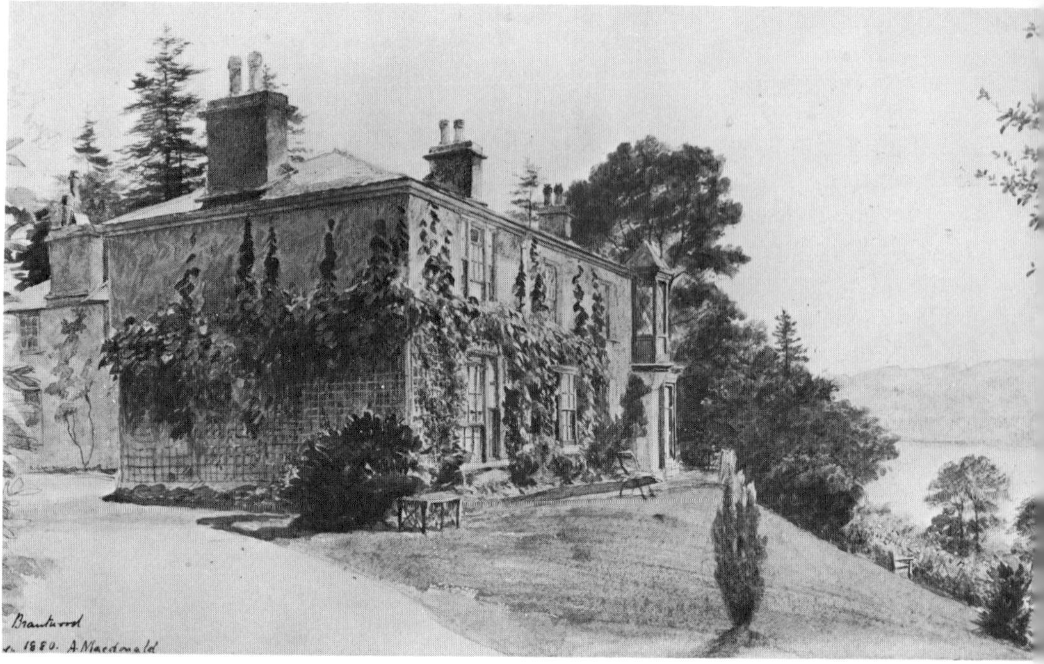

Brantwood in 1880

Watercolor by Alexander MacDonald (1839–1921). Courtesy Ruskin Museum, Coniston.

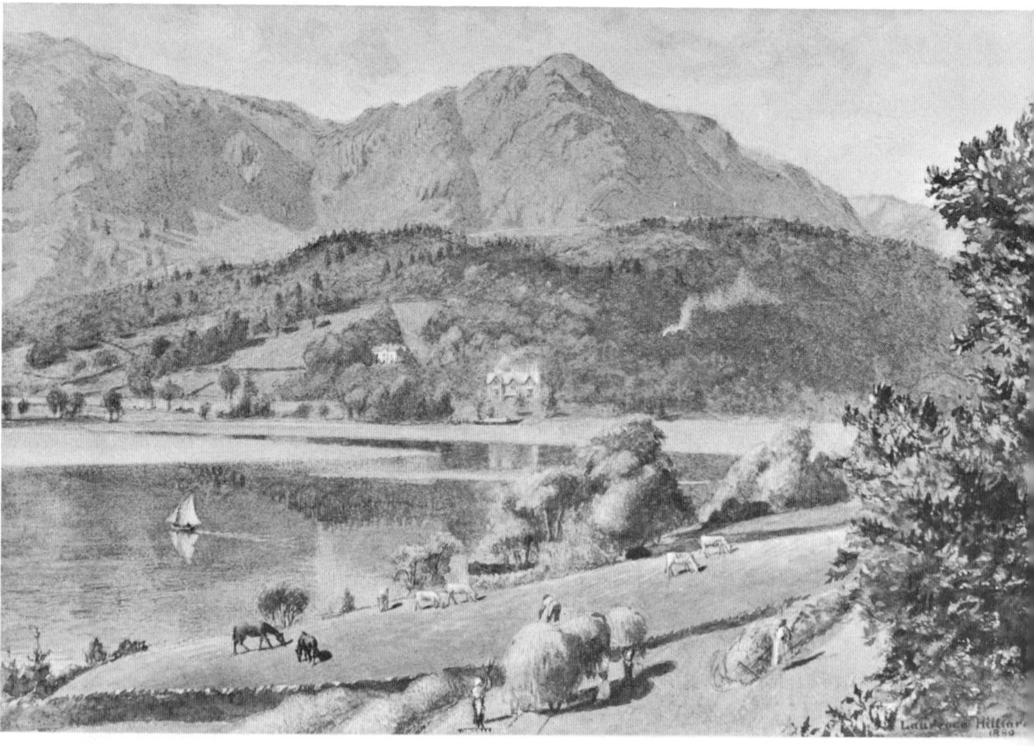

The View from Brantwood in 1880

Watercolor by Laurence J. Hilliard (1855–87), showing The Thwaite, the Waterhead Hotel, Wetherlam, Yewdale, and the Old Man. Courtesy Ruskin Galleries, Bembridge School.

"I've got a letter (which for his lordship's sake had better never been written) from the Bishop of Manchester," Ruskin informed the Reverend Malleson. "I send the letter with my reply this month to the *Contemporary*" (*Works, 34,* 239; letter of January 5, 1880).

The early weeks of January were therefore devoted mainly to the Bishop, with certain pages of the manuscript bearing "witness to the labour of the file" (*Works, 34,* xxxvii). And this "Rejoinder" was, in all, a bit of business smoothly executed. Ruskin avoided a consecutively reasoned argument by framing his letter so that its body consisted of 15 footnotes, lettered *A* through *Q*, in which he shrewdly attacked one and another remark made by his antagonist. In time the Bishop would say that these notes sounded to him like the "ravings of a lunatic," which he would therefore leave unanswered (*Works, 34,* xxxvi). He might better have said, as Cook and Wedderburn observe, that if there is to be an argument to purpose, there must be some common ground on which to meet, with commonly accepted premises. "I'm very nearly done with toasting my bishop," Ruskin would tell Miss Beever; "he just wants another turn or two, and then a little butter" (*Works, 37,* 307; letter of January 1880). In the Diary he notes, on January 20: "Get to my Plato Stopped by the Bishop since the 9th." On January 22: "frightfully tired with finishing Bishops letter."

Late in February, with the Bishop duly toasted and *Fors* sent off to Allen, to be followed by his revision of *The Seven Lamps* (its 1880 Preface dated "February 25th"), he was ready to formulate his reply to a lecture upon the physical evolution of snakes which he had heard Huxley deliver on December 1 at the Royal Institution. Preliminary reading for his rejoinder (scheduled for delivery on March 17) had been under way since shortly after his return to Brantwood (see entry for December 28, 1879), and before the end of January the lecture itself had been roughly sketched forth (see entry for January 22). After another few weeks, the Diary gives a pleasant glimpse of an evening when he sat reading aloud, from the *Antiquary,* as Laurence Hilliard and Arthur Severn prepared the visual aids (see entry for February 21 and *Works, 26,* 330–31). Do what he would, he subsequently explained, the material took on a comic cast, as though he were speaking in no more than "badinage" of Huxley—for example, when he elaborated upon the evolutionary course (spiritually speaking) represented by "Dove to Duck [to Serpent]—Coo into Quack [into Hiss]" (see entry for January 22 and *Works, 26,* 306–07). Staging the performance (as yet by no means an "old man"), he would leap to the top of the desk upon the lecture platform, to serve as one of the three standard-bearers of the outstretched skin of a boa constrictor. About to leave for London, or perhaps even after reaching Herne Hill, he had sent a note to thank "Dearest Doctor" Dawtrey Drewitt for the "viper skin" which had arrived "in the nick of time." "I'm not myself at all," he continued, "and fear the whole thing will be—grovelling. I don't mean that I'm actually unwell—but out of heart, and that is not a state to lecture in" (unpublished letter of March 1880; Pierpont Morgan Library). Nevertheless, the lecture, as delivered, was so amusingly effective that he was requested to repeat it on the 23rd, with the demand for tickets on each occasion out-running the supply.

Returning to Brantwood, Ruskin could rejoice because, with "plenty to do," he was greeted by sunshine (see entry for April 2). Since early in January, he had been working beneath "Manchester smoke—with the usual deviltry of cloud moving fast in rags" or with the whole sky an "Abyss of darkness" as the "hell-fog" remained "unbroken" (see entries for January 8, 9, February 29). Setting forth to deliver his lecture, he had felt "unable for all I've to do. . . . ¶But the curse on the sky is my chief plague— If only spring *were* spring! But its too hard on me, this devil in the wind and clouds and light" (see entry for March 12). Even so, his concern over such phenomena was more objective than it had been during July-August 1879, and fortunately this was not another year when the months of summer were dominated by the plague-cloud and "Darkness." As he would tell Miss Beever in September, writing from Chartres: "The sunshine is life and health to me" (*Works, 37,* 325).

Planning the next round of his work, he knew that at present he should not venture to "exhort, and rebuke." "Please recollect," he explained, refusing some request made by William Morris, "that I am old, ill, and liable any day to be struck crazy if I get into a passion. And, therefore, while I can still lecture—if I choose—on rattlesnakes' tails, I can't on anything I care about" (*Works, 37,* 315; letter of May 27, 1880).

Nevertheless, he was determined to produce much disparately useful work. "Within two months of longest day," he noted in his Diary on April 23, "—I must try and turn every hour to gold. It will be my own fault if not." No more than incidentally he had in mind the six letters (dated March 21 through June 18) to an anonymous friend who had requested a "paper" on the "Function and Formation" of *A Museum or Picture Gallery,* published in the *Art Journal* of June and August, 1880; the Preface (dated "April 29th") to *"A Joy Forever,"* about to be reissued as Volume IX in the Series edition of his *Works;* the Epilogue (dated "June 1880") that was promised Malleson for the appearance of his *Letters to the Clergy* in book form; and his recent lecture, *Living Waves,* to be readied for publication in July, as Part VII of *Deucalion.* Centrally, he was committed to writing the *Elements of English Prosody* "For Use in St. George's Schools" (issued in October as the third volume of his *Bibliotheca Pastorum*), together with the series of essays based upon the novels of Sir Walter Scott, *Fiction, Fair and Foul,* for June and subsequent publication in the *Nineteenth Century.*

Merely "planning" his first Scott paper during early April, Ruskin turned at once to writing out his *Prosody* as the "little school-manual" he had promised—as long ago as 1877—in his Preface to *Rock Honeycomb* (*Works, 31,* 114). "What I am going to lay down in this Prosody," he now told Henry Swan, "are the eternal laws of time and measure—which all language must, in perfection, obey; and which it violates only to express certain humours or likings of each nation which only the writers of that nation can explain. The eternal law—and the degrees in which *English* words obey it are all I have to do with" (unpublished letter of June 18, 1880; present whereabouts unknown). By July 22, as he noted in the Diary, the book (which turned out to be, to him, most disappointing) was "nearly finished." Already he had recognized that though work was "getting done," it was "not of the best" (see entry for July 6).

The essays on Scott had been in fomentation for about a year (see Diary entry for June 28, 1879), partly, it may be, because he could identify himself with the writer who, in one group of novels, had shown "characters of strength and felicity which never more appeared after [he] was struck down by his terrific illness of 1819" (*Works, 34,* 288). Some months ago, rereading Lockhart's *Life,* he had remarked: "Scott . . . feeling himself fast going to pieces at 54—and here at 61, I am just thinking of pulling myself better together! D.G." (see entry for June 23, 1879). By now, however, he was well aware that he had not regained the level at which he could work before he himself had been analogously "struck down." Furthermore, he notes, when Scott no longer had the physical strength required for writing, he had resorted to dictation: "the affectionate Laidlaw [besought] him to stop dictating when his audible suffering filled every pause. 'Nay, Willie,' he answered, 'only see that the doors are fast. I would fain keep all the cry as well as all the wool to ourselves; but as for giving over work, that can only be when I am in woollen' " (*Works, 34,* 288). For himself, toward the end of May he could but ask: "Heaven grant me wisdom and strength to spend these lengthening days well, and not to fear the shortening ones. But what Heaven means by letting me see my way to so much, and make my way to so little—Heaven must explain to—whom it chooses, in its own time. One thing I get more and more sure of—that the Devil is rampant—everywhere" (see entry for May 25).

Increasingly, the June-August-September installments of *Fiction, Fair and Foul* reveal the strain. As a first article for the series, the opening essay was well designed, except for the lengthily tangential close devoted to "the merely verbal characteristics of [Scott's] style" (*Works, 34,* 292). Having promised this paper for June publication, he was noting in the Diary on April 26: "I very languid yesterday—perhaps a little overworked on Scott." Three days later: "I seem to find my head today more confused than usual, and am obliged to give up my Scott work—and take to serpents—or perhaps to nothing— Perhaps my own fault—in forcing myself to begin thinking in the morning,—or perhaps—the mere chance of thoughts not falling right—as often has happened in my best times." Within a week, he was "at work . . . on

St Ronans [Well], and the disease of Scott. May I use the many warnings I have had, to better purpose than lately, while my eyes and mind still serve me" (see entry for May 4). Four days later: "Did much, yesterday but not well,—must take care. Scott giving me far more trouble than I expected—but that is no new thing. Take 'heart of grace' to it—and to all things—if I may." Although by May 10 the essay was no more than about half finished, by May 14 he could state: "Scott, first paper, done and off,"—with its tangential conclusion perhaps too readily, or necessarily, supplied from some material in manuscript which chanced to be at hand?

The next two essays show a slackening intellectual control, perhaps together with a loss of interest. Turning to the second paper, he could not direct his mind to continued work on Scott, who, in the next two papers (September and November), crops up no more than sporadically. On May 10 (the birthday of a Father who had greatly admired the poetry of Byron), he decided to make the second essay an "article for Byron against Browning," only to have this essay become an amorphous discussion of "Scott, Rime, and Wordsworth," as his thoughts about "Prosody" and the significance of rhyme crowded out his thoughts about Scott before the paper veered into an attack upon Arnold's recently published appraisal of Wordsworth—the (tellingly deliberate?) epithet for Arnold being "Silver How" (*Works, 34,* 318; the delightful *Silver How* could, of course, seem like no more than a slip for *Fox How,* as the name of Arnold's residence).

To be sure, he had undertaken to do more than could be managed. As he remarked in the entry for May 24: "This morning my head so full of crowded thoughts about Museums—Prosody, Clergy, Snakes, Scott, & Byron—all in hand together—that I don't know what to do." With the second essay due for August publication, he was noting, in July: "feel Byronized and jaded today,—must shorten sail"; and, next, "Scott and Byron work very bad for me without any doubt" (see entries of July 12 and 13). Before he left for London, the third article, only slightly less amorphous than the second, was sufficiently in hand to be completed at Herne Hill for September publication. The fourth, probably completed in October while he was visiting the Gales, embodied an account of Barbarossa which would have been more appropriate to *The Bible of Amiens* (by then under way) than it was to his analysis of either Scott or Byron.

Thus working in response to that Command with which, for him, the year had begun, he may already have known the discouragement reflected in a Sermon to be delivered, some years hence, to the boys of St. David's School, Reigate. Sketched forth in rough draft, it is preceded by a paragraph in which he comments: "Written in the small hours of night when 2 sermons were demanded on Sunday & only given [to his 'Connie'] after much pressing," he being aware of its "many imperfections" but "unable to resist aught she asks" (preserved among the "Hilliard Papers"; Pierpont Morgan Library). Speaking of biblical characters whom "we can understand," he dwells upon Elijah:

> Here we have him as one of ourselves—overworked, overwhelmed—the strain of anxiety too great —— the thought of loneliness over powering him—the importance of his work —the sense of failure —— He lays himself down & for one minute he gives way—gives way to despondency— He *cannot* bear it— It is too much— Usque quo Domine— How long O Lord how long— Let me die. Let me die ——
>
> . . . This scene of Elijahs— Other men stronger than ourselves—men loved by God—men whose characters stand out in our lives like beacon lights toward which the mariners steer with aching arms & beating hearts while the sea around them rages —— If they have had moments of weakness, we must not lose heart— Heart lost—all lost.... As they had strength sent to them so shall we —— If they had sinned & been forgiven so shall we. . . .
>
> But for a few minutes let us think of this scene of Elijah's on the Mountain top— . . . What a strain it must have been —no friends, no sympathy—seemingly so little success— Then the juniper—the loss of heart, of pluck—the prayer to die— And what was God's answer— Not in the strong wind —not in the earth quake—not in the fire but in the still small voice— "What dost thou here Elijah' [I Kings 19:12–13] —despairing—faint-hearted—throwing up your work in life

—— It is enough—now O Lord take away my Life— I am not better than my Fathers —— I even I only am left —— The piteousness of that cry —— the heart broken accents of that voice ——

But God's answer to Elijah was the comfort that is given to every man—"Go & do thy work"— Do thy work bravely & all else shall be sent thee —— You will find it true as you grow to be men— Work—real work—honest work—never so humble, never so insignificant in the sight of the world— That is the path that leads to God— That is it that drives away anxiety & brokenness of heart. — "Blessed is the man who has found out his work let him ask no other blessing" —— [Carlyle, *Past and Present,* Bk. III, chap. 11]

. . . This lesson we would teach you— What ever happens —Work— Take the duty, the work, nearest at hand & work at it conscientiously—fearlessly— . . . earnestly—bravely. Work is the kindest gift God has given to us— Many lives would be unable to bear but for that work— It brings comfort. It brings occupation— It brings sympathy— . . .

Yes—let the last words that some of you hear from this place be words begging you to see the nobility & holiness of Work—begging you to realize [that] to Work without the thought of results is what God demands —— What dost thou here Elijah? —— 'O Lord I am broken hearted—' —Go and work..... Work— Try & crush self— . . . as you grow up to be men you will understand that the nobility of a man's character is gauged by the nobility of his work—. Not by its results—not by its fame and popularity—but by its earnestness by its sincerity—by its thought for others—by its devotion to God— None know whether the same chance may ever come again— "Work while it is day, the night cometh when no man can work —" [ibid., chap. 12]

In addition to what Ruskin wrote for publication, there had been the usual endlessness of private correspondence, with many of these letters addressed to individuals who had sought his help even though they were not among his personal friends. And there had been the usual scattering of Public Letters, all of which

Alexander Wedderburn was now gathering for December publication as *Arrows of the Chace.* Time and thought, as well as money, had also been unobtrusively invested in his acquisitions for the Sheffield Museum and in his more general supervision of affairs connected with the Guild. Locally, he had been beneficent in his dealings with his many friends among the folk of Coniston, while giving pleasure to those who, in turn, could give him joy through their mere presence in his home.

Although "I can't have any visiting" (as he had told the Reverend Malleson), Frances Colenso, back from Natal, became his guest for about a week, and Martha Gale and Constance Hilliard had made visits more prolonged. Laurence Hilliard was there as his secretary, and Sara Anderson had returned to them in June. From time to time Arthur Severn's brother Walter, Alice Rathbone and her "lover," Annie Somerscales and her sister, Mrs. Ritchie, Lady Edwardes, and J. R. Anderson were entertained. Across the Lake were "Susie" and her sister Mary Beever, or Miss Rigbye, with whom to talk at tea, and by summer he had reached the point of planning his adventure into France, which, a year ago, he could scarcely have hoped to see once more.

Hence, two days before he left for the preliminary twelve days to be spent at Herne Hill, his entries in this unit of the Diary end. The December entries to be made after his return to Brantwood belong no more than formally to the year 1880 and will therefore be discussed in connection with the brief unit of this Diary which introduces the developments of 1881.

January 1. Read, for beginning of day, my morning diary of Oct. 2, [18]77, page 47 Read the Titus texts,[1] with comfort.

January 2 Friday Clear sky to south—& moon. I ⟨utterly jaded and feverish with nearly sleepless night and crowding thoughts,—wonderful in sudden call upon me for action—and I so feeble but must answer a little Thankful for the clear guiding—see the new Fors begun yesterday⟩[2]

January 3. Saturday Woful wild—and I much depressed, in shame of not taking up my task—in memoriam—rightly.[3] But had good from St Louis psalter last night, and saw my way to dealing with Bishop. this morning I read my diary of the great days—and am led to the αχαπητος p. 69.[4] — This is the Salute the friends by name.[5] But I look, by Fors order this morning, first, at the 1st epistle III. xiv— We know that we have passed from death unto life.[6]

1. Namely, "these things speak, and exhort, and rebuke" (Tit. 2:15). See entry for November 2, 1877, which is on page 47 of the MS. Ruskin now gives the wrong reference ("Oct. 2") because in the MS page 47 is headed "October," as the word which caught his eye.

2. Published in *Works, 33,* xxvi. The March 1880 issue of *Fors Clavigera,* Letter 88, is headed: "YEA, THE WORK OF OUR HANDS, ESTABLISH THOU IT" (Psa. 90:17). As originally written, this Letter begins: "1st January. 1880. The group of ten years, in the beginning of which these letters began, will I trust, not close upon *their* work undone, though it may very easily close upon mine, done to the end allowed me But the check I received in it two years ago I hope is rather to be read as a sign that no more was needed for my purposes than—(which was my first interpretation of the lesson,) that I was too feeble—and faultful—to carry it through" (page of MS in the F. J. Sharp Collection).

3. That is, "in memoriam" to Rosa La Touche, January 3 being her birthday.

4. The "Beloved," or St. John. See the last sentence of the entry for February 19, 1878, which is written on the right-hand page 69 of the MS.

5. From III John 14—read, doubtless, as words from Rose: "But I trust I shall shortly see thee, and we shall speak face to face. Peace be to thee. Our friends salute thee. Greet the friends by name."

6. Apparently he had seen his "way to dealing with [the] Bishop" because "Fors" had directed him to the verse: "We know that we have passed from death unto life, because we love the brethren. He that loveth not his brother abideth in death" (I John 3:14). In his "Reply" to Ruskin, the Bishop had stated: "What I

January 4. Sunday. Yesterday at last a Sunset—pure green blue—and flamingo clouds divine and dazzling and quiet and quiet purple clouds on the Old man—grand as on Olympus— This morning utterly dead rain mist again—and I as dead myself. The want—for a whole winter—of one pure sunrise! unbelievable and horrible—but fact. how we bear it is the wonder—

January 5th. Monday,—and indeed I dont bear it, but, though Ive had a good night—⟨came down—at ¼ to nine—into the dark room with drenching fog over all heaven and earth⟩[7] in a quite woful and helpless state. I[']ll get a few needful letters done rather than Plato.

January 6. Tuesday. ⟨This is quite—as far as I can remember, the most miserable January I ever passed—Today, pouring small rain—after a yesterdays unbroken fog, and miserably dark.⟩[8] — Yet I may be thankful that after a sleepless night,—nearly, I can still see the blue lines of this paper, without spectacles.

I[']ll do my Plato today, anyhow.

January 7 Wednesday. Yesterday Rain all day—today, drenching fog, the room feeling like a well. —Cold hanging on, ever since the magic lantern—26th Dec. now nearly a fortnight. The idiocy of poor old Dawson[9] in cutting all my hair off—and mine in letting him, at bottom of all.

January 8. Thursday ⟨Deadly fog-rain these three days, without a gleam— today—Manchester smoke—

---

do expect to find, in relation to my duty to my neighbour, are those unalterable principles of equity, fairness, trustfulness, honesty, which are the indispensable bases of civil society" (*Works, 34,* 402). In his Rejoinder Ruskin asked: "Has your Lordship *no* expectations loftier than these, from severer scrutiny of the Gospel? As for instance, of some ordinance of Love, built on the foundation of Honesty?" (*Works, 34,* 411).

7. Published (with minor changes) in *Works, 33,* xxviii.

8. Ibid.

9. Henry Dawson, who had been his servant as long ago as 1837, when he was a Gentleman Commoner at Christ Church.

with the usual deviltry of cloud moving fast in rags, with no wind)[10]—I with as much cold in head as a fortnight ago! — yet I was better last night, and have slept well, and have thoughts—for the Bishop!

January 9 Friday. The hell-fog unbroken—and I awake at 4, if not earlier lying thinking in the blank darkness— Not asleep early, neither yet I don't feel tired—but fretful and despairing and can't go on with anything—but pull my lips, and stare at the pitch cloud—and wonder if its the Devil—or the Bishop of Manchester or me, that it's sent for.

January 11. Sunday. The hills visible at last but the sky one curtain of lifeless grey—more deadly and depressing to *me* than the fog itself. But yesterday—after lying awake from 4, I got up in the old way at 6, and got on with Bishop—and then, in the thickest of fog, walked Mat and Agnes[11] up by the mines on the steep cleft cascade, which was lovely with ice on its heather, sugary and delicate beyond expression and found myself springy and well! — Rowed over lake home, and this morning, slept till Seven! Cold not gone, but merely remnant now—and harmless— Just a fortnight see Dec 28–9th, since it began and fog for a week, after the sunset on Rosie's birthday.

January 12 Monday. Yesterday was lovely in afternoon—cloudless—but misty, and sun setting red,—Helvellyn scarce visible— Climbed Furness Fell [12] with girls, rowing first to Fir island—view from crags at top quite noble: but I feeling

10. Published in *Works, 33,* xxviii.

11. Martha Gale and probably Agnes Stalker.

12. As Miss Gnosspelius explains, "a Ruskinian name for the fell above Copland's Barn, or 'Grange.' Properly speaking, *Furness Fells* (always a rather vague term) comprises all the fells (and mountains) in High Furness. But the bit that Ruskin seems to have referred to when he said '*Furness Fells*' (or '*Fell*') is Heald Brow."

nothing— [Bishop of] Manchester on the brain, —to which I must now set myself. It is frosty—and the sky of course one leaden veil—touching tops of hills— 'Morning' is a thing now impossible, and the oppression of this to *me,* unspeakable—and greater in its now accepted and almost unconscious burden.

January 14. Wednesday, I believe, but did not think I had missed entry yesterday. I got up early, and gained little by it.

Frost—hard, these two days—but not a ray of sunshine—and letter to Bishop dreadfully hanging fire.

January 15 Thursday. A little sickly sunshine streaked through fog on the hills clear night corrupted into dim day as the sun rises

I ought really now to begin noting some of the details of my dream of two years ago—of which one part was brought back to me as I lay awake this morning, in connection with my present fight with the B[isho]p of Manchester: of the more or less ruling idea in the dream, that two Bishops had been sent—after digging a hole for them, to the center of the earth to see if as astronomers said—they really could go on and come out on the other side; that these Bishops had agreed with each other to bring up a false report in favour of Scripture—that the British mob having discovered this false report, was minded to lynch the Bishops, who thereupon secreted themselves somewhere—and became byewords of iniquity to be extinguished—so that the cry "Bishop him"—became synonymous with that of Damn him, or Hang him—in the popular mind, and this went on till the very birds took up the cry—and sang "Bishop him" at the dawn of morning at my window.

January 16 Friday. Awake since ½ past 3—but with quite

useful thoughts, for Bishop—and for serpent lecture—but of course now tired. — Polar world —gold mines and Terra [*sic*] del Fuego[13] make me melancholy also.

I go on with my dream. A great deal of it passed at the top, though more at the bottom of this episcopal pit— One most tormenting scene at its mouth—a deep funnel, was the election of a new Bishop by some kind of ballot at the bottom of it, and *mouth* of the pit I recollect only the emotions of a thrilling and passionate contest about it—in which two amiable women were chiefly eager—and that they and I, and the right side people, were in some way cheated—and saw with astonishment and terror —(for some awful fate was at issue on the election—) an hypocrite & false Bishop ascend from the funnel and display himself at the top with bland assurance to the acceptant people as the elected one.

January 17 Saturday. Rosy light on snow at last—but not pure—and heavy clouds about—coming up after the stars had burned like torches all night— I was very thankful to see the Pleiades go down over the top of the Old man—and Orion low in the west and south once more

January 18th Sunday. Candles again at half past eight, but very thankful I am to see with them, after a good nights sleep, (—and blue lines without spectacles,)—though I must have been dreaming of my business—for I was being told by somebody that 'money' meant 'a heap'! It is indeed

13. See Hartwig's *The Polar World*, pp. 230–39 (describing life in the Siberian goldfields) and pp. 493–515 (describing the natives of Tierra del Fuego, or "Fireland," on the south side of the Strait of Magellan). In *Usury: A Reply and a Rejoinder* Ruskin illustrates the "beneficent influence of recent commercial enterprise" by quoting Hartwig's account of the effects of smallpox and alcohol upon the Indians of Canada, thanks to the great French and English fur-trading companies in the early days of competition (see *Works, 34*, 418–20).

false information—yet the dream is helpful—for it 'reminds' me—that actually I've never looked what money *does* mean! and now looking—I find it—in the root—μνημοσυνη! the mother of the Muses! [14]

January 19 Monday. Clear rosy dawn and sunrise at last—after starry night— I very sleepless—or dreaming of business—that Murray was dead and my check returned and the Luca lost,—yet my eyes now clear—only I don't care to set to work at anything

Yesterday went to see Susie—and found her bright and clear and full of play—and Shakespeare[15]

January 20 Tuesday. Intense frost—but yesterday divine and pure all day long— today—misty but likely to clear. An entirely new condition of hoarfrost on panes, in nearly vertical column—thus [sketch] each white column being a cluster of speculae as below—now curved. This lower sketch the real size.

Slept well last night, and down in good spirits. Get to my Plato Stopped by the Bishop since the 9th

January 21 Wednesday. Clouds look like thaw but frost still sharp. I lying awake since five, thinking over the

14. "'Mnemosyne,'" Professor Konrad Gries explains, "is the goddess of *mneme*, memory. *Mneme* is the short form of the Indo-European root (*m* plus vowel plus *n*) that appears also in *mental*, Latin *memini* (I *remember*), and Latin *moneo* (I *advise, inform, warn*). The root means *to put in mind, to cause to think.* At Rome Juno had a temple, the capture of which by attacking Gauls was prevented, one night, by the cackling of her sacred geese. The temple was consequently named the temple of Juno *Moneta*, Juno the warner. In later centuries, the official mint came to be located in the basement of this temple, and coinage and coins also came to be spoken of as *moneta*. Hence French *monnaie* and English *money*, as well as *monetary*."

15. To supplement her *Book of Reference to Remarkable Passages in Shakespeare* (1870), Miss Beever may have been at work upon "that Shakespeare guide" to which Ruskin refers in a letter of 1878 (see *Works*, *37*, 236, where the publication of Miss Beever's *Remarkable Passages* is ascribed to 1871). On the other hand, she may merely have been rereading some play for personal pleasure.

great dream, which I am ashamed to find is beginning to pass from me—and that too, in one of its most wonderful parts—the great contest between the Devil and—Georgie! [16] (who represented throughout the adverse queenly or even archangelic power,) for the Kingdom of the world. I dreamed that every seven thousand years it had to be run for in a chariot race—and that the Devil won always, because he knew some way of overlapping at the end of the last round, and counted the turns so that he always must win. This is the part that has got dim to me; but I thought that the secret had somehow become known to Georgie and that she raced him, and won.

January 22 Thursday. Calm lake and clearing sky,—after threatened snow, coming up in dawn after a marvellous moonlight at 3, and I frightfully tired with finishing Bishops letter—and the following thoughts crowding on me— today at coffee read the story of founding the Russian empire in Polar World [17]—too awful—and planned for lecture—on snakes. The seer—οφις —that sees and holds its tongue—the lark—latet alauda, latet anguis[18]—one, mute, the other heavenly voiced. The speechless forked tongue? — a double tongue never *can* say anything—Basilisk sight. The Evil Eye. If thine eye be evil! *Robin* without an eye, in Modern Science—so owl! — Then Rod & Serpent slavery of rod—or of subtlety? — Cadmus—teeth—then Two Horse Guards! Q[uestion] fangs? of London! Dove to Duck—Coo into Quack. Woodwalk into ground waddle,—and water dabble—

16. Georgiana, Lady Burne-Jones, 1840–1920.

17. See Hartwig, *The Polar World,* "The Conquest of Siberia by the Russians," pp. 206–17.

18. "The lark lies hidden, the serpent lies hidden." There seems to be no specific connection between these words and the lecture, "Living Waves," as published.

Then the colours. Hunts doves—Turners. Duck variegation—vulgar violent. — But the main point Speckle—Stigma. Spot. Clouding. Wings like a dove— *you* don't want wings and rest—you want bellies—and lots of going on them[19]

January 23 Friday. Dreadfully jaded today from sleepless and sad night of wonder, moon—scarcely more than half full—blazing in on me—I never saw more dazzling—from 3 to ½ past 4 when she set, and I scarcely slept afterwards. Natal [20]—America—Venice—and my own life—all seeming alike ruinous—and no heaven above

January 24. Saturday. The most gushing day of wonderful teaching and coincidence Ive had for—since Christmas of 1876[21]— Chiefly in invention in bed, of the definition of modern Deity for Fors.[22] Then—Fanny Colenso—wearing mourning—Then, my agates come from Pankhurst[23]— my photographed asps from Burgess, and my letter about Whistlers picture from Glasgow! [24] Now I must write my Fors bit at once

19. In these jottings one finds "Living Waves" in embryo. See *Works, 26,* 295–330 for the lecture in its final form (published July 1880).

20. Ruskin's thoughts had turned to Natal because Frances Colenso (see B.S. and Letters, IX) had reached Brantwood on January 22.

21. For the communications from "St. Ursula" which began on Christmas day and continued for about a week, see Introduction to 1877, pp. 27–28.

22. Contrasting the feudal and modern age, he stated in *Fors Clavigera* of March 1880: "The creed of the Dark Ages was, 'I believe in one God, the Father Almighty, Maker of heaven and earth'; and the creed of the Light Ages has become, 'I believe in Father Mud, the Almighty Plastic; and in Father Dollar, the Almighty Drastic'" (*Works, 29,* 388).

23. The mineralogist Edward A. Pankhurst (d. 1912, aged 73) of Brighton shared Ruskin's special interest in silica, and the engraver Arthur Burgess (d. 1886, aged 42), as Ruskin's salaried assistant, was evidently making photographs to be used in the lecture on snakes, for which he also prepared two of the drawings to be displayed (see *Works, 26,* 331; *37,* 319). "Six sheets of photographs for binding up with [the 'Living Waves' chapter of] *Deucalion* were issued" (*Works, 26,* 295n.).

24. A correspondent, "J.A.," is said to have told him that at an auction sale in Glasgow "the" Whistler painting which had caused the libel suit of 1877 had aroused "but languid interest . . . and at the sale fetched only a few pounds." "I

January 27th Tuesday. Fanny Colenso here since Thursday,—told me much that puts all else out of my head—Hard frost—and the everlasting fog back again but I better, and doing good in Fors, and on birds.[25]

January 29 Thursday. Down late after quite overwhelming tumbling in on me of thoughts about History of Iceland in Polar world,[26]—and sane old Horace—and new Natal business—and a more or less sleepless, half dreamy night,—dreamed of Miss Hill,[27] of all people! Now thick mist—not fog, but snow on hills seen through it

January 30 Friday. A little sunshine—dirty buff coloured clouds, and tawny ones, and feeble white behind—all changing and flickering and flying—restless and useless and defiled— Steady fog all day yesterday—dry nasty biting wind—yet just above freezing! took girls[28] to Colwith force—nice tea in cottage. Slept well and read wonderful Franklin expedition and Parry[29] and planned Lion and Cock beginning of lecture.[30] — Recollected a forgotten—totally—bit of dream—that Georgie began by wrongly distrusting me, thinking I did'nt want to get out of some enclosure or under some bar when I did—and her first mistake brought on the misery—more &

---

am sincerely obliged by your letter," Ruskin replied, "and much more pleased by its contents than perhaps some of my friends would think it virtuous to be." (*Works, 34,* 544; letter of January 24, 1880). Which one of the controversial Whistler pictures had been sold for "only a few pounds" is not known.

25. "The Dabchicks" was under way (*Love's Meinie,* Pt. III, 1881).

26. See Hartwig, *The Polar World,* chaps. 5–7, from which passages are quoted in "The Dabchicks" (*Works, 25,* 120–21)

27. Octavia Hill (1838–1912), the friend and social worker who since 1864 had managed slum property in Marylebone which he had inherited from his father and with whom, publicly and most unjustly, he had quarreled shortly before his illness of 1878 (see *Works, 29,* 354–60).

28. Presumably Martha Gale and Frances Colenso.

29. For the Arctic voyages of Lieutenant W. E. Parry (1790–1855) and Lieutenant John Franklin (d. 1847, aged 61), see Hartwig, *The Polar World,* pp. 392–422.

30. A plan to be discarded, no published lecture having been thus begun.

more—and it went on afterwards by her coming to disentangle me from some net—and my being forced to get entangled again—till she thought I was doing it on purpose, and left me indignantly and despairingly

January 31 Saturday. Nearly pitch dark, fog two miles thick or so—shaky wild diabolic wind and thaw.

— Slept well,—after nice game of shuttlecock with Mattie—and had all manner of successful thoughts for Dragon lecture,[31] but too many,—as I took my coffee—and now feel a little tired.

February 18 Have been at Sheffield since the 10th, and am more thankful to get back than ever yet.

The days not diaried were overwhelmed in doing new Fors, which has been done twice over, and inevitable fatigues and confusions

February 19th. Thursday. Wild wind and rain— Did good bird work yesterday and slept well— Mattie writing Fors out for me a great help.

See entry for this day two years ago!

Ασπαζου τους φιλους κατ' ονομα [32]

February 20. Friday. A little light at last—through rain, and I see my opal and my books are getting into order, and my strength at present gaining

This was the great day really, two years ago.

Strange, that I should not have marked it otherwise than by the entry next morning, "Up, like Sir Charles Grandison," and the House at Newbridge.

February 21. Saturday. Light soft, but broken—never any dawn. I sleeping better and happy in bird work. Alice Rathbone[33] came, and we made up our quarrel in the wood. A busy day—ending with

31. That is, "Living Waves"—"dracon, or dragon" meaning "The beholding" snake (*Works, 26*, 302, 332).

32. III John 14: "Greet the friends by name" (echoing the first sentence for February 19, 1878: "and all the calling of names").

33. See B.S.

nice Antiquary reading to Joan, Mattie, Arthur and Lollie drawing Sea Serpents.[34]

February 22 Sunday. Yesterday fine at last, nice work on ouzels and in wood with Mattie and Alice with her lover at dinner very nice— Sleep broken by fancies of going to a great scholastic institution—and then—I forget what. How vast a quantity of brain motion is useless

Today—shower and sunshine very sweet—snowdrops lovely everywhere Luca della Robbia a great comfort to me in the corner

February 24. Tuesday I see the 22nd was the last day I wrote on, two years ago Down today in bright morning, with much work satisfactorily in hand and more in order than for many years Yesterday took Paton[35] to call on Miss Rigby[e] and Susie.

February 25 Wednesday. Soft rain and healthy rain clouds. Down in good heart to my dabchicks, flints—and snakes—on the whole enjoying everything much more than for a long time. The month very mild. Note that I had a settled roughness of throat coming on every night at Sheffield keeping me awake sometimes with coughing—now quite gone without any cold in head following.

February 26. Thursday. — Slept well—with intensely clear dream of going to an old Saxon castle, in its own time—almost a cottage castle, with lovely successive courtyards and exquisite view from battlements—with brook springing in valley—all clearly seen, and thought of as a Walter Scott like scene. ⟨So much of life⟩ gained ⟨out of the night⟩[36]—it seemed, and I am fresh for my birds

34. Lecturing at the London Institution, he would exhibit three drawings by Arthur Severn and two by Laurence Hilliard.

35. Sir Joseph Noel Paton (1821–1902), one of the "Edinburgh artists" who had wanted to meet Ruskin as long ago as 1853 (*Works, 12,* xxvii).

36. Published in *Works, 33,* xxviii.

now. Wild wind—with blue sky and sun in breaks—but mostly gloomy

February 27 Friday. — Grey cloud and snow—*never* a dawn —the very sense of the word 'morning' fading into merely 'getting up.' Alas—how one threw one's mornings away once—and nobody to warn one! — Read Orphic hymn to Nature yesterday in afternoon. — recollect the great line

πικρὴ μὲν φαύλοισι, γλυκεῖα δὲ πειθομενο ισιν [37]

Came just now in looking for it in the Hymn to Justice.

February 28 Saturday. — Still wild wind and rain—assuredly the *∂λυκεια δὲ πειθομενοισιν* [the "sweet to those who believe"] was not written for this climate Wind squeezing in at every cranny, and raging at the leaves, and rasping at the water in swirls like a puff adder gone insane.

February 29 Sunday. Entirely black and dismal wind and rain— The never by any chance seeing a fine morning—how much less a dawn or sunrise is a more calamitous change to me from the continual sweetness of Denmark Hill in the old day than I have even myself any idea of. The Abyss of darkness in the *whole* sky today, without fog—is quite awful

March 1. Monday. The old story, wild wind and black sky,—scudding rain and roar—a climate of Patagonia instead of England, and I more disconsolate—not in actual depression, but in general hopelessness, wonder, and disgust than ever yet in my life, that I remember, as if it was no use fighting for a world any more in which there could be no sunrise

March 3 Wednesday. The same yesterday—the same today— On Monday evening I had a bad little attack of inflammation in the left eye,—which did not yield as usual to brandy and water,—

37. "Bitter to the evil ones and sweet to those who believe" (Hymn 9).

but, not reading in bed next morning, seems to have gone off—to my great comfort.

March 4. Joanie's Birthday. Thursday. A gleam of light presently overcast and I more down, and dim eyed than usual—and give up my Plato having my mind on Saxon coins.

March 5 Friday Since last Friday one continued storm and today worst of all—one drift and drench, and the bank cascade larger than ever yet I saw it in wildest snow thaws and storm together.

March 6. Saturday. A little better—but sky all covered, not one ray of sun all yesterday, and I much down today, yet slept well—and dreamed pleasantly enough of a mountain walk. Deeply interested in Saxon money, and Roman weights Have to find out, at this time of life—what a pound is! and how it came to be so.[38]

March 7. Sunday. A little sun, and calm lake, but the clouds foul, and I very languid and with sense of fatigue in head and eyes,—perhaps more—shortbread at tea than any thing else, but I did too much yesterday—diagram in afternoon.

March 8. Yesterday at last a perfect day. Sunshine entirely pure, and sky cloudless. Owl cried at night—waking me out of a dream which was entirely sad at the moment of waking Q[uestion] made so by the owl's cry? Notable!—and set me gravely thinking today, which is bright, also. Two fine days—and lake perfectly calm, D.G.

Composed my rhyme for Saxon Tower,[39]

38. "The pound, called by the Saxons Tower pound, being weighed and answered for at their Tower . . . of London, weighed 5400 troy grain; the ora, or Tower ounce, 450 troy grains" (*Works, 30,* 278–79; from "Note on Saxon Money").

39. "Ounce of comb in Saxon hive,
Count it ten times forty-five:
Pound of grain in Saxon store,
Count it hundreds fifty-four
Count ye true in Saxon tower
Pound by ounce, and day by hour" (*Works, 30,* 279).

weight and time—as I dressed this morning, and have got it written down with satisfaction—Again, D.G.

March 9. Tuesday. Yesterday up Dow crags at last with Mattie and Lollie,—a perfect day of sunshine—but ponderous smoke all round—Whitehaven—Yorkshire and Lancashire all under one brown curtain— Too horrible to be at present thought of As I came down, stayed behind on the level moor, Mattie & Lollie going on to get tea ready at Kate's. — Perfect calm, and I very thankful to be able for such a walk—feeling no serious fatigue—nor, today the least stiffness,—after sound sleep. Yet I am sad—I think with weight of unanswered letters and lost or ill done things — certainly bilious a little and heavy headed if not hearted. The morning suddenly frosty—closed into low cloud—has now opened into sweet cloudlessness.

March 10 Very sad— stay—it is the 11th. Thursday—after long sleeplessness,—not able to manage my mind. Read by good chance, just now—the entry for April—1879.* Strange that such a dream should not have more impressed me.

* Q[uestion] Ap[ril] 8th? [40]

March 12 Friday. A dull—nay, black sky again—*all* covered and blotchy — I bilious and wretched and unable for all I've to do, yet curiously last night, bathing in a dream which began with finding a lovely old pond filled up and being built over,—but ended with a real sweet deep bath in the stream of it—coming out in another place.

But the curse on the sky is my chief plague—If only spring *were* spring! But its too hard on me, this devil in the wind and clouds and light.

40. This query appears in the margin, as though added at a later date.

April 2nd. on Monday 15th March up to London,—lectured on 17th and 23rd. Back here yesterday in lovely sunshine—the first time these—four years I should think. Got home in sweet sunset,—very thankfully down to my work, well, today, though it rains,—but I have plenty to do.

April 3 Saturday Two years since I began to wake from the long dream, down well to work—though with bad cold in head & throat, merely, I think, the effect of east wind or fatigue. —Primroses and violets just in sweet beginnings, and periwinkles beaming in my ivy bank, made me happy yesterday

April 5 Monday. Yesterday showery and sunny, very lovely, but I shut up with bad cold and languid and misby[41] today, weather also wilder. But work getting on

April 6 Tuesday. — I never recollect quite so dismal lassitude as came on me last night—after a day of putting in order, which meant pulling old MS and letters out in heaps, mourning over lost life.

Today better—cough very tiresome at night—now relaxed. Out, in spite of it, yesterday chopping, and pulling down branches from the long neglected upper wall

April 7. Wednesday. Second anniversary of coming down into my study. Had a most wonderful series of clear, and rather naughty dreaming last night, in fits of sleep disturbed by violent cough, old Bear[42] coming in for a large part of them—and tiresome servants who put rooms in order which

41. This word, meaning "miserable," also occurs in the "little talk" often used in letters addressed to Mrs. Severn and other mother-figures.

42. Possibly Mrs. Severn, referred to as "the Bear" during Ruskin's illness of 1878.

I had only left for five minutes, and meant to come back to directly,—producing unspeakably provoking and disappointing consequences.

Very thankful to be down to my Plato in fair strength—my eyes seeing blue lines comfortably though the day's gray—not plague-gray—but April gray—with broken spray cloud— Some smoke and mischief mixed in it but on the whole, healthy

April 8 Thursday. Cold much better—but like last at Sheffield irregular and unaccountable—and more in throat than head—giving every variety of choke and grit.

A lovely clear morning found me stupid and not able to enjoy it. No appetite for dinner, this last week, and great languor after eating nothing! — Sound sleep—yet Eyes feeble too today.

April 9. Friday Cough nearly gone, but a frightful languor on me, after two days of setting in order, and reviewing useless accumulation of rubbish, in Venetian sketches—old letters—unfeeling and stupid—books never read,—plans never followed—and the question What to do now, with the last time—entirely vague to me. Eyes much dazzled yesterday with evening sunshine —though the slender birch leaves on the blue did me good. But I am entirely down—and must take warning never in future to use my strength as soon as I get it

April 10. Saturday. Got into heart by doing a bit of good painting yesterday, but eyes in an influenza sort of puzzlement still, and no appetite for dinner. Cough passing away in hoarseness, scarcely any cold in head, but lips very sore! a new thing (Joans also) with keen north wind—she says. I've been out in winds sharp enough to cut one in two, without lips getting sore

April 11. Sunday. I am not enjoying this spring a bit—

Much my own fault—but partly, Lily is ill and Joan obliged to take care of herself[43]—and I with more feeling of irrevocably gone energy, and hopeless plans, than ever yet. The putting in order of Oxford things bad for me Drew—successfully however on oak leaf yesterday however— Little thankful!

April 12 [44] Monday. Much depressed in the wood yesterday, but Lily got quite well in the evening, and put us all right. Well up to my work this morning

April 13.[45] Tuesday. Planned in bed the introduction to critique by Croxted Lane, and then the study of the two *perfect* living characters—false and true of Fair Service and Moniplies—one a venomous—one a wholesome plant but both stingy, with the cockney corruption of the Mill on the Floss—underminded for mined—no real fun in this—but the greatest in Andrews and Fair Services dialect—pure provincial.[46] ⟨I always get into heart again when I see my way well into a thing⟩[47]

For Museum paper,—that Mr Whizz and Mr Fizz, Mr Slop and Mr Pop—Mr Gas and Mr Brass, may take themselves and their apparatus out of the way[48]

April 14. Wednesday. Glorious moon last night new—going down over edge of mountain— today—frosty and clear and sweet and I ought to be in

43. Violet Severn (1880–1940) would soon be born.

44. Above this entry he wrote: "ARENA, for Mrs. Firth."

45. The upper margin of this page is headed: "NOVELS. MUSEUM," above which he wrote "STENHOUSE'S Illustrations to the lyric poetry and Music of Scotland"—which would have been useful in connection with his pending *Elements of Prosody*.

46. The first "Scott" essay, for *Fiction, Fair and Foul,* was under way—to be published in the *Nineteenth Century* of June 1880 (see *Works, 34,* 265–302).

47. Published in *Works, 33,* xxvi.

48. The gist of some observation which would not be included in *A Museum or Picture Gallery: Its Function and Its Formation*—the series of six letters to be published in the *Art Journal* of June and August, 1880.

high spirits my work getting on well yesterday—better than I ever hoped. But I am a fool—and am worst when I should be best.

April 15 Thursday. Half through April. But mind much better—and I saw the April light on the clouds from my bed in comfort

April 16 [49] Friday. A lovely clearing of tender blue and soft warm cloud, moving south above against north wind below has changed into grey and sullen threatening of rain. I have done some good prosody[50] at breakfast, but eyes feel quivery and weak. I suppose my own fault. I never let them rest rightly.

April 17 Saturday. I had no notion this week was so far on. Oak leaf painted so as to serve[51]—but not half what I should like to make it—

Sun—this morning, but impure and it was all black at dawn.

April 18th Sunday. A quite wretched dark dry-misty colourless day— here is April two thirds gone, and I have not had *one* April morning It has the ghastliest effect on my whole soul and temper,—which—fairly cheerful enough externally, are, within me, more cast down and cheerless than ever in my life—not for myself but for the Godless and Sunless Nature and people round me.

April 19 Monday A filthy evening of blasting blackness—followed by as filthy a morning of rain. But I got my study into perfect order, yesterday at last! with much cramming of letters into

49. Above this entry he wrote in the upper margin: "30th July, 1793 Scots wha hae [namely, *Bannockburn*] composed by Burns in a thunderstorm near Gatehouse (Kirkcudbrightsh[ire)]."

50. *The Elements of English Prosody,* "For Use in St. George's Schools. Explanatory of the Various Terms Used in 'Rock Honeycomb,'" would be published in October 1880, having been promised in 1877 as "a little introduction to English prosody" to supplement his editing of the Psalms of Sir Philip Sidney (see *Works, 31,* 132n.).

51. There is no published record of this drawing.

drawers— more hope of their extrication so than out of heaps on the table.

April 20 Tuesday. Grey mist as usual. Study in perfect order is a kind of sunshine in doors,—and I wonderfully well on the whole. Compare—for possibility of good weather, page 1, here, May 7–9, [18]76, and recollect how the cold I had on the 5th, of this month went gradually away, not teazing me by getting into my head. I begin today my separate MS of notes to these two first books of Plato. 4th June [18]79 to April 19th, [18]80,—(with continual interruption) — I may get the whole done yet—if I keep courage!

Write to Fred[eric]k Harris, 22 Canwick Road Lincoln, of his Turner copy[52]

April 21. Wednesday. I think this way of making memoranda, with gaps at the end of each day, will really do, at last! and I shall be able to glance back at each days province.

Drenching rain with south wind— I up in good heart—planning paper on novels,[53] to be set about today. Yesterday sunny at two oclock— hard work picking out rock from playground corner.

April 22. Thursday. Mr & Mrs Barratt called and were very sweet. — Lolly had to run his boat aground in the gale— Herdson drenched,—and I dreamed of coming down Simplon in lovely deep snow—(—if only I could invent such wreaths when I'm awake!)—with Joanie—and with no breakfast—and Joanie insisting on returning home again— Came down to an English looking inn where I took all the wrong people

52. A young artist, not known to Ruskin personally, whom he instructed by correspondence until 1887 and whom he befriended in 1886, when Harris lost his position as a master in the Government Drawing School at Chesterfield. In the Diary a tiny sketch identifies the "Turner copy."

53. Chap. 1 "[Scott]," *Fiction, Fair and Foul.*

for the landlord, and was so angry at Joanie and Lollie for wanting to bring two great trays of plums and cherries into the house, that I upset them all into the gutter in the middle of the street.

April 23 Friday — Within two months of longest day—I must ⟨try and turn every hour to gold.⟩[54] It will be my own fault if not. Anemone and primrose—totally divine now in my woods. Joanie well—Arfie well—for the first time this many a day, and I able to paint and think—not badly, still. D.G.

April 24. Saturday. Thorough wet—and general dampness and downness in the house—and in me—though I've done some good thinking in bed on modern novels. I ought not to be severe on them—for I'm sadly like one, myself. Wretchedly sleepy and good for nothing last night both Joan and I.

April 25 Sunday. Sunny, not pure, but we have had lovely afternoons with glistening sun on tufts of dawning foliage in the misty woods opposite

April 26. Sunny, with snow on Helvellyn—or at least hail, from last nights scudding and towering thunder-clouds. I very languid yesterday—perhaps a little overworked on Scott, as I feel little inclined for morning walk in north wind.

April 27 Tuesday. A lovely morning at last—perfectly calm at six though now windy. I had a restless night however but not an unpleasant one— I remember of it only dancing with delight at having found a Greek scholar who could elucidate my passage in Plato.

April 28. Wednesday. Sound sleep, after an afternoon walk round the anemone hills—and by Susies wood and cherry trees, too sadly lovely, like a divine dream of youth and peace.

54. Published in *Works, 25,* xxviii.

April 29 Thursday. After a days rest, as far as one rests in paying visits—and a more or less sound sleep—and—on our drive to Ambleside—⟨unnumbered sights of lovely things,⟩[55] I seem to find my head today more confused than usual, and am obliged to give up my Scott work—and take to serpents—or perhaps to nothing— Perhaps my own fault—in forcing myself to begin thinking in the morning,—or perhaps—the mere chance of thoughts not falling right—as often has happened in my best times. I shall do a bit of Plato, and then take to my serpents

April 30. Friday A perfect morning at last! — dawn rosy—with frost mists—and ever since cloudless and calm. Primroses on my own rocks, beyond dream beautiful, and I able to draw with comfort and success sitting out by my waterfall—at ½ past 5—to ½ past six—last night—then watching sweet sunset. D.G.

May 2nd Sunday. I cannot understand how I omitted this, yesterday— Continually fine weather,—two more afternoons on my drawing! and a ⟨Paradisical walk with Joanie and the children among the anemones,⟩[56] finished the week I early to bed—after dinner!

May 3 Monday. Reading St Ronan's well, for the first time—with infinite sadness—but all redeemed by S[is]ter Clara—gave me clue to much— Scott always himself in drawing noble persons.[57]

Read a lovely bit of Roger Ascham[58] too—

55. Published in *Works, 33,* xxiii, where the excerpt is misdated "1879" and combined with words taken from the entry of January 2, 1880.

56. Published in *Works, 33,* xxii.

57. In his published criticism Ruskin does not refer to the character of Clara Mowbray as in any way redeeming "the entirely broken and diseased *St. Ronan's Well,*" written in "the time [1823] of extreme weakness" (*Works, 34,* 292, 289; from *Fiction, Fair and Foul*).

58. In the *Fors Clavigera* of June 1875 he had given in facsimile two passages to show the "black letter" of his 1571 edition of the *Schole Master.*

and now to Plato— Grey morning but yesterday one glow—all the day till sunset—which clouded in faint-wind-driven films of rose and grey.

May 4. Tuesday. Fine—after grey yesterday. I early at work in bed on St Ronans, and the disease of Scott. May I use the many warnings I have had, to better purpose than lately, while my eyes and mind still serve me.

May 7 Friday. Yesterday Ascension day, I finished as Fors would have it—the writing out of In Endless bliss:[59] the title being given me as I thought over it in the morning, not knowing what day it was. Radiant and perfect time in the wood, with anemone and primrose at brightest

New Servant came. I cross and bad in evening. I get for motto this morning μακαριος ὁς μεν σκανςαλισθη [60]

May 8 Friday — Saturday, I mean—(a bad beginning —for a sunny morning with birds singing!). Did much, yesterday but not well,—must take care. Scott giving me far more trouble than I expected—but thats no new thing. Take 'heart of grace' to it—and to all things—if I may.

May 9th Sound sleep after good painting in quite divine afternoon in wood—wake at ½ past 4, but slept afterward through intensely pure sunny morning—utterly ashamed of myself.

Got for text a comforting one—see the day in

59. As he had recently told Coventry Patmore: "I have been putting chords of music lately, such as I can, to Herrick's 'Comfort [to a Youth That Had Lost His Love]':—

'In endless bliss
She thinks not on
What's said or done
In earth.

Nor doth she mind,
Or think on't now
That ever thou
Wast kind'—

fearing only that it is too true" (*Works, 37,* 314; letter of April 20, 1880).

60. "Blessed is whoever does not take offense" (see Matt. 9:6 and Luke 7:23).

R[ose]'s book,—but it should have gone on to —in whose spirit there is no guile.[61]

May 10 Monday. My Father's birthday shall begin the real writing of Scotts life in the pleasant half of article for 19th century, and I planned in bed what would have as much delighted him—the second article for Byron against Browning[62]— Soft light rain—too soft and light for the country's need— My stream all but dry— I could'nt get a clean tumbler dip out of it yesterday to paint with—except at the pool.

May 11. Tuesday. Worked hard at Scott yesterday and effectively—but can't get on! and mustnt diarize.

May 14. Friday. Dressed in cloudless morning, and down to coffee at 7; as yesterday and the day before— Scott, first paper, done and off,—and all manner of beauty around me in the perfect spring— the oaks a shower of new gold.

May 15 Saturday. I really had no idea what day of the week it was. Yesterday to Colwith force, with Connie, Lollie & Arfie, Arfie skipping about like a goat! [63] Walter[64]—not as merry as I hoped, came in the afternoon— we trotted home to receive him, double quick Exquisite weather — I out before 7, to meditate over finish of prosody,—but am too languid for Plato

61. "Blessed is he whose transgression is forgiven, whose sin is covered. Blessed is the man unto whom the LORD imputeth not iniquity, and in whose spirit there is no guile" (Psa. 37:1–2).

62. The contemplated "second article" became the third and fourth papers of the series, in which Ruskin used the poetry of Wordsworth, rather than of Browning, for contrast in his characterization of Byron as one of the "greater souls" who could feel, in depth, "Compassion" for humanity. In his library he preserved "his father's *Byron*" (*Works, 34,* 698).

63. Arthur Severn suffered chronically from rheumatism.

64. The artist Walter Severn (1830–1904), Arthur Severn's brother and president of the Dudley Gallery of Art. He was particularly interested in reviving, in England, the practice of needlework and embroidery, which would receive attention in Ruskin's concluding letter, of June 10, on *A Museum . . .* (see *Works, 34,* 257–62).

May 16 Sunday. Rather beaten—partly, from overwork—partly from over-port—partly from bad teeth. Woke at ½ past four—in dazzling day,—my poor little stream now only a few drops—the bright pool—stagnant.

I did not get on better yesterday for missing my Plato.

May 19th. Wednesday. — And since Ive had to miss everything! out all day, on Monday with Arthur up the hill between the two Langdales— Yesterday to see Mrs Firth, Mr Harrison & Miss Wilson[65]—Kingsley[66] staying with her. Mallesons note today— I hasten to say that we are beginning to think it has been a mistake, that instead of S[carlet] F[ever] it is only nettle-rash or *rose*-rash! that has given us all this trouble. The doctor gave out his dictum and he will not like to retract—that will be our difficulty if there really has been a mistake!

May 23 Sunday. Down in good time, with nervous pain in arm,—but resolutely facing against disorder. Rain at last makes order feasible.

May 24. Monday. Rain all day yesterday felt like a rest. This morning my head so full of crowded thoughts about Museums—Prosody, Clergy, Snakes, Scott, & Byron—all in hand together—that I don't know what to do[67]— Plato gone to the wall altogether Fors gave me such lots about Scott today—in bed at breakfast that I shall have to get some set down, anyhow

May 25 Tuesday. Heaven grant me wisdom and strength to spend these lengthening days well, and not to

65. Possibly the Mary Wilson whose name appears, in 1884, upon the list of Companions of St. George.

66. The Reverend W. T. Kingsley (see B.S. and Letters XXVII).

67. His next article for the *Nineteenth Century*, purportedly on Scott, would show the strain, while also indicating that his work on prosody was in the forefront of his mind. By now his serpent lecture was being reshaped into the essay "Living Waves," and he had promised Malleson an Epilogue for his *Letters to the Clergy*.

fear the shortening ones. But what Heaven means by letting me see my way to so much, and make my way to so little—Heaven must explain to—whom it chooses, in its own time. One thing I get more and more sure of—that the Devil is rampant everywhere. Mr Steel, no —Speed—or some such name brought me news yesterday that the hope of humanity was to make the dead speak, out of barrel-organs—instead of the living out of their lips.

May 26. Wednesday. Putting in order again, for journey! [68]

May 28 Friday. Down in good time—seven not yet struck —a little giddy in head with lots of thoughts— but lively, and I begin with Plato rightly. Yesterday the plan of posting journey all broken off by my laziness, but I think rightly.

May 29 Saturday. — In bed to breakfast—but well, & after good sleep, though deeply awestruck by seeing poor Mr Bowness[69] on his agonizing deathbed.

June 1st — Oh me—I had thought it was the last May! but its Tuesday Dazzling bright, after useful rain yesterday and cuckoo loud in the woods I sent off W[illia]m Conqueror to Sheffield— and must follow him with Harold [70] today, if possible.

June 2. Wednesday. Better work doing this year than last, though I'm still in bed to breakfast,—but got lovely things out of Creasys Saxons[71] and

68. In 1876 he and the Severns had greatly enjoyed a posting tour through the countryside in an old-fashioned carriage—an adventure which they were now evidently planning to repeat.

69. Possibly the blacksmith John Bowness. If so, his agony was prolonged: aged 62, he died on January 4, 1881.

70. He would give St. George's Museum three silver pennies "of William the Conqueror," one designated "Harold (of Hastings)"; (see *Works, 30,* 268–71).

71. Sir Edward Creasy's *History of England from the Earliest to the Present Time* (1870). Sending a "Noble of Edward III" to St. George's Museum, he would refer to passages in Creasy's *History* as he described the coin.

planned watercourse at Sheffield See first days of June last year giddiness in head, now scarcely troubling me— See names of mountains—p. 107, June 7th—Eaglet and Bracelet. Add now St Anthony's crag, opposite the Warder, the Tiger just seen over it— while the Lion ends the Bracelet. There ought to be a name for the rounded mass that hides Weatherlam [sic] top.

June 3. Thursday. Slept well—after seeing the grandest red sunset we've had for years,—on the mysterious clouds which have stood, one over the Old Man, the other over Wetherlam against North East wind, for twenty four hours changeless. The most wonderful forms of them were on the evening of the first of June—sulphurous milk blue films washed over brick-red gray—in agatescent zones the like of which I never saw before—with definite shadows as sharp edged as windmill sails always telling as darkness[72]—the light being diffused—not as light rays on diffused darkness,—the cloud edges forming against the wind as fast as arborescences of silver, in an electrically driven solution—but always in the same place—driven away to the left as they threw themselves out to the right, red bars crossing the whole When I woke at ½ past 3 yesterday morning, the same clouds were there, with ruby of dawn on them, see sketch in [blank space] held their own all day against heavy showers and diffused grey beneath them—and came out congressing in the blazing sunset of last night—past all description.

June 4. Friday Bright, but with sharp north wind. I have to add to the note above that the fixed cloud was gone next morning, the third,—and

72. Illustrated by a sketch, followed by a second sketch to show how the edges formed "against the wind."

the day gradually became cloudless blue—increasing in heat up to glorious summer—Lollie and I basking on the beach—(unable to do more, I! chopping too much for me [)], and the mountains dazzling bright and blue sky over moors—quite heavenly. Joan panting with heat all the evening—though the sky had clouded. But now it is fresh and sharp sunny north wind and my fire—on a small scale pleasant. My head full of Danes and Northmen.[73]

June 5. Saturday. The new lawn to be finished today. Great notions in my head of history for Museum, —and I begin examination of my great German MS.—in die Natalis Domini[74]

June 6th Sunday. Diddie came back yesterday—I find my last note of her being here on 12th Sept[ember] day of walking back from Mrs Firths in rain

Now to make the best of the month of long days.

June 10th. [Viz. Wednesday, June 9] Thursday. My brain is too busy again— I had no idea I had been neglecting this book! I began always with the Lectionarium— Called Lollie at 4 today to see the dawn, but slept afterwards

June 10. Thursday! — Above date a mistake! and I've gained a day! and yesterday was well spent too —on clergyman's epilogue[75]—and I hope to do my museum today—and make every minute of it as good as gold. It's something to be old, after all whether for wine—or a man—if one has body, and the other, soul.

June 11. Lovely weather—and nice investigation of fish-

73. The reading which would lead to his adventures into history, in the opening chapters of the *Bible of Amiens* (Part I, December 1880), was under way.

74. Identified by Mr. Dearden as the "*Lectionarium Secundum usum diœcesos Augustinæ*, c. 1160, which Ruskin bought in 1880 from Quaritch for 500 gns. and sold in 1884 to the Guild for the same price." For a description of the MS, see *Works, 30,* 256–57.

75. See Epilogue of *Letters to the Clergy*, dated "June, 1880" (*Works, 34,* 215–30).

pond—and work getting on—of course, one inch where I expected six, but getting on.

Never heard the Cuckoo so clear and constant as in the warm sunshine yesterday.

June 12. Sunday. Planning museum all day with Mr Doubleday.[76] Quite dreadfully tired and sorrowful—but up to coffee this morning, D.G. and in good heart.

June 13 Monday. Rested yesterday utterly, indoors, and got good sleep, and feel stupid, and good for little— Note tendency to inflammation in eyes this morning now gone off—but watch-worthy.

June 16th Wednesday. Dates and everything wrong on last page,—too many things in hand again, nothing goes right unless I have my Plato properly in the morning. Try again today. Great excitement last night, on Lollie's boat drifting away in grand storm, dragging her anchor.

June 17 Thursday. Awake at ½ past three, and now my eyes dim— Must lead a new life somehow—for it is a lovely day, and my eyes have no business to be dim.

June 18 A dazzling day, seeming to make my eyes swim with its brightness—but compare miserable 17th & 18th June last year! Yesterday quite idle in divine sunshine all day rowed over and walked through clover fields—and had tea with Miss Mary Beever.

June 20. Sunday. — Late up, but with many useful thoughts of Byron and Wordsworth—and curiously helped by coming on the mediocrity of Roscoe,[77] before unknown to me.

76. The architect William Doubleday (1846–1938) of Birmingham. Contributing a guinea to the Gift of the *Splügen Pass*, Mr. Doubleday had written A. W. Hunt: "Were every one who has received profit and pleasure from his pen and pencil to contribute in proportion to the benefit conferred on them, John Ruskin would be as rich as he is honoured and beloved" (unpublished letter of April 29, 1878; F. J. Sharp Collection).

77. Probably William Roscoe (1753–1831), a Liverpool attorney and historian

June 21 Monday. Wet, after thundrous heat. — I terribly beaten yesterday,—and can't keep the heaps of letters down on table:—making me wretched to look at them, but down to coffee in good—type—time! I meant but was thinking of revise of Serpents, to be got done this morning if possible

July 5th Monday. Actually a fortnight without diary—Could not have believed it! — Today, though Ive had a nasty cold in head—in good heart, getting on with Scott, and my Broadlands book and missal found by Mr Gatty! [78] We went on Thursday the 24th to Lake side inn, returning on Saturday to meet Mr Gatty, and I neer began diary again

July 6. Tuesday. Very low and stupid with continual reduplicate cold—unconquerable—absolute patience needed and instay. Work—getting done, but not of the best.

July 7. A wretched day, yesterday, all sneeze and linger —wretched night—waking at 3, but slept after, and better now—finding out much of Ca' Ira and Marseillaise[79] at breakfast in bed

Wednesday—last of Joanie for a little while —Yesterday Annie Somerscales and her sister at dinner

July 8 Thursday. Joanie going away makes all wretched —but have worked out some lovely bits of Byron and my cold is better—but lags on, nearly three weeks old. — No—fortnight — it came on upon Thursday the 24th at Lakeside.

---

who wrote verse with diligence (e.g. *Odes and Songs Saluting the French Revolution*), inclusive of the happily exceptional nursery classic *The Butterfly's Ball and the Grasshopper's Feast.*

78. Probably Charles T. Gatty, of Liverpool, who may have found the missal which Ruskin at first believed that he had left at Hawarden (see entry of February 14, 1878).

79. Using a passage from Carlyle's *French Revolution,* he makes these two "songs of wrath" a high spot in his rather rambling second paper for the *Nineteenth Century* (see *Works, 34,* 315–17; from *Fiction, Fair and Foul).*

July 9 Friday. Cold much better, and fancy good—Byron and Scott working in nicely—but too much to manage in it—as usual.

July 11 Sunday. Missed again!—but got good Byron work done, yesterday and new hopes for Sheffield Museum.

Can't get up to breakfast just now. I sleep well and dream, if at all, not unpleasantly but always wake about ½ past 3 and begin sleeping again —in ¼ of hour towards 6, today quite sound at 7.

July 12 Monday. Awake again after Yorkshire cakes at Mr Bells, and feel Byronized and jaded today, —must shorten sail. Perfectly divine walk by the green oatfield in soft west wind up to Bells, the trees in living emerald—the gardens all glow and scent—campanula & pansy.

July 13 Tuesday. Still very languid and enjoying nothing. — ⟨Scott and Byron work very bad for me without any doubt— some letters too have made me angry, worst of all.⟩[80]

July 14 Wednesday. — Yesterday—drove to see Susie and then chopped down half the wood behind lodge, a good riddance— Ate trout—Cucumber —Duck—pease—stuffing—currant tart custard—raspberries—and cream—with a lot of port and sherry—and dreamed—rather pleasant dreams, about gathering pretty Alpine flowers: —of course the people they were gathered for—did'nt get them—but that was their loss as much as mine—and *they* had'nt been eating currant pie.

July 15 Wonderfully low, swelled cheek; and breakings out on lip! very unusual with me. — On the other hand my eyes are good—blue lines all clear though morning utterly dark

I believe this is partly green pease—partly

80. Published (inexactly) in *Works, 33,* xxvi–vii.

Scott article—partly accounts partly the weather. Must fast—and—what else I can.

July 16 Friday. Just made acquaintance with the lodge kitten—the sauciest I ever saw yet!—thanks to Lockie's[81] education I suppose. In doors all day yesterday but got lots of accounts and stone sorting done and was'nt tired. Pouring all day—now fine—but misty

July 17. Saturday. Yesterday Mr Malleson and his niece—pleasant,—and nice day, but very hot. Campanulas and black currants the staple of garden, now with Sweet William and blue bells trying to be seen.

My face better, and, on the whole as I walked on Terrace in sunshine, yesterday how much to be thankful for—& ashamed of myself in possessing.

July 18 Sunday. Can't get my diary written for the kitten—obliged to put it out at last. Whereupon I suppose it will occupy itself in mewing— Mr Macdonald came yesterday in sweet evening after fearful heat—ruining our expedition to Colwith force,—Lollie getting ill with it Fierce thunder and rain all night—now more or less open and calm.

July 19 Monday. Wet yesterday all day, but I got on grandly with puttings in order and classings of books and shelves, and coins. Today a clear morning—broken down—no good in weather after the violets fade

July 20 Tuesday.—Drove with Diddie and Mipie to visit Victor and Tora,[82] yesterday and did accounts &c well and coins— Out early this morning—comparing violet fiction of spring to fungus fiction of autumn.

81. For "Lockie," see B.S.

82. That is, he visited Mr. and Mrs. Marshall with Sara Anderson and Mrs. Severn.

July 21 Wednesday Yesterday out sketching with Marshalls, imprudently—and fear I have caught cold again! sense of relaxed throat—and relaxed spring—but also—up playing chess late last night—and long asleep this morning all irregular. Things enough in head however, to finish both Prosody and Fors[83]

July 22 Thursday Yesterday Mrs Ritchie in afternoon very nice—and I got Prosody nearly finished—and minerals finally looked over and pasted up. But am very bilious and dim this morning. Q[uestion] — Potatoe soup at lunch—strawberries at tea—or too much head work? or all?

A lovely morning and roses all out.

July 23 Thursday — (Friday, I mean) Languor *seems* less in grey day, because one does'nt expect to be in spirits—but if the sun were shining I should feel I was ill.

Sound sleep always however—and on the whole pleasant dreams— a very odd one last night of people gathering fruit—not their own —and giving me melons which I wouldn't have.

July 24 Saturday to Sheffield, to Regin[al]d Gattys.[84]

July 25 Sunday. Walk down valley, see house

July 26 Monday home again

July 27 Tuesday at accounts, all day

July 28 Wednesday Drenching rain all night and now —too dark for accounts. But I see my blue lines! and am on the whole well, though always waking at 3, for an hour at least.

July 29. Thursday. Same again! but thought over my Byron to some purpose and slept to coffee time

83. Another "Letter" of *Fors Clavigera* would be issued in September.

84. Son of the Reverend Alfred Gatty (1813–1903), author of *Sheffield: Past and Present* (1873), the Reverend Reginald Alfred Gatty (1845–1914), Rector of Bradfield from 1869–88, "had a unique collection of prehistoric flints, and in that particular branch of archeology he was considered an authority" (obituary notice, *Rotherham Advertiser*, March 14, 1914). "Bradfield Rectory" appears under his name among the addresses listed at the front of the Diary.

Black day, and I rather blackish all the summer flowers always now rotten with rain. Only the Docks triumphant, and the Ferns—but all my poor raspberries—fruitless—or worse—with ruined fruit, doleful beads of hopeless grey green.

July 31. Saturday. Still can't sleep—had to get up and write thoughts last night—after taking less tea and a long walk. — I hope it is currant pie and green pease, not tea, and will be resolute—next month— Dropped my book and crushed it—for ever and aye—a true diabolical time it is to me;—for a minute afterwards, I came on Marc Antonios terrible Nymph and Satyr[85]—the nymph with denlolium? hornshaped shell in her hand. Burnt it out of my way—a type of Renaissance—enough for all

FIRST OF AUTUMN [August 2] I have long felt that the proper division of the year, took February for a Spring month. The old calendars took my own birthday, the 8th, for the beginning of Spring. I have my own reasons,—and think there are some which other people should have, for counting the 2nd of February as the First of Spring[86]

'Today' it is the 2nd of August

August 3. Tuesday. After a hard days work at Byron—and Susie in afternoon—and too *little* dinner—and a worrying note or two—I did'nt sleep till four and woke again at five—again at six—yet less uncomfortable than I used to be in 1855—in the

85. Probably *Le Satyr surprenant la Nymphe.* ". . . the works of Marc Antonio [had] been so degraded by the baseness of his character that they became one of the deadliest instruments for the corruption of taste throughout Europe," he had remarked in the *Catalogue of Rudimentary Series* for the Ruskin Art Collection at Oxford (*Works, 21,* 185).

86. On February 2, 1866, Ruskin had asked Rose La Touche to be his wife. Asking him to wait three years for her answer, she had implied a "yes." "It is eleven years to-day since the 2nd of February became a great festival to me," he had remarked in the *Fors* of March 1877 (*Works, 29,* 66).

sleepless nights,—and my head full enough now! —with finish of the Holy Land bit in my paper —and Apollo and the Python.[87]

Now—thats very wonderful— I open my Fathers Bible at the 16th of Numbers—and my eyes fall first at the word 'Python' of my note at the top of the page[88]—this the instant after I had put this book aside, open, to let the ink dry

August 6th Friday Pouring—and pouring yesterday in morning—and ⟨in afternoon the most overwhelming wonderful hours of unceasing prismatic light like a painted window in heaven—pale but intense and—in one or two cases, even deep, rose colour passing into orange, barred, or interstained, with pale emerald green, passing here and there into blue; but not violet except in some dark grey clouds which became violet by being touched with the ruby,—these very rare and small—like Turners lightest spray of dark touches in Flint Castle All this on the edges above the sun, at about 12—15$^{\theta}$ above him,—he—some 20$^{\theta}$ above horizon, and all the sky interwoven with muslin and netting of divinest cirri cloud, over infinite shoals and sands of mackarel cloud,—but all flying, failing, melting—reappearing—twisting and untwisting,—faster than eye could follow—and—after some three hours of this play, (—5 to 8)—ending in

87. For the "Holy Land bit," see his discussion of Byron's "Carnage . . . / Just now, behaved as in the Holy Land" (*Works, 34,* 326–28; in "[Byron]," *Fiction, Fair and Foul*). To him Apollo's contest with the Hesperid dragon, or Python, primarily signified "the strife of purity with pollution; of life with forgetfulness; of love, with the grave" (*Works, 7,* 420; from *Modern Painters, V*; see also *Works, 20,* 339–40 and Pl. XVIII, *Apollo and the Python,* in *Aratra Pentelici*). Now, more specifically, the Apolline conquest of corruption was probably attached to his thought of Byron's hatred of injustice.

88. "The earth swalloweth up Korah and his company" is the theme of Numbers 16. No comment by Ruskin appears above the chapter, Mr. Dearden states, in either of the two Bibles which belonged to Ruskin's father and which are now among the books in the Ruskin Galleries, Bembridge School.

two great ranks of storm cloud—lower pale against higher dark—or backing of dark, the latter with long locks and tresses as of hair at its edge—and both overlying the range of hills exactly like the Hesperides dragon[89]—ending northward in clear sky, against a black monster cloud—half dolphin—half tiger—[which] rolled and rose—and finally toppled & tumbled, the face of it, or where had it been a beast, the face would have been, falling forward like a gloomy and slow avalanche and melting as it was torn down or dragged—into nothingness.

I believe these swift and mocking clouds and colours are only between storms. They are assuredly new in Heaven—so far as my life reaches. I never saw a single example of them till after 1870.)[90]

Last night pussy petted me to sleep in the loveliest way— I never knew what a cat could be, neither! till now, almost more tender in little subtle ways than a dog. But their tongues are terribly rough for licking!

August 7. Saturday. — Awake early, and by lovely—but devil spoiled—sunrise, saw my way—I think—finally—into my Byron paper, with better resolution than for many a day, D.G.

August 8 Sunday. Held pretty well too—during the forenoon—! Today—much lessoned about being thankful for what I have—and enjoyed my Turners, strangely, and did much good thought —of Euphemy before breakfast.[91]

89. Namely, in Turner's *Garden of the Hesperides* (for the dragon, see *Works, 7,* Pl. 78).

90. Published (with minor changes) in *Works, 34,* 23n.

91. The contrast between "blasphemy" and "euphemy" is made a theme of the two Byron papers, leading to his final definition: "the 'phemy' or 'fame' of the two words . . . signifies broadly the bearing of *false* witness *against* one's neighbour in the one case, and of *true* witness *for* him in the other" (*Works 34,* 366).

This is the last entry for the summer, Cook and Wedderburn having misdated

December 14th 1880. Tuesday

After four months at Chartres—Amiens—Canterbury, London I have just been carrying out the resolution above spoken of, by some due gratitude for my little bed room, which is now thus arranged. Fireplace wall

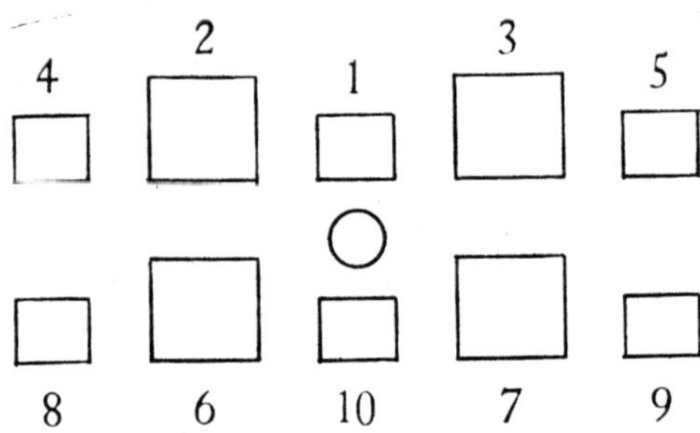

1. My Fathers Conway
2. Goldau.
3. Zug.
4. Rouen.
5 Mont Cenis—i.e. Turin from Superga
6 Leicester Abbey
7. Carnarvon Castle
8 Florence
9. Nemi
10 Vesuvius

With Hunt's peach and nuts for brooch.

Over Bed

11 12 13

14 15 16

11 Constance	12. Faido	13 Coblentz
14 Flint	15 Bolton	18 Salisbury

(as of 1880) the sentence which they quote from the entry of August 11, 1879 (see *Works, 33,* xxii).

Opposite Bed. 19 [ ]

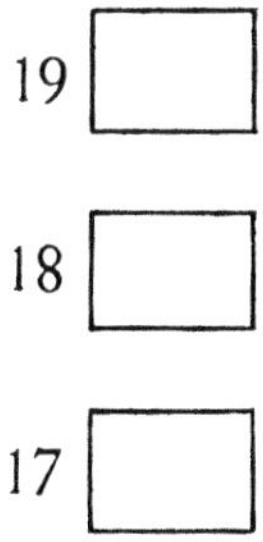

17. Richmond Surrey

18 [ ]

18. Gosport

19 Fluelen. 17 [ ]

(And beside window, above bathstand [92]

20. Heysham. 21 [ ]

21. Old Savoy

20 [ ])

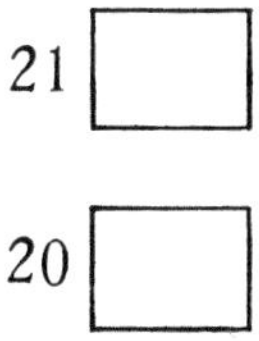

There are thus a series of my Father's Conway and 20 Turners, all such as I would have chosen out of all he did; except only the Richmond, which is sacred nevertheless as his own dwelling place! [93]

December 15. Wednesday. Heavy snow and leaden fog. Read Ephesians, 1, 2 (Chapters 1 & 2)[94] carefully, and some of my Greek MS again

92. Referring to Items 20 and 21, Ruskin notes (probably in 1883): "Altered, see back leaf." On the preceding page (or "back leaf") he records the 1883 arrangement of these pictures (see entry of September 2, 1883).

93. In 1884, showing W. H. Spielmann these pictures, Ruskin said: "There are twenty of Turner's most highly finished water-colours representing his whole career from this one, when he was quite a boy, to that one, which he executed for me. There is not one of them which is not perfect in every respect. . . . Here you see what is probably the most beautiful painting of fruit that Hunt ever did, and it hangs among the Turners like a brooch. Yes, I hold this to be the finest collection of perfect Turner drawings in existence, with one exception, perhaps" (*Works, 34,* 669–70).

94. Ephesians 1 he had called "the great chapter of praise to God the Father" (Diary entry of January 29, 1878). Then, in chapter 2, St. Paul voices his joy that through God's mercy the Ephesians have been awakened unto faith in Christ, the Corner Stone: "And you hath he quickened, who were dead in trespasses and sins" (v. 1).

December 16 Thursday. — Yesterday a dreadfully confused day, black cloud and snow outside I have got my study into order today and there's some sun on the hills.

December 17 Friday. Glorious moonlight all morning—after eclipse which I did'nt see— No matter.

— Now glorious dawn, cloudless, but I tired and stomachic—for once—not my own fault,—unless by eating a fig after dinner. Figs certainly not good for me, that I'm clear about. Keep so much for gained.

December 18. Saturday. Yesterday wholly clear—like the 19th, last year, and I at work D.G. but enjoying it little. Spoiled by Paris! Q[uestion] Am I right here—or at Amiens—or at both, if I will?

December 19. Sunday. Frost, wild bitter wind raging from the *South.* Raging black sky. Ones life passing by candlelight, and between bed, soup and warm water.

December 20 Monday. Pitch dark again—without fog, mere heavy cloud Read, at coffee—to my utter amazement, the beautiful life of the emperor Claudius.[95]

Melancholy scorn of myself making it gloomy —yet vital knowledge of things—inconceivable before Must find out where Sirmium[96] is at once.

December 21 Tuesday. Rich snow on hills down to moor—and now almost cloudless amber sunrise on them (after some lovely though imperfect rose) keeps me from any work—but I am listless and valueless after a stomachic night—a glass too much port—with no rest after dinner, and much

95. Doubtless to his "amazement" because he had found it in Gibbon's *History* (*1*, chap. 11), which he heartily disliked. Characterizing Claudius in *Valle Crucis,* Ruskin refers to Gibbon's account of this Emperor who "best exhibits the new virtue of *Justice in pity* instead of anger" (*Works, 33,* 215).

96. The once great city on the Save, about 80 miles west of Belgrade, in which Claudius I was born and died.

excitement of new thoughts (after some alarmed ones about loss of golden box, happily found) and Jamie here telling of Egypt.[97]

December 22 Wednesday. Pitch dark again—and snowing, likely to be so all day I very tired and low all yesterday even in the brightness—better today!

December 24 Friday. Rain for ever and ever—perpetual blackness—wind—mixed frost and thaw—nasty flies all over my bedroom, and sad Devils work in all letters and business as I never saw! Always before Xmas, I seem to get this kind of lesson

Bad sense of cold in throat, last night suddenly, but compare entry at p. 175 for the 26th last year; and I'm still writing without spectacles, though by candlelight.

A little blue sky appearing above!

December 25. Christmas curiously ignored in Rosie's book—and the text is—In the world ye shall have tribulation! but be of good courage—*θαρσειτε*.[98]

Sunny, though with north wind—wickedly to the west! scattered clouds, and sprinkled snow to shore

In my first mornings look about me, found out the meaning of Turners font, under the church of the Splugen.[99]

And—at this moment only— I think of the cross on the bridge of St Martin! [1]

97. In July, returning from Egypt, J. R. Anderson had sent Ruskin "some photos of statues of the Early Empire and of Architecture." "I am so very thankful to know you're at Keswick," Ruskin had responded, "—and not in a pyramid—or the Valley of Diamonds, or the gardens of the Hesperids—or of the Queen of Sheba. . . . ¶—Come and see me now as soon as you can" (unpublished letter of July 18, 1880; Baillie Institution Library).

98. St. John 16:33—viz. Christ's parting words to His disciples. The phrase "be of good cheer [or courage]," Ruskin observed, is more forceful than the Greek "Be bold."

99. In Turner's picture a mother holds her child upon the ledge of this "font," called the " 'Bains' at foot of Church on Rock in *Splügen*" in Ruskin's diary entry for September 23, 1881 (*Diaries*, p. 1002).

1. Namely, the cross in Turner's *Sallenches,* a drawing which Ruskin also called

December 26th Mon—no, Sunday!

A perfectly full dawn and sunrise on brightly sprinkled snow—dazzling and in some ways, more curiously overpowering me than the black weather I've been suffering from My eyes seem unused to it. Also I found in my walk yesterday that I was ⟨much beaten and tired, and must positively take to the rocks and grass again for a while.⟩[2] I must do a bit of St Genevieve[3] though, first.

December 28th. Tuesday. Yesterday out before breakfast and then long walk in snow—½ past eleven to ½ past 4. Result. The worst night I've had for years—mixed cough; heart burn—bilious melancholy, and feverish sleeplessness,—leaving me now—not beaten by any means, but feeling the room and entire ground floor damp and wretched, as well as it may be under utter black sky with masses of thawing snow—three inches deep all round.

December 29th. Wednesday. Quite laid up with cold black day

December 30 Thursday

December 31. Friday. Last day of my year—such a divine dawn! the purest I ever saw here. Snow everywhere.

---

the *Bridge of St. Martin's* (*Works, 13,* 401). Commenting on the *Sallenches* and the *Mont Blanc* when he completed the *Notes on His Drawings by Turner,* he remarked: "St. Martin's Bridge with the cross on its keystone has been principal in Turner's mind in both these last two sketches" (*Works, 13,* 471).

2. Published in *Works, 33,* xxviii.

3. To be used in *The Bible of Amiens,* chapter 2 (published in December 1881).

1881

The entries which were resumed on December 14, 1880, after Ruskin's return from France, are continued from January 1 through February 19, except for the week of February 5–14, during which he was, however, still at home. On February 20 he was overcome by his second attack of the "delirium," under which he suffered until March 22, when he returned to his study to write letters. On April 8 he made his last entry for 1881 in this manuscript, having filled all but one of the right-hand pages preceding those which had been reserved for an index to the volume. Hence on September 15, when he was ready to resume the keeping of a diary, he used an empty section of what is now Bembridge MS *xxi*. The daily record of his life at Brantwood through the autumn of 1881 and during 1882 has therefore already been published.

The chief interest of the present unit of the Diary (inclusive of the entries for December 1880) is that it provides the immediate background for his second "serious illness." In this respect, the pending attack differed from the first in not overtly indicating its approach through the daily jottings. Whereas in 1878 he was manifestly living as though in a Waking Dream during the better part of a week before his mind was overwhelmed, the present record remains under rational control until it stops abruptly—two days, he would recall, before the "month of terrible delirium" began (see entry for April 8). More explicitly, as Laurence Hilliard would tell Norton: "He was taken ill (seriously) on Saturday the 20th [sic] February" (unpublished letter of March 2, 1881; Harvard University Library), his condition having caused Laurence Hilliard to telegraph Mrs. Severn on Sunday, the 20th, urging her "without fail" to come at once from Herne Hill with her husband. "It must be *very sudden*," Mrs. Severn wrote Mrs. John Simon on Sunday evening, "as I had an excellent report of him yesterday" (letter of February 20, 1881; see Letters, XXXVII, sect. 2).

The illness itself, as Ruskin told Dr. John Brown, was "much more definite in its dreaming than the last one, and not nearly so frightful" (*Works, 37*, 348; letter of March 29, 1881); or as he phrased it, writing Norton: "I've been much more gently whipped this time and have learned more" (*Works, 37*, 345; letter of March 24, 1881). The main theme of the conflict between Good and Evil, as an overall characteristic of these periods of "wild sleep"—manifested in 1878 through "the great definite Vision of the contention with the Devil"—now became "quite narrowed" in its "demonical vision." More specifically, there were "much meaner visions of dragons and spectres in the room with me—made out of the folds of curtains or bedclothes or what-not" (see entries for February 2 and 5, 1883); and "sometimes, the black window at night filled with white phantoms" (unpublished letter to Dr. John Brown, August 8, 1881; Yale University Library). Such apparitions may have been related to his smashing the panes of a bedroom window, although when asked why he did it, he explained: " 'it was a signal to be given at Windsor Castle—of breaking a spell of witchcraft'—but, added he, 'I've killed the third witch at last' " (letter from Mrs. Severn to Dr. Simon, March 9, 1881; see Letters, XXXVII, sec. 2). He himself would recall "the dreadful part of suspecting Joanie and then of her dying, just before my own fancied death—very awful—and to be remembered in perpetual wonder and fear" (see entry for February 5, 1883). Often, however, he was a difficult patient, venting his hostilities upon his attendants and Dr. Parsons (who served as his only physician during this attack) and even threatening "Joanie" herself—sometimes, in letters of later years, called "the Dragon." A conviction that he was not "master in his own house" was evidently at the core of his anger, though at another extreme, he would lie down beside Mrs. Severn, calling her " 'mama'—& himself 'a little donkey boy' " as he awakened from sleep (letter from Mrs. Severn to Mrs. Simon, March 9, 1881; see Letters, XXXVII, sect. 2).

Other experiences ranged from the frightful through the relatively prosaic or somewhat comic to the supreme in beauty. There was "the terrible fire-dream in the streets of London" (see Diary, February 2, 1883), with a "vision of the burning moor, and of the burning women in ballroom" (*Diaries,* p. 1118; December 28, 1885). There were the troubles with his publisher, George Allen: "*you* were especially tiresome and—unfortunate—dragging me first and yourself next into all manner of scrapes" (unpublished letter of March 22, 1881; Columbia University Library). There was the morning "when he shut up the cook in his room saying she was the Queen kicked out," and, after her release, asking: "who has dared to send the Queen off guard[?]" (letter of March 26, 1881; see Letters, XXXVII, sect. 2).

The attack was "brought on," he told Norton, by "my beginning family prayers again for the servants on New Year's Day—and writing two little pieces of collects every morning—one on a bit of gospel, the other on a bit of psalm." This led him into "a long meditation on . . . the later Acts of Apostles" (with their account of the preaching of St. Paul, helped by his performance of miracles and guided by visions) and "on the work of the 'other seventy' " whom Christ sent forth, two by two, to preach His gospel and to whom "the spirits [were] subject," as is recounted in the first part of "Luke x." Thus "[I] got in my own evening thoughts into a steady try if I couldn't get Rosie's ghost at least alive by me, if not the body of her" (*Works, 37,* 355; letter of April 26, 1881). And so the Dream began by his "setting out [barefoot] to walk to her grave" (see entry for February 3, 1883).

Thereafter, within the delirium, Rose would reappear. Four years hence, specifically referring to this illness as he planned a chapter of *Praeterita,* he noted that he must tell the never-to-be-recounted "story of Rosie's cup" (*Diaries,* p. 1118; December 28, 1885). In his entries for 1883, however, he is more definite about what he calls "the period of highest exaltation": "I thought I had a kind of crucifixion to go through—and to found a farther phase of Christianity and that Rose was as the Magdalene to me This part of the dream, I think, began . . . with the hearing [of] the seven guns fired in heaven, as the end of this dispensation—a curious and ludicrous confusion of them in my mind with the notion of guns heard from Windsor." There was also the episode of Rose's "coming with her mother"—a fantasy interrupted, ominously, by the cry of an owl (see entry for February 3, 1883; see also Letters, XXXVII, sect. 2, March 9, 1881). Before long, he would be asking Mrs. La Touche: "I told you of my dream, didn't I? How I set out barefoot to go to Ireland? and how you and R[ose] came here instead? I CAN'T understand how so extremely rational a person as I am can lose their wits, and still more, how they don't know they have lost them at the time. ¶ I do think if I were to go crazy again for the *third* time I should know I was so" (unpublished letter of August 20, 1881; see Letters, XXVIII, sect. 3).

Apart from Rose, his emotional and imaginative retreat into the past had evidently begun during the autumn while he was traveling in France and also writing the first chapter of *The Bible of Amiens* for Christmas distribution. Entries in his Diary, together with a letter of December 31 to the Reverend Faunthorpe (see *Works, 29,* 557), confirm what he subsequently told Norton: "at Christmas time I was not myself—the over-excitement of an autumn in France leaving me much pulled down" (*Works, 37,* 335–36; letter of January 20, 1881). In the first chapter of *The Bible of Amiens* he explicitly refers to the "old times, when one posted from Calais to Paris," and proceeds to portray the landscape with an eye upon the chalk and limestone terrain which had impressed him when he was sixteen (cf. *Works, 33,* 36 with observations of 1835, in *Diaries,* pp. 4–7). Then, too, through his account of Amiens he had resumed the type of work which had filled his heart and imagination when he was in his prime, particularly during the years devoted to his historical interpretation of the architecture of Venice. Now Amiens became "the French River-Queen" or "Venice of Picardy" so magically deft in her needlework that she could "match herself against Penelope" as her cathedral with its spire, like an arrow, rose from amidst the 50 "smoking chimneys" to proclaim that there was "no manner of profitable work" excepting that which was founded on the Christian faith. As he handles the description, it is as though the characterization of this Cathedral had become strangely synchronized with a characterization of the Margaret Ruskin (also associated with the fine needlework through which her eyesight was hurt) who had fashioned the abiding values of her son. Back in London, with his first chapter completed, he had entered in his Diary a tribute to his mother to replace the inscription which had originally appeared, in Croydon, on the memorial tablet of "Margaret's Well," after which he immediately noted: "And 'to-day' I have got the name of my Christmas book. / Our Fathers have told us. / Sketches of the History of Christendom / For Boys and Girls / who have been held at its fonts. / Part I / The Bible of Amiens" (*Diaries*, p. 995; November 30, 1880). As J. D. Rosenberg has observed, it was particularly Proust who felt "the miracle of Ruskin's animation" of Amiens and its cathedral (*The Darkening Glass* [New York and London, 1961], p. 209).

His own *recherche du temps perdu* had found further expression when, returning to Brantwood, he had almost immediately rearranged the 20 Turner drawings in his bedroom, with his thoughts now directed especially toward his Father, in "some due gratitude" (see entry for December 14, 1880). Why otherwise would he now have arranged this "collection of perfect . . . drawings" so that *Conway Castle*—the watercolor made by John James Ruskin as an Edinburgh High School student—became central to them all? Thus without words he once more could say that the Father who "*sometimes would not give me this, or that*" had nonetheless given "*not only all these drawings, but Brantwood—and all else*" (*Works, 13*, 485).

Immediately beneath the *Conway* (fondly associated with his Father's entertaining tale of a fisherman, continued from morning to morning) he had placed *Vesuvius, in Eruption*. Autobiographically, this was the first Turner drawing he had ever seen—probably in 1830, when it had been reproduced in *Friendship's Offering*. Then, as he recalled, "I used to feast on that engraving every evening for months, and return to it again and again for years" (*Works, 13*, 428), until, in keeping with what was typical of his imaginative contemplation, the two-coned mountain might readily have come to signify to him his own Mother in a phase of Wrath, to be appropriately complemented when he saw the "cool" *Vesuvius, in Repose*. By 1878 he had acquired both these watercolors, entitling them *Vesuvius Calm* and *Vesuvius Angry*.

And now, between the paternal *Conway* and the probably maternal *Vesuvius*, he had placed "like a brooch" (*Works, 13*, 670) a *Still-Life* ("Peaches, and Nuts") by William Henry Hunt, of the Old Water Colour Society, whose *Doves* (always "Dead") had adorned the Herne Hill breakfast room of his childhood. Strictly middle-class, or "plebeian," in his interests, background, and appeal; unblushingly blind to "instructions" and, in his "detached and sharply defined" touches, "always frank and clear, to a degree which might seem not only imperfect, but even harsh or offensive, to eyes trained in more tender or more formal schools"; his hand skilled through "unceasing practice" as he used simple means with "unbiased directness of aim at the realization of very simple facts"—Hunt had as his motto "Love what you study, study what you Love" and had shown "what real painting is" as he produced "pieces of art . . . at once so sincere and so accomplished" that, "in modern days," there was nothing else of the kind (*Works, 14,* 373–84 passim; characterization of Hunt in Preface to the *Notes* of 1879–80). Surely, as thus analyzed, the practice and achievement of Hunt as a painter would seem to have been notably analogous to that of the Mother Margaret, who, as remembered by her son, had trained her child into docility and interminable "obedience"—this being a resemblance which Ruskin himself was not likely to have missed when he hung that *Still-Life* "like a brooch" between the *Conway* and the *Vesuvius Angry.*

Yet before long, despite the "due gratitude" to his Father, experiences with the bookseller F. L. Ellis had reanimated rankling memories freighted, as ever, with resentment. During February a number of Scott manuscripts became available at auction, and Ruskin directed Ellis to buy, as his agent. Instead, Ellis decided that the manuscript of *Guy Mannering* was being sold at such an extravagant price that he refrained from out-bidding the representative of James Pierpont Morgan, leaving Ruskin "speechless with indignation" as well as afraid that he might lose, likewise, the manuscript of *St. Ronan's Well,* which he particularly desired. This novel, he would explain, was "preeminently characteristic of the condition of clouded and perverted intellect under which Scott suffered, at intervals, ever since his first attack of gout in the stomach. These two attacks of *mine* have been wholly on the brain—and, I believe, conditions of merely passing inflammation. But the phenomena of the two forms of disease are intensely important to me, in relation to my future treatment of myself" (*Works, 37,* 346; letter to F. S. Ellis, March 24, 1881). Because of *Guy Mannering,* "I am *really* angry with you for being so much of a Papa," he was telling Ellis a few days before he became ill (*Works, 37*, 342; letter of February 16, 1881). As to *St. Ronan's Well,* "Dear Papa Ellis," he implored, "Do *please* get it anyhow for me this once," signing his letter "ever your loving / SON GEORGE"—"George," of course, being his adopted name as Master of the Guild (*Works, 37*, 342–43; letter of February [1881]). As a young man, he had been so repeatedly galled by his dependence upon the bounty of a father who sometimes could seem to take pleasure in petty manifestations of power that in later years we find him recalling, during a period of derangement, how John James (saying that he had a "Wife to be looked after," to whom, he charged, Ruskin had been "cruel") had refused Joseph Couttet "ten and sixpence" for "an absolutely unique bit of Titanium" which "I coveted . . . dreadfully." In the course of this story he remarked, "My Father grudged me minerals as much as pictures—so odd—and so foolish of him" (MS material, presumably designed for *Dilecta,* in the F. J. Sharp Collection).

The death of Carlyle on February 5 (ambiguously commemorated in the Diary by no more than a cross) may have been a precipitating cause of the collapse—Carlyle having been, for some time, the acknowledged "Father" of much of Ruskin's intellectual life and, in their personal relationship during later years, also frankly his "Papa Carlyle." To the death of his Father, Ruskin had reacted not with grief but with a self-reproach which found expression during later years. In one mood, discussing his initial reaction to the death of his Father, he had said: "My father had been dead to *me* in all the inner and deep senses of death—for many years——not that he knew that—but things to *me* are just what they were" (unpublished letter to Mrs. Hewitt, April 23 [1864]; Pierpont Morgan Library). Analogously, he now explained: "The death of Carlyle is no sorrow to me. It is, I believe, not an end—but a beginning of his real life. Nay, perhaps also of mine. My remorse, every day he lived, for not having enough loved him in the days gone by, is not greater now, but less, in the hope that he knows what I am feeling about him at this—and all other—moments" (letter to Mary Gladstone, February 15, 1881; in *Letters to M.G. and H.G.*, p. 70). *Past and Present,* he would tell George Richmond, "was the only book I could get help from during my illness, which was partly brought on by the sense of loneliness—and greater responsibility brought upon me by Carlyle's death" (*Works, 37*, 361; letter of May 20, 1881). Probably referring to his conviction, during the delirium, that he was called upon to found a "further phase of Christianity," he told Norton that the "result" of "some strange passages of dream . . . is mainly my throwing myself now into the mere fulfilment of Carlyle's work" (*Works, 37*, 345; letter of March 24, 1881).

Restored to sanity, he turned almost at once, prematurely and rather ineffectually, to his work, which by April was under way to his own deeply hopeful satisfaction. "I am all right again—in the head—very dark yet in the heart," he was telling Lady Mount-Temple by March 23. "The issue of the matter is that I must be much alone this summer, and am gradually breaking to Joan the necessity of my being so" (letter of Wednesday, March 23 [1881]; see Letters, xxx). By the end of the year, retrospectively, he would ask Mrs. La Touche: "I wonder what you and Joanie call being 'good'? I call being good, to think of the past—& hope for the future—& then I go mad" (J. H. Whitehouse, "Ruskin in Old Age," *Scribner's Magazine, 62* [December 1917], 742; letter of December 5, 1881).

January 1. Well in health, and not poor in hope—D.G. —a little anxious at having no letter from Arfie Began Gospel of St Luke with servants and my work—tracing of Amiens and read some Douglas Virgil.[1]

January 2. Sunday. Roast ham and raisins gave me a nightmare of fancying Joan going to tumble into the fall of the Rhine—four times as high as it is—and then two long sleepless hours, in which however I've done some good geography[2] and other matters, and can see my blue lines by candlelight without spectacles. Cold gradually working off.

January 3 Monday Could not have a sadder morning for the birthday. Read entry for last year, but am much more dead, myself, in this one. I see it is the Octave of St John.[3]

January 5. Wednesday. It is infinitely strange to me that I *can't* keep this book regularly—resolve as I will!

Yesterday pleasant work in wood. Marshalls and Mr. Darwin[4] at dinner.

Snow very lovely in wreathed cloud over calm lake yesterday but I always feel in my study chilly now, in morning.

1. Ruskin considered Bishop Gawin Douglas' *Aeneid* one of the great translations, to be named with Chapman's *Homer*. On Christmas Day, 1880, he had sent an inscribed copy of this "English Virgil" (1553) to the students of Whitelands College. For them to "study every word of it," he now told their Principal, the Reverend J. F. Faunthorpe, "would be an education better than any living queen's" (*Works, 29,* 557; letter of January 2, 1881).

2. Presumably for chapter 2 of *The Bible of Amiens* (issued December 1881), with its reference to "All the maps of Germany which I have myself the privilege of possessing" (*Works, 33,* 62).

3. In other words, the birthday of Rose La Touche chanced to fall upon the "eighth day" after December 27, the festival "Day" of St. John the Apostle.

4. Probably William E. Darwin or George Darwin, Charles Darwin not having made his "second visit to the Lake country" until June 1881 (Litchfield, *Emma Darwin, a Century of Family Letters 1792–1890, 2,* 246).

January 8. Saturday. Have been wofully ill and despondent, these two past days,[5] the loveliest I have ever seen at Coniston in winter! Out all day yesterday into long half moonlight—with bad attack of my worst bodily weakness[6] as I walked. Slept well and am cheerful and up to things this morning!

January 9 Sunday. Yesterday another lovely day of sun and calm, and I did much but had nasty and terrific nightmare of a puppet serpent, which suddenly came to life—⟨grotesque,⟩ like a clown, but ⟨terrific and inevitable⟩[7] — Also, of bathing in a deep pool, with some one holding me—and of rather pretty but saucy country women passing close above—pretending to be greatly astonished and shocked.

16th—Sunday— 23rd, Sunday—

January 28 Friday — Thaw and darkness after some twenty five days of splendid frost—ending on Wednesday the 26th with the loveliest and most perfect hoar frost, and entire calm on frozen lake— Lolly skating out from Joannas bay into deep water—safe to go over if we had had time, in the afternoon. All manner of wonderful and beautiful things—alas now fast passing away I myself languid—weak—nervous and stupid—beyond precedent

February 4th. Friday. Revising Sketchbooks "Siena Green lane. Oak. Virgin's bower. Rose. Blackberry. Poppy Mullein.["]

5. On Thursday, the 6th (Old Christmas Day), he nevertheless had given a dinner to 315 Coniston children and, accompanied by Mrs. Severn and Martha Gale, had greeted them with an "Address" (see *Works, 34,* 632–34).

6. Probably a reference to the rupture for which he was subsequently treated by Dr. John A. Kingdon (see B.S.; see also the Thomas Pebardy Letters, XXXIII).

7. Published in *Works, 33,* xxviii.

[February 5th?] [8]
or
[February 14th?]

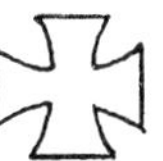

February 15 Tuesday. Yesterday found inscription on first leaf of the book Mr Ellis[9] gave me, by accident as I was showing Mattie where Punch was, and afterwards, the last thing in the afternoon, Giotto's St Louis,[10] which I did not know I had.

German band, coming immediately afterwards, plays Home, sweet Home, [“]The Keel row” and “Is there room for Mary there”

February 16 Wednesday. Yesterday called on Mrs Sly,[11]

8. The cross between the entries for February 4 and 15 could have been appropriately used to signify the death of Carlyle on February 5. Hence Ruskin's memory was probably mistaken when, in 1883, he noted in his index to this volume, under “Health”: “The cross at p. 240 [that is, beneath the entry for February 4, 1881] indicates the coming on again, upon St Valentine's day of the forms of coincidence and imagination which were the prelude to my second illness. My first begins on the same day, at p. 62 [see entry for February 14, 1878, designated “St. Valentine”] (previous ill health shown for several days before) and the prelude state lasts till the 22nd, seven full days—in the second it seems to last only till the 19th but I was about the house and at dinner sometime after that—I suspect the prelude was six or seven days in all the cases. (Written from + down, 22nd July [18]83).” In the index this + appears in the margin, two lines above the beginning of his comment on “The cross at p. 240.”

Thus, curiously enough, the symbolic cross can seem to signify, dually, the loss of Carlyle on February 5 and the loss of reason which he himself dates from the 14th. Writing his diary in 1881, however, he was scarcely aware of his pending loss of reason but was poignantly aware of the loss of Carlyle.

9. Ruskin's “always helpful friend,” the dealer in rare books and editor of Chaucer for the Kelmscott Press—Frederick S. Ellis (1830–1901). In 1870 his firm had published, in a remarkable edition, 25 copies of D. G. Rossetti's *Poems,* one of which (probably the book to which Ruskin now refers) Mr. Ellis had presented to Ruskin. For the “inscription,” see *Works, 34,* 699.

10. Evidently some reproduction of Giotto's *St. Louis,* in the Santa Croce Chapel, Florence. Discussing this fresco, Ruskin had called St. Louis “the type of a Christian king” and “the most interesting saint of all saints—for *him* [Giotto] to do for us” (*Works, 23,* 354, 296; from *Mornings in Florence,* 1875).

11. Mrs. Elizabeth Sly (d. June 27, 1889), keeper of the Waterhead Hotel after her husband's death in 1880. (“Inasmuch as Joseph Sly was buried on Nov. 19, 1880, according to the Coniston Parish Registers,” Miss Gnosspelius notes, “C. & W. must have misdated the letter to the Rev. F. A. Malleson, ascribed to Nov. 19, 1879, in which Ruskin refers to the death of Mr. Sly” (see *Works, 37,* 300).

Father Gibson[12]—Mrs Bell and Mrs Inman,[13] and rowed across lake home—hitting south of harbour exactly without minding what I was about,—having written letters that gave me much to think of—Miss Gladstone,[14] Francie, (no—she came in afternoon,)[15] and telegraph to buy at Reginald's hillside—[16]

Then in evening—found chipped galena and thought over it[17] Waked at 1/4 past two, and read Proverbs xxxi.[18]

February 17th. Thursday.

Yesterday. Received Froude's letter[19]—did what I could of business in forenoon, ordered squills which Herdson asked for, narcissus of Vevay, and Cranberries.

12. The Reverend Father Henry Gibson (d. 1907, aged 80) served the Roman Catholic Chapel in Coniston from the time of its construction, in 1872, until 1886.

13. By now the W. D. Inmans were presumably the tenants of Coniston Hall, occupied during the 1870s by Mrs. Routledge, the widowed "farmer" who had proposed to repay in geese the £300 which Ruskin had lent her (see Collingwood, *Ruskin Relics,* p. 25; identifications provided by Miss Gnosspelius).

14. Ruskin's letter to Mary Gladstone (see *Works, 37,* 341) shows him to have been pondering the death of his "Papa" Carlyle, with a transference of the "remorse" elsewhere expressed when he reproached himself for having been what, retrospectively, he considered heartless in his treatment of his own father.

15. Evidently meaning that a letter had arrived from Frances Graham, to whom he had sent his love in the letter to Mary Gladstone.

16. Presumably a telegram to F. S. Ellis to buy some Scott MS, offered for sale, at Hillside, by Reginald R. Cavendish, youngest son of the Earl of Clare.

17. From boyhood he had dreamed over his specimens of minerals, often discussed in his work with undercurrents of personal allegory. It would be characteristic if now, having "found" the specimen of "chipped galena," he had "thought over it" as though it were a counterpart of his own damaged self. Specifically, W. G. Collingwood recounts how "for years" Ruskin had been "wretched because his great and glorious specimen" of galena—a "big, black, shining crystal"—was flawed ("chipped"?) by "an angular notch" which, one day, he realized had probably been made by a crystal of calcite once embedded in it. "His galena had not been damaged . . . and life was still worth living" (*Ruskin Relics,* p. 173).

18. "The words of King Lemuel, the prophecy that his mother taught him"—primarily a characterization of the ideal woman. Ruskin may have turned to this chapter because he had been thinking about Mary Gladstone, whom he called his "little Mother" and who, from the start, had seemed to him to be "a very 'perfect woman, nobly planned' " (*Works, 37,* 263; letter of October 22, 1878).

19. For Froude's letter of February 13, expressing his regard for Ruskin and describing the aftermath of Carlyle's death, see Letters, xiii.

Began final arrangement of mineral cabinets.

After lunch, answered Froude wrote to Ned, and Janet,[20] who[se] letter came also in the morning, to Diddie and Susie

Then drove to have tea with Mr & Mrs Herdson, and walked home, in the snow and fog.

Met Mattie

Then before dinner in the study found out meaning of Lemuel.[21]

The night very strange,—could not sleep, but at last got to sleep by counting resolutely up to seven hundred, articulating the names of the numbers.

February 18th. Another very sleepless night in which I could'nt help thinking too much; and it seemed very long: partly because I was impatient to get to my Saussure[22] in the morning (Mem[o]—begin "today" MS. of it with Mattie:) and when I got to it I was too dreamy to read it.

February 19. Another—it seemed to me, *quite* sleepless night, but I fancy I dozed in the morning; shaky & nervous now—but not ill that I know of— Enjoyed my Saussure immensely, at breakfast,—but more my Miss Edgeworth last night—first and second chapters of Ormond quite marvellous to me in their fineness of finish.

20. Doubtless Janet ("Jessie") Leete, with whom he was in correspondence at this time. She was the "young . . . governess" to whom he accredits his having undertaken *The Bible of Amiens,* in response to her request that he "write some pieces of history which her pupils could gather some good out of" (*Works, 33,* 21).

21. In Hebrew, "Lemuel" means "devoted to God" or "Godward."

22. H. B. de Saussure, *Voyages dans les Alpes* (1796)—the book for which he had asked as a present for his fifteenth birthday. In *Modern Painters, V* Saussure is called "my dear master" in geology (*Works, 7,* 164), and in *Praeterita* he is designated "Papa" (*Works, 35,* 162).

[April 8th] And then came on just a month of terrific delirium again. — ⟨On the 22nd March,⟩ (see large folio book) ⟨I was down in my study writing business letters—and yesterday the 7th April, the third anniversary of my coming down to study after my first illness,⟩ see above, page 203,[23] ⟨I was working in the wood for good three hours,⟩ (one before lunch, and two and a half in afternoon) ⟨with as good strength as I've ever felt.

The First Primrose out, too—no bigger than this [sketch of petals in outline]—but very delightful.

And the first soft sunshine of the year—lasting into far twilight⟩[24]

But Note—in these fine spring twilights there is no *glow*—only tender pearly light

23. Entry for April 7, 1880.

24. Published (with minor changes) in *Works, 33,* xxviii.

1883

Having reached home on January 4, after almost a year's absence, Ruskin began again to use the Brantwood Diary for the daily record. During 1883 he would leave home only to fulfill engagements to lecture at Oxford and, for ten days, to revisit Whithorn Abbey and the homes of Sir Walter Scott. Hence, specifically, this Diary unit records his Brantwood life from January 6 through March 8, from March 25 through May 9, from June 22 through September 23, from October 4 through October 12, from November 28 through January 1, 1884.

Although no longer expressed in so many words, his determination to serve others, chiefly by resuming his work in its various branches while also guarding his health, is probably the main interest of this series of entries. At Herne Hill, during March 1882, he had suffered his third mental breakdown, from which he had recovered under the care of Sir William Gull—a friend and colleague of Dr. James Oldham, the father of Ruskin's goddaughter Constance. Pathetically enough, on March 5 he had appealed to Lady Mount-Temple: "Darling φιλη Please come and look after me here tomorrow or any day, as soon as you can. I'm afraid I'm going off the rocks again—and it looks to me more like a terminus than the other two times" (see Letters, XXX). In this third illness, he would note, "the vision was mostly very sad & personal, all connected with my Father" (see entry for February 2), though more immediately he had written Mrs. La Touche: "But what a simplicity of a Saviour? you are—quite the Prem[re] 'Ingenuito' of Saviours, to think that I should live without work or merely by looking at things! These fits of illnesses are all *accidents* (what an Accident is—God knows—not I) not in the least consequences of my general work: and I rather fancy the three of them are all I'm meant to have. They were all of a piece, and, Ireland and *her* 'Rest' has had much more to do with them than my English work. I'm a little shaky yet" (see Letters, XXVIII, sect. 3, April 5, 1882). By "Easter Monday" he had been able to return to his work (Collingwood, *Life*, 2, 516). "I need not tell you it has been no small pleasure to me to be able to serve Mr. Ruskin," Dr. Gull had remarked, "and I am sure that his satisfactory recovery will be a cause of thankfulness to all. ¶We may confidently expect many years of usefulness for him" (letter to Constance Oldham, April 14, 1882; in M. E. Spence, "Ruskin's Correspondence with His God-Daughter Constance Oldham," *The John Rylands Library Bulletin*, *43* [March 1961], 5).

By autumn this prospect could command Ruskin's own hope. Early in August, accompanied by W. G. Collingwood, he had reached France, en route to Italy, and toward the end of September, despite misgivings recurrently expressed in his Diary, he could tell Mrs. Severn: "I am deeply thankful to find my mind unchanged in any traceable way by my grave illnesses. I am not more irritable, nor more melancholy, except for the definite cause of being older, and what is left to enjoy is more deeply enjoyed and wondered at" (unpublished letter of September 26, 1882; Harvard College Library). Probably enclosing this letter, Mrs. Severn had informed Norton: "I am rather happy about the Coz at present—and thank Heaven when these terrible attacks are got over—they do not leave him shattered either mentally or bodily . . . — Sir William Gull saw him frequently all through last spring's illness—and assured us, he *might* never have another attack, or he might—but he did not dread any softening of the brain—or actual disease" (unpublished letter of September 30, 1882; Harvard University Library; for letters of 1885 from Dr. Gull to Mrs. Severn, see Letters, XIX). His self-confidence having gradually increased, by October 22 (writing Mrs. La Touche), he had announced that he was "doing some good drawing, *so* good in fact that having occasion to write to Oxford today, I sent word if they liked to have me for Professor again for a while they might" (from a paragraph omitted when this letter was published by Miss Young and therefore, next, by Cook and Wedderburn; see Letters, XXVIII, sect. 3). Within a month he was acknowledging letters in which his Oxford Drawing Master, Alexander MacDonald, had reported "the more or less general wish to have me again at Oxford for a little while" (*Works*, *37*, 421), after which he thanked Canon Henry Scott Holland: "Your kind words to myself come hopefully to me, at a time when I do not know if I am right in thinking of the completion of work interrupted by humiliating failure of mind and body, yet which it seems to me my proper task to complete, if I may" (letter of November 22, 1882; in Stephen Paget, ed., *Henry Scott Holland . . . Memoirs and Letters* [London, 1921], p. 106).

Back in England, to the friend and secretary who had been constantly with him for more than a year, he could seem "to have quite recovered his health, and to be ready for reëntry into public life" (Collingwood, *Life*, 2, 522). On the day after reaching Herne Hill, he had faced a large and enthusiastic audience at the London Institution as he gave the lecture to be entitled (autobiographically?), upon publication, "Mending the Sieve." "And Ruskin flourishes," Burne-Jones could rejoice, "—gave a lecture on Cistercian architecture the other day that was like most ancient times and of his very best, and looks well—really looks stronger than for many a year past" (*Memorials*, 2, 133; letter to C. E. Norton, December 1882). Planning ultimately to use this lecture as a chapter in *Valle Crucis*, Ruskin had made St. Benedict—"Captain of the Host" of "working saints"—together with St. Bernard of Cîteaux, his heroes of the hour: St. Benedict, who had determined "that Christian men ought not to be hermits, but actively helpful members of society: that they are to live by their own labour, and to feed other people by it to the best of their power" (*Works*, *33*, 237); St. Bernard, who, within 25 years, having gathered about him "a few more fiery ones, of his own sort," had placed "more than sixty thousand Cistercian monks, at work on any bit of trenchable ground they were allowed to come at" (*Works*, *33*, 248) —"the Benedictine gospel" having been "the proclamation . . . of useful labour as man's duty upon earth, and of the Sun of Righteousness as his Lord in Heaven" (*Works*, *33*, 239). To Ruskin as Master of the Guild of St. George, these two saints, in spirit and practical endeavor, might seem compositely to have epitomized his own *alter ego*. ". . . there is one word that is true for the feeblest of us, and for all it should be enough," he had concluded the lecture. " 'Let us labour joyfully while we have light. The night cometh;—but thou knowest not what shall be on the morrow' " (*Works*, *33*, 249). Next, as though in a complementary conclusion, he had recorded: "Last day of 1882. I close this year's diary in even health, I trust of body and mind, with much hope and power still left to me, and all kinds of blessings, D.G." (*Diaries,* p. 1046; December 31, 1882).

At Brantwood the year began with two months of quiet work as he readied various enterprises for spring publication and planned the Oxford lectures to be delivered in March and in May. On January 17 a telegram from Dr. Acland officially confirmed what Ruskin had known since before the end of November: "once again welcome to Alma Mater" (see entry for January 17 and *Works, 33,* xlv). It found him keeping in contact with local friends (Ethel, Fred, and Laurence Hilliard), welcoming the Andersons ("Jamie" and his bride "Emilie"), conferring with Mr. Rydings upon business of the Guild, and completing his work on the edition of *Modern Painters, II* which would be issued in April, to be followed by Francesca Alexander's *Story of Ida.*

During October, while in Florence, he had met Francesca and her mother, having been introduced by their mutual friend the American artist Henry R. Newman, who had told him about Francesca and "her book," *The Roadside Songs of Tuscany.* "Mr. Newman had been in love with my book for a long while," Francesca would explain (Swett, *Letters to Francesca,* p. 371), and Ruskin, after his first sight of the drawings of flowers and peasants used to illustrate the songs of the countryside, which Francesca had been gathering through the years, had decided to acquire it (paying Francesca £600) for the Sheffield Museum.

Immediately, too, he had responded to her account of the life of her friend Ida, who became to him the "Maid of Fésole." She was a maiden who was like a Rose La Touche, idealized, in having died (when she was only 17) with such perfect acceptance of God's will that she had not even seemed to feel her physical suffering through the months during which she awaited death with absolute peace and unfailing happiness. Moreover, Francesca had made a drawing in which she portrayed the spiritualized Ida sitting upright against her pillows, with eyes closed and face enframed by the rays of the setting sun: in her features, as well as in her complete peace, this Ida resembles the Rose La Touche-like St. Ursula shown by Carpaccio as she lies asleep upon her bed, enframed by light and dreaming that she is approached by the Angel of the Lord (cf. F. Alexander's Ida in *Works, 32,* Pl. I, and Carpaccio's St. Ursula in *Works, 27,* Pl. VIII). And now, through the teaching of Ida, he had received as though it were a message which might have come from Rose herself: "It will be as the Lord pleases: He knows what He does" (*Works, 32,* 25). Supported by this knowledge, Ida had shown, through her own life, that it is possible to be so entirely acceptant of God's Will that one is also trustingly acceptant of whatever may be one's lot, including the loss of one's beloved.

Returning to the Alexanders on the day after his first visit, Ruskin (Francesca recounts) "said a good deal about my story of Ida, which he had just read, and quite took my breath away by proposing to take it away and have it published. He said it would be a very good religious book . . . especially from the absence of all sectarian feeling in it" (Swett, *Letters to Francesca,* p. 376). Hence he went back to England with her story and her drawing of Ida asleep "in the last ray of Sunset," leaving the manuscript of *The Roadside Songs* for her final touches. By mid-January he was noting in the Diary: "Got most of 'Maid of Fesole' corrected and sent off—for press, and the 8th Chapter of Deucalion" (see entry for January 14).

This chapter of *Deucalion*—"Revision"—was one product of the work he had been doing to prepare the new edition of *Modern Painters, II,* which, in 1881, he had said would be reissued through partial publication (see *Works, 25,* 122–25). For many years the evangelical assumptions upon which he had based his analysis of beauty in the volume of 1846 had made him feel that *Modern Painters, II* was the only book which he had ever written that, with his consent, would never be republished. Even in 1881 he had planned to issue no more than "the analytic parts . . . with perhaps an additional note or two, and the omission of the passages concerning Evangelical or other religious matters, in which I have found out my mistakes" (*Works, 25,* 123). Presumably because such cutting had proved to be impractical, he had resorted to the stream of notes which characterize, venomously and disruptively, the first volume of the 1883 edition. These notes (two of which are dated "Pisa . . . 1882") had evidently helped to keep him occupied while he was traveling with W. G. Collingwood, and presumably account for the Diary comment made at Pisa: "Here once more, where I began all my true work in 1845. Thirty seven full years of it: how much in vain! ¶How much strength left I know not, but yet trust the end may be better than the beginning" (*Diaries,* p. 1028; September 26, 1882). In other words, as an immediate result of the "true work" begun in 1845 through his discovery of the Campo Santo frescoes (see 1883 Epilogue of *Modern Painters, II*), he had written this book in which his aesthetic theory had been cast in the mold of the evangelical creed to which, in 1846, he had still all but unquestioningly subscribed.

Why, then, reissue a "beginning" to which he himself now reacted with such scorn? To answer this question was a function of the *Deucalion* essay "Revision" and of the pending Preface which he found it difficult to write (see entry for January 29). Having highlighted the limitations in the knowledge of his young manhood and, through the footnotes, especially the "wrongness" of his evangelical beliefs, he was concomitantly convinced, he now explained, that he had been fundamentally right in having assumed that there is in actuality some Creative or Governing Power (or Living Spirit or Divinity), to man incomprehensible, who manifests His attributes through what is Beautiful, such Beauty being visible only to those who are obedient to the Moral Law (see *Works, 4,* 4; *26,* 334). Moreover, he still approved his initial thesis that this Beauty, with all the knowledge of things unseen to which it is conducive, can be known only through the "theoretic" or "contemplative" faculty—that is, through the "intellectual imagination" with which all men are endowed and which gives them the capacity for intuitive apperception of "God's majesty and providence as revealed through his works." (The burden of Psalm 104, which was in the forefront of his mind while he was engaged upon "Revision"; see *Works, 26,* 344; *Diaries,* p. 1022; September 6, 1882). And since this was a "higher" faculty than that represented by the strictly rational thought which had led to the discoveries of "modern" scientists who triumphantly investigated the material world, gaining knowledge which "almost without exception" turned out to be destructive when practically applied, he was reissuing this "imperfect essay" in which he had first proclaimed the faculty that had become increasingly—and how dangerously—potent within his personal life.

Meanwhile, remaining critically self-observant, he refused to "force" his productivity (see entry for February 11). Mundanely, he was at first badly bothered by an abscessed tooth, but toward the end of February he could note with satisfaction: "Doing a lot of good work too—and on the whole wonderfully well" (entry for February 23). As part of this "good work," he had selected and catalogued 100 minerals for St. David's School at Reigate; and he wrote—chiefly, one infers, for the students at Whitelands College, where he had instituted the May Queen Festival—the sentimentalized "Lost Jewels" (to be issued in May, as Letter 90 of *Fors Clavigera*). As Master of the Guild, he had resumed his activities in behalf of St. George's Museum, which he had always hoped would attract the ironworkers of Sheffield. Analogously, during the summer he would send his annotated contributions ("hard work") to an exhibition designed to raise money with which to buy books to be used, mainly, by the quarrymen of Dalbeattie (see entry for July 12). While he had "power," he had resolved, he would make use of his "blessings": according to the Gospel of St. Benedict, as he had said, "Christian men ought . . . [to be] helpfully active members of society."

Early in February he began to plan the lectures to be delivered at Oxford, without feeling called upon to exert himself. As he had told the Reverend Faunthorpe, rather too inconsequentially: "I have only taken the Professorship again in order to keep my hand on the helm, not to talk. They will be quite content to hear me read *Proserpina* or anything else I am doing" (*Works, 37,* 434; letter of January 24, 1883). In the same spirit he told Lady Simon that, so far as he could discern,

> there are no symptoms of any return of the illness which—these three times, has seized me in the spring; and what I propose to do at Oxford will be merely the turning [of] the general current of my work in that direction. I am well assured that without effort, I can write as many [illegible]

> lectures for them as they will expect, in the year,—if I feel too dull I shall read things written before, which will be quite as useful, and which in the proper Theory of Professorship, it is the real duty of the Professor of any science to do—not at all to pursue new discoveries. (February 10, 1883; see Letters, XXXVII, sect. 1)

Nevertheless, in actuality he prepared *The Art of England* series, in which he called attention to the talent of contemporaries who, professionally, were helped by his interpretative appraisals of their work. Each lecture would be available in printed copy before its delivery, and in all of them he was careful to avoid extremes of blame or praise.

Before leaving Brantwood to meet the first of these engagements (four lectures being scheduled for the spring), he experienced a "frightful fit of despondency and dread" (see entry for March 6). Yet he was still fully able to delight an audience at Oxford: after his first lecture, the "undergraduates cheered no end, and Baxter said the people going away who couldn't get in [around 200] were like a church coming out" (*Works, 37,* 440; letter to Mrs. Severn, March 9, 1883). Consequently arrangements were made to have him repeat the performance, whereafter every lecture was scheduled for two deliveries, with Alexander Wedderburn sending a full account of each to the *Pall Mall Gazette*. The second lecture having been no less successfully delivered on May 12, Swinburne turned from "this evening's" paper to say, in a letter to Burne-Jones: "I never did till now read anything in praise of your work that seemed to me really and perfectly apt and adequate. I do envy Ruskin the authority and the eloquence which give such weight and effect to his praise. It is just what I 'see in a glass darkly' that he brings out and lights up with the very best words possible; while we others (who cannot draw), like Shakespeare, have eyes for wonder but lack tongues to praise." (*Memorials, 2,* 132; letter of May 15, 1883.)

Returning to Brantwood, he soon began to enjoy with Joan the presence of houseguests, Kate Greenaway being the first to arrive. She had known him initially through *Fors Clavigera*: "I longed for each evening to come that I might lose myself in that new and wonderful world" (M. H. Spielmann and G. S. Layard, *Kate Greenaway* [London, 1905], p. 223; letter of 1896 to Violet Dickinson). Through the display of her drawings included in the Fine Art Society's Exhibit of 1879, he too had found a uniquely new world of masquerading little girls, sometimes accompanied by virginal mothers, which he would call her "Dance of Life." All but immediately he had begun their correspondence by writing the long and whimsical letter in which he expressed admiration for "your gifts—and your graces, and your fancies, and your —yes, perhaps one or two little tiny faults" (*Works, 37,* 307; letter of January 6 [1880]). Almost three years later, in response to her Christmas Greeting of 1882, he had announced: "I *must* come to thank you, there's no writing what pleasure your note gives me. When may I come—" (unpublished letter of "Christmas day, 1882"; Pierpont Morgan Library). Hence, on December 29, 1882, they had met (see *Diaries,* p. 1046; December 30). In a letter of later years she confessed: "before you came I thought so much of your coming that it got to be really a pain, and I said I almost wish he was not coming. But then the first moment I saw you, I was glad—so glad" (Spielmann and Layard, p. 208; undated letter).

By February it could seem right to call her "My dear 'Kate' ": "I beg pardon—but I really can't call you anything else, since I've seen you: —now—when can you come and see mountain spring? . . . April would be best" (unpublished letter of February 18, 1883; Pierpont Morgan Library). Therefore, in April, she arrived as a guest who rather surprised herself by spending almost a month in a wonderland she left as a woman (now 37) who, apparently, had fallen in love.

Through a letter headed "Brantwood," she would leave an account of these days: "After breakfast I am allowed (which is a great favour) to go into the study and see all sorts of beautiful things, with little talks and remarks from Mr. Ruskin as he writes; then we go on drives, walks, or on the lake till tea-time. Then it is dinner-time; then he reads us something nice, or talks in the most beautiful manner. Words can hardly say the sort of man he is—perfect—simply. . . . I do not know yet when I shall come home—they want me to stay a month, but I shall not stay nearly so long as that" (Spielmann and Layard, p. 113; letter to Mrs. Edmund Evans [April 1883]). Subsequently: "Everything is confused, I never know date or day. I'm always looking at books or pictures. I am absorbed in a new world altogether" (ibid.).

Henceforth, when lectures took him to Oxford, Ruskin would arrange to call upon Kate after he had made his way to London to attend to other business; and between-times, for as long as he remained well, he faithfully responded (if through only a few lines) to her letters. These are said to have been almost always decorated by a sketch—sketches she continued to make, for his pleasure, upon letters sent to Brantwood all through the years when he himself was no longer able to reply. About a year after her death, answering a letter in which C. E. Norton had urged the need to supervise, with care, Spielmann's use of Ruskin's letters to Kate Greenaway, Mrs. Severn would observe: "the tiresome point is the letters on KG's side especially to JR savour of much deeper feeling than ordinary friendship and of course his letters to her are very affectionate beginning 'Darling Kate' etc. Now don't you think it will be wise to let the world think it was only an ordinary friendship, and suppress the idea that it meant anything else? — or what?" (unpublished letter of July 24, 1902; Harvard University Library). Next, we are told that it was *Ruskin* who destroyed all the letters, except one, which he had received from Kate Greenaway before 1887! (see *Works, 36,* cv).

Yet despite the folly of such destructive protectivity, Ruskin's letters to "Darling Katie" (of which 592 are available in the Pierpont Morgan Library—around 1100 pages in all) clearly show that she did not disguise the love which he had initially evoked and that he did not respond in kind, although there was always great tenderness in his deeply affectionate regard for her. Consider, for example, a letter of September 1883, written just after he had been at work upon his will, helped by C. E. Norton. In her last letter Kate had evidently asked when he would be able to reach London after his next trip to Oxford. He would not be in Oxford before October 14 or 15, he replied,

> and must stay here [at Brantwood] till then—*can't* get to London till towards the 20th but *must* be in London at that

time And don't think I shall put anything before seeing you when I do come, for I feel this affection you bear me puts me in a place of most solemn trust over you—but I do hope you will manage to get it put into a more daughterly and fatherly sort of thing, for indeed, Katie,—part of the necessary work with this American friend [Norton] was recasting some bits of my 'Will'—and just think what a sad Katie you would be,—as things are with you now—if—you had'nt me to write to you any more. Now be a good girl, and try to get into a quieter—I do not [mean?] less deep—feeling to your poor old —Master

Ever your loving JR (Unpublished letter of September 10, 1883; Pierpont Morgan Library)

Or, quite directly: "—— You sweet Katie, its a very wonderful thing to have made any woman love one so——but its *awful* too—for what is to become of you!" (letter of "Friday morning," written on Herne Hill stationery, in an envelope stamped "London, April 25, 1884"; Pierpont Morgan Library.)

By the end of June—having returned in good health from the weeks of May spent in Oxford, followed by three weeks spent at Herne Hill—he was welcoming Charles Eliot Norton, whom he had not seen for ten years. En route to the Continent, where he hoped that Ruskin would join him before the end of the summer, Norton had landed in Liverpool, the more readily to reach Brantwood for a visit of no more than four days. Too gloomily, 30 years later, he would recall having found Ruskin already "an old man, with look even older than his years, with bent form, with the beard of a patriarch, with habitual expression of weariness, with the general air and gait of age" (*Letters of John Ruskin to Charles Eliot Norton, 2,* 165). In reality he had found a friend whose shoulders, prematurely, had begun to stoop and whose appearance had been radically changed by the moustache and beard (still trimmed) which had been permitted to develop after his illness of 1881. While at Brantwood, Norton more realistically observed: "Ruskin has aged a good deal in these late years. He looks as old as he is,—sixty-four. He stoops a good deal; but he seems physically well enough, and his mind is as active and perhaps as vigorous as ever" (*Letters of Charles Eliot Norton, 2,* 150; letter to his children, June 28, 1883).

In September, Norton would return, probably for two days, after which Ruskin told Kate Greenaway: "if he outlives me, [he] will have the editing of all my private MSS—as Froude of Carlyle's" (unpublished letter of September 9, 1883; Pierpont Morgan Library). It was an ironic decision in view of Ruskin's abiding admiration for, and Norton's pending condemnation of, Froude's editorial and biographical work for Carlyle. (For Ruskin's defense of Froude, see Viljoen, *The Froude-Ruskin Friendship,* pp. 138–46.) By 1886, when Norton launched the first of his attacks upon Froude, Alexander Wedderburn had been asked to share the responsibility of being Ruskin's literary executor. Assuming office in 1900, Norton would state: "If it depended upon me, there would be no further word of Ruskin or about Ruskin given to the public. Enough is known. He printed or allowed to be printed far too much. . . . He was a kind of angel gone astray; meant for the thirteenth century, he got delayed on the way, and when he finally arrived was a white-haired anachronism" (*Letters of Norton,* 2, 291–92; letter to Sir Leslie Stephen, March 28, 1900). Shortly thereafter, sanctioned by Alexander Wedderburn, he and Mrs. Severn were reverently making a bonfire of Ruskin's letters to Rose La Touche—according to Wedderburn "perhaps the most beautiful things he ever wrote" (*Works, 35,* lxxvi).

As yet another most meaningful house-guest Mrs. La Touche was entertained during the last week of July. In days of old, through her implacable opposition to having John Ruskin become the husband of her enigmatic Rose, she had been very largely responsible for the agony endured by her daughter as well as by Ruskin. After the death of Rose, she remained in correspondence with Mrs. Severn, to whom she expressed her sympathetic anxiety, in 1878, because of Ruskin's illness (see Letters, XXVIII, sect. 1). Thereafter they frequently exchanged letters until, in 1881, she evidently (see below, p. 469) had asked "Joanie" whether Ruskin would forgive her, whereupon he had resumed his correspondence with her and, during July, had welcomed her to Brantwood. Then he gave George Allen her address, with the request: "Please at once send a 7th Deucalion (serpent) [viz. Pt. VIII, "Living Waves"] to Mrs. La Touche . . . and be very careful to send her one of the earliest copies of everything I bring out to the same address" (unpublished letter of August 20, 1881; Columbia University Library). Her inquiry about "forgiveness" must have been presented to Joan after Ruskin's illness of 1881, during which he had set forth, "barefoot," to visit the grave of Rose, only to have it evolve, within the "dream," that Rose and her mother had come to Brantwood (see entry for February 3, 1883). Several months after his recovery, speaking of his "last illness" in a letter to Lady Mount-Temple, Ruskin said: "The visionary part of it [the 1881 "delirium"] was *half* fulfilled—as soon as I was well enough to make it safe for me, by Lacerta's coming to see me and finding—some manner of comfort (not to me comprehensible—but I was glad to see it,) in being with Joanie and me" (Bradley, *Letters of Ruskin to Lord and Lady Mount-Temple,* p. 379; letter of August 2, 1881). Providing more tangible evidence of this first visit, after Mrs. La Touche's return to Ireland he remarked: "I'm wild to see that mossy Foxglove of your's but I'd rather not have any seed lest our foxgloves should take to playing any such tricks! I am so glad you found things to gather here, and enjoyed yourself" (Whitehouse, *Scribner's Magazine, 62,* 740; letter of July 22, 1881).

In 1883, just before he lectured at the home of Mrs. Bishop (Mrs. La Touche's cousin and intimate friend), he suggested: "And perhaps I might see you at Brantwood again this year" (June 4, 1883: see Letters, XXVIII, sect. 3). Whereupon Mrs. La Touche decided that her husband should now accompany her to Coniston. "Darling Lacy," Ruskin had replied, *"PLEASE do* come both. It would be so lovely to think of you being over at the Waterhead, just beyond the calm water. I never heard of such a lovely plan, and I've *SO* much to ask you about birds and things" (June 30, 1883; see Letters, XXVIII, sect. 3). On July 17 the La Touches had consequently arrived to spend a week at the foot of the "calm water," after which Mr. La Touche returned to Harristown, leaving "Lacy" to spend the next week at Brantwood with Ruskin and Joan. ". . . indeed I should like to have you forgotten and left behind," Ruskin had agreed, "and I'll keep you carefully until you're telegraphed for. But I don't quite see why the Master should go back and look after *his* hay. It's selfish. *We've* hay here to look at, and hood umbrellas over the cocks of, if that would do any good" (July 6, 1883; Letters, XXVIII, sect. 3). Readily enough she had explained: "The 'Master' will forget me for a week, but he can't possibly forget his hay. Of course he's selfish, and the Lancashire is not the same to him as his own Irish hay. He wants to see it 'saved'; and to command the Salvation Army that does it. . . . ¶I don't care, and I like your hay best, because there are all sorts of geraniums in it" (Young, *Letters of a Noble Woman*, p. 89; letter of July 1883).

Reaching the Waterhead in time for tea (she told Miss Young), "we found a note of most cordial welcome from Brantwood, and they said they would come and see us at 3 to-day, but Mr. La Touche wants to see the Professor first in his own home. So we are going to walk over there, and I hope they will take us back in their boat" (ibid., p. 90; letter of July [18], 1883). After another two days: "We are having a heavenly time, and the 'Master' is more delighted with this place, and the joys of Brantwood, and the enthusiastic welcome they gave him, than he has been for a long time with anything." The "Professor" had in fact been "delightful" while giving Mr. La Touche "a reception worthy of the Prodigal Son" (ibid.; letter of July 20, 1883).

Her own week of enjoying those geraniums which were peculiar to the Lancashire hay had been so satisfying that, accompanied by Miss Young, Mrs. La Touche repeated the visit in 1884, when, one morning at breakfast with Ruskin in his study, she read aloud a letter he had just received from Francesca Alexander, which contained an account of the peasant Polissena. In the absoluteness of her trust in God's Knowledge and Love as from day to day He directed the course of her life before receiving her into Heaven, Polissena could appeal to Ruskin as yet another Rose. Concluding "The Peace of Polissena" chapter in her tales of *Christ's Folk in the Apennine,* Francesca would say "that our Lord spoke of certain people whom He would *make His abode with*—well, sometimes I think that perhaps she [Polissena] is one of those, and that He is always with her; she seems like it" (*Works, 32,* 265). "You don't know how strange it was that Rosie's mother read that letter," Ruskin replied. "I never told you that it was chiefly the mother that separated us, and I have been in such bitterness of soul against her as you in your goodness never could so much as conceive. Two [factually, three] years ago, she wrote Ivan [a misreading of Joan] asking if I would forgive her. But I *had* forgiven her, though she did not know it, on Christmas day of 1876 at Venice. And *she* is happy, though how I cannot conceive, in being here" (Swett, *Letters to Francesca,* pp. 77–78; letter of August 23, 1884). Mrs. La Touche had indeed been so happy that, accompanied by her grandchild Florence "Rose" Ward (the 19-year-old daughter of Rose's sister Emily), she returned in 1885, helping through her presence to precipitate the collapse by which, despite some further (albeit sporadic) activity, Ruskin finally was broken.

Now, however, he did not seem to suffer from the strain of being her host, and at the more superficial level of his being he doubtless received help from her knowledge of botany and the quality of her pleasure in flowers and herbage. "Darling Lacerta," he had immediately answered her letter of thanks, "It is very wonderful to me that I can do all that for you, being so dead myself and full of all sorts of fears and sadness, but the things I care for are good, and the sympathy we can give each other in caring for them is indeed good for us both. I am so glad that you were happy in that way in looking over Francesca's drawings" (letter of August 2, 1883; see Letters, XXXVIII, sect. 3). On the same day he was telling Kate Greenaway that he was not on the train in which he was supposed to have been traveling toward London: "[I] have been drawing Veronica on a fresh cut sod all morning. I find I can't and mustn't leave my mountain flowers just now—if I don't carry my Proserpina a bit forward this year, she'll never see the good light more and I've been so interrupted by inevitable visitors this last three weeks that everythings thrown out of gear" (unpublished letter of August 2, 1883; Pierpont Morgan Library).

Continuously overshadowed by the threat of a relapse into insanity (surely his worst fear), he could nevertheless feel heartened as he found himself able to enjoy his life throughout the summer and well into the autumn. Occasionally, of course, there were days when he was depressed and sometimes he had special reasons for alarm—succinctly indicated, for example, by the Diary entry made shortly before he set forth to resume his duties at Oxford: "Sadly fevered and overstrained [during] these last days [at Brantwood], but guarding myself carefully" (see entry for October 11). Yet from day to day he was no longer tormented by that "plague-cloud" presence of smoke; and he found pleasure in a wide range of relatively casual guests—the biblical scholar, Professor Gregory of Leipzig being followed, for example, by the Margaret Cox, daughter of a "Master Mariner," who, with two other Companions of St. George, helped him to celebrate his mother's Birthday (see entry for September 3, 1883).

Yet above all he depended on the writing through which he still could forget himself—sometimes to be unrealistically satisfied by the result. As he told Mrs. Alexander toward the beginning of July: "I cannot rest wholly—I get morbid and ill if I try to, and I am really well at present in carefully ordered work" (Swett, *Letters to Francesca,* p. 35; letter of July 14, 1883). Through such work, he told Miss Beever more specifically, he wanted to have his four *Art of England* lectures published with an epilogue and index, to prepare a report (long overdue) for St. George's Guild, and to produce "as soon as possible" new issues of *Love's Meinie, Proserpina, Deucalion,* and *Our Fathers Have Told Us* (see *Works, 37,* 461; letter of July 21, 1883). Already he was working "against time, with general vexation the result" (see entry for July 25). By the end of September: "I am almost giddy with the quantity of things I've in hand at present" (*Works, 37,* 467; letter to Kate Greenaway, September 25).

By mid-August he was making it his business to prepare the report for the Guild through which he would show how much money had been contributed, since 1881, by the Companions of St. George, and how, as The Master, he had spent it upon acquisitions for their Museum. The citizens of Sheffield had recently expressed, through their Mayor, their willingness to finance the construction of a building which would more adequately meet the present needs of St. George's Museum—a prospect which could precipitate him into assembling data related to the financial affairs of the Guild. In the Diary it would suffice to do little more than repeat "accounts," "accounts," "accounts" as a tangible record of how "I lost myself, day after day, among spitefully irreconcilable sums, and sorrowfully unintelligible scraps of memoranda" (*Works, 30,* 69). Before long, however, he could tell George Allen: "I'm sending Jowett [the printer] today a magnificent piece of St. George account work—" (unpublished letter of September 11, 1883; Columbia University Library). As a "Report" from The Master, this work would not be issued before January 1, 1885, but in its "main matter . . . [it] was ready for publication before Christmas of 1883" (*Works, 30,* 69).

Meanwhile, he was not neglecting other projects. A "new number" had been "finished" for *Proserpina* (see entry for August 8), what he called his "final papers on agates" had been planned for *Deucalion* (see entry for September 8), and before he left for Oxford, another letter for *Fors Clavigera* (on Scott: Letter 92, "Ashestiel," published in November) and *Valle Crucis* were well under way. With so much in hand, he abandoned his plan to launch, at Oxford, *The Pleasures of England* as a new series of lectures. They would be delivered during 1884. For the present he had decided merely to enlarge *The Art of England* series by discussing the work of those, especially Du Maurier, who contributed to *Punch,* and of the English artists, exclusive of Turner, who had established landscape painting as a genre. Working "against time," he could give these lectures without making any special effort. "The Fireside" lecture upon *Punch* had probably been planned for spring delivery, to be put aside so that he could substitute his "Fairy Land" lecture as a tribute to Kate Greenaway, and he could readily round out the series by discussing, with autobiographical overtones, old friends such as Copley Fielding and George Robson.

Returning to Brantwood satisfied by the success of his concluding lectures, he at once resumed his work on *Valle Crucis* and on the *Roadside Songs* (to be issued in April 1884, with a Preface dated January 1, 1884). Additionally, to support some local cause, he prepared a lecture on Sir Herbert Edwardes (see entries for December 5 and 22) and also greeted the Companions of St. George through the "Christmas" Letter 93 of *Fors*. During these weeks he himself was suffering from the pain caused by a rupture. But though this affliction was a worry and sometimes, physically, a "torment," it did not aggravate his "fear"; in the Diary, for example, he would note: "feeling very well but groin-pain worse than ever" (see entry for December 4). Making his last entry for the year: "Down . . . in fair health and good heart, D.G. with infirmities for which—there may be use if I will—" And as his first words for 1884: "Very thankful to be spared to see the light, and begin the labour, not unhopefully of this New Year."

Diary on return to Brantwood, January 4, 1883

[January 6th] Epiphany, 1883

It will be well I think to make my diary now always an index of the old ones, keeping regularly a page for each day[1]

Down to work in good health and power, though after a sleepless night nearly, partly nervous, partly too much on mind, returning here after a years absence all but 16 days,—the day before yesterday

January 7. Sunday Down to work in good health—among more treasures than I could use in fifty years. — Yesterday Ettie, Lollie, & Fred, came over from Mrs Slys and were happy I, fairly so—but for weather. Fog today, but whitish and breaking a little as it dawns

January 8. Monday. Up in good strength, and a clear frosty morning. Yesterday a white fog on lake, but clear above, and sunny quite calm, and hills beautiful, only smoke always now at horizon[2]

January 9 Tuesday. Slept well—though after extremely unsatisfactory day of idleness in sunshine, gnawed by wish to do—everything

Note that sun sets, when seen from the gate into upper field, behind the point A [on a line which is drawn to show the contour of the hills against the horizon] of the opposite fells, on the 8th of January and on the 9th it had got to B.

January 10 Wednesday Yesterday more or less fine, but

1. This entry, made on the left-hand page opposite Ruskin's entries for May 7–10, 1876, is followed by two notes which indicate how he planned to "index . . . the old ones": "1 of weather, note opposite 8th & 9th of May—with 11th and 12th / 2 of Health, pages 1 and 2, throughout!"

2. From the prosperous "Iron Works" (see Map A).

looking over old MSS of my lectures, I made myself completely wretched

A good night, with some vestige of rational reflection and resolution has put me nearly to rights.

I see by p. 9, l[eft] of Broadlands that Macdonalds[3] children are now,

Alexander	20
Nellie	18
Maggie	15

For preface to II Vol M P. Note on Man's use and purpose—quoting, end sentence of Advent sermon (from St Augustine[)]

Explain Plato—(Aristotle I meant [)] [4]

Close of section on Theoretic faculty, p. 346. The whole end and aim of my labour to shew that no supreme power of art can be attained by impious men, and that the neglect of art as an interpreter of divine things has been of evil consequence to the Xtian world [5]

January 11. Thursday. Made no entry—so busy framing Turners &c, but got into heart—and set to work on Loves Meinie again[6]—and had walk by quiet lake with new moon clear—in twilight.

January 12 Friday Good and quiet night—found Cun-

3. In the Broadlands Diary (Bembridge MS *xx*) he had noted: "[Alexander] Macdonald's children / Alex. 13 / Nellie 11 / Maggie 8," dating this record "1st Jan[uary, 18]76" (from information supplied by Mr. Dearden).

4. See sect. 7 in 1883 Preface to *Modern Painters, II* for Ruskin's comment (or "note") on his pronouncements in the first edition (1845) upon "Man's use and purpose" and for his translation of "that great sentence of Aristotle's" (*Works, 4,* 7) with which he had concluded his discussion of "Typical Beauty" as apprehended by the "Theoretic Faculty" (*Works, 4,* 145). In the 1883 Preface he did not, however, quote the sentence from St. Augustine.

5. For this sentence, as originally published, see *Works, 4,* 211 (the "p. 346" being a reference to the passage in the first edition of *Modern Painters, II*).

6. Whatever he wrote, henceforth, for *Love's Meinie* would remain unpublished. For passages left in MS, see *Works, 25,* 175–84.

ninghams "Diddle-dee" berry—in first reading. Q[uestion] excellent subject for Oxford! [7]

BIRDS, opposite, 4th[8]

January 14. Sunday Dark—every day, all day long.

Raining all yesterday — Put everything in lovely order for Joanies coming back—and this morning, have lost my pen!

Serves me right for forgetting to take Susie hers. Can't write with this thing—modern pen-stick

Yesterday Got most of the "Maid of Fesole" [9] corrected and sent off—for press, and 8th Chapter of Deucalion[10]

Now—what an odd coincidence it is— I look—*after* writing this—to opposite page—and find entry there on pen-distress! [11] —nine [sic] years ago.

Foolish enough—the dream entry opposite[12]— Is the storm on lake Down's alarm?

January 15. Monday

Rain all night—but slept well, after uncomfortable Sunday—(black fog and cold—I shivery and valueless)—helped by Italian medicine—

Thought over Francesca's tale and began a new Fors, I hope with the moral of it.[13]

7. In the Falkland Islands "the Upland geese are very partial" to the Diddle-dee berry (Robert C. Cunningham, *Notes on Natural History of the Strait of Magellan* [Edinburgh, 1871], p. 158).

8. See entry for June 4, 1876.

9. The title initially planned for Francesca Alexander's *The Story of Ida.*

10. Namely, Part VIII: "Revision" and "Bruma Artifex," which became chapters 2 and 3 of *Deucalion, II.*

11. See entry for June 8, 1876.

12. See entry for June 10, 1876.

13. At the beginning of the next *Fors*—Letter 90, "Lost Jewels," issued in May 1883—Ruskin repeats his fundamental thesis that "the wealth of a country *is in* its good men and women, and in nothing else" (*Works, 29,* 424), which is perhaps implicitly, though by no means obviously, the "moral" of Miss Alexander's account of the peasant Ida, "buried in the poor people's burying ground at Trespiano" (*Works, 32,* 36).

January 16 Tuesday Finished all I could of Cochin cock I had best begin notes for Meinie, this time, here. Note *colour* going out of Cockscomb—as it Dies—I mean, as the dead body dies,—so mackarel [quicker?] Dolphin, *in* dying Q[uestion]—all gone in dolphin as in sunset—, in death.

But cock's comb from scarlet to dead blue purple in three days.

Separation of Wing feather in vultures and crows— How far typical? in Austrian black eagle accidentally.

Oppose to sweet Domed nestling cover. Give partridge death from Ulric the Farmer[14]

January 17 Wednesday ⟨Yesterday at evening, came Aclands telegram, announcing reinstated professorship "Dear friend may all good attend you and your work in this new condition, once again welcome to Alma Mater.["]⟩[15]

January 18. Thursday. The Loves Meinie note, on the 16th, scrawled in pure haste—but I must take care of my old tricks—doing too much at once

Perfectly drenching rain all yesterday—and I sorted—into disorder again

See "using up the brush" [16]

14. None of the ideas recorded in this entry appeared in published form. In Jeremias Gotthelf's (Albert Bitzius) *Uli der Pachter* the body of a "partridge" is found after a terrible hail-storm: "It was a brood of quails; the mother had probably wanted to flee with her little ones into the nearby bushes. When she realized that it could not be done, she had gathered her young ones, who had followed her, once more under her gleaming wings and thus had died with them" (Paul Siegfried, ed., Collected *Works, 3* [1849], 283).

In *The Laws of Fésole* Ruskin had used the partridge to exemplify "a class of birds . . . in whom the function of the wing is essentially, not flight, but the protection of their young. ¶. . . there is nothing in arrangement of plumage approaching the exquisiteness of that in the vaulted roofs of their expanded *covering* wings" (*Works, 15,* 339).

15. Published in *Works, 33,* xiv.

16. Mrs. Severn's remark about the sunset described, on the opposite page (see entry for June 25, 1876).

January 19 Friday White mist—going to clear, probably.

See weather entry opposite [June 26, 1876] for possible light of new moon

Of Light—conf—sorts now known, Magnesium—Lime and electric.

Natural living phosphoric

——— dead ———

January 20 Saturday Very jaded after a dreamy night —in which I saw pretty things, moonlights and hills and had to send Collie to see a picture which I could'nt—&c. The business of Concert—and Joans cold for the last week, much disturbing me

January 21. Sunday Yesterday for once a lovely afternoon quiet and entirely clear Walked from the Thwaite to Waterhead, and by the cross road to Yewdale returned by Coward's and under the rocks of the Yewdale angle, to Kate's and had tea

Walked in clear moonlight to Waterhead, and saw Lollies drawings. Drove back with Joan

Today wet as usual

January 22 Monday. A frightful night of ugly nightmares —(not monstrous) but that I was getting bald, and that Miss Wakefield couldnt sing my music, &c. all of humiliation—caused, I know not why, unless by drinking Aleatico.[17] Now, mist—as dirty as nightmare over everything and I, 'blackened in heart'—open at the entry for August 14th—1879, p. 157!

January 23 Tuesday Steady fog all yesterday today sulphurous black cloud over the whole sky—glass standing at set fair all yesterday if anything, now a little advancing Must mark its degrees now. Today ——— 30 3

17. A sweet red muscat type of wine, known in England in Chaucer's time.

Bad dull toothache with much depression all yesterday fought with it till 12 last night then slept well till Annie came at ½ past six —and am much better this morning

January 24. Wednesday Drenching rain—on the hills snow—smoke-darkness above

Toothache better—passed into chin-ache, and beard ache, and stiffness of teeth with sense of their being all got into wrong places Yesterday in cold wind & dim sunshine to Hawkshead Saw Mr Hawkrigg[18] in bed—and the Billiard room at the Institution! came away much puzzled what to do or say. terrible sense of exhaustion in evening.

Glass gone back to 29. 9

Dreams. See opposite [entry for July 25, 1876, as italicized], ugly after pleasant day, and get parallel cases—pleasant after ugly Conf entry above—Jan. 22—but I have no account of Jan 21st, only I recollect thinking *it* had been rather pleasant, as I was considering the dreams

January 25 Thursday.

[Marginal note] Compare Jan. 25 1878 at page 50, and [Jan.] 26 page 52 Same feelings in myself.

Snow down to Trinu. set. Sal [19]— Bitterest squally west wind—wild and vicious—down

18. "There have been Hawkriggs at Hawkshead ever since I can remember," Mrs. Gnosspelius writes. "This would have been some villager who had been struck down by accident, ill-health, or other trouble and possibly called to Ruskin's attention by Dr. Parsons. One does not have to be reminded of how tender-hearted J.R. was in his encounters with such cases."

19. "*Trinucleus seticornis* (Salter) was the name in the 1880s for a fossil trilobite found in certain ridges of the Coniston Limestone close to Ash Gill Quarry [see Map B]. The fossil gave its name to the ridges which formed a useful landmark by which Ruskin measured the coming and going of the snow as he looked out of the Brantwood windows" (information provided by Miss Gnosspelius, who found the name "Trinu. set. Sal" used by W. G. Collingwood in notebooks which record the geological investigations he was making for Ruskin during 1881–82).

low out of the valleys, as usual Plague cloud drifting steadily above at its usual rate—quite independent of the wind below, and more southerly, crossing it at about this angle [diagram] Why does one never see squally motion in clouds?

Note of Kathleen, opposite [entry for July 30, 1876], criticising my drawing, she was then an entirely sweet and very interesting girl of 12: since utterly spoiled by 'society' Recollect her meditative speech as she turned her tea cup, worthy of her Grandfather. "The cup turns round, but the tea does not."

January 26 Friday Awake since three—with a gale such as I've not yet seen, or heard—forcing me for the first time since Ive been here, to put shutters up and draw curtains—to get a place without draught—and even so in vain—the wind flickering in at every chink—keeping my bedroom carpet in a dance—and scooping up the lake in twenty places at once in whirlwinds and flying columns of spray Glass a full semicircle back—risen 23 from 30, 3, but mostly yesterday, now at 28 4 ½ and the wind as cold as it is fierce. Snow deep, now and down half way from Trinu set Sal to the lake.

January 27 Saturday. Host of letters Black sky, steady snow

January 28 Sunday Steady rain washing away the snow —which fell two inches deep yesterday—all gone up to Trinu set Sal again Slept well,— and face better but very prickly and fidgetty —and more not worth writing

Glass up again to 29 6

January 29 Monday An extremely bad, nervous, restless night, with quick low pulse, much waking and much dreaming, but not painful dreams.

Mouth very painful at first, got better—but Im swollen and hard all over chin—and sore at roots of hair everywhere but chiefly beard

Pouring rain all night now grey cloud and wild wind but some chance of clearing

Glass gone back to 29.

Indoors all yesterday as the two days before, and much over-thoughted—but got rest with natural history.

Took Seidletz powder this morning before coming down and must try to finish M[odern] P[ainters] preface, which has much worried me

January 30 Tuesday. Black—universal drift and drizzle of wretched small hail—half thaw half lying in mess. it was clear moonlight at 3—but always the devils work begins in the morning Vile plague wind with it from the south. Glass—not looked at. Dark with four candles now—after being full daylight ten minutes ago—the fitful passion of it all so mean and beastly.[20]

Sent for Dr P[arsons], yesterday afternoon —had tooth out and gum lanced and am much better sleeping till 3, waking then quite lively—but now, tired—chiefly however by this demon-blackness— I've never seen it more closely spread, but it *can't* last

Gone into snow, now!

January 31 Wednesday At last—a cloudless sky and calm lake—after violet and rose dawn. Having found out, for the first time in the night, the power of the mind in commanding sleep! and, this morning (with the vase of first primroses on the table by the globe) getting one of the strange floods of sudden teaching by

20. In the index at the end of the MS this paragraph is particularized under "wind," with the comment: "Plague—very important."

opening at p 47 [November 2, 1877] on the reference to Titus [ii], following that up—and now to complete it—I open at p 46! for the contrary warning.[21] Then fullness of help in the comparing of Titus and Timothy, bearing mainly on my M[odern] P[ainters] preface quite marvellous.

— (That study being chiefly on the word διαβολος without even looking at the opposite
A
page!)[22] Comment written Feb 1st, 1883.

And that I should'nt have written a word of it!

Our poor Lucy Tovey died on the evening of this day.[23]

February 1 Thursday This seems to me a better notation than any, yet,—but I shall change that next month, I suppose.[24]

Frost with fog, but getting brighter, as my

21. The "p 46" reference is to the entry for November 1, 1877 (actually, on page 47 of the MS), which would have directed him to I Timothy 4:12–14. Titus 2 begins with the *positive* behest: "But speak thou the things which become sound doctrine," and concludes: "These things speak, and exhort, and rebuke with all authority." *Negatively,* Timothy is warned: "Neglect not the gift that is in thee" (I Tim. 4:14).

22. I Timothy 4 begins with a reference to those who, "in the latter times . . . [will give] heed to seducing spirits, and doctrines of devils." Then "the Devil" is called "the adversary" (I Tim. 5:14). On the page opposite the present entry the words "in having proof of an Adversary" are conspicuous, having been written in the margin (see entry for August 4, 1877). Although his "study" of "the word διαβολος" is not reflected in the 1883 Preface, what is meant by "the Devil" is discussed in "Revision" as an essay which effectually complements the Preface of 1883 (see *Works, 26,* 345–46).

In the present entry the capital *A* above the word "page" probably signals the capital *A* in "Adversary," as written in the margin on the opposite page.

23. As though added at a later date, the record of the death of Lucy Tovey (see B.S.) appears in the upper margin, in ink darker than that used for the body of the January 31 entry.

24. The year is now noted in the upper margin instead of on the first line, with the date of the month placed in the margin at the left rather than at the right—a practice followed until the entry for March 1.

own mind also, though much foggier than yesterday: but with steady gain

How strange that the entry about good spirits, yesterday is set opposite that of evil spirits,[25] the most definite in my diaries, and quite forgotten in the after sickness but of strange and helpful significance *now.*

I begin today the first notes for new Oxford lectures, in my old book of Myths! [26] all seeming ordained and pointed out—for I only wanted a blank one, and found *this* put beside my two old ones; and its entries ending with Daedalus and Deucalion[27]

[February 2] Friday, Candlemas. (Black Sky raining steadily into universal snow.)

How often have I resolved to try for nobler life on this day, and always fallen back to the wretched one (conf. opposite, just now underlined)[28]

And now—how am I even forgetting the lessons of my three illnesses, of contention between good and evil! I will try to fasten some, here—after noting for todays gift, the recurrence of the text to me as proper head of all to be taught or learned by me. "If ye live after the flesh ye shall die, but if, &c. [ye through the Spirit do mortify the deeds of the body, ye shall live.]" [29]

Well—the first thing to be noted of those

25. See entry for August 4, 1877.

26. "The Book of Myths," Mr. Dearden explains, "is now Bembridge MS 45. It is a large foolscap, suede-bound volume containing on pp. 1–76 notes on Greek Mythology; then on p. 77: 'Notes for resumed Oxford Lectures [*The Art of England*]. Begun Feb. 1st 1883.' These extend for six pages, and then on p. 83 are some notes on Daniel. The remainder of the volume is empty."

27. Deucalion, Ruskin states, was central to "the myths of the betrayal and redemption" (*Works, 26,* 98, 335; from *Deucalion*); Daedalus was the "great type of the practically executive craftsman, and the inventor of expedients in craftsmanship" (*Works, 20,* 351; from *Aratra Pentelici*).

28. See words italicized in entry for August 11, 1877.

29. Rom. 8:13.

three illnesses, that in the first there was the great definite Vision of the contention with the Devil, and all the terror and horror of Hell—& physical death. In the second, there was quite narrowed demoniacal vision, in my room, with the terrible fire-dream in the streets of London; in the third, the vision was mostly very sad & personal, all connected with my Father. Enough, for 'to day'

February 3. Saturday. Black Cloud—heavy south wind—fitful rain

Going on from last page—observe that the sad part of the third vision, and the terrible, was all in its beginning and crisis, but, as soon as I began to get better, I had the delightful notion that Ruth[30] had been Rosie's nurse, and that she had hidden Rosie away and was going to bring her back to me, and I was expecting Rose every evening to come to tea—and watched the different doors of the nursery—and then when Ruth or Martha[31] came in, instead—bore it as best I could, waiting always for tomorrow.

In the second vision, here, the first part of it was my setting out to walk to her grave—the second part, her coming with her mother, and the interruption by the owl's cry.[32]

Recollect the Madeleine part.

(The Madeleine part was, in the 1880 [sic]

30. Ruth Mercier (see B.S.).

31. Presumably the housemaid, Martha Ray, whose name appears, with those of Baxter and Herdson, on Ruskin's listing of expenses for 1884 (F. J. Sharp Collection).

32. In the index to this volume he enters "Owl," with a reference to his entry of "March 8th 1880" and the comment: "most notable, corresponding with the darker dream in the beginning of illness of [18]81." To him the owl's cry signified impending evil. In *Praeterita,* for instance, he speaks of the "owl's cry" while he was at Crossmount (*Works, 35,* 428), connoting that he had then become engaged to E. C. Gray.

illness, I suppose, the period of highest exaltation, showing the exact connection of pride with insanity— I thought I had a kind of crucifixion to go through—and to found a farther phase of Christianity and that Rose was as the Magdalen to me This part of the dream, I think, began [—] but all beginnings and each are confused [—], with the hearing the seven guns fired in heaven, as the end of this dispensation—a curious and ludicrous confusion of them in my mind with the notion of guns heard from Windsor.) 6th Feb[ruary 18]83

February 4 Sunday ¼ past eight. Full daylight and noble brown sunshine on Yewdale Crag. Pretty. Robin and Chaffinches at dining room window

Almond blossom of Florence on my study window.

I wonder how much good I can get done today. I've always hitherto counted what I could'nt do.

Slept curiously well last night, after drive round lake in constant rain, and call on Susie.

February 5 Monday I've only three days more to be '63' in! What a youthful period I shall think it—if I live to be 73.

Yesterday the bright morning changed to drizzling steady rain mist—which ran off my hat on the moors as if it had been a gargoyle.

Slept without once waking from 11 to 6, a wonderful night for me, and I think with little dreaming, except about more or less pleasant travelling.

The notion of guns, in the first dream—was quite constant, through great part of the dream—(1878) I was shot, myself, twenty times over, and was attendant on a desperate artillery man who fired batteries of ball and grape into opera-houses and shot whole audiences dead at a discharge. I have greatly forgotten the long and complex tortures of this fancy (Ash Wednesday, 1883) but observe generally that all the grand and melancholy mountain visions, and the idea of a Kingdom possible to me, and lost, beyond the great imaginary mountains from which I was at last restored in mercy to "my own Coniston" in humiliation and thankfulness, belonged to the first dream: the much meaner visions of dragons and spectres in the room with me —made out of the folds of curtains or bedclothes or what not, to the second; which had also the dreadful part of suspecting Joanie and then of her dying, just before my own fancied death—very awful—and to be remembered in perpetual wonder and fear. (30th March, [18]83)

February 6 Tuesday A very bad night, lying patiently awake from ¼ to two till past 4, and then dreaming of rail stations and 'works' on the way to Chamouni Did some useful planning though for Oxford Wrote 16 useful letters yesterday.

Actually some blue sky—*after* a smoke cloud morning

February 7 Ash Wednesday All black—and has been raining, but Ive had a good night, after wet woodcutting and finding my favourite anemone place under charcoal burners scarred circle,—and getting into general despair of the place. Must do a chapter of Love's Meinie to get back some spring of heart

February 8 Thursday Grey fog and rain—partially breaking over the Bracelet Yesterday a singularly good day. At breakfast, read beginning of 3rd Vol[ume] M[odern] P[ainters] with great pleasure, and planned poetry lecture, No 2, for Oxford.[33] Then got the class Alca[34] arranged for Love's Meinie, and in doing so, found all my young poetry behind Buffon. Next—got letter from Mrs Alexander,[35] about my Christmas sermon in Fors. Next—letter from 'Alice in Wonderland' [36]—showing me that I must publish my young poems! [37]—lastly—walk to Peel Island in calm sunshine, and have happy quiet hour on the rocks opposite it— next—present of Milton and Elder wine from the Thwaite—and edition of Scott, come for Hawkshead, looked over in evening. Got study in perfect order, and so to bed and slept quite soundly, D.G. Conf. 8th Feb[ruary] 1878 p. 60

February 9th Friday A clear frosty dawn, now as the sun is near rising covered up, and opened again, with cloud rising from the lake, dull grey—off and on at intervals of two or three minutes! A bad night after a weary day of pitch black rain, and 43 letters, 37 in morning—6 in evening, to meditate on,—many very charming,

33. Lecture II, "Mythic Schools of Painting: E. Burne-Jones and G. F. Watts," to be delivered on May 12.

34. A species in the Family of Alcidae, the Auks.

35. Mrs. Lucia G. S. Alexander (d. 1916, aged 102), widow of the American portrait painter Francis Alexander (d. 1880), and mother of Francesca (1837–1917), of whose life and work he would give an account in the first of his lectures on *The Art of England* (March 1883; *Works, 33,* 282–84). For letters interchanged by the Alexanders, Mrs. Severn, and Ruskin, see Letters, I.

36. Daughter of Dean H. G. Liddell, "Alice" (Mrs. Reginald Hargreaves, d. 1934, aged 82) had become famous, as of "Wonderland," by 1865. Ruskin had known her father since 1836, the Dean having then been a tutor—he himself a Gentleman-Commoner—at Christ Church.

37. Soon, however, he would be telling Henry Swan: "Of my poems, I never allow a copy to get out—that I can burn—their extreme folly and stupidity is beyond all words—they are nothing but nonsense rhyme" (unpublished letter of May 18, 1883).

but nearly all needing thought and several unreadably written. Mrs and Miss Alexanders the great joy of the day, and Miss Emily B [38] the chief worry, with good Mr Faunthorpes[39] optimistic answer to Miss Irvine.[40]

February 10 Saturday Rain—but soft, and with whitish cloud—some faint sunlight through it, but the plague cloud scudding under it from the south at twice its usual pace

Yesterday the bitterest cold wind on the lake, after calm, rising in five minutes, with black cloud of the worst plague, from the south and driving me into Mr Mellys harbour.

Some drivelly cold in head these two or three days—and knees stiff! Slept well however, till 3, and from ½ past four on, last night.

February 11 Sunday Sound sleep, after good writing day's work but evening wasted in chess and on Punch, only I won't force myself to work, now—waste time or not. Better waste it well than sick

Some dim blue sky with scudding cloud, but getting darker, and I am utterly horror-struck and hopeless about the weather. The Plague wind now *constant* and the sun virtually extinguished

Things do seem getting better today though, as the day breaks.

February 12 Monday Sound sleep, after a perfectly quiet day, indoors except at sunset,—too cold with western squalls: but sunshine through hail and pretty rainbow almost on the lawn.

38. Probably Emily Brooking (see B.S.), who was about to resign as a member of St. George's Guild.

39. The Reverend John P. Faunthorpe (see B.S.).

40. Edith Irvine of Tunbridge Wells was a Companion of St. George whose periodic contribution of £1.0.0 was faithfully reported in Guild accounts, she having also been a contributor to the Gift of the *Splügen Pass*.

Saw the sun go down for the first time since Jan. 9 having missed, as every year we do, all the sunsets which would be so pretty in the hollow of the valley towards Torver: it is now half way up the hill on the right of it, and in a week, will begin to climb Dow crag. May I make the most of the lengthening strides.

Today, south wind, heavy gray scud over all the sky and steady rain.

See weather opposite[41] and my folly in not more using it.

February 13 Tuesday Drifting snow cloud, after pouring rain nearly all yesterday. Did not get out, but much good work indoors

The most interesting opposite page leads me back to Broadlands book.[42] See notes p. 36, l[eft], of Library Catalogue[43]

Note also, this page [of Broadlands Book] begins the Ave translation, from R[ose']s psalter.

> Hail, thou that art from
> everlasting to everlasting
> King of all creatures and
> Judge of all Laws.[44]

February 14 Wednesday. St Valentine's

Yesterday a good day generally with much

41. Entries for September 17–19, 1877: clear, calm days with "perfect" sun.

42. See entry for September 24, 1877, with its account of how he opened, by "chance," to the entry for October 22, 1875, in the "Broadlands Book."

43. Probably a reference to what is now Bembridge MS *xiii,* in which, however (Mr. Dearden states), pages 36–62 are missing.

44. "The beginning of the Ave translation faces page 51 of the Broadlands book, opposite the entry for 22 October, 1875," Mr. Dearden explains. "The translation was made from an illuminated MS which Ruskin gave to Rose. It is PSALTERIUM DAVIDIS ET HORAE, French, *c.* 1300. This MS, now in the library of Major J. R. Abbey, is inscribed, 'Posie with St. C.'s love, 3 January 1862.' After Rose's death it must have been returned to Brantwood because, in July, 1875, Ruskin was making an extensive textual analysis of it in his *Diary.*"

good done, yet I discouraged and irresolute—

St Valentine's has usually been a good help to me I am very thankful to find myself writing, by candlelight, and seeing my blue lines, without spectacles

February 15 Thursday An entirely good night not waking till 6, though scarcely out at all, yesterday —mostly at mineralogy for Connie,[45] with Ethel playing La fille du Reg[imen]t at tea. Finding my classical music dictionary a great help to me. Today, really bright light above, though plague cloud on the Old Man.

February 16 Friday Fair—and some gleam of sunshine —lakc calm.

Birds singing—and I have had a singularly peaceful night after visit to poor dear Mr Hawkrigg. What a close of life—to a man so good, active—and capable

The opposite page[46] a terrific one of warning and memory Joanies illness on 5th [October 1877]—only the prelude to her real suffering—but she knew though she told me later what real danger she was in

The crisis 8th October [18]77, on next leaf.

J. Campbell.[47] Letter containing terrible accusation against Cambridge men, and queries about use of spirit-media.

February 17 Saturday Nearly pitch dark again and rain as usual.

Some watery sunshine yesterday and everybody said, 'What a lovely day'

I see on 5th September 1877, I went up the

45. A reference to the gift of minerals to be presented (with a printed catalogue dated 1883; see *Works, 26,* 491–513) to St. David's School, Reigate.

46. Entries from September 28 through October 5, 1877.

47. Unidentified.

Old man in afternoon, and came down and across here to harbour in two minutes under the hour and a half—page 34. — today, I feel stiff in the knees and a little numb in left foot —(old sign)[48] and have lost sadly in the five and a half years

February 18 Sunday. Rain all yesterday clearing sullenly now.

Began first Oxford lecture in the morning, yesterday. Rossetti and Hunt [49]—not ill, but after Hackstoun's[50] coming in afternoon, got discouraged and all wrong. Played chess, and found the lovely Miss Alice in Punch, who will be a text for Leech's part in the lecture.[51]

Slept fairly well, but curious nightmare of losing my fathers travelling bills in my confused desk. woke with pulse quick and all out of order.

By the way, had been reading my wretched, short, disorderly diaries of 1870 to 72.

That's a terrific entry, opp[osit]e for the 13th [October 1877].

Some pretty pale sky now over Yewdale Crag.

February 19th Monday Quite clear frost, much snow on

48. At Lucerne, in 1861, Ruskin had been hurt by some remark in a letter from Mrs. La Touche, whereupon his "left foot up to the ancle [had become] quite white and numb for half a day after: without however taking away any power of action [from] it" (unpublished letter to John James Ruskin, August 24, 1862; Yale University Library).

49. Lecture I, "Realistic Schools of Painting: D. G. Rossetti and W. Holman Hunt," to be delivered on March 9.

50. William Hackstoun (1855–1921) of Glasgow, who was soon to leave for France to make drawings for the series of architectural sketches to be placed in the Sheffield Museum. In 1881 Ruskin had obtained permission from the trustees of the Guild to pay Hackstoun an annual stipend of £120 for work to be done under his direction.

51. See Lecture V, "The Fireside: John Leech and John Tenniel," to be delivered November 7, 1883. "The most beautiful sketch by Leech throughout his career, and, on the whole, in all *Punch,* I take to be Miss Alice on her father's horse" (*Works, 33,* 360; "Miss Alice," as Cook and Wedderburn note, is a slip for "Miss Ellen" in *Gone Away!*).

the higher hills down to Leathes Water[52] level and nearly cloudless sun, though the rose-red was exactly stopped by cloud at sunrise! —so wonderful—one day in fifty capable of it—and on that day, cloud in the east for that quarter of an hour!

Slept well—but dreamed *again* about money difficulty waking at ½ past 3, but sleeping again

All yesterday was more or less beautiful and I had a divine quiet walk in absolute calm of morning on the opposite shore, in the field with the edge of rocks.

February 20 Tuesday Pitch-dark,—south wind and rain; but a really lovely forenoon, yesterday, calm, clear, mild—and glowing warm with sunshine! —everything looking lovely. Rowed Ethel over to the rocky field, where it was absolutely still and heavenly, and the Old man looking his grandest over the group of wild larches—and not a house in sight, except Brantwood at its prettiest In the afternoon up the moor with Mr Jones and have good hope of leasing the pet rocks at last.[53]

That was a bold reading 'as to myself'—on the opp[osite] page! [54] —leading on into —phrenzy—yet how much nobler than most of my sanity. Found, following out opposite

52. The other name for Thirlmere. It was "in use in the 18th century but was obsolescent when J. R. was writing, by which time the name, *Thirlmere,* was in use on Ordnance Survey Maps," Miss Gnosspelius notes.

53. The "pet rocks," Mrs. Gnosspeluis remarks, were probably on the land of Major Harrison, with Mr. F. M. T. Jones of Ambleside acting as Major Harrison's agent. If so, they signify the piece of property which Ruskin would call "Naboth's Vineyard" because he had for so long desired it enviously. (Mr. Jones' name and address appear in the front of the Diary; he is also mentioned as Major Harrison's agent in letters from Miss Rigbye to Mr. Goodison, in the F. J. Sharp Collection.)

54. Entry for October 23, 1877: his reading the 1st verse of II Apocalypse "as spoken to myself."

entry under 25th [October 1877] exactly what I needed for my Fors work today, planned before I rose! [55]

February 21 Wednesday Rain yesterday and again to-day. Jamie & Emilie[56] came and we had a nice afternoon; but I did'nt get any fresh air—and woke at four—thinking however usefully of minerals—lectures, & the new Fors.

See the terrible bit for Fors, opposite.[57]

February 22 Thursday ⟨Y[esterday] a fearfully dark mist all afternoon, with steady south plague wind of the bitterest, nastiest, poisonous blight, and fretful flutter— I could scarcely stay in the wood for the horror of it.

Today, really rather bright blue, and bright white semi-cumuli, with the frantic Old Man blowing sheaves of lancets and chisels across lake,—not in strength enough or whirl enough, to raise it in spray, but tracing every squalls outline in black on the silver grey waves, and whistling meanly, and as if on a flute made of a file.⟩[58]

February 23 Friday Slept well, after tea with Ettie and Lollie at Low Ground [59]—hearing of Water Ouzel.

55. His discovery of the "correspondence of *attribute with MESSAGE,*" as noted in the entry for October 25, 1877, seems to have no bearing on the content of any issue of *Fors Clavigera* subsequently published.

56. The recently married Mr. and Mrs. J. R. Anderson.

57. Presumably the entry for October 29, 1877, which is marked by double lines drawn in the right-hand margin opposite the passage about how, in his dream, men used for fuel "flesh and bones, *hands of children, especially.*" Issued in May, the next *Fors* would be Letter 90, "Lost Jewels," in which the destruction of children by their parents, through selfishness, folly, or neglect, is made the central theme. In the essay, however, Ruskin's treatment of this theme is quite untouched by the primitive intensities of feeling manifested by the dream.

58. Published in *Works, 34,* 38. In the index to this volume Ruskin calls these sentences on the Plague Wind "the finest piece of description."

59. Ruskin's abbreviation for Low Bank Ground, the present home of Ethel Hilliard.

Doing a lot of good work too—and on the whole wonderfully well

February 24 Saturday Yesterday rather nice, very lovely part of afternoon—sun on the opposite shore, careering high over the little crag which he set behind on the 9th January. — But never cloudless to the hill edge. — I can't even guess where he goes down.

Slept well, and up in fair spirit—having finished the Fors on 'sorts of girls' yesterday.[60]

Planned ideal mineral collection for schools this morning

100. Quartz, with Gold.
100 Felspar and Mica
100 Calcite and Fluor.
100 Metals.
100. Gems.

The quartz includes agate and opal; the Felspar and mica must include the Epidotes & schorls, and the Calcite,—some few of the mixed things zeolite and the like, with one or two of Barytes.

February 25 Sunday Entirely cloudless, with warm sweet quiet light, which came full glow at sunrise, and made me—to my great wonder, deeply melancholy, with the strange sense of the dream of return of departed youth and a departed world

Compare entry p. 61, 11th Feb. [18]78

February 26 Monday Soft flaky raincloud moving slowly —showing hills through rents in the old way —showing me how totally prevalent the plague cloud, sooty and furious, has been— for this is quite wonderful and lovely to me. Fast now—alas changing into the other.

Yesterday quite lovely all day! though with

60. Namely, Letter 90, "Lost Jewels."

irregular gusts of cold wind, settling at last west— Rowed to Peel island and back under shore—saw first springing hyacinths And was—pensively happy but in evening, tired and sad,—none the better it seems now! Yet slept well—and dreamed of a pretty blue eyed girl vowing eternal fidelity to me at parting—which so moved me that I came away without my hat!

February 27 Tuesday Black dry plague cloud of chimney smoke flying hellishly over the whole sky. — Yesterday the afternoon one bitter chill of grey plague.

Slept well—though after weary & discouraged evening, and mean to have a grand letter-clearance being in no humour for better work

Note the leaving my long table, opposite, 26th Jan[uary 18]78

February 28 Wednesday White wet mist, but bright. Sound sleep, and generally good health this morning—but little in my head.

Yesterday indoors all day and wrote heaps of letters, getting things off mind

March 1 Thursday. My old way is the best after all for dating I shall have fixed my system, by the time I can date no more

Yesterday a quite lovely day of balm and sunshine, all lost to me by Mr Rydings coming! and a thoroughly bad night—by my own thoughts. Got to sleep at ½ past twelve, and a sweet deep red sunrise revived me but I am still sad, and discouraged.

March 2 Friday. Yesterday up the Old Man once more —stiff and slow but not tired, and slept from ½ past 10 to 6. D.G.

March 3 Saturday. Yesterday entirely cloudless, after misty morning. Called on Susie—crossed the quarry-field to Waterhead, walked over to

Tilberthwaite then by rocky streamlet bed up Yewdale Crag, and returned over its tops in dazzling sun fixing a view of Coniston water from beyond White Ghyll, as the best we have, and one of the loveliest scenes in the world Dazzling sun, literally, my eyes feeling it more than of old, my limbs heavier—yet I felt more myself than for many a day, and was not tired The Entries on the two following leaves 56, 57 [31 January, 1 February, 1878],—are very solemn warnings not to over-rate appearances of strength— Only 21. days then before my mind totally failed 21st February, p. 71.

March 4 Joanies birthday. Sunday.

Yesterday entirely clear and calm from sunrise to set, today perfectly cloudless also. And I—amazedly, sadder and heavier than for many a day the beauty of all things making my own age and decay more manifest to me.

A stomach sadness and dimness of eyes, or rather swimming and faltering of them plaguing me also—and this after long walks and rest.

And discontent and failure of hope in heart.

And heard owls cry last night though faint and low.

March 5 Monday. Cloudless, yesterday all day long. Cloudless today—and I, more than ever melancholy! though in fair enough humour for work this morning.

Yesterday in afternoon went to see poor sweet Mr Hawkrigg

Very sound sleep, except for an hour between 4 and 5.

March 6 Tuesday. A quite frightful fit of despondency and dread came on me, yesterday the result of three days lovely weather! It is today bleak and broken and I am better. Sleeping well through all, except yesterday a bad nightmare of running away from people through heath and marshes, and my head and eyes have troubled me, more in the clear sweet light than in darkness and candlelight Opposite, Feb 5, [18]78, much the same thing! and see farther on, Sunday the 10th.

March 7 Wednesday. Bright, though with cold wind and after good sleep, I am fairly up to work. Sleep really sound and dreamless but I'm a little anxious about eyes again, a sort of trembling and missing in them—partly, I believe, from having too much thought and writing to do, and not enough keeping the eyes to their own simple business Using spectacles too much also, perhaps, by candlelight Room in excellent order, lecture well enough forward, but drawers, many, yet in bad mess.

March 8 Thursday. Sun bright on snow down to lake —and more coming in wild black squalls, with sun between—and I've to fight my way to Oxford somehow, with poor Baxter ill. We must do our best both,—this time, anyhow. — I very well, D.G.

Gave 1st lecture of the new Professorship, on

9 March. —
and repeated it on the 10 Went up to London on

11 Monday, and pretty nearly wasted all my time till the 24th, Saturday. Diary resumed over page—on 25th.

2145. March 25 Easterday.

Back yesterday from London. The 2145. being the days counted hence till Im 70 For interval from March 8 to this, see page 120 back to 118 of foreign diary for last year[61]

2144. March 26 Easter Monday

Bright sun on snow, and lambs in field

I down in fair health and strength. Five years since that first phrenzy fit—but note that at page 65 [February 17, 1878] where the record of the bell ringing is, I seem all right again.

2143 March 27 Easter Tuesday

Gloriously bright—but frost! I—fairly well, but altogether despondent and moody: not without fear of faster failing in strength than I know My wrist feeling weak in rowing and chopping. Q[uestion] rheumatic?

Slept well and had more or less pleasant and curious dreams—of wanting stall at theatre—only one left in the middle,—taking out a lot of silver to pay, and finding half of it pretty old coins, which some Eton boys behind me helped me to decipher, or rather, deciphered when I could'nt.

2142 March 28 Wednesday. Intensely clear after rose-purple dawn. — I fairly well—yet sad and listless —and feeling as if I walked in dream, that sense of darkness in light too which I used to have at Oxford (Abingdon)[62] All stomach, I fancy, the continued cold affecting the vital power. Certainly I'm neither overworked nor over excited! now! I chopped wood—or merely sorted bills for Sheffield, all day, yesterday.

61. While in London, Ruskin had calculated: "Supposing I could work till I was 70—five years and 327 days left...2152 days" (*Diaries,* p. 1048; March 18; see also July 28, 1879).

62. Probably in 1871, when, enjoying the walk or drive to and from Oxford, he had spent part of the spring at the Crown and Thistle Inn of Abingdon. For him this was a period of grief and special strain (marked by the death of Nurse Anne, the ebbing strength of his mother, and the agonizing stress in his relationship with Rose La Touche), during the course of which he first had publicly proclaimed his awareness of the plague cloud (see *Works,* 27, 132–33).

The opposite entry [February 17, 1878] is of what was a very wonderful day to me

2141 March 29 Thursday Gray—though not gloomy—small close hail over all places, white on the beach, and pale on the already too pale grass, lambs and mothers standing disconsolate in middle of field, as I never before saw them

I fairly well—trying to dance the 'Perfect cure' [63] as I was dressing—but poor Baxter really quite ill, yesterday and I'm anxious about him.

2140 March 30 Friday Black rain, yesterday and today and I very good for nothing Vexed just now in looking back, to see how scrawled this years diary is, in many places

2139 March 31 Saturday. More or less bright with broken plague-cloud—some bits of real summer, yesterday after the rain Slept well—but am much depressed and nervous about new symptoms of nervousness. These bodily ailments go on and off however, seemingly without cause,—but resolved to try a little Arabian fasting—confirmed by the various accounts in Esther[64]— To think of the poor Sheik, blessed in sip of dirty water, and I—perhaps the reverse in my amplitude of sherry & port

2138 April 1 Sunday. Slept extremely well, taking no wine after dinner, but was very languid in evening Found, this morning, old Willoughbys[65] pres-

63. See J. H. Stead, B.S.

64. See especially chapter 14 of the Book of Esther (in the Apocrypha), with its account of the fasting and prayer of Queen Esther as, "in fear of death," she "humbled her body greatly" (v. 1–2). The "Arabian fasting" probably connotes the "Barmecide" feast of Shacabac (in the *Arabian Nights*), "wherein the courses are indeed well ordered, but the dishes empty" (*Works, 12,* 388).

65. Sir Willoughby Jones (1820–84)—"only lately, to my sorrow, dead," Ruskin would remark, in *Praeterita,* as he named the friends whom he had met as "fellow-scholars" at the school of Mr. Dale (*Works, 35,* 82–83).

ent of Epictetus, and read some with advantage[66]

Great fog—but not gloomy yesterday in afternoon—sweet clear sunset. I walked on the garden terrace, with many thoughts of the first illness. It is always lovely and awful to me, to watch the sunset there.

2137 April 2 Monday. Bright, though misty and a little frosty. I lost all the loveliness of a quite perfect sunset yesterday, in evil thoughts and am depressed today, but now depressed always. Yet took no wine after dinner, and slept well, and hope there's really nothing the matter with me, except that this Oxford work is'nt so much restful or comforting as my birds or stones—which however, will come, I hope in due time.

2136 April 3 Much dreaming last night—but not painful —though perhaps produced by vexation about Baxter and his family.

Thought out Oxford school system to some poor conclusion as I dressed—and got my Severus period of Rome[67] settled at coffee.

2135 April 4 Bright and calm, and I fairly well—and full of all sorts of useful notions for Oxford—but joyless; and vainly trying to bring myself to a right sense of my position and power—and duty.

Every day, anyhow, *some*thing now is usefully done, D.G.

2134 April 5 Wet, but warm and calm. Birds singing.

Yesterday a very bad day generally but I

66. For Ruskin, Epictetus was preeminently the slave "poor and sick in body, and beloved by the Gods" (*Works, 6,* 22; from *Modern Painters, IV*).

67. The years 193–235 A.D., during which the dynasty founded by Lucius Septimus Severus (reigned 193–211) controlled the destiny of Rome. Ideas relevant to *Valle Crucis,* which he intended to publish in 1884, were evidently now in germination.

got globe sketched [68] and Susie called on, and had nice letters—and did some grim business, and 'saw'—Herdson and Martha! [69]

Now see p 78 [70]

In the opposite entry, which with that below is all on the night [February 22, 1878] preceding my first great illness, the words of my Venetian gondolier were a subsequent interpolation: all the rest is left as written

2132 April 7 I missed yesterday, going out for early morning walk—quite lovely but I felt idle and melancholy

Began 4th lecture on Fairyland [71] and got some good business done Today still fine but misty. Yesterday was lovely all day

See opp[osite] 17th Jan[uary 1879] of sunset.

2131 April 8 A quite wonderfully long night's sleep and no dreams, but I felt sadly heavy and breathless yesterday in climbing High Cross. Not *tired* for I got to Dr Parsons' without the slightest sense of fatigue, but so inelastic and slow on the hill [72] Quite clear again today after red

68. Ruskin's design for the revolving, or "celestial," globe to be constructed by W. G. Collingwood and placed in the Coniston schoolyard so that the children who climbed into it would "see a blue sky pierced for the greater and the lesser lights, and painted with the constellation figures" (Collingwood, *Ruskin Relics,* p. 10; see also *Works, 32,* 286).

69. Martha Ray.

70. In MS the April 5 entry appears on the left-hand page 74; the next entry is made on left-hand page 78. The blankness of left-hand page 75 helps to dramatize the blankness of the "opposite" page except for its heading: "February,—to April [1878]—the Dream." Left-hand pages 76 and 77 had already been partially filled by miscellaneous data, such as addresses and money "In hand" for St. George's Guild.

71. Lecture IV of *The Art of England,* "Fairy Land: Mrs. Allingham and Kate Greenaway," to be delivered on May 26 and 30.

72. "The walk from Brantwood to Dr. Parsons in Hawkshead by High Cross and back would be about 7¼ miles with a total elevation climbed of some 860 feet," Miss Gnosspelius comments.

sunset—but with much smoky mist, so that I thought it would rain, and today though clear of cloud, the frost mist very heavy.

2130 April 9 Monday. A really perfect morning after a week of fine weather! Up on the moors and on into Grisedale, yesterday must really go out this morning

2129 April 10 Tuesday Out nearly all day, yesterday crossing moorland into Grisedale. Not a bit tired, there and back—but no spring in walking, and much shortness of breath.[73] Still—*that* might be dealt with by sound training if I had time! On the whole down to work today in good heart,—and expecting Joanie— D.G. for all

2128 April 11 Wednesday. Brought Joanie home, with Miss Greenaway[74]—yesterday from Ulverston, they arriving happily by ½ past 4 train, and reaching the foot of lake in quiet, though too grey sunset. Today calm, but cloudy and somewhat threatening

2127 April 12 Thursday Yesterday quite fine—after chilly morning,— rowed Joan and Miss Greenaway to call on Susie—rowed in waiting to Waterhead, and thought of old times.

New moon setting among many stars when I went to bed.

2126 April 13 Friday Yesterday entirely lovely. walk with Joanie and Miss Greenaway from tarns, by

73. "On this walk," Miss Gnosspelius observes, "going up past Lawson Park and along the paths over the top of the moor, and then down into Grisedale and coming back the same way, the distance covered would be about 5 miles but the elevation climbed about 1150 feet. Hence he climbed a good deal more on the Grisedale walk, without covering the same mileage. But the walk of April 8th over High Cross was taken on 'made' roads mostly; the walk to Grisedale was over footpaths and cart tracks, and was probably taken more slowly with more stops for botanizing and geologizing by the wayside, for which there are fewer opportunities on the roadway to High Cross."

74. For letters from Kate Greenaway (1846–1901) to Ruskin and the Severns, see Letters, XVIII.

cascades.[75] Ethel, Lolly and Fred at dinner.

Rather nightmary dream of being beseiged by naughty little boys, and running after a redhaired thief with Baxter. Woke with bad taste in mouth.

Opposite [February 6th, 1879]—see good resolutions for 1879 how much more I ought to enforce them now!

2125 April 14 Saturday. Lovely morning—but I jaded after restless night hurried telegram about Glasgow rector-ship[76]—and exciting talk in day with Miss Greenaway; too full of topic.

2124 April 15 Sunday Yesterday up Yewdale stream with Miss Greenaway, and showed her the white rose tree on the roof of the Cottage by the brook.

Today wet, but I up with good notion of work for fairy lecture.

2123 April 16 Monday. Very tired, yesterday and eyes bad—heavy head, &c.

But slept well,—(yet with one nasty piece of nightmare)—and saw my way and duty better this morning. D.G

2122 April 17 Tuesday. Long long awake last night—but slept sound, and find things coming beautifully by help of Herrick asked for by Miss Greenaway.[77]

2120 April 19 Thursday On Tuesday, walk with Kate Greenaway up to moor and round by the farm-road to see primrose and anemone opposite Low Bank Ground Yesterday wet all day. Connie, Harry,[78] and Ethel to dinner—a wonderful evening.

75. Tarn Hows?

76. Ruskin had been (or was being) nominated as an Independent candidate for the Lord Rectorship of Glasgow University.

77. Acknowledging her Christmas greeting of 1881 (*A Day in a Child's Life*), he had expressed special pleasure that she had illustrated one of Herrick's "Graces for Children" from *Noble Numbers* (see *Works, 37,* 383).

78. "Connie's" husband, the Reverend William Henry Churchill.

2119 April 20 Friday. Yesterday a grand day, but too much done— Walk with Kate to Coniston Hall & Farm house, drawings to be made!

Slept well, though after exciting music—Land of the Leal.[79]

2118 April 21 Saturday*

Yesterday Miss Greenaway drawing Coniston Hall!

Lily came with Scrappy[80] in evening—Harry and Connie in forenoon

Got right notion for finish of Jones lecture,[81] in showing of Romance of Rose.

* Sorrowful news from India[82]

2117 April 22 Sunday A wonderful morning of help—from Arthur Helps! and Orpheus[83]—and thoughts of my own, on Edwards not interpreting Chaucer as Chaucer—nor Rossetti Tennyson as Tennyson—nor the 19th Century Rembrandt, Christ as Christ.[84]

A fine dawn—now all plague wind—frightful black rubbed down over all

2116 April 23 Monday This week will be then

23,	24,	25,	26,	27,	28
M.	T.	W.	Th.	F.	Sa.
The next,					
30.	1	2	3	4	5.

79. The Land of the Loyal (father, mother, nurse, Rose)—a song by Caroline Oliphant, Baroness Navine.

80. "Scrappy" is identified by the name VIOLET, printed in capital letters above this entry. For her mother, "Lily," see Mrs. William Kevill-Davies, B.S.; see also Letters, III.

81. "Mythic Schools of Painting," in which Edward Burne-Jones' designs from Chaucer were referred to no more than incidentally.

82. Possibly news of someone's death, as is suggested by Ruskin's use of a cross.

83. Quotations from Arthur Helps' *Friends in Council* and from the Orphic "Hymn to Earth" helped him to round out (most loosely) the May issue of *Fors Clavigera,* dated "23rd April."

84. Doubtless a somewhat ironic reference to John Everett Millais, whose *Christ in the House of His Parents* "first showed me the beauty of extreme minuteness and precision" (*Works, 37,* 428; letter of December 28, 1882).

The third

7	8	9	10	11	12
M	T	W	Th	F.	Sa

If I leave punctually on Wednesday 9th it will do.[85]

2115 April 24 Tuesday Yesterday a terrible day of north wind and discovery of horrid things; slime in streams &c Today, snow on Old Man

2113 April 26 Thursday. Happy work with Kate Greenaway, who gave me yesterday the dancing children—All kinds of plans in my head for her.

2111 April 28 Saturday. Better in health than for many a day, D.G Yesterday morning found the map of Palestine in French expedition Awake long—thinking over plans—and calls, and warnings.

Curious! I was going to write that I saw my way somewhat,—and now—behold the entry on opposite page—last line [of March 15, 1879]

Strangest of all, now looking for passage in Plato for Oxford (Burne Jones lecture) I come on, καταγύσιν περαινει and my own note VIII. 112[86]

2110 April 29 Sunday. Well—whether I win my battle this time or not—clearly I cant escape it—for the helps and the hindrances come like hail—Yesterday I had five hours of variously exciting or painful talk from 5 to 10, evening,

85. To deliver at Oxford, on the 13th, his lecture on "Mythic Schools of Painting."

86. Looking for the passage in Book VI of the *Laws* which he would use in his pending lecture (see *Works, 33,* 302), Ruskin had chanced on the words περαί νει κατα φύσιν ("he executes according to nature") on the page which contains the annotation he had made in 1879: "If I could bring my own work to an end, as I began!" (see March 2, 1879, n.40). In 1837 he had published his essays on *The Poetry of Architecture* under the nom-de-plume "Kata Phusin." "I could not have put in fewer, or more inclusive words, the definition of what half my future life was to be spent in discoursing of," he would remark in *Praeterita* (*Works, 35,* 224).

when I had to give in: and the first thing this morning, finding the precious bit in Friends in Council about money and the Bible[87]

2109 April 30 Monday In for it indeed— Yesterday after writing last page, comes down poor Joanie, announcing Violet Kevill Davies illness[88] and all our plans broken up · Lay long awake this morning, and am jaded now, but I hope still quite well, D.G

2107 May 2 May-day. Yesterday wholly bright and the brightest letters I've ever had, from Ned, of Avallon—and music of St. Jerome.[89] Up to mines and waterfall with Kate Greenaway; and found Lily's Violet out of danger in her illness, humanly speaking. D.G.

2106 May 3 ⟨Thursday Above bit of Horace [the "definition of a gentleman"] comes in now providentially, for close of lecture on classic art.⟩[90]

Yesterday a terribly confused and overtasked day, but slept well till three and am up in good heart, D.G

87. Presumably a reference to Helps' essay on "Despotism," in which a sardonic discussion of how the value of money is lessened by discoveries of silver and gold is followed by the statement: "Even in affairs that are purely secular it must be admitted that the Old Testament is a mine of wisdom. . . . As every word requires to be pondered, I will read you part of the chapter of Samuel, in which he declares what will be the doings of this king whom the people demand to have set over them; and I am sure you will say that, if it had been written yesterday, it could hardly be more applicable than it is to the present state of human affairs" (*Friends in Council,* Ser. IV, pp. 205–12, in 2d edition of 1859).

88. "I am sorrowfully appalled at the consequence of our poor little Scrappie's visit to us," he would soon tell Kate Greenaway. "—*You* ill of all people!—what should I have thought if I had known that I was to be the instrument of this discomfort and harm to you" (unpublished letter of May 20, 1883; Pierpont Morgan Library).

89. Burne-Jones' "letters" on these topics are not available.

90. Published in *Works, 33,* xxiiin. "Horace's definition of a gentleman [—] Est animus tibi: sunt mores, et lingua, fidesque" appears at the top of the page opposite Ruskin's entry for April 10, 1879, the present entry being therefore placed beneath the "definition." The lecture on "Classic Schools of Painting" would begin with Ruskin's comment on "the single line of Horace which sums the conditions of a gentleman's education, be he rich or poor, learned or unlearned" (*Works, 33,* 306).

2104 May 5 Saturday. Perfect morning, but cold.—Things going well, but too many

2103 May 6 Sunday Yesterday at Peel island with Kate and Lily and the wonderful American, Mr Clarence King,[91] at dinner, came and overwhelmed me.

Slept ill—and rather jaded now, but full of useful thoughts.

I copy the note at Milan so long lying about, at last

Dante and Galileo are on each side of the door of
the "Specialità in mantelli scialli, &
setorie [sic]" of Signor Molinari Marliani
Galearzzo Visconti and Vettor Pisani over the Caffè
Ristorante di Fiumagalli e Compagnia
Giovanni da Procida presides over "Edizioni
Musicali, Casa Filiale a Napoli"
Marco Polo over "grande assortimento di Stoffe Nazionali
ed esteri" and Pier Capponi over "abiti per signora" [92]

2102 May 8 Tuesday. Yesterday the loveliest calm and clear morning I ever saw at Brantwood to my memory,—at two, north east wind came on violently with black cloud and today, the mountains are thick with snow half-way down—and all below—grey rain! Kate Greenaway went home yesterday,—I fear not much wiser for her visit (April 10th to May 7th.)

91. For Clarence King, see B.S.

92. Presumably data which Ruskin had gathered in Milan (last visited during his trip of 1876–77), recording the whereabouts of likenesses of Italian notables—e.g. those of Dante and Galileo decorating the doorway of the "Specialists in mantels, shawls, and silks," and that of Marco Polo above the "great assortment of clothing materials, national and foreign," with Pier Capponi presiding over "outfits for ladies."

2101 May 9 Wednesday. Awake at 3, but slept afterwards, waking always with very pleasant dreams, as the morning brightened. Three or four there were—now forgotten, but a new experience to me.

2057 June 22 Friday On the 10th May I started for Oxford. Slept at Matlock got to Oxford on the 11th through Coventry and Kenilworth Lectured at Oxford on the 12, 16, 19, 23, 26, and 30th and in London, at Mrs Bishops,[93] on Tuesday, the 5th and since have been working on Oxford galleries, till Tuesday last the 19th June, when I went by afternoon train to Worcester, next day to Hereford and Llangollen, and yesterday, home here, Joanie arriving with the children and Clennie[94] at 1/4 past 7—trains punctual, mine 3.40, her's 6.30 all well, and my 44 days well spent

D.G.

Now see p. 212.[95]

2056 June 23 Saturday. Sunny, but thundrous and misty with heavy dew—clearing now, 9 oclock gradually, I hope into a day for drawing— Saw my way, I trust, in quiet morning walk, and hope to carry forward Oxford work in foreground leaves this autumn.

2055 June 24 Sunday. Leaving three lines for any future comment, I may utilize all the pages now.[96]— Yesterday painted in wood, and got midge plagued. Tea late—bad nightmare, curiously

93. Mrs. W. H. Bishop (see B.S.).

94. Marion Maclellan (see B.S.).

95. In MS this entry is written on the left-hand page 104. On the next left-hand page the translation of the first two books of Plato's *Laws* starts, to be continued to the end of page 211. In the upper margin of the left-hand page 212 Ruskin notes: "Continue Diary of 1883 from p. 104."

96. Meaning that he will no longer reserve a whole page for the entry of one day. By July 24, having reached page 221, he evidently decided that if the remaining pages in this volume were to suffice the year, he could no longer afford to leave even three blank lines between his entries.

consecutive and rational—a quarrel between two cabmen ending with one being pitched down six or seven steps with a crash on his head, and the other carried off by the police.

2054 June 25 Monday. Reading rule of St Benedict in Mont Alembert[97] with great comfort and help at coffee-time. The quantity of good now possible to me if only I can be what I ought to be—! but it seems to get more difficult every hour.

2053 June 26 Tuesday. Called on Mrs Harrison[98] yesterday and met Flora,[99] in heavy thunder after heat. Pouring, now.

Read with great joy, Mont Alemberts life of Cassiodorus,[1] at coffee-time Now must try and get a new Love's Meinie on way.

2052 June 27 Wednesday Sunny, but with dirty and threatening clouds.

Norton arrived at Liverpool yesterday—expected today!

2051 June 28 Thursday Norton came, yesterday at 3:40 with his son, and it was a very wonderful evening with them and Flora.[2] Today, wet, of course and I bothered much with paper for Horsfall[3] about Manchester.

97. Charles Forbes René de Tryon, Comte de Montalembart (1810–70), *Les Moines d'Occident*, Bk. IV, "St. Benedict."

98. Probably the mother of Major Benson Harrison (see Dorothy W. Harrison, B.S.).

99. Flora Shaw, Lady Lugard (see B.S. and Letters, XXXVI).

1. In *The Monks of the West* (New York, 1905), Bk. V, pp. 348–53.

2. Writing to his "children," Norton said that at about four o'clock Ruskin had met them "on the platform of the station,—his heart unchanged, his welcome as loving as a welcome could be, and in an instant the ten years had gone, and we were talking as if we had met last week, so familiar did our voices seem to each other" (*Letters of Charles Eliot Norton, 2,* 149).

3. His Introduction (dated "28th June, 1883") to T. C. Horsfall's pamphlet *The Study of Beauty and Art in Large Towns* (*Works, 34,* 429–34). It was a bothersome bit of writing because, as he explains, many of his beliefs differed from those of Mr. Horsfall, whose "principles" he nevertheless considered "true and sound."

2049 June 30 Saturday. I can't think how I missed yesterday. I had pleasant walk in afternoon with Charles, to the mine-stream valley I want a name for it, having got Turner Catalogue[4] and Benedict lecture[5] posted first.

2048 July 1 Sunday. Yesterday lovely walk up to tarns[6] and down by cascades with Norton—Flora—and Eliot I not fatigued, though rowing with Eliot for stroke to and fro the Waterhead Tea [with Marshalls] at Monk Coniston, unsatisfactory

2047 July 2 Monday Yesterday Grey, and I dismal,—but always sleep well and with no painful or ugly dreams

Norton has to leave today

2046 July 3 I'm really getting quite tidy *at last*! after forty years of diarying[7]

Norton left at ¼ eleven—and I had a nice afternoon tidying with Flora

July 4 Wednesday 2045

July 5 Thursday 2044

2043 July 6 Friday—so much for my tidiness! [8] but one *cannot* keep right with anybody extra in house.

Weather constantly thick and thundering, sometimes clear in the evenings, but *never* happy or right for a quarter of an hour at once

4. Possibly, in proof, the Turner section in "The Ruskin Cabinet at Whitelands College" pamphlet, these notes having been dated "February 8th, 1883" (see *Works, 30,* 352–55).

5. Probably the lecture, "Cistercian Architecture" (delivered at the London Institute on December 4, 1882), the full text of which was set up in type and, in the December 1883 issue of *Fors Clavigera,* announced as "forthcoming" (*Works, 29,* 474); first published as "Mending the Sieve," in *Verona and Other Lectures,* edited by W. G. Collingwood.

6. Tarn Hows?

7. For three pages, entries neatly penned have been neatly separated by three blank lines.

8. The dates July 4, 5, 6 form one group because he had failed to make entries for July 4 and 5.

2042 July 7 Saturday. Down in time to good work after a somewhat restless & troubled night—but seeing my way into Petrels[9]—and Benedictines! [10] D.G.

Wasted the afternoon, yesterday after too much lunch with Mr Barr[at]t

2041 July 8 Sunday. Down after most valuable bits of reading in geography of America, to study in the perfection of order;—and with pictures perfectly placed, and eyes, D.G. wonderfully well. — see above, p. 121 [entry for June 28, 1879], and heart—more or less at peace. Nice visit yesterday of Mrs Marshall & friends and in evening some coins got in order!!! once more

2040 July 9 Monday Clearing after rain. I down to work in perfect—as far as I can judge, health, for my age, and—circumstances—and hoping to be very useful yet. D.G.

2039 July 10 Tuesday. Of course all that fine state of things fell away, yesterday and I've had a bad night, awake from 2 to ½ past 4 and then a frightful dream of being pursued by a centipede serpent, flat headed and about twenty feet long, with crab-like legs—which after first running from, I perforce faced, on which it recoiled, and changed into a small dog, which I caught, and was strangling, when I woke all jaded and fevered—got gradually to rights but of course am not well now. Read America in morning, and planned Autumn lectures on Alfred to the Black Prince[11]

9. In a chapter for *Love's Meine* which reached the stage of proof, the Petrels appear as one main group in his classification of the Long-winged "Knife-Bills" (see *Works, 25,* 183).

10. Probably for use in *Valle Crucis,* which was planned as Part VI of "Our Fathers Have Told Us." His special interest in the Benedictines would be reflected in his Oxford lectures of 1884 on *The Pleasures of England.*

11. See *The Pleasures of England,* Lecture II, "The Pleasures of Faith: Alfred to the Confessor," October 1884 (*Works, 33,* 439–57).

2038 July 11 Wednesday Pouring swash of rain, with variable filth of fog.

Slept well, but woke at 4 and worked out some history and perspective in head.

2037 July 12 missed—hard work sending drawings to Dalbeattie[12]

2036 July 13 Friday Hardly slept since two, and am tired and feverish—but greatly enjoyed cataloguing coins with Joan.

2035 July 14 Saturday Mrs and Miss Wakefield and Dolly Bloomfield [*sic*][13] made the afternoon very happy to us, yesterday—being itself entirely pure in quiet sunshine which was *awful* to me after the plague clouds month of victory—So also a quiet clear dawn today after sound sleep.

2034 July 15 Sunday. I never passed a healthier or much happier day than yesterday arranging coins with Joan—seeing windhover on moor—taking Joan up to see anagallis in evening—and I hav'nt slept but from ½ past 11 to 2, and 5–7 of full constant nightmare!!!

2033 July 16 Monday Fits of darkness and rain—Heather all blighted, and raspberries. Conf. entries for August [14th through 17th] 1879, p.p. 157 158 Slept better, and down in good heart, but mouth sore and head giddy

Read in Macdonalds Diary of an old soul the verses for 3rd Jan and Feb. 8.[14] D.G.

2031 July 18 Wednesday. Read at coffee, the two ⟨marvel-

12. As a patron of the Industrial and Fine Art Loan Exhibition (July 12–August 3, 1883) held under the auspices of the Dalbeattie Mechanics Institute, Ruskin contributed ten of his own drawings, a number of architectural photographs, and a "rare and costly book full of steel engravings of Egyptian architecture" (*Kirkcudbrightshire Advertiser and Galloway News,* July 13, 1883, p. 5). This exhibition was designed to raise money with which to buy books for the Dalbeattie Library, which met the needs of workingmen. For Ruskin's notes on the drawings and photographs sent for exhibition, as reported in the local press, see pp. 343–45.

13. For Dolly Blomfield, see B.S.

14. George MacDonald (see B.S.).

lous passages by Mont Alembert)[15] on the monks in the forests—and Ireland,[16] and hope to get them translated and printed without delay.

Yesterday at the Marshalls'—seeing sketches—sorrowfully enough

July 19 Thursday. Yesterday R[ose']s Father and Mother came to see me.[17] D G.

Read today,—first beginnings of St Patrick.[18]

2029 July 20 Friday R[ose']s Father and Mother up the fell with me, to see anagallis on my cranberry bed. Lacerta found quantities more.[19]

2028 July 21 Saturday. Wrote some good botany yesterday overwhelmed with thoughts about it in the night, now tired! must do Sheffield accounts

2027 July 22 Sunday Indoors all day, sorting, yesterday and slept far better than after outdoor work.

Planned lectures on Saxon M.S. and Turner as scale of measurement in English art,—to be called Elf-land,—and What, Cloud-land? or 'Memory.' [20]

15. Published in *Works, 33,* xlviii.

16. For the "marvellous passages" describing the "famous Druidical forests in which the sacrifices of the ancient Gauls were celebrated," see *Monks of the West,* Bk. VI ("The Monks under the First Merovingians"), par. V ("The Monks and Nature").

17. For an account of this visit, see Introduction to 1883. For letters from Mrs. La Touche to Mrs. Severn and Ruskin and from Ruskin to Mrs. La Touche, see Letters, XXVIII.

18. For "the legend of St. Patrick," see *Monks of the West,* the opening of Bk. VII ("St. Columbanus.—The Irish in Gaul and the Colonies of Luxeuil").

19. "Rosie's father and mother have been very happy here!" Ruskin soon would be telling Norton, "and her pet flower anagallis tenella, a capricious thing like herself, and wholly uncultivatable, has come in gushes all round the rock edges of my moorland garden" (unpublished remark in letter of August 2, 1883; Harvard University Library; for the context of this passage, see par. 2 of the letter as published in *Works, 37,* 464).

20. Doubtless ideas related to the first and last lectures delivered at Oxford during the autumn of 1884. In Lecture I of *The Pleasures of England* Ruskin would characterize the Saxons, speaking of the drawings in their MSS (see *Works, 33,* 436–37). Unable to complete the series of lectures he had planned, he concluded

2025 July 24 Tuesday Calm lake—and sweet briar heavenly—but grey and gloomy sky, and I a good deal like it!

Called on Susie, yesterday and L[acerta] rowed me back.

In afternoon, Mr Thomson[21] of Huddersfield.

July 25th Wednesday, 2024, [2]6th, 2023, [2]7th, 2022, all work against time, with general vexation for result

2021 July 28 Saturday Most lovely yesterday walk on moor with L[acerta] picnic the day before with childrens tea. how happy I ought to be! Slept well last night but dont know what to do first.

2019 July 30 Monday. Very languid and wretched all yesterday but slept well and am up to work today, and it ought to be happy work, on lovely things,— I read beginning of diary in 44, yesterday and find I was just as dismal then as now!

2018 July 31 Tuesday Slept well and feel well, D.G. and ought to—be no end of good—yet—if I use gifts rightly

2017 August 1 Wednesday Slept well—but was sadly tired and languid yesterday. Gave up idea of going to London I scarcely know if rightly or wrongly.

2016 August 2 Thursday It will depend on what I do with the leisure I have gained. Up today in good health and all things open to me—it seems, more & more D.G.

Read in T[estamen]t—but with puzzle the end of Job, xxxi—never enough noticed

---

with a lecture on "Landscape" (never published), to which the titles here suggested would probably have been appropriate to his interpretation of Turner's work. (For this lecture, as reported in the *Pall Mall Gazette,* see *Works, 33,* 532–37.)

21. George Thomson (see B.S.).

about LAND [22] Read also the beginning of Brantwood book. [Virtually?] May 25th 1875, of which gather, the notes on Epistacy p. 1, the account of 28th May clouds, [p.] 5, and note beginning of collects, Lincoln Psalter, [p.] 6[23]

2015 August 3 Friday A morning of perfect calm and sunshine—garden quite lovely—cloud resting clear of the Old Man, casting shadow I slept well, but am languid Dreamed on Aug[ust] 1st. of lovely colours on clouds, distinctly seen, and enjoyed

2014 August 4 Saturday Slept entirely well, all night long, and yet feel quite good for nothing, as I did all yesterday also—Pulse curiously slow—sometimes stopping for a moment. now steady, but low.

2013 August 5 Sunday. Drew well yesterday and got on with plants, a number of F[lora] D[anica] coming with just what I wanted in it, & my Veronica officinalis the first plate[24]

Slept well,—dream't of pretty ladies and finding real crystals of Ice, quite a long time spent in studying them—octahedrous six inches across—it never occurred to me in

22. "If my land cry against me, or that the furrows likewise thereof complain; If I have eaten the fruits thereof without money, or have caused the owners thereof to lose their life: Let the thistles grow instead of wheat, and the cockle instead of barley" (Job 31:38–40).

23. See entry of May 11, 1875 (*Diaries,* pp. 844–45—where "812" should read "81 l[eft]" for "notes on Epistacy"; of May 29, 1875 (ibid., p. 846) for "account of 28th May clouds"; and of June 3, 1875 (ibid., p. 847) for "beginning of collects" (Mr. Dearden explains that in this entry of August 2, 1883, "the Brantwood book" must be what Ruskin usually calls "the Broadlands book"—namely, Bembridge MS *xx*, which begins with May 10, 1875).

24. The last issue of *Flora Danica. Icones plantarum . . .* (1761–1883), a series of engravings of the flowers of Denmark, Norway, and Sweden, contains the *Veronica officinalis* as Plate 248. Ruskin's drawing, to which he refers in a letter of August 2 (*Works, 37,* 464), is a study of the leaves of the plant. It was placed at Oxford as No. 298 in the Rudimentary Series (*Works, 21,* 234) and appeared as an illustration in an 1885 installment of *Proserpina* (see *Works, 25,* Pl. XXIX).

dream that ice was'nt cubic. A more painful part, about probing into depths of an old well, followed, perhaps suggested by kitchen-range being out of order!

Down in good heart for my Menthae.[25]

A lovely morning, *brown* clouds on mountains—white cirri above

2012 August 6 Monday Slept well—but spiritless now,—failing with drawing yesterday— Raining at last—and its quite pleasant.

2010 August 8 Wednesday Raining hard, and I'm more cheerful than in fine mornings. — Very dismal all yesterday enjoying nothing but got new number of Proserpina finished.[26]

Joanie left on Monday for H[arris]town.[27]

2009 August 9 Thursday. See entry for 2nd. I have made little of my leisure yet—except making myself ill, which I seemed to be yesterday extremely, and was very sad, lying awake at one in the morning. Better now D.G. hopeful of much teaching from Mr Gregory[28] in all sorts of ways.

August 10 Friday. Better—but very idle

Friday 2008. — Sat. 2007. S[un.] 2006 Monday 2005

2004 August 14 Tuesday These last have been bad days, but I got good accounts done yesterday and am in order today. D.G.

25. His studies of the salvia, dead nettle, and thyme are assembled in Plate XXVIII of *Proserpina* to illustrate the "Menthae."

26. Probably chapter 6, "Monacha," of *Proserpina II*. This chapter contains his discussion of the "Menthae" and was evidently under way in 1883, although not published until May 1885 (see *Works, 25,* 473–82).

27. The home of Mrs. La Touche, near Dublin, where Mrs. Severn would spend two weeks.

28. The biblical scholar Caspar René Gregory (1846–1919) of Leipzig, author of *Canon and Text of the New Testament* (1907). He would now tell Ruskin that 1463 was the "true date" of an illuminated manuscript (an Old Testament, in Greek) which Ruskin had ascribed to the tenth century (see *Works, 34,* 701).

2003 August 15 Wednesday Yesterday got on with History[29] and accounts, and slept well D.G.

It will be curious, and awful, to come below 2000— let me see if the count is right, thus far.

Why,—I have miscounted grievously. There are now only 148 days left of this year —then five whole ones—1725 and 39 in 1889, altogether only 1912 How I got my number of 2145,[30] at p 62 [March 25] I can't think—but even taking that, there have been 144 days since, so I have missed count of two Today, by that count would be 2001, which I'll go on with—as it is so

2000 August 16 Thursday. Yesterday a very bad day: but I got on with accounts, and hope to finish them off now before any thing else.

1999 August 17 Friday Yesterday got on with accounts & heard wonders from Doctor Dallinger,[31] making him happy and a *very* nice girl with him

1998 August 18 Saturday. Nice day yesterday at accounts and minerals.

Theres no satisfaction in keeping count of a wrong number—and as I have made the mistake in the encouraging direction, I[']ll take the hope of it, and count now to the end of 1890 which, counting 7 years clear without leap years, will be 2555—and adding this day, 18th Aug. and to end of year, 135 days the

29. Beyond Montalembert, Ruskin was reading widely in Church history, with special thought of the "Studies in Monastic History and Architecture" which he was planning to present in *Valle Crucis*. (Misdated June 25, 1883, the words "Getting on with my history" have been published presumably as a quotation from this entry; see *Works, 33,* xlviii.)

30. He had more immediately obtained this number by carrying over into the present Diary the numbering which he had begun in another volume (*xxiii* of the Bembridge MSS) while he was in London on March 18, 1883. For his initial calculation, see above, entry for March 25, 1883, and n.

31. The Reverend W. A. Dallinger (see B.S. and Letters, XI).

sum will be 2690, which I will take for this days count—and so downward

2689 August 19 Sunday. Slept well and down in good heart, for accounts! and minerals. D.G.

Read life of Addison at coff[ee]— I see he died at 47! warned by shortness of breath, which I've been feeling more than I like, lately myself.

2688 August 20 Monday Slept well, after good long woodwork in afternoon, and much mineral ticketing

2687 August 21 Tuesday. Not a good day yesterday and I languid this morning, but quite eager to get to accounts! Gathered gooseberries in the morning yesterday and did but little in afternoon

2686 August 22 Wednesday Not a good day yesterday neither and bad dream of long walk through grassy marsh to find Flora's Mr Evelyn I come down with grand resolutions about finishing accounts

2685 August 23 Thursday. A better day, but I good for little, accounts getting on however, and useful letters written

Dreamed of being in a great passion in the kitchen about a stale egg, afterwards the servant thinking I had gone crazy again. Then, of my Father, and his introducing me to the sweetest & prettiest girl I ever dreamed of.

2685 August 24 Friday. A better day, yesterday. Walked through loveliest hayfield with Clennie & the children to receive Joanie from Ireland!

D.G.

2684 August 25 Saturday Well, I am getting always a little tidier in diary, anyhow.

Long talk of Harristown yesterday at dinner — very wonderful Dreamy night—but slept till Mary[32] came. much about long

32. Probably the servant Mary Jane Fleming, who seems to have been charged

roads, not to be traversed in time and a great caravan—and great buildings— Comfortless

2683 August 26 Sunday. A bad day and worse night, with singularly loathesome and terrific dreaming. Never was more thankful to wake Compare entry above, 8th Ap[ri]l [1883] page 79—and consider the causes of change.

2682 August 27 Monday. Weather breaking, after another week of loveliness, hardly any plague cloud and lovely delicate sunsets.—Out of doors all day yesterday and slept well. D.G.

2681 August 28 Tuesday. Wonderfully well today after good sleep, D.G. Tea to discuss Irish lover!—Libbie[33] tomorrow, ½ past two

RENAISSANCE — see opp[osite] at bottom of page.[34]

2680 August 29 Wednesday. Lovely music last night from our Border Mary[35]—but woke with headache Gone now and leaving me lively for accounts!

2679 August 30 Yesterday broken weather but quite lovely in afternoon for walk with Libby Bell to the undiscovered glen!

— Sunshine on green field behind Coniston Hall, divine as I returned Very well this morning.

2678 August 31 Friday I had a bad day however and got terribly confused over Botany and accounts. Slept pretty well and up to work now.

2677 Sept. 1 Saturday. Slept wonderfully well and have

with forwarding his mail during several weeks of 1880 which he had spent in France, and who received a letter signed "Yr. faithful master, J. Ruskin," calling her to account for having sent him "seven packets of letters, every one underpaid" (unpublished letter of October 23, 1880, addressed to "Mary Jane Fleming, Mr. Ruskins, Brantwood, Coniston, Angleterre"; Ruskin Museum, Coniston).

33. The daughter of William Bell who "married a gamekeeper called Percival—the Barratts' man—and lived all her life in Coniston," Mrs. Gnosspelius recounts.

34. See the concluding sentences of entry for July 31, 1880 (viz. the burned Marc Antonio *Nymph and Satyr*, as "a type of Renaissance").

35. Presumably (Augusta) Mary Wakefield.

put my room in order for my mother's birthday. D.G.

2676 Sept. 2[36] Sunday Down to morning work in good health, and far-reaching though subdued hope. D.G.

The arrangement [of the bedroom Turners] now, (Zug and Fluelen gone!)
My mother's Birthday. 1883

1 My Father's Conway
2. Goldau
3 Faido
4 Dinant
5 Rolandseck
6 Gosport
7 Flint
8 Rouen
9. Vesuvius calm
10 Vesuvius angry

11. Constance 12 Heysham 13 Coblentz
14 Devonport 15 Bolton 16 Salisbury
17. Eggleston
18 Dudley

19 21

and beside windows

19. Farnley Avenue 20. Farnley stream
21 Farnley 22. Richmond Yorkshire

20 22

2675 Sept. 3 Monday Margaret Cox and Emmeline Miller, with her brother came to see me yesterday and made me very happy[37] I woke

36. The first sentence of this entry, written on the left-hand page 229, is immediately followed by the entry for September 3. "The arrangement now" is given on the left-hand page 233, opposite the entry for December 14, 1880, with its analogous record of the arrangement of the pictures in his bedroom.

37. Three recently acquired Companions of St. George, from Liverpool (see Margaret Cox, B.S.).

languid, at five and sad, but thought usefully in the two hours and set to work on the next Fors, already well begun[38]

2674 Sept. 4 Tuesday. Yesterday really very happy with sailing yacht for children in Jumper—and Margaret and Emmeline at Dinner and tea—but violent attack of indigestion this morning!

2673 Sept. 5 Wednesday. Did nice piece of Fors and accounts—planned more and read Scott in lovely autumn morning. Down to work after sound sleep in good heart.

2672 Sept. 6 Thursday. I've gained a day—! of the month—anyhow. I dated all letters yesterday 6th. Woodwork with Alic in golden afternoon, but as usual much of its gold lost, to me, and today—regular Coniston drench

2671 Sept. 7 Friday Yesterday Found my mothers diamond brooch—and Wisie's letters, and more than her's, and today open, in looking for Hawick, on page 96 above—with all its entries, and 97 opposite—cannot be read too often.[39] Norton expected today, and all going well for me, except my own mind, which is very ignoble and unworthy, just now.

2670 Sept. 8 Saturday. Not quite so bad as 1884,! yet. —[40] Dreamy, this morning but in the right way, after sound sleep, and happy time with Norton last night. Planning now final papers on agates for Deucalion[41]

38. Doubtless Letter 91, issued in September 1883. On September 11, 1883, Ruskin wrote George Allen: "and I'll send Jowett [their printer] the whole new Fors, which I finished on Sunday, as soon as Mr. Wedderburn can get it copied. I've got well to work on Valle Crucis, and shall have the number finished I hope by end of week, and I'm sending to Jowett today a magnificent piece of St George account work" (unpublished letter; Columbia University Library).

39. Page 96 contains the entries for March 13, 14, 15, 1879. For the "opposite" page 97, see March 17, 1879, n. 55.

40. In the dateline he had written 1884, corrected to read "1883."

41. Left unpublished, if ever written.

2669 Sept. 9 Sunday. Yesterday planned bequests to Bodleian, and had much happy sense of beauty of my upper field, walking there in evening sunshine. — Slept well, and today happy in Lucca and Pisa and in all other fields of present work.

D.G.

2667 Sept. 11 Thursday Yesterday Norton went away, and the day was discomfited, but the 'will' arranged, which was a piece of good work[42] Today, Glorious sunshine and I begin Valle Crucis,—in actual text. Birds singing, one cloud only, calm in the clear sky on Wetherlam. Exquisite sun and shade on the field. One cow lying in the shade like one of our alabastor cows from Matlock.[43]

2665 [sic] Sept. 12 Wednesday An entirely divine day, yesterday. Sailed from Bells boathouse into Brantwood Harbour in Jumping Jenny, (Must finish study of personal character in Saints)—in the sweetest possible summer breeze and sunshine. Mary Wakefield—Alic, and Arthur all off down the lake; the children & Clennie on the rescuing party in afternoon to pull becalmed Arthur home.

I wonderfully well and enjoying myself! Began Valle Crucis, yesterday to purpose. To-

42. From Brantwood, Norton had written: "I find Ruskin in excellent condition, —steadier, less excitable, more equable than when I saw him nine or ten weeks ago. I have had a very interesting, but a very touching day with him; touching because his solitude is so great, and because the past is a sad retrospect and the future a sad prospect for him. ¶ [I shall leave him with no assurance of a continuance of his present sanity, and with a certainty that I can do nothing for him of the much that I might do were not the ocean between us.—Thanks to Columbus!]" (letter to Dr. John Simon, September 8, 1883; published in part in *Letters of Charles Eliot Norton, 2,* 156, the passage in square brackets being supplied from the letter in MS, now in the Harvard University Library).

43. Presumably decorative figures acquired during his boyhood. To buy "a trifle from Matlock" seems to have become a family byword (see *Works, 35,* 267).

day entirely divine rose purple dawn. Sun now on all, and calm lake

2665 Sept. 13 Thursday Yesterday good in morning—worried from lunch till eleven at night, and quite jaded today— Yet slept fairly, only dreaming little teazing dreams; Affairs of new will extremely mixed in vexatious trifles also, and unmanageable—*not* trifles.

2664 Sept. 14 Friday Absolutely perfect morning from dawn, on, and I well beyond my memory, and planning abstract of laws of Fesole for handbook,[44] with other matters—D.G.

2663 Sept. 15 Saturday Yesterday the most lovely and on the whole, happiest day Ive ever passed here, — all day out, in morning on moor by myself —meditating on oatfield and glacier marks—in afternoon, the childrens picnic opposite Peel Island.!!! No words for the beauty and sweetness of it.

Slept perfectly well, only waking a little at three, till Annie came. Found wonderful things in Scott Vol III of Life[45]

2662 Sept. 16 Sunday. The day got wrong, later on with thinking over will, and tiresome letters. Too much chatter at dinner, and above all, festering indignation at the nonsense in Knowledge,—and other bad feelings. Foggy now—but calm and birds singing

2661 Sept. 17 Monday Yesterday a bad day,—yet on the whole—coming out right and I down this morning with more thoughts than I could write in a year, and have had a nice time with my ruby silver. D.G.

2660 Sept. 18 Tuesday Yesterday wrote well, and at Coniston school.

44. This project did not find its way to publication.

45. His ten-volume (1869) edition of Lockhart's *Life of Scott,* marginally annotated throughout, is now in the Ruskin Collection at Bembridge School.

2659 Sept. 19th Wednesday. Down to coffee! and fairly well, though much tired and threatened with sore-throat last night, lying awake at one oclock, rather frightened and feeling very helpless

D.G.

May as well read the life of Claudius again, see opp[osite, entry for December 20, 1880]

2658 Sept. 20 Thursday. Curiously giddy, today, though down to coffee in right time from intense anger and disgust with various people, yesterday. How difficult also to fix one's thoughts, when one is angry. must try, for emperor Claudius.

2655 Sept. 23 Sunday Terribly over-thoughted, and though down every day to coffee, missing this! Today, found in the Persone's Tale, all I want about dress for women;[46] — and have lost my Broadlands book! The strangest loss I've ever had!! Wonderfully sad all afternoon, but slept well

2644 October 4[47] Thursday. Back to my home with deep sense of its blessedness, D.G. and knowledge worth the ten-days toil, and more

Monday to Abbotsford.

Tuesday, at Melrose

Wednesday. Storm at Abbotsford

Thursday. To Laidlawstiel

Friday. to Ashestiel and Traquhair.

Saturday to Kenmure Castle. Sunday, walk in glen.

Monday, to Whithorn.

46. See sects. 26–27 of the *Parson's Tale* in the Skeat edition of Chaucer. In essence: "Now as of the outrageous array of wommen, god woot, that though the visages of somme of hem seme ful chaast and debonaire, yet notifie they in hir array of likerousnesse and pryde. I sey nat that honestetee in clothinge of man or womman is unconvenable, but certes the superfluitee or disordinat scantitee of clothinge is reprevable." Ruskin, however, seems not to have used for publication whatever he now may have had in mind.

47. In the upper margin he notes: "Ten days in Scotland. Sept 23–Oct 4."

Tuesday to St Ninian's cove
Wednesday, home.
Saw Dumfries on Saturday on the way to Kenmure

2642 October 6 Saturday. A quite glorious morning Much happiness with Alic Alice & Maudie,[48] yet I have bad wakings at 3 or 4. But this opposite entry [December 25, 1880] helps me[49]

2641 October 7 Sunday A lovely walk up Yewdale crag, yesterday gave me more faith—or rather conviction, as to my real strength, but I have got into a bad habit of waking at 4, which leaves me languid for morning work—and still more—afternoon!

2637 October 11 Thursday Sadly fevered and overstrained, these last days here, but guarding myself carefully. Divine soft blue sky over Old Man on Monday we had the lovely picnic at Peel island; more beautiful than words can tell—

2636 October 12 Friday Much better. Slept sound all night
Got best bit done of Ashestiel [50]—drew pillar for Alice
Must get through blots to clear paper for tomorrow[51]

2599 Nov. 28 [52] Wednesday. And tomorrow never came! for the book. Today, back from Oxford after good work—by carriage from Ulverston—home at 7 ¼ on Monday. D.G.

2597 Nov. 30 Friday. Yesterday dreadful head-cold and eyes

48. Doubtless Alice and Maud Bateman (see B.S.).

49. A line is drawn to indicate the concluding words—his thought "of the cross on the bridge of St. Martin's!"

50. For the November *Fors Clavigera:* Letter 92, "Ashestiel."

51. The part of the page on which this entry is written has been splotched by ink from the opposite entry.

52. In the upper margin he notes: "North and 13 Days in Oxford. Oct 13–Nov 26 See Monday 15th Oct. in Lucca book p 117." (See *Diaries,* pp. 1049–51, for the Oxford entries; conjecturally, p. 1033 for the Lucca entry of 1882.)

streaming all day, but got good work done—good sleep, and up now to time—and see my blue lines well by candlelight without spectacles. D.G.

2596 Dec. 1 Saturday. A lovely warm-coloured morning for Joanie to go away in! — My Cold quite better, and anxiety about groin pain relieved.[53] D.G

2595 Dec. 2 Sunday Yesterday a very bad day, Joan going away,—and my groin pain returning very plaguily. Up the moor in fine—nay in exquisite morning sun, like a dream. But the sunset lurid and strange Arthur has noticed more than one such, lately, almost terrible.

2594 Dec. 3 Storm all day yesterday. Working at Francesca's book,[54] & pain much better, D.G. Now, chilly wet morning and I set myself to Business to begin the week

2593 Dec. 4 Tuesday. Cold gone, virtually and I feeling very well but groin-pain worse than ever, yesterday, making me very anxious.

A fierce storm last night rounded into bleak, but clear north wind. I set to business again—wrote 20 letters yesterday.

2592 Dec. 5 Wednesday. Lovely clear morning. The pain much relieved yesterday but again this morning threatening. But slept well, after consenting yesterday to lecture on battle of Kincyree! [55]

2591 Dec. 6 Thursday. Pain very bad yesterday, all the afternoon, but slept well and it seems gone

53. See entry for January 8, 1881.

54. *Roadside Songs of Tuscany,* to be issued in 12 numbers (1884–85), Ruskin's Preface being dated "Jan. 1st, 1884."

55. Delivered on December 22 at the Mechanics Institute, Coniston, to be incorporated in *A Knight's Faith* (1885) as chapter 1, "Introductory," and as part of the Conclusion (see *Works, 31,* 385–95, 505–06).

this morning. Otherwise I am wonderfully well and getting on with useful work in all directions. D.G.

2590 Dec. 7 Friday. Pain much relieved, yesterday, and slept quite soundly, with much enjoyment in work and plans. D.G.

2589 Dec. 8 Saturday Quite horrid pituita cold again, and the pain far from right, though I trust better. Slept fairly well, but prologues and epilogues on my mind.[56]

2588 Dec. 9 Sunday I hope, better though troubled with tiny cough and occasional pain. Writing without spectacles by candlelight, yet see the blue lines [word illegible] enough. D.G.

2587 Dec. 10 Monday. Slept well, but pain very threatening and bad all afternoon, and today beginning already! I find I can pump with it, but not cough, or sneeze, scotfree.

2534 Dec. 13 Thursday. Getting on grandly with putting in order, but the great gale of Tuesday night threw us all out of gear.

Wild black wind again today. cant see to do anything

2553 Dec. 14 Friday Pain bad this morning but general health curiously good! Read "the Decline of Life ["] with encouragement but also horror at the possible diseases!

Very happy yesterday with Hackstoun's drawings

2552 Dec. 15 Saturday Pain still bothering but all else going wonderfully well. D.G.

Except the weather, wind never having ceased since Tuesday. a little slack now—but dark & bitter.

56. A reference to his "Christmas" Letter 93 of *Fors Clavigera,* which is entitled "Invocation" and which concludes with a section headed "CHRISTMAS POSTSCRIPT." He also told Kate Greenaway that he was "busy on a Christmas Fors" (unpublished letter of December 10, 1883; Pierpont Morgan Library).

Lecture. (Genius & Instinct) Animal's modes of Fear. Bramble's of the Storm. Crab's —at St Pauls, in panic if thrown into sea,— but at Lido, ready to fight Paulizza. Their —'Conception' of Austrian officer. (Compare Murrays nonsense about ideal of Landscape!)

Viol[l]et le Duc's wonderful drawing, with *no* genius.[57]

2551 Dec. 16 Saturday (—no, Sunday) (Only thinking of something else for a minute, not forgetting day.) Yesterday got walk to Copland Grange[58] —found its side blown down, begin to think I'm a little in the same way myself—for the pain worries me,—yet I am in better spirits & doing better work than usual,—and more useful. D.G.

2550 Dec. 17. Monday. A bad night, after one of my best days! notable. Eyes bad this morning too, when I want them most, to see I hope a lovely dawn. More than I deserve, but it seems coming

2549 Dec. 18 Tuesday. Woke early—½ past 3 and have had uncomfortable and anxious morning, hope to forget it in work. — D.G. as Beatrice degli Ontani says, thankful for pain[59]

2548 Dec. 19 *Yesterday much put out with steel* and leather, learning what penance means; no doubt sent because I wanted that knowledge. D.G.!

57. No lecture which developed these ideas seems to have been delivered. In the long succession of Ruskin's dogs, Bramble was now at hand for observation and companionship. Paulizzi was the Austrian officer with whom Effie had had a flirtation while she and Ruskin were in Venice in 1851–52. The "nonsense about . . . Landscape" is probably a reference to some passage in one of John Murray's *Handbooks,* although something said by his assistant, Charles Fairfax Murray, may have been what he had in mind.

58. Ruskin's name for Copland's Barn (see Map B).

59. Beatrice Bugelli (see B.S.).

Beginning of new phase of decline in life, for me.

2547 Dec. 20 Thursday — very uncomfortable this morning—with various galling and fretting—not pain, as I used to be tormented when a child How one forgets torment! but it is best, so, in some ways

Wild wind, the wind that blew all our trees down, rain as thick with mist as grey soup.

2546 Shortest Day. Friday. Discomfort and pain much abated D.G.

2545 Dec. 22 Saturday. I had an anxious evening though, and most sad thoughts in the night, as I lay awake partly in over-fatigue about Herberts lecture.[60] Q[uestion], how much of anxiety for *him*—Edwardes—how much small vanity for myself?

2544 Dec. 23 Sunday — Pain much less, and general strength good, but thoughts extremely sad.

Got lecture given—but very badly, the 'luck' going all against my work in the most Diabolic way in the last day or two.

2543 Dec. 24 Sunday (Monday I mean) Bad nightmares all night of vulgar accidents.

Christmas Monday. Pain much reduced. Very sad last night, but happy with Saussure and plans today All good about me. D.G.

2541 Dec. 25 Tuesday. Very sad, and uncomfortable,—stomach mostly wrong—but Im little else than stomach now. But slept well. D.G.

2539. Dec. 27 Thursday A dismal Xmas time for me—with many deep pleasures and prides stuck in the mud of it like garnets in Honister whin-

60. "The Battle of Kineyree," to be delivered that afternoon. It was a "most difficult subject," he told Kate Greenaway. "If I fail it does'nt matter—but if it goes well, it will be nice." In retrospect, "it was [about] the management of Indian gypsies and banditti—and was I think rather interesting" (unpublished letters of December 21 and 26, 1883; Pierpont Morgan Library).

stone Miss Greenaways gift the greatest I ever had, for the personal pleasure it gives me[61]—the Birthday book, a great pride, tempered by the portrait.[62]

Dec. 28 Not at all well and horribly fidgetty and uncomfortable. Got much in order, yesterday however.

2537 Dec. 29 Saturday Fifth day of fog, unbroken and now black. Indoors all yesterday, I yet slept from 11 to ¼ past six, sound, dreamless,—and healthful—D.G.

2536 Dec. 30 Dense fog, smell from drains. Baxter ill, I with pains in stomach.

2535 Dec. 31 Monday Down to finish Fors,[63] in fair health and good heart, DG, with infirmities for which—there may be use if I will—see over leaf [64]

I shall not take up too much of index space by noting that yesterday I went up by the farm to top of Furness fells, & down by Copland Grange 3 hours walk in all,—untired, though breathless in going up.

Supplementary Note

The Dalbeattie Exhibition, 1883

Speaking of the Ruskin drawings which were on display when

61. On Christmas morning the "marvellous" drawings had arrived, and Ruskin had "no words," next day, with which to tell her "how marvellous" he thought they were. "No one has ever done anything equal to them in pure grace of movement—no one in exquisiteness of dainty design." He was sure they would be valued "endlessly and everywhere if I can get them engraved the least rightly—the sight of them alters one's thoughts of all the world" (*Works, 29,* xxvi; letter of December 26, 1883).

62. *The Ruskin Birthday Book* compiled by Grace Allen and Maud A. Bateman. Its frontispiece was a portrait of Ruskin engraved by William Roffe from a photograph by Elliot and Fry (ca. 1882) (see Frontispiece to *Works, 29,* and xxviii.

63. Letter 94, issued in March 1884, is dated "31st December, 1883" and is referred to as "this last *Fors* of 1883" (*Works, 29,* 478).

64. He has reached the end of page 243 and the rest of this entry, followed by that of January 1, 1884, is written on the page, headed "A," which begins the section of the "Ledger" reserved for his index to this volume.

the Industrial and Fine Art Loan Exhibition opened at Dalbeattie, *The Dumfries and Galloway Courier* reported:

> The Professor also contributes five sketches illustrative of the proper treatment of material in sculpture. From the letter which accompanies the exhibits we learn that these are (1) Egyptian and Greek work, both of finest time in granite, marble, and clay. The upper sketch is of small work in terra-cotta, real size, Greek, best time, showing the use made of ductility in pinching out projecting ornaments. The one beneath is the exactly reverse treatment of incision in granite, keeping the relief as shallow as possible (a profile section at side). The lateral sketches are of light and shade in fine Greek marble work, broad and delicate at once. (2) Granite sculpture, Egyptian head of Anubis (below painted of the real size from sarcophagus in British Museum). Above first chalk sketch of head of jackal (stuffed, British Museum) to show the writhed lower lip which is dwelt on in the sculpture, the expression depending on the most subtle management of simple incision. (3) Hard marble, Verona, central drawing 12th century, lateral drawing 15th century, showing the rounded breadth of masses and softly modelled surfaces with no sharp edges. (4) Greek marble, Pisa, in font of baptistry, 11th century. Sketched font to show the beautifully varied treatment of the sway of leaf up and down, and mode of turning the angle—all freehand work of finest style, real size. (5) Greek marble, Avallon, France, 12th century. Finest style freehand, but less varied than the Pisan work. The lines of main curvature superb in style. About one-sixth size of Capital.
>
> (July 17, 1883; p. 2)

A second installment of material had been received from Ruskin by July 20, whereafter the *Kirkcudbrightshire Advertiser and Galloway News* reported:

> As we briefly mentioned last week, Mr John Ruskin sent in an additional lot of his beautiful sketches, photographs, &c., and as these are not included in the published catalogue for

the information of those interested we give Mr Ruskin's own notes. The additional specimens commence with

No.

6. Greek marble, Venice (6th century, brought from St. Jean d'Arc), showing the finest freehand design, nat one curve or leaf resembling another. Very sharp in relief; undercut a little in places.
7. Hard marble (Pisa), 12th century. Flat in surface, and nowhere undercut. Entirely splendid in design.
8. Hard chalk (Abbeville, France), 16th century. Style founded on wood carving, and only possible in soft and tough stone, but first-rate of its kind.
9. Fast study, for sculpture, of currant-bud opening in spring. Three times size of life.
10. Finished study of oak leaves in autumn to show general variety of contour fixed by frost.

PHOTOGRAPHS, taken under Mr Ruskin's superintendence except Nos. 14, 15, and 16.

11. Hard limestone. Northern porch of west front, Rouen Cathedral.
12. Hard limestone. The keystone of inner moulding in the same porch.
13. Hard limestone. Herodias counselling Herod. (Part of the figure subject in same porch.) The other guests discreetly turn away, partly looking at her daughter, who casts a somersault in the middle of tympanum. (See No. 11.) The execution of St. John the Baptist on the right (also in No. 11), and Herodias receiving his head from her daughter. The servants under the table represented as almost children—partly a traditional practice from Egyptian sculpture, which always by what is called "conventional," *i.e.*, "agreed upon" principle, marks inferiority of rank by diminution of size. I cannot make out the small broken figure. It looks as if it had been a dog begging. It adds greatly to the composition by carrying out the sloping lines towards the centre, emphasized by the left arm of Herodias.

14. Hard chalk. West front of Rouen Cathedral—late 15th and early 16th century. The north porch, represented in Nos. 11, 12, and 13, is seen on the left, buried under the pomp of the later eclipse. When I first saw this façade fifty years since the two buttress pinnacles on the right and left were as rich as the two central ones, but a little more decayed. They were pulled down to be "restored," and put up again in blank blocks—all, of course, for the sake of the job. The modern stonecutters could easily cut out the blocks, and the builder got his commission on putting them up, but of course nobody could carve them when they *were* put up—nor would the town have paid for the carving; so there they stay till they moulder like the others—the façade being thus ruined for ever. The modern clock and lamps are conspicuous defacements of what remains of it. The figure standing in the doorway shows the scale.
15. Finest style of French woodwork (exterior) Abbeville, 16th century. The small white Madonna in the niche over the doorway is, of course, modern. The winding external staircase was a principal feature in most of the important houses of French cities. Many examples remain in stone. At Chartres there is a wooden one of extreme beauty going up to the top of the house and terminating in a peaked roof.
16. Finest style of French woodwork (interior) Amiens, 16th century. See p. 7 of "Interpretations." (Bible of Amiens No. 4.)
17. Six 4-foils of base of Amiens Cathedral. Hard limestone, finest 13th century. (Bible of Amiens, p. 42.)

Above — The Tower of the Flock.
Jonah escaped from the sea.
Elijah and the captain of fifty.
Below — Under vine and fig tree.
Jonah under the gourd.
Ahab and Obadiah.

18. Six more — inside Cathedral porch. (p. 42, Amiens.)
Above — Nahum ii., 8 — "There is none that returneth."
Daniel in Lion's den. (p. 41, Amiens.)
Ezekiel and the wheels.
Below — The Burden of Nineveh. Nahum i., 1.
Daniel and Belshazzar. Daniel v., 5.
Woe to the bloody city. Ezek. xxiv., 6.

19. Six more. (Amiens, p. 43.)
Above— The Lord strikes Ethiopia. Zepaniah ii., 12.
I waited for the Lord. Habakkuk ii., 1.
Thy princes and thy great ones. Micah iii., 17
Below — A place for beasts to lie down in. Zeph. ii., 15.
Habakkuk ministers to Daniel (Apocrypha).
Untimely figs. Nahum iii., 12.

(July 27, 1883, p. 4.)

1884

2534 January 1 Tuesday. Very thankful to be spared to see the light, and begin the labour, not unhopefully of this New Year.

Collie and Dorrie[1] very happy with me: and the shepherd above me on the moor, happier *for* me.[2] Began day with my large new Diamond and Forbes's map of Mer de glace[3] and read the four different gospels of the Resurrection. Now begin on Francesca's book

1. After her marriage to W. G. Collingwood, Edith Mary Isaac (1857–1928) of Maldon, Essex, was known as "Dorrie" to her husband's friends. She was a trained musician, as well as an artist who specialized in painting flowers and miniatures. At this point, coming to Brantwood to help Ruskin through her presence, she had been married for no more than six weeks.

2. This "shepherd," as Miss Gnosspelius specifies, doubtless was Mr. Wilkinson of Lawson Park, to whom Ruskin appears to have given money during the Christmas season to help offset the various losses which the Wilkinsons had suffered, as described in Ruskins' "A Charitable Appeal" of 1884. In this public appeal Ruskin speaks of having "partly reimbursed them for their loss myself" (see *Works, 34,* 654, where Cook and Wedderburn substitute "the Watkinsons" for "the Wilkinsons" as the name which appears in the MS Preface to the Collecting-book, now in the Coniston Museum).

3. The *Mer de Glace,* as charted in J. D. Forbes' *Travels Through the Alps* (1845), had been central to Ruskin's championship of Forbes' glacier theory in the controversy with Tyndall. For the map, see *Deucalion,* Pl. XIII, in *Works, 26,* facing p. 160.

Miscellaneous Entries

1873

[The following entries appear upon pages cut from *Diaries* and preserved in the F. J. Sharp Collection.]

May. 1873 — Oxford

Oxford. 6th. — Monday.

I begin this for my Oxford and travelling diary.

Left Brantwood on Thursday. Friday, disturbed and failing at lecture on swallow. Saturday in doors all day. Yesterday only out to see Alice [Liddell?], and get a little walk—chanced on Canon Dixon at lunch. — Half sleepless night.

Read this morning part of the Νεκυομαντεία, [*Nekyomanteia,* more commonly known as *Nekyia,* a title given to *Odyssey XI*] to my great comfort, and delight

Oxford. 7th May — Tuesday

Lecture yesterday satisfactory. Bright now.—little morning walk, meditating on mist— Look at [my drawing of Rock at?] Maglans and my Father's portrait—long: very full of thoughts and plans

Herne Hill 8th May. — Wednesday

Yesterday busy at Oxford. M Bolet—and men at work— Up talking with Professor [William?] Smith, then—[dentist] Mr Woodhouse—

Then, Home, and find Pussie [Mrs. Severn] well, and cheerful.

Today,—up in showery morning, a little headachy.

Oxford. 9th. May. Dates above all wrong. This is Friday morning. Tomorrow my Fathers birthday. If he could have known that yesterday his son should have come down to Oxford—one of its most honoured teachers, and with one of the Princes of England [Leopold]. That his portrait would be over my door—and a Titian beside it.

Salt Hill. 11th May Sunday

My Father's birthday was spent pleasantly on Italian drawings and lecturing to Eton Boys! how he would have rejoiced.

Today grey morning in old inn at Salt Hill

21st. Wednesday.

Sadly broken up just now, but getting Oxford room in order. [His copyist, Charles Fairfax] Murray at SIENA Casa Dominici. Via del Casato. Mrs J. H. Allin, 5, little Pulteney St St James's.

Dr Henry Ongar, 46, Regent Sq. W.C.

11th June. Herne Hill.

Yesterday down to Carshalton [Spring, dedicated to his mother]—and disgusted & discouraged— Feeling of cold came on last night at Metaphysical.

Black East— No—South—wind! deadly

12th June Corpus Domini 3.45. 8.15

Yesterday. A terrible day, at Croydon and Carshalton among destruction and misery.

Sleepless night mostly.

The grand long day, ¼ before four, to ¼ past eight of sun, made partly unavailable—*all* sad.

15th June. Sunday
Yesterday at Carshalton, with mamie and Papie [Mr. and Mrs. Hilliard]. Inscription printed for my mother's memorial —but wrongly. Dreamed of R[ose] that she was still hard and cruel in heart, but that she came to me—and gave herself to me—as sweetly in body as Cressid to Troilus, in Chaucer's verse.

I never had such a real vision of her before, in a dream.

Better & wiser in mind this morning than usual.

Herne Hill 17th June. Tuesday
Heavy cold upon me, and every sort of practical despondency. Worst, the perpetual darkness of the sky. At Leadenhall market yesterday watching ducks, which refreshed me.

19th June. Thursday
On the 17th in at Arundel, talking to an audience of nine people Yesterday to Cowley [home of the Hilliards] by Richmond. today, up early, see sunrise at 4: joylessly.

20th June. Friday.
Terrific day of hard work, yesterday, correcting index to Fors. Mr Gale and Martha in evening. Today— Grey heavy sky and I as leaden.

1878

[While examining books in the Brantwood Library (ca. 1930), the editor transcribed the following Diary entries of 1878 from an otherwise blank page of Volume 1 in a set of Bacon's *Works,* the present whereabouts of which remains unknown. For Ruskin's account of the trip during which he had this book at hand, see his entry for August 22, 1878; *Diaries,* p. 976.]

12 Aug[ust] Monday—walked down from Malham Tavern House to Malham—sketching a little at top of Cove. Arthur [Severn] leaves me.

13th Tues[day] Work quietly and well—after strangely bad night (stomachic)—on geology of Yorkshire in my square room at Malham

14th Wed[nesday] Wet, working successfully today on cubic Malham Cove for Fesole

15 Thurs[day] A thoroughly good day, yesterday on Deucalion in morning and the Cove, showing my best sketch hitherto, in the afternoon. Cloudy to-day. Doubtful if to go or stay

16th Fri[day] Ingleton—walked over Malham moors yesterday afternoon— today ten miles from Settle—and evening here quite fresh, and up to anything but writing—books at least, letters I can do.

17th Sat[urday] wet at Ingleton

18th Sunday, up at Ingleton.

1840

[The pages which provide the following "abstract" of entries in the Diary of 1840 (from which 34 pages "have been torn out": *Diaries,* p. 83n.) were probably cut from a volume of the *Diaries* which belongs to the period during which Ruskin was preparing to write *Praeterita.*]

1840 (Abstract begun—of course left off at 3rd page.[)]

Sept. 23rd. Rouen. Diary 2. p. 10

With Father & Mother, and Mary.

Think St. Ouen finest thing I ever saw in my life.

"Corsaire rouge," before window, my mother says "like overgrown grasshopper" Cafe de la Place, already spoiled. Walk down Turner's avenue—on other side of river. 11. 2.

Sept. 24th By Louviers to Evreux. p. 13, 14 saw both for first time.

(it was in starting on this journey that the old

Abbeville landlady said, "Quel dommage que vous ne prenez pas de potage. Le potage est *si* bon."[)]

Sept. 25. From Evreux to Chartres.
French nobility building "niches" instead of chateau. 15. 1.

Sept. 26th. Sketched at Chartres in choir, in the morning.
Stayed at "Grand Monarque."
Then, this day, to Orleans.

Sept. 27th. Sunday. Orleans.
Window in cathedral "like phosphorescent starfish" 19. 1.

Sept. 28th. Monday—Blois.
Sunset interesting, p. 22.

Sept. 29th. Tuesday. Blois.
Sketched cortile of palace.

Sept. 30th. Wednesday. Tours.
Seeing Amboise on the way.

Oct. 1st. Thursday. Tours.
Sketching in morning, describe St Julien in a way I suppose fine. 27.

Oct. 2nd. Friday from Tours to Chateau-roux
Late in.
Curious bit of road. 28. 1.

Oct. 3rd. Saturday. Chateauroux to Gueret.
Not in till twilight. 30.

Oct. 4th. Sunday at Gueret

Oct. 5th. Monday, to Aubusson.
All page 32 very good.

Oct. 6th. Tuesday, from Aubusson to Pont Gibaud
Aubusson. p. 33. well described.

Oct. 7th. at Pont Gibaud. walk to mines
Galena note p. 35

Oct. 8th. Thursday. Pont Gibaud to Clermont.
Account of Clermont, p. 37.

Oct. 9th Friday to Brioude.
No notice of Brionde, but valuable matter at p. 38.

Oct. 10th. Saturday. Brionde to Le Puy

1887

[The two following entries appear in a black "Cash-book," in the F. J. Sharp Collection, which contains other material relevant to the year 1887.]

Hythe Sunday. 11. Sept. 1887

Yesterday, made the acquaintance of the Captain and his men, on board the rough-sea barge lying high and—not dry—on the mud of Folkstone Harbour.

And obtain the following measures taken by the men themselves with great delight, with my old architectural tape, —thank God, in service once again, when I never expected to unroll it more

	Ft.	In.
Length, within *timbers*	74	
Length of hold for wood	48	
Beam	18	6
Main-mast at bottom	5	
— — at top	2	8
Heel of bowsprit	1	11
The main-mast is of pitch-pine		10
— top — — white pine	2	3
Lengths of spars		
Main-mast	38	
Top. —	32	
Mizen —	12	
Point Sprit	59	
Mizen Sprit	22	
Bowsprit	28	

The point sprit *was* 61 ft long, but the master had two feet of it cut off.

Trafalgar Sq. Wednesday. 28th Sept. 87

Spent an entirely bright day in Nat[ional] Gallery, yesterday—and am greatly humiliated by the beauty of everything. Met Peter Bayne, who really does care for me, and made him happy by confessing that I began to enjoy Canaletto. D.G.

Part Two

Selected Letters

I

The Ruskin-Alexander-Severn Correspondence

[To the letters from Ruskin to Francesca Alexander and from Francesca to her "Fratello" which have been published in *John Ruskin's Letters to Francesca,* ed. L. G. Swett (1931), the following can now be added from the F. J. Sharp Collection. In this collection there are also many letters (1885–1906) to Mrs. Severn from Francesca and from Mrs. Alexander.]

1. *Ruskin to Francesca Alexander*

Brantwood
Monday [late 1880s]

Darling Sorel

Don't you think it was—to say the least—*cool* in you when you know how fond I am of colour—to paint that gray plate for me all over grey brambles? Dont you know that bramble in Latin is 'Rubus'

I always have my morning bread off that plate—and coffee out of my rose cup beside it—and the plate looks fearfully dismal.

I walked good three miles yesterday, mostly on the lakes shingly shore—macadam shore rather like this [sketch of very rough terrain] as far as you like. Was'nt a bit tired—and looking for minnows nearly all the way—and did'nt see *one!*

Jane Anne was [holding?] my 'chopsticks' on Saturday I saw she was'nt minding what she was about—and had to keep her up to it— after about half an hour—says she—all of a sudden

'Father got a howl yesterday'

R[uskin] — Got one—what do you mean? shot it?

— Jane — No—brought it home and we put it to kill the mice.

— How big is it?

As big as a hen—

What colour?

White and brown—

It turned out her mind was set on whether I'd like it for a present. I said I should, immensely but she must look after it for me—and I did'nt want my mice eaten

So its agreed—and Im going to pay her brother, Willy to clean etc its cage—and teach it manners.

Ever your lovingest Fratel

Brantwood
Easter [18]87

Dearest Sorella

I never saw a more perfect Easter Sun, and your Asiago letter is invaluable to me—chiefly of all the bit about your Grandmother and the Irish servant, but I am badly down myself, with withering of East wind, and feel like Jonah,—and I want to know what became of Jonah—for thats whats going to become of me, I suppose I'm doing a little Proserpina and branch work from it and am not as far as I know, unwell—but very sad, and my eyes flickering—and in the state in which they see vermilion brown-gray—and blue, black-grey—but the [newgreen?] outside is irresistibly visible

I can only write this poor word today, and love to Mammina

Your sick—gourdless—Fratello

Brantwood
Monday 4th April [1887] [1]

Sweetest of Souls.

This Asiago letter is invaluable—to me, as well as to the readers of [Christ's] Folk and what 'I shall like still better' in the next—what *can* it be!!!

It describes scenery and people of which I had not myself the least idea—and the pieces of history are delicious—proving my continually reiterated doctrine of trust in race.

Those about your own ancestry with mamminas letter to Joan, are treasures also— You shall of course see whatever use I make of all, before publication— The III part should soon be with you it is most delightful to *me*! —the 4th will begin with the toybank story and go on with detached pieces—chiefly the 'going home' of Signor Rossetti.

I am keeping well, and have gone back into my botany for fear of too thrilling interest in Folk I hope Proserpina will be more complete than for the last two or three years seemed possible, but

1. The pending Part III of *Christ's Folk in the Apennine* was issued on June 7, 1887.

really the use of what is already done will be trebled—if I can do half as much more.

— I can't get my class interested though—half as much as I expected—probably because I have only pictures, not the real flowers. They are more interested in learning what I give them to learn well, than in the meaning of what is learnt—and are as eager over a vulgar fraction as over the gracefullest of flowers.

Joanie has enjoyed being alone with me and hunting all the buds that are opening But she leaves me on Thursday and I must get on by myself for about a fortnight when I shall have somebody to take care of me again I hope

— but we'll have some chats before then

Ever your lovingest Fratello

Brantwood
1st May 1889

Darling Sorel

I never thanked you for the beautiful last rispetto— they are every one prettier than the last, it seems to me—only I don't allow the jealousy— the right feeling is that one would like all the world to see and rejoice in the loveliness—and to know in ones own heart all the while that it could never change or fail from being one's own.

I have passed through nearly all the visionary part of this 'illness'—(if it is to be called so) and am out in the daily world again among the anemones,—but 'the Enemy' has sown long grass all through my violet and strawberry beds,—there's nearly two years growth of grass, just where I don't want it—and the way the wretched gardeners neglect all the places I care for, when I'm away—and grow nothing but staring hot house plants, ruining me in coals and smoking all across the lake—is enough to make St. Benedict swear,—let alone a poor sick soul like mine

I'm going to write K[ate] G[reenaway] & give her a May-day word of thankfulness for all she has done and is doing.

— And ever so much May—to Mammina

And Im your—really very happy —— —— and so's Joanie I think today*— Fratel

* Her boys have gone off to school but she's very proud of them!

Brantwood
Sunday —— 12th May, 1889

Darling Sorel

You will never write of things too high for you—but you *do* sometimes write of things the least bit too low— at least—you sometimes *teaze* your poor Fratel by writing of pretty girls going to be married—when *he* is tempted in the saddest way by wishes that he were young again—instead of having to think so constantly of all he must leave—for an unknown land

— But Sorel dear, I am really getting better—for this spring—even the doctor says—though it's no business of his!—hes sitting opposite me while I write

so this must go.

Ever your lovingest Fratel

Brantwood
Sunday   1st July 1889

Dearest Sorella

I have just got your quite lovely letter—telling me the good report of oculist—the best brightness that could come to me—and I think oculists know their science well,—and indeed as I look over all the beautiful work you have done there is reason enough for rest—and with your power of happiness in all sweet things and kind creatures you will only enter into a wider heavenly world than that of flowers. What you tell me of dear Piero [Mazzini, his gondolier] is altogether beautiful— I think his the sweetest face I ever saw—of *mans*   There are surely better times coming for the world, for assuredly gentleness & love are increasing, and in deeper and more subtle ways, than ever was possible in the great war times.

Dearest love to mamina— I don't know what [she'd] say—or Marina either, if they had to feed me just now—for I have taken a fit of caring for nothing, and what is worse of lazy bed-keeping half awake—which would at any rate relieve you from all dread of my doing too much. — I don't recollect having done anything these last three days—but Joanie has been away—called by sad occasion into Scotland, and I am nothing without her—nor any body else in the house—the streams are all silent, for the drought has withered them from the hills, and the birds have stopped singing and think only of eating strawberries— How fearfully short the sweetness of the summer is.

Joanie will be back tomorrow I trust—but sorrowful enough—(one of her favourite (dead) sister's daughters having died suddenly at school) I am trying with what poor wreck of me is left to show her a little how I love her.

— Much love to Raffaele & Angelo—and their sweet wives.

Ever dearest Sorella

Your lovingest Fratello

J R.

2. *Francesca Alexander to Ruskin*

Venezia
Di 27 Giugno 1889

Mio caro Fratello

I hope today that nobody will come in, and that I can have a quiet hour to write, for as usual, I have many things to say, besides two or three rispetti. And, first of all, I have seen Piero Mazzini, who kept his promise and came back again. He is looking well, and seems overflowing with gratitude to you; but, more even than your generosity to him, he likes to dwell on the happiness of seeing you again, last autumn: he was never tired of going over and over again the most minute circumstances of your meeting with him; but, after the first moment of recognition, he says: "It was all a confusion. I had no eyes to see with, for the too great joy!" Teresina is well now, with the exception of her eyes, and they do not grow any worse, and the doctor thinks they will finally recover. He (Piero) has put himself at the disposition of your friends, as you said; and they have already been out once for a sail, to the great pleasure of everybody. And the next thing I want to tell you is about myself, and I know it will please you. We have been to see an oculist, Dr. Gosetti, about my eyes; and he assures me that there is nothing the matter with them, excepting that they are weak and tired; and that this will pass, with time. He even says that I shall be able to go to work again, after a while, if I follow his directions, (which I certainly mean to do!) I don't mean to set my heart on his prophecy coming true; but I am very thankful for the hope. Meanwhile, until it does come true, you will have patience if I send you a good deal of crooked blind writing to read.

I am having a very idle life just now, which is a contrast to the drive that I usually live in; and for the present I really like it, and feel as if it might be making me fit to do some sort of work again, one of these days. Before breakfast I weed a little in the garden, and attend to the house-keeping. After breakfast, I go out all by myself, to buy fruit, and other little matters, for the day, and have a lovely walk in the fresh morning air, always ending with half an hour in the Church of S. Stefano, which puts me in tune for all day. I do not meet very aristocratic company there, at that hour: the congregation usually consists principally of servant girls, from the mountains of Cadore, Carnia, or Friuli, in their contadine dresses, often with market baskets in their hands. But they are very devout and quiet, having no doubt risen early and driven through a good deal of hard work to earn time for those morning prayers; and it makes one feel better to be with them. (For, devotion is contagious, like most good and bad things.... is it not strange, when one thinks of it, how few things are *not* contagious?) But Fratello, I can't tell you how pleasant those morning walks are; and every day I see many things that I should like to tell you, only they seem too trifling. The shopkeepers, of the less fashionable sort, are just taking down their shutters at that time, and one of my amusements is to look in to each shop as I pass, and try to judge a little of the occupants, by seeing what pictures are on the walls. One has a Madonna, with the King and Queen on her right and left; another, Garibaldi, and various engravings of battles (in which the Austrians are all being conveniently killed, or running away) but no Madonna at all.... he is probably a republican free-thinker. One elderly man, (who sells fruit in a pretty little shop, all open to the street, and made into a sort of bower with green oak-branches,) has his Madonna opposite to the door, with a little lamp burning, and, usually, a bunch of carnations before her. On her right, hangs a large lithograph of Garibaldi; and on her left, a most remarkable one, of a french soldier, with a sentimental face, very large eyes, and a figure of which I can only say that it is a powerful sermon on the evil of tight lacing, walking triumphantly, with lifted sword, over the body of a fallen austrian. And, without any want of respect to french or italian heroes, I wonder sometimes whether the Madonna, if she knew anything about it, altogether likes the company she is in. One very old man and his wife, who sell vegetables, have (with, I believe, truly devotional feeling) festooned their Madonna tastefully with bunches of onions! I have been wondering today whether one reason of the considerate manners, and kindness to animals, which I notice in the Venetians, may not be the influence of St. Mark's pigeons. This morning, when I came out of the church, there were several of them outside of the door; and I stopped to throw down a handful of corn for them. Down they swept, from all the roofs in sight,... in a moment, I had a great flock, crowding and fluttering about my feet. Then I became aware that somebody had joined me; and, looking up, I saw rather a rough looking, weather beaten old woman, standing beside me. She had left the well for a moment, and held her copper pail, half filled, in her hand. She looked very poor, and as if she had led a sad, hard life. As our eyes met, she accounted for her presence, by saying simply: "We love them!" And when I came away, she was still watching the doves, quite happy in seeing them pleased. Then I crossed the traghetto: a pleasant looking old man, apparently a sailor, in a very clean checked shirt, came up as we were starting, said, "Would you permit me?" and finding I was willing, stepped in, and sat down at the opposite end of the boat. He was carrying home the materials for a vegetable soup, in a red cotton handkerchief. All the way he did nothing but look critically at the sky and water, and talk audibly to himself about the weather, until we reached the landing, where he held the boat in place with one arm, and gave me the other to step ashore. But the paper cuts me short in the middle! Goodbye and love from us both.

Your affectionate Sorella

[Airolo, August 1890] [2]

Mio caro Fratello,

It seems like a very long time since I have written to you: I have always been afraid lest my letters should fatigue you; but

2. A number of letters addressed to Mrs. Severn show that in 1890 Francesca spent the month of August in Airole, in this letter discussed as her present place of residence.

now, as I hear from every one that you are so well, and gaining strength every day, I think perhaps I have had patience long enough; and it is indeed with a thankful heart that I take up my pen again! Joanie said that you were pleased to hear of our coming to Airolo, and so perhaps you would like to have me tell you a little about it, (though I think likely you have seen it yourself, as you know Switzerland so well.) For the present, I have not recovered from the first sense of strangeness, and perhaps a little home-sickness, which came over me at first sight of this neat, prosperous, very un-italian little town; but I am growing more into it every day, especially as the people are all so kind and friendly. But the country about is extremely beautiful, and almost realizes the wish expressed in that rispetto which I once translated for you "The stones all crystals that you tread upon!" Really, the shining stones in the roads and walls are a wonderful sight, being all full of little crystals, that glitter in the sun as if the dew were upon them! The mountains are grander, higher, more savage and less lovely, than those about Abetone; (but perhaps they only less lovely because they are not old friends, like those!) the flowers, pretty much the same, but less abundant; the climate.... Well, today is the first of dog days, and we have had a snowstorm on the hilltops close above us, and as I look from the window, I see that the snow is beginning to fall again! But the stones are beyond any that I ever saw for beauty; and Edwige [Gualtieri, her servant-friend] keeps filling her pockets with them, to take home to the children. She is very happy here, especially in the church; and came home yesterday delighted with the sermon about "Pharisees and republicans." Later there was a procession, from our church to one in the next village, and I went out myself to see it, and Edwige and I fell in behind, and walked all the way after the others, up a pretty winding foot path, through lonely green fields full of bluebells and buttercups, among great thickets of wild roses in full blossom; with the narrow valley, and the impetuous, green, foaming river, dropping farther below us at every turn; and the mountains rising higher around us. First walked a man carrying a tall cross; then the priest, a venerable looking man, with a kind, saintly face, and silver hair; and then the choir of little boys, and one or two men, all chanting the litanies. And then came all the long procession of women, headed by a dark-haired, italian looking girl, carrying the Crucifix, with a scarlet canopy that fluttered in the wind. Some carried babies, or led little children by the hand; all joined in the singing, (including your Sorella, for there was no resisting the example of their devotion!) and in the pauses of the chants, they recited prayers, with deep feeling. The clouds which brought the snow today were already settling down on the hills; but now and then a flash of sunshine broke through them, and lighted for a moment the gay silk handkerchiefs of the women, making them look like a long border of flowers. But I can never describe to you the sweetness of that chanting, with all those soft women's voices in such perfect harmony, and the distant rushing of the river heard through it all! And surely no congregation ever had so grand a church to pray and sing in: it seemed a great deal more devotional than any church with walls to it; and I know that Edwige felt this, for she said to me as we walked home: "I think the Lord Jesus likes the prayers that are made in these little lanes!" And, (that no class of inhabitants should be un-represented) there was a very well behaved brown and white dog, who chose to go in procession with the others, and seemed to enjoy it. The animals seem to be an important part of the population here, and are most lovingly cared for, and are very pretty, intelligent and affectionate. I wish you [second folder missing]

Lugano
Di 8 Luglio (1897?) [3]

Mio caro Fratello

I am afraid you will have no Sunday letter this week! I can't tell you how sorry I was not to write yesterday, but a letter came from Florence on some business which it was absolutely necessary I should attend to without delay, and it took me the whole day long, and left me tired out at night I will not tell you about it, for fear that I should do as I did last time, when I filled up all my precious permitted four pages with the history of the traghetto cat! But when I tell you that yesterday was all passed in writing, and walking, and seeing people, all to secure the exemption of Edwige's eldest grandson from conscription, (from which it ap-

3. In stationery and in handwriting this letter exactly resembles a letter sent to Mrs. Severn from Lugano on July 27, 1897.

pears he will be exempt, in virtue of a law about a widow's eldest grandson) and that this young man has an invalid Father, and has just secured a good situation, which he will lose if taken in the army, I am sure you will say I did right, even in neglecting, for once, the Sunday letter.

I was very sorry to leave Venice, and feel somewhat home-sick for it still; we had such a beautiful visit there this time! I had almost dreaded seeing it, after two years of absence, but it is in no way changed. As I told you once before, Madonna Povertã is the last patron saint of Venice and she takes good care of it. The Venetians have not money enough to disfigure their beautiful city as they would like to, and as the Florentines have done theirs. It never looked more lovely. We saw many old friends there, among them Sig. Boni, who was there for a few days, and talked and asked about you with the most affectionate interest, as he always does. He had been making a great study of the statue of S. Teodoro, on the column in the Piazzetta, of which he gave us a wonderful history. Only think, it is made of pieces of other statues put together the head being the most ancient part, greek, of parian marble. . . . But never mind! This is a more interesting subject than the cat, but I don't want to fill up my letter with it, for all that; and you will read sometime what Boni is going to print about it. What I really want to tell you is, that Italy and we have been very, very near to losing him altogether, and that his life was saved by a very wonderful providence. I do not know if you saw in your english papers about the terrible land-slide, or rock slide, at Sasso, between Bologna and Porretta. You may remember the place, a great, terrible precipice of rock, looking like a gigantic fortification, towering very far up into the sky. The other day a great mass of the rock broke away from the mountain side and fell, crushing everything in its way, and burying completely the railroad track. The train, if it had kept good time, would have been buried with all the rest; but it was exactly *half a minute* in retard! And Boni was in that train. Now that we are here, I am glad that we have come; for Mammina seems better and stronger in this air than I have ever seen her since her illness, and has taken liking to the place. We are very pleasantly situated, quite in the country this time, among beautiful trees, and overlooking the lake just at the end of the garden. What a succession of pictures the lake makes, in all the variations of wind and calm, of sunlight, twilight and moonlight! But here I am at the end of my paper; and I wanted to tell you some of Edwige's sayings, but they must wait till next time. (I have taken some larger paper, but it is not half large enough!) Much love from Mammina and your

Sorella

3. *Mrs. Severn to Mrs. Alexander*

Brantwood [4]
17th Nov[ember], 1886

Beloved Mammina

I am so glad you have written to me openly on the Millais subject—because I may be of some comfort & help in the matter to you—having heard all details from trustworthy sources—& your Figlio has often talked quite openly to me about it all— so did his mother, whom I dearly loved—& whose sense of duty *was so great,* that I am positive she was ever most indulgent & kind, in all ways to her son's wife— it was not a marriage either she, or her Husband ever approved—especially as about a week before the marriage he had to pay £12,000 for the Father's debts (Mr. G[ray])—this first startled your F[iglio] into seeing the marriage was one of convenience— at the time E[ffie] made love to him (to save her Father from disgrace) she was already engaged to another man in India, (who was broken-hearted by her desertion of him) at her school she was known amongst her companions as '*lying* Effie'!—(this I knew from one of them)—she was *most ambitious!* —the compact was, that for the first year of their life nothing should happen, as he had much travelling & work—& wished to run no risk of babies— after that he had no desire to live otherwise with her—but was always most generously kind & indulgent to her & her family— his old nurse's evidence *was* that from a baby he always exactly seemed like other *children* (boys)—up to 12 when she had constant care of him. I well know to what you allude, having known several cases of such obstruction, where operation *has* been necessary—but never heard it breathed in connection with

4. In the upper left corner of this letter Mrs. Severn wrote: "Please burn— for yourself." On the envelope Mrs. Alexander wrote: "Most private, but I had finally permission to keep from Mrs Severn."

him. I *have heard* that wicked untrue story of his having agreed about the then Mr. M[illais] he took him to Scotland—& directly he became suspicious spoke to his wife— *she* said there was *nothing* & no cause for it—but *he* (M.) burst into tears—(an admission of *his* feeling!)— that very day your Figlio got him to leave them—and believed all was at an end! —but they kept up a clandestine correspondence till she ran away— she volunteered that examination— the day she left (on the pretext of paying a visit to her people in Scotland, where he was to join her)—he saw her off —& almost her last words were, can't you give me some more money?! —that evening she returned her wedding ring—& signed herself Effie Gray! —saying she had left him for-ever— His Lawyer asked if he'd have her back—saying he could oblige her to come provided he would live with her as other Husbands— He said *"never"*—tho' added he could on these terms if he liked— he had been *so* unhappy latterly with her he was thankful to get rid of her— *she* expected large damages—& got a *farthing!*

Dr. Parsons has just been here—and I asked him having a good opportunity—the question once more [à propos of Kathleen Olander?]— he answered with even more firmness than once before that marriage would be *the* very worst thing—& the most dangerous to his health—quite out of the question— he came to me afterwards—but had not had time to enter into any detail with him, but on his saying (an old joke) 'well have you advertised for a nice girl for me yet—Dr. P[arsons] said—certainly not!—and you know I consider *that* form of excitement *the* worst of all for you'—

Miss Anderson has gone home, but I will forward F[rancesca]'s letter—

I have been writing in an odd corner, with a very bad pen—forgive confusion.

Your ever grateful loving

Figlia

I consider your F[iglio] *much* better, & more himself the last few days—

[In 1888, accompanied by Detmar Blow during his last trip to the Continent, Ruskin visited the Alexanders in Bassano while they were staying with friends in the Palazzo Rezzonico. At the end of nine days he unexpectedly departed, leaving Francesca and Mrs. Alexander as troubled as they had been surprised by the abruptness of his farewell. By December he was in Paris, where he became so seriously ill that Mrs. Severn was summoned to conduct him back to London. Meanwhile, she had sent Mrs. Alexander the following letter.]

Brantwood
Sunday
Oct[ober] 28th 1888 [5]

Beloved Mammina

I am writing this part of my letter last—after extracting all the bits from my Di Pa letters that I thought might be of interest to you—& what you asked me for—the between dates 29th & 30th Septr—& 1st 4th 6th & 7th Octr—he either didn't write—or only a tiny line—& nothing in the few letters I have of these dates with any allusion to you—or what would interest you—chiefly home business matters to advise—or tell me about— I had not before leaving time to arrange his letters consecutively—hence the rather promiscuous sheets of paper—having written down from each letter as they came anything bearing on his Rezzonico visit—

The enclosed "Angelina" letter may be precious to Francesca—it was amongst your's I had to destroy so cruelly! — Alas! I am so grieved for all the sorrow & distress that has come to you from the loss of so many precious friends—

"Sallenche[s] 12th Sept I have written a line to Francesca to thank her for invitation. I really go to Italy to see Mammina & her: and would'nt, but for them" —

on 23rd Sept 88 *Milan* He writes

["] I find myself so miserable in Italy—and so much feebler, my ancles swelling—and a languor on me such as I have not had since Abbeville—and scarcely there." ——

From Milan he wrote to me—"I have written to Francesca that I have no power of doing any work now at Venice—and she is welcome to what she cares to have of the fag end and aches of me! —

5. This letter is headed: "Back from the Bectives—& lose no time in looking over Di Pa letters— Arthur still at Kirkby Lonsdale—."

that however—poor as the gift seems, I may be able to help her in some things, and be advised and comforted in others—very differently in giving her all my time peacefully, from the best that could have been if I had tried for any work of my own"

Pal[azzo] Rezzonico 27th Sept 88 Bassano

"we got here in all comfort—Francesca and the Count Pasolini (Silvia's husband) meeting us, and there are no words to tell all their kindness—and the beauty of the place— Ah, if I can but live and keep well, to make the people who love me happy a little longer! — But the days are so short—and they fly so fast—and I don't know the least what plans will come out of the multitude that Mammina has formed for me— She is entirely wonderful— Francesca's face is very beautiful, when one sees it quietly—["]

"Bassano Friday 28th Sept There never were such kind or sweet people, in a moment, and Mammina says they all like me, and can't think of my going away; and my Sorella is far sweeter and dearer than I expected—"

Bassano 2nd Oct "I was led on from step to step—& now I don't know how ever I am to get back again—but it seemed to me I owed it to my Sorel—

["] The people here are exquisitely kind—and the Countess Silvia is simply St Cecilia herself—and she is so kind & sweet—and I am in agony because I don't know how to thank her or do anything to please her— Her mother watches everything I eat just as Doanie would" ——

In next letter he says— "It is impossible to say *how* kind these people all are to me—they take me to see gardens and picture galleries, where the ladies of the garden, and directors of the gallery come out to do me honour, and show me everything—and I don't know what to say nor how to answer—and I've no energy to write or employ myself" —

Bassano Wedy 3rd Oct 1888 "They say I am looking better since I came but I think it is only the sort of flush that settles on me from shyness and never having anything to say— Mr Blow is entirely happy but then he can run & play with the children and speaks German well so that he can get on with the Countess Silvia, and Mammina likes him for being so attentive to me, and he is always radiant" —

Then I don't seem to have any letter of 4th Octr but have one dated Bassano, Friday "5th *Sept*" but of course he *means Octr* which shows *slight* unsteadyness of mind & beginning to my great surprise at once "Darling own Doanie / I felt it absolutely necessary to come to some close of the sort of life I was leading here—receiving all sorts of polite and kind attention from people to whom I could not say a word in return" —

I feel certain that a sudden dread of illness came upon him—& he determined, even at the risk of being rude—& seeming ungrateful—& misunderstood, to leave so abruptly—believing anything was better than the risk of alarming you—& if you compare the *languor* he complained of at Milan—the little effort & delight of his coming to Rezzonico may have caused a feeling of collapse—I have known him like that before

---

he writes on 8th Octr from Venice— "I have the most lovely letter from Bassano— how people can care for me as they do is inconceivable to me—but they really all were miserable in letting me go—

["] I begin to think my chief gift is in making people *unhappy*— certainly I am a mere burden to Detmar, here at Venice —for I forget all I knew about it—& don't care to—& can't learn it over again—and my old favourite pictures are nothing to me" —

In this letter he asks me not to be frightened as if he were getting back into the state he was in at Sandgate—adding "there is no fear of my breaking windows or throwing coals downstairs—but I am very heartsick for my Doanie" Ever since, his letters have been more or less depressed—& full of sweetness to me—& longing to see me—& I do hope to be with him again *somewhere* by the middle of Novr —& I am glad to hear that there is no chance of Mr Blow leaving him—

I *quite expected* a course of depression to follow the excitement at Beauvais & Paris—& am only surprised it did not come sooner— Possibly the pleasant little time at Bassano—& looking forward to it, warded it off—& prevented it's being so severe—much love to the beloved Sorella from your devoted & ever grateful — Figlia —

4. *Mrs. Alexander to Mrs. Severn*

Rezzonico. Bassano.
12. October. 1888.

Mia amata Figlia,

Many thanks for your kind and most interesting letter of the 9th and for all the trouble you took about those letters. I am more grateful to you than I can tell, and you would not wonder if you knew all my reasons which I will tell you some day— I was not influenced by caprice, and you must trust me, even when I appear to be so— Do not let your D.P. know it, but I am very sorry about his visit here, all the more that he had expressed his intention of remaining with us all the time he spent in Italy. As for the family here they considered his presence both a pleasure and a favor, and they received him simply as one of themselves, there was never an additional dish on the table. I only hope they will not torment him by urging him to return, though I am sure they would not wish it unless he did— His change of feeling was great and sudden after he received some letters— We shall probably never meet again. F[rancesca] understood his parting to be a final one— If, as you say he went on in the same way about both Miss O[lander] & Miss W[arren?] he probably was not well at the time, and I hope no serious harm has been done him. Miss O's parents appear to be good people, though in an inferior class of life, and have no idea of taking him in, and indeed will insist on the daughter keeping her "testa esaltata" within due bounds. Your D.P. seemed perfectly well, and fairly strong, he took little naps easily, as I remember my own Father did at his time of life, but a short one always rested and refreshed him—and I fancied long conversations fatigued him— He took one quite long walk to Bassano without fatigue, and had planned several more, when his change of mind came so suddenly. He says he does not intend ever to reside in England again, so you will not have him to write about, but I hope I shall not quite lose the great comfort and pleasure your letters have given me but that from time to time you will write me of yourself and your dear ones, and I am sure you will always preserve for me your affection which is more precious to me than I can tell you, all the more that so little remains to me, so few of my early friends now remain. Dear love to you, your kindest of husbands, and your blessed children from F. and

Your affectionate and most grateful
Mammina.

5. *Francesca to Mrs. Severn*

Di 29 Gen[naio 1900]

Dearest Joanie,

I cannot tell you how much I have felt your kindness in writing to me so soon, and in the midst of your own great sorrow and confusion! I wanted to write to you yesterday, but it was so dark that I could not, (you know that my eyes are none of the best,) and now, this morning, comes your second most precious letter! All your words are full of comfort and blessing to me; especially when you tell me that his later years were rendered happier by knowing us. What I owe to him, of happiness and of usefulness, the Lord only knows! His friendship has been one of the great blessings of my life. And now that he is gone, I think you and I will be nearer to each other than ever. I am glad you insisted on having him laid where he wished to be; though it is very natural that the english should wish to have him in Westminster Abbey. I, for my part, could have wished to have him laid to rest in Italy, the country for which he did so much! But it was right that he should choose for himself, and it seems more fitting that he should be in a peaceful country place, where the flowers can grow about him, and the sky look down upon him. I will send you a little wreath of wild olive in a few days, as soon as the weather is dry enough for me to go out and gather the branches; it never loses the leaves, and it grows on my terrace. I should like to send it for his birth-day. I should like, in the autumn (for this is not the season) to send a little rose bush to plant near his grave, if there is any room for it: it is against the law, but I can send a very little one, hidden in a box of flowers. But I cannot see to write more, and there is so much more I want to say! How well I understand the terrible emptiness just now in your heart and life! You were more than a daughter to him, and he knew it. Goodbye! Dearest love from the Mammina first to you, and then to all, and my love also, and a kiss for Lily and for you, from your ever loving

Sorella Francesca

II

SARA ANDERSON TO MRS. SEVERN

Brantwood
Thursday
[October 18, 1888][1]

My own Di Ma

Besides what I enclose "Old Cheyne Walk" etched by Arthur Severn has come, & a bill for the same gentleman, which I've put in your business drawer.

Mrs. Talbot is going to drive over after all, & hopes to arrive about 12, & it's now past 11, but I've freshened the dining room flowers & some new drawing room ones, & seen your children, who are well.

The Birthday boy had a very happy day yesterday & was so good. We had 'cool 'oom [school room] tea; Alice and I as guests; bread and butter, leading up to jam, muffins, biscuits (Mrs. Baxter's gift) & the cake decorated with flowers. Herbert was told that he must look after Susan, who sat next to him, so when he saw her plate empty he said "Eat more Susan. Have plenty to eat," & such sentences, much to the delight of the devoted nurse. Your rowing of Violet has done much good, so far. We have had reading aloud the last two nights, which is less fatiguing than railroads, or shooting parties. Your letter to me is *rivets,* stay out your week, see everything, and take mental notes on Mary Stuart relics. I am fascinated.

I find I sleep much better on a quiet evening! That doesnt

1. The first two letters can be dated through references to the birthday (October 17) of Herbert Severn (1882–1955) and to Ruskin's having left Venice, homeward bound. Mrs. Fanny Talbot was a wealthy Companion of St. George who had been most generous in supporting projects launched by Ruskin as Master of the Guild.

sound complimentary, but you'll own we have lived hard this last fortnight.

I said goodbye to Ethel [Hilliard] yesterday, & called on Susie [Beever], who has a terrible cold. And oh Joanie she is so anxious for me to meet & love Mrs. Howard, who she says is a "special person." She is specially obnoxious to me. I dont quite know why, but I cant like her! It's awkward, as Susie wants us to become London friends! Oh my!

Baxter writes his wife that Dipe is "very nice, but in his low way," which to ears not acquainted with the professorial depressions, might convey a somewhat different meaning. They are leaving Venice, because too many people were calling, but Baxter didn't know where they were to go to.

Your loving
Diddie

Baby [Herbert] delighted with your letter & A[rthur]'s drawings, but I couldn't be shown the former, as the envelope was a cartridge bag with string through letter & all!! Income tax paper come for Dipe.

Brantwood
Saturday
[October 20, 1888]

Darling Di Ma

I have spent all morning darning, as all my stockings had "honey-combed heels."

Mrs. Talbot wouldn't stay over last night because they're going to Barmouth today, & they wouldn't go except by the 7:20 which was too early. I think she and Miss Atkinson[2] both enjoyed their visit: they both left many messages of thanks to you & regret at not seeing you, & Mrs. Talbot left her love over & over again for you. I told her how very sorry you were to miss her. *What* a plucky woman. Of course it was misty all the time, tho' very lovely, but no Helvellyn! However there was no lack of beauty.

The children are well & good. We had story telling last night, & Baby volunteered one. Judge my feelings when, after telling me

2. Blanche Atkinson (1847–1911), a Companion of St. George who had been devotedly attached to Ruskin since 1874, was now also a Companion of Mrs. Talbot, with whom she spent the remainder of her own life.

how a nurse & child had been shot by a soldier & how a search-party went out to find them he said, "There was a *dreadful* smell, and,—what do you think? — it was the nurse & child dead. And it was dark, & they couldn't see, & they stepped on their bodies["]. They must have heard some cheerful talk.

A box of pears & grapes has come from H[erne] H[ill]. There was a sound of merry rattle when one lifted the box, & a good many of the grapes had burst from their moorings, & were quite spoilt. The pears are quite sound, & will keep for some days, & there is a quite large dish of grapes all right. Baxter writes that his master seemed sad at leaving Italy but is very well. He is off wintering at Paris, at present, & talks of coming "home," but not to Brant[wood], tho' where else his home may be he has not confided to Baxter.

I'm glad you're staying out your week, but I shall be glad when you come back.

Your loving
Diddie

A Grosv[enor] Gal[lery] private view ticket was Hannah's [Mrs. Allen's?] only enclosure.

Brantwood
Thursday
[October 17, 1889] [3]

Darling Di Ma

All well and good. Baby [Herbert] supremely happy with store book, for which he sends love & thanks. They got a walk before the rain came on: it is now pouring hopelessly, & I daresay you will have a call from Lunefield today, deploring with sniffs that Arthur is missing the "tints" I hope you are having a good time, wet or dry. Dont forget a single detail of interest.

Naina's dance went off well. The bridegroom had to play, which seemed hard, & Susan said "The music wasn't very good, Miss." She and (Winn?) had plenty of friends there, & got on very well. The only grave face was Barnes's, who objects on the score of

3. The date can be ascribed because in 1889 Herbert Severn's birthday fell on Thursday. Among the children Gussie, Naina, and Nora were daughters of Barnes, the Barratts' coachman. Susan was the Severn "children's maid," Ruskin had told Francesca in a letter of 1885 (Swett, *Ruskin's Letters to Francesca,* p. 103).

Naina's youth it appears. Though Nora is supposed to be the family beauty Susan thought neither she nor Gussie could compare with Naina, who looked very pretty & very happy. I can see that Madonna face pink & smiling. Can't you?

I send you the outside bit of Agnew's note! I mean a bit of the envelope.

I'm so sorry about Dipe's depression. I read his letter, as you said.

Your always loving
Dido

Brantwood
"Soonda"
Dec[ember] 13, [18]91[4]

Darling Di Ma*

A. Thanks for the Severs cheque. I'll attend to orders, & Baxter also sends thanks for his cheque.

B. I've retained brougham for the 18th. Its lovely to think of seeing oo, & to have the boys & Lily thrown in, as it were. Let me know about ordering the carriage to meet you.

The Di Pa is well, but not down yet, & with that my news & business comes to an end, & I want to write you something which has been in my heart for so long, & which I feel I ought to write to you, lest I might not be here if ever troubles arose about the Di Pa's will, tho' I hope much you will be spared such.

I have, as you know, seen him many times when he was in a very excited state, as well as when he was really ill. It was always more difficult to manage him then as he was suspicious of everyone. But he used to talk to me a very great deal, & it was always my endeavour to prevent what came about when I was not there, namely his leaving Brantwood, or making any public quarrel with you & Arthur. I knew well that the instant he was himself again he would turn to his Joanie.

4. The "Mr. Barker" in this letter was identified on the MS, through a pencilled note, by Mr. F. J. Sharp, as "Mr. Charles Mylone Barker, President of the Incorporated Law Society." The "Fleming episode" occurred in 1885, when Ruskin, upon the verge of another collapse, wished to leave Brantwood because of anger against the Severns and was encouraged to make the break by Albert Fleming, whom he had convinced that his grievances were substantial.

And this is what I want particularly to say: that in all his abuse of you his idea was to make over Brantwood & his money to you. And he never varied from this, that Brantwood was to be ultimately yours and Arthurs, "The Severns," he used to call you.

Then should any question arise as to that unhappy deed of gift, I can only say that I was here when it was drawn up & I am indeed one of the witnesses, & I can also bear witness to the intense impatience of the Di Pa for Mr. Barker's coming, & the equally intense thankfulness when it was settled.

One more point & I have done. I can tell how, after the Fleming episode, when the Di Pa was at home again with you & me, I have seen him sitting at his study table with his head between his hands groaning "Oh why didn't Albert see that I was mad!"

My Di Ma, if I have hurt you by dwelling on these dreadful times, please forgive me. Only we have so many proofs lately of the uncertainty of life, that, lest I should be cut down suddenly, I write this for you.

I don't know what value it would have in a court of justice, perhaps none, but I send it on the chance of its being useful, tho' with the hope that you may be spared the necessity of using it.

Your loving
Dido
Sara Anderson

*so *very* sorry about telegram.

III

Lily Armstrong (Mrs. W. Kevill-Davies) to Mrs. Severn

4 Highfield Terrace
Leopold St
Leeds
Sunday [1878]

My darling Judy

I have *just* seen the enclosed in a paper. I *do* hope it is not true. Send me a line at once if you can, to say how you all are. I should be so very very sorry if Darling Birdie was ill. My fond love to him. I would have written you since I came here but my darling Father has been and is *so very* ill I have not had the heart to write to any one. I wont bother you with a long letter now until I hear from you.

Ever your loving
Lily

IV

Correspondence with Miss Susan Beever

[Four letters from Ruskin to Miss Beever and nineteen letters (three incomplete) from Miss Beever to Ruskin are in the F. J. Sharp Collection. There are also 31 letters from Miss Beever to Mrs. Severn, most of which were written during Ruskin's illness of 1878 as notes sent in response to Mrs. Severn's constant, if not daily, messages about Ruskin's condition.]

1. *Ruskin to Miss Beever*

Brantwood
3rd Jan[uary 18]75
(Rosie's 26th Birthday)

Darling Susie

So many thanks for the nice note, and the 2nd subscription— Your accusations of your own dullness would be cruelly ironical if you ever could be either cruel or *under-minded.*

— Thats a new useful adjective of mine—but awkwardly like a blundering 'undermined.' (All the better—the two words meaning two phases of the same thing.)

The book [*Frondes Agrestes,* issued on April 28, 1875] will be soon ready,—but I've had to rearrange one or two passages— Susie had got some of the tailfeathers stuck in the wings—which really would'nt have let the bi[r]die fly.

Ever your affectionate J R.

Brantwood
[January? 1875] [1]

My Dearest Susie

1. This date is indicated by Ruskin's reference to "our book"—namely *Frondes Agrestes.* In a letter dated January 25, 1875 he announced: "Here's our book in form at last" (*Works, 37,* 158).

Again a black day! — When I came to Brantwood I was prepared for any quantity of *wet*: but not for this dry or nearly dry black 'London-best' fog— Is it not a new, or at least a late—curse on our modern England, Susie? —from which you & I and the birds and flowers, must all suffer with the wicked—like the cattle of the Amalekites.

— I am so glad you like the birdies. Don't be anxious about them; take care of the little sitting rock kingfisher and the hoopoe —but in general, you may let anybody who *likes* them look at them in perfect comfort— A torn edge or dropped spot of anything is of no consequence— they are quite replaceable plates— and will be roughly used by me, when I come to use them.

They are Italian, Lombardic, birds—incomparably better drawn than Gould's.

Agrestes means what Scott means by 'wild wood'—the leaves of trees that grow at their own pleasure, as opposed to cultivated fruit trees, orderly poplars or elms,—or cared-for parks. But this meaning belongs to the word accurately only in this place. Latin is a powerful, because a poor, language,— its words are servants of all work, and you must always look carefully at the place each is in—before you know what it is doing. Ever

Your affectionate

J. Ruskin

(Now for our book—) —still I've two days work on it—but you'll like it better, I hope.

I've just got a Fors on hand which I do seriously hope will help to soothe & refresh our dear Doctor [John Brown].

What a lovely Bee Envelope.

Brantwood
Michaelmas 1886

Sweetest Susie

I am very thankful to be opposite you again, but still extremely dead in leaf and dry in pith. Thankful also to have enjoyed some jumping sea and cloudy spray—to have seen that there *are* sunsets to be seen, and to have made the acquaintance of Seven very amiable young ladies—three kind Squires, two good boys, and two pretty little girls,—three, I should say counting the booksellers shopgirl on the Morcambe parade,—besides having the luck to net Agnes Greg [possibly Gregg or Grieg, the Rose Queen of Cork High School in 1888], whom you know, I think?—for Brantwood itself.

But my writing is not the least fit to be read yet! — I'm so out of practice with the fortnights idleness.

So no more at present from your loving

Cat

Brantwood
St Valentines [18]87

Dearest Owlette

I was thankful to know of your betterness from Joan—and of your pleasure in daffs—as always in daffing. I like the yellow tufts about the fields—but never care to gather one. I have some anemones from Florence which are marvellous in their exquisitely nervous trembling & veining of colour—violin playing in scarlet on a white ground. But I get more and more melancholy in spring, feeling that—the anemones of this spring are *not* those of the last—and if anemones have no souls—why should *I* have any? — Also—I've not one Valentine—no Sunday post. I got one from a little 'Diamond Eyes' yesterday—but I wrote back it was'nt fair, before the day, and the Sapphire eyes [Margaret Burne-Jones] must have their chance. I dont know if the postman will find her! I directed

"À Mlle

Mlle aux Yeux Diamants"

Is it Libby Newby [by 1898 an Infants Mistress in the Coniston Parochial School] who brings you word of our Saturdays at een? She is an intense bit of country life herself,—but does'nt care much for botany lectures. — Certainly we do get on slowly. All last Saturday's time went in trying to define the difference between a grape and a gooseberry!

— I am myself meditating on the uses of turpentine, and why fir cones don't grow into pineapples!

On the whole—I'm fairly myself—and not beside myself—as far as I know—

and ever your devotedest Phoca

2. *Miss Beever to Ruskin*

Coniston
Thursday
[December 1873] [2]

My dear Mr. Ruskin

May I write upon this sea-green paper—manufactured of course on purpose for Neptune & a little of it granted to me as a special favour because I love the sea & many of the wonderful things that come out of it— The Hermit crabs for example— May I tell you what *funny* things they did in a shallow Tank which I had once upon a day?—

You know that they always live in a borrowed shell & in one suitable for their size. I always had a few empty shells of different sizes, in the tank, ready for use. To watch the crab choose a new house was most amusing— He took hold of the edge with his claws—his feelers vibrating in the most wonderful way—his stalked eyes *glaring* pulled the shell to him felt it all over, then put his claw into the depths of it, lest there should be a lurking enemy—then fixing both claws upon the edge, he jumped out of the old shell into the new one with the swiftness of thought—seemed settled in it, & then finding something not quite comfortable jumped back again into his old shell. Altogether the most crafty little being you can imagine—(lawyers must have developed from Crabs—) It is a curious fact that these crabs have nearly always, a beautiful kind of sea-worm living with them in the shell —called I think, a Nereis—(spel't wrong?)— To see one of these Hermits sitting in his borrowed shell, holding a tiny mutton collop in one hand & tearing fragments off with the other, & putting them into his mouth much quicker that a boy does gooseberries is very entertaining—but of crab, q: s:— I did not know I was going to say anything about him—please to lay the blame upon the marine paper. I am so glad that you liked the [kissing?] the plants—and I am sure you liked the violets near the well— I send the old book—ashamed of the untidy marks I have made that I might remember which passages I have copied for you—

2. This letter is in an envelope dated by Ruskin "Dec. 73." The "two dear little feathers" were probably the two "Studies" in watercolor which Ruskin sent her on December 7, 1873 (see *Works, 38,* 250).

If you would accept of this old book if you would—if you would—you would add another drop of pleasure to the copious draughts you have poured out before, to the great refreshment of little Susie. I find from an old man, that I came to wrong conclusions about the Bannock Stones. The fact is, that there used to be an old bridge—built of *cobble* stones—& the men who built it, lived upon Bannocks & butter & *so* it came to be called Bannock Stone bridge. A servant, the sister of our housemaid, has sent me by post such exquisitely lovely flowers & such sweet Heliotrope that two senses are delighted— Will there never be any more of that pretty tale—nor of Sir Walter Scott? — I am almost faint for lack of them— Last night reading Richard 2—I was amused by the poor unhappy Queen calling the gardener "Thou old Adam's likeness"— I do not think Adam would have been much flattered. I have some of the "Pomps & vanities of this wicked world"—to impart to the beloved Jo*anie,* as regards Miss Hopwood but I must reserve them & not presume to talk to you about such things— I may just say, that the fog drove them away from London three days sooner than they intended—and that the wedding is to take place on the 14th of Jan[uar]y— Would it be bad taste to have those two dear little feathers put into little frames with the narrowest moulding of dead gold? —

A third kind of Titmouse has come for winter food— The Cole Tit—such a compact, neat little bird, dressed in very good taste in quiet colours. It is so very delightful that all these dear feathered fowls, think they may come whenever they please, & be sure of a heart's welcome— Some look almost in the imperative mood if I do not help them at once & sometimes I really have to *run* for food. This is such a bright day of continuous sunshine I have just picked up a poor weak old fly, & put it in the window Being a rather weak old fly myself, I have—sympathy. But how I am writing, just as if I had known you all my life— at any rate I have long been wishing to know you—though I never thought to receive such kindness as your's— My Sisters send their very kind regards.— Will you give our love to dear Mrs Severn— I hope soon to write to her. May I say,

Your affectionate
Susie

Please give our very kind regards to Mr. Severn— How the precious Baby [Lily Severn, b. 1873] will bask to-day.

April 9 [1874] [3]

My dear friend,

I have just been pleased by seeing a Blackbird enjoying with schoolboy appetite, portions of a moistened crust of bread which I threw out for him, & his fellow creatures— How he dug with his orange Bill—even more orange than usual perhaps at this season of the year— At length the Robins have built a nest in the ivy, in our yard—a very secure & sheltered place, & a very convenient distance from the crumb market— Like the old woman, *he* sings with a merry devotion—& *she* thinks there never was such music —as she sits upon her eggs he comes again, & again, with every little dainty that his limited income allows—& *she* thinks it all the sweeter because *he* brings it to her— Now & then she leaves her nest to stretch her wings, & to shake off the dust of care—& to prevent her pretty *'ancles'* being cramped— But she knows her duty too well to remain absent long, from her precious eggs— Now another little note from Dr. *John* [Brown] & he actually begins, My dear "Susie"—& ends, "Let me hear from you soon— Ever your's *affe[ctionat]ly*"— Also he says, "It is very kind in you to let me get at once close to you"— The rest of his short letter (like you he was busy—) is nearly all about *you*—so of course it is interesting to *me*— he hopes you are already getting good from the change—& I indulge the same hope.

April 10. Brantwood looked so very nice this morning—& *decorated* by the coming into leaf of the larches I wish you could have seen them in the distance as I did— The early sunshine had glanced upon them lighting up one side, & leaving the other in softest shade—& the tender green contrasted with the deep browns, & grays, stood out in a wonderful way & the trees looked like spirits of the wood, which you might think would melt away, like a white lady of Avenel— A wretched description— Dear sweet April still looks coldly upon us— The month you love so dearly— Little white lambs are in the fields now—& so much that is sweet is coming—but there is a shadow over this house *now*

3. Second folder missing. Ruskin is now in Italy, having left Brantwood on March 23, 1874.

[the illness of her sister Margaret]—and also, my dear, kind friend is far away— The Horse Chestnuts have tost'd away the winter covering of their buds—& given them to that dear economical Mother earth—who makes such good use of everything, & works up old material again in a wonderful way—& is delightfully unlike most economists   The very soul of generous liberality Now some of your own words—so powerful as they are— You are speaking of the Alp & of the 'Great Builder'—of your own transientness, as of the grass upon it's sides—& in this very sadness, a sense of the strange companionship with past generations, in seeing what they saw— They have ceased to look upon it, you will soon cease to look also—& the granite wall will be for others &c. &c. My dear friend was there ever any one so pathetic as you? —& you have the power of bringing things before one, both to the eye & to the mind— you do indeed paint with your pen— Never was anything more true [& keen?]— Hence that strange, & sometimes fatal *charm* which there is in all things as long as we wait for them, and the moment we have lost them; but which fades while we possess them. That sweet bloom of all that is far away, which perishes under our touch. Lovely! Now I have a photograph of you—not a very satisfactory one—but still I am glad to have it, rather than none. It was done at Newcastle on Tyne— Were you in search of something of Bewicks?

April 14 [1874][4]

I sent off such a long letter to you yesterday, my dear friend. Let me be glad with you that you have had that bit of sugar— Do not be so sad— I am sorry you are so lonely   it is not good for you. Did you think of your own quotation from Homer, when you told me that field of yours was full of violets? But where are the four fountains of *White* Water?—'through a meadow full of violets & parsley'— How delicious Calypso's fire of finely chopped Cedar! — How shall I thank you for allowing *me,* Susie the littlest to *distil* your writings. Such a joy & comfort to me—for I shall need *much* very soon now— I do so thank, & love you for it. I am sure

4. Published in *Hortus Inclusus* (1st ed., 1887, published by George Allen at Orpington, Kent), pp. 156–58. The year 1874 is indicated by references to plans for *Frondes Agrestes,* to Ruskin's "safe progress" as he traveled on the Continent, and to Miss Beever's grief because of her dying sister Margaret.

I may say so to *you.* I rejoice again & again that I have such a friend— May I never lose him never prove unworthy of his friendship How I wanted my letter—& now it has come, & I have told our Dr. John [Brown] of your safe progress so far— I trust you will be kept safe from *everything* that might injure you in any way. The snow has melted away, & this is a really sweet April day—& *ought* to be enjoyed—if only Susie *could.* But both she & her dear friend must strive with their grief. When I was a girl (I was once) I used to delight in Pope's Homer— I do believe I rather enjoyed the killing & slaying—specially the splitting down the *Chieves!* but when I tried to read it again not *very* long ago, I got tired of this kind of thing— If *you* had only translated Homer! Then I should have had a feast— When a schoolgirl going each day with my bag of books into Manchester I used to like Don Quixote & Sir Charles Grandison with my milk porridge. I must send you only this short letter to-day I can see your Violet field from this window— How sweetly the little Limpid would tinkle to-day—& how the primroses are sitting listening to it & the little birds sipping it— I have come to the conclusion that Bees go more by *sight* than by scent— as I stand by my Peacock with his gloriously gorgeous tale all spread out, a Bee comes *right at it* (very vulgar but expressive) & I have an Alpine Primula on this window stone brightly in flower—& a bee came & alighted—but went away again at once—not finding the expected honey— I wonder what you do the live-long day—for I know you & idleness are not acquaintances— I am so very sorry your favourite places are spoiled— But dear Brantwood will grow prettier & prettier under your care. I have not an envelope Must get some— Your loving—

Susie.

April 18 [1874] [5]

My very dear friend,

This morning I read about the *grass* in your book—& it was so lovely that it threw me into a state of delight—& I exclaimed aloud. But I won't tell either you or any one else what I said— There some one else can *teaze* as well as 'Ruskin' What an ex-

5. Second folder missing. Ruskin is now in Rome.

tract it will make for the book—leaving out the passages marked by you, as—Fanciful! or to be omitted. I'm in a rather bad humour this morning—& have written a rather *fierce* little letter to some one who does not understand me I have had such a kind note from dearest Joanie—& she says I must *not* send any more stamps for my letters to *you,* but—it seems scarcely right that you, you dear Chalced[on]y should pay postage both ways—& I have just secured some 6d stamps— What must I do? —for Joanie speaks rather *commandingly*— I see some ladies have been attacked by ruffians in or near Rome— *do please* be cautious—though *my* saying this will be no lump of sugar to you—as I am not eighteen! — I have what you called the grotto agate on my table to-day. Those white lines as if done by a ruler—& *why* did they remain white—when the rest was stained? — To-day we have a little more warmth, but with rain. No Swallow yet—but Starlings are building over my window & it is so pleasant to watch their upward & downward flight— They go so swiftly & joyously that you would wonder how they could draw up suddenly as they do—& they seem to think that scarcely any time must be spent in recreation though at times *he* sits upon a topmost bough of an oak tree & shakes his wings, & whistles, & chatters for very joy—his feathers shining & gleaming in the sunshine as if he were distantly related to an Opal! — Did'nt you look like a benevolent being when you gave me *my Opal!* your face radiant with the joy of giving pleasure—and it *is* a delicious thing to do—but some people neither understand giving, nor receiving pleasure—& it is that kind of thing which made me write the cross note I spoke of— While another dear friend writing about a little sum which I owed her for some oranges, better than those we can get here, says delightfully 'What is that between thee & me'? — Oh, the warmth is so delightful if only, one's mind were at ease—& it *ought* to be— I see the Gondola is launched. I suppose she has had to endure a coat of paint— We are greatly hoping that the Marshalls will not come yet— We much wish for quietness now. This is a very poor letter, but I think I will venture to send it. I've lent our young doctor "The Queen of the Air"—& he is reading it with interest—but feels that it requires much attention—so I quoted to him what you say—'What costs time to select—will require time to understand.' — he really has an enquiring mind—& has for such a long time been wishing for your 'Stones of Venice'—that I am seriously contemplating giving him the new edition—as a mark of my sense of his kindness & feeling attention to my sister [Margaret] For you see he cannot buy it himself—just beginning *for* himself—& engaged to marry when he can make a house. Does the dear professor like this scheme? Should Susie have told him? She likes to do—[end of the first folder]

20th April [1874] [6]

the sweetest wallflowers— The gift of a poor man—& so, doubly sweet— I hope you will have many wallflowers in the new garden— I love to stand by them & to have their sweetness wafted to me— As regards letters both you & Dr. J[ohn] B[rown] have for the present forsaken me—poor Susie! — She must wait as patiently as she can—but she feels a great blank— This is an April day—the 20th I have just bought two little plants of 'Gentiana Verna'— They are on my window stone & one is in flower—& what a blue! Oh, to see them in patches in their own homes—as you have done Now I *hope* you are safe & well You are remembered in the best way every day by,

Your loving Susie

May 1 [1874] [7]

I cannot longer refrain from writing to you my dear kind friend—so often are you in my thoughts— Dearest Joanie has told you I doubt not—& I know how sorry you are & how truly you are feeling for your poor Susie— So *knowing that,* I will say no more about my sorrow— There is no need for words— I am wishing oh, so much to know how you are— quite safe & well I hope and able to have much real enjoyment in the many beautiful things by which you are surrounded— May you lay up a great stock of good health & receive much good in many ways—& then return to those who so much miss you, and by whom you are so greatly

6. A stray page. Within the period of Miss Beever's friendship with Ruskin, before the death of Dr. John Brown (in 1882), 1874 is the only year during which Ruskin was on the Continent in April.

7. Published in *Hortus Inclusus,* pp. 162–64. For both this letter and the one which follows, the year 1874 is indicated by the opening references to the death of Margaret Beever, on April 21

beloved— Coniston would go into your heart, if you could see it now—so very lovely The Oak trees so early, nearly in leaf already— Your beloved blue hyacinths will soon be out—and the Cuckoo has come—but it is long since Susie has been out She only stands at an open window—but she must *try* next week to go into the garden & she is finding a real pleasure in making extracts from your Writings, *for you*—often wondering, will he let that remain & hoping he will— Do you ever send home orders about your Brantwood? — I have been wishing so much that your gardener might be told to mix quantities of old mortar and soil together—& to fill many crevices in your new walls with it— Then the breezes will bring fern seeds—& plant them or rather sow them in such fashion as no human being can do—when time & the showers brought by the West wind have mellowed it a little —& the tiny beginnings of mosses will be there— the sooner this can be done the better— do not think Susie presumptuous — We have hot sun—& a *very* cool air, which I do not at all like. I hope your visit to Palermo & your lady have been all that you could wish— Please *do* write to me— it would do me so much good—& so greatly refresh me— This poor little letter is scarcely worth sending—only it says that I am your loving

Susie

May 8 [1874]

I must thank you my very dear friend. Sympathy so full, so true —so quietly & briefly expressed, must be balm to a sorrowful heart— I fear I am more & more sorrowful beginning more to realize my loss— There now, no more —— When your lovely letter came I was writing an extract from your 'Modern painters' —the volume you lent me— I have nearly gone through it now —in *obedience* to your kind *command* or rather permission It has been such a help & comfort to me, turning my thoughts & leading me in paths of beauty 'Green pastures'—'Still waters'—and this morning, about your being '*let out* of the Chaise to run up the hills'— How happy that expression, 'let out'— why I can see you bounding along full of joyful gladness—having no thought for the Morrow —— full of pleasure, all with the charm of novelty— & really those fells are so very fine, that even I in my old age, was delighted when passing under & among them about a year & a half ago— Besides their real grandeur (for grand they are) it is wonderful how without a tree, or a rock, or a bush such pleasant sensations of beauty can be conveyed to the mind— *William* has said it all in a few words, 'Turfy mountains, where live nibbling sheep' What a William he was, & *is!* don't I love him very dearly? Dr. John Brown (*bless him,* for he is very good to me, & so very tenderly & considerately kind in my sorrow) sent a note to be inclosed to you, so I forwarded it at once to our dearly beloved Joanie— Really if I were not so old, & a few other *ifs,* I would make a pilgrimage to Edinburgh to see this same *dear John.* Brantwood, your poor forsaken Brantwood—looks like a bird's nest now, so hidden by trees with 'their new foliage on'— Yesterday the Lake was perfectly smooth—(I will not say like a mirror because everybody says *that.*) But oh, we have a return of such cold, 'discomfortable' weather—& Susie when her eyes are quite used up, with reading & writing, feels as if she did so want someone to open her heart to—some one with whom to hold pleasant converse— nearly all shut up in herself—it is not good for her I think. Is it think you? Will she live until you come home again? & if so, will you let her see your beautiful drawings with which you are now occupied? — Really at Coniston there is no one who *really* suits me, save you & Joanie— There are one or two who are very kind to me, but do not exactly understand me—(how can they? for I am such a very strange being & so unlike people in general, that I do not even understand myself & would in some respects be glad indeed to be very different—but I cannot however I try.[)] William Youdal has just sent some such lovely Lake Trout for sale How I wish you had them. They are just in season now— Alas! one of my Peacocks had had the number of eyes in his beautiful tail sadly reduced—a dog tore them out ——

This is no proper answer to your so kind & so interesting letter —but I hope to write again ere long. Do take great care of yourself— I was carrying your large book upstairs one night and fell *up* not *down*—yes, both up & down & came full *bang* (how refined!) upon my forehead—poor me—& the other day I had such a fright & horror a dog having been worrying my poor fowls, that I have never been right or well since & it has made me wretchedly nervous. —

The hawthorne is in bloom now I have a piece on my table— & Lilies of the Valley—& the white narcissus—all so very sweet & pleasant to the eye also —— next month the Roses will come What flowers *you* must see & you do, & *must* & *shall* love them always notwithstanding all you say to the contrary. The dear little birds still find the markets high this dry, cold weather, & come to Susie for their daily bread—but they are so shy—so different from what they were in winter, when she was so much to them—that it is evident their affections are (for the present) bestowed elsewhere— dear little things, it is all right— they *Mean* no unkindness—& are simply doing their duty. Much as I love to have a letter from you, I command, entreat, exhort, that you will never teaze yourself to write when you are weary, or busy about other things— I must reserve remarks on the double Fors, until another letter—for I have been so busy with the extracts, that though I have gone glancingly through them I have not yet studied them.

Goodbye my dear kind friend

Your loving old Susie

May 18 [1874] [8]

My dearest friend,

I've just been reading Ps[alm] 65— do read it again it is so *very* lovely, & the very soul of poetry— 'The valleys stand so thick with corn' &c. All so cold still with us in our England. My dearest old Pussie is so very affectionate this morning, that she will scarcely let me either read or write— if I whisper a few words when reading which I do sometimes she leaves her easy chair & comes to ask me what I say—& rubs her dear old head against me. I have just given the Squirrel his little *loaf* (so you see I am a lady) & he has bounded away with it—full of joy & gladness— I wish that this were my case—& your's—for whatever we may wish for that we have not, we have a variety & abundance of loaves. Oh, that dear Dr. John Brown my friend tells me that she called at his

8. The year 1874 again is indicated by Miss Beever's references to making extracts for *Frondes Agrestes* during days of sorrow.

house the other day, & saw his *only* grandchild a perfect Idiot! Imagine if it is possible to do so, what that must be! — My friend says, Dr. J. Brown was made an L.L.D. a few days ago, & the enthusiasm of the people about him was extraordinary— Though the Duke of Buccleugh received the same honour at the same time, he was scarcely noticed— When Dr. B. appeared, it was some minutes before silence could be had— Dr. B. was as white as paper— He is strung too fine—so are you—so am I— a medical man told me so— Now *joy!* a letter from you— so kind, so good in you to remember again your poor Susie— What *you* express about your Mother, is just what I am so often feeling about my dearest Sister—& all in vain—too late— I have been copying a sentence or two with just the same feeling, from your Volume 3, of Modern painters— What must I do? — I have made all my extracts from that vol[ume]— & have *ignobly* borrowed Vol[ume] 1—which will not have so many in it I think being so much on art— Where must I turn for volume 2—&c. &c. for I should like to have all ready when you return unless my eyes fail altogether—& I can scarcely write this poor letter—& feel rather anxious about them. The Lake was so calm this morning & a boat left such a long streak behind it—a fishing boat I think— Dearest Joanie tells me she goes to Liverpool to morrow— I think I will venture to send this 'on the sly', as you say— Your poor old Susie is very, very grateful that you care for her, or her letters—& can scarcely tell why—but she *does* thank you from the very depths of her heart—& hopes you will never feel differently for that *would* be a terrible sorrow to her—oh, so great!— Not being able to use her eyes *enough* she has far too much time to think—& that works badly, & she was so nervous last night that she scarcely knew how to bear it— it is really terrible. I have asked Dr. J. Brown whether he would like photos of your house, & the picturesque breakwater— *He* calls you 'Our Genius'— Cannot you give *him* a name? Shall we call him our Pole-star? I do wish that you & he & I, did not suffer so much, but *could* be at least moderately happy— I am sure you would be glad if you knew even in this time of sorrow, when all seems, 'dull flat, unprofitable'—the pleasure & interest I have had in reading your Vol[ume] 3. I study your character in your writings—& find so much to elevate—to love, to admire—a sort of education for my poor old self—& oh, such beauty of thought & word— [end of folder one]

May 14 [1874][9]

My dearest friend,

Your letter yesterday did me so much good, & though I answered it at once, yet here I am again— A kind woman from the other side has sent me the loveliest group of drooping & very tender ferns, soft as of some velvet belonging to the fairies & of the most exquisite green—& primroses—& a slender stalked white flower—& so arranged that they continually remind me of that enchanting group of your's in Vol[ume] 3, which you said I might cut out— What would you have thought of me if I had? Oh, that you would & could sketch this group—or even that your eye could rest upon it. Now you will laugh if I ask you whether Harpies ever increase in number, or whether they are only the "old original"— They quite torment me when I open the window, & blow chaff at me— I suppose at this moment, dearest Joanie is steaming away to Liverpool One always wants to know now whether people accomplish a journey safely. When the Blackbirds come for soaked bread, they generally eat a nice little lot themselves, before carrying any away from the window for their little ones— but Bobbie, 'Our little English Robin'—has just been twice, took none for himself but carries beak-load after beak-load for his speckled infants. How curious the universal love of bread is— so many things like & eat it—even flies—& snails! — You know you inserted a letter from Jersey about fish— A lady there tells me that formerly you might have a bucket of oysters for 6d & that now you can scarcely get anything but such coarse kinds of fish as are not liked—& she has a sister a sad invalid, to whom fish would be a very pleasant & wholesome change This is really a sad state of things—& *here* the railways seem very likely to carry away our butter and it is now such a price—quite exhorbitant— Why did I put an H in? Is it to prove the truth of what you say, that ladies do not spell well? — A letter which I once wrote

9. Miss Beever's statement that she is now 68 years old indicates the year 1874. This letter was published, through the words "a cruel *East* wind," in *Hortus Inclusis,* pp. 164–67. For the passage within angle brackets see *Works, 37,* 102n.

when a girl, was a wonderful specimen of bad spelling— ⟨May 15. I have found such lovely passages in Vol[ume] 1. You do float in such beautiful things sometimes, that you make me feel I don't know how! — How I thank you for ever having written them, for though late in the day, they were written for *me,* & have at length reached me— You are so candid about your age that I shall tell you mine! — I am astonished to find myself 68—very near the Psalmist's three score and ten Much illness, & much sorrow, & then I wake up to find myself *old*—& as if I had lost a great part of my life— Let us hope it was not all lost— I think *you* can understand me when I say, that I have a great fund of love, & no one to spend it upon—because there are not any to whom I could give it *fully* and I love my pets so dearly, but I *dare not* & cannot enjoy *it* fully, because—they *die*—or get injured—& then my misery is intense. I feel as if I could tell *you* much, because your sympathy is so refined & so tender & true— Cannot I be a sort of second Mother to you? I am sure the first one was often praying for blessings for you—& in this at least, I resemble her— Am I tiresome writing all this? — it just came & you said I was to write what did— We have had some nice rain, but —— —— followed not by warmth, but a cruel *East* wind.⟩ What a wretched thing that is— It must be first cousin to the Harpies A Harry-longlegs was outside a windowpane last night, so I fetched a lens, & examined him— he has lost one leg, but did not say how & had at each side what I suppose must be *poisers* to steady him in his flight [diagram] — how dare I even make that wretched attempt to send to you— I thought he had lost one of his feelers too—but he suddenly displayed a second, poor fellow, so weak am I, that I suppose I *wasted?* a grain of sympathy on him. The gifts I have had to-day, are, Wallflowers, & Stocks— Many are very good to Susie—& "Once upon a time["] a "Genius"—gave her an Opal—& a rock crystal, & such a number of other lovely things— Tell me *please* why that Rock Crystal gives me so much pleasure— It seems so very refined, & somehow it's transparency seems different & more beautiful. There was a smoke ascending from Brantwood this morning—were they airing that dear old marble? — I shall 'win a smile' by saying that? — I've had a very rare pleasure this morning—a letter from Mr. Severn—such a very pleasant one—& he said he had heard from *you* the night before. It seems they do not go to Liverpool until Saturday— I *do* think he is going to sketch *that* CHAIR & the Baby— I wonder what *you* were like when *you* sat in it— I would some one with a skilled hand had sketched you—& that I had it! — I daresay your poetical feelings were working in you even then & that you did not see & feel things just as other children did—— are there no remembrances of your childhood? —— Did you eat your porridge in the same way that other Babies do? Suddenly interrupted here. A knock at the door. Enter Miss Rigbye— so glad she did not come sooner, & *smash* all my ideas— Your loving

Susie.

[1874?] [10]

Even yet, my birds want so much bread— I do believe the worms are sealed up in the dry earth & they have many little mouths to fill just now—& there is one old blackbird whose devotion to his wife and children is lovely. I should like him never to die he is *one* of my heroes. And now a dog which calls upon me sometimes [is] at the window—& I point kitchenwards, & the creature knows what I mean, & goes, & gets a good meal. So if I can only make a dog happy (as you do, only you make your's to live with you & I cannot do that) it is a pleasant thing— I do so like to make things happier & should like to put bunches of hay in the field for the poor horses, for there is very scant supply of grass—& too many for the supply. I have luxuriated in the juice of two oranges— do you indulge in such things? I only take the juice— Must I send you some *Bismuth lozengers?*

Your very loving
Susie

Brantwood looks so still & patient, & what a silence for that dear old Marble! ——

10. Published in *Hortus Inclusis,* pp. 161–62. The page of MS was placed in an envelope which contains the letters of 1874. Ruskin would not return to Brantwood until December 22, 1874, having reached Herne Hill on October 22, after six months on the Continent.

Saturday evening
[July 17, 1875][11]

In my own den once more my dearest & kindest friend— Ah, if you could quite know what this afternoon has been to me! — Mary [Beever] thought me late home—but indeed I took no note of time— I never do when I go to Brantwood & I fear, I fear I am very thoughtless & I *ought* not to have remained so long but it was so delicious! & so unlike any other joy I ever have—& other things seem so different— I'm delighted that you have lent Chaucer to me. But oh, I forgot that lovely greenery that you gave me—but dear Joanie said it should come— How fast we crossed the lake— The air was very refreshing, & Lily [Severn] was in a state of such pretty excitement—& your young friends are so nice—& how happy you are making them—& how happy you made me, only, that I can never be quite happy when my dearest friend is not so It was so delightful to hear you read those beautiful things— I wish I *could* thank you as I ought— And how troubled I am when I think how lonely your heart is—the heart which desires to make all around you happy! — I fear my poor Lucy was disappointed—but I think she said she would come again— How delightfully kind it was in you to come for me *your own* self! But my heart is too full to say any more to-night—

Your loving Susie

Thursday [1875][12]

I am so much better my dearest friend—& I have been in the garden, & got up some little seedlings of "Geranium lucidum"— There will be plenty more in a little while but at present the remaining ones are too much infants to be removed— *one* of these tiny plants will be enough for *one* crevice in the wall. The dear little Sedum (you *must* think it a darling) will like a situation like that in which the "Erba"—is— I heard from my Cousin to-day She had seen Mr. Anson—but she did not think the garden

11. Ruskin noted that "Susie" was at Brantwood on Saturday, July 17, 1875 (*Diaries,* p. 853), when the "young friends," W. G. Collingwood and Alexander Wedderburn were his houseguests.

12. This letter and the one which follows are dated through the references to *Proserpina,* of which Part II has been published (issued August 1875) and Part III, chapter 5, "Papaver Rhoeas" (headed "BRANTWOOD, July 11th, 1875") is under way

robbery was a pleasant subject so she asked no more—but she says that such things are common— early on the morning of Sunday, gardens are entered & the flowers carried away & apples were stolen in the autumn & carrots,—in other gardens. I have just been to look at the little Bird's nest— It is lovely in it's simplicity— some old wood is leaning against a wall & there they were, perched upon the top—& the old birds came & *stuck* to the side of the nest & little beaks were widely opened, & the mouths all lined with yellow satin! such clean darlings! — You see I have ventured [through a marginal sketch] to try to give you an idea of the curious way in which the nest is perched. The children were chirping, & set so high up in the nest that they will probably fly tomorrow morning— It has done me so much good seeing this pretty sight—& I look upon the parent birds with *reverence*. There they are, doing their duty in their appointed fashion— How I love them! & how I wish they knew it—for I would not watch them long, for it made them uncomfortable. I cannot tell you the intense joy this little bit of domestic happiness has given to me— it has soothed me in a wonderful way! — And now another great slice of happiness Your dear kindest note— I do think your notes are nicer, & nicer, every day!—& I feel immensely honoured & grateful A caller has been! & there was no one at home but poor little Me—so I had no chance of "pouting." —— So I bore it as well as I could. I'm delighted that you think me so naughty— it *is* so pleasant to me to be so— You really *are* like Samson's wife when she tried to get *at* his secret—& you become the Meekest of the meek, & say "*please* tell me what I said["] &c—&c So I suppose I must be meek too & indulge you at my own expense— Well then you know I was so absurd as to propose some old fashioned plants to you—*really* in the simplicity of my heart—& only thinking how nice they would be, (for I am so fond of them myself)—but when you said, (rather awfully—) "If *you* will manage *my* garden" I was in the Valley of humiliation in a moment—& felt most wretchedly small!—& felt too that I had *seemed* officious! — There now you have it all!—but I *was* very unhappy—& vexed with myself— I am always saying something I ought not to say do try to pity me & to forgive—for you know I am but a child!—& I fear a very wayward one, but I will tell Joanie how well I have behaved to-day, & how brave I have been— I really *am* an astonishment to myself, & feel a considerable amount of stuckupishness! — The lady [Miss Waterhouse] who was a Quaker "once upon a time"—must be just about arriving at Coniston & I hope she has brought her book of wild flowers with her— She is always very, very good to me— The Mother, & two other daughters & a son came too—but I do not *much* know any but this one & the Mother—& she is feeble. The lovely bit I spoke of, *is* in 'Proserpina'— I nearly fear to name it to you— You have been speaking of 'Geranium lucidum'— "I suppose the scarlet leaf colour is a kind of early autumnal glow,—a beautiful hectic, & foretaste in sacred youth, of sacred death" [*Works, 25,* 263]— I hope I am not wounding you—but I did in a moment think of *her!* [presumably Rose La Touche] ——— ——— ———

My dearest friend, my prayer for you is, that you may come & *abide* under the Shadow of His wing—& there find, *rest*—

Your very loving
Susie

Tuesday Mor[nin]g [1875]

To come crouching like a Spaniel, my dearest friend, would seem to be making my poor epistle of yesterday, of too much importance—*but* I was sorry not to speak to you this morning!—& *you* believe me? Did'nt Mr. Malleson deserve to lie awake all night with indigestion? I did not see him being engaged with 'The Antiquary'—but from what I know, you must have astonished him—& were no doubt superlatively naughty! — How engagingly pretty that little Water-lily is in that engraving from Turner in Modern Painter's— I forget the name of the place & am too idle to go upstairs to look, but to my thinking, there is inexpressible charm in it— I am enjoying Chaucer very much— it quite amuses me— it is so quaint & has such original ideas—but I have not read much yet— How absurd it was, that when I turned to look at his portrait, I somehow expected an old man—& was quite taken by surprise to see such a handsome face—& such merry looking eyes— I wonder whether he was like this portrait— I am sure you wish that this season of gloom would pass away —but how terrible the floods in other places! I hope our turn will not come— A last brood of robins (for the season) has come out—little brown, speckled, things fluttering about, & scarcely able to fly—with Daddy, & Mammy in very shabby clothes, dancing attendance upon them—& administering green caterpillars— Does anybody ever give you one? or me? — Don't I see your sketch of the yellow Poppy? — Mary [Beever] says it is no longer called a papaver C[ruciforme] but Meconopsis C[ambrica]— I am going to edify Miss Waterhouse by lending her the second No. of, "Proserpina"— I shall of course take her up to that Scarlet Poppy! and if she is not enchanted, won't she fall in my estimation? It was this lady who saw some of Mr. Severn's paintings at a gentleman's home in the South— I have forgotten his name— Mr. Severn was a 'Child of the Mist'—last evening. I saw his boat sailing pensively, after a dreamy fashion— I wondered that there was breeze enough to make 'The Lady Joan' exert herself at all— You were speaking of "Howls" one day— how wonderful it is, that their feathers are so *very* soft, so that they can glide along noiselessly, so as not to alarm the poor little mice which they strike with their claws— but you don't like *'Howls'*— neither do I—but I *do* like Owls— Don't you wish that men and boys in general were like sailors—who are generally very unwilling to molest land birds, being superstitious about it, & thinking that it brings ill luck—

Do let me bring before your mind's eye—a lovely shrub, or tree—an "Althea"—twelve to fifteen feet high, & thickly covered with *pink* flowers, much like those of the hollyhock but rather smaller— every day through the summer, Humming Birds flock to these blossoms & hang & sip round & round there, but never still. This is in Alabama— Am I tiring you? or may I tell you about the sparrows I used to watch from our garden, before the ivy was stripped from the end of Miss Rigbye's cottage, and a Magnum Bonum Plum placed instead— It was a *fashionable* place of resort as a lodging, for innumerable Sparrows. The incessant chirping at bed-time attracted my attention to it. Perhaps the birds were telling each other the events of the day, such as where they had found the ripest peas—or the finest corn—but I fear that like many human beings, they were each trying to get the best place— I hope I am not slandering them—for I do not understand their language—but the sounds were very suggestive of squabbling—gradually the clamour became less & less—until it ceased altogether—perhaps because their last song was, "We're aw [all?] noddin"— "The hours come, & the note," & it is such a kind one —& it makes me both happy & unhappy!—and it is so dark that I can scarcely see to write— Miss Waterhouse has been to call—& I lent her Proserpina—& made her read the bit about the Scarlet Poppy—and she did *not* fall in my estimation, for she thought it beautiful—but you know having once been a Quaker, she is not so ecstatic as I am— how I wish the next number was finished & would come by post to morrow— I directed her attention to the laurel leaf too— how happy she is to be going to read it for the first time, in all its freshness & beauty— I shall certainly *not* undertake to manage your garden, until I know what wages you give, it is the refinement of cruelty in you to mention a subject which gave me so such pain. And on Saturday, I said something which I wished I had not said, (I always do) but I will not tell you what it is—even if you say, 'Please'—a hundred times! — there! — I'm so sorry this weather tries you so much— The gloom is *very* depressing—& I feel almost as dull as I often do when there is no one in Brantwood & I have no one to tell my thoughts to—& nobody to care for them when I do tell them—Mr. Chapman called to-day, & I used him as I did Mr. Malleson yesterday, left him to the two Marys [her sister and cousin], who were both more equal to things than I am—& I was so wicked, for I saw Mr. C[hapman] coming, & never told them— I don't mean any harm about him—but three to *one,* is generally too much, & it is very dull to be like "The Silent Stars which wink & listen" —— I am very like a little boy I once knew, who was often ill & therefore irritable he used to say, "I wish I could be good! — I can't be good— I *wish* God would make me good"! — I often get into little scrapes you see—& am rather impetuous! Do you remember that you once called me "—a little eager thing?[")] but really the things you have said about *me* are —— —— —— just what one might expect from you I don't think either you or Lucy, are much addicted to repentance— Did Mr. Parsons, (how can *you* endure anyone with that name) take off any of his restrictions. *Did* Dr. Brown send you a copy of "Raeburn"—? I find today, from a letter from my friend Miss Watson that *she* wrote nearly all of it— Dr. J[ohn] B[rown] though wrote the life— This Miss W[atson] is a brave woman— she was asked to write prefatory remarks for an edition of Hogg's poems— She says, "I have got a paper this morning in which my &c. &c. gets a severe handling— I just take the bite & the buffet we't— do you know that Scotch proverb, meaning take the good with the bad. I am always the better of being told my faults— it is wholesome—though it may not be pleasant" — Another blot! & I cannot see to transform it. I hope this long note may be counted for yesterday's & to-day's —I thought you might not like what I had said yesterday & I should not have gone to sleep happily if I had sent it—but the poor thing was in it's envelope, & I let it live until bed-time—& then I made spills of it! — I *could* not write another then—& had to open Joanie's envelope to apologize— that was why her note was addressed with a pencil— Please give my love to her—& I will not write to-night—as she kindly gave me leave not to do so— I really think Lily [Severn] must not be taught too much— her mind for the present should have a milk diet— I thank you from my heart for permission to speak to you of *her*—! ——

Your loving Susie

Feb[ruar]y 23, [18]78 [13]

My dearest friend—

This sheet of paper came, inclosing some letters, you had had to read—& the fancy came over me to try whether your paper was pleasant to write upon—& the spirit of mischief makes me enjoy the thought of your surprise, when you see the date! *MY* 'Fors'— told me to do it \\!// Did you know that I had one? — Some flower pots are upon the window stone. Bobbie came and stood upon one, expecting to find "Micaceous particles"—though not exactly the same kind as those which compose the Matterhorn! "Poor little mica flake!"— he found none, & was surprised, & no doubt whispered to his little Self, "Miror" ["I wonder"]— Then he came close to the glass, & stood upon his tip-toes, or, tip-claws,

13. This letter, written upon Brantwood stationery, was evidently a response to the "rather odd" note which Miss Beever had received from Ruskin while he was succumbing to insanity on February 22

& looked in perhaps to see if "the child Susie," was there— She was, & you may be sure that she did not let him look in vain— "darlingest," darling. These sample verses about a sparrow [a printed "What the Sparrow Chirps" is enclosed] came to me to-day—& I think them so pretty—that I send them to you. Two horses have been hard at work ploughing the wet sticky ground, this week— To-day they have a holiday & their *spirits,* as well as their legs, have *run away* with them, & they have been playing such antics, dashing to, & fro, & kicking up their heels in a frantic manner— Then one threw itself upon the turf, & rolled & rolled!! & rolled!!! — how it would refresh it's spine! The cook has just uttered some magic sounds at a distance & my dearest, sweetest, cleverest Pussie has flown out of this room, knowing that it meant dinner!

> This happy Puss has all her wants supplied—
> And so she never needs to be a thief,
> She likes all meat that roasted is, or broiled,
> But strange to say, she will not eat *boiled* Beef!!!

There's no accounting for taste. If a cat may look at a King she may surely have a choice as regards diet— She thinks Salmon, & Turbot excellent!!! but few things can equal a Mouse, in her estimation. A milk diet is all very well but she prefers cream! *William* knew this, & said—"He takes instruction as a cat laps cream"—or words to that effect— Surely I must have been as the Quakers say —— but No—I won't say it! it *might* be naughty—! for I had written this first sheet before Baxter came! I *am* desperately wicked to-day & was half inclined to say something about "Baxter's Saints Rest" —— How come you frighten me so about your Valentine You can deliver your own love messages—or— send Baxter round with them— your note is such a remarkable one that I cannot answer it while *Bee* [Baxter] is waiting—

Your very loving
Susie

My note is rather odd too— you were a sort of Cat-kin when you wrote your's— I shall try to harden myself— you don't say whether you shall Shine here tomorrow? — Do give me notice if you intend—as they do of American storms! —

Wednesday evening[14]
[Summer, 1878?]

My dearest friend

Do remember that you are never to write to Susie when you are not well, or when you are busy, or tired. I hope that this so very lovely day is doing you real good. I think a series of such, & as much out the doors exercise without fatigue as you can take is the best restorativc for you. Don't bathe your pen too often in that Black sea— Joanie has been lecturing me a little, & insinuating that I am to be chastised for one thing or other. Poor little me! I will try to bear it patiently! I had the pleasure this morning of helping to take an envelope off a scarlet poppy —The lovely— "crumpled" dress inside, was so wonderfully packed— This moment, as I write, I wonder whether the expansion of the scarlet (what must I call it? no right word comes to me) then let it be *scarlet,* is caused by *sap* flowing through the veins—*because* when a butterfly comes out of the Chrysalis, it too is folded up in the most perfect manner, & gradually as the wings quiver they expand & shall I say, come into flower? but this is only a sudden thought —& you know you always tell me to write what comes— So, when I write things worthy of chastisement—am *I* to blame, or *you?* — I am sorry to be too much tired to-day to get enough of the delicious air— I saw the first group of slender harebells in the grass to-day—& I want to go to them & speak to them—so dearly do I love them— It is a meditative day. "Sweet day so—" &c—& then comes, what comes to all sweet things, "Thou too must die!["]—& the dear summer is passing away so fast—& how few real summer evenings we have had! — Perhaps Joanie would tell you that she saw the *white* headed Robin. I cannot think what caused it—for no moulting ever looks like that—but the little being seems well—& carries off food for it's infants— Now tea, stopped my pen & after tea, it was no use struggling any longer, for I felt that I *must* go down to the lawn to those dear slender bluebells—& they did me good I knew they would—& most people would think me absurd & affected, if they knew how I love

14. The concern over Ruskin's health expressed in the opening sentences suggests that this letter was written while he was recuperating from his illness of 1878, or possibly of 1881.

them—but *you* will not think so—*you* never despise Susie! —— & she is very grateful —— and all this day a certain feeling of hope, & happiness about you, has hovered about her!

What a wonderful colour this little feather is, which I have just picked up, upon the lawn & what a lovely bit of down! — I want you to read a psalm to me some day. Will you? Your reading affects me very powerfully— Does this man's character please you? —

"A true swinker, & a good was he,
Living in pees, & parfite charitee
God loved he best with all his herte
At all times, were it gain or smerte
And then his neighbour right as himselve
He wold thresh, & thereto dike & delve
For Christes sake, for every poure wight
Withouten hire, if it lay in his might."

How I wish there were hundreds of such men! — I should scarcely have a sufficient stock of reverence to divide amongst them— Such men are what some one calls, "God's Gentlemen"— What think you? What a multitude of lovely things there are in the sky tonight! —& how delicious the stillness & the great calm! Mary Youdal sent me to-day a great handful of *white* shall I say *blue* bells—such pretty little things—growing after a lowly fashion. What pretty little vetch like yellow flowers, in little tufts, are out just now— I don't know their name— What then—"Every Godfather can give a name"— You who speak of ladies nursing cats—what would you have said if you had heard me talking to my Selim— I found him eating a fly—smacking his lips over it—didn't I say to him "And thou hast killed it! — What if this fly had a father & Mother?" — All in vain, I made no impression on him— he will be a flycatcher to the end of his days—& he has no more respect for what Mr. Severn calls, "The domestic fly"—than you have for Clergymen's wives! I should like to say something very naughty to you, & I cannot think of anything bad enough *ie.* of a suitable kind! —— But do try to be a good Professor &

take care of yourself for the sake of those who so love you, & mind you always think as kindly as you can of

Your very affectionate
Susie

June 24. [18]80

My dearest & kindest friend,

Once more I am like Cordelia & can *say* nothing! — If anything here below *can* be perfect—my enjoyment was—yesterday! — It was truly a day to be remembered— The one drawback was, that your great goodness to me tired you! — I had heard of the carpet in the new dining-room—but when I was thinking things over last night—I found that I had never even seen that there *was* a carpet!—and what was much worse, though I had just a glance at a marble chimney piece of a *lovely red* marble? I forgot to look at it again & this I regret—but with all that I *did* see, this may be excused? — My Mind is quite in a maze yet! I was wondering last night how it was that though I felt such tender pity for that lovely Pigeon of Hunt's, I did not feel anything for the snail! & I think from the look of it, it had died too! *Why* did I feel so much for one, & nothing for the other? — Well—the Pigeon could have loved me! —there was a *soul*—a heart! —a much higher intelligence— Is *that* the right explanation? — What with all the beautiful works of art, inside the house & the exquisite scenery outside—no wonder that I could not grasp everything! and those blue Violets haunt me! — The whole atmosphere of the place is so different from any other All so refined! —all with such a sweet grace! — Something to charm the mind & the eye, everywhere!——giving one such a feeling of delight— That picture of the Doge impressed me much—as being very fine— But you *know* that if I might choose from *all* the precious things— —— that little Boy in the white frock & blue sash [Ruskin, as painted by Northcote] would be to *me* SUPREME! Such blinding tears keep coming as I write— And oh, that lovely profile [presumably of Rose La Touche] you showed to me in the Study— *It,* & what you said afterwards about the holy life, entered into my soul — and after you had waved your hat to us in the boat there was something in the quiet manner of your walking away that touched me very much— And I hope & pray that you may be rewarded Seven fold for all your quite unspeakable goodness to Susie. But I must cease talking about *this* for I shall not be fit to be seen— & people will wonder what is the matter! — Imagine though my surprise, when Joanie opened her mysterious basket, & let out that little flock of lovely China! *Blue* Bantams! —& that *you* have used them! I need not tell you what that is to me and for this too—I can only give you—"Thanks"—the exchequer of the poor — And they *are* so pretty & the blue so sweet —— I shall never dare to use them, for fear they should get broken—to say nothing of the desecration! —— Mr. Cooke was so very grateful for your criticism—which he felt so valuable— I think he wished me to tell you this— And oh, his real, honest delight when I gave him a Bust Photograph— You made *him* very happy yesterday—& for that too I thank you —— I hope you are well to-day

Your very loving
Susie

Jan[uar]y—11—[18]82

My dearest friend

Your hand-writing grows more, & more beautiful— it is quite a treat to look at the note I had from you last night—even if it were only for the copper plate—but—there is such a sparkling of wit in it, as rivals an Opal in its flash & brilliancy! How delicious it would be to share, "The music of the spheres"—with Dr. J[ohn] B[rown] without mentioning any name—though of course I shall not let "the delicious secret out" to anyone —— but it seems too good for my private eating! A very *tiny* book of extracts came to me from Dr. J. B.— Many of the extracts are from *you* —w[hic]h of course gives the wee bit bookie a great charm— Several extracts are from "Ethics of the dust"—& the others I suspect are taken from *our* well beloved little "Frondes"— One of the choicest little books of the age! —for every word in it is your's— Dr. J. B. has written in the little book—

"To Shakespeare's & Ruskin's *Susie*"—

Is'nt that a delightful inscription?

There are some extracts about St. Francis—his preaching, & how the swallows interrupted him—well known to *you*— Do try to lose your cold—& when you can spare yourself, come & see me —for I cannot tell you how much I wish to see, & to talk with you once more—

Your loving
Susie

[December? 1883] [15]

My dearest friend,

A young man who keeps the fish & fruit-shop in the village is quite distressed because he thinks his father will wish him to be at home in Millom, on the day of your lecture ["The Battle of Kineyree," to be delivered in Coniston on December 22, 1883]— Miss Tolmie who teaches him sometimes, has written down what he said—& I inclose it for you[16]— I think it is quite touching— I hope you are better. Dr. P[arsons] said he was going to see you— I think Mary [her sister, d. December 31, 1883] very feeble to-day Dr. P. said she was much the same—but I felt that he said so, to quiet me— I hope your lozengers will come tomorrow I heard from a friend to-day about a cousin of her's, only *seven* years old— She was ill but not thought to be in danger & she said to her mother, "I have often heard May say, 'In my Father's house are many mansions' & I never understood what it meant till now —& I *know* that Jesus has gone to prepare a place for *me*—& when it is quite ready I shall go to it"— These were nearly the last words she spoke. She fell asleep, & thus passed away—

Oh, my dear friend would that you & I could become as little children for such is the kingdom of Heaven—

Your loving—
Susie

n.d.[17]

My dearest friend,

Mary had the blessing of seeing a litle bit of Paradise to-day.

15. The approximate date is indicated by Miss Beever's references to the "Battle of Kineyree," and to the feebleness of her sister Mary.

16. Enclosure: "I may never have the opportunity again! I should like to be able to say, perhaps 40, or 50 years after this, that I had once heard John Ruskin give a lecture! People don't know that they've got him now! but they will worship his name by and bye!"

17. Inscribed by Ruskin: "most precious."

A Robin brought his beloved onto the window-stone & fed her as tenderly as if she were a newly hatched baby. And she opened her mouth & gave herself pretty airs—just as if she could'nt possibly feed herself! and no doubt everything *he* gave her tasted doubly sweet! — Don't you wish that you & I had seen it? — I have something curious to tell you that happened when you were in London—but I reserve it— You gave me ever so much happiness yesterday—

Your loving
Susie

V

DR. JOHN BROWN TO MISS SUSAN BEEVER

[The following two letters were evidently given to Ruskin by Miss Beever. They are accompanied by the last page of a letter which was probably written to Ruskin.]

23 Rutland Street
Edinburgh
30th July 1881

My dear Susie

How are you? & how is our dear Genius & Friend? You will tell me. I fear Carlyle's death must have shaken him—& these sad things about him & his wife, which should never have been known must have grieved him Did you read Miss Gordon's letter to Carlyle—she was Blumine in "Sartor"—bidding him a final farewell—if not, get it—it is in Froude's paper in last 19th Cent[ur]y It seems to me a perfect letter— How are your eyes? & your—which self? & how is Mrs. Severn? My Isabella is very thin & pale—has more soul than body— I have been refreshing myself with the Arrows of the Chace—he is "Lord of the unerring bow"— Tell me some books to read— I have lost all appetite for reading—almost— I am like a leech that bites but doesn't fix— I read Cymbeline & The Winters Tale & a lot of the sonnets lately— you know his "infinite variety"—his infinite richness & yet how tiresome he sometimes is, just as nature is— My biggest & best love to our friend—

Yours ever affect[ionate]ly
J. Brown

23 Rutland Street
Edinburgh
[1881?]

My dear Susie

Thanks for yours— I am sorry for the eyes—the windows of the soul—& of the heart too— Try a wash of Boracic Acid— Thanks too for that beautiful letter of our Genius's— What a faculty! — He writes just as nobly & sweetly to you & me as to the great world which listens to his Diapason *Concentus omniscus*

[no signature]

23 Rutland Street
Edinburgh

& staring at Nature & doing her best to read her, in colour. A daughter of our late Sol. General And[re]w Clark— Is there any engraving of the Marriage of the Virgin by Fra Angelico? I heard this day week in a little Baptist Chapel, in a wood up the hill from Pittodery a most excellent sermon—on "What is that to thee. *Follow thou me*" I am more and more convinced that the essence of Xianity, of righteousness & of all goodness, is in this— in following the Christ—in thinking, feeling & acting (within our human limits) as he would have done.

Dora has got to the second edition—& Lady Minto agrees with you as to the winkle & the daffodils—

Y[ou]rs ever affect[ionate]ly
J. Brown

VI

Rawdon Brown to Ruskin and to Mrs. Severn

1. *To Ruskin*

Casa della Vida
20 June 1869

My dear Ruskin,

Believe me that your message however imperfectly translated, was perfect in as much as it produced the effect desired by you; for it rendered Lorenzi-Velludo—(the vice-Librarian his firm friend and adviser) and me, thoroly happy as it would have distressed us all very much if your *supplementary* contribution to the history of the Ducal Palace, had in any way dissatisfied you— It would have been a bad return for such munificence.

I am glad Borromeo's note amused you: by all means keep it. He will be delighted to hear how much trouble you have taken and are taking about HIS copy of the "Stones"— MY copy, I lent on Wednesday last, to Charles Alexander, Grand Duke of Saxe-Weimar Eisenach, who paid me a visit incog. as *"Comte di Cella"*; speaking very good English, and he returned me many thanks for the loan of your books. He introduced himself as the friend of Mad^e^ de Goethe—the daughter in law of the great German writer and was very courteous and well bred.

Yesterday I sent a second revise or summary of the letters about Hawkwood it is more intelligible than the first, and was written expressly for insertion in "the English in Italy"; but the work had escaped my memory, and it was by mere accident that I discovered the lost & forgotten sheets, so I sent them at once, hoping to save you trouble—

The weather continues cool & pleasant thanks to constant heavy showers, which the astronomers account for, by spots on the face of the sun, so tho' fond of his light, I cannot but wish this cutaneous disease to last until autumn; by so much the more as this state of the atmosphere, enables you to do your work pleasantly—

Ever your most affectionate
Rawdon Brown—

Casa della Vida
3rd Dec[ember 18]69 [1]

My dear Ruskin

I am so glad Richard II pleased you, and that you do not reject the other references. Some Frenchman said, that any book which induces thought and reflexion, is an important book: it is universally admitted that all *yours,* have that merit; and now-a-days when every body knows every thing—and a great deal more —I like you all the beter for taking credit to yourself for *"igno-*

1. This letter and the two which follow are in an envelope inscribed by Ruskin: "M[r.] Brown / Derivations—Bully, &c. / Precious— / Final service of Hawkswoods men."

rance", an assumption which I shall henceforth couple with Montaigne's motto, "Que sais-je?"

I quite believe in your rare power of analyzing expressions; and am of opinion that the chronology of words—I mean the DATE of their introduction into any language—is no less worth knowing, than their etymology. My passion for *Venetian* derivations makes me think that we owe many of our words of the 13th 14th & 15th centuries, to the Galley-crews, who frequented Galley Quay in Thames Street, and Southampton water. For instance *"noon"*, from *"nona"*, the Venetian chimes which were struck daily from the Tower of St. Marks when the sun was *due south.* How much more sense and meaning are contained in this word than in it's synonyme,—*"mid-day"*, derived from the French *"midi"—"south."* We may suppose that originally the words *"c'est midi"*, signified *"the* [*sun is in the*] *'south'* ", *not* that it was the middle of the day; but our people—talking from EAR and not from *sense* converted *midi* into *"miday."* Again, as I told you last summer, the French word *"goutte"* signifying a disease, a *drop* of acrid humour distilling downwards and corroding the system, conveys a meaning: it's English synonym, *gout* is gibberish. A Venetian Ambassador (Francesco Contarini who lived to be Doge) at Rome, early in the 17th century, styled the malady *"una discesa di catarro"*; an explanation which might be advantageously pondered by Physicians. The Venetian word *"mangano"*, is evidently the root of our *"mangle"*, the etymology of which, Johnson does not attempt, tho it is much needed; as a utensil for *smoothing* linen, cannot be said to *mangle* it. The Venetian word "mangano", is explained, thus *"mangano macchina nota, sotto cui si lustrano e amarezzano le tele e i drappi avvolti su i subbii."*

You say nothing about Caldera's drawings: do enquire whether Messrs Smith & Elder have received them; and ask McCracken about your cases by the Steamer *"El dalia"*, which—I know for certain—got safe to London some time ago.

I enclose a letter received in October from Jessica before her return to Paris: it will amuse you. I told her in reply, that the Liverpool *"Revival"*, proceeded from *Wig-wam* scenery amongst the nuggets in California, or from some view from the windows of Queen Pomaro's drawing-room at Otaheite; and that the "Merchant-Princes" of Lancashire made their money in the savage *west*—those of Venice in the gorgeous *East;* the train of thought of the two races being illustrated by their buildings. You see I *crib* your theories.

Tell me how your Mother and Cousin are.

Ever your's affectionately
Rawdon Brown

Do you not believe that the BEST of any language, are derived from *common* parlance rather than from classical authorities? It seems to me that the decadence of the Italian languages, dates from the establishment of the *refined Academy della Crusca* in 1691—

Venice
13th Dec[ember 18]69

My dear Ruskin,

From *"fishermen"* to pilots, there is but a step, and on the 12th March 1588, an indenture was made in London between "Matthew Byrde of Lymehouse in the county of Middlesex, *marryner* on th' one partie and John Ghise of Venice, Pursser of the good Shipp called the Gallion Patti of Venyce, now *SURGINGE* at an anker at Gore-ende near Margatt etc", so that, to "an honest diligent and expert pilott" (as Byrde is styled elsewhere in the indenture) we are indebted for the *first* use—in *our* language—of this expressive, swelling, and sonorous VERB— The word is often used *substantively,* by Shakespear, and Johnson shows, that Spenser and Milton made a *verb* of it; but the "Faery Queen", was not published until 1589, so my working *sailor,* was in advance of the *poet,* by one year. All seamen and all Venetians—from the highest to the lowest—knew the values of order and discipline—they were oligarchical NOT republican, and thoughts, induced by raging seas and this beautiful city; took such effect upon them, that their phraseology was rarely ignoble; so my love for it does not blemish my toryism.

Did I ever tell you the etymology of the substantive *"Bully"?* — Johnson supposes *"burly"—"bulky"—"bull-eyed"—* The Venetian word *BULO*—signifies—*"Bravo"—"Cagnoto" "Sgherro" —"Tagliacantoni"*—Do you not hear the crew of roaring *"bullies",* at Galley Quay in Thames Street?

I am glad your sea-borne things have at length got safe to Denmark Hill; Toni also rejoices, and wishes to know whether the contents of the cases, agree with the inventory already sent to you through [Tiln?], and of which he (Toni) kept a copy—

I am afraid these land-carriers are robbers; and poor Caldera is in despair; the other day or rather 3 weeks ago, I sent a parcel to my sister who has never received it, and some photos destined for Jessica seem also to have been stolen.

Let me know whether the artillery-men at Woolwich are staunch to the good cause. Do you know a Capt[ai]n Brackenbury who is one of the professors there, and was correspondent for the "Times" with the Austrian army in 1866. At the close of the campaign, I saw him here, and he pleased me: he was a good Austrian.

I did what I could for the Brookes, tho' in truth it was but little; they are amiable people and therefore took my good-will, as it was meant—

Ever, my dear Ruskin

Affectionately your's

RB

Casa della Vida

16th Jan[uary] 1871

My dear Ruskin

As you know me well enough to believe in my hearty wishes for your well-being, at all seasons, I delayed answering your kindest of letters announcing the pamphlet, until able to say that it had reached me, which is not yet the case, and I think the mis-chance may be explained by the accompanying notice from the P.O.

You are as usual affectionately considerate about my feline attachment & I try to take comfort, and foster the hopes you hold out, that my Jew's extortion, will spoil his market, by so much the more, as Bembo told me last week, that the Duke of Bordeau is unable to obtain a hundred thousand francs for Ca' Cavalli, altho' he disbursed that sum for the garden alone!

Would that you were here at this moment— I think I could say a word or two, to reconcile you to the autumnal BLIGHT; the force of habit is very great, in almost all men, and increases with age; if you acknowledge this, you will comprehend my meaning;

and when we meet, I will explain myself more fully; Borromeo says you have promised him a visit in the spring, so I hope it will be soon.

What you say of Hawkwood reminds me that I have just printed a paragraph showing that after his death, the disbanded English soldiers transferred their services to— guess again —— the prostitutes of Rialto! and turned *"Bullies"!* So much for hero-worship. Who are we to admire or place trust in? Do you remember Bonifacio's "Strage degli Innocenti" at the Academy? — I think I have discovered that the principal figure, represents one Lodovico da L'Armi, a Scelerat employed by Henry 8 to murder Card[ina]l Pole at Trent in 1546— He was a "character", and good or bad, he attracted attention, and the artist's vanity or love of fame had taught him that human nature is curious and inquisitive rather than moral and laudatory, even at church or in a national gallery— I wish you would write about Titian and his times—

I am glad you were pleased with the Bentincks, by so much the more, as they most certainly appreciated, the flattering except made by you when accepting their hospitality

My love to Miss Agnew.

Ever your most affectionate
Rawdon Brown

Casa della Vida
15th December 1881

My dearest Ruskin

I am like an infant learning to write, and the letter to which your's is so kind a reply, was half a day's painful work, but encouraged by Toni, when I told him it was destined for you so he rejoiced yet more, as I added that you had taken the Pope under your protection.

In reply to your complaint, that there is nothing in the first volume of the Venetian calendar, of the 12th & 13th centuries, the apology for this omission may be read at pages viii–ix, PREFACE; and pray bear in mind that my extracts from the Venetian archives, are limited to facts, hitherto unpublished, and connected directly or indirectly, with England.

I gratefully accept the assurance of your affection, under whatever title it may be conceded me, even under Cardinal Manin's [Manning's] red hat; and tomorrow I will deliver your kind message to Parini.

In the time, believe me ever,

Your most affectionate old friend,
Rawdon Brown.

2. *To Mrs. Severn*

Casa della Vida
1st July 1880

My dear Mrs. Severn,

Your most comforting letter arrived on the 14th June, when I sent to London immediately for "the 19th Century", and "Art Journal" of last month, which came two days ago, and delight me.

I desired the bookseller, whenever these periodicals contain articles by the same pen, to let me have them without delay, and as Lady Castletown, who loves Coz heartily chances to have just now come here, one of her many daughters, by name Mrs. Huffington Smyth, I sent last night for her perusal my two copies on "Fiction" and "Museums" that she might let her mother know the author's determination not to die poor, and after long sufferance, to bring publishers to equity and justice, from which resolve, I trust he will never again swerve.

To pair with Doge Gritti I have now *a negative* made from a portrait by Titian of one of his contemporaries, Giacomo Loranzo, who was ambassador in England from 1551, to 1554, the portrait having apparently been painted in July 1575, when he was elected Procurator *"de supra"* of St Mark.

Of this *negative* (*senza ritocco*) I now send a *positive* a mere ruin, but a grand one, with best love to him, and to you, from your most affectionate old friend

Rawdon Brown

Poor dear Toni is my usual assistant in packing and ordering photos and all other domestic arrangements, but alas he has been very ill of late, and the extreme heat, forbids the Lido voyage; nor is the little Doggie "Cici" quite herself; we often talk of you & Coz, & to both he is grateful for your remembrance, Lorenzi likewise returning thanks for it.

Again goodbye, and may God bless you and yours.

Casa della Vida
13th May 1881

My dear Mrs. Severn,

The consolation you so kindly sent me on the 8th, arrived yesterday, and corresponds to that staunch friendship which you have long shown me.

To return to what you wrote me last June I sent instantly to London for *"The Nineteenth Century"* and *"The Art Journal"* which at once convinced me that the Publishers knew what they were doing, though I sent you no congratulations, our mutual thoughts on this success being known to each other by sympathetic electricity.

At present I *most peremptorily* forbid your cousin to write to me, and rely on you alone for occasional notices of him as it is necessary for his mind to be quite at rest for a few days, that it may recover it's pristine vigour.

I translated what you wrote last, word by word to Toni, whose grief till that moment, kept pace with mine and he now sends his hearty rejoicings.

Pray let me also know how Mr Severn and your children are, and believe me to be always

Most affectionately your's
Rawdon Brown.

VII

Burne-Jones to Ruskin and to Mrs. Severn

[The following letters from Sir Edward Burne-Jones have been selected from the 32 in the F. J. Sharp Collection which were written between 1862 and 1889. Two of the four letters addressed to Mrs. Severn have also been included among those in which Burne-Jones discusses his appearance as a witness for the defense in the *Whistler* vs. *Ruskin* trial.]

The Grange
North End Road
Fulham, S.W.
[November? 1876] [1]

My blessedy

Who am I to instruct you about things: I darent press you about the matter at all for sometimes I feel a minority of one— and certainly I have espoused the unpopular side— it was popular for a time & some of my friends were ashamed of it for that reason and now its so unpopular that many are ashamed of it for fear— and I dont want to drag you into unpopular causes without need— I do feel patriotic though—so much so that of all things I want my country to be noble—and I'm sorry when it dins its interests into the ears of the world, & sorry when its unjust— I think it very unjust to Russia now—very very—but so mad that it wont hear reason—& horrible blind war may burst out of some little accident any hour— all this is unworthy of a big strong people— I think all along we ought to have remembered one only thing— the relief of those unhappies whose history we ought to have made it our business to learn, and our duty to succour them—lucky & happy as we are— I'm not a Russophile I know so little of them— I feel that up till to-day they have not departed from their high promises and that with our help mankind may for ever owe them its sincere blessing— to morrow it may be different but who has provoked it from the first we taunted them with hypocrisy, were happy in their defeat, depreciated their success—judging of the nation generally from the acquaintances and friends I have

I might say that depths of ignorance were at the bottom of all this—but its ignorance that six hours of reading could enlighten if they would, but they wont. Its too late now to say more to

1. A letter (with the second half of the first folder missing) in which Burne-Jones discusses "The Eastern Question," having undertaken to enlist Ruskin's support of the foreign policy of Gladstone, in opposition to that of Disraeli. Partly in response to Burne-Jones' solicitations, Ruskin became one of the Convenors of the "National Conference" on the Eastern Question held on December 8, 1876. "All your letter is very precious to me," he thanked Burne-Jones, on December 8, 1876. "I am greatly amazed, for one thing, to find that I can be of use and value to you in this matter—supposing myself a mere outlaw in public opinion" (*Works, 24,* xxxviii).

them they wont be just—they might be they are strong enough— in any righteous matter they are as invincible as Greeks at Marathon—but they will

[The second half of this folder has been torn off.]

son's or his own life in the quarrel— so base to get others to do our butchers work.

it is a steam & devil-driven land & you are right, and I am in a hurry to see the awakening that must come— the gods take it more patiently—only the punishment falls on the simple folk and the scoundrels are so happy.

a little league that at present hasnt 3 names will be started to protest against this coming war—and while it lasts to labour for the return of peace— it will be execrated at first but will grow in numbers after its originators have been vilified or otherwise crucified enough—but I wont ask you to join us seriously as I did when I could show you Carlyle with us: and I dont know whether you might think it might compromise St. George. — I mean I cant judge & of all things cannot [bear?] to press you about things— Enough for me that with all my heart I more and more love your work and acknowledge its truth.

I dont think I should ever like dear to have anything I write to you printed because I take no pains with it & write gladly & eagerly to you without measuring words a bit— I shall look forward with great eagerness towards the March Fors.[2] — This is the fever month, God send March may not be the war month. O my sweet oldie what a comfort you is to sore eyes— Yes I heard of your expedition to the Circus & was very unhappy.

ever your loving

Ned

What an incoherent letter but it is writ in agonies of toothache & I can think of little else

The Grange

[July 29, 1878][3]

dear blessed one

2. See Letter 75, March 1877 (*Works 29,* 60–61), for a Ruskinian version of what Burne-Jones has been saying.

3. On July 28, 1878, Ruskin had dined in London with Mary Gladstone (see *Works, 37,* 254).

We were very glad of your note to say that you had neither caught cold nor been tired: I had a note by the same post from Mary Gladstone asking me to meet you at dinner last evening: and I would have rushed off gladly, but Swinburne was to come to me—and I see him now very rarely and am very glad when he does come, that I may show him a little friendship— poor little thing what friends he might have had— he came so late that I was dressing to go to you.

if you come any morning to wander through my poor work you will tell me first wont you? on Wednesday for an hour or so before lunch I draw from a very lovely damsel—& if you came you could tell Frances [Graham] and make her unhappy and green with jealousy (and serve her right & serve her right)— well, not quite: but to watch pretty things, is good for our old eyes—thine and mine— Meantime I am much happier for having seen you—if ever you go away it wont be the same world ever again to some of us—& I think Italy will be so heartbreaking I should never go there again—but now for a time its happy— give Joan my love & Arthur— ever thy old

much battered but stubborn

Ned

British shyness makes it impossible to speak out one's heart about you face to face—but you do know how you are loved in this house. its fun having that Sapphira [his daughter Margaret—1866–1953]—but Georgie [1840–1920] is simply awful about it—we are not to praise her nor buy her hats & feathers nor watch her at all—never—and she is to be brought up absolutely unconscious of self

[sketch of two hands thumbing nose]

This is a vulgar emblem
but it's true

The Grange
[October 1878] [4]

Written 3 weeks ago
My Very Blessed

4. Arranging to visit Mary Gladstone at Hawarden during October 1878, Ruskin had expressed his hope that he might then see Burne-Jones as a fellow-guest (see *Works, 37,* 260–61).

It wasnt to be this time for me—but we are to meet at Hawarden yet and have a little season all to ourselves. I'd got leave from Dunira [home of the Grahams] and was getting ready when Mary's note stopped me—& she's quite right. last night I saw little Harold Rathbone [son, b. 1858, of Philip Henry Rathbone of Liverpool] but could only talk a minute or so with him—and when I asked about you he said you would work too much & that you were as hard at it as ever, which seemed likely to be true: be careful for all our sakes— my creed is this, many a day, that you are the most important living thing, and I get more and more sure of it—when you were ill and I thought you would die I felt bitterly what a change it would be for me— though I love my work and life, & have Georgie and baby & friends all good to me it never again could have been like it was for me: nobody else is in the least bit like you and it will never happen again in this world So dont work much— Why shouldnt you come sometime and Stay a bit with us— There's a little prophet's chamber ready in a moment, and your man could lodge opposite, one minute off—and you should have a room to work in and peace and crumpets we would plan things and be happy. And we'll talk about that scheme of painted chapel and I'll help with all my might anything you want. Good bye. dont answer my letters because there's nothing to answer—only if Joan could spare you a bit one time you come to London it would revive my youth, & really it would be quite silent here for you.

Your old Ned

[The Grange?]
[early November 1878] [5]

dear dear Joan

[Seven lines inked out.]

I havent seen Arthur yet, that is since Wednesday—but on your letter I telegraphed to him to come across to me or to meet me

5. Burne-Jones is now preparing to testify at the *Whistler* vs. *Ruskin* trial, to be held on November 26–27, Ruskin having told him in a letter of November 2, 1878 that the lawyers had been referred to him as the chief witness for the defense (see *Works, 29,* xxiv). Burne-Jones was embarrassed because the condemnation of Whistler for "Cockney impudence" in the *Fors* Letter 79 of July 1877, which led to the suit for libel, had been eloquently complemented by Ruskin's praise of his own power and achievement as an artist (see *Works, 29,* 159–60).

in town & I will go first to our lawyers and then [inked out]. [Then?] I want to send my blessed oldie something to amuse him and make him forget this ugly rubbish— he shall not be left alone in the matter— hundreds of us are eager to do something and only want to know what— his praise of me in the same article makes it at first sight funny for me to appear—but I shall if they think I can do one halfpenny worth of good: fatten him & make him eat & make him laugh, and rouse him & tell him a great thing as he is must be bright & strong for all of us— my courage is altogether a fictitious one, founded on nice things he has said in consequence of which I strut about and am prepared to-day to stand on my head before the clubs in Pall Mall if it can be of the least good to my friends— read to him bright things "Sky neighbourhood" in the Uncommercial traveller and "City churches" I wish Georgie was with you to help make fun— I will lend her if you would like it— as to Georgie I assure you dear Joan Boadicea was a milksop and a Miss in comparison and as for the mother of the Gracchi I must be pardoned for smiling— As for the Roman empire she would have made slight work of that and then we shouldnt have to bind up Gibbon pompously, to look like part of—a gentlemans library. When I'm low Georgie whips me up as the cook does a cream & I become fit to present at table, with a curly froth on the top of me. A most vigorous woman!—now in her prime—& capable of arresting the corruption & decrepitude of an empire—except ours which not even Georgie can manage: dont lose heart dear but take care of him— he's the biggest thing we have.

ever your affe[ctionate]
Ned

The Grange
[November 26, 1878] [6]

6. At the trial, the witnesses for the defense testified on Tuesday, November 26. As a witness, Burne-Jones reminded himself of Mr. Winkle who, at the trial of Mr. Pickwick (outrageously sued by Mrs. Bardell for £1500 damages because of breach of promise), was supremely inept: confused and confounded by the lawyer for the plaintiff, he was at once "reluctant" and "too-willing" as he provided the witlessly honest "evidence" through which the cause of his friend was irreparably damaged. Next, as a friend of Mr. Pickwick, Tracey Tupman was "driven to the verge of desperation" by the "excessive badgering" to which he was subjected (see *Pickwick Papers,* Part II, chap. 34).

Tuesday the Horrible-th

O my dear oldie I was like Nathaniel Winkle after all— they wouldnt ask me the questions I wanted them to ask— they would not ask me about you and what you'd done as I wanted—and I don't know *what* I said and their counsel turned all I said so that I didnt know it again & I never spoke out louder than one does to a friend in my life, and I dare say I was most unwise—and I was very nervous and it all felt dreadful— I wanted to say things about you and they gave me no chance— I wanted to speak of the Irving picture & it wasnt there & they didnt ask me, and now Im back feeling just like Tracey Tupman did— they wouldnt give me a chance to stand up for you— dont answer for I am always your loving

Ned

[The Grange]
Northend
[November 27, 1878] [7]

My dear Joan

I enclose a fourth part of a half penny stamp which I do in justice think I owe to my blessed oldie for any possible injury I may have done to his cause— Serjeant Parry [Whistler's counsel] made it seem that I said what I hadn't and the only paper I have seen this morning makes me say what I never did for one moment say and this may possibly have increased the damages— I hope my dear will not be offended at my offer to help in what I feel is a national cause— it was very ugly work, & I trembled a good deal, and wasnt very articulate and my tongue clave to the roof of my mouth (—no it was too hot & dry to cleave to anything) and Frances Graham was there to laugh when I stumbled and I dare say I spluttered and was ridiculous but as I said—I would stand on my head in Pall Mall for him and I did what was pretty much the same.

Serjeant Parry said something which was not in the morning's paper— "Is an imperious autocrat on his throne to issue edicts which shall bring ruin, irretrievable ruin gentlemen on a humble

7. Found guilty of libel, Ruskin was sentenced to pay a farthing damages. At the end of this letter, the forefinger of a carefully drawn hand points to one quarter of "a half penny stamp" which has been pasted upon the page.

industrious & gifted gentleman" yes—he said *humble* & he said *industrious*— my oldie will laugh when he sees me discourse on atmosphere and praise Whistler for it— it was really very hard for me to attack him—and I said harmful things of him which I believed, and qualified it with all the praise I could think of which also I believed—and he wont think I failed him in a pang of mercy that came over me.

And now Oldie must be my second when I fight my duel on Calais sands the weapons I shall choose for I shall be the challenged party— the seconds must determine if the affair is to be to the utterance in which case we use pots of oil paint— in a slight affair—distemper —— in either case I select prussian blue as the most effective weapon I know. — tell us some fun & tell Arthur I *must* have my 5 vols of Modern painters back—for the price of them is rising & will rise now fabulously

Your aff[ectionat]e
Ned

The Grange
[November 1878] [8]

dearest St C.

I suppose you know that people arent going to let you have one penny to pay over this business— you mustnt interfere because people are longing to make a little demonstration about it. When Morris & I talked of the chance of your losing we didnt mean that the matter should rest there but—we are determined you shall not pay one penny & you wont baulk us will you? I dont know who has started the affair at the Fine art Soc[iety]; but they have only just anticipated other friends that I know and thousands for anything I know—so sit still and play— I think it was a triumph really, & was better than I expected I did feel it rather dreadful to say things against another painter, because I dont run them down much even in private do I—and often I feel as if I didnt

8. In reference to the £386.12s.4d "costs" of the trial, paid by 118 contributors. Now addressing Ruskin as St. C(rumpet)—the pet name used by Rose La Touche, Burne-Jones again recalls the *Bardell* vs. *Pickwick* trial, in which only Sam Weller (undismayed and imperturbably good-humored) was able to cope with the lawyer for the plaintiff—for example, through his remark that as prosecutors Dodson and Fogg had most generously "taken up the case on spec" and had agreed to "charge nothing at all for costs, unless they got 'em out of Mr. Pickwick."

know much about it all— I asked them not to call me because you had praised me and people would laugh—but each counsel made capital out of the fact in a way they only understand I suppose. — I envied the witnesses the day before who came to praise & I did feel ill & miserable over it all & am sleepless & sick of painting for a bit— it was all so hideous—made to seem hideous by the lawyers. — I asked them to examine me on two points only What you had done for art these 40 years past—and on the right of freedom in criticism but I suppose they knew their business— I told the truth as well as I could under the hardest conditions I ever had— I was frightened of their wigs and sterile faces— I suppose Watts and Leighton and others will blame me a good deal and will think I neednt have volunteered— I hear Rose who is Whistlers lawyer took the matter in hand on the principle of Dodson & Fogg—so you need not feel magnaminous ab[ou]t Whistler— we wanted a Sam Weller sadly— Georgie read me the Pickwick trial the night before and Morris carried me metaphorically in his arms to the door of the Court— if they had called on him to give evidence he would have spoken in the unqualified way that Frith [of the R.A., another witness for the defense] did— I could not truthfully do quite that— here comes my model & I must work. tell me someday if the whole thing has bothered you, much— I like to hear that you were merry about it. — never answer my letters but only write when you have a mind—

Your loving Ned.

The Grange
[1883] [9]

St. Valentine his foolish day

dearest & best oldie

Morris, like other men of vast genius, wont do anything that is proposed to him: on my bended knees so to speak have I besought him to try experiments on glass, & make his own little bits—just as you say, the dark got by depth of itself—, on bended knees, with piteous words—and he wont. he gives many reasons against it, admirable as rhetoric— *I have urged him when he wants a*

9. Ultimately 14 windows for the Whitelands College Chapel were designed by Burne-Jones and executed by William Morris. Dated by the reference to Ruskin's age in the following "letter No 2."

deep ruby to steal his wife's gold ornaments & boil them up and make a red for himself— he wont, he wont: and so if you and I could have a kiln (a little one we could keep in the parlour) we would make little bits to our hearts content: as it is, he used the mean, thin, trumpery cylinder sheets of tinted speckled rubbish sold by the glass blowers—and does, I think, wonders with them, & I believe sometimes depth is got by doubling the glass—but I know that he often bewails his fate and dreams that in heaven glass will be much thicker: and I think so too:

Meantime I will ask him, & even get him to write to you about it—a great task, but possible

But I have a notion that in an old abbey, they made their own glass in bits—dear deep blobs and picked out the bits they liked & fitted them about, & broke the cartoon-designer's heart (if ever they had such a person) by contempt of his outline, & were happy.

Proserpina bides, my dear, I havent begun her yet— I am practicing my art— one day I mean to paint a picture

And so you are now at Coniston & I hoped you were in London —and that comes of being rich & having more houses than one, that I never know where you are. in the next life all my friends shall be poor & live next door to me

Your old old
Ned

The Grange
[February 14, 1883]

This is letter No 2

my dearest oldie

Morris has just come in—

He had gout & was contrarious

Can you form an idea of how contrarious a great man can be? No? then to proceed.

it seems I wrote great folly to you this morning—& that glass neednt be thick & that ancient glass isnt thicker than ours—and that laying glass behind glass however fascinating is not a safe process because of the unequal strain on the leading of the window—

And he will send you a memorandum of his experience & a box of specimens.

and he says to talk to you face to face is best—but I feel aged this morning because of the nature of great men, who are so trying— if one could but do without them!

And he said XIV cent[ur]y glass is less thick than 2 centuries earlier—but it may have been gout that made him say it— you cant tell about great men I assure you.

it was my fault for saying *that glass ought to be thicker for he instantly said "thinner you mean."*

But he will send you his experience and that is all that is wanted.

Good bye. You wont like my picture at all this year: but you will like all I do henceforth when this is finished.

Art thou 64? — I dont think it— we will always be between thirty and fifty and choose the year we like to be— to-day I am fifty, because Morris wouldn't let me have it all my own way in talk— tomorrow I will be thirty if I can

but always I am

Your loving
Ned

The Grange
Tuesday
[March 13, 1883][10]

My own blessed—

When will you come? fix any day and any hour (not tomorrow) and what will you say about me? shall you say I do all I ought not to do, & wont be guided, and am obstinate & nasty—& tiresome—and I'll write you out a list— alas! I have wrought much folly in Israel and my pictures are many. I'll make a list of them—the chief ones and send it you.

When is the feast day you want it by— I'll do all I can about the Cross. You shall talk it over with me when you come & tell me why hawthorne and how much work is to be in it.

Yes heaven demanded a victim & smote my Morris with gout—he is very cross— it has made him much less Christian than he was before—but he mends & I will remind him of the glass—

10. Ruskin is now preparing to lecture on Burne-Jones in *The Art of England* series, and Burne-Jones is preparing to design a gold cross for the May Queen at Whitelands College. For Ruskin's reply to this letter, see *Works, 33,* xlvi.

indeed I knew he ordered the sample to be put together for you —but I will see to it—and tell me when you will come—& will it be morning or noon. I am working very hard to get 2 pictures done for this spring— one is the Wheel of Fortune— you wont like it— one is six little boobies sitting on a seat that I call the "hours" you will like it perhaps a little bit it was nice seeing Joan the other night & we made merry, yea, even in the very presence.

Now goodbye—& I'll do what I can to make the cross pretty but I dont like the form of a cross—do you?

Your loving
Ned

I'm so glad you are going to say a word about me—in my own country—that is Oxford. — I feel very happy about it & it's a surprise.

But forebodings as of the approach of doomsday are upon me if you saw the pen with which I have written you would marvel

[sketch of a feather with a pronged point]

[The Grange?]
[April? 1883] [11]

Dearest St C.

Not to keep the St waiting I send a sketch of the Shield [of St. George] for you to comment on before I draw it out further— if it will do I shall draw every oak leaf sharply & neatly & do the acorns tidily—but perhaps it wont do— it is such ages since I drew patterns that what little faculty I had seems gone— Morris does it all so much better that I have no courage about it— all lines would be of equal strength—in the shield and all— I dont think a cross a pretty shape & so I have rather left it to be dug for by the faithful & theres a thing at the top of the shield that I wanted to be a grassy earth but it looks like a plum pudding. — oak seemed right for that Saints garland— the label needn't be if you have nothing to say—& if finally its bad I will try again at once—

& let us design in this way together— you take my rough notions & amend them & I will do what I can to yours.

11. This letter, written in pencil, ends with a penciled sketch of a staring and despairing Burne-Jones, and is contained in an envelope upon which Ruskin has written: "Ned's miraculous portrait of himself."

I think you quite right about the edge of the florin. next week I will try to get one side (the Michael) done for you— I feel the right way would be to hammer one out myself & get the fat-raised-up-lumps that make such things happy— outline is little help & I think in nothing but outline now—for love of Florence—

I wanted to go on Thursday to you—but am shut up with cough that shatters me to bits— Joan says you patted my withered back— did you? I should like so to see what you said—for I cling tightly to the skirts of your love

ever your old Ned

[sketch]

Rottingdean

May [1886] [12]

O thou dear one, and much too good for this world—

They have brought me here to rest, Georgie & Mich [Margaret] —but as it is written, there is no rest for the wicked—and I dont like being made to rest, and having my paints taken from me—

I have been writing incessantly to you, in a spiritual sense— I wrote after every number of "praeterita," a long loving letter full of praise—such as we like to get, we men—and especially I wrote a very long letter, which I suppose never reached you since I would not stoop to ink & paper after Joan's visit—all in praise of Joan and her ways, lauding & magnifying them— —no, it is clear that you dont know when I write unless I stoop to this vulgar materialism, & use ink, paper and letterboxes.

I was very full of Joan for a time— she brightened me, lifted years off my bent old back and made my countenance to shine— but she had to go away—to exacting Arthur and exorbitant thee —and I got used to it and grew dull again—and duller & duller till they brought me here to mend.

Are you on good terms with Mich? I never knew— she is a sibyl of dark counsel & hidden ways— I hope you are on good terms with her.

But at present there is nothing I am half so happy about as about 'praeterita'—and nothing I dread so much as its coming to

12. In the upper margin of this letter Ruskin has written: "Read carefully Its all nice."

an end—or getting on too fast— doo 'ee linger over it and dont speed— there cant be enough of it—

No need to answer this my dear— its true what I said, I often indite letters to thee while I work, & you are more & more in my life as time goes on—but I never could write letters—

Your ancientist and affectionatest of Neds

The Grange
[1886] [13]

Blessedest—out of all comparison with any other competing blends.

I'll see to the grasping desires of this priest— neither do I know a bit what he means, for he has written to me too—but dismiss it from your mind & I will see to it.

It is thirty years ago since I first set eyes on thee in Gabriel's studio—Blackfriar's bridge, — I had known him a month or so and was playing with him one day when you came in— it was in 1856— that was my Annus Mirabilis— in the eye of the parochial register I was 23 years old—but looking back in the calm of old age I see that I was a month old—& that those 23 years are not to count—

I'll be what age I like, & have been born when I like, & presently I mean to come out with my own 'praeterita' & you musn't fail me or express surprise if you find me stating that I have been a pirate and an arab before I settled down—

You wont tell, will you? and if you write about me do cheat a bit & pretend—

Adoo—my dear—but who has been a-despising & rejecting thee?

ever thy ancient Ned

The Grange
Sunday
[July 21, 1889]

dear Blessed Oldie

I would often write to you if I were sure my letters wouldn't

13. This letter is enclosed in a folder of Brantwood stationery upon which Ruskin has inscribed: "Ned. No dates—but 1886. Thirty years since he first saw me 1856, therefore. Praeterita—II VII."

come amiss—or make you feel you had to answer them, but when we get sad news of you I dread writing & have no heart for it & so the time goes—but I want you dreffle bad, often. Did Sarah Anderson give you my message? that I sorely want you to play with, that at present I am exceedingly good, so douce & suave that there must be an outbreak presently—for it cant last like this, long, and we ought sometimes to see each other— just now I couldnt be obstinate, I would give in to everything you said—and praise mountains and upper cirrus, and admit that I have often painted very badly & do all you like.

This is Georgie's birthday [b. July 21, 1840]— She is thirty four, but looks only thirty two—a magnificent Georgie who has attained to Nirvana (however it is spelt—dare say its Nịṛ ẅ ạṅạ̈, yes that looks right) and she surveys the world from China to Peru and my flounderings with pitiful indulgence—but I am ninety four and get so old & more and more crumpled up, & my knees crack when I go up stairs, & bend the wrong way when I come down the same, & now is the time for that philosophy I stacked so carefully for old age, & where is it all? But I want you constantly my dear and have nothing of you. — I believe you would come if I didnt paint pictures—& really I would not if I could help it—

And yet the one that I am doing now!!! Gaspar, Melchior & Bathazar— it looks sometimes as if it would be a pretty carol (not this morning when I hate it) but sometimes— do you remember ages ago [1862]—in Milan it was, when in the impidence [sic] of youth I said I liked the subjects of the shepherds best—& you straightway blew me up & said "No, Ned, they had everything to gain by coming, and it was greater grace in the Kings to leave their Kingdoms & come"—at which I was abashed & fell to thinking— so I am taking great pains over the Kings & have repented.

And the other day I thought of thee, when I saw such a book—gospels written on purple vellum in humped up fat gold letters—so straightway I was minded to go to the Pope & be received into his fold. My dear, we ought to belong to a church that writes its Gospels in gold on purple vellum— Every kind of purple that Tyre could devise, from indigo purple to rose purple— let's go, on the condition the pope makes a great fuss of us & sings, himself, in his finest cope— Georgie won't join us, needs reasons for things & in that way constantly imperils domestic peace—but if the pope himself would chant a special mass for us, (& I should like it in the Latuan if its all the same to him) will you come?

Phil [Ruskin's godson, now 28] is working thoroughly & I think you would have a word of praise for his pictures—full of care & finish—on a small scale as to size & chiefly on panel—& chiefly portraits it is the greatest comfort to me & sometimes when he has made light gleam through a window in a dark room, & painted the motes & made the light palpitate I do straightway go & make a window in one of my pictures, with light also streaming through.

Most days I see Margaret [m. John Mackail, 1888], through her merciful goodness to us, & this is all about me that in the least matters

Oh my Oldie—I have written this clearly so as not to trouble your eyes "No, Ned it is anything but clear" you say— Good bye—& never answer my letters if there is anything else to do—& put all mine into the fire "because of the Angels" but especially because of the devils— love to Joan always.

Ever your ancient Ned.

[sketch of Ned disconsolately seated with his pallette on his knee before a canvas, with spectacles strewing the foreground]

VIII

The Reverend Charles Chapman to Ruskin

The Parsonage, Coniston
July 2, 1881

Dear Mr. Ruskin.

The meeting for Monday is the monthly one agreed to be called for eleven.

If you and the other Gentlemen will kindly help in all needful attendance until other arrangements can be made for carrying on the conduct of the school, SO AS TO PRESENT A BLOCK, I think it would be desirable.

Yours ever faithfully
Cha[s] Chapman

[Ruskin's reply, "I[']ll come," appears in ink at the end of the letter, which was returned to Mr. Chapman in an unstamped envelope addressed by Ruskin: "The Rev.[d] Charles Chapman / Coniston.]

IX

FRANCES ELLEN COLENSO TO RUSKIN

The Grange
North End Road W.[1]
13th March 1880

My dear Mr. Ruskin

I put my answers to Mr. Herbert's questions upon a separate sheet, as Joan said you might wish to forward them. I have no desire to with-hold my name, but I fear the very name "Colenso" will be enough to prevent the Colonial office paying any further attention to the subject. I have no belief in Sir M. Hicks-Beach, who seems to me to have systematically shirked every question brought before him which might, if investigated, oblige him to take any action inconvenient to himself. The officer who told me what I relate on page 467 of the printed chapter which I send you with this, was a Capt[ain] Elliot, (of Lord Gifford's party.) He, of course, had nothing to do with the orders except to obey them, & he allowed me to copy from his note-book the orders which he received & jotted down at the time.

We were on friendly terms then, & he knew I intended to make use of what he told me, but later on we differed very decidedly, & I should not like to get him into trouble, unless it were necessary. His superiors will be very much annoyed at his letting out their mis-deeds, & there are many ways besides direct ones, of punishing young officers, from whom the rules of the service make it very difficult to obtain information.

However I leave it to you to decide as you think best.

I am very anxious to begin work at the Slade School after Easter, if you will allow me to do so, but am still awaiting the permission I desire.

My brother & I have taken a tiny little house close by here, which, as we are persons of the very smallest means, we are going to furnish for ourselves in economical ways (learnt in Natal) which will rather astonish some of our London friends. I am

1. The address of "Ned" and "Georgie" Burne-Jones.

very glad to be settled for a time so near dear Georgie, who is as good to me as a real sister, & comes next after Dora to me.

We are all wondering whether we may not soon have the great pleasure of seeing you here & I remain

Yours very affectionately
Nelly Colenso

The Grange
21st March [1880]

My dear Mr. Ruskin

I have never tried nor even wished to get you to take an active part in Zulu matters because I have always felt that your own work is already too heavy.

But when you were here the other day you told me that you really are moving in a matter connected with Zululand & are keenly interested in it.

May I venture to make a suggestion, leaving it to your own wise decision?

In the matter which you have taken up,—disgraceful as it is to the British name—there is nothing actually to be done except to show *how* disgraceful it is, & perhaps, to strike another blow at the Conservative war-party.

But there is a crying injustice going on, which *can be* remedied & if you are really going to throw the great weight of your voice & influence into the S. African scales, I feel that I must bring this before you, that you may know what can be *done*.

We cannot bring the dead to life again, nor wipe our injustice and treachery from the memories of the Zulus, but we *can* restore to them their King, to whom they have proved their devotion beyond a doubt.

We have him in captivity which will slowly break his heart. (There is an account in "Temple Bar" for February or March which shows this.) Yet it is acknowledged by *all* except the few personally interested in asserting the contrary, that there was *no* reason for what we have done, & that the man is innocent.

It would therefore be right. But also it is palpably expedient as well. The Zulu people, though temporarily crushed, are still strong. They have now cruel injuries to avenge, & bitter hatred for the whites. Sir G. Wolseley's "settlement" is a farce, from which anarchy alone *can* result. By our border raids upon the Zulus we have sown bad blood between them & the Natal natives— Zululand is split up into a number of chieftainships under ill-chosen heads. When Sir G. Wolseley's iron heel is removed there will be endless trouble, & there is now no strong hand to control the Zulu nation, as Cetshwayo [spelled "Cetywayo" in enclosed clipping] did for so many years, during which he prevented the slightest offence being committed by his people against the English, whose friendship he has always looked upon as essential to his well-being. Were we now to restore him to his people, to rule them again under some wise restrictions, we would have done the one thing possible to atone for our past crimes, & to avert the retributions which will otherwise surely come.

Both he & they would be grateful & will actually have received *one* lesson in forbearance & humanity from us to weigh against the many we have brought them of another sort.

Sir Bartle Frere & his party would die rather than lose their victim, & my Father would willingly die to obtain his release, although in point of fact I believe it would add some years to my Father's life to succeed in that, so deeply has he taken it to heart.

I have just read a letter from Sir Bartle Frere, in answer to Edward Durnford's most temperate & reasonable request for justice to his dead brother's name. I felt sure we should get no satisfaction, but the reply is even *more* false, mean & cruel than I expected. It has made me quite ill with indignation & pain, & I long for the day when some public recognition of that dear & honoured name shall fling the falsehoods of those base men upon themselves.

It was a great pleasure to see you, even for such a little minute the other day, & we are looking forwards to Wednesday.

I wanted to tell you how I find in art—even the little I can do—the only anodyne for pain, & in the possibilities before me the one happiness left to me. When I am trying to paint or draw I am happy, & sorrow is forgotten. I can even bear to look forwards to living many years before I get leave to go where I want to be, if those years can be spent thus.

I cannot tell you how good they are to me here.

I hope you are not leaving London yet awhile, for I do so want the honour of receiving you in my own cottage, & we cannot get into it for another ten days.

I hope Mr. Severn is better—& remain

Yours very affectionately

Nelly Colenso

P.S. The enclosed newspaper slip is what I wrote at the time about the Zulu King, which will be less troublesome to you to read in print.[2]

X

W. G. COLLINGWOOD TO RUSKIN

Gillhead
Windermere
March 4, 1888

My dear Mr. Ruskin

It has been on my mind for some time past to write and wish you well, and to say that "Modern Painters" is going rapidly through the press: and that I am looking after it to the best of my ability,—a little overwhelmed—and a great deal proud of my responsibilities: I hope it will turn out that this book will do as much good to the present generation as it did in the past— the generation needs it as much, and the practical truth in it is as true as ever.

We are very well and happy in our quietness—but that means that I have nothing in the way of news to bore you with.

We remember you often and often, and I remain always

Your affectionate

W. G. Collingwood

As I don't know where you are, I take the liberty of asking Miss Anderson to address the letter—message rather.

2. Enclosure: Letter *To the Editor of the Natal Witness,* dated August 20, 1879. Title: WHAT TO DO WITH ZULULAND. Signed ENGLISH, with "ie / F E Colenso" beneath signature, in inked script. The letter begins: "Sir, — Will you kindly give publication to the following suggestion? If we have not already captured Cetywayo we expect to do so immediately, and on every side is now discussed the question, 'When we have got him what shall we do with him?' "

XI

The Reverend W. A. Dallinger to Ruskin

Wesley College
Sheffield
May 24, 1886 [1]

Dear Mr. Ruskin

I read your letter with much interest. I agree very fully with what you say. I feel quite sure that all the joy and enlightenment that might be derived from the study of Nature, with the observant eye used normally, is very far from reached: and I am equally certain the mere curiosity and straining after the unusual diverts many from the healthy observation of Nature as it lies all around us. On the other hand I have known many instances of minds wholly indifferent to nature, until some unusual path—such as the microscopical unfolding of the hidden beauties of some "common" object,—has suddenly and intensely directed such a mind to it, and close and delighted observation has followed.

That there may be an enormous amount of "priggishness" and conceit in the most useless kind of "observation" with the instrument I am perfectly certain; and I have to encounter evidence of it every day. But my contention is (1) that supposing the mind to retain a healthy interest in the *visible* world of life and action, the disclosures we are able to effect with fine, and constantly improving lenses simply intensifies the awe and delight of the mind in the wonder and beauty of nature; and expands and deepens the idea aroused by the word beauty: (2) although in doing this we encounter what may seem the *unlovely,* as for example the *putrefactive organisms* or their now demonstrated congeners the *Pathogenic* organisms of living viruses of certain diseases yet (a) they are not unlovely *in themselves,* and are as perfectly adapted to their sphere as a swallow or the grayling are to theirs. While (b) Immense advantage is secured to our race by knowledge that has a practical bearing on its material health and welfare.

I admit, with painful consciousness of its existence, the peril to

1. The first of the eight photographs which accompany this letter shows (presumably) the Reverend Dallinger himself, with his "camera" or "microscope," drawing what he sees.

all true knowledge of mere specialism; and I see leering by, the still more odious peril, of supposing that because "so much" is known to us that therefore we know *every thing*; and have stripped away the mystery of the universe. But is not this the folly of men—their mental arrogance and impatience of the infinite and indiscoverable? and after all does not the prolonged *contemplation* of true knowledge engender ultimately in the leading thought of the race a most living reverence and a truer faith? I can imagine an answer from you that would utterly negative my undertone of hope: but if we confine ourselves to a concrete case may it not be shown that there is at least a hope that this may be so? By way of illustration I send with this some Photographs of my transparencies of minute objects as drawn by a special process of my own—a very simple one—*upon glass,* by means of a fine *camera lucida.* All the objects except Plate I are enormously magnified; and some of these very transparencies you saw projected upon the screen at Oxford. What seems to me of moment is (1) that the objects reveal unexpected beauty and adaptation; and (2) there is much to gain to human progress in the facts.

I send Fig. I, Plate i merely because it was painted the exact size of the photograph, in India ink, from life, by *a boy* who taught himself all that he really knows; and because it shows the exact process by which the *camera lucida* drawings are made.

Figs II and III plates ii and iii are the ultimate grains of a siliceous earth or chalk: the "earth" is dissolved in acid and the powder under the lens is shown in the photographs: only these are a few out of thousands of varieties. As you know they are minute skeletal envelopes of the lowliest animals. It seems to me that "more of reverence in us" dwells as we look upon such a lump of chalk with such knowledge added.

Plate iv gives a selection of the eggs of Butterflies and moths: and what enhances their beauty is the *use of it*; their spines and carving all serve to secure the ultimate end for which the egg exists. But without any further advance I want to disclaim any *art* in these drawings. They are strictly true to what the eye sees—or appears to see—and even the apparent imperfections of perspective are such as the objects reveal.

In Plate v I show highly magnified *parasites* of Birds—Epizoa.

They are very minute as a group—not so large any of them considered individually as the egg of the smaller moths. Yet these also as I stated, deposit eggs, the magnified images of some of which are shown on Plate vi. The upper parasite in Pl[ate] v for example produces the floral egg seen in the uppermost position in Plate vi. And these drawings will be clearer for the use of a lens.

Again in Pl[ate] vii you have the greatly magnified image of a *mite*. You observe the beautifully reticulated scales round its little body: these are for protection: it lives during this (its immature or "nymphal" state) in danger of being crushed. To counteract this as it grows and casts its skin, in the fashion common to the group, instead of throwing its "old clothes" away, it makes use of them by changing the material in the process of Ecdysis into the exquisite scales given in the drawing: and each *row* of scales is the result of a separate ecdysis. The scales are as elastic as steel, and as light as pith! and by their means a scale armour is provided securing adequate protection. It seems to me that as a phenomenon and as a fact this must be interesting and beneficial. Finally I call your attention to Plate viii where you find on the left the scabbard and stings of a Bee; one sting is protruding beyond the point of the scabbard, the other is withdrawn: they used a fair lens such as is used in the picture galleries to bring them out. Beside these, on the right, is a piece broken off, to about the same length as the sting scabbard, from the point of a *cambric sewing needle* and magnified by the same lens. This tells it's own tale: to me a most instructive and valuable one.

Now I do not ask you to oblige me by accepting these drawings because they have *any* artistic recommendation. I love art too much to suppose it: but I should be glad that you should have them as examples of honest effort to reproduce nature as seen under the best lenses; and as showing to some minute extent, why it is, that with a very profound love of nature, art and Poetry, I still love to delve amidst the minute realm with such aides as mans ingenuity has devised.

Pardon me for this obtrusion; but the kindliness of your letter led me to feel in some way that you might understand me better—not but that I know that *that* is of the least importance to you: but it goes along with a view of the whole question of such studies; which from *my* point of view, I think it valuable to have your judgment of, however pronounced.

I look with deep pleasure upon your continued labours, and I trust your health will long be continued to afford you the pleasure which I am convinced comes to yourself, and is certainly produced in multitudes by your writing.

Believe me

most sincerely and respectfully yours
W. H. Dallinger

Mr Ruskin Esquire D.C.L.A.

XII

Lady Edwardes to Ruskin

[Lady Edwardes was now at work on the *Memorials* of her husband, published in 1886, while Ruskin was now reliving his past through the writing of *Praeterita*.]

Wootton Hall
W. Ashbourne
Derbyshire
Friday 4th Sept[ember 1885]

My dear John

I am so happy to see your handwriting again—but you must not write anything for me—for I feel that it is *pain* not pleasure to you just now—(and this *I would not* be the one to bring this [sic] to you!) — I can *quite* understand it—and sympathize with it—for I often feel, in my desolate life, that this *living in the past* —takes a great deal of *strain;* and often I feel as if I were writing with my very life-blood— But I like it better than anything else I find to do—and should like to get into some out of the way & quiet place, and do nothing else. (How difficult it is to do anything without being absorbed in it.) But it is all right for me— I only write this line again, to say—you must not trouble yourself or think any more about it—but let me use any words of your's (if I find them already written—) At any rate I'm glad I *asked* you—if you won't worry yourself at all about my request. Ever y[ou]r very affectionate

Emma Edwardes

My love to Joan if she is with you

XIII

J. A. Froude to Ruskin

[This letter is included as a token of the 65 letters (1862–93) from Froude to Ruskin and Mrs. Severn in the F. J. Sharp Collection—these letters having been already published in *The Froude-Ruskin Friendship,* ed. H. G. Viljoen (New York, 1966)].

5 Onslow Gardens, S.W.
Feb [ruary] 13 [1881]

My dear Ruskin

Your letter assures me that I have not lost your regard as I feared, and as you are now [Carlyle having died on February 5] the only person left in this world, for whom at once morally and intellectually I have a real esteem, you may guess what this assurance is to me—

As to your coming to see me, I must not steal your time from those to whom you think that in special ways you can be of more use than you can be to me— Only believe that there is no face whom it would give me more pleasure to see, & no voice more cheering to me to hear than yours—and do not mock my poverties by saying that you have nothing to teach me— Those two hours which you once gave me in the South Kensington Museum left me richer in new knowledge than any two hours which I can remember. Censure me also publicly or privately when you see cause. No censure of yours falls lightly on me. I know that in what you say there must be *some* truth at any rate, and I endeavour to lay it to heart.

"I pray thee do not mock me fellow student."

Next to your good opinion, I value most your reproofs.

The whole of the last fortnight has been like a miserable dream —from the "reporters" who came clamouring at Cheyne Row for "the full particulars of the death bed" (this is fact) to the scene at Ecclefechan, the ground covered with melting snow, the family attending in form but speaking neither to Tyndall nor to Lecky nor to me. No "Minister" present, no order or solemnity or attempt at such, some thirty curious grown spectators—Journalists most of them—and a mob of schoolchildren boys & girls, some hundreds I suppose, pushing and shouldering as if to look at a wild beast show— Such "maimed rites" I could not have believed in if I had not witnessed them. One Edinburgh fellow told me kindly that Carlyle had been a considerable *"mon"* and that there should be a subscription to put up a stone to him in the Kirk yard —as if it was a great condescension on his part— He said that the Rectorship had been a great honour to Carlyle &c. &c.

I told him that a thousand years hence only two Scots would be known to mankind; Knox and Carlyle—on which he left me, I suppose thinking me mad.

I cannot account for the attitude to us of the brother James Carlyle and his sons. I should have set it down to shyness but that Mary's husband Alex Carlyle [Carlyle's nephew] was there and would have introduced us if there had been a wish for it. I shall send you in a few weeks the "Reminiscences" in which English Stupidity can hardly fail to see what C[arlyle] personally was—and what *She* was—

As to the Biography no one but you can give me any advice worth having— So you must not refuse to let me have an opportunity of talking it all over in full with you— I have no real friend left in this world, unless you will be one.

This is all sickly and sad stuff I will trouble you with no more of it.

We are trying to get some appointment for Alex. Carlyle from Government, and we shall perhaps succeed. We have also an idea of buying the old house for him and Mary if we can get it on reasonable terms— But we keep this secret lest the price should be raised upon us—

I had to refuse Westminster Abbey peremptorily. He had insisted that he should be taken to Scotland—

Haddington ought to have been the place, but some difficulty was raised—(I know not what) a few years ago.

And Ecclefechan was ordered instead.

Yours ever affect[ionate]ly
J. A. Froude

XIV

Helen Gladstone to Ruskin

[Now Vice-Principal of Newnham College, Helen Gladstone wrote the following letter as an answer to Ruskin's letter of February 24, 1887 (see *Works,* 37, 655).]

North Hall, Newnham College
Cambridge
March 18—1887—

My dear Mr. Ruskin

We cannot thank you enough for the beautiful books— they are even more beautiful than the last set, because they include the large Stones of Venice & other treasures (among others, Dame Wiggins), & because they are full bound. We have put one set, including the best bound ones, in the College Library, to be used in that room & never removed except by special permission, the other set in the Duplicate Library attached to this Hall, from which the students may freely borrow them to read in their own rooms— We do thank you very heartily for your kindness—Library Committee, students, & all—

We shall be delighted to have the loan of any drawings from St. G. Guild, & perhaps some may be brave enough to try & copy them. You ask what practice there is in elementary drawing— I hope you will not think us Philistines & heathens when I tell you that the College has not provided instruction in drawing— it is simply that students who wish to *study* it chiefly would naturally go to Art schools where they could be far better provided for—& those who wish to study other things chiefly have not time while they are here to *work* at drawing— indeed this does not mean that they do not care for it. I think it is an almost necessary example of the working of "the ascetic principle of division of labour."

I have waited till I could tell you that I am sending to Mr. Jowett a copy of the Superiora story. Our term is just over— I am going to Hawarden to be with Mary & Harry for a few days—

Yours gratefully & aff[ectionate]ly
Helen Gladstone

XV

Mary Gladstone to Ruskin and to Mrs. Severn

1. *To Ruskin*

10, Downing Street
Whitehall,
Nov[ember] 26, [18]84

My dear Mr Ruskin,

Will there be any hope of your being in Oxford next week, & are you still too much bothered by the "infernal" station horn to see me?

There is a little story which takes 10 minutes to read aloud, & I have promised its author, a girl, some day to read it to you if you would consent— it is just for you to see whether she ought to persevere in that line. I think it a lovely tale, but what she wants is a word of encouragement or discouragement from you. If the former, she would throw all her soul into trying to write, if the latter she would just give it up & do her best in other ways— I know you would love her if you knew her— I do not want to bother you, you know, but it would be so delicious if you would make an assignation with me   I shall be staying at Keble College— You were a very wicked St C. to call my Father's speeches a Wind Bag— But I forgave you directly, because of what you said to me once before—[1]

If you come, we must have a tete & Lavinia [Talbot] & Edward [Burne-Jones] may only come in at the end to give us some tea, & before they come in I will play as much as you like—   Three cheers for the Pall Mall's reports of your lectures.

Y[ou]r ever aff[ectionate]
Mary Gladstone

1. In a conversation with M. H. Spielmann, published in the April 23, 1884, *Pall Mall Gazette,* Ruskin had called Gladstone "an old wind-bag" who "uses his splendid gifts of oratory, not for the elucidation of his subject, but for its vaporisation in a cloud of words" (*Works, 34,* 666). See his letter of October 23, 1880 (*Works, 37,* 328–29), apropos of his having called Disraeli and Gladstone "two old bagpipes," for the remarks which had now caused Mary again to forgive. On November 28, 1884, he noted in his Diary that he had been made "very happy" by a letter from her (*Diaries,* p. 1088)

10, Downing Street
Whitehall.
[1884?]

My dear St. C.

What a darling little letter— First I dont know which days you are engaged. But I will find all out from Lavinia Talbot who will be in London Sunday & Monday. And then I will write again & take you at your word— It will be quite delicious to see you

Y[ou]r ever aff[ectionate]
M G.

Hawarden Castle,
Chester.
23 Nov[ember 18]87

My dear Aprile,

I want to tell you that this is my birthday, & that my nicest present is Hortus Inclusus, & in it you say I have forgiven you even "that second naughtiness," so I want you to forgive me my first naughtiness [or] whatever it is that has made you silent to me for so many months, & to show you forgive me by fulfilling your promise & giving me the second Volume of Praeterita— my last letter perhaps you never saw. I think it is in the bundle labelled "needing particular attention", tidily pigeon-holed "in a business-like way."

I love all the letters to "Susie"—but I wish I had had the looking over of the proof sheets & not left "pies" for "pics" Who ever would have called a picture a PIE, not even a printer I should have thought— I don't dare write any more

Your ever always affecti[onate]
Mary

And if you do write will you direct to me under cover to "Roy" He is my collie & everybody knows him.

2. *To Mrs. Severn*

73 Harley St.
28 March. [18]78

Dear Mrs. Severn

I have been wanting so much to write all the time but did not like to trouble you till your kind message gave me an excuse—& so a week ago I wrote to you & sent it to Frances Graham to enclose it but she & Mr. Burne Jones read it & would not send it, because there was a word at the end which they both thought might be unacceptable— it was only that my mother who has had great experience of illness was so anxious about the quiet—& I did not think you would be offended as you would know it only came from thinking so much & anxiously of Mr. Ruskin; you would never think it was because she thought nobody knew enough about nursing. It was chiefly because we had a case of the same kind in our family. 9 weeks of fever & delirium & brief moments of consciousness—& it *was* so tempting to speak to her during those moments, & yet so all-important that we should not. I remember then how eagerly we used to listen to anything we could hear of other cases of the kind, & how thankful we always felt for any hints of caution. And so I feel sure you will not mind my saying this, even though you know it all by heart. We have been thinking & hoping & praying all the time with all our might my father takes the deepest interest in the accounts & we always hear anything there is to hear from Dr. Acland or Mr. Cowper Temple or Frances. Nothing gives one so much faith I think as Mr. Ruskin's own beautiful words about prayer— how hard & how sad & weary it must be to you this long waiting & the hopes & fears— forgive my writing such a long letter & don't *think* of answering it, if you will say you did not mind my writing to somebody you are naturally writing to I shall be sure to hear. Meanwhile we think of you with such sympathy & of Mr. Ruskin with reverent love & faithful prayer.

Y[our]s very sincerely
Mary Gladstone

XVI

Mrs. Goodison to Ruskin

[Ruskin is now in Sandgate.]

Coniston Bank
Coniston, Ambleside
Feb[ruary] 21st [18]88

Dear Mr. Ruskin

I most heartily thank you, not only for your very kind subscription, received safely, but also for the kind sentiments in your letter expressed about my interesting studies— You express so exactly what I feel. "New pleasures" continually arise—& "the materials are so infinite—and so clear." I feel very pleased you have been sufficiently interested in me—to write me these sentiments —& I shall treasure them.

My good husband has indeed been enjoying good health & has been very active & busy about many things, but unfortunately on Sunday last he fell near Mr. Hilliards house on some frozen snow & now he is in bed, again, & has to use crutches if he moves, for his knee which has always been tender doubled up under him when he fell; I hope it may soon pass off but anything the matter with his knee has generally been very tedious.

Coniston is very quiet, & the snow lies about in light drifts, but it is not particularly cold.

My husband begs to unite his kind regards with mine—

Believe me dear Mr. Ruskin

Y[ou]rs very faithfully & respectfully

Annie J Goodison

XVII

Frances Graham (Lady Horner) to Mrs. Severn

35, Grosvenor Place S.W.
April 10th [1878]

My dear Mrs Severn

How kind of you to ask me— I have sent this morning a small quilt as you directed— It isnt nearly, not nearly as nice as I should like it to have been—but I couldnt get a nicer one in that size *ready* made, & as you wanted it so very quick I thought I'd better send a nasty one immediately—

If it doesnt quite do, I could have one made in two days & then I would see it was lovely— Please—if there's anything I can do ever, you will know how I shall love to—

I am so glad to think he is better

Yours aff[ectionate]ly

Frances Graham

Will you shake it at the fire when you take it out— the heat makes the feathers swell out & get light—

XVIII

Kate Greenaway to Ruskin and to the Severns

1. *To Ruskin*

11. Pemberton Gardens
Holloway, N.
24 July. 1883 [1]

Dear Mr. Ruskin

Here is the drawing finished at last for you, I seem to have been so long over it, having to wait for the models, and there is such a difference between a drawing and a sketch— will you remember it is only half a drawing I mean it wont look right until the colour comes on it—and will you tell me a little about the colouring, is it to be shaded up or a flat work—deep colors or faint—and any colour I like, or *RUBY GREEN* and *PURPLE* You will have to help me if it is in any of those

The little Girl who sat for the small Girl in the drawing would interest you greatly— she is 7 Years Old— she comes to me and goes home again all by herself— she looks so tiny that the traincar men think she wants to run at the back instead of being a passenger— she told me the facts with much indignation and 7 years old— I cant think WHAT he can be thinking of.

She also scrubs rooms, buys the dinner—and talks of doing her steps, meaning she cleans the doorstep, but theology is her great point— Heaven is very real to her, at least the fact of there being a Heaven—and angels forever in her mind— the Clouds are the outside of Heaven. it occurred to her the other day that she might step on the moon, and break it— Oh my—she said what a bother I should get into

Is it wicked to draw Jesus's cross with steps leading up to it— My Freddy (her brother) does it— he *can* draw *nice* he did a horse standing by the side of it. I cant draw a horse—at least I can draw its *tail* but not its mouth, and its eyes, and ears, and its back

Is it wicked not to pray. My cousin says if you are a good Girl, and don't tell stories, and mind your mother, you neednt

1. This letter is contained in an envelope inscribed by Ruskin: "K.G. on her delightful 7 yr old model."

say your prayers at night— My mother says you never go to sleep in Heaven— Jesus can see all over the sky—cant he— he peeps down between the clouds and looks at your books.

Her name is Mary, and she has a Cousin Mary so to distinguish the Virgin Mary she calls he[r] Jesus's Mary I cant write it properly, it doesnt seem the same as the pretty childs voice saying it— I would like—if such a happy time ever came, that you came often to tea—so that I could spare a little of the precious time to someone else—Id like to have her to tea—dressed in big Mob Cap and little white Frock. You would be delighted she is so pretty and a real darling

Ah yes you must not write to me when you are too busy or if it bothers you in any way, —only—if it can be not so *many many* days— I will try and never be any trouble to you, but I was so miserable and so ill I could not work. I wish I was greater and better. I hope you know. I truly wish it.

I hope you are not working too hard now— I often wonder what you are doing now— how much I used to like hearing the little bits as you went on— The dreadful Tyrant—I send my love to the Tyrant tonight—there are such pretty Golden little clouds passing the window—though haven't there been some terrible ones—tawny and [Boil?]ing black, and didnt I see the daemons drifting by. You may have a whirl of them soon. I saw them as they [sped?] over the Gloom. Goodbye

Kate Greenaway

I dont send you any sketch because the drawings and sketches are not good friends.

50 Frognal
Hampstead N.W.
15th April 1887 [2]

My. Dear. My Dear Dinie—

I am very sorry to hear your sad news, and sorry too, for the shock to you, just now—when you are not well—it is very sad— how often it seems to happen—to people who are—not strong— I dont think it does for them to go away like that—they want the

2. On April 11, 1887, returning on the yacht *Argo* from the Dardanelles, Laurence Hilliard died.

things they are used to—it makes the third I have heard of in such a little time —— I'm very sorry for All of you—but Dear Dinie I hope you wont trouble about it more than you—can help —though I know—you are very grieved —— Poor-dear ———

Yes Dinie—I'll be very good— I dont think I've been—naughty —have *I*—

My Pope—has come —really—I think I did it very badly—it looks so different—to the Copy—

I'm doing the steps [of] one of the Pipes to day—it's getting on, but they have a great deal of work in them, so many figures and so much background ———

A fortnight and the Academy opens— it doesn't seem possible —I suppose it is being so unspringlike

My Grape Hyacinths are little [Combs?] now—of exquisite blue-purple tipped at the top, so lovely to paint the one running into the other in that way—

You say you are much the same— I wish dear—you—could—begin to feel better—but I hope it wont be long now before you do—

Oh, Dinie Dear I'm afraid you are very grieved and troubled over this— I am so sorry for your sorrow, and for theirs —— poor, Dear Dinie—

I think the air is softer this morning—as if it were another sort though Eddie told me it was so Cold when he first went out that his lips were frozen together— why he could have thought that is a mystery

do you know lung-wort a curious little Flower—some pink some blue on the same plant— the dear Wall-flowers are coming out fast now—and lots [of] little shoots showing—

I do so wish I could say things to Comfort you—but you tell me to be so quiet —— but Dear I may hope you are better to day and if you have it so mild—you will go out and that will do you good —— Good bye my Dear Dear Dino— may all things bless and Comfort you Dear

With all my love

†
† Katie †
†

[In pencil] Poor, dear thing *I know* you are very very sad over this

2. *To Violet Severn*[3]

24th Nov[ember] 1884

My dear little Violet

The naughty little Girl gave her little Sister a very hard slap on her arm— I sent you a picture of her to show You. You see the place is VERY, VERY red—

She was *never* so cross any more—not on any other days—and she let her play with her dolls just when ever she liked—and she gave a beautiful Dolls tea party and—let her little sister pour out the tea—and—their mama was So pleased to see them So good and happy that she bought them a lovely NEW doll *each,* and a beautiful new Chair each for their lovely dolls to sit down—and two lovely Cradles for them to go to bed in they had Pink Satin Curtains—and—a Crimson satin Counterpane and then some new Cups and Saucers—with Pink roses on them and the little Girl[']s was just like her Sister's.

And they were *very very happy*—and Gave tea Parties every day—and were never Cross or cried any more—

I thought you would like to know all about it and the next time I come to see you I hope you will show, me *your* Doll.

With much Love

Yours respectfully
Kate Greenaway

3. *To Mrs. Severn*

39, Frognal
Hampstead, N.W.
22nd Jan[uary] 1900

Dearest Joanie—

I can hardly believe it but I cannot be grateful enough that since death must come—that it came painlessly ——— and He deserved no Pain ———

It was a great shock yesterday afternoon. The Samuels called and said they had seen it in one of the Sunday Papers—but I did

3. Violet Severn was now a four-year-old, her sister Lily being ten.

not believe it in the least I thought the report of his Illness had got about—but when they had gone—I went out and got a paper and then from what it said I became doubtful—and this morning I have your and Lilys letter— I know so well how you feel and how things seem years ago. Thank you very much for writing for I know how much you had to do I will write again ——

It is a great shock I feel it—very much— My dearest love to you

Your loving
Katie

24th Jan[uary] 1900

My dearest Joanie

I am very sorry For You I know, the Crowds of letters Y[ou] would be sure to have and the work it makes for you to do, I hope You wont get over tired—

I have sent a little bunch of Violets He and I had so many associations with them I Feel He would have liked me to send that.

My very dearest love to you

Your loving
Katie

Do not trouble to write me at Present. I know so well—How Fearfully tired You will be

27th Jan[uary] 1900

My dearest Joanie

One Feels all one can say is of no use— nothing is but time— and it is merciful—that is—I knew I should Feel it—but I did not know that I should Feel it like I do—but nearly every morning and evening writing little bits of my letter—I am so bitterly sorry that the last two years have been such difficult ones to me, that I had so little time to draw For him or write properly. I might have done so much more—but I was always hoping things would get better and I would have more leisure —— but you see it is a necessity I do my work. I am so dreadfully sorry when I Feel I might have given Him more pleasure—

As You ask me— Personally I did wish For Westminster I

never thought it would be anything else—but I think you are right to do what you think right— — what we really think is beyond our own will—. We can none of us alter our real thought—and we ought to follow it ——

I know what You must Feel— I know how desolate it must Feel to You— I hope You will keep well— I am afraid you will be very tired and done up— I am most grateful to you about the Flowers— I should have sent a wreath, but I Felt he would like the others best— I wanted better ones but I could not get them though I went to Covent Garden I wanted Violets because we always had Violets when he came to tea— He would like to have my Flowers if he could *know*. I thank you for putting them near—

I should so like to make him some beautiful Memorial I should like to design him a tomb, all Girls and Children and Angels—with Flowers growing at the top He would like it I wish I could do it later on— You know he used to say when he saw Della Robbia He thought my things best—and when He saw mine He thought the Della Robbias so.

My dearest love to You.
Your loving
Katie

XIX

Dr. William Gull to Mrs. Severn

Croftinloan
Pittsbury
13 Aug[ust] 1885

Dear Mrs Severn

Your letter reached me yesterday— I should desire to advise much care in the use of Sedation Opium & the like. Your kind medical friend will I am sure pardon my saying this— Time and food are the main measures for the patient's recovery. There may be room as there was in the last attack for some opium but I remember that then I had my doubts as to the good it did Please not to lay more weight on this caution than it needs as I can, not being at hand, form no more than general opinion & no criticism at all. Food: wine & time I shall be glad to hear either from you or your medical friend how matters go on

I am resting here for some weeks.

If Mr Ruskin can receive a message give him this from me that I hope he will be a child again (now) & let nature nurse him by your kind hands

With thanks for your letter & kind regards I am

Yours v[er]y faithfully
William N Gull

Cresswell Hall
Morpeth
Northumberland
July 29, 1886

Dear Mrs Severn

Give my kind regards to Dr. Parsons & say I hope he will let me repeat that food & alcohol (in such form as he may find best) are the means we must still rely upon. Drugs are out of court for a nervous system so weak & sensitive

I know Dr. Parsons will forgive my thus writing for he feels as I do

Yours very truly
William N Gull

XX

Ada Hartnell to Mrs. Severn

69 Falmouth Road
New Kent Road
13th April 1878

Dear Mrs. Severn

I rejoice greatly and thankfully in the good news— It is most kind of you to send it—for you must be fully occupied, and have a host of people to satisfy of so much more consequence than I am.

I hope Mr Ruskin will be very idle—and—as widest charity—take great care of *himself* for a long time to come.

I shall go happily now to see the pictures, whenever circumstances will let me—

But we have had an extraordinary rain—the next street was impassable on foot. The water came through my roof in both rooms, and the basement is still flooded. I have sore throat and much coughing in consequence. But I have already been out several times this year.

I walked up Regent St. on one of the days when Mr. Ruskin was so very ill. Looking carelessly at some photographs in a window, I was quite startled to see his face. It was a better likeness than either of the two I had before—but not—I think *very* good — I bought it—and laid it away reverently thinking I would rather see it uncovered when he got better. It is a great blank to have no Fors—but there is the University Magazine to come this month—and today I have some *poems* of Mr. Ruskin's that (except one) I did not know of before. If they have never been printed but for private circulation, I wonder if it is quite right to quote them to enrich an article—but I forget that Mr. Ruskin may have given permission— Does not Lord Leetrim's murder emphasize very terribly what he said about Ireland in March?

I hope Mr. Severn is better. With many thanks I am

Very respectfully yours
Ada Hartnell

XXI

Sir Arthur Helps to Ruskin

Vernon Hill
May 8 [18]59

My dear Ruskin,

I duly received your letter, but scarcely knew what to say about the extracts you sent me. They are nobly and beautifully expressed, as it seems to me everything is that you write. But I have studied somewhat the results of war, and I am horrified at them. Of course a 'noble' war may be a fine thing for a nation; but, my dear fellow, there are not many noble wars; and even when they begin from a good cause, they soon degenerate into ignobility. Still, I am willing to hear with all tolerance anything that can be said on the other side, especially when it is said by you.

As to my work, it is a few essays & conversations—not of much credit, & which it is hardly worth while to publish now. I send you a fragment, which, however, you must, if you please, return to me not later than by Tuesday's post. You will understand the meaning of Ellesmere's essay.

I am afraid there is no chance of my seeing you before you leave. When do you propose to return?

Most cordially yours

AH

Alice desires to be kindly remembered to you.

Kew

Jan[uary] 12th 1871

My dear Ruskin

Your letter in the Daily Telegraph of today is excellent

I have to thank you for the first number of "Fors Clavigera" There are many admirable things in it; but it itself is the thing which I most admire. That a man who has the highest capacity for art, and for enlightening other people about art, should turn away from his own proper work because he cannot put up with the misery of the poor people by whom he is surrounded, is one of the noblest examples that can be offered to the world now.

If I were not your friend, if indeed I had never seen you, I should be very much drawn towards you by this exploit of yours, which especially wins my heart.

It is a lesser matter, but I am very grateful to you for having taught me to see many things that I should never have seen without it. I am afraid you have taught me to be more critical, and so have taken away some pleasure which I should have had in inferior productions. But, as an American would say, the balance is greatly in your favour, and I am always

Yours affectionately

Arthur Helps

Alice to whom I am dictating this begs to be cordially remembered to you.

Privy Council Office

Feb[ruary] 6 [18]74

My dear Ruskin

Alas! it is impossible for next week. I am engaged to the uttermost. Among other things (Pity me!) I have to take the chair at a great public dinner for the Clerks & Warehousemen of London—at which I mean to say some things that are in my mind.

Yes: you are very great in aphorisms, and in what, for want of an English word, I must call aperçus. In description, too, in the present time you are unrivalled. But I maintain that your specialty is in looking hard at things, and seeing more in them at once than the rest of us do.

If I were asked, in one of these competitive examinations, who is able to compete with you as regards this power, I should get no marks for that question, for I really do not know of any one to put by your side

Alice moans over the last numbers of the 'Fors' not having been sent to us; and I moan ditto to her moanings.

By the way how truly you speak about what should be our feelings to our fathers.

Enter lots of people

Ever your affectionate
ARTHUR HELPS

XXII

LAURENCE AND CONSTANCE HILLIARD TO MRS. SEVERN

[The particularly beloved "Connie" and "Laurie" can be represented, even though inadequately, through the following letters.]

1. *From Laurence Hilliard*

Cowley [Rectory, Uxbridge] [1]
Sunday
[December 22, 1878]

My dear Joan

A merry Christmas to you, and all at Brantwood, and a Happy New Year when it comes— I daresay you are expecting to hear from me, but you know how evil I am & how anxious not to add to your correspondence— I had a fearful drive to Windermere

1. Laurence Hilliard, as Ruskin's secretary (1876–82), had evidently left Brantwood to spend Christmas with his parents in the Cowley Rectory. The letter can be dated through its reference to Florence, Arthur Severn's 15-year-old niece, who had been asked to stay from November until Christmas at Brantwood, where she had been articulately critical of "Laurie Hillard's manners," as well as so unhappy that she finally burst into tears, sobbing forth her desire to return to her parents in London (see Birkenhead, *Illustrious Friends,* pp. 271–73). In its top margin the letter itself is decorated by a pensketch of birds.

that day in the open carriage; my gloves, which had been wet the night before, from sailing, froze as I went along, & I could not wear them. Then there was a bitter fog at Ambleside, & I nearly cried for cold before I got to Somervells. However, I soon recovered, & had a nice skate in the afternoon at Kendal. The frost here continues unbroken, & we have 3 inches of fresh snow fallen during the day. My Missal cups have come back from the firing, & seem very nice.

Oh! I left my best go-to-meeting Lincoln & Bennett in the cupboard in the sideboard in the Hall— you *will* be good to it, for it cost *Mints*! MINTS!! All my masses of Luggage got home safe—

I suppose Florence has departed— If not you may give her my love, supposing that she still recognizes my name—

The trees are so lovely with the snow on every twig. Is Arthur back, yet?

Love to Lily & the others & of course Mr. R.

Yours affect[ionate]ly
Laurence J[ermyn] Hilliard

2. *From Constance Hilliard*

Home [Cowley Rectory]
Tuesday
[February 22, 1881] [2]

My darling Joan

I got home safely yesterday and sent a little note to Arfie, as I thought he would be lonely at breakfast this morning and also I wished to make it up! & also I was afraid I had said *too* much about Papa—when I came home & found him *so* well again— All our thoughts are at Brantwood today—*yearning* for news of darling Cuzzie I went to the post but alas there was no letter & we do not like to bore you with telegrams I thought of you so often last night dearie—& this morning—arriving *so* tired & wondered how you would find things going on— It is all so sad & Brantwood seems so *very* far away— We can only pray—& have faith in Gods mercy—

Mammies best love, & many thanks for the dear little cat in

2. This letter can be dated through the references to Mrs. Severn's having been summoned from Herne Hill to Brantwood by telegram on Sunday, February 20, 1881.

the basket. *How* good you have been to me Joanie dear— you have made a new creature of me—& I have come home so well & refreshed— Only, yesterday was an awful termination to such a delightful visit, & I felt for you *very* much—but could not trust myself to offer any consolation My dear, dear, love to him, & Laurie, & you— Ettie went to Maidenhead yesterday so I am the only Child at home, & very busy. You will let us hear some-how? I daresay Loll will write today.

Ever your lovingest sister
Connie

Stone House
Broadstairs
Monday
[January 22, 1900]

My own Darling—

I am asking Ethel to have me—on Wednesday— I feel I *must* be at his Funeral—the *Last* of him— You will not blame me? — If I can have one hug from you after it is all over, it will be worth anything— I shall sleep at our Club [presumably Low Bank Ground] tomorrow night

My heart is *ever* with you my own darling

Y[ou]r Con

XXIII

Mrs. Hilliard's Last Letter to Ruskin

[The following letter was written two days before the death of Mrs. Hilliard, a victim of tuberculosis. For Ruskin's response of May 13, see Constance and Mrs. Hilliard, B.S.]

Cowley Rectory
Uxbridge
May 12 [1882]

My darling Cuz,

I have many troubles just now—myself the worst of all—but through it all I feel in the uttermost depth of my heart that to have such a blessèd friend as you is worth living for through anything— Lately I have been ill in a way especially disagreeable to my nature—so weak, & low & despairing that to lie down & shut my eyes for the few minutes my cough allowed me, was all I wanted—nothing but the feeling of the cruelty to Ethel has made me try to sit up—& smile—& pretend that I wanted to get better— I DO for her sake, but weary nights & tiresome days make it hard to bear the trouble of living for myself —— still when she gave me your letter to read this morning I felt better & more thankful, & less naughty—& got up an hour sooner, & am really enjoying writing to you— the books have not come yet—but the idea of your having thought of me & sent them—makes me happy.

My husband has had slight pleurisy [d. May 30]—about which he has made a fearful fuss—& is still in bed, though the doctor has given him leave to get up— our garden is a most lovely sight full of flowering shrubs in their greatest beauty & profussion [sic] & the Wisteria like a perpetual lilac fountain all over the house I am glad you have plenty of nice girls, to amuse you—and hope you will go on gaining strength & spirits— Laurie writes word that it is *very* cold in the north—and his *bronchial tubes* are troublesome, but he has a better appetite & no doubt is getting all right again— he will be only too glad to come home at any moment if he thinks you have any thing for him to do—

You must miss Joan dreadfully, but I hope Martha [Gale] is able to comfort you a little— I think she is quite *one* in a thousand of girls—so useful, & wise, & unselfish.

I saw in the paper that you had given Prince Leopold as a wedding present—a Copy of your *last* work, & as you always have so many in hand at once I wondered what it was. Oh! do take care of your precious brain & do *not* write too much— it is dreadful, that what you do for others is harmful to yourself— nobody else is worth your hurting yourself for—

I am so thankful for the sunshine & brightness—as I know it helps you—but I wish the wind would keep out of the North East — we have got it hard to day—but a beautiful blue sky & blazing sun-shine—

Ethel joins me in kindest love to you & Believe me darling Cuz

your ever loving & Grateful Mammie

M. St A. Hilliard

How grieved I am to see the death of Dr. John Brown, mostly because I fear it will grieve you

XXIV

M. B. HUISH TO RUSKIN

[This letter is in an envelope upon which Ruskin has written: "Subscription to Whistler Costs," and is accompanied by a list of the names of those who subscribed—118 in all.]

The Fine Arts Society
148, New Bond St. W.
28th April 1879

Dear Mr Ruskin

I have the pleasure to inform you that I have today paid to Messrs. Walker & Martineau the sum of £386. 12. 4 being the amount of their bill of costs against you in the late action of Whistler v Ruskin.

The subscribers wish me to add that they have contributed their offerings in a great measure as the expression of their opinion, that your lifelong, honest, endeavours to further the cause of art should not be crowned by your being cast in the costs arising out of that action.

I have taken the liberty of appending a list of their names & I am sure that they all join with me, in hoping that you may long be spared to disseminate by your writings the doctrine of honesty in art.

Believe me to remain
Very truly yours
Marcus B Huish

XXV

ALFRED WILLIAM HUNT TO RUSKIN

1 Tor Villa
Campden Hill
Kensington W.
Nov[ember] 2 [1873]

My dear Ruskin

I have been at home long enough now to regard my Coniston life from a proper distance—a distance of time which makes me know how happy I was there and how much your kindness did to make me happy. Perhaps I may have to thank you yet for something which won't make me happier—but that will be just as I use it—namely an advance in Self-knowledge which makes me look back upon all old work with a very calm settled horror, and upon all work to be done with a very grave seriousness. It is all very well to try to find out what is within one's power— *Nothing* is— in any drawing small or large—well or ill-designed—there comes a desperate difficulty when you try to give pure bright colour and sweet wholesome tone—

I saw some pictures in Liverpool as I was passing through, and have seen some since in London which make me despair about pictures altogether— At a private view at the Dudley the other day I felt myself out of place & I shall have to remain so here in London whenever art is talked about.

You were terribly right about the foreground of my large picture in the R A. Only the stones were utterly unlike those of the Yewdale beck—black moss adding to the confusion of them.

Margaret [Mrs. Hunt] and I are pleased with the Spectator's article upon her novel. What she will write hereafter (after the next) will I hope have a better plan and a moral meaning. It's a fashious thing meddling with art at all—

I grudge the glaciers the space which you have cribbed from Scott in Fors to give to them. There is a great 'demand' for those dignified old-world manners of Mrs. Ogilvie's time—

How I wish I could be a Tory! I am heart and soul a hero-worshipper— I think I allow for a greater variety of modes in which my born governors of their fellow men are to exercise their power, and longer time for them to spend in gaining it, than you do.

Surely Philip Sidney must have been sorely exercised in mind about his relations' deaths! and either ashamed of them as justly punished or driven to question the right of those who kept their heads to have their government called divine. Visible power when once attained with all its trappings must have had an overmastering hold upon men's imagination in those days.

Margaret sends her love to you. The children [Sylvia, Violet, and Ruskin's goddaughter Venice] are all well— Violet will send you her love herself.

I thank you again most sincerely for all the delight for which I am indebted to you. What splendid sunsets those were which I watched from Brantwood. I own that I have a true pleasure in writing to you of it even only for the sake of signing myself

Your most devoted disciple & friend
A. W. Hunt

I hope Mr & Mrs Severn are quite well— I wonder whether I shall ever see that very charming young lady Miss [Constance] Hilliard again.

XXVI

MRS. KENDAL TO MRS. SEVERN

[No address]
[1880?] [1]

You dear:

Thank you so much! I thought you guessed when you were here with y[ou]r friend Mrs. [Williams?]. — I hope she guessed & has not attributed my not calling to bad manners entirely! —— My little business comes off in June. Thanks for the little pills— & the ticket dear. I look forward to hearing the Professor with delight! —so sorry you will not be there. Take care of yourself above all things— I am a miserable object when like this—& horribly nervous!

Fondly, with love
Y[our]s ever
Madge

145, Harley Street. W.
[early 1880s?]

My dear Friend

How good of you to think of me. I wish whenever you come to the theatre you would send y[ou]r card round, and then I could at any rate see & speak to you for a few minutes.

How are all y[ou]r dear children. My boy has been indulging in *Mumps,* [a re(al)ly?] painful uninteresting thing. I send you a Song. Sing it sometimes for my sake. Will you?

1. In view of the compliment to be paid to Mrs. Kendal in "Living Waves," Mrs. Severn may have given her a ticket for this lecture, delivered at the London Institution on March 17, 1880. She herself was expecting another child, Violet, b. August 28, 1880.

Please remember me most cordially to the Professor—& with our kindest regards to the Hubby & love to y[ou]r dear Lily

Y[ou]rs al[wa]ys aff[ectionate]ly

Madge

XXVII

Ruskin to the Reverend William Towler Kingsley

Brantwood

18th Feb[ruary 18]86 [1]

Darling Kingsley

I am no end glad of this talk about the scratches [presumably made by glaciers] and tempted to go at it again as hard as ever,—but I am at work on a little account of native metals, & must not go into the other furrow,—but I shall forward your letter to my dutiful & loving G. Collingwood who is working out all I want,—I fear I did not send you his Savoy Alps. — they are ordered down to you by this post— He spoiled his cuts by putting too much in them, but the book is very valuable.

Ever your lovingest

J R.[2]

1. This letter is bound in a copy of the first edition of *"Our Fathers Have Told Us," Part I. The Bible of Amiens.*

2. The first paragraphs of Kingsley's reply to the foregoing letter help to explain the next letter from Ruskin:

South Kilvington

March 10, 1886

My dearest Ruskin

I sent back the 'Alps' as you gave me a copy a year ago.

There is one fatal defect in the honey theory; honey clings to plates, ice on the contrary slips more easily than anything, due to the fact of the heat caused by friction penetrating only a very very short way, & so causing the ice to slide on a film of water.

In the machines for cutting iron, the tool is made very heavy & urged with great pressure and slow velocity and at the same time kept wet to prevent the excess of heat at the cutting edge; if the tool is light, used with little pressure or with rapid motion, the tool is ground away & the surface to be cut is left with very little abrasion.

Now a rhomboidal rock of felspathic porphyry 50 feet long (of which there are plenty in Wales) and fixed in 2,000 feet thick of glacier seems to have all the heat conditions of a tool for cutting in the highest degree. You can see in Wales plenty of ice ground rocks extending on both sides of the vallies, & then the nicks cut out by the streams in these ice ground rocks; these nicks are quite insignificant,

Brantwood
[March? 1886]

My dear William Kingsley

I would'nt have believed that in this epoch of glacier study anybody could yet write such a piece of utterly damned nonsense as your saying about the honey 'theory'— Do you suppose that Buckland Forbes and I—dont know that honey sticks to plates? — The honey—law—has nothing whatever to do with the adherence —though I should like to see you move the ice on *my* rocks today! [(]Forbes statement is no theory—but was a demonstrated fact forty years ago—) I never wrote with more contempt of any blockheads or any absurdity than I have always of all its opponents

——— I

Your idea of 2000 feet of glacier ice is as false as of 2000 feet of sea, moving as a body.

——— Goodbye for today

J R.

XXVIII

Mrs. La Touche-Severn-Ruskin Correspondence

[Section 1 represents a selection from the 64 letters in the F. J. Sharp Collection from Mrs. La Touche to Mrs. Severn. This group as a whole includes most of the letters which were published, in whole or in part, by Margaret Ferrier Young in her privately printed *The Letters of a Noble Woman* (London, 1908), copies of which are not likely to be found beyond the British Museum and the Library of Congress. Section 2 contains the only unpublished letters from Mrs. La Touche to Ruskin which, to my knowledge, have survived. Section 3 presents heretofore unpublished letters which I transcribed while at work among the manuscripts once gathered in the Brantwood Library and which have been impossible to locate after the Sotheby dispersal sales of 1930–31—during which they may have been permanently lost.]

---

rough saw marks, rarely 20 feet deep where the ice marks run up to 1500 or 2000 ft. I do not mean that the ice has cut down the 1500 or 2000, but the lines of action visible in such places make the water work look like a scratch. . . .

1. *Mrs. La Touche to Mrs. Severn*

Tuesday
[1878][1]

Dearest Joanie

I cannot tell you how much I feel for you— I am so afraid you will be worn out— It is so good & kind of you to write me—but I ought not to expect it— I go back to Ireland by the night mail this evening— How strange & touching that he should think my poor Child near him— perhaps she is— Who can tell?

I know you are overwhelmed with writing, & nursing—& a thousand other things— I won't ask more than a word—to Harristown—in a few days' time— My cabobs [Mrs. Bishop, her cousin; see B.S.] is glad to know she can always get the latest news in Bond St. The papers seem to give pretty accurate reports, & even in Ireland I shall not be left in the dark— Love to Arthur— Think of me always as your loving & sympathizing Vice-Mother

M La T

Harristown
Tuesday [1880?][2]

Dearest Joanie

Fag's oo's ee? I was so glad to get y[ou]r letter— Oh Joanie do tell me about the pinguicula— is it possible that it was the Irish one, the Grandiflora one, that was growing so thickly? & if so, I want very much to know whether it continues to be Grandiflora, the Spanish form of the plant, or is reverting to the common pinguicula. Tell me— I'm every day more & more interested in that sort of people, & less in the human sort (unless they are my old friends— I *hate* my new ones) You can't think what a joy the things you & that delightful Miss Beever sent me years ago, have been to me ever since— The yellow pops have quite established themselves & colonized all over the place—the Sedums & saxifrages have all thriven & spread—but the most wonderful

1. Dated by the references to Ruskin's illness. In 1878 bulletins informed the public about his condition.

2. Conjecturally dated through Mrs. La Touche's reference to "the new Sweetness"—presumably Violet Severn. Miss Young published the first paragraph of this letter as the last paragraph of a letter dated July 5, 1880, and part of the second paragraph in a letter dated June 1879.

thing of all is the Orange Hawkweed "Grim the Collier" The one tiny plant you sent me is now a great tuft, & I counted 50 heads of blossom on it! The only thing that has not done well, was a very interesting Convallaria. It sends up four leaves every year to show it is alive, & that is all it does— The Oak & Beech ferns are very strong & well, but "keep themselves to themselves" & don't spread—

Do you remember "Tommy Hare" who was Rector here in *your* time? Well, he has expanded enormously both in person & position— the former I do not wonder at, for his powers of eating were always tremendous— the latter is more strange, for he had very little other power to speak of— Anyhow, he is now Dean of Ossory, & lives in a nice old Deaney house in my native town of Kilkenny, & I have been staying with those merry brown hares, & while there, I went to look at Desart, my old home. It was the very strangest sensation—like a dream. You know it was the woods & shrubberies of that place that taught me, in my solitary childhood, to care for Nature as I do—with a love that goes on growing till it has left little room for anything else— Well, I can't tell you how strange it felt to be there again— All the time between now & my 12th year seemed blotted out— And everything, as well as myself, was entirely changed & totally unchanged at the same time (in Ireland this is quite possible) The dear old place had gone to utter ruin as far as its lawns & pleasances & walks were concerned— The hand of man had not touched them for years— All the familiar walks were obliterated—the stones of the terraces & balustrades were lifted out of their places by seedling trees— The greenhouse had fallen in & was all a tangle of passion flowers from within & ivy, ferns & honeysuckle from without—flowering shrubs trailed & twisted & caught at one another across what used to be trim avenues— the old lawns were waving meadows in which there was less grass than tall hyacinths purple orchises & white columbines, all nodding & dancing with a perfect revel of joy, that nature had at last taken the old place to her heart, & man had abandoned it— Rabbits & hares scuttled about, & sat up & stared at me— The place was alive with birds— It was a poem— There was something very sad about it, from the human side—

but yet I never saw a place look so beautiful—or so stately & calm— It is very unlike other places, particularly now! It has haunted me ever since & I am longing to go there again—

The Master has been giving himself a holiday at Oban—but returned on Thursday. Rose [Ward, her granddaughter] & her *very* nice governess are here—& are very happy & companionable— Rose [now 14] is a delightful child—but I don't find that she has any talent for anything, tho' full of intelligence & a wonderful natural tact & discretion—& such a perfect temper—& she takes no sort of interest in *herself*—either her clothes, or her "inner consciousness." This is, I think, a singular blessing—

You will be sorry to leave y[ou]r Paradise in August—but I hope the new Sweetness will make up for everything. *Do* go on advising y[ou]r friends & everybody else to go to Glengariff for their honeymoons— I hear Eccles' Hotel there, is more perfect & home like than ever—& there are 5 miles of lovely walks belonging to it—& a Library in it— I'm interrupted & must stop— love to Arthur.

Ever y[ou]r loving vice mother
M La T

8. P[rince] of W[ales] Terrace
[home of Mrs. Bishop]
Tuesday
[February 22, 1881][3]

Dearest Joanie

We are all so grieved— My cabobs sends her love— she & I & all of us are anxiously hoping for one little line to tell us how you found him— Is it the same illness as before? I fear it must be serious, as you were telegraphed for—but I trust there is a change for the better— I can't write to you about other things in this sad uncertainty—but let me have one line— tell me you have not knocked yourself up—& with much love I am

Y[ou]r very loving V.M.
M La T

3. Written from the home of Mrs. Bishop and dated through the reference to Mrs. Severn's having been summoned to Brantwood on Sunday, February 20, 1881.

Harristown
Friday [July? 1881][4]

Dearest Joanie

The basket & oo's little letter are come—& yesterday I had a nicy [sic] letter from St. C. & I'll write to him when I am not cross, which today I am, because I have to go to a garden party at [Gilltown?], & I thought something would happen to save me, & it has'n't happened— I wish I lived at the back of the Old Man, everyday I find Bœotian festivities more and more hateful— I can't sleep the night before & three nights after, a Bœotian gathering, with sheer nightmare of disgust— So the Begone—ias [Begonias] knew St. C. did'n't like them, & broke themselves up— Everything we don't like does'n't break up, unfortunately—either hard frosts or human institutions— Alice & I sat up half the night trying to make three [Kilcullen] Dorcas [Society account] books agree. She is now gone to Mrs. Wakefield [Treasurer of the Society] with them not agreeing a bit— I suggested pretending they did—but it seems this was unprincipled— So you have got my cabobs & her Flopsy [daughter Florence, now 27 years old] — When do they go to their "other friends?" —& what are you all doing together? The sweet little Lacerta [Lizard] that appears every sunny afternoon on our balustrade is a daily excitement— I find the creature *is* known in Ireland & was supposed to be overlooked by St. Patrick. Of course he had the sense to overlook it on purpose— It eats flies & is growing visibly fatter— Its name is "Zootoca Vivipara"— I hav'n't a notion what the Z word means— but I am in hopes it is going to explain the V. word itself— How are the Cimabue Bennet's five [i. e. the Bennett sisters] My love all round—altho' I'm not in a good temper—

Ever y[ou]r loving V.M.
M La T

Queen Hotel
Chester
Saturday [July 14, 1883][5]

4. Dated through the reference to Mrs. Bishop, who visited Brantwood during the summer of 1881 (see Bradley, *Letters*, p. 379; letter of August 2, 1881).

5. She and Mr. La Touche reached the Waterhead Hotel on July 17, and after his departure, she spent a week at Brantwood (see Diary entries for July 19 ff.).

Dearest Joanie

We are getting so impatient— I'm tired of sitting all day in Mr. Bullen's [dental] chair with my mouth full of fingers. But this is to be final, & I must give him the time now which I ought to have given him in April on our way home [from Mentone]—only that the Master was not well & wanted to get back— I do trust we shall escape Tuesday afternoon & get to Paradise [Coniston] that evening— Not *quite* Paradise, though, until the following week— Won't we jabber? & won't I listen? —& I'll do my welly best with the coins— We have such nice rooms here at the back, looking into a very green & coloury convent-like garden, & all our windows curtained with greenery; there is really a great deal to see— the clutching & clinging of the clematis & Virginia creeper from day to day, & the groping of long twigs for something to catch— are so interesting to watch— Also the ways of the sparrows—& in the evenings swallows come & circle about, until the bats join them, when they retire, finding the company no longer select. The poplars sway & bend about in a manner which looks quite affected —& behind them stands a church spire which seems to say "you don't see *me* going on like that—"

I'll write again, my Joanie, tomorrow or Monday— Love to St. C.

Ever y[ou]r loving v.m.
M La T

Harristown
Easter Monday [1884] [6]

Dearest Joanie

Fag's oo's ee? I guess oo's now at Herne Hill— I wrote to St C— a few days ago, & now I've sent a note to Herdson to thank him for the sweet little plant of the blue loveliness. It was so beautifully packed, and arrived perfectly fresh. I am only waiting to plant it out in my playground till this horrible east wind ceases & there comes a little kindly rain which is tebbily wanted— Oh Joanie I would so like to be sitting in your pocket (it must be a large one) to talk about 50 things— are you & Arthur & St. C. making nice plans for coming to Ireland! & we'd have a better time

6. Dated through the reference to Prince Leopold; d. March 28, 1884.

than last year [when Joan and Arthur Severn, accompanied by the Marshalls, had been her guests]. I'm more angry with that Exhibition Committee than I can say—so I'll say nothing— It was too sad about Prince Leopold. Is it wicked to say that one can't help thinking sometimes that the wrong people die— "Taken away from the evil to come" is what good people say—& yet I always think, in such cases as Prince Leopold's less evil would come if they were left, & naughty people taken away— Bœotia is wildly Bœotian just now— Races are going on all over Ireland, & the P[ercy, her son] & A[nnie, his wife] Co. tearing after them, & visiting in all the most rackety houses, & having rackety people staying with them— We hardly ever set eyes on them, they are always "on the batter"— Their financial condition is mysterious, for 6 months ago they declared they could not possibly live at Newberry, nor anywhere but in an extreme back settlement in Canada—& now they announce their intention of remaining at Newberry, & they seem quite regardless of financial considerations— When they went on a visit of a week to somebody down in Cork, they took two horses & three servants with them! Punchestown is next week & then the whole county goes mad— Major Borrowes is on his way back from a trip to Tripoli! — Somehow one feels so free and comfortable when he is away— Mrs. Wakefield [her friend and closest neighbour] gets on very well with her adopted family now, & they & Miss Young often come here & play with me—& sometimes we have tea-parties, & devouring of jam & short-bread, & when the summer comes we will have outdoor diversions— the jam will be so much better with caterpillars falling into it, & midges add so much to one's enjoyment, & damp grass is so much better than a dry chair to sit on, when one is under 13.

I don't know *that* Mrs. Hewitt who had not the civility to write to Arthur again—but Mrs. Wakefield told me someone else was painting the child's portrait— she did not tell me who, & she did not seem pleased about it—

She is now making my life a burden to me with her bewildering Dorcas accounts, which it is my business to put into order & show results—but oh if you could see the way the other ladies keep their books— Blots, erasures, & corrections of figures, done by writing the right figure over the wrong one, *so* [illustrated] so that I defy anyone to know what's meant— I don't believe an Irish woman in any class of life can do anything with *finish* & accuracy— I try my very best, & wish my colleagues would do the same—

Tell me how oo is—& Arthur & St– C– & all the [five] Sweetnesses My pussy cat has still only 5 kittens— The naughty cat tried not to have a sixtth— & *succeeded*—& was very ill— oo would'n't do sus a ting? oo vill be dood?

oo's loving v.m.
M La T

Harristown
Tuesday [August? 1884] [7]

Dearest Doanie

I wonder if oo's come back from oo's visit yet— Please I want to pay for my nice candlesticks, which arrived all right— Could oo get the man to send me his bill? & telly me how oo is, & all the dear Brantwood news— It now seems like a dream—such a lovely one! I mean my visit there—& St C. was so sweet to me—so was oo—& Diddie, & everybody— I'm longing for Pye [Miss Young] to come back that I may have some one to talk to about it all, who can listen with pricked ears, & respond with quick tongue— The Master listens with awe & respect, but he does'n't know the pecious [sic] little jokes, &c &c— I hav'n't much to telly oo— Life is rather stupid— The P. & A. [Percy and Annie] are in Dublin seeing the horse show, & on Saturday they are to go to Howth (Lord Howth is one of the dissolute companions) & the end of next week they come home— I have excellent accounts of Ernest [Ward, son of Emily La Touche] from Jersey, the doctor there affirms that there is nothing wrong with his heart, but he has outgrown his strength— he is over six feet, a good height for 17— He is to come to Ireland next month, & go first to Castle Ward (Lord

7. Dated through the reference to Mrs. La Touche's having been a guest at Brantwood, where she had spent most of August with Miss Young. Having welcomed her on July 28, 1884 (see *Diaries*, p. 1077), Ruskin wrote Francesca on August 23, "And *she* is happy, though how, I cannot conceive, in being here" (Swett, *Letters to Francesca*, p. 78). While there, she had met Eva Layton (1859–1949), whose singing of duets with her sister Constance, Ruskin much enjoyed. The Laytons had been spending some weeks in a near-by farmhouse.

Baiyor's) & then come here. I have been to see my pussey cat, she seemed rather in despair, her governess was having holidays, her nurse has been packed off for misconduct, & the five little girls were all running perfectly wild, with only a rough Irish girl to look after them— She was tying up a great cut in little Olive's leg, & she told me Joan & Norah had fallen out of the pony trap & Joan had hurt her head a good deal— She seemed rather mishy altogether, & was looking high & low for a good nurse— She wants an English head nurse— Do you know of one? There's a great difference between the condition of her five kittens & yours! The Norah one who is a little older than your Violet, is to have the ligaments of both her knees divided, & be kept on her back for some time, the doctor says if this is not done she will gradually lose all powers of walking— So altogether the poor Cat was less cheerful than usual— The Linaria Purpurea of which you gave me the seed, is in bloom, & is ever so pretty—& I've got lovely carnations from the Paris seed, I could send you cuttings of some, but unluckily a good many have produced *no* side shoots, & some only one or two. I've got some sunflowers as big as King Arthur's Round Table— I have not seen many of the neighbours yet (& don't want to) I've refused a few garden parties. The Breretons (the people at whose house the concert was) have one next Wednesday— I won't go— The hot weather went away quite suddenly on Sunday last, between the two services, & we were all baked in the morning & iced in the afternoon— Today is so cold & showery— Mrs. Wakefield expects me to join her at a picnic at the Waterfall, but I have sent to say I won't— My playground looks rather wild & weedy— I see a sad necessity for having everything dug up & a lot of manure dug in— very soon I will send you some wild poppy seed, & some Victoria Cross poppy seed, you must sow them where you mean them to live, poppies are sleepy & hate being woke up & transplanted—except the perennial sorts— I wish our railway was finished, the navvies are getting troublesome, fighting & robbing one another & being brought before the Magistrate, all over blood & mud & bruises, when he is in the middle of his dinner. (This of course is the least of it) And the poor river is running quite turbid & Thames-like, owing to the making of cement for the embankment wall at the railway bridge— She will run clear again when that is done— Goodbye my dearest vice bairnie, love to St C— I'll write to him as soon as the sun shines— I hav'n't got a Miss Eva Layton to look at, with the sun in her hair, & the cloudiness makes me cross! Love to Diddie—

Ever oo's loving V.m.
M La T

Harristown
Feb[ruary] 4th 1897

Dearest Joanie

It was delightful to receive such a booful long letter from my vice-bairnie, telling me all the things I most wanted to know, I did not answer it the minute it came, but waited for a nice wet afternoon when I should have no duties & no interruptions at last it came. At least I pretend it's a wet afternoon, but it's only a grey damp one & I won't go out. It's most interesting to hear all about my vice-grand-children— I can't imagine you with two boys at Oxford—but you have not told me what their professions are to be—or are they to have any? Your little Herbert must be a real joy and blessing— He can't be like Henry VIII now, as St C– used to say he was— What a delightful school he is at, & I believe the air of Broadstairs is wonderfully healthy— he will almost be sorry to leave it for Westminster— I've nothing the least amusing to tell you. We are both outrageously old [she 73; he 83] & have become a pair of grumpy hermits— The Master is as active as ever, & walks all over the place, poking into everything that concerns farm, stables, garden &c—out in all weathers, & never buttoning his coat—but he has grown very deaf, and trying to hear always gives him a headache— So that we have got into very solitary ways & never see anyone. The people about here all think of nothing but sport, varied by as much gossip & scandal as they can invent or collect, & I am truly thankful that I am not expected to be sociable— I can hear very well, but would much rather not hear the kind of conversation that goes on when Bœotians get together! The P[ercy] & A[nnie] Co. still live at Newberry— They adopted some years ago a little nephew of Annie's, one of Lady

Saunderson's 10 children. Sammy is now 13, & at school at Eastbourne, but spends his holidays at Newberry & belongs entirely to the Co. I don't think him a very interesting little boy, they are training him into a regular sporting character. Ernest is working very hard in the South & West—inspecting model farms, teaching various agricultural arts, distributing animals & poultry & looking after roads, bridges, &c— very useful work—but he gets provoked sometimes when people won't keep their appointments or pay their debts— In Ireland we are quite regardless of all that sort of thing! & Ernest is extremely English in all his ideas & has a great sense of duty & of going through with whatever one undertakes— Well, I was telling you that the Master is as active as ever— I am *not,* though ten years younger. I like to sit still & knit petticoats for the Needlework Guild—or read foolish books— Walking out is a good deal of trouble—& I catch bad colds pretty often & always seize upon that or any other excuse, for sitting in peaceful solitude—but I still have my black ponies & drive them on fine days aimlessly about the roads, never, or hardly ever, paying a visit— This place [the burned house, re-built in 1893] is quite unchanged, except that the house has only two stories instead of three— the garden is just the same, except that it seems to me to be several miles off! The Clematis & Gloire de Dijon still cover the wall, half strangled by the Virginia creeper—& the river runs before the windows sometimes rippling among its rocks, & sometimes, as now, rushing down in a turbid flood— that is what happens when the snows melt on the Wicklow hills— Give Lacerta's love to dear St C— I am so sorry to hear he has a cough & is not as strong as he was— I hope by this time Arthur has come back to you without the "flu"—& Lily too— I wonder who lives at the Thwaite now? & what new wonders are growing in your garden? My cabobs is I fear quite an invalid now, tho' better than she was— She is not able to be in London at all now —& was quite knocked up by a little excursion to Dieppe in the summer—

It's always a joy to hear from you my dearest vice-bairnie— You don't forget your loving old fossil V.M.

M La T

2. *Mrs. La Touche to Ruskin*

Harristown
24th April [1884] [8]

Dearest St C—

I don't like you to have either one "bad influenza cold" or seven pets. But I like you to go & comfort the Duchess of Albany, if it won't be too much for you. And while you're at Herne Hill you're to do, say, eat, & drink, everything Joanie tells you— She's quite pet enough for you— However, I think I'll allow you the Cabman's daughter—if you'll tell me more about her. But as you say, I do think seed diamonds are nicer—, & seed that grows flowers nicer still— I'm so glad to have Santa Zita from my dear good Santo C— And I'm looking out for the cloud lecture— Our doctor says we have still got what he calls "Ruskin's plague cloud" over our heads— He is so delighted at your having recognized its plaguiness— We have had weeks of rainless gloom & bitter cold— Now & then the sun breaks through to keep us believing in him —but the grey curtains close across his face before he has had time to warm anything— My playground is hard & sorrowful. You know your gardener sent me a lovely little plant of that pretty blue thing with a long ugly name— I hope it will thrive when the weather changes, which it must soon do— I wish one's friends would'n't be each other's enemies— I'm thinking of the jackdaws— I liked to see them holding Synods upon the lawn, but they have formed themselves into a Society for the Suppression of Flowers, & this morning they have picked all my pansies, & young shoots of carnations, & big oxlips, & left them on the ground to show the purity of their motives as compared to those of the slugs, who eat what they destroy— Victor—(he's my dog) brought me with pride a dead leveret yesterday— I wish these kinds of misunderstandings did'n't happen— I wish I could make all the creatures like each other as much as I like them— (I don't mind their *eating* each other— that arrangement works well. —)

8. Dated through the reference to Ruskin's pending call upon the Duchess of Albany, at Claremont, on April 25, 1884, to express sympathy after the death of Prince Leopold (see *Diaries,* p. 1064) and to the "Storm-Cloud" lectures, published during May 1884. Inasmuch as "The Ballad of St. Zita" would not be published before July, he had doubtless sent her, perhaps in proof, a copy of the poem which he had received from Francesca.

The Master sends his love— I would like dearly to come & see you again—& so would he if he was once got to move out of this —but it is'n't easy to dig him up— I have no particular root—

Oh St. C— I want to know, why can't I get the "Diary of an Old Soul" by George MacDonald — Joanie sent me a copy of the title-page, & I wrote to the address given & enclosed a stamped envelope directed to myself for the answer (I asked the price of the book that I might send the money) but no answer ever came. Is there a Mr. W. Hughes, 32 Beaufort St—? I've been reading some of G. MacD[onald]'s latest books— There are lovely things —mixed now and then with ghastly ones—& impossible people —but nicer than possible ones. Goodbye dearest St C—

Always your loving Lacy

Harristown
Nov[embe]r 4th [1884] [9]
too late for post because tiresome visitors would'nt go away—

Dearest St C—

I was so glad to get your little note—& I was going to write to you this very day, before it came—for I wanted a word from you —& thought to myself that you could'n't possibly write because a chit had hold of your right hand & a minx of your left— For even at Oxford I suppose there be chits & minxes— And I thought perhaps a soft snap from Lacertine teeth might make you let go one hand for a minute or two! I shall be more than grateful for the lecture, & won't leave home without telling you where to have it sent— I believe I am going next Monday to the Grampians at Tunbridge Wells, & to London with them, in a week or two— The Master sends you his love, he is so delighted because I have got him the first four numbers of Francesca. Please are you going to give the lectures, in London, this winter, about which you were talking to Diddie & Joanie when I was so happy at Brantwood last August?

9. Dated through various references: Mrs. La Touche had reached Brantwood with Miss Young on July 27, 1884 (see *Diaries,* p. 1075); the expected copy of "The Storm-Cloud of the Nineteenth Century" had arrived; the first four numbers of Francesca Alexander's "Roadside Songs" had been issued April–October 1884.

I have got your two plague-cloud lectures— & Miss Young (Pye) & I, have been reading you very mindfully these winter evenings, & meeting in sheltered corners among the dead leaves, to talk about summer & Brantwood. Your sweet old Susie (you may keep hold of *her* hand) sent me some little Iris roots that were much too pretty to bury—little sleek fluted things like Moorish pinnacles (or domes that come to a point) of the loveliest silky texture & pale tawny colour like a baby's hair— I *have* planted them, but regret to spoil them by making roots go down & a shoot go up— All wrong of me I know— Now I must stop talking— It was nice & dear of you to write to me—

Ever your loving
Lacy—

Harristown
April 30th 1885

Dearest St C—

Here I come again. Do you wish you had'n't whistled? And do you really want to know about Punchestown Races— They are the annual Saturnalia of this country, & are considered more social than sporting— I don't know why— They are not very business-like as races I believe— Not as much of a turfy Stock-Exchange as races ought to be— But I believe as an exhibition of fine clothes & fine people they are highly laudable—& the date is a sort of era in the year— People say "My first-day Punchestown gown" & "My second-day P. bonnet"—& the Sunday before is Punchayesima Sunday, & the faithful sit pining for the Sermon to be over that they may rush out & compare notes on their preparations for running with impatience the race that is not [sic] set before them— Some of the races are for farmers, in order to keep them in good humour & favourable to fox-life & patient of crushed crops & broken fences— But most of the races are ridden by "gentlemen" They are "steeple-chases" (but there is no steeple & no chasing) They gallop over about 4 miles in a ring, across fields, some grassy & some ploughed; & they jump over ditches, banks, rails &c—& there are always some men & some horses hurt— There are enormous greedy luncheons in tents & iron huts—& much jollification, & money lost & won, & no sense from beginning to end— The farmers rather despise it all, except a few—&

the Nationalists denounce it as the amusement of the "idle blood-suckers" but this year the presence of the Prince & Princess gave it renewed importance, tho' the steady rain that fell both days was enough to quench Vesuvius, & destroyed thousands of smart frocks & bonnets—& spoilt my holiday; for I generally have a real good time those two days, knowing that every creature is safe out of my way— I'm glad it's over— Percy rode & won a match with some other fool—

Are any of the 40 books you are writing & editing such as the likes of me would understand? Is there any more of Proserpina? But I won't bother you with questions. For when you are not busy, it's playing in the garden you should be (with Bramble, not with a minx) & not writing letters— I wonder if my red poppies are coming up among your yellow ones— The Jackdaws that send Missions to my playground are worse than ever this year— They are John Knoxes— They won't allow anything pretty to develop itself— I've got beds of anemones—& these horrid clerics walk round & peck off the petals of every red & pink blossom— They have agreed to tolerate the grey & purple, & are divided in opinion about the white— I am obliged to cut off all the bright ones before they open, & let them bloom in water— But a squirrel came into my room the other day, so a deputation of jackdaws would not surprise me— Now you *do* wish you had'n't whistled!

Ever, dearest St C—
Y[ou]r loving
Lacy

Harristown
June 16th [1885] [10]

Dearest St C—

Praeterita is—or are—delightful— I hope there will be a great deal more about those earliest days— It's good for the public to read about a righteous education when it's result is before them, & when education now is often so unrighteous. But how *could*

10. Dated by the reference to her contribution to the "Tablet"—namely, a Public Letter of June 1885, condemning fox-hunting as a "cruel and dehumanizing" sport (see Young, *The Letters of a Noble Woman,* pp. 109–13). Inasmuch as the first three "Parts" of *Praeterita* were not issued until July 1885, she had presumably been reading them in proof.

you learn the 8th chapter of 1. Kings! I too had to learn chapters when I was very small—but not so many as yours, & not all the same— I did not like it much, but what really drove me wild was a commutation of the chapters-task, into that of daily learning three quite unconnected verses—a Prayer, a Precept, & a Promise, out of a horrid little book with a tucked flap, called the Threefold Cord. It was that little book that caused me to run away at day-break on a summer's morning with a blanket & a burning glass—to secure warmth if nothing else—with no other intention than to become a Wild Woman of the Woods; but returned (from half way up a tree) on being respectfully told by a footman that break-fast was ready— Did you ever want to be a Wild Man, & were you ever naughty & violent? I think not, for you had the great natural gift of patience, & your surroundings being harmonious tho' somewhat stern, were calming in their influence. I never was allowed any thing good to eat either, but still I always thought the flowers were for the fruit, till you taught me better— You say you never were afraid of anything— That astonishes me, with your imagination & perceptions— I was horribly afraid always—not of any *thing*—but of what I saw *behind* my eyes when certain Terrors were before them—such as a white dressing gown hanging up, not one whit less terrible for my knowing what it was. And a narrow street at Brighton with high chimneys out of whose tops I knew that wicked ghosts' heads were sticking tho' I never even *thought* I saw them—& a fearful agate ring that my aunt wore, the stone had a ring of white round it & I thought it was The Evil Eye— Were you not afraid of Ugliness, or did you never see any?

I've found no more minx flowers lately— But I'll soon write again— Did you like my scold in the Tablet?

Ever your loving
Lacy

Harristown
June 23rd [1885?] [11]

Dearest St C—

The minx-letter is very nice— I like minxes that found societies to befriend Living Creatures—& I'm glad you let her go shrimp-

11. Only the first half of the first folder of this letter has survived, preserved in an envelope inscribed by Ruskin: "Lacerta / Very valuable, on Education."

ing. About cruelty in children—ask mothers, nurses, & schoolmasters— I am afraid it is a deep rooted tendency in undeveloped uncultured humanity, whether nation or infant— The exceptions are daily getting more numerous, & the tendency would die out entirely in a generation or two if it was never allowed to continue in the adult; so that no child could be born of cruel parents, or see cruelty allowed— The little brother of Pye's pupils—four next November—is as nice & carefully trained a little boy as can be, but he loves to pull the ears of the little dog & make it squeal— He knows perfectly that the squeal has the same kind of cause, as his own outcries when his finger is pinched— He knows he is "hurting poor Judy" but he *will* do it— His brother, aged nine, has what may be called *attacks* of liking to tease *him*— The next, a girl, aged 11 has *no* cruelty in her, & is essentially a "mother-hearted child"—but the low development tells in other ways, she is very stupid at lessons [end of folder]

Harristown
Thursday
March 29th [1888] [12]

Dearest St. C.

Yes I am alive; & the more alive for having seen your handwriting again   But I'm laid up with influenza & can't write a nice letter— You ask me where I am— I am by the Liffey, & hav'n't been out of Ireland for more than a year. Yes I'm sure there will be nice things in Vol III [of *Praeterita*]. Only don't make yourself ill with too much writing—& I'll do as you tell me in writing to Joanie; but don't say she is wicked, she is so fond of you & anxious that you should be well & happy; & if she can't realise things that are real to you, that's not her fault— Believe me she will never bring any mischief on us— And I am always your loving

Lacerta

3. *Ruskin to Mrs. La Touche*

[The present whereabouts of the following letters in manuscript being unknown, it has been impossible to check the accuracy of the transcriptions originally made or to supply passages which were not copied at that time.]

12. Dated through the reference to *Praeterita,* Volume III, of which chapter 1 was published on May 19, 1888, a year when March 29 fell on Thursday.

And please I think you'll be more comfortable in being able to growl when you want to, without even Joanie's seeing it unless you send her messages; so have your say about what you like, dislike, or think wrong. Only, don't talk to me 'of thinking.' I never trouble myself to think. I either *know* a thing or don't. I don't know whether you or Grampus [Mrs. W. H. Bishop] are the wrongerer.[13]

but I'm ever your loving St. C.

Brantwood
9 Aug[ust], 1881

Dear Lacy!

That's Him! the crested stork I mean, to a dagger's point. What eyes you have! but I wish they could see more into hearts, then you would not ask absurd questions. As if I had time to tell you about visitors, or cared about any visitors! except swallows and snails and lizards. You might just as well ask auld [Elshie?] to write you a court circular; all the foxglove news is delicious to me but you must tell me some of those laws of the links. I'm doing a very serious bit of classification principle for the next Proserpina, and I want you to set down unvexed and uncompelled by any question or thoughts of mine, your own knowledge first and impressions next, of the relations in wild flowers between SPECIES and LINKING as distinguished from Hybrids, i.e. I call the common Burnet a true LINK between roses and grasses. But this foxglove is not a link but a curiosity. I honour and love and pity the links, but would throttle the curs and the Botanists together all in a string, as Ulysses did his maid servants, if I could.

Ever your loving, J.R.

Brantwood
13 Aug[ust], 1881

Dear Lacy

I find the Irish post comes in the evening. Lest anything stop me tomorrow, I answer the gravest question tonight. What *I* should do, if I had either a son or daughter, I know not. But I do

13. Concluding paragraph of letter of August 3, 1881, omitted from the letter as it was published by Young, in *The Letters of a Noble Woman*, and consequently by Cook and Wedderburn (see *Works, 37*, 372).

not think there is any question respecting the principle of Paternal duty; in *any* distress, in *any* shame, the parents' door should be open to the child. But he never should pay its wilfully contracted debts. Steady refusal would put an end to incalculable vice and misery among youth of wealthy Christendom.

....I think you will find more in my serpent lecture which I ordered to be sent you. Grampus was very nice, but why on earth should you be jealous of her; do you think I have no friends of longer standing?

Ever your loving — St. C.

Brantwood
20th Aug[ust], 1881

My dearest Lacy

The first part of your letter deeply 'concerned' me (I was going to say 'grieved' but I'm past grief) only I do not understand it because if parents and trustees refused to pay debts, what would the Bankers and Jews do....

It is nice hearing you call Joanie "My Joanie." It is a great shame she and Arfie don't go to see you. I told you of my dream, didn't I? How I set out barefoot to go to Ireland? and how you and R[ose] came here instead? I CAN'T understand how so extremely rational a person as I can lose their wits, and still more how they don't know they have lost them at the time.

I do think if ever I were to go crazy for the *third* time I should know I was so!

Ever your lovingest St. C

Herne Hill
5th April, [18]82

Darling Lacy—

...But what a simplicity of a Saviour you are—quite the Prem^{re} 'Ingenuite' of Saviours, to think that I should ever live without work or by merely looking at things! These fits of illness are all *accidents* (what an Accident is—God knows—not I) not in the least consequences of my general work: and I rather fancy the three of them are all I'm meant to have. They were all part of a piece, and, Ireland and *her* "Rest" has had much more to do with them than my English work. I'm a little shaky yet, and had much better look at square things than Round! I will write more legibly D.V. in a day or two.

Ever your loving
St. C.

Herne Hill
23d June [1882] [14]

My darling Lacy—

What's the use of having my photo when you never write me a word? Does Joanie say I'm not fit to be written to? or haven't you anything to say? or do you think my last little note nonsense and that I had better not write any more? Partly I am of that general mind myself, but I am doing crystallography just now, and some diamonds of Lacerta wit would brighten the study considerably. I was showing Froude the Rosie photo the other day, and he said it was more French than Irish. You know old Owen said she was "pure Circassian." I must not go and describe all my Irish saints from it at that rate, but there *is* a fair Irish real type, as well as a dark, isn't there?...Tell Flopsy I'm having music lessons and turning my master's hair grey (what is of it under his wig) and *he* vexes my poor little soul by taking all the points out of my compositions because they're consecutive fifths or some other such sinfulness.... You really must send me a little letter every now and then, while I'm here all alone. I never was so dull yet in all my life (and it's saying a good deal) but I've nothing now to look forward to except arranging the Sheffield Museum! For this year at any rate. Next year, if I live, I'll try to paint a Swiss village if there's one left. I wish you could get a glimpse of the goings on at Brantwood. Joannie seems so happy in them.

Ever your loving St. C.

Lucca
October 22, 1882 [15]

My dearest Lacy,

I've been carrying a letter of yours dated "Saturday" a good

14. In 1882, after his third illness, Ruskin spent June at Herne Hill. By now he was well enough to have addressed the Arundel Society on the evening of June 22.

15. Opening paragraph omitted by Young, in *The Letters of a Noble Woman*, and therefore also by Cook and Wedderburn (see *Works, 37,* 416–17).

while about with me. I hope it's of this year. I think you might write me word oftener that you weren't shot; and it's about time I should begin to send you the same news of myself, for I go walking among the woods here, and continually meet picturesque figures with long guns. They are content hitherto to wish me a pleasant evening and go their way. But I . . . am doing some good drawing, *so* good in fact that (having occasion to write to Oxford today), I sent word if they like to have me for Professor again for a while they might. I've been quite amazingly rational lately and believe I'm getting stout, after all! I'm writing today partly because I thought you'd like to know about Oxford, partly because I'm beginning to think of coming home. Joanie seems going on very well and perhaps by the time I get back there'll be room for me somewhere. But a line to...Pisa would still be safe, and after the end of this month to Annecy.

Brantwood
4th Feb[ruary], 1883

Darling Lacy:

There's more natural history in your little finger than in all my books. That summing up of elephants is inestimable, and for the metaphysics of aesthesis, the pins point holds them on it.

What a lovely bit of peacock sentiment that is; but I can't write a word today. Please *tell* me how long 'a few days' is at Chester. I wish you'd stay in Chester instead of going to [illegible]. (I once had the woefullest walk there I ever had in any town.) But you could go to watch seabirds for me on the Welsh coast, and come here every week to tell me about them. Not the Finch's but the Petrels . . . What *do* the wretched lands people mean by its walking or running on the water with its feet? Tell me if the pretty niche in Chester's Sacristy is still safe.

Ever your lovingest—St. C.

Herne Hill
19 March, 1883

Dearest Lacy

I'm so thankful to have you at a place I know, and care for and can fancy you at, and feel that you are within reach and will really get a letter out of the post, and I think even already there will be squills and the beginnings of primrose and other blessednesses about Montreux, and the mountains will be at their divinest, and all the streams. But more than all this I hope you will find out my poor little Alice Bennett who has lost her pet sister Florence only a fortnight since and will be so thankful for a little kindness and she's worth it, so meek and simple that she'll be like a little bird to you. I seem to be nearly quite well again and was able enough for anything I had to do in Oxford and there seems a great deal to be done there now for they are glad to have me back. Things are so changed and I'm changed not a little also, chiefly in having more sympathy with modern life not quasi-steam but in its activities and hopes for larger and more levelled multitudes. There are such numbers of nice people now if one looks for them, and assuredly some great reaction must take place against what is brutal and cruel in Socialism, and new codes of dealings with the poor.

Ever your lovingest St. C.

Herne Hill
4th June, 1883 [16]

Dearest Lacy

I've got everything in order for the feathers tomorrow, and I hope Grampus will have pleasure out of the order, and her own trouble and kindness. I have some pretty things to read which will remind *you* of old Italian days. I owe you infinite letters, for one of yours is worth infinity of mine. But I think you ought to get into the habit of writing whatever you would like to say to me, knowing that I listen and am grateful, even when utterly silent. I have had nothing to tell you lately but what would have made you anxious for me. Now after tomorrow I am through all my promised work and have only to correct the press of the two last [Oxford] lectures and you'll have them directly. And perhaps I might see you at Brantwood again this year and if I cannot, still you will care to know what I am doing abroad, and be perhaps—I do hope—a little proud of me and help me about birds and flowers which I shall expect you always to write half the chapters about now. And we may have some bits of autumn sunshine yet.

Ever your loving St. C.

16. On June 5, at the home of Mrs. Bishop ("The Feathers"), Ruskin lectured upon drawings of Francesca Alexander. The last two sentences of this letter have been published as the conclusion of a letter of June 22 (see *Works, 37,* 457).

Brantwood
30th June, 1883

Darling Lacy

PLEASE do come both. It would be so lovely to think of you being over at the Waterhead, just beyond the calm water. I never heard of such a lovely plan, and I've *SO* much to ask you about birds and things. That Jackdaw and the pinks are beyond delicious!!!!

Ever your lovingest St. C.

Brantwood
6th July, 1883

Darling Lacy

It's lovely for you to send those orders to Joanie for the 14th and indeed I shall like to have you forgotten & left behind & I'll keep you carefully until you're telegraphed for. But I don't quite see why the Master should go back to look after *his* hay. It's selfish. *We've* hay here to look at, and hood umbrellas over the cocks of, if that would do any good. How wonderful that awe of yours about deserted rooms. I feel it very distinctly, but nothing ever affects or disturbs me to the point of preventing simple action & my fear, as distinguished from awe, is only of really dangerous things in broad daylight.

The nearest thing to a tremor I've ever felt was in crossing a glacier once by myself after fresh snow; & I never sail here on squally days, but have been many a time alone at night in ghostly places, & saw in my delirium relly tebby things indeed without being fitened, though suddenly in one phase of it I found myself reduced to shameful cowardice: which you would never have been; but that's different from nervous imagination.

You've set me at my birdwork again with good heart.

Ever your loving — St. C.

Brantwood
2 Aug[ust], 1883

Darling Lacerta:

It is very wonderful to me that I can do all that for you, being so dead myself & full of all sorts of fear & sadness; but the things I care for are good, and the sympathy we can give each other in caring for them is indeed good for us both. I am so glad you were happy in that kind of way in looking over the Francesca drawings...Recollect my new name for the common pedicularis, Monacha Rosea, but I want an English one I can't say Rosy Aucbrile, or Eremite.

Dear love to the Master.

Ever your loving St. C.

Brantwood
3d Jan[uary], 1884
[Birthday of Rose]

Darling Lacy

I am so very happy that you like your books & like the old signature and like *me* and that you can send me the Master's love too. Many very lovely things happen to me always at the New Year now, and I have got some work done which will I believe be of more use than ever anything I've done yet, and I'm pretty well but I can't keep up with the pace of things. I hope to send you a chat when you've got out of the Babel and some more books and things. Dear love to the Master & I'm your both's loving old St C.

Herne Hill
2nd March, 1884

Sweetest, nicest, oppressedest Lacy (to have her Hazel taken away!)

I've been longing to answer that dicious letter ever since. Haven't had a moment. I suppose I ought to write to Flossie [Florence Bishop] herself, but I don't quite know how, because she's such an ineffable little duck (I *mean* gosling) to think that there could be any collision or displacement or effacement of Flossie by Lacy. She might as well accuse the North Star of extinguishing her. [end of page] I began on a single leaf by accident. Perhaps it will just do to send her that and say no more! But you may say further if you think well that all my *young* pets are being extinguished now as fast as I can manage it, only it's like sparks in tinder there are always some in the corner yet. But I find pets are incompatible with the authority and air of a philosopher and —Abbot, and with one's general peace of mind and conscience beside. I've got two coming to sing to me this afternoon but it couldn't be helped. Very seriously, I can't waste any more time at Brantwood flirting though I don't yet see my way out of it in London. Flossy doesn't care for the Interpreter's Hour a bit and I must vegetate as utterly as may be to make up for the rather heavy overwork which must it seems to me last through the spring. I've books on hand which I must carry on while the thoughts are yet with me. Francesca's especially needs extreme care and acute reflection. How I've scratched this, forgive and I'm ever your poor

Archigosaurus

Herne Hill
4th May, 1884

My darling Lacy

Joanie has just been reading to Arthur and me your lovely account of Punchayesima Sunday, etc. It's very bad for Arthur who immediately feels "westerly" but very useful to me who have been in a bad fit of putting up with things and hoping the best, lately, extremely weakening and demoralizing.

...I caught cold almost the day after I left [Claremont] and have been shut up since, but hope on Tuesday to get home and to start fair for the healthy summer as far as the plague wind will let me. I was so very glad to hear of that good clergyman's observing it but then wonder that other people don't. Here it is raging now with rain and mixed fog. I don't know what to make of anything, but seem myself at present to be able to give many people a good deal of pleasure, and Joanie never looks as if the plague wind had any hold of her or any manner of mischievous thing. I'm looking forward with great pleasure just now to a little bit of new experience in life, one of my best pets [the invalid Ada Dundas (see B.S.)] is going to be left in my charge while her mother goes to Ireland for a week or so. I'm very proud and I think the girl will be very happy and much the better for it. Her mother is to bring her and stay a day or two just to see she's all right. Later in the summer I've a French art critic [Ernest Chesneau] with his son coming to stay. The father is commissioned by me to write Turner's life and I mean to take him and the son if he's nice to Farnley and see the drawings there again myself. Later still I've two nice girls [probably Eva and Constance Layton] coming with their mother, a widow whom they support as well as themselves as music mistresses. I'm going to get them cheap lodgings in a farmhouse and they're to sing to me among the hills. (Now don't be jealous!) and I'm ever your old Arch-Saurus

Brantwood
14th June, 1884 [17]

Darling Lacerta—

...I'm writing twelve books at once—at least confusing myself in writing six between the lines. Proserpina is most in my head—a grammar of Silica chiefly in hand—Songs of Tuscany; a seventh Oxford Lecture—and the planning a life of Turner with a lively Frenchman—who talked all day long, here for three days, —20 letters a day at breakfast, all shrieking for instant reply, four artists to direct the work of, in Italy,—Oxford school to direct here, and an interesting young sculptor [Conrad Dressler] to chip into shape himself, as he was modelling me, have sufficiently filled what time I could give to work in the sunny days of May, while my lecture on Sir Herbert Edwardes begun carefully at Christmas and my two numbers of Our Fathers, lie helpless in a back drawer....Dear love to the Master and I'm always your poor old Saurian St. C.

Brantwood
1 May [18]85 [18]

Darling Lacy,

You have made me very happy this May day; but what a strangely simple childlike Lacy it is—with all its wit—to take what I wrote about those books au serieux like that, and be frightened at it! — I really never meant a word of blame, or a suspicion that you did not care for them. And I *did* take the silence all for my own fault, as it was: for I knew if I whistled, I could get a letter

17. In my record the following few words of summary replace transcription at the beginning of this letter: Joan, who had recently returned from London with the children, is really herself again.

18. Written in answer to Mrs. La Touche's letter of April 30, 1885, with its description of the races. For Ruskin's "whistle" letter of April 28, to which she was responding, see Whitehouse, *Scribner's Magazine, 62,* p. 747.

directly, but indeed I was ill and weary beyond [illegible] all Christmas time, and dared not add the least to the letters that were of consequence to me, but wrote and thought the least possible—with good results for I am fairly well again now, and very thankful for Lacy's turn of its head at a whistle.

How dear of you, again, and like a child, to think I meant you really to tell me of the races! I gave you that commission as the last you were likely to fulfill.

Grampus is being no end of good, too—and I'm like to be spoiled between you

Dear love to the Master

Ever your devoted and loving

St. C.

Herne Hill
May 15, 1885

Darling Lacy

Ive been writing to Grampus, so of course I must to you too—It's very pleasant, and I'm wasting my morning—thinking of pleasant things—instead of doing disagreeable ones, which they say one always should.

I never have, when I could help it, but don't feel disposed to recommend my example to others in my autobiography

I want to know how the Master is—and I want to know if you know what the story of St. Christopher means. The Master wouldn't allow it meant anything would he. I want to explain it a little on Francesca's telling of it, and I find I haven't the least idea what it means myself....[19]

Ever your loving St. C.

Brantwood
8 July, 1885

Sweetest Lacy

With deep thankfulness will I call her Wisie [doubtless Florence Rose Ward] and be her Di Pa. Come as soon as ever you can,—

19. In the conclusion (in my record merely summarized) Ruskin speaks of how "Lacerta" gives him constant help on *Proserpina* by making suggestions and reading proof, and he refers to sending her installments of *Praeterita,* in proof, as they come off the press.

the heath is going to be wonderful this year—and I want some looking after, for I have been tired and sad lately—chiefly because I have not been at books but on the hills in sunshine, feeling that my days for them are gone.

Ever your loving St. C.

Brantwood
8th March 1887

Dearest Lacy

It's a lovely day, and I wish you were here caressing the little green things that are coming up everywhere, and me a little too.

So you never got that horrid letter I wrote you. I wonder how it got stopped—or if I ever wrote it except in my head. I had such terrific Irishdreams at the beginning of this last illness—very beautiful and wonderful too. But I made sure I sent that letter.

Send me word how the Master is.

I heard that Ernest [Ward] was asking at Cirencester the other day how my wood-girl was getting on. I wonder how he knew about her.

Love to Rose [Ward], if she cares at all for it.

Ever your loving
St. C.

Sandgate
14th April [18]87

Darling Lacy

I am so thankful to find myself strong and cheerful in work again; and the part of the III vol. [of *Praeterita*] that I was at pause about, coming, I am sure now, rightly. Joan gleams about prettily in various places— φιλη only in the parallel numbers of Dilecta, beginning with "Ara Coeli"—which is parallel with Rosie's chief number, L'Esterelle which follows the one on my own "Mont Velan"

It will all come out, if I live, with whatever I have in me of the best, at least—a little expressed so that it may explain what I have done or tried to do, and writing it seems to lift the smoke from the hills and bring sunshine on the sea.

I am drawing a good deal for it, too, retouching and completing old Swiss work.

And we may do some Proserpina together yet! you & I, provided you resign yourself to pet my *minx* flowers if I choose.

Ever your lovingest St. C.

Love to the Master.

XXIX

Victor Marshall to Mrs. Severn

15, Cranley Gardens
[as of January 25, 1900]

Dearest Mrs. Severn

I send these little simple wild flowers because all the grand hot house flowers that I might have had do not seem to be *his* as these always have been.

God help dearest friend through today. I shall be *with* you, at the Abbey service—

Y[ou]r loving
VM

XXX

Correspondence with Lord and Lady Mount-Temple

Ruskin's letters to the Mount-Temples, in the F. J. Sharp Collection, were made available to John L. Bradley, for inclusion in his edition of *The Letters of John Ruskin to Lord and Lady Mount-Temple* (see, therein, Letters 3, 4, 12, 159, 168, 171, 174, 176, 200, 214). Not until after this book had been published did it become evident that the present whereabouts of the following letters remain unknown. While studying Ruskin manuscripts at Brantwood before the Sotheby sales, I transcribed them, unfortunately without pausing to proofread the copies which I have now added to the items collected by Mr. Sharp.]

1. *From Ruskin*

Morning of the last whole
day at Denmark Hill
[28] March [1872] [1]

Dearest Isola

No, I can't come to Broadlands I'm going to Araceli. Not that I care about Araceli now, nor anything else. The sense of ended life is so complete since that child [Rose La Touche] left me.

I'm very busy, for other people however—and fighting, and rather proud, which is pleasant. — I'm falling from bad to worse —in temper and character every day—indeed—which I sometimes think is a pity. Still—what I *do* is for the best, that I'm sure of. By the way, are *you*, receiver of angel's visits? — What *are* you doing—till midnight, when you write to your poor friends?

Tell Mr. Clifford that I'm quite sure any grown up angel, I can't answer for the absurd little unfledged ones, but any angel of that size, would object to being waited on by a page with his eyes turned up like a fish's.

Ever your affectionate
St. C.

[Oxford]
23rd evening [November 30, 1872] [2]

Dearest Isola—

All went well at the lecture. I had a long walk, over bare hills under the sunset afterwards where I have not been for thirty years.

I was thinking of writing a line of Political Economy to that child,—before five P.M. next Saturday—to explain to her that it is not intended that women should make men pay twelve years of their lives to have the last six made happy—if ever they count on a last six—but the usury is too heavy. I was lecturing on Albrecht Durer today. I am like him (in my weak way) in many

1. For the date, see *Diaries*, p. 721; for Edward Clifford's portrait of Mrs. Cowper-Temple, see *Works, 37*, Pl. II, facing p. 36.

2. On November 30, 1872, Ruskin delivered his lecture on "Design in the German Schools of Engraving" (see *Works, 22*, 390 ff.).

things. He died at fifty-seven of being teazed by the presence of his wife. I suppose I shall die at fifty-seven of the absence of mine. She *is* mine, however, now—isn't she—absent or present? That's always something—

Ever your loving St. C.

Brantwood
17th Feb[rua]ry, [18]73
Morning

My dearest φιλη

Thanks for the little note— write to me of anything that interests you—and don't be troubled for me any more— you have had trouble enough with us. My life here is good for me, and would have been too happy, I suppose, if—

As it is, I am not unhappy—only half dead—in the quite literal and true sense— But I'm glad to know exactly where I am, which I did not till I was alive again for that gleam. Do you recollect a long while ago, in the Academy meeting me when I had another gleam, and calling it "my resurrection face." By the way I don't like the Dudley Gallery picture— you are immensely nicer than that. —[3]

Brantwood
[October 1873] [4]

My darling φιλη

I'm so thankful you're still hearing from that child. Can't you get her to write to me again? She need never fear my having any more hope, either, in heaven or earth—but she might give me some peace— the very beauty of the heavens, and earth only torments me, now, not for want of courage, but because there is— the dead wild rose always in my sight instead of it. Now my sight, too, is getting dim, a little. But I've done some work—good and bad—in its kind, since I saw you. I'm coming south to Oxford on the eighteenth to give ten lectures twice over—on Val d'Arno, four days a week for five weeks, if I'm well enough—and I think

3. For the rest of this letter, see *Works, 37,* 62, and Bradley, *Letters,* p. 343.

4. Ruskin reached Oxford on October 21, 1873, to deliver his *Val d'Arno* lectures (see *Diaries,* p. 763)

they're coming rather nice. But if she won't write to me, won't I pitch into the Florentines for making their lilies red?

Ever your loving St. C.

Herne Hill
Dec[ember] 31 [1873][5]

My dearest φιλη

I called in Stanhope St. the other day—but you are never anywhere, what are you about down there. Just now I'm more beaten than I thought I should be, at the beginning of the New Year—the sense of the fearfulness of the battle with Python and Mammon is heavy on me. I had no notion of how horribly girls would be persecuted who believed in me. Two of my chief disciples are being tormented out of their little lives; I wish you would ask one of them [presumably Blanche Atkinson, now 26 years old] down to Broadlands for a couple of days— She's an entirely fine creature belonging to a vulgar set, and not in affectation or morbidness, but really like a linnet born among ducks' eggs she's entirely wretched; and her people peck and buffet her all day long— she has been pretty—once— but she is worn to death and faded away— She would not be troublesome to you except from extreme diffidence and terror of speaking to a great lady—but you would soon put her to rights. Of course I should be gone to Brantwood when you come to town. So if I don't see you till next New Year's day I'll write you from Araceli.

Ever with love to William
Your loving St. C.

Christ Church College
22nd Jan[uary 1874?][6]

My dearest Isola

I much doubt if you would think it an escape if you knew more

5. At the end of December 1873 Ruskin was at Herne Hill (see *Works, 37,* 77); he returned to Brantwood on February 23, 1874, and on March 30 went to the Continent for seven months of work.

6. Since there is no evidence that between the years 1870–76 Ruskin was in Oxford on January 22, this letter was probably written at Herne Hill on Corpus Christi stationery. The year 1874 is suggested by Ruskin's references to Rose, who —ominously ill—had come to London to escape her parents by staying with her maid at the Palace Hotel.

of my mind and its present course of fall and cowardice and helplessness. I am not sure how long it will stand under its present laws of work; for myself I believe *any* form of distress associated with the distinct and personal care of a creature I loved would have been better than this mechanical life, of which the horror is deepened by the daily increasing sense of the uselessness of what is remaining of good in it. My own belief is that a distinct form of insanity connected with her bodily health is on that child. But when I think of this as the end of a life spent in prayer and seeking to know God, according to her light—and as the result of a foolish father's care, and a wicked mother's cruelty, and a true lover's love—the World problem is not in the least made clearer or kinder to me. When you have any rather prosy people at Broadlands and don't mind having one more at the table, I wish you would write a line to this poor and faithful (for the present) girl or middle aged woman, whom I told you of—saying that you want to talk to her of the Queen of the May plan and that she is to come down to Broadlands—for two days— she has some eight or ten thousand pounds to will (or give it may be) and I've given her a plan about appointing three Queens of May —between seventeen and twenty-one—every year to have the dispensation of the charity. That's all you need to know—you'll hear the rest from her, pleasantly for you both and for William— for you'll like this girl for being a true disciple—

of your poor lonely St. C.

Brantwood
22 Aug[ust 1875?] [7]

My dear Mama

It is very nice to get letters from home, and such pretty ones, and I am going to practise my writing very carefully, that you may be able to read my letters very easily, because I should like to write home very often.

Dear Mama, I will try to learn back some of my french and Italian, to please you. — Indeed, I do sometimes read a little of

7. Mrs. Cowper-Temple (who became Lady Mount-Temple in 1880) seems to have adopted Ruskin as her "little boy" during August 1875 (see Bradley, *Letters*, p. 360).

that French which—the people used to write before they *were* French, you know, mama—only I don't know what they were and surely you would say it was very wrong to spell—que, ke,— How funny those two words look together—mama— Just like qu-ack. Do you mean me to know all that the ducks and geese say, mama, as well as the other birds—or do you only mean, birds that sing, and all the bad birds croak and scream,—and that God never makes the bad birds any better? Why doesn't he, Mama? Oh dear, I remember I ought to have spelled him—He, I mean with a capital h, only I hope God won't mind. You wouldn't mind, mama, not being spelled with a capital m, and I don't know, now, whether spelled should be spelled or spelt, and now I want to go and do some lessons before breakfast—and I'm your poor—puzzled—affectionate little boy, J.R.

and *little* St. C.

Herne Hill
4 Dec[ember 1875] [8]

Dearest Grannie—

(I'll try to come down and keep my day) What an insufficient thing one's life is. And mine scarcely *is* life just now, the darkness [illegible] me. But I got well through my lessons at Oxford people say, and I shall be so glad of my holidays.

Much love to papa and Juliet [her adopted child] and also Miss Munro ["Annie," Juliet's nurse].

And I'm ever your poor little John Ruskin

Rosie's birthday
[January 3, 1876] [9]

Dearest Isola—

Are you better—and where are you—and where is She? I said I would not ask, neither will I, on any day but this—nor any

8. In 1875 Ruskin had reached Herne Hill on November 30 after having delivered twelve lectures, at Oxford, on the *Discourses* of Reynolds (see *Works, 22,* 492), and on December 10 he began to enjoy his "holidays" at Broadlands.

9. Rose La Touche had died on May 26, 1875. Ruskin spent January 5–12 in Peppering (see *Diaries,* p. 880). At Broadlands, on December 14, 1875, he had received "overwhelming evidence" of personal immortality (see *Diaries,* p. 876).

one else than you— I would wish you a happy New Year—but what are years to you—or me, if things are true.

Love to φιηος

Ever your loving St. C.

Write ℅ F. Dawtrey Drewitt Esq., Peppering, Arundel

Herne Hill
20th Jan[uary 1876] [10]

Dearest Grannie—

My lessons are very hard just now, and I don't like them at all; and I can't get my holidays, and I'm not neglecting my darling Grannie, but thinking of her every day; —that's not the same thing as writing though; but that's what my Grannie used to do for her little boy. But it's very terrible here. I can't get home [to Broadlands] just now; the people here in—London want me, and I must go to Oxford next week— How long does Grannie stay at Broadlands? —perhaps I could come the week after next? I got two such lovely photographs from auntie at Brighton last night you know I said I wouldn't ask questions—but I can't understand why nobody tells me anything.

Ever with dear love to Papa—
Your loving little boy—St. C.

Brantwood
20th February 1878 [11]

Darling Isola—

I couldn't understand, till last night—why I had put the "beautiful Island" in my Oxford school series in the cabinet illustrating the "Sentiment of Landscape." Now wasn't it odd that *I* didn't think of *that*. And wasn't it odd *you* didn't think—who came into the room? — Well look here—the last message but one I got, last night—was "They of Italy salute you." Nero—you just write to that little Duchess, and tell her, she's to pick up sticks in Italy—for *Pollys* put the kettle on and we'll have tea.

Pollys a vulgar word—very—but Duchesses picking up sticks

10. In 1876 Ruskin was in Broadlands on January 30, and in Oxford on February 4 (see *Diaries,* p. 883); in the Diary entry for December 20, 1876, see also the reference to his having received two photographs.

11. This letter contains remarks which also were made in Ruskin's Diary entry for February 20, 1878.

must learn low English. And look here. Ask that little beauty from Cheshire if she remembers my nearly "boiling over" at *Breakfast*. And see Punch for boiling over generally, and Goodbye for 'today.'

Ever your lovingest St. C.

Now here's a little postscript for yourself if—φιλος won't be jealous. He was once, wasn't he when he stopped me from using *his* pet name Well—I won't venture to take quite the end—but I will—in this beginning of things—venture *for once* on the Beginning— "Georgia"—do you recollect giving me a kiss over Juliet's head as you were nursing *her?* — May I have another today?— You can just put a little cross where it is, in your next letter.

Brantwood
12th May [1878]

Darling Grannie—

I am able at last to write you because I really can tell you, I'm going to be a good little boy and have holidays all the year round—as all good little boys ought. (I told them so, in my last lecture at Eton—and that only old gentlemen should go to school) So I'm amusing myself with my flowers, and apple blossoms (and such an old crab-apple as I've got—you never did see:—) It's just like me, really and truly—but I can't tell you why today, for I mustn't go on talking of myself. Else—I should have to tell you of sad things in that illness—a very wonderful and terrible one—much more so than the Doctors knew. But *you* know, I never had much favour for THEM. If I had had my senses, I should have called for my beautiful Nurse again [she herself had nursed him at Matlock, in 1871]— But as it was—I had nurses I didn't like—of my own imagining, and they wouldn't let me have even my own poor Joanie! who had a rather awful time of it! poor sweet— I really don't think I shall—be naughty more nor have naughty illnesses—as long as I live. I'm not going to eat any cake, Grannie—nor read any more nasty books, nor write them, except just a little Proserpina and so on— And you won't send me to school again— Please Grannie? and I'll be your obedient little boy all the year round— I don't quite know if I'm St. C.—still— I was ashamed of myself and grieved R[ose] so, you *can't think!* and I mustn't yet awhile. So I'm only your poor little boy. Dear love and thanks to G. — Always —

[signature not transcribed]

Brantwood
Wednesday 23d March [1881]

My dearest Isola—

I have just read your last Thursday's letter to Joan. I am all right again—in the head—very dark yet in the heart, and passing through an experience of which I imagine you and φιλος know more than any one else can. The issue of the matter is that I must be much alone this summer, and am gradually breaking to Joan the necessity of my being so. There are on *her* side, partly real, partly imaginary difficulties, in many kinds—but as soon as I *am* alone—I shall pray φιλος and you to come and stay two or three days with me. *You* probably can get news of me of most authentic nature without letters from anyone here. If not, wait quietly till *I* write again.

Dear love to φιλος—

Ever your loving St. C.

[Herne Hill]
5th March [1882]

Darling φιλη

Please come and look after me here tomorrow or any day, as soon as you can. I'm afraid I'm going off the rails again—and it looks to me more like a terminus than the other two times. Joan's not well, neither, and we all together want a good look and word in season.

Ever your loving St. C.

I've been working hard on Ara Coeli and find the first Popes people whom one would gladly climb the steps after. Also I've been very wildly forgetting Ara Coeli and everything and perhaps am only getting another flogging—but this is a very nasty one. Love to φιλος—

P.S. Monday

I am better—and have no good time to spare you *today,* but

please answer this fixing your own time, to come, tomorrow, or Wednesday— no telegrams to be sent, or asked for.

[Herne Hill]
21st May [1882]

Dearest Isola—

I haven't been able to stir this week—except for business—or some sad inquiries for sick friends. Are you still going to stay in town? And please would you be so very good as to tell me how one addresses Italian Princes. I've got suddenly to my great surprise and discomfiture—mixed with complacency—of course—into quite an affectionate correspondence with the old Prince—of Mantua and Montferret, and don't know what to say in beginning my letters.[12] Love to William.

I'm keeping pretty well and doing some crystal work—which has got put off and off ever since that lecture.

I've got a new photograph for my nursery.

Will you come and see it some day?

Ever your loving St. C.

Brantwood
27th January [1886][13]

Darling Grannie,

It's too bad of you going and having big parties and weddings and Princes of Waleses, and neglecting your poor little boy. I haven't had a word this—year—and I'm getting so naughty and spiteful—and Mary Gladstone's gone and got herself married—and Joan's got a cold and I'm *so* lonely. Your *very* poor little boy.

2. *To Ruskin*

Broadlands
Friday [1875?][14]

Dearest St. C.

I could never tell you how deeply touched I am—& today I have only time for this line.

12. For a letter of April 2, 1882, to the Prince of Mantua, see *Works, 34,* 561.

13. Five days hence, Mary Gladstone married Harry Drew.

14. Probably written before August 1875—the year 1875 having been penciled upon the MS.

I can hardly believe that you are going to do me this favour—& that you really care for me so much!

Never doubt that I can be other than yours most gratefully and lovingly, φ

[Broadlands]
Oct[ober] 4, [1875][15]

My dear John—

I gratefully sign & ratify your projected treaty of alliance defensive but not offensive— We are each to move in our own orbit of work & occupation & to collide into juxtaposition only when our circles touch naturally & without constraint— But we agree always to be in sympathy though not always in society & it will be a great delight & advantage to me to have as much of your company as you can give me without interfering in any degree with the work of your mission in life—

I'm starting for Portsmouth & leave Isola to add all that is necessary to say before you arrive on Wed[nesda]y.

Ever y[ou]rs aff[ectionatel]y
W. C. Temple

Broadlands
Monday [October 4, 1875][16]

My dear little boy,

I am very glad you are coming on Wednesday— You will find poor Mama very sad and poorly—but I know you will be very good & quiet and you may be a great comfort to her.

I am so glad you mean to go to bed early.

Mama breakfasts always in her own room—as she is tired of a morning—& you can either have yours in your day nursery—or with the other children at 8-30 downstairs—

You will dine with me when we lunch at 2—& have tea at 5-30—& some supper in the nursery before going to bed—

15. On October 6, 1875, writing to C. N. Norton from Broadlands as his "new home," Ruskin said: "The Temples have given me a room here for my own, and leave me to stay in it in the evenings instead of coming down to their late dinner—" (*Works, 37,* 181). He was their guest from October 6–25 (see *Diaries,* pp. 864–67).

16. For Ruskin's response of October 5, 1875, see Bradley, *Letters,* p. 36.

— I shall allow you full liberty at home—as I think it is good for boys to find their own occupations & amusements, and as Papa & I are both always very busy we shall not expect you to be a great deal with us—tho' I trust we shall have some good times together Let me know my dear child by what train you come—and we will send a carriage for you.

Your loving
Mama

Broadlands
Wed[nesda]y [October 27? 1875] [17]

My dear St. C.

Your letter went to our hearts— We are so thankful to have been allowed to cheer you a little bit—and to us it was an *immense* treat to have you here—

Wicked unbelieving St. C. to have doubted us before! — If you are ever so wanting in faith again you shall be put in the lowest Inferno—but I think you will rise to Paradise—& be *"Pyramidal"*—

Yes, we truly *love* (not *like*) you & we want you—& expect you to be very kind to us! — It will indeed be so to come to Curzon St.—& you will come back here I hope whenever we are here, & you are inclined to have country air & be kind to us—

[Illegible]—this evening—for we go up tomorrow—& I am in an uncomfortable skurry.

Ever y[ou]r affect[tionate]
φ.

9 Cheyne Walk
Tuesday, Aug[ust] 13, [18]89 [18]

Dearest St. C

I should like to do anything to please you, and I sympathize very much in your admiration for Mr. Froude— I must tell you

17. Probably an answer to the letter which Ruskin (having returned to Herne Hill on *Monday*) presumably wrote after his Broadlands visit of October 6–25, 1875.

18. This deeply black-bordered letter (William Francis, Baron Mount-Temple having died in 1888) is in an envelope postmarked "Au[gust] 13 [18]89."

how much I enjoyed your last Praeterita with the lovely sketch of your dear Joan— It seems to me as perfect as anything you have ever written!

I am just leaving Town for a few days. Do write to me again.

Ever your loving

φιλη

Babbacombecliff,
Torquay
[1890s] [19]

His Grannie loves him more & more—

Babbacombecliff,
Torquay
Tuesday, Feb[ruar]y 7, 1899

One line to express his Grannie's fond & hearty wish for her dear little boy that tomorrow may be the happiest of all his birthdays & that all succeeding ones may go on crescendo to eternity's end now he has called out the love & veneration of all his Earth mates

[To Mrs. Severn]

[No address]
January 21, 1900

I have just received the tidings of my beloved friend's transfiguration. Loved from my earliest days and to be mourned till my latest. The world will always be the darker without him, and, oh, how I feel for you, his sister, his friend, his child.

XXXI

Constance Oldham to Ruskin

[The following letters from "Connie" to her "G.P." (God Papa) have been selected from the 40 which are included in the F. J. Sharp Collection. Most of these letters were written during the first half of 1888, many of them having been specifically dated in manuscript. One by one, as of 1888, they were prompted by the desire of Ruskin's "G.D." to send him a daily message while

19. This message was written on a small black-bordered card in penciled script, which indicates that it was written during the 1890s.

he was living alone at Sandgate, futilely hoping thus to be able to escape another relapse into insanity.]

Walpole
Chistlehurst
[1886 / 87?] [1]

My G.P.

Oh, but I *was* glad to get a G.P. letter this morning, for breakfast! Thank you, G.P.—

And it's like my G.P. to think the letters get nicer, when I've nothing but such dull little bits of every day things to tell him that I'm always afraid he'll be bored.

And mother is writing to you about the [hand-knitted] *Sox!* and you're not to think of them EVER [underscored by four lines in the shape of a pyramid] again. I think she'd be a funny sort of mother if she wanted you to wear things that weren't comfortable, —to please her! And I think my G.P. had better send them back, and we'll find someone else they'll be useful to; or else I know every time my G.P. goes to the drawer he'll have a fit of compunction.

That's cos oo's *So* Toopid, oo know.

— G.P.,—does you know? I *used* to write good grammar *till* I wrote so much to you, and now I never can! THERE,—oo demoralizing G.P. Did you *ever* hear such a Saucy accusation, before?

Do you know, I'm so puzzled by what to do! A long while ago, now, some one told me of some poor Italian exile, who was teaching some English girls Italian; and they got tired of the exercises; and one day, for pleasure, merely, brought him a translation of part of the Songs of Tuscany; and directly he read it, he burst into tears, exclaiming 'Ah, but these *are* my people!'—and wanted to know where they had found it; and made them translate every word of it to him, listening often in tears. I told Miss Alexander about it; and she sent me a copy of 'Ida' in Italian, to send him; —but I don't know who he is, and I am *so* sorry. Perhaps I shall be able to find out. I have written to the friend who I think told

1. Conjecturally dated in view of Ruskin's having edited Francesca Alexander's *Story of Ida* in 1883 and her *Roadside Songs of Tuscany* during 1884–85.

me the story, and I hope she will know, but she did not know him, herself. For it would give him such happiness, it would be too sad to miss it.

— I was thinking afterwards, how stupid it was to speak of having you & Switzerland *together,* in those drawings. — For, in essence, one could never know you,—either of you,—apart. — And if you *knew* the blessing of your Swiss drawings,—loans, and gifts—to your G.D.—you'd be a little glad.

Me *loves* oo, and me's oo's own

G.D.

Saturday
[November? 1887][2]

My own G.P.

I *began* writing to you a long while ago, and then I didn't write you a nice letter, so I tore it up! Isn't that a shame? Now you'll want to know what was in it, and I won't tell you!

But I've such a lot of things to tell you, without, and to answer in your letter, that I don't know where to begin. The lovely Praeterita was here, & the Christ's Folk: precious, beyond saying, to your G.D.; and more especially, that you ordered these for me.—What *lovely* friendships you have had, G.P.! —you *have,* my G.P. —for they've only begun, yet, have they? — Dr. John Brown the most pathetic of all. His never seemed a nature that could have *borne* this world at all: perhaps not even for as long as he did, but for you. Oh, G.P., if your friends have been some comfort to you, WHAT have you been to them? And then there's the *lovely* Joan bit—which went to my heart,—it is,—if I may say so,—so *true.* I have not seen her for some time, now, to my sorrow; —but when last she was here, the light of her face seemed to show, not so much what she has been through, as *how* she had been through it; and often & often, the look of her eyes comes before me, and I know she will fail neither you—nor herself.

Yes, Praeterita is full of pain to you, I know. If we could but *save* you the pain— Sometimes I wish—you will not misunderstand your G.D.? —you had never begun it—for it seems to me

2. Conjecturally dated by the references to the content of *Praeterita II,* chapter 2, issued on November 8, 1887.

it must be more trying to you as you go on. — But perhaps there is more happiness to you, too, in it,—in parts of it, at any rate, that your G.P. knows: who is apt to feel the pain of anything that hurts her G.P. so much that it is difficult to think of the other side. And it has certainly *given* pleasure and help to hundreds, and *you* will care for that most. The Christ's Folk is lovely, as always; but I have not read that *thoroughly* yet, I have been so busy; I am looking forward to it tomorrow. And at the beginning of the week, I hope to be able to begin to index your letters. I do enjoy doing that; for the letters' sake: and to feel of a *little* use to my G.P.

Yes, I thought you would be interested about the music. It is really very good. Have you written to Townsend, I wonder? SHAN'T I be cross if he doesn't send me the letter! Though I *have* one or two of my own! on *music,*—and sunsets, too.

And *how* kind of you to take all that trouble about St. Christopher. It will be the greatest treasure in the house.

There, they've come for the letters! and I've only time to tell you, I've been thinking & thinking, since the cold came, if there was *nothing* G.D. could make or find for her G.P. to keep him warm,—(*out*side—*in*side, I think he must be, with such shield of love to send him) and this morning, G.D. saw these gloves, and thought *they* would be just right! G.D's worn a pair like them for five years: and they're *delicious:* so warm, and *leaving you the free use of your fingers.* So G.D. sends them, for Sunday greeting: and Lily sends her love: & Lang, too, (and its worth having!) and so *would* mother, only she doesn't know I'm writing. And

I'm your lovingest

G.D.

[January 1888] [3]

[first page missing]

that, myself; and I wanted you to *want* me to have it! But *this* [Bible] is a far deeper treasure to me, really. — I don't think you *could* have given me anything I should care for so much,—too

3. Dated through references to the chromolithograph of *St. Jerome in His Study,* published by the Arundel Society in December 1887 (see *Works, 24,* lvi), and to the letter written to Kathleen Olander (see *The Gulf of Years,* ed. Unwin, p. 24).

much to be able to *say* any more about it. But I'm *so glad* my G.P. knows.

And oh, G.P. the drawings! HOW you do spoil me! You don't know a BIT how I *love* your drawings; not a bit for YOUR (!) sake, except by the way, and because I know what my G.P. was happy in;—but for their own, and much more, for the Divine nature they teach me to see. My G.P. always manages to draw things *before the Fall.*

— I've had such a lot of lovely things come to me lately! What do you think mother gave me on New Year's Day? The new Arundel, which we, having been busy, had let lie by, unopened; and did not know what it was; and it *was,*—Carpacchio's St. Jerome in his *Study,* the Arundel calls it—in Heaven, my G.P.— Only I don't think in Heaven he'd be all alone. At least I hope not,—but yet, to me, infinitely more beautiful in that light.

And I was *so* happy in it, that Mother gave it me! Aren't I spoilt? —and as to the doggie—Mother says she can't imagine how any one drew that, who did not know my Cuddie—it is so EXACTLY his expression—of *back,* as well as head! And if anyone had *spoken* to him, when he was eager like that, he'd have flung a little sharp bark over his shoulder *at* them for interrupting, and been 'Attention' again, in a moment.

But *how* lovely, Mr. Anderson's thought, that we know no more of the Divine Love, than the doggie of St. Jerome. So of course Carpacchio had to put in the dearest doggie he could find.

Here's lunch, and I've written all this, and almost forgot to tell my G.P. I wrote to Kathleen [Olander] yesterday (such a duck of a letter!!) to ask her if she would come down tomorrow or Saturday, but of course I have not heard yet. Think of forgetting that! Well, it's all *your* fault, G.P. When oo write me letters like today's, and send me things like these: how *can* one think of Kathleens, or any body else's—except one's G.P.?

Me's oo's lovingest, *gratefullest,*

G.D.

Has my G.P. any *pens?* [4]

4. She sometimes gave him points to place in the holder of his Sir Walter Scott pen.

Walpole
Chislehurst
19. Jan[uar]y. [18]88 [5]

My own G.P.

Such a lovely idea has struck me: I *must* tell you! You were saying you liked and had been looking out for, the Doggie bits in my letters; and then I remembered I had never told you much, if anything, of our Family of Seven dear Doggies, whom we used to have all at once. And of course they were as individual as possible, and each had his own little ways and character; and if you *like,* I'll begin now, and tell you something about each! *Would* you like?

I should *like,* if it didn't bother you, to send you a photo. we had taken of all the seven together, just for you to know whom we are talking about: for it was only a rough one, and didn't do any of the dear things justice.

I've been puzzling which to begin with; but I think I'll tell you what the family consisted of, first. They were of all sizes & kinds. First, was Juno, whom you knew. Lang bought her at Oxford when she was a week or two old; and afterwards, when she was still too young to swim, jumped into the river after her, she having slipt off a raft into the water. Next came Punchie: a big, thick, brindled fright of a faithful bull terrier, with a face like a dissenting minister's: also Lang's—(*not* the dissenting minister's face!—); then Pepper, *politely* called a Dandie; then Gy-p, a foolish, morbid, sentimental Skye; then 'Fat Fan,' a delicious little black and tan, pure bred, and *fully* conscious of the fact; then, the love of my heart, Tiny-wee, a little person who didn't belong to us at all, but made up his little mind he would like to live with us, and came and sat persistently on our doorstep in Brighton till we took him in:—a 'Squire of some degree' he was, half Skye, half rough Scotch, terrier; — he never stopped dancing & laughing all his little life, nor shaking his pretty tasseled ears; —then, Lorloo, or Dollie, a Maltese Lion Spaniel, who weighed five pounds and a half;—and rushed furiously at the cows when they put their heads over the garden fence.

5. This is the first of at least two letters originally placed in an envelope which Ruskin inscribed: "Connie on Doggies." In a letter dated "26 January, 1888," she continued the present account.

That was our family; and except Dollie, we used to take them all out for walks together.

Next time, I'll tell you about Dollie, who had wits and heart enough for Juno: but today I will finish with telling you of a little doggie who belonged to our gardener, and lived at the lodge, after the Seven had gone to the Happy Hunting Fields, alas. He couldn't get as many walks as he liked, so he used to watch for me as I went out at the gate; and then dance up to me and ask leave to go for a walk. Of course I was very glad of his companionship; but all the way, though he followed perfectly, he always kept at a distance, with an air of 'I'm not going to be supposed to *belong* to YOU!' If I turned a corner and called him, he pretended not to hear, but trotted after me as soon as he considered he had asserted his independence. When we got back to the lodge, he used to dance up to me, jump up against me, and say as plainly as possible, 'Thank you for my walk:' and then trot into the lodge. The lodge garden was at the top of bank above & behind the house; so by it, he used to climb on to the roof of the outhouse, and sit there to watch down the road till his master came home in the evening.

He was a very nice little dog.

There, G.P.—that's enough for today. But I *could* tell you such lots of doggie stories, if you like!

Tell me if you *would* like to see the photo,—or the other things;—or to have the stories; and me's oo's lovingest, Looking-forward-to-*your*-Doggi*est*

G.D.!

Walpole
Chislehurst
7. February. 1888.

My own G.P.

I don't think any G.P. *can* want a letter from his G.D. for his birthday: because he knows it is one of the wonderfullest, blessedest days of the year to her, without telling.

And she can't wish better things, nor those more earnestly, that day, than every day; because *every* day begins a new year, of love, and trust, and thankfulness, and prayer, in, and for, her G.P..

Only perhaps on birthdays like tomorrow, the thankfulness is deepest—

— And I am so very, very thankful you have Joan with you. — My G.P. wanted her,—and I trust you will hear all the big things,—and all the *little* ones,—you care for most, at this opening, please God, of new years of blessing and mercy.

My G.P., I know tomorrow will try you a little: and I can't *bear* that,—or anything—to hurt you— But my G.P. *knows*—and you will tell him that, too,—that he is more & more precious to us with every year of life; —and you know, he can't judge of that, one bit, for himself! We know LOTS better than he does, there.

— And if there *has* been pain, my G.P., the one thing we *could* not have borne, would have been, not each to have our share; and my G.P. mustn't grudge,—nor even fear,—for us,—what we treasure so,—must he? — And tomorrow, that we had once hardly hoped for, seems now so full of hope and mercy, straight from God. — We *will* be happy in it—together,—won't we?

— And G.P. will have such lots of people with him! — Joan, that he knows of,—and G.D., that he doesn't, and the Sorella [Francesca Alexander], and lots more. I don't believe he'll be alone one minute! — And he'll have to tell his G.D. afterwards if he got nice letters—and love *her* a little bit, too—

His lovingest

G.D.

Mother sends her dearest love & wishes to you for all good.

Walpole
Chislehurst
23. Feb[ruar]y. [18]88.

My own G.P.,

You *would* be jealous of my Pollie if you could see her, now!

First of all she insisted on my letting her out, when I didn't want her, because I wanted to write to you! and then, on sitting on my desk; and these are her beak marks on my paper, where she ran off with it! I am only able to write now with one hand; the other she has cuddled into,—oh dear, she got out at that minute, and walked over the letter, and now she is sitting, toes together, and feathers up, staring, like Athene's owl! Oh dear, here's her head on the paper now! and she's so jealous of the pen! — I should have given her to my G.P. LONG ago, (though she *was* given to me!) she's such a duck, only I think she'd bother you too, and sometimes whistle & talk too loud. — She keeps making little sort of *whines* if I don't talk to her, and rubbing up against my hand. — She's gone off to sit on a chair at last! — My G.P. I *would* like you to have her so very much! but you know you wouldn't like her to walk about over your books and papers; and cluck like a hen, or yelp like a dog, just at the pretty ending sentence of Praeterita? And she wouldn't be happy, nor show you her pretty ways, if you *didn't* let her out, and pet her no end. I *wish* you had a doggie, for *he*'d put himself out of the way when you wanted; and be a little friend all the while. I am very interested to find out how far a pollie can be trained to do as it is told; and how far it is capable of a doggie's unselfish sympathy. Not much, I fancy.

Pollie quite knows if I tell her *not* to do a thing, and is fairly obedient. She was tearing a paper just now, so I said 'Pollie'!, solemnly. 'Well, what are you doing?' *she* said, at once!

Did I ever tell you about the chickens that were so jealous of my hat? I had a little brood I had made great pets of, and directly I went into the yard they all came running & flying up. Then someone gave me one of the hats then worn, made of a pheasant skin, with the head in front. One day I went into the yard with this on. Up came the little Houdans as usual; but I had forgotten the hat, and couldn't think what excited them so. They walked round me, on tiptoe, craning their necks, and staring; and presently they began to half climb, half fly, up me; till two reached my shoulders, and then they flew at the pheasant's head, pecking it furiously. They couldn't keep their balance, poor little pets, and slipped off, so I don't know if they would have found out it wasn't a real bird.

Wasn't it pretty of them?

— I left Pollie in possession of the town, there, & when I came back she had torn up three cheques, and made a hole in my pocket book! So I scolded her, and gave her a little flap with the cheque book: at which she gave a human laugh!! But she is now sitting, looking very penitent, on the edge of my desk.

— I'm so very glad you got the plates safely [a gift which Connie had arranged to have sent by a former landlady in Switzerland]: and so *very, very* glad my own G.P. likes them so. — And the honey, too. It *does* make G.D. happy when you like any thing she gives you—

But oo, Horrid, naughty, Teaze of a G.P. to tell me that, & not send me Kathleen's letter to see! *Me* won't write *oo ANY* nice letters, if oo's so naughty! oo may do on Kathleen's!

Now *me*'ll plague OO. —*Lily* says—oo don't know oo's G.D. *one bit! There!* Me wonders what she'd say if she knew oo meant to get a Polly to study her by! — Me can't think of any thing else horrid to say, so me thinks me'd better stop! But *OH,* what a Love of a letter oo'll have to write oo's G.D. next time.—IF [underlined four times] oo want her to ove oo any more!

———

I'm glad that was a *man's* letter. It puzzled me, because of the Cordelia; but it was a man's *letter*—and nicer, so.

Oh dear, here's Pollie again!

Me's oo's—
Pollie-ridden—
G.D.

Me does *OVE* oo's letters!

Walpole
Chislehurst
28. Feb[ruar]y. [18]88

My own G.P.,

Oo's G.D. was *quite* penitent for teazing her G.P. long ago; and *would* have written quite meek yesterday, only she was in town shopping, and couldn't. (I went to choose some curtains, and didn't like the great bunches of flowers they showed me. So I asked if they hadn't any artistic patterns. To which the man replied, 'Oh no, Miss; *Art* has quite gone out, and *Flowers* have come in!')—

My G.P., it wasn't *worth* teazing you about! It was only that oo's G.D. has a bad habit of never speaking of anything that hurts her—or that she much cares about, even;—and sometimes that makes one lead a *double* life, so to speak;—especially, perhaps, in letters. And one day, when we were talking of sundry *old,* & *past,* worries that I had never told you,—chiefly because I wouldn't give my G.P. a pin's weight more bother, for all the world,—Lily made that naughty speech. — But I don't think even Lily knows quite what the perfect trust of Silence is; and that even though I'm sometimes sorry, myself, there's *any*thing you don't know, it really matters very little whether G.P. knows things that come into his G.D's life, or not, while there is not a thought that came from them that G.D. would ever *wish* to keep from him. I don't *know* what it feels like, to *want* to keep anything from you: but well enough, the longing that you should know me better than I do myself, and put me right when I'm wrong. — That was all, my G.P. —

I meant to have told my G.P. a lot of other things that we'd both care about, today;—but there isn't time—only one thing I must tell you, a thought of the Bishop of [Turin?], I saw quoted. "Christ says, 'Take my yoke upon you.' You remember the figure, the *double* yoke, for the two oxen. Jesus puts Himself in the place of one, prepared to go patiently by our side up the great field of the world, and there is the other place vacant— 'My yoke,' He says."

Your lovingest
G.D.

Walpole
Chislehurst
14. May. [18]88.

Oh, my G.P. — I don't know a bit *what* to do! If I write to my G.P., I think, 'Perhaps he wants to be without letters,'—and if I *don't,* I think, 'Perhaps he had an empty breakfast plate today,' —and it seems wrong, *both* ways,—and G.D. is *so* puzzled what to do! — And I didn't mean to write to you today a bit, only I'm so cross I thought I would! — It's such a good reason, that, for writing to one's G.P., isn't it? — But I've been printing [i.e. typing] the Rosie letters;—and I *hate* the look of the print, and I don't know what *you*'ll do! So now I've put them away, disappointed; and thought I would grumble a little to you, instead.

Because writing may be faithful,—or real print, perfect;—but *type*writing is neither! — Please be a little cross, too, G.P. —

— What shall I tell my G.P. today? About the thrushes' nest, close to the library window, too high to see *into;* but in which one can *feel* soft, warm, fluffy things? — or the other family of somewhat older baby thrushes, whom one meets out for walks, with Papa and Mamma, to keep them in order?

— I think my G.P. *would* be pleased to know what a lot of people recognized him in Church, and were *so* pleased to have him there. And other peoples who weren't there that day, and can't get over the loss,—one, who came on Saturday to beg I'd *promise* to tell her next time. She'd just been reading the Ethics, and been so happy in it,—and to think she'd missed *seeing* you! So my G.P. gave happiness to others than only his G.D.

I'll be very thankful when my G.P. can rightly write to me again, without tiring himself, but not *till* then, for I mind the silence most because I know a little what it means of suffering to you—

Only you won't think any more, if *you* want to write, that it *saves me* not to hear, will you? For indeed, *that* thought hurts me most of all.

Your lovingest
G.D.

Walpole
Chislehurst
22. May. [18]88.

My G.P.

Here's just a tiny little word for my G.P.; but you know nobody *could* have anything nice to say such a horrid day. — We'd a lovely sky all yesterday, with grand gathering thunderclouds; and then in the morning they massed together into leaden gray, in the east; the low sun shining on all the fresh spring green of the trees *against* them, and forming a scarcely defined, evanescent rainbow across the darkness: *so* beautiful.

So today the sky's tired; and is as sulky and dull as it can be;— dirty, formless, grey all over—(don't you think gr*a*y is a colour—

grey—is—Smoke?); and all the pretty leaves and Flowers look sad and disappointed; and Molly is asleep, and Inee, too; and nobody is awake but two starlings on the lawn:—and apparently, as many worms!

It's not often there's nice news in the paper, but there really *is,* today. I wonder if you saw it? About the oil-fuel? — They say they have now discovered how to use steam from oil for steamers and trains: and that it makes no *smoke,* and of course, no black dust; and that in America, where they have tried using oil-gas for fuel entirely in one of their towns, from being one of the blackest and dirtiest in the country, it has become the brightest and cleanest possible; and that the scientific men have discovered that this oil is generated by the normal action of the earth's forces, so that the supply is never likely to fail: and they are also finding out how to construct monster tanks to store it, and steamers to bring it, to countries which have not a native supply. — "On the eve of an Oil age," the article finishes;—which doesn't *sound* so tempting;—but if it cures the smoke, and gives us pure skies again, it will indeed be a discovery to be thankful for, won't it?

Is my G.P. better, yet, G.D. thinks?

Me's G.P.;
G.D.

Walpole
Chislehurst
2. June. [18]88.

My own G.P.

I am SO sorry! — I *could* only write you just a tiny word yesterday, just that your plate shouldn't be empty; and now I find there was a mistake, and it was never posted,—not even that little scrap,—"and so the Poor Dog had *none!*"

Well, it wasn't worth having:—only you wouldn't have looked for a letter and not got one. But I hope you had lots of nice ones from other people, and then you wouldn't mind. (Of course I HOPE you *did* mind, a little, any way!)

Oh, my G.P., I was so *very* glad to get my G.P.'s letter—and that he liked my children:—and that the winds do *not* keep him awake. It is *better* so, really, my G.P.,—even in all the weariness. And doesn't my G.P. know YET that the want of good news was the very reason his G.D. *should* write to him? — while you like it? oo naughty G.P! oo knows *quite well,*—it was 'all p'etend.' G.D. peets! [repeats?] — And when the good news *comes,*—won't it be beautiful for us *both?*

And my G.P. do you know,—it was three years yesterday since you came to us that time, with Lily— — and a little while ago, I was dreading this week, so; and now you have given me that precious two days, that can never be taken out of my life again—that has *added* three years, in its own way, to my life—

And last night, when I went to bed; and was thinking of that, and looking at my new Lucerne (which came home, framed, *yesterday,*—I was so glad!) and with my Bible—and thought of all that meant, of mercy and restoration to my *G.P.,* as well as to us, who love him,—I felt how little we can tell of the mercies and hopes of the future, any more than of its sorrows. — Such beautiful surprises God gives us,—doesn't He?

— The frame for my picture came home yesterday, as I said; and I framed it; and this is how they hang, now, over my mantelpiece. [diagram to show how the following pictures are grouped] 1. My G.P. / 2. Grindelwald / 3. Winter Lucerne / 4. Summer Lucerne / 5. Strawberry plant / 6. Brantwood. / There's a gallery to have at the foot of one's bed! Roslyn hangs over my davenport, near the window, because it won't [last?] in stronger light than there.

And oh, G.P., the winter Lucerne *is* so lovely! The *cold* of it,—but the real Swiss *living* cold,—(not our black death.)—*silent life.* The intense, suspended, and yet present, *life,* that is so wonderful, there.

They are a real possession, and treasure to me, those drawings, —more than I can *tell* you, only G.P. always knows! — For they are Switzerland itself, and G.P. himself,—and the two *together*—are nice!

I'd a nice day at Blackheath. All is going on happily and well. There was a cricket match in the afternoon, so I sat on the heath and watched it; but "Gay's Hospital" went in first, and I came away before our boys' innings.

It was very nice, driving home; there was such a beautiful, drifting sky. And then I had a long chat with Townsend's coachman; and found he had lived nine years on Ashdown Forest, and knew Crowborough, and Nutley, and all that lovely world, well. His father lived forty years in one family; and when he was too old to drive any more, his son,—this one's brother,—went to them.

This is the first day I have written out-of-doors, this summer, I think: it is so warm, and *such* a sky! *What* skies we have had lately. Last night I was tired— I had had such a busy, driving day, and not had time to go out, or *look* out; and then in the evening, I sat out and watched the evening sky. It wasn't quite sunset; but [Thomas?] was driving his flocks home,—and such a number he had,—and I suppose because it is spring,—such a *lot* of little lambs! — and the light was low enough for their fleeces to change colour,—to *darken,*—as they went, so that no two looked alike; and then round the [sun?], he had left some of his sheep, having too many to look after all at once, I suppose,—and these got pale gold.

It was so still, and beautiful: — and I wished my G.P. had been here.

I was *so* glad of your letter!

Your lovingest,
G.D.

XXXII

DR. PARSONS TO DR. SIMON

Hawkshead
Ambleside
28 March 1878

Dear Mr. Simon

I write to tell you of a new phase, & I am sorry to say an unpleasant one in my poor patient, viz., what we have been dreading so much, refusal to take nourishment. He had chloral once last week which acted well. On Monday afternoon last he had a *very* lucid interval from 2 p-m to 9 p-m, & had a good night's sleep On Tuesday morning he *was as bad as before,* and from Tuesday evening about half past five refused to take any food, although coaxed to do so. I thought it well *not* to *force* him to take it, & yesterday afternoon he asked for & ate his orange as usual but would take nothing else. Last night when I saw him, I pretended to be very cross with him, *when I saw coaxing was of no avail,* & so got him to swallow a *teacup full & a half* of milk. After I left he was very restless, so Mr. Hilliard gave him 20 grs of Chloral at ten minutes to twelve, after which he slept until seven or eight oclock this morning, but after waking refused food. When I saw him about 9.30 a.m., he still refused to take anything. So as he had been 36 hours or more without nourishment except the cup & a half of milk I had administered the previous evening, & I could make nothing out of him by gentle means I thought it necessary to employ force, so with Baxter holding his hands I forced him to swallow from a *feeding* cup about half a pint of *new* milk, with an egg beaten up in it. I am going to Brantwood again this evening, & hope to find his mood changed, but if he still continues to refuse food, I fear I must telegraph for you tomorrow, & hope you may be able to come down so that we may consult what is best to be done under the circumstances. He has not been noisy but very restless & anxious to get out of bed, & when he is allowed to get out, will not remain quiet, or have his trousers or stockings on & soon wants to get in again. I thought it best to write you this hurried scrawl, which I hope you may understand. With kindest regards believe me to be very sincerely yours

George Parsons

Mr. Severn is better. Shall write again tomorrow if I have not to telegraph. There is no sign of exhaustion yet.

G.P.

Hawkshead
Ambleside
29 March 1878

Dear Mr. Simon

Thanks for your telegram received this afternoon about one o'clock when I returned from my "round"— I saw Mr. Ruskin again *last night,* & heard he had had a good dinner, & was very quiet, & to some extent rational during the afternoon. He would not have any tea, but when I asked him he said he would, & took some. He did not have any Sedative & only had about one hours sleep during the night but was quiet This morning he had a large cup of milk, but would *not* have any breakfast, & was when I visited him very restless, throwing the bedclothes off, & incoherent, but talking very little. You may perceive from the above that at present we have "tided over", the difficulty of refusing food, but how long we may do so I cannot of course prognosticate. I am going to see him again this evening. I am sorry you are so busy; as I fear in the case of an emergency you are the only person who could help me & *the Severns,* as any help I could get from *Lancaster* or *Carlisle* would be of no *practical* use to me *under the circumstances,* as the advice from either place would be I feel sure, "Send him to an Asylum." It is you who can advise, *generally as a friend* as to *arrangements,* that alone can give material aid, if the worst comes to the worst. Help *purely medical & professional* I don't think we require at present or are likely to do. However I trust we may be able to "carry on" until the 18th of April, as soon as possible after which I should like to see you, unless a decided change mentally should occur before then, which I fear is not likely. I forgot to mention in my previous letters that I had again tried the Hypophosphite about a fortnight since, but I *thought* it produced excitement so discontinued it. I allow my patient to sit up every day he seems inclined to do so & *will remain at all* quiet, but he is so *quietly* restless, not *noisy,* that he is sometimes very difficult to manage. The whole tone of the mind is perhaps quieter than it was some days since, but I fear when I have said this I have said all. *I* have *never* seen the *very lucid* intervals his attendants describe, nor has *Baxter* or *Herdson* his two *most dispassionate* nurses, & I fear *we three* are agreed there is not *very much* mental improvement & that too glowing descriptions of such intervals must be received with reserve—

With kindest regards & many thanks believe me to be very sincerely yours

George Parsons

Hawkshead
Ambleside
13 April 1878

Dear Mr. Simon

I saw a newspaper cutting to-day in which it stated that a few friends of Mr. Ruskin's had bought the "Pass of Splugen" picture to present to him, & inviting anyone who wished to join in the presentation to apply to you or Mr. Cowper Temple. As I think you know my regard for Mr. Ruskin, you will not be surprized at my wish to be allowed to *join* in this little attention; & although unfortunately I can only *afford* a *very small* subscription, I should feel very much gratified, if I might be allowed to contribute my "mite." Will you kindly let me know if I may do so? My patient is I am glad to be able to report going on far more favorably than I had dared to hope, gets out every day, & the weather up to today has been beautifully fine for him, but I told him this morning not to allow the rain to keep him in; knowing how essential outdoor exercise & distraction of mind, especially with *natural* objects (which he admires so much) are for him. He eats well, but cannot sleep without the "Chloral." tried it last night for a time, but had unpleasant dreams & finally took it. I shall be happy to see you, & I think you will him, on Friday or Saturday next. With kindest regards

Believe me to be very sincerely yours

George Parsons

Hawkshead
Ambleside
16 April 1878

Dear Mr. Simon

Very many thanks for so kindly & promptly answering my inquiry. I enclose check for one pound as my small offering—The Severns know of the intended gift, for it was they showed me the newspaper paragraph about it, but they have kept it secret from the Professor. I saw him to-day, he is going on very well but rather inclined to be despondent about himself & for this I anticipate *your* visit, & way of talking to him will be the best remedy. With kindest regards & again very many thanks believe me very sincerely yours

George Parsons

XXXIII

Thomas Pebardy to Ruskin

22 Greville St.
Hatton Garden
Oct[ober] 29, 1887

To John Ruskin Esq
Morley's Hotel
My dear Sir

If I might venture to offer you advice on the matter of the rupture, I should urge you to think as little as is possible about it, and to place full reliance in the power of your medical attendant (Mr Kingdon) He is a man possessing great knowledge of the malady, and can offer you all the Skill of a very intelligent and experienced mind, in addition to which his knowledge obtained from the treatment of some (*many*) Thousands of Cases enables him to appreciate the most minute intricacies of individual cases.

I have had the pleasure of his acquaintance for a period of a quarter of a Century, and know exactly what he is capable of doing.

During the period of such acquaintance I have not slumbered, and if my opinion is worth your consideration? I should like to say that with care and time I see no reason why your rupture should not be brought under controul—

Constant use of the instrument, is however *imperative* to accomplish such a result.

Your Friend Miss Greenaway's House is situated within a few Hundred Yards of the rear of mine, and from her window a very pleasant view is obtained of Hampstead Church spire surrounded by pleasant old trees, and the remains of green fields, not yet disfigured by the Builder.

I apologize for giving you so much trouble in deciphering my name. It is now spelled Pebardy,—a corruption of Peabody—a change in orthography not wisely made by my late Father. — So if I am favored by further correspondence from you, either method of addressing me, I might say would be correct.

Yours Faithfully
Tho[ma]s Pebardy

XXXIV

George Richmond to Arthur Severn and to Mrs. Simon

1. *To Arthur Severn*

20, York Street
Portman Square. W.
[February? 1878]

My dear Arthur

Your letter of this morning has filled us with the deepest anxiety & sorrow.

I had not heard of Johns illness, till now.

I have telegraphed to ask you kindly to let us know about him. Please let us have one telegram [as you?] write he is so ill I would come at a moments notice if I could hope that my presence would be of any use

I dare say you have let Acland know, and it is a comfort to feel that you have the support of the presence of his old & wise friend "The Simon"

We are sure that with dear Joan & you on the spot that every thing will be done that affection & skill can supply & I pray God that our dear Friend may soon be restored

Ever aff[ectionatel]y y[ou]rs
G. Richmond

20 York St
March 7 1878

My dear Arthur

"A somewhat better night", little as it is, gives hope of continued improvement, however slow.

I have not written the last 2 days, because I know you must be overwhelmed with letters, and I go daily to Bond St. to get the Telegram

But I shall ask you to send me one line not only to tell of dear John, but also of your own Father.

A Postcard is all that you need send, but for that I shall be very grateful.

I hope you all keep up, during the nursing & that Joan does not overdo herself.

Ever aff[ectionatel]y y[our]s
G. Richmond

20, York Street
Portman Square. W.
August 13, 1885

My dear Arthur

Thank you very much for your touching and deeply interesting letter about our dear friend.

I fear this illness will shake him very much, but with loving care from Joan and you, & skilled nursing, please God he will be himself again

Any communication from dear Joan or you will be very precious to me, and as you kindly say you will keep me informed of any "change of importance" I shall rest contented & hopeful without troubling you to write often. I feared from a letter that he wrote to Julia Robinson when he was in [illegible] that he was getting nervous & strange.

He has been very much on my mind and in my heart, of late, for the 3 numbers of "Praeterita" have revived very vividly many old & dear recollections

When he is able to receive a message please give him my love. I am glad that brightness came over him when Joan went in to see him, for one of your trials at these times is, that those whom he loves most at other times, when these attacks are upon him, he hardly recognises with pleasure

Is it not so?

Give my love & sympathy to Joan & believe me always

Affection[ate]ly yours
Geo[rge] Richmond

2. *To Mrs. Simon*

20 York St
Port[ma]n Sq
April 15, 1878

My dear Mrs Simon

I think the thought does honour to his friends who originated it, of presenting the coveted drawing of the "Pass of the Splugen" to dear John on his recovery.

I am much obliged by your invitation to add a stone to that which might have been his "Carni," but happily is not.

We get excellent accounts from the Severns, & I wrote to the Professor a day or two ago.

Y[ou]rs very truly
Geo[rge] Richmond

XXXV

Miss Rigbye to Ruskin and to Mrs. Severn

[The first two letters, to Ruskin, reflect the personality and interests of Miss Hariette Rigbye at the age of 75. The fourth letter is in an envelope inscribed by Mrs. Severn: "Last precious letter from our beloved Miss Rigbye." It was written two days before Miss Rigbye died.]

1. *To Ruskin*

Lausanne
3d November 1886

Dear Mr. Ruskin

I am very grateful for your kind expressions of regret at my leaving Coniston, where however I hope to find you when I return & when the few months of our usual wet-*blanket* winter are over; & hope also to find you unharmed by its continuance. I am very glad also to know that if at opposite poles in some ways, I may claim to be very near you in others, for I do most entirely appreciate your great & constant kindness to *myself* & all with whom you have relations, & in other ways, though necessarily at a greater distance, I most heartily admire what I am so little capable of imitating, but feel happy that I can *understand,* & this has been for *many years true,* with regard to you. And now I trust you *are* enjoying your *own* way, & seeing all around you as beautiful & happy as you can desire, the green house filled with most lovely blossoms, as I once saw it, & the blotched leaves serving as a background to their more transparent colors— I had almost forgotten Carpaccio, & my audacity in venturing to disclaim admiration of his work— you must overlook it & just say—"she does not understand anything about it"! which is probably true. *"My own way"!* for many years I scarcely knew whether I had my own way or not—for my dear friend's way was my way, and my way was HER way! — I suppose now I *have* my way, but it is greatly influenced by knowing what hers *would have* been—

We have had unusual weather here much mist & damp, very unlike the old Switzerland which was my home for so many years: I hear the *heat* has been almost insupportable this summer; this place, as so many others, is now full of memories for me; I ask after so many I have known here & receive constantly the same answer, "departed"! —& the younger generation I scarcely know, but in other ways I see great improvement, & especially in the greater comfort & ease of the poorer classes, not however I fear in better feeling *between* the classes, which would be desirable. Since I began writing the weather has cleared & the grand beauty of the sky & Lake & Mountains makes one feel it strange that in such scenes, so much that is regrettable & sad can exist.

Miss Tolmie sends her grateful thanks for your kind remembrance of her and joins me in many good wishes & kind messages to you & Mrs. Severn & all your home party. We shall not leave this for 2 or three weeks & then go on to Italy whither in Italy we don't quite know. Believe me affect[ionate]ly & gratefully y[ou]rs

Harriette Rigbye

Capri
Italy
12th Jan[uar]y 1887

Dear Mr. Ruskin

Besides the treat of your interesting letter, I have to thank you for your kind thoughts about us & our fate. We have now got to a perfect paradise of beauty, & I think a healthy place, which Castellamare was not. it was dreadfully damp. Mount St Angelo overshadowed too much, and so south Italian nuisances were all the more difficult to escape. The Mountain walks were bordered by high walls leading from village to hamlet, the sun never penetrated into them, there was a small part of one road which led through a wood but no sun could ever get there— the only walks which we could take with comfort were into the Campania in the direction of Vesuvius, these had to be preceded by a plunge into the town which was always most objectionable & especially so of late when it was never dry, the compania gave us sunlight—& pretty views of the mountains round of which I could sometimes get a sketch in sepia in a little drawing book, but I must say a word of Vesuvius. I admired it much more from Castellamare than from Naples, I was continually in great admiration of its beautiful lines, it *was* also more substantial & rose from the plain at its base more majestically, the lower peak was of a better form, at Castellamare we saw it on the *right* of the crater— altogether at Naples it seemed to me more like this. [sketch showing the two peaks in outline] from Castellamare more thus [sketch] We saw it once with the cone covered by snow. We endured Castellamare for a month & I got a view of the little port & town from the Sorrento road, the only drawing I could do besides 2 or three sepia sketches from the plain. The weather was bad Mt. St Angelo continually pelted us, & storms of hail & rain thunder & lightning hardly ceased. We left last Friday & came to Sorrento in the usual storm of rain; a boat (steamer) professes to leave Naples 4 times a week for Capri calling at Sorrento on the way, but as it only starts when it has 15 passengers, & never starts at all with certain winds it is always *un*certain, & we were not hopeful of its arriving the following morn[in]g. — It came however & an hour's passage brought us here. Do you know this island? it presented itself to us something like this [sketch, outlining the main contour of two hills] on the north side. In the hollow between the hills is the village of Capri to which a winding road leads from the port, where are some fishermen's houses & hotels: just beyond the village are the best hotels with a southern aspect. The De'barcadère on this northern side is the only one for a steamer to come near, & for the *"Barques,"* there is one other port (Niccola Marina) on the south side. The hills are all crowned by the villa-palaces of the Emperor Tiberius— there are 12 in all & these ruins cover a large space they are untenanted—not like some of the ruins of the ancient Stabia at Castellamare which are mostly converted into modern habitations, there is a world of Rocks here, all beautiful and falling perpendicularly into the Sea except at the two points I have named. The walks are beautiful & delightful, though of course many of them are very rough, but today we went along a carriage road round Mount Solaro, & were quite enchanted by the beauty of the scenery & the views all round [In the sketch] I have marked this road under Solaro a zigzag road at first, & then passing along & round the perpendicular towers of rock that fall into the sea. Italians have always been the first masons in Europe & this road is admirably built up & protected so that one has no feeling of insecurity while walking over it at such a height, it led to another village of Anacapri. Wherever vegetation could appear it was myrtle, & near to Capri there were a few Stone pines & oaks, but the olive is the most abundant here, & the trees are not fine like those of the Riviera. We saw Vesuvius & all the Bay round to Ischia, & at one point of our walk we could see the bay of Salerno. The Stone pines when not planted in a straight line, I think, are very beautiful but the maritime pine I admire much more. They do not grow here. I have written of this Island as if you were not acquainted with it & perhaps you know it well, but probably Mrs. Severn may not have seen it— We have here the sun, almost from the moment it rises till it sets, & the "couchait" I am told is very beautiful frequently. The village here compared with Castellamare is a pattern of cleanliness, they actually sweep the little streets! This island is not volcanic but all Limestone & therefore dry. Miss Tolmie was hardly ever free from face ache at Castellamare, & has nothing of it here. Your Peaks & Matterhorn must bring many pleasant sights; I wonder if you have all the Titmouse families at Brantwood, the large & little blue kind, & the *coal Titmouse* black & grey & the longtailed Titmouse & the Marsh Titmouse. I have seen them all at the Thwaite. The little blue is the cleverest & the most dandyfied of them all. I have often watched it at work on a bit of meat, together with a Blackbird pecking at a potato & driving it away & rolling it down a slope in a vain attempt to get something off it— not so the little Tit, he knew better, he placed one little claw on his meat, & pecked it to pieces immediately.

What a charming benefaction you are devising for girls, & how well, not to admit of *oil painting,* which is such a ready medium for *Pasticci!* The manipulation is so much easier than water-colour! Perspective lessons I remember once being much interested in & especially in the building up of winding Staircases, &c. A striped blanket folded will give something of the same kind. I am sorry to hear of such a severe winter, sorry I mean for those who have passed through skating times already, for a hard winter is not good for health, then, here we have a temperature of an English September. I beg very kind love to Mrs. Severn & the children in which Miss Tolmie joins me, as also in much kind regard to you with our best wishes for a happy & prosperous year & that you may have as much satisfaction in your benefactions to others, as they will certainly receive from you. Believe me most gratefully y[ou]rs

Harriette S. Rigbye

2. *To Mrs. Severn*

[Thwaite Cottage]
Wednesday

Dearest Mrs. Severn

You are too good to make us participate in your good things, mushrooms & peaches, the two favorites of my Mother in fruits & vegetables, & I inherit her taste; Frances [Tolmie] also I think seems to share with enjoyment. So many thanks! I will send back the Box with this note: What tempests of rain & wind I sympathized specially with Lily pray tell her with my love for the spoilt garden party she was to have gone to, perhaps you did go, but it must have been a little disappointing & I felt sorry for Mrs. Barrett. I don't remember ever to have met with disappointment of that kind when I was young, & outdoor picnics were so frequent; only once in an excursion across the Lake of Geneva did we meet with a contretemps, we had hired a large sail Boat & got across—about ten miles, very pleasantly, but then a furious north wind arose & prevented our attempting to return & we all had to walk some miles to get night accommodation & our boat was taken along the shore the following morn[in]g. When we re-embarked & got home, the weather was splendid! & it was all very delightful except *Sortes arrangements!* I have been delighted by the account of the welcome given to the French-Fleet The Queen is *always courteous,* & she seems to have been specially so on this occasion; Miss Tolmie is raking the walks, after the Hurricane! but I took out one of your delightful peaches, of which I had only just been apprised, for I thought the box was filled with mushrooms! & Frances could not resist it & laid aside her rake. One good thing will I hope result from this Hurricane. I found the wall in the corner going up to the little gate, had been thrown down, a sign that the Trembling Ash Tree in that corner had been shaking at the roots, so I spoke to Atkinson & found that he had been to the Steward to tell him it was not safe & should be cut down. I have been for some time very anxious about that tree, & I hope now it will be removed, it is dying. Have you any disasters among y[ou]r tall trees? — a willow tree near the farmyard has been uprooted & the road is under water at the head of the Lake besides a large portion, *more than I have* ever seen here. with both our loves & thanks always

very affec[tionate]ly y[ou]r's
Harriette Rigbye

[Thwaite Cottage]
September 22 [1894]

Dearest Mrs. Severn

I find you have been kindly enquiring after me & dear Lily, & Violet, enquire so kindly, but I must really protest against your all giving yourselves so much trouble. I am really *not ill;* I suffer occasionally & am quickly losing that's fast recovering—& no longer in the slightest degree—*interesting*— Mad^e^ Schmid takes care of *that* every time I apply to her she does wonders! & now I hope soon to be quite free from all troubles, & ready to set out on the journey, so *pray* don't give yourself *any trouble about me!* H[erdson?] tells me you would like some *Turn-up orange lilies.* I have some for you & also the *common orange Lily*—they are all ready for you. Then some Belladonnas you must have to give Mr. Ruskin his Bouquet, & there are too, very fine Peonies those which come up well above the foliage of a *beautiful color;* there are some Phloxes too but, they *smell!* The Fern I showed you a *marvel* of Tolypodium, some St Brunos lily, & very lovely Spirea Palmutu do you like my clematis over the door? because, if so, your gardener could I am sure take *cuttings,* it wont transplant. Your own lovely yellow Rose is quite *delightful.* have you one? — it—too—will not I think transplant. Have you Scherosytylis? there is of that too, & the *Japanese lilies* there are also, these plants should be taken before we start, for next year, it would be risky to take them as we shall probably go earlier, I send the names of these plants that you may see if they will give you pleasure to have, but your *own* corner which you mentioned may perhaps be already too full! so I will not say more but you will next time you come to look at things. Always with many thanks for all those enquiries &c &c &c I remain most gratefully y[ou]r's

Harriette Rigbye

XXXVI

Flora Shaw (Lady Lugard) to Mrs. Severn

Greenhill
Thursday 27th[1]

Dearest Joanie

I am so glad you liked my Blue Eyes but you must forgive me if I say that you've all got very bad taste if you really dont think her fifty times prettier than me. Still it is *very* kind of you to think anything half so nice about me and though I know you would very soon change your mind if you knew anything at all about Blue Eyes I thank you all the same.

Do you know I am half afraid I shall not see you as I had hoped to do in about a fortnight for my aunt with whom I was to have rested a few days on my way through London writes to me that she fears she will not be able to have me because her pet dog is very ill and is occupying the bed that I was to have had.

I am so disappointed because I had been counting on seeing you and Mr Ruskin then; and I had made in my own mind a nice little plan for one day. I thought that Mr Ruskin would let you have the carriage and that you would come and call for me at my aunt's and that you would drive me to Marshall & Snelgrove that we would choose the little ones' winter dresses together and then that we would go back to Denmark Hill and dine there with Mr Ruskin. Now wasnt that a nice little plan and there is that

1. This letter is in an envelope inscribed by Ruskin: "Flora — Doggie" instead.

poor old Tiffchen gone and got ill and spoilt it all. Poor doggie it is worse for him though than for me. I daresay you will drive down to Woolwich and have lunch with me and the children, and a good chat, some day, wont you? Please. We are going back to Northampton tomorrow. I shall stay there about ten days or a fortnight and then go home, if I am strong enough. This place has done me wonderful good in many ways, and since I have got a kind of steel corset that the doctors ordered I can sit up and walk a little, though without it I cannot yet sit up at all. I do not know where Mr Ruskin is, at present, so if he is near you will you tell him that my address will be at Castle Cottage again. I hope you and "Arfie" are both quite well; that seems to me the nicest thing I can wish to anyone now.

Your very affectionate
Flora. L. Shaw

XXXVII

Ruskin and Mrs. Severn to Sir John and Lady Simon

[In the first group of these letters Ruskin expresses his friendship for Lady Simon as his Pre-Raphaelite "Sister" and / or "Sibyl" and for the "Brother John" whose advice as a physician became important during periods of mental illness, as is indicated by letters in the second group, addressed to the Simons in 1881 by Mrs. Severn.]

1. *Ruskin to the Simons*[1]

Denmark Hill
6th December, 1871[2]

My dear Brother John

It is good for me now to know I have a brother—for I felt very much more lonely yesterday afternoon, when there was no more pain or sighing in that little bed in the room off the passage

1. The Ruskin-Simon letters represented in the F. J. Sharp Collection begin in 1862, although only those between 1871 and 1895 are included in the following section.

2. On the death (December 5) of Ruskin's mother, with a reference to the death of his father, in 1864, as "that other dark time."

to my study, than I thought I ever could have felt—more. It ended at 1/4 past two. The days before were very woful—much worse in some respects, than what you saw, when you were with me in that other dark time— Else I should have asked you to come, sometimes.

— I have kept myself well against it—and as far as I know—am still well enough, and ever your loving

J Ruskin

She wanted you to have her largest diamond ring. I think Jane [Mrs. Simon] will like to see you wear it—if you would. Love to her.

Herne Hill
6th Dec[ember 18]79

My dearest brother John

Jane tells me that the dark time when the great Honouring is to be no more possible but in memory, is coming to you—as it came—and remains for me—every day darker, since you first comforted me through the sudden stress of it— how little then I knew what its long weight would be. — But I have a thousand things to reproach and shame myself for, and mourn for in the pain they gave my father, with a grief far worse than the shame—while you have only well done duty to him, and his unhindered and untortured pride in you,—for the after-glow of your twilight time.

I will come, assuredly, to see Jane and you—as soon as I can get out of the house again— I was necessarily exposed to more cold than I could bear, not once nor twice lately; and though not in any way seriously colded, am just in the state when if I exposed myself farther, there would be mischief: and I am staying grimly at home—till to stir would be safe. Tell me what times would be available for me on Monday or Tuesday; if any— I hope to get away from town towards the end of the week.

Herkomer has done a most precious drawing of me; and Boehm a bust of extreme and, more than perhaps I quite like—historical—veracity,— it is like a cast from life.

I greatly rejoice in the better personal acquaintance with both the painter and sculptor.

— I meant to put their personalities in postcript—but it would have been a formalism, for I know you will both care for them

Ever your lovingest
Brother John

[Herne Hill]
Tuesday
Jan[uar]y 31, 1882

My dearest S.

It is very delightful to find John and you so well, and happy, in Boo [their adopted daughter, Jane Faulkner] and in her husband, and I'll come for a happy afternoon with you soon. I am not able now for evenings; this last illness has left me enough to carry me through the morning and its business, nearly as well as of old—if less fervidly, perhaps more wisely; in the evenings I am able for little. One of the saddest forms of decline in me is the loss of interest in reading. Very few books have much charm left for me, but I am thankful that I still care for the clouds and rocks. I am getting a lovely model of the Coniston fells made,—six inches to a mile, and am greatly surprised to see how well they look on a quite unexaggerated scale. The old Swiss models used to be always at least double the true scale in height—and an Alp scarely looks itself unless you make it so—but the lower Cumberland hills don't appeal to the imagination, and look no worse in sculpture than in reality. Of a series of *leaf* models, undertaken at the same time and going on prosperously I will bring you a pretty specimen

Dear love to John
Ever your loving J R.

[Herne Hill]
23rd Feb[ruary, 18]82

My dearest S.

I have just sent for the Doctor! (Dr Elliott.) to give me some cough mixture—having caught—incomprehensibly and I believe merely as an inevitable epidemic, a chest cold which needs nursing. I have had to throw up all engagements—for a week in advance—as well as those of the last 3 days, and although I hope, and have every reason to think, that I shall beat the mischief itself by the end of the week, I do not mean to go out in the evening again on *this* London visit— I have to be up again in the end of April—and must leave for Brantwood now as soon as I am able. You know that I am sorry not to see more of the friends who care for me—but I am too thankful to be still above ground—and able still for my essential business, to care much, myself, for mere talk—so long as I am assured of their sympathy in my work. But I wonder what made you say that, the other day, about my becoming a Roman Catholic? So far from that, I've all the difficulty in the world to keep the least rag of Christianity any more about me—against the East wind.

Ever your loving JR.

[Herne Hill]
15th April, [18]82

My dear S.

There was a lovely dawn at four, this morning— I am thankful that even after this illness, I can see skies nearly as I used to.

— You will see little sky at Edinburgh: When it was really the mouth of a triple crested volcano, it was not more sulphurously wrapped in the blackness of Hades than it is now by the doom of its own children. But, on a breezy day, if you drive round Arthur's seat—(and can stand the perpetual cracking of rifle shots from the valley where Jeanie Deans milked her cows) —you may get still the idea of the true—the Romantic—the *Only*—town of Edinburgh,—sloping from its Castle down to its Holy-Rood Chapel,—Palace—and—once, sweet fields and woods at the feet of the basalt crags. There is not—never has been—never can be—any other "*Edin*burgh" than that Ridge of rock with the buildings left yet upon it of Scotts time & earlier. — Modern *Sawney*-burgh—the New Town—with its achievements—its Mock temple of Pallas,—its decoratively Castellated Gaol, its Gothic [extinguisher?] over its Scott—its railroad run under its Academy—and its chimney as high as Strasburg spire—half as high as Arthurs Seat—is simply the most brutal piece of human impudence extant—in the ruined cities of Europe— An Englishman, at the worst, when the modern devil gets into him—becomes only a bloated Sausage of other people's ideas—but a Scotchman is blown up like a bagpipe—and modern Edinburgh is the screech of him—for the last fifty years.

— It is best you should be prepared for this, at once—

Understanding so much—take Marmion with you *in the large print octavo edition,*—(I[']ll get you one and send it today, if I can.) — WALK—down the Canongate on a day when it is mild enough to stand here & there—and look and think— You will have people enough to show you the castle— its *rock* you will see for yourself to be one of the grandest masses of basalt in volcanic Europe— But, be sure to give yourselves time to see Roslyn, and Craigmillar,—and for Scott's sake the view from Blackford Hill—and for 'the Antiquary's' sake—the place where once was 'Queen's Ferry' It used to be a pleasant drive—and I imagine is so still.

If—either going or coming you could stop at Dunbar, its rock-coast is in the deep water *chines* of it, to me most impressive—certainly strange and worth—an afternoons rest. Tantallon I have never seen—and wish *you* could. — I can't write more this morning—only—though you will have plenty of people to plague—or help you—in Yorkshire—please remember that Fountains is one of the few places still *lovely,* in the spring, it must be heavenly—and that both Pontefact and Selby are worth *baiting* at—if no more. Newark castle is very nearly my favourite Castle ruin in England—if it had not been spoiled by its surroundings—Southwell minster is pretty but much overrated its carvings being botanical *without imagination.* I would much rather spare time for Grantham,—(have you seen Coventry?) *DON'T* get stopped at York—and perhaps—in order to enjoy the smaller things properly it would be wise even to avoid Lincoln. Durham, it's needless to talk of,—it is so blasted in cinders— Keep clear of it

Ever your affect[ionat]e, JR.

[Herne Hill]
Dec[ember] 21, [18]82

My dearest S.

I fear I have lost a pretty letter from you—for this one which is to prevent my answer, is all I have had. — But my little nursery is in great confusion, and I may find the first one under heaps of love-letters and crystallography which—illustrated variously by Christmas cards & diagrams—are falling about the floor in avalanches, if ever I try to move anything.

But you must really not ask me to come out in the evening I find nothing so harmful to me as talking at dinner—simply because I either swallow things whole, or don't eat, and I am always jaded the next morning. You all, who care for me, must be content to see me doing what I can in my own old furrows—and you must take care not to let me break through the rules for health which have been now for forty years, becoming more & more imperative

Dear love to John

Ever your affect[ionat]e

JR.

Brantwood
10th Feb[ruary 18]83

My dearest S.

Curiously, this morning I was writing some account of my proceedings in old times, by way of addenda to the new 2nd Vol. M.P.—and specifying the Mont Blanc from les Tines "in the possession of M[s] John Simon" as the best extant example of my way of study at that period.

Yes, I hope you were quite right, (as you usually are,) in feeling that I was in healthier state when you met me at the Institution, and I hope that both John and you will have some pleasure in reading the number of Deucalion ["Revision"], which coming from the printers today to me, I send on to you the first of my friends who will see it. You will I hope think my power of *rational* writing not impaired—and you never were among those of my friends who thought that in that kind I had little to lose.

When you see the drawings made in Italy this last year, I hope you will think my power not lost in hand, either. But my general bodily strength is now finally impaired, and I found a six mile walk the other day, the first the weather has allowed me for a month, quite as much as I was able for. I trust however that as yet—there are no symptoms of any return of the illness which—these three times, has seized me in the spring; and what I propose to do at Oxford will be merely the turning the general current of my work in that direction. I am now well assured that without effort, I can write as many [illegible] lectures for them as they will expect, in the year. — if I feel too dull I shall read things written before, which will be quite as useful, and which in the proper theory of Professorship, it is the real duty of the Professor of any science to do—not at all to pursue new discoveries.

It is true also that there are very general signs of better acceptance of what I can do, than ever before, and that, if for the first time in my life, I can exercise a little discretion, power is certainly offered me of doing much good.

But these promises are very like the kind which the Fates have a trick of holding out to men, near the end of the Thread; and certainly, the fear of Death was never closer to me, or sadder—than it is now, day by day; —nor the Hope of any good thing, beyond Death, more dim.

In the meantime, I am building a new house for Joan—and making my own little one very tidy; and studying the habits of Mother Carey's Chickens— Can anybody you chance to know in London tell me who Mother Carey was?

— Dear love to John, and I am (with most egotistic trust in his regard & yours—as this letter well shows!)

Ever your loving John Ruskin

Brantwood
8th July 1885

Darling S,

It will be a beautiful autobiography if it is dated thus out of my head & heart! with no corrections—

— But I *do* wish the picnic had been in 42!

I thought I had painted that rock with you sitting by.

— *Is* it dated 42? I am confused between 42 & 44.

Im doing some bits of 'word painting' which I think are as good as they used to be, (*at least*) but perhaps its only a cormorants idea—

You'd better give Francesca away—any how,—you esprite fate that you are!

Ever your—pitying— JR.

Brantwood
20th Dec[ember 18]85

My dearest S

I cannot enough thank you for this most precious letter, (—but how you could have put off writing it to me, for an instant, I can't think!) And it will be of invaluable service to me that you tell me, as you find time & power—anything that comes into your head or heart about my Father & Mother—of whom *I* knew scarcely anything but the foibles; and never valued the affection. My own cruelty to them is now altogether frightful to me in looking back.

Very little of the deeper calamities of all that chanced and mischanced to us, will be shown in Praeterita It will not the least be 'Confessions'—nor even, in pleasant things—far analyzed. — it will be what the public may be modestly told to their own benefit—no more. But it is quite *vital* to my doing even so much as this rightly, that *you* should tell me what you knew and felt about them both.

I shall not alter a word in the already written chap VIII, that occurs about my mother, & there is a good deal; but in chapter IX, *with your leave,* I shall give your letter nearly entire—only mind that [you] write with the certainty of my never using anything or word as you do not wish.

Love to John, always, (Wisely)!

Ever your—also wisely—loving

J.R.

Brantwood
12th Feb[ruary 18]86

Dearest S

I am so very thankful that John and you have so much pleasure in these pieces of travel. If I am spared, I hope to do Geneva and Chamouni—and some bits of Thun and Lucerne—just enough to be borne by the general public,—and indeed, giving the due space to accounts of friendship & of thought—there will be scant room for description except as it is a part of thought.

So many thanks for the little hint about poor Eliza [Fall]— Yes, I knew she cared a good deal for me— she was much more of a poet than girls are usually,—but what a quaint oldmaidishness in her always,—and what an odd thing old maidishness is. Old bachelors are always intelligibly crazy, like me,—but Eliza was so indefinably—unmarried.

What a wonderful book that is of John's! I'm so glad I wrote and asked him about it.

I think happily of you safe in Kensington Sq—in case of a mob in the highway. What a lovely nook it is. I want to know what John and you would do if you were King & Queen.

Ever your lovingest J R.

Brantwood
16th Jan[uary 18]87

Dearest S.

I'm *so* glad of your letter—and P.S. and the long Turner[3] one and all—but Im just planning the whole third vol—and teaching schoolgirls here music—of a Gregorian cast—to sing Dame Wiggins to—and cant possibly write more than this—today—except—See over

Vol II

Chap XI. L'hotel du Mont Blanc (St Martins)
XII. Vevay

Vol III

Chap I. [unspunnen]
II Juliets Tomb
III *L Hotel del Union*
IV— &c &c &c.

One chapter was to be

'Count Godfrey's Cliff[']

but it can't be, because of Godfreys cordial—

Forgive my confounded pale pen— Dear love to both of you.

JR.

Then—there's Mornex / The Dome of Parma— and other pretty things

3. Note by Lady Simon, at top of letter: "Sydney Smith— / I didn't mention Turner perhaps he means in a previous letter to Joan.

Sunnyside
Orpington, Kent
2nd May [1888][4]

Dearest John

If only I knew how I am,—how thankfully would I tell you, but from day to day all things change with me. The bodily ailments indeed seem entirely conquered,—but the wanderings—(I will not say totterings, yet—) of mind & heart continue—complicated with real difficulties in discerning what is best—or—of ways all dangerous, the best fenced,—which for the present are too many to tell of. The best that I can say of myself is that I love all my—friends, & lovers—better than ever, and am more grieved daily for the grief I cause them

Dear love to S.

Ever your faithful & affect[ionate]
Frater John

Brantwood
3rd March, 1894[5]

Dear Lady Simond

I am so grieved that you are feeling unwell—but Joan thinks you would like a little word from me—only I cannot write as I could once—but I must tell you how we think of Kensington and its dear days and I never think that any work is so good as Sir John's— if only I had learned better from it and I am his and your loving brother John

Brantwood
12th Oct[ober] 1895

Dear Brother John

Your beautiful note has given me much happiness— it is wonderful to see your steady writing and to know that you think of

4. In the upper margin this letter is dated 1888, in blue pencil.

5. Through the kindness of the late F. J. Sharp, this letter and the one which follows have been already published in facsimile, in *Ruskin's Scottish Heritage* (facing p. 57). The letter of 1894 is in an envelope addressed: "Lady Simond [sic] / 40. Kensington Sq. / London." The letter of 1895 to "Brother John" was probably sent to Sir John Simon as an enclosure in a letter from Mrs. Severn. It remains within an unstamped envelope addressed in Ruskin's, by now, almost microscopic script: "Sir John Simon, KGS / 40 Kensington Sq. / W."

me still so affectionately and of Joan—for taking care of me—but— much blessing to you both.

your loving
John Ruskin

2. *Mrs. Severn to the Simons*

[The following letters tell the story of Ruskin's illness of 1881 and thus complement the group of letters, now in the John Rylands Library, addressed to Dr. and Mrs. Simon during Ruskin's illness of 1878 (see Spence, *Dearest Mama Talbot,* pp. 77–95).]

Herne Hill. S.E.
Sunday evening
[February 20, 1881][6]

Dearest Mrs. Simon

I came here to settle various household troubles—and to take Lily back—and meant to ask *when* I might have the great pleasure of coming to see you—but alas!—I have to-day a telegram from Brantwood saying I must without fail start back again to-morrow morning, as the Coz is ill— I have heard no particulars—and am sadly perplexed—& have at once to upset all my plans—& go off by first train in the morning—

To add to my trouble Arthur is at Heyford with [his twin-sister] Eleanor—but I have sent David [presumably David Fudge] there—in the hope that if possible, he Arthur may have time to go with me—tho' I fear not— The telegram is from Laurie Hilliard whom I always can trust to tell me if there is any cause for alarm about my darling Coz— It must be *very sudden*—as I had an excellent report of him yesterday— I shall of course let you know how he is when I get there—

Always your's—& Mr Simon's loving & grateful

Joan

Brantwood
Monday
[February 21, 1881]

Dearest Mrs Simon

I am sadly grieved to tell you that the poor Coz is ill again as

6. The date is indicated by Mrs. Severn's reference to the telegram which recalled her to Brantwood and by the fact that in 1881 February 20 was a Sunday.

he was before, with a breakdown of brain— it is in every way similar to the last attack—but as yet, without such violence & malice—

Fortunately our past experience enables us to know what is best to do— Arthur & Laurie Hilliard are here—& Baxter Herdson & Downs— if necessary Arthur will get a trained nurse—

Of course we are anxious if possible to manage without it's becoming known—& therefore do not wish it made public—

I am miserable at ever having left him even for so short a time —for I guard him daily with the most jealous care— Heaven only knows whether this *could* have been prevented— I fear not under any circumstances.

He is much more rational on the whole— If Mr. Simon wishes it, I could send details—

Today I am very busy—so many things to arrange—& people to see after—so you will excuse more—& believe me always

Your loving
Jo-an

Arthur & I arrived last night—

Brantwood
Wed[nesday]
[March 2, 1881]

Dearest Mrs. Simon

All goes on as well as we can expect— he has more frequent intervals of consciousness— *most* unfortunately I have sprained my ankle—& Parsons says I must remain in bed for a week actually the Coz came into my room yesterday to convince himself it was'nt a sham—& was *wonderfully himself*—indeed *almost* quite so—& then went back to bed— his night was not very good but he's very quiet today— ever your loving Joan

Brantwood
Wednesday
9th March 1881

Dearest Mr. Simon

I'm ashamed of my stupid mistake in having put your wife's letter in Mrs. Marshall's envelope—& Mrs. M's in her's—tho' glad you gleaned the present state of our troubles here—& I'm very grateful—& glad to have your precious little note to-day, before sending you a long one, Arthur & I having agreed it would be better to put you in possession of details as to the Coz's present state—as we are anxious for your approval of what we do—considering you always as his, & our best friend, & medical adviser—

Well—the last few days he has been—(as you warned us might be the case before) in a very difficult phase—insisting on being dressed—& about, in the house—giving absurd orders—& insisting on being Master—until Arthur has been obliged to take the reins in *his own hands*— poor fellow (Arthur I mean) is always *on the spot,* night & day, unwearied in his attention to the poor Coz—& with five nights, as well as days of nursing, I fear he may get ill—but he won't listen to this! —

I will go back to last Thursday [March 3] when he (the Coz) got up & dressed—& was *so much* his own self. he came into my room—& had tea—& was read to—& I really thought in every way *so much* himself, that he might remain so— He however insisted on being alone in his room—& we agreed to this, having watchers close at hand outside— he would not take any sleeping draught—saying it made him have horrid dreams—

On Friday morning when Baxter went in, he was again full of delusions—ordered his clothes out of the room—& did'nt dress or get up all day— it was my birthday—& the evening before, when he asked the date, he said, "then tomorrow's your birthday"! —& he hoped we might spend it happily to-gether—but alas! *on* the day—he was not at all himself—& never remembered anything more about it—& at night would not allow any one *in* his room—so they listened & waited outside—

On Saturday morning he dressed—& went down to the study (not attempting to *do* anything) (reading or writing I mean) & in the afternoon he smashed a pane of glass in his bedroom—& swore at everybody he saw—ordering them to leave the house—he was found kneeling in the hall "to receive Cardinal Manning"! —& insisted that the Duke of Argyle—& two ladies "one being Rose" were coming to dinner—& everything was to be in readiness—& we were all to dress in our best to receive them— he was furious at their never appearing—and accused *us,* of preventing it—

On Sunday morning he was tolerably quiet—tho' he smashed another pane of glass in his bedroom exactly next the former one— when later on, he came into my room—& seemed tolerably himself (completely dressed) I asked him *why* he had done it? —and he said "it was a signal to be given at Windsor Castle—of breaking a spell of witchcraft"—but, added he, "I've killed the third witch at last" — I said "that was a good thing—& there was the end of it—& she wouldn't bother him any more["]—to which he said "he was'nt so sure of that—& he might have yet to suffer a great deal for having done it" so I comforted him—& begged him to promise he would not break any more windows— I was so afraid of his catching cold—(and he never has since) then he became *almost* himself—& said he was tired—so Arthur with my persuation got him to lie down on the sofa beside me (I being in bed—) & wrapt him up—& he fell fast asleep— how I thanked God for that! — he woke much refreshed in about half an hour—wandering a *very* little—calling me "mama"—& himself "a little donkey boy"! —but quite calm & sweet—& went to his room saying he'd come back & have tea—which he did in about ½ an hour & enjoyed it, with Arthur & me—in my room—(I being in bed, with my sprained ancle[)] — then I got him to lie down again on the sofa—& Arthur left us quietly alone—& the poor Darling lay quite still for an hour & a half—& *may* have slept a little— he was *so* much himself that he had tea-dinner at 7:30 with Arthur, Laurie, & Martha Gale in the dining-room— (wandering a little but not much[)] — then they all came up, & for an hour I read "Ormonde" (Miss Edgeworth's) aloud—& he seemed to enjoy it & spoke very sensibly about Ireland as it was, & now is— then about 9-30 he went to bed—*would* be alone—& *wouldn't* take his draught—& had a pretty quiet night—

All Monday he insisted upon being master in his own house—& would have no orders obeyed but his own—*would not* take food —so I got up—& hobbled in & tho' he was very angry he promised if I'd carry his dinner with my own lame foot he'd take it— I did, & he dashed it all at me, swearing, & ordering me out of the room— Later on, he rang & ordered soup—sherry—mince collops— bread—& ate all up heartily—& then tea bread & jam— as yet he has taken his food well—on the whole— he seemed after all this food wonderfully himself—& in the evening sent an apology to me for his rude behaviour— he *would* see the cook & parlour maid —& said the latter was to take his coffee in the morning I should have before this told you that at about 2 on Monday morning it was raining hard & very stormy & the card-board panes blew out —& made his curtains fly about—& he got up & called Arthur who was at hand & put all right—

Of course we've tried to humour him all we can—so the maid went with his coffee at seven—& was ordered out at once— this was yesterday *Tuesday* morning— about 8 he was quiet & Arthur went to bed & Baxter went on guard— very soon a terrific row began—& knowing Arthur had gone to bed in the little room at the top of the stairs I got up to hobble & call him (Mattie Gale sleeps with me) — as I opened my door I saw the Coz dressed & standing facing me half way down stairs. he screamed out to me "don't move another step or I can't be answerable for your safety —but I'll do what I can, with the Queen's help" I walked on, calmly saying don't be afraid! "I'm all right—& only going to call Arthur" he had shut up the cook in his room saying she was the Queen kicked out. Baxter & Laurie & the entire household became terror stricken till Arthur appeared— I released the cook— the Coz flew to his room (I was in the passage) saying "who has *dared* to send the Queen off guard["]— I said quietly "*I have*—she's the cook—breakfast's an hour late—& we're all starving & she must go & get us some food"— He was *furious* & said soon indeed we *would all be starving*—& was making a rush (I fear to strike me!) shouting "I *will* be Master in my own house"! to which I answered "If *you* are incapable of being master—I *must* be mistress!["] & had just time to escape into my room— very soon Arthur appeared—but ever since he has been very violent if anyone goes near him & was eager to go to the Thwaite yesterday —ordered his out-door boots & a carriage,— Arthur told him he couldn't have them— ever since he's been furious at everybody—& we found letting him go about the house an impossibility —so Arthur had to show a bold front—& be quite firm— now looking after him is easier—but for the peace of the household we resolved it would be wiser to have a trained attendant at hand—& so have telegraphed for one to be sent—by Dr. Luke—& expect the attendant tomorrow— We have put off as long as we could—& hope you will not disapprove of what we have done—if so, it would be a relief to Arthur & me if you had the goodness to send a line to Dr. Luke saying you know all the circumstances of the case, & approve of what we have done? — his address is

Dr Luke
37 Albernarle Street
Piccadilly—W.

Arthur of course told Luke about you—I mean knowing all about the Coz—his former illness &c—& Luke of course knew well about you. Today Coz has as yet—(now it's *3*) refused food— Much love to Mrs Simon—& forgive my troubling you so much—

ever your loving & grateful Joan

Arthur says that what he would rather like would be your telling Luke that we are people to whom the care [handwriting changes into that of Arthur Severn] (The Baby has just come in! and Joan is of course quite gone! so I must go on!) What I mean is that it would be just as well if Luke could hear from a man like yourself, that *we* Mr & Ms A Severn, are or have a right to the position we are holding towards the Coz. & & &— You see at present he has only heard this from *me,* and although I was quite able to explain our position towards the Prof[essor]—still I should like him to hear it from you—just a line.

Brantwood
Friday
[March 11, 1881]

Dearest Mr. Simon

Arthur & I are both *most grateful* for your great goodness to us—

We so entirely agree with *all* you say! — and as yet have not taken the attendant near him—because I'm thankful to say Baxter is again in favour—& Laurie says he has just heard the poor Coz tell him that he's "a high born Irish gentleman & Catholic—& shall be his Premier"!

Well—our Darling had 4 hour's natural sleep last night—& is now having some real clear turtle soup—

Even if we never introduce the attendant at all, it is already an immense comfort having him in the house—

It is so very dear of you to have written to Dr. Luke for us—& to give me such kind advice about my ankle— I came down stairs yesterday—& saw my lambs for a little who came through the new dining-room window! Dearest love & thanks to your wife for her sweet note—

Always your loving & grateful Joan

He is very quiet today & Dr. Parsons seems to think more favourably of his state—

Brantwood
Monday March 14 [1881]
3-45

Dearest Mrs. Simon

I do hope your precious eyes are better—

I have little fresh to say about the poor Coz— he is much the same—

I have just been with him for an hour—& his mind wandered sadly— Arthur & Laurie Hilliard were terribly abused—but as he talked he much enjoyed eating *8* oysters, & some turtle soup—

He eagerly asked me to order a carriage for him—saying the only chance for my remaining here in safety, was for him to live 'on the other side of the Lake[']—

He looks well—& speaks in his own firm natural voice—which makes it all the more distressing he insists *he's all right* & we're *all* wrong—& now he hates the sight of Parsons—& he suspects everybody & has the wildest fancies—

It almost breaks my heart— I'd rather hear him jabbering nonsense—than *seeming* so much himself, & yet so insane— This is of course for you both— I send *no details* elsewhere—

Herdson the gardener—could no longer sit up at night—with swelled legs—so the attendant as a trained nurse takes his place—& manages very nicely—

always your loving & grateful

Joan

[Brantwood]
Tuesday
[March 15, 1881]

Dearest Mr. Simon

I wish I could give you a better report—but the poor Coz continues much the same— no apparent change for the better, or worse—

He is very quiet, & we believe has natural sleep in the night—

If things go on as they're now doing, I can see Parsons would much like your opinion—should you really have the immense goodness to come & judge for yourself—but at present he thinks it better to let things take their course till we see the result, say a fortnight hence—

Dr. Acland has of course offered to come if we wish it—and we particularly do *not* wish it—

I used my ankle a little yesterday—& it is more painful since, & Dr. P[arsons] says as you do, I must rest it all I can for some time—

The Coz has, as before taken a great dislike to Dr P[arsons] so he did not see him today in case of a scene—& irritating him unnecessarily—

Much love to both—ever your grateful

Jo-an

Brantwood
[Monday]
21st March 1881

Dearest Mr. Simon

You will both I know rejoice to know that the Coz has continued so rapidly to improve that I think we need not fear any further relapse at present—

He was down stairs yesterday—& got out in the afternoon—& from having eaten fairly well, all through the illness is not weak—

I can hardly realize that our anxiety is ended so suddenly—but I'm sorry to say tho' he seems quite well mentally, just as last time —he is *very* naughty—& refuses to believe *how ill,* he has been—& abuses us all to-day for our treatment of him— it is a very uncomfortable phase *for us*—& I trust will soon pass

He little knows the intense anxiety & sorrow for him we have had this last month! —

Always your most loving & grateful

Jo-anie

[Brantwood]
Sunday
[March 27, 1881]

Dearest Mr. Simon

It is *so very* good of you to write so kindly—& so often—& I *never can* thank you as I wish—

The Coz, thank God, goes on *so well* was himself all yesterday—& in the evening he had dinner with us in the dining-room —& no one could have discovered *any oddness.*

This morning a few cobwebs want sweeping off his precious brain—he insisted on writing today to the chief manager trustee of St George Mr Baker—to resign the Mastership—& have the Affairs of the company wound up—adding he'll never more have *anything* to do with it—all this "off his own bat"! —& I'm heartily glad if it *is* carried out—

Our dearest love to you both. He asked me in the most knowing way what *you'd* think of his getting over this attack so soon!

Your devoted & grateful friend

Jo-anie

I write hurriedly for early post—

[Brantwood]
Sunday morning
[April 3, 1881]

Dearest Mrs. Simon

I am so thankful to tell you that since I last wrote the Coz has daily got better—& now seems *himself*—and it's like waking from a horrible nightmare to find all the clouds had silver linings—

He won't hear of our going! —& all seems getting back to quite the old happy footing between us— he said he could'nt in any way account for his strangely varying moods—

I can't tell you *how much happier* we now are—or *how* grateful for the sweet sympathy & support you have both given us—

In haste for early post—

Your loving
Joan

Brantwood
4th April [1881]

Dearest Mrs. Simon

It was very *very* good of you to write me such a sweet long letter— I value your goodness in doing it very much—& can't settle to anything until I have sent you my most loving thanks—

The Coz, & Arthur were both much interested in what you said—especially about dear Boo, in whose happiness we all greatly rejoice—& also in all you say of Eliot Norton—

We all laught, the Coz in particular, (quite in his old way!) at your saying 'daffodils is *in*'! —they certainly are not *out* here! —but *in, very much* IN, in *bud,* I mean! —& the moment they *are in,* in the sense *you* mean, I look forward to sending you some—which I *should* have done without any reminder—& as for primroses! —well, *they* seem *months* off! — If the ground has'nt been covered with snow—we've had, & have now, the most bitter, biting, bleak north-east wind, with hard frost, that shrivels up one's very ("gizzard" Laurie Hilliard would say!) soul! —but it's fine, & in some sheltered parts of the wood, where the sun shines the Coz chops branches—& as this occupation keeps him warm— it's a great blessing— Did I tell you he is growing a beard & moustache! —it must seem very odd to his friends—to *us* the growth has been so gradual, we hardly seem to notice it now— it saves him much trouble but he has just asked me with some concern what's to be done if he gets a cold in his nose! — this does'nt seem at all a pretty prospect—& is evidently a puzzle to *him*—tho' I told him I had no doubt people *were* just as liable to colds in noses *with* as without! —

He feeds *very* well—on oysters & turtle daily—tho' "*not* at his own expense"! — (how wicked of me to make such base jokes!—) Miss Susie Beever insists on sending regular supplies of oysters from the Liverpool market—& a rich old lady (a Mrs Talbot) who has been very generous to his St George schemes—&c—sent me a big check imploring me to get *anything* for him, as the greatest favour to her—& as another friend sent a pint of turtle which he gloried in—I've continued the extravagance! — this of course is all entre-nous—

The crowning cause to rejoice has been that the Coz promised he'd see Dr. Parsons the first time he came (after vowing that no power on earth would ever induce him!) & Dr P[arsons] who came just now, *has* been received as of old—& is at this moment in the study with him to my joy, & his! —

How entirely right every word Mr. Simon has fore-told about the poor Coz! —

I'm sure he'd be glad *now,* to have a line from either of you—

I can hardly realize that all the horror of a bad nightmare is ended— I try to forget it as fast as I can—& really feel quite happy again—tho' for a week we were all exquisitely miserable—every hour revealing some fresh dagger—that *appeared* to be *from* my poor Darling himself—& tho' I *knew* it was'nt, he had *reasons* always to give—that had so much foundation—& he never listened to one word of explanation or opposition—& we were all before him as *crushed worms! Did* you ever see that in Punch? — "the missus my Lord"! — How nice all you tell us of the poor Taylors—& [Wycliffe's?] promise of success as an artist I can't think what you mean by a [Sedgwick?] Norton [spirit?]! — If it's adverse in any way to *you,* it's *wrong,* & ungenerous—& indeed!

Much love to both—ever your loving

Joan

Dr. Parsons just gone— he had a quite *pleasant* interview with the Coz

XXXVIII

Annie Somerscales to Ruskin

3, Leicester St
Hull
14th April, [18]88

My dear Master,

A hundred birds are singing amidst the budding trees in our delightful garden, which Frank has at last got into fair order. Easter, and April are encouraging seasons, and I think, perhaps, I may find the *Master* again. If only there were some ripe garden of Araby, for his feet! Some enduring spicery and balm of precious comfort instead of these thin seasons of reluctant bloom.

I am glad you are beside the sea! There's a changeless monotony of strength, I think, in the great pulses of the tide. Nothing to excite or distract in sea scenery:— Delicious dreams of ships, on far off tracks. Sheltering rocks between the world, and a fairy strip of borderland, where one seems to have alighted from nowhere. It is wonderfully nice I think,—(if there's plenty of *lon*[*e*]-*liness*—only to be beat, in fact, by Juan Fernanderz or Tahiti.

On Monday is my birthday and I cannot venture on the new year, comfortably without the Master's blessing. But for all that, you need not write, if not in writing mood. I shall still know that I have as it were touched you, and feel myself strong.

I'm very old [46], *getting* to be that is, and I begin to feel a sort of separation of body and spirit—to find that my real self is gaining sweeter life,—while yet, I cannot but know that physical life is declining. But I am perfectly well and strong and am dying for summer and holiday rambles and freedom.

I should so much like to know what you are doing or thinking, and how you feel about things. I wonder whether you will be at Brantwood, in July? I should not like to go to the hills—if the Master were not there. — Every thing is lowered in tone of beauty and interest,—has no *spirit* life,—when I know you all away from the sweet valley of Coniston Water. It is not that I am venturing a hope of seeing you, my dear Master; that's an extra & special delight belonging to life's few lov[e]liest islands; —but it really would help Sophie and me to decide about our holiday haunt, to know what part of the world the Master would be enriching with his presence, in July.

I hope my words do not read like thoughtless ones. To the Master I always speak from dearest affection and sweetest reverence, and I am always, your loving servant

Annie Somerscales

Part Three

Background Sketches

[June 30, 1876] SARAH ANGELINE ACLAND

Sarah Angeline Acland (1849–1930) was Ruskin's godchild and the only daughter (with seven brothers) of his intimate friend Sir Henry Wentworth Acland (1815–1900). She was an expert photographer, and some of her studies of fishes, in watercolor, were placed in the Ruskin Art Collection at Oxford. On February 2, 1919, she wrote Mrs. Severn: "I still have the doll which he gave me when I was four years old and which the then Mrs. Ruskin dressed for me. The cradle I gave to a favourite niece but I could not part with the doll" (unpublished letter; F. J. Sharp Collection).

[September 20, 1877]

JAMES REDDIE ANDERSON

At Oxford, J. R. Anderson (1850–1907), of Balliol, had led the students who, in 1874, had repaired the road at Hincksey. Next, in Venice (1876–77), he had assisted Ruskin in the study of Carpaccio. Returning to Edinburgh, Anderson abandoned his preparation for the Scottish Bar because of failing health and, in 1877, settled with his mother at Lairbeck, Keswick. Here, having married his cousin Emilie Marianne Anderson in 1882, he spent the remainder of his life in quiet study interrupted by trips (largely motivated by his interest in painting and architecture) to Greece, Egypt, Spain, Sicily, the Holy Land, and, again and again, to Italy. The only child of the Margaret Reddie who married Andrew Anderson, M.D., President of the Glasgow Faculty of Physicians, he would greatly puzzle some of his distinguished friends by his unwillingness to publish. His "Story of St. Ursula," compiled for Ruskin, was issued in the *Fors Clavigera* of November 1876 (*Works, 28,* 740–44), and in 1879 his essay on Carpaccio, "The Place of Dragons," edited by Ruskin, appeared as chapter 11 of *St. Mark's Rest* (*Works, 24,* 370–400). Seven lectures, given to the Keswick Literary and Scientific Society and edited by friends, would be privately printed and posthumously published as *The House of Bondage* (1908).

Anderson once laughingly said that the only money he had ever earned was a guinea awarded him in one of the Academy competitions for the epitaph to Ruskin: "He taught us / To hold / In loving Reverence / Poor men and their work, / Great men and their work, / God and His work" (A. R. MacEwen, Preface, *The House of Bondage and Other Lectures* [Edinburgh, 1908]). He himself would be commemorated by a sonnet:

In Memoriam

J. R. Anderson

Obiit March 26, 1907

You, who in Balliol day at work were seen
    With him we called "the Master"—him who bade
    Us toil at Hincksey with the pick and spade
To give poor men a pleasant village green—
Who, later, here in Crosthwaite's vale serene
    Lived out your student life, and plied your trade
    Of seeking Thought, Art, History, Faith to aid
The quest for Truth that grew with quest more keen—
Is it for nothing that your heart has given
Such strenuous work for wisdom, not for fame?
    Nay, other worlds shall gain your stores' increase,
The seed you gathered yet shall fruit in Heaven,
    And here your memory be a man of Peace
Who, loving light, toiled on till morning came.

R. D. Rawnsley

(Reprinted, in *The House of Bondage,*
from the *Westminster Gazette* of April 2, 1907)

Within the realm of Ruskin scholarship (except for comments by Cook and Wedderburn which are limited to the obvious), this self-effacing friend has been totally ignored. In 1883, writing the *Bible of Amiens,* Ruskin still would turn to him as "my general investigator" (*Works, 33,* 171 n.).

[June 9, 1876] SARA ANDERSON

A cousin of James Reddie Anderson (see B.S.), Sara Dunlop Anderson (1854–1942) first appears in Ruskin's Diary of 1874 as "Sarah"—a spelling which she herself never used, although it appears in the registry of her birth. Now she had come to help

Ruskin by transcribing the Psalms of Sir Philip Sidney to be included in *Rock Honeycomb* (see *Works, 31,* xxxi). From around 1882 until 1891 she assisted him as a full-time secretary, later serving Rudyard Kipling in this capacity. At other times (after 1891) she did secretarial work for Burne-Jones, Sir Henry Roscoe, Lady Ritchie, George Moore, and Meredith (although she never actually was the secretary of Meredith, as Charles Carrington states in his biography of Kipling). "She may be described as having been a super-secretary," Sir Sydney Cockerell recounts:

> She also was a super-friend. . . . Ruskin and Kipling placed her on a pinnacle among those who had served them. Kipling once declared to a mutual friend that she was in a class by herself, and that merely by the tone in which he pronounced the word "Damn" she knew exactly the kind of letter to write. Being on terms of intimacy with her employers, she . . . was possessed of many secrets which, however valuable as "copy," were very safe in her hands. Her lively understanding was happily lit up by a sense of humour, and she had an appreciation of their foibles, as well as of their genius, their strivings and their achievements. But after the great ones had departed, Sara Anderson never came into the open, never wrote down what she knew, never lectured or broadcast. She lived on serenely in retirement, enjoying literature, music, memories, and most of all conversation with surviving friends. (Obituary Notice in *The Times,* October 30, 1942; written by Sir Sydney Cockerell, who, in a letter to the editor, spoke of Miss Anderson as "one of my dearest friends from 1887 until her death")

"She was a unique character," Mrs. Gnosspelius comments; "she had what one remembers as a *depth* of understanding and integrity; she was completely sympathetic without ever losing her balanced sense of fun. One felt that she had the very highest sense of responsibility—and yet was never pompous, never prosy, never censorious—and to call her a faithful friend merely outlines the bare idea of the easy, comfortable taking-up-of friendliness, perhaps after years of absence. She had a voice of great charm, and a manner to match. Dear creature—"

[April 21, 1883] Lily Armstrong [Mrs. William Kevill-Davies]

In the *Ethics of the Dust* (1865) Ruskin had portrayed Mrs. Kevill-Davies (d. 1931, aged 79), née Lily Armstrong, as the 12-year-old Winnington schoolgirl who became for him a very special pet and, for Mrs. Severn, a special friend. Daughter of Sergeant Armstrong, M.P. for Sligo, Lily lived in Dublin so that, in 1868, when Ruskin went to Ireland to lecture on "The Mystery of Life and Its Arts," he spent (with Joan Agnew) a few days in her home, vainly hoping that with her help he might find a purchasable house, which could become his own home, within the vicinity of Rose La Touche. Lily had seen Rose "often lately," Ruskin told Mrs. Cowper-Temple in 1868 (Bradley, *Letters to Lord and Lady Mount-Temple,* p. 131), once finding her strapped to her bed in a nursing home (Leon, *Ruskin,* p. 391). Until 1875, when Rose died and when Lily, "a young Dublin beauty," married "a dashing Guardsman," Captain William Trevelyan Somerset Kevill-Davies, of the 17th Lancers (Spence, *Dearest Mama Talbot,* p. 56), Ruskin and Lily frequently interchanged affectionate letters. In 1873 the Severns had expressed their regard for her by naming their first child "Lily" (Sheila Birkenhead, *Illustrious Friends. The Story of Joseph Severn and His Son Arthur* [New York, 1965], p. 228). Now, in 1883, Lily appears at Brantwood with her own child—"Scrappy." Her portrait, as drawn by Ruskin in watercolor, appears in Derrick Leon's *John Ruskin.*

[August 10, 1877] The Barratts

"Holly How, Coniston," Mrs. Gnosspelius comments, "was the home of the Barratt family, who had established themselves early in the nineteenth century as mining engineers. They worked the local copper mines with great success, bringing prosperity to Coniston and wealth to themselves. The 'nice old couple' were probably William Barratt, who died in 1879, and his wife Sarah, who died eight years later."

[October 6, 1883]

Alice and Maud Bateman

Alice Annette Bateman (1850–1934) and her sister Maud Agatha (1846–1918) were daughters of the surgeon Dr. Henry

Bateman, who had died in 1880 (aged 74), leaving his widow Elizabeth (whom he had married in 1845, when she was sixteen) with £60,000 and 12 children (there had been 13, all-told). By 1883 his oldest daughter Maud was a Companion of St. George and with Grace Allen (now twenty-five) was arranging *The Ruskin Birthday Book: A Selection of Thoughts, Mottoes, and Aphorisms, for Every Day of the Year, from the Works of John Ruskin, LL.D,* of which George Allen would publish 3000 copies in December 1883. For Ruskin's birthday, for example, they chose a sentence from *The Stones of Venice*: "The whole difference between a man of genius and other men, it has been said a thousand times, and most truly, is that the first remains in great part a child, seeing with the large eyes of children, in perpetual wonder, not conscious of much knowledge—conscious rather of infinite ignorance and yet infinite power; a fountain of eternal admiration, delight, and creative force within him, meeting the ocean of visible and governable things around him" (quotation for February 8).

Maud's youngest sister, May Geraldine (1872–1938) would pay tribute to what Ruskin had meant to her childhood:

> He told us things simply and naturally just as our father had, with the same exquisite frankness, and understanding. He never made the mistake . . . of 'talking down' to us. He chose words which sang in our hearts and were all the more magical and entertaining because we didn't always know their meaning. And when he made stories in stones for us, we had no idea that we were being taught. . . . A slab of quartz in his hands was a faëry casket of marvels: we loved to see the veins of fine gold running through the Blue Chalcedony—the very phrase was an inspiration. . . . Walks became quests under his guidance; the country, a storehouse of secret treasures; every cliff a wonder of the world. . . . Taken to some new place, you were on the rim of who knew which thrilling phase of the unknown? Geology was no science, but a golden gateway. The seashore was God's mint, and the whole world His Book of Lovely Wonders. ("My Friend John Ruskin," *Catholic World, 119* [1924], 460–61; first published in *Black and White,* January 27, 1900)

At Brantwood, during later years, as W. G. Collingwood remarks, Ruskin in turn would find joy through the singing of "the Misses Bateman" (*Ruskin Relics,* p. 156).

[October 31, 1877] PETER BAYNE

Peter Bayne (1830–96), editor of the Edinburgh *Witness* and the *Weekly Review,* had been pilloried in the May *Fors* of 1875, in which Ruskin had published what he considered a smugly self-satisfied and monumentally obtuse letter that Bayne had sent to him in defense of "usury." Personally, as Ruskin had proceeded to explain, Bayne was a most worthy man, but "mischance [had] made him take up literature as a means of life," and he had become "one of the unhappy modern mob," in temper insolent and irreverent, who could not read with comprehension so much as a sentence written by Shakespeare or Goethe (whose names Bayne had invoked), not to mention Xenophon, Plato, Horace, Moses, David, and their kind (*Works, 28,* 321–23). The general annoyance caused by the well-intentioned Mr. Bayne dated back to 1859, when Ruskin's father, never respecting his son's judgment in the conduct of his own work, had strongly opposed the writing of Public Letters; nor had it helped that this "accursed idiot" had then refused to publish three such letters, addressed to him as editor. Paradoxically, in 1879 Bayne would issue *Letters from My Masters—Carlyle, Tennyson, Ruskin.*

[May 16, 1876] SUSAN BEEVER

Ruskin's intimate and very special friend, Miss Susan Beever (1806–93), lived in Thwaite House, diagonally across the Lake from Brantwood, with her sister Mary (1802–83). Here a "Cousin Mary" (d. 1908) was also sometimes to be found (see, for example, *Diaries,* p. 1080; September 10, 1884). Ruskin's friendship with the "Ladies of the Thwaite" had begun in the autumn of 1873, when Miss Margaret Beever (1805–74) still was of the household.

The garden of the Thwaite was notable not only for its asparagus, ferns, and flowers but also for its fruit trees, cultivated to attract the birds who might become Miss Beever's individual friends as they fed upon her window sill. It was her pleasure reverently to watch and love all forms of life as a keenly observant naturalist whose observations were combined with the richness of fantasy and tenderness in humor which characterize her letters. Ruskin also received pleasure from her watercolor studies of plants and of birds: "Those drawings of yours are quite marvellous," he thanked her for one group of sketches. "You might have done all that Bewick did—if you had had to work for bread, poor wee Susie! " (unpublished letter, n.d.; Pierpont Morgan Library). Or again: "It is no wonder, when you can draw like this, that you care so much for all lovely Nature" (*Works, 37,* 164; letter of [1875?]). Samples of her studies have been preserved in the Ruskin Museum, Coniston, and in a sketchbook, marked by Ruskin's bookplate, at Bembridge.

In 1870 she had published *A Book of Reference to Remarkable Passages in Shakespeare;* and in 1874, during months marked by the illness and death of her sister Margaret, Ruskin had helped her to compile the "Readings in 'Modern Painters' " known as *Frondes Agrestes* (1875). In later years she asked Albert Fleming to make the selections, published as *Hortus Inclusus* (1887), which represented the "nearly two thousand" letters in her Ruskin correspondence (Introduction, *Hortus Inclusus* [London, 1887], p. xi); subsequently Albert Fleming received about 900 of her Ruskin letters as a bequest (*Works, 36,* cviii). In the Coniston Churchyard she and Ruskin rest, commemoratively, side by side.

[February 9 and December 24, 1879]

William Bell and His Children

William Bell (d. 1896) of Haws Bank, whose boathouse was across the lake from Brantwood, had a joiner and builder's business, which means that he was a master craftsman. Helped by the boatbuilder Mont. Barrow, of Windemere, he constructed the "Jumping Jenny," as designed by Laurence Hilliard. He had four children—Joseph, John (b. 1854, who carried on the family business and was for many years the Coniston Registrar of Births and Deaths), Polly, and Libbie (or Libby, who married the Barratt's gamekeeper, Frederick Percival).

"I remember Libby well," Mrs. Gnosspelius recalls:

> she was what Coniston would consider rather "superior" and her children are likewise. But Libby was always ready to talk about the old days when she and Polly used to row across the lake to see the Professor, and spend a day in the hay-field or on the lake with the younger people. Polly did not marry; and I remember how Mrs. Severn used to depend on her in all sorts of domestic crisis and need— "Polly will come and cook for me," if she were alone at Brantwood for a time, and I recall even now her little grimace when she would add with her rich chuckle, "Polly is a dear girl but such a bad cook! " At afternoon tea parties Ruskin could always count upon Polly and Libbie to take care of the children and to serve them their food.

Made "J.P. by Mr. Gladstone's last government," William Bell was known as the "leading Liberal" of Coniston, which caused Ruskin to tell John Bell that he would like to call "and have a talk about politics." In the Diary he notes that on December 24, 1879, he was "at Mr Bell's" for what was probably the meeting described by W. G. Collingwood:

> Now the carpenter was used to Conservative orators and Liberal arguers, but he knew that Ruskin was a different sort of man; and all day long before the hour fixed for the visit he was in a greatly perturbed state of mind, walking up and down and wondering—a new thing for him—how he should tackle this unknown personality. At last the distinguished guest arrived. He was solemnly welcomed and shown into the parlour. The door was shut upon the twain. The son . . . who felt he had brought into contact the irresistible force and the immovable post, waited about hoping it would be all right, but in much trepidation as the sound of talk inside rose from a murmur to a rumble, and from a rumble to a roar. At last his father's well-known voice came through the partition in no trembling accents: "Ye're wrong to rags, Mr. Ruskin!" Then he knew it *was* all right, and went about his work. And after that Ruskin and "ald Will Bell" were firm friends in spite of differences. (*Ruskin Relics,* p. 24)

Subsequent diary entries adequately indicate that in Mr. Bell and his family Ruskin had indeed found "friends."

A similar tale is told by a countryman who remembered when Ruskin "and yan they cawd Bell hed a crack about politics and sec-like, and William clapped Perfessor on t' shoulder—he was vara friendly wid him ye kna—and he said, 'Well, to my waays o' thinking, for aw your conservative talk and writings and what not, thoo's as radical as t' best on us.' And Perfessor leuked oop wid a smile and smacked his hand intil William's, and he said, 'Well, well, you're not so far wrong efter aw' " (Rawnsley, *Ruskin and the English Lakes,* pp. 70–71).

[July 28, 1877] THE BENNETTS

Ruskin knew four of the Bennett sisters: Alice, Florence, May, and Rose, daughters of Robert Bennett, a prosperous wine merchant of Liverpool and Birkenhead (which would account, inferentially, for his having been in possession of letters from John James Ruskin). Florence Bennett (b. 1859) died at Bournemouth from tuberculosis on March 5, 1883, expressing her wish that her personal estate of £2900 (as stated in a document connected with her will) be given to St. George's Guild. Probably in 1877, listing the Companions of St. George in Volume XX of the Diaries, Ruskin had noted: "Not yet Companions—but may be: Florence Bennett, her mother [Susannah, d. January 23, 1868] dead nine years" (from a transcript provided by Mr. Dearden, supplemented through the help of Miss Vera J. Ledger; the list of Companions is undated). While visiting an "invalid sister" (presumably Florence), Rose (aged 25) was to be "accidentally drowned," on June 27, 1878, at about 10 P.M. because she had apparently sought relief from the unseasonable heat by taking a swim in Morecambe Bay (from accounts of her death provided by local papers). In September 1882 Ruskin wrote Miss Beever, from Genoa: "I am very glad to hear of those sweet, shy girls [designated Florence, Alice, and May], poor things. I suppose the sister they are now anxious about [viz. the consumptive Florence?] is the one that *would* live by herself on the other side of the Lake, and study Emerson and aspire to Buddhism!" (*Works, 37,* 411; see also letter to Mrs. La Touche, March 19, 1883, Letters, XXVIII).

"Alice and May," he added in March 1887, were "still sometimes at Coniston, D.G." (*Works, 37,* 411 n.).

[June 22, 1883] MRS. W. H. BISHOP

A daughter of the wine merchant Thomas Edmondson, Mrs. Bishop (1821–98) was a cousin and lifelong friend of Mrs. La Touche, with whose help she translated the *Meditations of Mrs. Augustus Craven.* In 1849, as the widowed Hannah Windham, she had married the stock broker William Henry Bishop and had had one child, Florence, who in 1905 (aged 52) became Mrs. Hubert A. Burke. On June 5, 1883, in Mrs. Bishop's home, Ruskin addressed about 200 people (among them Lowell, Leighton, Burne-Jones, and Matthew Arnold), repeating the tribute to Kate Greenaway's art given in his Oxford "Fairy Land" lecture and then displaying, as a surprise, twenty of Francesca Alexander's drawings for the *Roadside Songs of Tuscany.*

[June 1, 1876] LOUISE VIRENDA BLANDY

Louise Virenda Blandy (1860–90) was one of the nine children of Dr. Alfred Addison Blandy (1823–95) of Hyde Park, a dentist who had spent his earlier years practising in the United States. By 1874, having become interested in Louise's talent for drawing, Ruskin had asked her father to permit him to direct her art education. In 1879 and 1881 Louise was exhibiting at the Grafton Galleries, and for a number of years she served Ruskin as a copyist. In 1888, already suffering from tuberculosis, she married Ronald (1861–1933), son of Ruskin's friend George MacDonald—only to die two years later, in Ashville, North Carolina, where her husband had become Headmaster in an episcopalian school, vainly hoping that for her the change of climate would be restorative. Her watercolor study of seven angels in Fra Angelico's *Resurrection* was preserved in the Sheffield Museum, and her letters from Ruskin are now in an album at Bembridge School. There is also a note she sent to Mrs. Severn during Ruskin's illness of 1878: "Deepest sympathy. I am wretchedly anxious. Give him my dear love" (unpublished letter of March 1, 1878; F. J. Sharp Collection).

[July 14, 1883] Dolly Blomfield

Dolly Blomfield, later Mrs. Gurney, was an intimate friend of Mary Wakefield, whom she had met in 1870, when Miss Wakefield was attending a finishing school in Brighton. Miss Blomfield was two or three years younger than Miss Wakefield (1853–1910), whom she is known to have survived. After Miss Wakefield's death she helped Rosa Newmarch to prepare *Mary Wakefield: A Memoir* (Kendal, 1912), in which the author consistently refers to Miss Blomfield as "Dolly *Blomfield*"—never as "Bloomfield." (For the identification of Dolly Blomfield I am indebted to Miss Gnosspelius, who found a copy of the Newmarch *Memoir*—a scarce book—in the Liverpool Reference Library.)

[January 13, 1879] Robert Bloomfield

Author of *Rural Tales, The Farmer's Boy,* and *Wild Flowers; or Pastoral and Local Poetry,* Robert Bloomfield (1766–1823) was called "the shoemaker-poet." "All my pictures are from humble life," Bloomfield noted in his Preface to *Wild Flowers.* Progressively descriptive of rural sights and occupations from "Spring" through "Winter," *The Farmer's Boy* is analogous, in content, to *The Seasons* of Ludwig Richter, reproductions of which Ruskin presented to Whitelands College.

[February 9, 1883] Emily Brooking

In 1900, after Ruskin's death, Emily Brooking would write a letter of sympathy (signed Emily A. Lyne) in which she expressed her fear that "after the lapse of seventeen years" Mrs. Severn might not remember the Emily Brooking who had not forgotten Mrs. Severn's kindness "in past days," when she had visited Brantwood and Herne Hill. Although "Mr Ruskin," she recalled, "was angry for giving up my membership in the St George's Guild," nevertheless, "I feel the best of me is due to his teaching" (letter of January 25, 1900; F. J. Sharp Collection).

[August 17, 1877] Rawdon Brown

Rawdon Brown (1806–83) had known Ruskin since 1849, when, as a resident of Venice engaged among the archives, he had given generous help on problems connected with *The Stones of*

Venice. Theirs was thenceforth an affectionate though not an intimate friendship, their personal contacts having been renewed during Ruskin's recent stay in Venice. In 1862 Brown had been commissioned by Lord Palmerston "to calendar those Venetian State papers which treated of English history" (*Works, 9,* 420 n.)—an assignment at which he worked for the rest of his life. He was "a generous old antiquary with strong prejudices and a tender heart; with a lover-like devotion to his friends, and a profession of hatred for all the world beside," as Norton characterized him in 1871. "Venice has been his only mistress, and to her he has given his life" (*Letters of Charles Eliot Norton, 1,* 405). Yet he always found time to entertain delightfully the many travelers who came to him as friends, or friends of friends, as well as to assist Ruskin through giving directions, corrections, or advice. Hence he became one of those mentors whom Ruskin addressed, often ambivalently, as "Papa."

[December 18, 1883] BEATRICE BUGELLI

Famous as an *improvvisatrice,* Beatrice Bugelli—called Beatrice del Pian degli Ontani (1802–85)—had taught Francesca Alexander many of the songs published in the *Roadside Songs of Tuscany*. Giving an account of her friend's life, Francesca Alexander states that Beatrice degli Ontani ended every story—even her account of the death of an unusually beloved son—with the words, "Grazie a Dio!" As Beatrice explained, "We must thank the Lord most when He sends us trouble, because that is when He loves us best" (*Works, 32,* 209).

[January 19, 1879] JAMES BURDEN

Toward the end of February 1879 Ruskin was "summoned to London to give evidence on a charge of forgery, variously painful to [him]" (*Works, 37,* 276; letter to C. E. Norton, February 27–28, 1879). Two checks had been forged by James Burden, "28, an engineer" (*Times,* April 1, 1879), whose name (spelled "Burdon") appears on the Roll of the Original Companions of St. George (*Works, 34,* 703). "I knew him well about three years ago," Ruskin testified at the trial. "I gave him work to do" (*Criminal Courts*

Trials, 89 [1878–79], Case 379). The first check, for £35, 10s., had been cashed on November 1, 1878, and the second for £10, on February 6, 1879, at which point Burden was arrested. "The bank authorities were long in tracing the crime," Collingwood recounts. "They even sent a detective to Brantwood to watch one of the assistants." Found guilty, Burden was sentenced to a year in jail, though "no sooner was the prisoner released," Collingwood states, "than [Ruskin] took him kindly by the hand and gave the help needed to start him again on a better career" (*Life,* 2, 509). As a model for such behavior, Ruskin could readily have pointed to Sir Charles Grandison.

[Jan. 23, 1880] FRANCES ELLEN COLENSO

Ruskin's interest in Frances Ellen Colenso (1849–87) was closely connected with his admiration for her father, although through her work of later years she herself gained his personal regard. He had met her and her mother at Winnington Hall during the three years (1862–65) which the Bishop of Natal had been forced to spend in England with his family, defending himself against charges of heresy. After Volume 2 of his *Critical Examination of the Pentateuch* had been published in January 1863, he was asked to resign his bishopric, after which he had spent months fighting against vilification before he was reinstated. Meanwhile, he had also been deposed by the Bishop of Capetown —a judgment which the Privy Council did not reverse until 1865. Mrs. Colenso, with the five children, had spent most of 1862 either with or near Miss Margaret A. Bell, Principal of Winnington Hall, as a personal friend of long standing, under whose care Frances remained as a student. Here, therefore, Ruskin had met her (probably in 1863, she then 14), when the persecution of her father, for whom Ruskin felt unqualified sympathy, was at its height.

Passingly, he next saw Frances in 1869, when her eyesight began to fail so seriously that her parents had sent her to London to seek medical advice—escorted by the two brothers who were about to enroll in Oxford and in Cambridge. "Fannie Colenso at dinner," Ruskin noted on December 23, 1869 (*Diaries,* p. 691), she by then having been in London for almost a year. Her personal admiration for him would be expressed in 1876, when she enrolled as an original "Companion of St. George."

Back in Natal by September 1870, Frances was as yet unable to resume her drawing of landscape (one of her chief pleasures after her stay at Winnington Hall), but once more she could throw herself into her work as a teacher in the "mixed" school she had established (for black and for white). Now, too, she began to show her interests as a writer, first by publishing *Two Heroes* (1873) under the pseudonym "Zandille." This book, of which no copy has as yet been located in any library of the United States, is called "a novel" in the *B.M. Catalogue*.

In her next book she was animated by the concern which, in 1874, had taken her father to England to plead the cause of the Zulus while particularly intervening in behalf of the so-called "rebel" chief Langalibalele, whom the English were holding in captivity under false charges while subjecting his people to cruelly unjust exploitation and punishment. During this trip Bishop Colenso spent an afternoon with Ruskin at Oxford (unpublished letter to C. E. Norton, November 23, 1874; Harvard University Library; see also *Diaries*, p. 825, November 24) and probably made the gift to which Ruskin refers in a *Fors Clavigera* Letter of 1875: "I never saw a rough diamond worth setting, until the Bishop of Natal gave me a sharply crystallized one from the African fields" (*Works, 28,* 434 n.). At this time, however, Ruskin was evidently less concerned with Colenso's mission for the Zulus than over the fact that Bishop Wilberforce had made it impossible for his own "dear Bishop" to preach while at Oxford.

Meanwhile, in Natal, using the pseudonym Atherton Wylde, Frances was writing *My Chief and I, or, Six Months in Natal after the Langalibalele Outbreak*. Several purposes are served through this account of a trip taken into native territory (that of the Putini tribe) by the fictional Atherton Wylde under the leadership of his "Chief," Colonel A. W. Durnford of the Royal Engineers, a friend of Bishop Colenso to whom it was "rumoured" (rightly, one would infer) that Frances Ellen was engaged (Wyn Rees, *Colenso Letters from Natal* [Natal, 1958], p. 330). As a newcomer, Wylde approaches the "blacks" with the false assumptions and racial contempt which characterized the average white settler and soldier. Centrally, however, Colonel Durnford, with his understanding of the natives, whom he treats justly because of his personal integrity combined with knowledge of the true state of affairs, epitomizes a leader in whom England could take pride, in contrast to the shame which Englishmen would feel could they but know the *facts* about the typical conduct of officers who acquisitively conquered the territory of native chieftains falsely charged with treacherous aggression. The travelogue itself portrays the consequent suffering of members of a tribe robbed of their cattle and their land, individually insulted, all-but enslaved, and repeatedly betrayed by promises that they would receive due compensation and care. In the Preface the narrator recounts how, in 1875, "he" asked Colonel Durnford to read this book in manuscript, only to be told that it must not be published while "My Chief" was alive. Hence it was not issued until 1879, Colonel Durnford having been killed in that year on January 22, when "an immense body of Zulus attacked a large body of English troops which had been left inexcusably exposed and slaughtered all of them" (G. W. Cox, *The Life of John William Colenso, Bishop of Natal,* 2 [2 vols. London, 1880], 479).

In September 1879, Frances returned to England with her brother Frank, perhaps also accompanied by a sister, to spend some time in London. *En voyage,* she conceived and began her *History of the Zulu War and Its Origin,* to be published in 1880. It was a book designed to tell the English nation the *facts* about the origin and conduct of this war as sponsored by a government which had been constantly misinformed by the South African Colonial Office and by leaders of the Nationalist Party in Natal. Many of the actualities had already been publicized through various pamphlets written by Bishop Colenso as a result of his personal investigations and first-hand knowledge of events. Reaching London, Frances appealed to Lieutenant Colonel Edward Durnford (brother of the deceased Colonel A.W.D.) for help largely based upon his personal knowledge of what had really happened in Natal in connection with this war—help which he provided so generously that he was named as the coauthor of this book.

By January 1880 she was spending a week at Brantwood as a guest who left Ruskin very much aware of conditions in Natal and of the responsibility of England for cruelty and injustice (see Diary, January 27, 1880). But Frances herself urged him not to add, to his already heavy commitments, the work which would be entailed by his becoming, publicly, a champion of the Zulus. Thereafter she corresponded with him about immediate problems related to their cause, hoping that he would visit her after she had settled in a "cottage" near the home of her dear friends "Ned and Georgie" Burne-Jones (see Letters, IX).

Her next undertaking was a book which, shortly before his death on June 20, 1883 (aged 69), her father had asked her to write as a sequel to her *History of the Zulu War*. She herself had returned to Natal, toward the end of 1881, wracked by a tubercular cough which had necessitated her living quietly as a convalescent. Nevertheless, in response to her father's request, she arranged to have Lieutenant Colonel Edward Durnford help her as a coauthor and launched into *The Ruin of Zululand: An Account of British Doings in Zululand since the Invasion of 1879*, its first volume to be published in 1884. About a year later she sent to England two-thirds of the manuscript of the second volume (1885) just before a gigantic grass fire, swept forward by a gale, destroyed the rest of her manuscript, together with her home. She thereupon decided to develop the lost chapters into a third volume. But this was not to be.

In 1886, disregarding the cost to herself, she eagerly responded when the Reverend Sir G. W. Cox asked her to come to England because he needed her assistance as he wrote his two-volume life of her father. And in England she remained, faithfully helped by the friendship of Mrs. Burne-Jones as her cough became steadily worse until, on April 29, 1887, in the Tubercular Hospital of Ventnor, death came as a release. As the Reverend Sir George Cox truly said: "Thousands for whose welfare she shared her father's toil and self-devotion will remember with lasting thankfulness the name of Frances Ellen Colenso" (*Life of Colenso, I*, xii). Before the end of 1887 Ruskin had formally presented to the nation, to be kept in the British Museum, the uncut, 130-carat "Colenso Diamond." To the Zulus the Bishop of Natal remained

SOBANTU, which in their language means "the Father of his people" (Rees, *Colenso Letters,* p. 258).

[June 29, 1876] W. G. COLLINGWOOD

In the spring of 1875, at a breakfast for Oxford undergraduates, Ruskin had expressed his wish for a good translation of Xenophon's *Economist,* and before the summer ended, Alexander Wedderburn (1854–1931) and William Gershom Collingwood (1854–1932) had been visitors at Brantwood, reading aloud their rendition while Ruskin sat reading the Greek.

Shortly after entering Oxford in 1872, Collingwood had been introduced to Ruskin by Alfred William Hunt, a friend of his father, the landscape painter William Collingwood (1819–1903). Though the young Collingwood had, himself, already exhibited landscapes, Ruskin was soon prodding him, disconcertingly, as a member of the Oxford School of Drawing. During the summer of 1873, he had made his first call at Brantwood, with his father. Next, he became a Hincksey digger and then, more strenuously (with Wedderburn), a digger of Ruskin's harbor at Brantwood, after their morning bouts, of 1875, with Xenophon. Returning to Oxford in 1876, he won the Lothian prize and took a first in "Greats." Leaving the university, he studied in London at the Slade School and in 1880 had his first picture hung in the Royal Academy. During 1881 he stayed at Brantwood as an assistant who became Ruskin's traveling companion in 1882. Henceforth Collingwood's help and friendship were important to Ruskin. In 1883, having married Edith Mary Isaac (1857–1928), he settled within call of Brantwood, in a Windermere fisherman's cottage, at Gillhead; here he lived until 1891, when he moved to Lanehead, Coniston, with his wife and four children—all the while painting, studying local history, and writing historical novels, and sometimes traveling, purposefully, in Ireland, Norway, or Denmark to gather material for *A Pilgrimage to the Saga-steads of Iceland* (1899) as he became a leading authority on the Norse settlements in the Lake Country and, more generally, in the North (from Obituary Notice in *The Times,* October 3, 1932, written by his son, Robin George Collingwood, then professor of metaphysical philosophy at Oxford).

Collingwood's 28 years of association with Ruskin are commemorated by his edition of Ruskin's *Poems* (1891) and *The Poetry of Architecture* (1893), the essays collected in *Ruskin Relics* (1903), and the official *Life* (1893), distinguished by its insight and dependability. Issuing *The Economist of Xenophon* in July 1876, Ruskin, as Collingwood recounts, "gave his translators the profits: 'It will keep you in raspberry jam,' he said, and I have had a postal order for my share regularly these nearly thirty years" (*Ruskin Relics,* p. 8).

[September 3, 1883]

Margaret Cox and Emmeline Miller

On her marriage certificate Margaret Cox (1851–1943) is identified as the daughter of Henry Thomas Cox, a "Master Mariner" —this being the occupation which Ruskin, in *Praeterita,* would ascribe to his mother's father, the so-called "Captain Cox of Yarmouth," who had been, in actuality, William Cock, the Keeper of a Croyden Tavern (see H. G. Viljoen, *Ruskin's Scottish Heritage* [Urbana, Ill., 1956], pp. 79–80). It was therefore strikingly appropriate that in 1883 Ruskin should have arranged to have Margaret Cox, with Emmeline Miller (as new Companions), spend the weekend of his mother's birthday within the Brantwood neighborhood.

As they would tell the story of their visit, on Margaret Ruskin's birthday he had sent a carriage to their lodgings at Mrs. Dixon's, across the lake from Brantwood, and when it reached his door had greeted them by "giving his hands one to Emmeline and one to Margaret" and saying, "I am very glad to see you, *very* glad—but do tell me which is which?" Then, in the drawingroom, as Clennie made the toast before the fire, they evidently missed the joke when the Master said that "he was teaching [Miss Maclellan] Scotch." But they thoroughly enjoyed his reading (chapters 25 and 26 of *Old Mortality,* they would recall, years hence), as well as Clennie's Old English songs and the duet which she played with Mrs. Severn. "The Master doesn't like Mendelssohn," said Mrs. Severn, probably not explaining that Mendelssohn's "Wait patiently" had been a favorite tune of Rose La Touche. It was arranged that Baxter should call for them next morning, in a rowboat, at Tyson's pier so that, again with brother Ernest Miller, they would return for lunch, after which Ruskin took them up to see his "little field of experimental oats" in Naboth's Vineyard and "the contrivance for irrigation on top of the rocky land."

In 1886 Margaret Cox became Mrs. Thomas Harley and moved to St. John's Cottage on the Guild land in Bewdley, where she and her husband (formerly a bookkeeper) turned "a piece of the yet unreclaimed Wyre Forest into a fruit farm" (Edith Hope Scott, *Ruskin's Guild of St. George* [London, 1931], pp. 64–79 passim). As Mrs. William Clibbert Stapledon, Emmeline Miller (1851–1935) became mother of the writer William Olaf Stapledon (1886–1950) and remained active in her leadership of the Liverpool Companions.

[September 14, 1877]

BENJAMIN CRESWICK

A knife grinder of Sheffield until his health began to fail, Creswick (d. 1946, aged 92) had gained the interest of Henry Swan through a bust of Ruskin made from photographs in the Walkley Museum, and visiting Brantwood on August 23, 1877, Swan had vouched for his talent. "After the first sitting of an hour," Creswick would recount, "the Professor asked me how many more I should require. 'Five,' I replied. 'After what I have seen of your work,' said he, 'I will give you as many as you want'——" (M. H. Spielmann, *John Ruskin* [London, 1900], p. 176). Before long, Ruskin was thanking George Baker, a trustee of the Guild, "for employing Creswick, who has the truest genius, though it will take time to develop in the direction of beauty. But St. George and you could not do a greater kindness than in fostering it" (*Works, 30,* 302; letter of 1878). Spielmann was led to understand that for four years Ruskin had paid all expenses for Creswick and his dependents.

In London, Creswick did some interesting work, including the head of Carlyle on the Cheyne Walk tablet. In later years he was a Lecturer and head of the modeling department at the Birmingham Central School of Arts. In 1879 his bust of Ruskin was presented to Prince Leopold, after whose death it apparently was returned to Brantwood, inasmuch as at the Brantwood disposal sales of 1930–31 it was acquired by W. H. Whitehouse, to become an item (by now somewhat battered) in the Ruskin Galleries, Bembridge.

[August 17, 1883]

THE REVEREND WILLIAM HENRY DALLINGER

The Reverend W. H. Dallinger (1842–1909) was Principal of Wesley College, Sheffield. Since 1870 he had been engaged in microscopic research "on the life-histories of minute septic organisms." President of the Royal Microscopic Society for four years and senior lecturer of the staff of the Gilchrist Educational Trust, he edited and rewrote the last editions of *The Microscope and Its Revelations* (enlarged in 1901). In 1887 he would publish *The Creator, and What We May Know of the Method of Creation.*

On May 21, 1883, as Sir Edward B. Poulton recounts, when Dr. Acland had taken Ruskin to hear Dr. Dallinger lecture before the old Ashmolean Society "on the least and lowest forms of life," Ruskin had

> had to listen while Dallinger described his beloved organisms "darting across the stage of the microscope with all the grace and rapidity of a swallow's flight." I heard Ruskin, as we came out, protesting against the comparison. I was Secretary of the Society at the time, and the following morning met Ruskin and the lecturer at breakfast at Dr. Acland's house. Ruskin said: "I could not help thinking at prayers, Doctor Acland, after last night's lecture, the words you were reading ought to be—'The works of the Lord are *little,* sought out of them that have *pain* therein.' " ¶"No." said Dallinger at once, "sought out *on behalf of them* that have pain therein." Ruskin made no reply; but the idea of microscopic life and microscopic structure had evidently irritated him. He did not forget it, and he was referring to one of Dallinger's lantern slides when he said, in a lecture delivered about six months later [November 7, 1883, Lecture v, *The Art of England; Works, 33,* 354]:—"but only last term we saw the whole Ashmolean Society held in a trance by the inexplicable dec-

oration of the posteriors of a flea." (*John Viriamu Jones, and Other Oxford Memories* [London, 1911], pp. 249–50)

Poulton continues by identifying the posterior decoration which Dr. Dallinger had displayed.

[August 8, 1879] CHARLES DARWIN

Darwin (1809–82) spent the month of August 1879 at the Waterhead Hotel, with members of his family—among them his son-in-law, Richard B. Litchfield, a founder of the Workingmen's College and Ruskin's friend. Though Ruskin's acquaintance with Darwin dated back to 1837 (they had met, as fellow guests, in the home of the geologist William Buckland), he had first felt Darwin's charm in 1868, when Charles Eliot Norton had arranged to have them spend an afternoon together in Keston, where the Nortons were spending the summer as Darwin's neighbors. Subsequently, Darwin's son William had married Mrs. Norton's sister, and now, in Coniston, as Darwin's daughter recounts, her parents "also had the interest and pleasure of making friends with Ruskin. I remember very well his first call on them and his courteous manner; his courtesy even included giving my father the title of 'Sir Charles' " (Litchfield, *Emma Darwin, 2,* 238). For his part, sending Darwin "a study of peacock's feathers" and a photograph of "the globe [drawn] in true perspective," Ruskin wrote Litchfield: "It has indeed been a great pleasure to me to be brought into some nearer and kinder relations with Mr. Darwin; but you must not think I did not before recognize in him all that you speak of so affectionately. There is no word in any of my books of disrespect towards *him,* though I profoundly regret that the very simplicity and humility of his character prevents his separating what of accurately observed truth he has taught us from the wild and impious foolishness of the popular views of our day" (*Works, 38,* 334; letter of August 1879).

[October 16, 1877] DAVID DOWNS

David Downs (alternately Downes; d. 1888, aged 71) was officially the "head gardener" at Brantwood, as he had been, initially, at Denmark Hill. His was, however, a varied career. In 1872, embarked upon "the first labour of St. George," in the center of

London he had supervised three broomsmen whom Ruskin had employed, for eight hours a day, to keep Church Lane clean. Two years later, when Ruskin left Oxford for Italy, he had remained watchfully in charge of the Hincksey diggers, as their "foreman." Sometimes Downs had traveled with Ruskin, so that in France, for example, he could see how flowers and melons were grown, and together, at Brantwood, they had planned and worked many an improvement upon the estate. During 1878 he would be sent to superintend the cultivation of St. George's Farm—a tract of land (originally called Totley Farm or, alternately, Abbeydale) acquired in 1877 in response to the request of a "Communistic" group of Sheffield workingmen who, at the start, had planned to own it ultimately themselves through annual payments to the Guild of St. George. Left with the property after various misunderstandings had caused this group to abandon the original plan, Ruskin decided to plant fruit trees upon what now was called the "Farm" of St. George, entrusting its management to David Downs. As Ruskin then explained to Henry Swan, the "Stewardship" at Brantwood had been

> reduced . . . to such simple limits that I can spare him for most part of the year. I mean him to live, for a while at least, at Abbey Dale [where he died, in his own home], whence he can make little flying visits to me, and ask me a question or two between whiles, as I chop wood; and in all matters respecting the management of the land, he is to have whatever authority I could have myself, if I were there, and deserves it much better, seeing he knows more about the business, and understands my mind, by this time, having lived twenty odd years with me, besides taking care of me when my mind was nobody knew where. (Unpublished letter of July 1878; present whereabouts unknown)

[March 10, 1879] ADELA ("ADA") DUNDAS

For many years Ada Dundas (*d.* 1887, aged 47), daughter of William Pitt Dundas, of Edinburgh (Registrar General for Scotland), was a friend by correspondence only—the *"wisest"* of such "stranger correspondents" because of "caring much and troubling little," Ruskin told their mutual friend, Dr. John Brown (*Works,*

37, 340; letter of 1881). He had first known her through her drawings, in 1860, when he had arranged for her to become a pupil of his protegé, William Ward. Placing "a little study of fruit and leaf, by Miss Dundas" in his Educational Series (1878) at Oxford, he noted that "in qualities of actual realization, without reference to those of design, neither Dürer nor any one else could do much better" (*Works, 21,* 146). When it was feared that Ruskin might not survive his illness of 1878, Miss Dundas had evidently told him (in a letter he cherished) about a public prayer given, in his behalf, in the churches of St. Andrews. Afflicted by curvature of the spine, she herself needed constant care. Yet in 1884 Ruskin was welcoming her to Brantwood, first with her mother and a sister for a few days in May and again, without attendants, in July—she having acquired a Kate Greenaway gown for this second visit, "just to please me!" (unpublished letter to Kate Greenaway, July 4, 1884, Pierpont Morgan Library; see also letter from Ruskin to Mrs. La Touche, May 4, 1884, Letters XXVIII).

[January 14, 1879]

Sir Herbert and Lady Edwardes

Ruskin's admiration for the work of Major-General Sir Herbert Edwardes (1819–68) as a soldier and administrator caused him to issue, in 1885, *A Knight's Faith* and, in 1887, to present the Edwardes Ruby to the British Museum. *A Knight's Faith* provides a condensed version, through direct quotation with interpolated comment, of Edwardes' *A Year on the Punjab Frontier—1847–1848* (2 vols., 1851)—a book which Ruskin had received in 1851 as a birthday gift from his father. Back in England during 1850, Sir Herbert had married Emma Sidney, a stepdaughter of John James Ruskin's kind neighbor and physician, Dr. George Grant. Having thus known the Ruskins since her girlhood, Lady Edwardes (d. 1904, aged 82) remained Ruskin's affectionate personal friend after she had settled in England as a widow. The entire record of her husband's performance as the young lieutenant who had subdued the tribes of Bunnoo without bloodshed and who, as a colonial governor, was motivated not by the proverbial desire to obtain "loot" but by concern over the welfare of natives who could trust him to be beneficently "just," aroused Ruskin's desire to show, through *A Knight's Faith,* "how a Christian British officer can, and does, verily, and with his whole heart, keep in order such part of India as may be entrusted to him, and in so doing, secure our Empire" (*Works, 33,* 473; from *The Pleasures of England*). Lady Ritchie would recall how, during the 80s, Ruskin's eyes kindled when she was with him in the Brantwood library and he showed her "some book of Indian warfare," quoting Sir Herbert Edwardes as he "spoke of the example which good Christian men and women might set in any part of the world" (*Records of Tennyson, Ruskin, and Browning,* p. 77). "All our after misfortunes in India," he told Kate Greenaway, "were caused by effacing and contradicting his work" (unpublished letter of December 29, 1883; Pierpont Morgan Library).

[February 9, 1883]

THE REVEREND JOHN P. FAUNTHORPE

In 1877, through his *Fors Clavigera* correspondence, Ruskin had become acquainted with the Reverend John P. Faunthorpe (1839–1924), Principal of Whitelands College, a National Training School for Teachers. By 1881 the Whitelands May Queen Festival had been established, with a gold cross (designed by Burne-Jones) for the May Queen, together with the annual gift of about 40 books by Ruskin, to be distributed among the approximately 160 members of the Queen's Court. For his part, the "good" Mr. Faunthorpe helped, practically, by reading proof for Ruskin, in final revise, and by making a general index for *Fors Clavigera,* separately published as one substantial volume.

[June 20, 1876]

MRS. JULIA FIRTH

Widow of Thomas Firth of Sheffield, Mrs. Julia Firth (d. 1919, aged 85) of Seathwaite Rayne, Ambleside, became the translator of Jeremias Gotthelf's *Ulric the Farm Servant,* edited by Ruskin (1886–88): "he told me a translation should be 'closely accurate or fearlessly divergent.' I made one which was very literal, but it did not satisfy me, and I did it all over again, comparing French, German, and my own English version. In the course of years I completed the work, and laid it, figuratively speaking, at the Editor's feet" ("A Few Words about Jeremias Gotthelf," *Igdrasil, 1* [1890],

20). Ruskin speaks of her as "one of the ablest and kindest of my women-friends" (*Works, 33,* 343 n.).

[July 8, 1876] John Edwards Fowler

John Edwards Fowler (d. 1901, aged 59) was an original Companion of St. George and founder of the Ruskin Society at Liverpool. In his will he calls himself a "Pattern maker," though he is said to have come from a family of some distinction (see Scott, *Ruskin's Guild of St. George,* p. 58—this book having been illustrated by Mr. Fowler's son, Harrison Ruskin Fowler).

[August 19, 1877]

Marion, Martha, and Claudia Gale

Claudia (or "Tottie," 1853–1943), Marion (later Mrs. James F. Clarke, 1854–1934), and Martha (or "Mattie," 1855–1926) were among the eight children of Arthur Severn's oldest sister, Claudia Fitzroy Severn (1829–74), who in 1852 had married Frederick Gale (1823–1904), a parliamentary agent and successful London barrister. Once a famous cricketer, as "The Old Duffer" he had become a well-known sportswriter, whose friendship Ruskin much enjoyed. On a gala day it was Martha who would launch Ruskin's "Jumping Jenny," wreathed with daffodils. She and Claudia, as Mrs. Gnosspelius remarks, "were always bracketed as 'the Girls' —Martha and Tottie." "You know I loved him dearly," Martha would write Mrs. Severn, after Ruskin died, and Claudia echoed, "You know what a delight we have always felt it to have known him," while their father recalled "his wonderful goodness to me & mine" (letters of condolence, January 22–25, 1900; F. J. Sharp Collection).

[January 18, 1878] Mary Gladstone

Mary Gladstone (1847–1927), later Mrs. Harry Drew, had met Ruskin through Sir William Graham, the father of her close friend Frances. From January 12–15 Ruskin had been the guest of her family at Hawarden, much enjoying his first visit in their home, though he had gone to them armed with a telegram to insure his safe retreat. "In some respects," Gladstone had noted in his *Diary,* Ruskin was "an unrivalled guest, and those important respects too" (Wyndham, *Letters to M.G. and H.G.,* p. v). As to Ruskin: "I thank Fors and your sweet sister, very solemnly, for having let me see your father, and understand him in his earnestness. . . . I have been grievously deceived concerning him myself, and have *once* written words about him which I trust *you* at least may never see. They shall be erased henceforward [for the passage to be removed from the *Fors Clavigera* of September 1875, see *Works, 28,* 403 n.]. . . . If ever you see them, forgive me, and you will know what it *is* to forgive" (*Works, 37,* 239–40; letter of January 18, 1878). To him she almost immediately became "St. Cecilia of Hawarden," and before long she would be receiving letters signed "St. C.," she having found in him her "Aprile."

[July 1, 1876] KATHLEEN GORDON

Kathleen Gordon, a sister of Mrs. Victor Marshall, was now "an entirely sweet and very interesting girl of 12," subsequently "spoiled by 'society,'" Ruskin would comment (see entry for January 25, 1883). More immediately, he would tell Lucy Drewitt that Kathleen "was being swept away into the wilderness of this world —(She's just fourteen and was a bridesmaid at one of these dreadful West End marriages the other day so I've given her up)—" (unpublished letter of 3 December, 1876; Pierpont Morgan Library). "Like Tora [Mrs. Marshall]," Mrs. Gnosspelius remarks, "she lived to a great age, becoming terribly eccentric and a great problem to her children; but like Tora, a youthful charmer."

[February 22, 1878]

FRANCES GRAHAM, LADY HORNER

Frances Graham (d. 1940, aged 85), who in 1883 became Mrs. John F. Horner, was the daughter of William Graham (d. 1885), M.P. from Glasgow. Ruskin had probably met her, after his return from Italy in June 1877, through their mutual friend Burne-Jones —who would profess to be sadly disconcerted when she married: "many a patient design went to adorning Frances' ways. . . . Sirens for her girdle, Heavens and Paradises for her prayer-books, Virtues and Vices for her necklace-boxes—ah! the folly of me from the beginning—" (Georgiana Burne-Jones, *Memorials of Edward Burne-Jones,* 2 [2 vols. New York and London, 1906], 130–31).

Meanwhile, during Ruskin's illness of 1878, Frances became active in soliciting contributions for the Gift of the *Splügen Pass*, a picture which her father offered to buy so that, through being acquired by some other collector, it would not be lost to those who wished to present it to Ruskin. A few months after his recovery, Ruskin visited the Grahams' home in Dunira, Scotland, where he saw the pictures which prompted him to write *The Three Colours of Pre-Raphaelitism* (November and December 1878).

Subsequently Lady Horner would recall how she had been a guest at Brantwood, probably in 1881 (during the months left unrecorded in the Diary):

> He was very fond of me and made me call him "St. C." always, as a pet name. . . . We used to go out on the lake and on the hills together, Ruskin always making a curious sort of love to me, and I wondering if I could care for him enough to spend much of life with him. He was often rather unkind and loved power; he was not tender by nature and we quarrelled constantly, but his talk was so delightful and his courtesy so great that I always came back to his lure . . . [He] had a passion for birch trees, and there was one up by a waterfall which he specially admired and used to apostrophize as if it had been a lovely woman. (*Time Remembered* [London, 1933], p. 55)

"But F[rancie]," Ruskin remarked, "was never more than a birch tree to me, and it didn't always keep march-music time" (*Works, 37,* 590; letter to Mary Gladstone and to Frances Horner, of May 15, 1887).

[July 28, 1876] PROFESSOR E. W. GURNEY

Mrs. Severn had arranged to have Professor and Mrs. E. W. Gurney rowed to Brantwood for a "high" or "meat" tea:

> we have not had a more delightful evening on this side of the water, and Ruskin was everything that is considerate and courteous and kind. He first showed us his literary and art treasures while there was yet light; had tea laid in the drawing-room that we might enjoy the lake; talked delightfully, with a slight twinkle of humorous enjoyment of his own extravagance, when he trampled upon all the existing ar-

rangements of society and augured its speedy downfall; read us bits of Cowley and Sir Philip Sidney, and, best of all, the preface, so far as yet written, to the edition he is to bring out of Sidney's version of the Psalms, full of humour and nice feeling; and instead of coming away at nine as we had proposed, we tore ourselves away at half past ten or later; and instead of walking home as we had arranged to do, the faithful Downs . . . insisted on rowing us back as well as over. It was pleasant to hear him talk of his master and of his own pride in appearing in person in the "Fors." The row back in the dusky light was an appropriate close to an evening so delightful in all ways. (*Letters of John Ruskin to Charles Eliot Norton,* 2, 134–35)

[May 20, 1876] MAJOR BENSON HARRISON

Major Benson Harrison (d. 1900, aged 80) was the child of Benson Harrison (d. 1863, aged 77) and of the Dorothy Wordsworth who, during her youth, had lived at Rydal Mount with William Wordsworth and his wife, as their virtually adopted daughter. (See also entry for June 26, 1883.) By 1871 Major Benson Harrison was living at Coniston Bank (see *Diaries,* p. 712; September 18) as one of the five estates (two in Coniston, two in Ambleside, one in Ulverston) which had been the property of his father. The land of Coniston Bank bordered that of Brantwood, so that "the Harrisons" of Coniston Bank (sometimes confused with another family of the same name) were Ruskin's nearest neighbors until they moved to Leamington Spa, where they spent the rest of their lives. They left Coniston in 1884, when Ruskin makes his first Diary reference to the Goodisons (see *Diaries,* p. 1075, July 28; see also Letters, XVI) to whom Major Harrison had "let" Coniston Bank, which in 1897 would be bought by Mrs. Severn from Major Harrison, as lake-front property which adjoined that of Brantwood. (For the foregoing information I am indebted to Miss Gnosspelius, who obtained it through an interview with a grandson of Major Harrison's brother Matthew, supplemented by data gathered from her study of tombstones in the Ambleside churchyard.)

[June 26, 1883] Mrs. Dorothy W. Harrison

The mother of Major Benson Harrison, née Dorothy Wordsworth (d. 1890, aged 89), often spent the summer at Water Park (the second Coniston estate, at the lower end of the lake, acquired by her husband), to return to Scale How, Ambleside, as her more permanent residence (information provided by Mrs. Gnosspelius). She is the "old Mrs. Harrison" to whom Ruskin refers in his Diary entry of August 26, 1886, when she told him how William Wordsworth, as though her father, had escorted her "to her first balls" (*Diaries,* p. 1132).

[February 22, 1878]

Constance and Mrs. Hilliard

The friendship with Mary Constance Hilliard (1852–1915), who became Mrs. William Henry Churchill in August 1880, was especially precious to Ruskin until her marriage, after which it became a relationship that held his deeply affectionate loyalty. "Connie's a little goose—" he would write Norton in 1883. "I never 'left' her—nor came back to her but I can't amuse myself with her as I could when she was 14—and I've lots of others who need serious *help*" (unpublished postscript to letter of April 16, 1883; Harvard University Library). Ruskin was then arranging a generous gift of minerals for her husband's school for boys, in Reigate, where the Reverend William Henry Churchill (d. 1936, aged 81) was a master whom students would not recall with affection (see Lionel Fielden, *The Natural Bent* [London, 1960], pp. 22–24). One of her five sons recalls having been taken to Brantwood when he was ten or eleven years old, to sit upon the knee of Ruskin as his godfather. At a Memorial Service in 1915 the boys of St. David's School would be told: "never forget . . . that mirth and glee which was one of her great gifts to the world" (E. W. Hornung, "The Angel of Death. In Memory of Mary Constance Hilliard"; pamphlet in the F. J. Sharp Collection).

Constance was a daughter of the Reverend John C. Hilliard (d. 1882, aged 61), of Cowley Rectory, Uxbridge, and of the sister of Ruskin's beloved Lady Trevelyan, who had died in 1866 while traveling with Joan, Connie, and her husband as Ruskin's guests.

Ruskin had met Connie at the Trevelyans' home in 1861, to be immediately captivated as she "glittered about" in her "extremely quaint and witty way" (*Works, 35,* 458). Two years later (when she was eleven) Dr. John Brown, of Edinburgh, had thanked her for sending him her photograph: "it is so 'awfully' (as young people now call very) good and like, the mouth especially, and the sly, prim, droll, quaint, queer, dear, funny, sunny look all over, which is EURZ" (*Letters of Dr. John Brown* [London, 1907], p. 163). Recalling the Connie of later years, Mrs. Gnosspelius writes:

> She was a sweetie; she had a heart-shaped face and a little chin that turned down. . . . Do you know what I mean? Some people's chins don't take an active part in the conversation; Connie's was as mobile as her other features. She had arched eyebrows and an animated, sympathetic charm, and she and J[oan] A[gnew] S[evern] were in many ways alike, especially when they were together. One felt that they were deeply in alliance. I can only have seen Connie once, and probably I was a mere brat; but I still have her in my vision.

Ruskin's friendship with her family followed, Connie's mother (née Mary St. Alban Tollermache, 1827–82) becoming Ruskin's "Mamie." On the day before her death from tuberculosis, he would write:

> Darling Mamie
>
> I don't know how to thank you for your lovely letter—or how to tell you the sympathy—I do not say, sorrow, with which I read it—for you are too brave and good ever to be sorrowed for—only rejoiced in—at all times—and through all trial. ¶—I do not know how much you have been to me, and always will be, for I cannot fancy what I should have been, without Pauline [Lady Trevelyan] & you, always holding me up and holding me straight—when my foot slipped most—and my way became dark ¶And now—it is more and more lonely— perhaps I shall see more starlight but I am very blind just now. (From unpublished letter of May 13, 1882; Pierpont Morgan Library. For Mrs. Hilliard's letter of May 12 [1882], see Letters, XXIII.)

[June 2, 1879] ETHEL AND FREDERICK HILLIARD

Ethel Hilliard, or "Ettie" (d. 1946, aged 87), had always been affectionately accepted by Ruskin as the daughter of her parents and the sister of "Connie" and Laurence. By 1883—her parents having died in 1882—Ethel was a resident of Coniston, where she spent the first year at Low Ground Bank with her bachelor brother Frederick (d. 1913, aged 53), after which, by 1884, they lived at Tent Cottage until 1908, when they went to the school of their nephew, J. Churchill, in Ascot. After the death of Fred, Miss Gnosspelius states, Ethel "lived in Canterbury (until around 1930) and then moved to Uxbridge, where she died."

"Freddie, who acted as a land agent to some big land-owner in Scotland, was often absent," Mrs. Gnosspelius writes, "and when present was amiable but speechless. Yet somehow Fred's occupation seems irrelevant to the story, these Hilliards [Ethel and Fred] being as it were a legacy from the *real* Hilliards, Laurie and Connie, the dear and treasured ones. Ethel was a dull and rather prudish person (you felt that she never forgot that she was a daughter of the Church)" who became

> a solitary spinster with a passion for gossip and a very sharp eye for passers-by. She loved company, and was a great one for "taking offense" if she imagined a slight. All the local matrons were kind to her (I think they pitied her) and my mother, Tora Marshall, and Joannie visited her constantly—and often came away rather ruffled, as I recollect. Except for her status as the sister of Connie and Laurie, I think she was a *trial.* But she was to be reckoned with, because she had a nimble tongue, and was a notable mischiefmaker. She was kind to us children, and loved us to visit her. I think she was the first person who tried to censor my reading: I asked her to lend me "Jane Eyre" and she solemnly refused. I think I was never, up to that moment [ca. 1900] so furious. I was about thirteen.

[June 13, 1876] LAURENCE JERMYN HILLIARD

Laurence Jermyn Hilliard (1855–87) had recently been appointed secretary "for St. George's correspondence," Ruskin had explained in the June *Fors Clavigera* (*Works, 28,* 633).

> A strange, bright, gifted boy,—admirable draughtsman, ingenious mechanician, marvellous actor; the imaginer of the quaintest and drollest humors that ever entered the mind of man; devoted to boats and boating, but unselfishly ready to share all labors and contribute to all diversions; painstaking and perfect in his work, and brilliant in his wit,—Laurence Hilliard was dearly loved by his friends. . . . He was Mr. Ruskin's chief secretary at Brantwood from January, 1876, to 1882, when the death of his father, and his own failing health, made him resign the post. He continued to live at Coniston, and was just beginning to be famous as a painter of still life and landscape when he died of pleurisy on board a friend's yacht in the Ægean, April 17, 1887, aged thirty-two. (Collingwood, *The Life and Work of John Ruskin, 2,* 489 n.)

[September 8, 1877]

Thomas Coglon Horsfall

Thomas Coglon Horsfall (1841–1932) founded the Manchester Art Museum and University Settlement. His plans to establish an art museum for workingmen had been discussed in the July 1877 *Fors Clavigera* (*Works, 29,* 149–57), and he had responded with a letter, published in the September issue (*Works, 29,* 195–96), in which he urged that Ruskin might be more effective if he would modify his tone and become more patient with the sins and sinners he denounced. This public interchange had been accompanied by a number of personal letters (*Works, 29,* 589–93) which had led to Horsfall's being welcomed as a guest at Brantwood.

[May 6, 1883]

Clarence King

A geologist and mining engineer, author of *Mountaineering in the Sierra Nevada* (1872) and *Report of the Geological Exploration of the Fortieth Parallel* (1870–80), Clarence King (1842–1901) was a memorably delightful conversationalist and companion. As John La Forge recalls, King had met Ruskin by chance at a picture dealer's, where they had "argued upon a number of points," Ruskin apparently having been delighted "by the value of King's remarks" (John Hay, *Clarence King Memoirs* [London and New York, 1904], p. 191). Describing King's "universal success" in England, John Hay recounts: "Ruskin took him to his heart, entertained him at Coniston, and offered him his choice of his two greatest water-colours by Turner. 'One good Turner,' said King, 'deserves another,' and took both" (ibid., pp. 129–30). In the Diary entry for September 2, 1883, recording the arrangement of the Turners in his bedroom, Ruskin notes: "(Zug & Fluelen gone!)"

[January 8, 1881]

Dr. John Abernathy Kingdon

Dr. J. A. Kingdon (1828–1906), a close friend of Ruskin's intimate friend Dr. John Simon, was "best known as Surgeon to the City of London Truss Society, to which he was elected in 1858, to serve the Society with all his energy for thirty years. . . . [He] was not an operator but was a very ingenious mechanician, and all the best improvements in trusses used by the society during the last fifty years came from him. He was very successful in reducing hernia" (Plarr's *Lives of the Fellows of the Royal College of Surgeons of England, 1,* 667).

For a letter of 1887, from Thomas Pebardy, urging Ruskin to have faith in Dr. Kingdon's treatment of "your rupture," see Letters, XXXIII. Mr. Pebardy's confidence in Dr. Kingdon's skill presumably was warranted inasmuch as, in undated material (F. J. Sharp Collection) which was written during a period of mental illness, one finds the following statement: "But I was made to understand by the healing of the rupture that I must now attend to my business, and I intend instantly [to] turn to my business letters."

[May 19, 1880]

The Reverend William Towler Kingsley

The Reverend William Towler Kingsley (1815–1916) was tutor and fellow of Sidney Sussex College, Cambridge, until 1859, when he was presented to the Rectory of South Kilvington, in the Diocese of York. In his drawing room he "hung a number of Ruskin's water colours, each covered with a little curtin [sic]. ¶ [He] was a tall man, with long hair, and shaggy beard. He was stone deaf, but built his own organs, and had two grand pianos in the small drawing room at the Rectory" (a note by C. A. Markham bound, with one of Ruskin's letters to Kingsley, in a copy of *Our Fathers Have Told Us*; F. J. Sharp Collection). An authority on Turner, whom he had known personally, Kingsley had been close to Ruskin, in friendship, for more than 20 years, and in 1878, when Ruskin was ill, he had prepared the "Notes" issued under his name as an Appendix to the seventh edition (May 1878) of *Notes by Mr. Ruskin—On His Drawings by Turner*. "No greater nonsense can be uttered than the story of Turner's saying that Mr. Ruskin saw things in his pictures that he himself had not thought of," Kingsley had then remarked, to Ruskin's delight (*Works, 13,* 535). Ruskin, in the *Notes,* had listed Turner's drawing of a jay as "The most wonderful piece of water-colour work at speed I have. It was given me by Mr. W. Kingsley, of Kilverton [sic], with many and many a precious thing besides" (*Works, 13,* 469).

[July 16, 1880] "LOCKIE"

The most attractive Lockie, who looked "as if she was meant to go into a [jewel] case herself" (*Diaries,* p. 1046; December 27, 1882), by now had evidently become a member of the household, as an assistant governess or nursemaid for the Severn children. She seems to have been still at Brantwood in 1892, when Gordon Wordsworth wrote Mrs. Severn: "I was sorry I never said goodbye to Herbert [by then ten years old] and his companion whom I only knew as 'Locky' " (unpublished letter of September 29, 1892; F. J. Sharp Collection). Mrs. Gnosspelius writes:

> I have only my mother's spoken word about this shadowy character. She [Mrs. W. C. Collingwood] told me an anecdote about a governess, nursery-governess or some such—naming Lockie *tout court,* nothing more; but my memory is perfectly clear on the matter. Her *name* may have been Lockie, since it is a perfectly good Scots surname; but more likely it was another of the interminable diminutives. I find

that other households in the 19th century were also addicted to this pet-name madness, but at Brantwood it really became a disease.

[July 16, 1883] GEORGE MACDONALD

Rose La Touche and Ruskin had had no more mutually intimate friend and advisor than George MacDonald (1824–1905), author of *A Book of Strife, in the Form of the Diary of an Old Soul* (1880). ". . . perhaps the days which have given us *Hiawatha, In Memoriam, The Christian Year,* and the *Soul's Diary* of George MacDonald, may be not with disgrace compared with those of Caedmon," Ruskin would say in an Oxford lecture of 1884 (*Works, 33,* 449). The book is written in seven-line stanzas, numbered so that each stanza marks the day of a month. January 3, Rose's birthday, is commemorated by the lines:

Sometimes I wake, and, lo! I have forgot
And drifted out upon an ebbing sea!
My soul that was at rest now resteth not,
For I am with myself and not with thee;
Truth seems a blind moon in a glaring morn,
Where nothing is but sick-heart vanity:
Oh, thou who knowest! save thy child forlorn.

For February 8, as Ruskin's birthday, one finds:

Thou wilt interpret life to me, and men,
Art, nature, yea, my own soul's mysteries—
Bringing truth out, clear-joyous, to my ken,
Fair as the morn trampling the dull night. Then
The lone hill-side shall hear exultant cries;
The joyous see me joy, the weeping weep;
The watching smile, as Death breathes on me his cold sleep.

[June 2, 1883] MARION MACLELLAN

Marion (Minnie) Maclellan (1863–1942) became governess to the Severn children in 1882 and spent 12 years at Brantwood. "Pretty, Scots, and well-educated, she was a favourite of all, and especially with Ruskin," Mrs. Gnosspelius writes. "When, as an old man, he became 'tiresome' or intractable, Clennie would be called from the schoolyard, and her quiet, pleasant voice soon would work a calming influence. There was a case of valuable minerals in the study and, the story goes, J.R. would press Clennie to take a specimen—the sapphire was a beauty—and she would accept it with pretty thanks, and retire. The sapphire was generally back in the case within an hour."

More immediately, one catches a glimpse of Clennie, "—a pretty young girl in a white woollen gown," during an afternoon of 1883, as she "made toast at the drawing-room fire, a charming performance," and then, with Mrs. Severn, played "a selection from Offenbach" for Margaret Cox and Emmeline Miller, as two Companions of St. George (Scott, *Ruskin's Guild of St. George,* pp. 69–70). ". . . our beautiful governess Clennie," who goes "to church . . . [because] she likes doing everything that is proper . . . and [has] inscrutable (to me) ideas about Sunday bonnets," Ruskin would remark in his *Letters to Francesca* (pp. 103–04). Her portrait in oil, painted by Arthur Severn in 1888, just before she left Brantwood, "is said to have been exhibited under the title 'A Lady of Skye,'" Miss Gnosspelius notes, "and to have prompted one critic to write, 'Then she must have been an angel.'" After Ruskin's death Mrs. Severn received from her a letter of condolence (F. J. Sharp Collection).

[September 20, 1877]

William Hirrell Mallock

W. H. Mallock (1849–1923) had recently published *The New Republic* (1877), in which with much sympathy and considerable insight he depicted Ruskin as Mr. Herbert. The first part of *Is Life Worth Living?*—to be dedicated to Ruskin—had just appeared in *The Nineteenth Century*: a "faultlessly logical article," Ruskin had remarked in the September 1877 *Fors* (*Works, 29,* 216). In the early 70s Mallock had been one of the undergraduates who attended "the Professor's" weekly breakfast parties at Corpus Christie, finding in Ruskin the one personality at Oxford, among the dons, to whom he could fully respond. ". . . at Oxford I grew to know [Ruskin] intimately," he states in his *Memoirs of*

Life and Literature (London, 1920), "and my sympathy with his genius never lost its loyalty" (p. 70).

[January 25, 1878]

CARDINAL HENRY E. MANNING

For many years Ruskin had discussed religious problems with Father (made Cardinal in 1875) Henry E. Manning (1808–92); in 1852, for example, both his mother and his wife had been worried lest, influenced by Manning (among others), he might become a Roman Catholic (see Mary Lutyens, *Millais and the Ruskins* [London, 1967], pp. 16–17; letters of July 26 and August 2). During the period (*ca.* 1860–75) marked by his repudiation of essential tenets in the Christian faith, including his belief in personal immortality, he would naturally have discussed what troubled him most deeply with this leader (from the first, a fellow member of the Metaphysical Society), whose intelligence and values commanded his regard. As one of Ruskin's readers, Manning had remarked that *Fors Clavigera* was "like the beating of one's heart in a nightmare" (*Works, 36,* lxxxvi; letter of 1873), and inevitably he would have rejoiced could he have been an agent in giving Ruskin the spiritual comfort of the Roman Catholic faith. Now, in the *Nineteenth Century* of January 1878, he had read "An Oxford Lecture," delivered in December, in which Ruskin had examined the "true or false" of Christianity from the point of view of a believer whose faith could seem to be at one with that of the "Venetian maid," St. Ursula (*Works, 22,* 534–36), and he had evidently written to inquire whether he was right in inferring that Ruskin had become a "Catholic."

[June 13, 1876] THE VICTOR MARSHALLS

Victor Marshall (d. 1928, aged 78) and Mrs. Marshall (1854–1936), née Victoria Gordon, were what Ruskin called "our own Squire and Squire's lady" (*Works, 25,* 102). Mrs. Marshall, as well as her husband, was a godchild of Queen Victoria. The family of Victor Marshall, Mrs. Gnosspelius relates,

> were Yorkshire mill-owners of liberal views and extreme wealth. Early in the century several brothers settled in differ-

> ent parts of the Lake District: one at Derwentwater, one at Patterdale, and one, James Garth Marshall, at Monk Coniston. These men were bringers of good-will, employment, and civilization generally, to the rural dales and their rough, untutored ways. . . . Victor settled in as the "young squire" after his adored brother's Alpine tragedy (as I recall old talk), and after a time at Cambridge, where he made many friends, such as Leslie Stephen and Hallam Tennyson. J. G. Marshall had married into the nobility (his wife was a Thynne, of the Marquess of Bath's family); and Victor was a god-child of Queen Victoria. He was an extremely interesting and complex character; my father was, in a way, a great friend of his, and in a still funnier way, I was too. Victor played the violin, wrote poetry, in interminable rhyming couplets, mostly satiric . . . but painting was his passion. In his old age he deserted his home, family, and everything he had, and lived in a Chelsea studio painting, playing the fiddle, going to an occasional concert—utterly detached from his former life. I used to go and see him there.

Mrs. Victor Marshall's mother, Mrs. Gnosspelius continues,

> was a Lady-in-Waiting to the Queen, who, a Gordon by birth, married a Gordon, of the noble Scotts family of whom Lord Aberdeen is the head. Hence, with all those Victorias about the Court, she was always called Tora. Now what is there to say about Tora? She was a charmer; she was a terror; she was as proud as—Lucifer. . . . She was an aristocrat and gloried in the fact. But she was an autocrat too. Tiny, with dark, sparkling eyes and a lively tongue, she was admired more than loved, I should say; but I think my mother, who was afraid of no one, loved her. Yet she was never "Tora" to any of her local friends. She lived to a great age [82], becoming more embittered, shrewish, and hating all her family [she had three children] so that her death was a release. But in her prime she was a *force* in the whole district; she had a *style* which was frankly envied and emulated by everyone. . . . Yet she was the proverbial "martinet." . . . Deportment

was the thing: stand up; carry yourself straight; no lounging, Dora; turn out your toes, Barbara; Emile, don't be so stiff! And her critical glance at a child's teeth and hair—rather like that of a vet, with an animal. — So her daughter [Mary] left her, and went to a nunnery, where she stayed for many years. Then, when her mother died, she returned to the world. "I only did it to get away from Marme," she explained; and took up dog-breeding, and lived alone for many years until one day she was found dead among her little dogs. George, the younger boy, was quite a little beauty; he went into the Hussars after a lively career at school, and he was killed in the first month of fighting—November 4th, at Ypres. That broke up the family for good; there was nothing left. . . . There are no Marshalls here now; and the last acre of the immense estate has gone into other hands. The mansion (just below my house), where we used to have the parties, is now a Holiday Fellowship resort.

[June 14, 1876] THE MELLYS OF CONISTON

Widow of Andre Melly, of Liverpool, Mrs. Melly (née Ellen Grieg; d. 1895, aged 85) lived at Lanehead, with her daughter Louisa, from around 1876 until 1891 (when Lanehead became the home of the W. G. Collingwoods). Her son George (1830–93), although a resident of Liverpool, was a frequent visitor and kept a boat in "his" harbor (see Diary entry for February 10, 1883). George Melly had sat in the House of Commons as M.P. for Stoke-on-Trent, 1868–75, and it was doubtless with him (rather than with his son, George Henry, as identified by Miss Evans), that Ruskin took a walk in 1884, "over moor," engaged in "parliamentary talk, possibly useful" (*Diaries,* p. 1069; June 2). The Collingwoods would remember the Mellys not least for their hospitality. "My parents," Mrs. Gnosspelius recalls, while providing identifications, "used to tell about the marvellous spreads which they were expected—urged—to consume at [the Mellys'] table: they would come away hardly able to stagger, and would then have to raise an appetite to make a good appearance at the Brantwood dinner-table"—about a mile up the road.

[February 3, 1883] Ruth Mercier

Ruth Mercier, swiftly established as "my favourite Ruth" (*Works, 34,* 502), had been sent by Ruskin's London doctor to attend him in the old "nursery" at Herne Hill during his illness of 1882. Some weeks after his recovery he had written C. E. Norton: "I got faster better this time, because Sir William Gull got me a pretty nurse, whom I at first took for Death (which shows how stupid it is for nurses to wear black), and then for my own general Fate and Spirit of Destiny, and then for a real nurse [who had nursed Rose and kept her alive and got her hidden from me] and slowly—and rather with vexation and desolation than any pleasure in convalescence—I came gradually to perceive things in their realities" (*Works, 37,* 405; letter of August 30, 1882, the words in square brackets being supplied from MS in the Harvard University Library).

In 1885 Ruth would be his guest at Brantwood (*Diaries,* pp. 1101–02; March 13, 15, 19), where, a few months later, she would be serving him again, professionally. Although there was "no better news *mentally* . . . ," Mrs. Severn then told Norton, "he is much quieter . . . Arthur is now here—and his old favourite nurse 'Ruth' " (unpublished letter of August 5, 1885; Harvard University Library). At the front of the Diary one finds her Kensington address.

[February 17, 1878]

Henry Wentworth Monk

Henry Wentworth Monk (1827–96) was a Canadian fruit farmer who believed that he had the gift of prophecy. Among his dreams was the restoration of Palestine to the Jews and "the establishment of a united Christendom with a central government and police force" (William Gaunt, *The Pre-Raphaelite Tragedy* [London, 1942], p. 59). For some time Ruskin had considered Monk "an interesting and somewhat pathetic example of religious madness" (*Works, 28,* 312; from *Fors Clavigera,* April 1875, in which he published a letter from Monk, withholding his name). Answering a letter of 1873, he had said:

I acknowledge the wonderfulness of much that you tell me

—but I simply do not believe that you can understand so much about God when you understand so little about man. You claim prophetic power. Prove to me that you have the slightest insight into the workings of my mind and heart, when they are not open to public inspection. If God wishes you to convince me that He is teaching you more than He is teaching me, and that it is my duty therefore to help you in your work, He could enable you to do so in ten words. But unless He does so, I simply do not assist you or condemn. I do not venture to judge you. You appear to me to be mad, but for aught I know, I may be mad myself. But I mean to do what seems to me to be my own business, and leave you to do what seems to be yours, unless you can show me that you have some direct message to me, authentical in special knowledge of me. (Richard S. Lambert, *For the Time Is at Hand* [London, 1947], p. 104)

Now, having received from Monk an appeal for the Palestine Restoration Fund, modeled on his own appeal of 1871 for the Guild of St. George, Ruskin sent a response which attests the imminence of his first illness: "I thank God for your letter; and Christ. For, as I interpret it, I am taught that you are brought out of the tombs—and I also, clothed, and in our right minds. ¶I send you your Palestine R[estoration] Fund paper signed. This is also written with Sir Walter Scott's pen. ¶I am ever, your faithful and loving fellow-servant / John Ruskin" (ibid., p. 112; letter of February 15, 1878).

[February 21, 1880] ALICE RATHBONE

A daughter of Phillip Rathbone, of Liverpool, Alice Rathbone (1855–1911) would marry William Moore, a pottery manufacturer, and become the mother of five daughters and a son. Mrs. Gnosspelius comments:

As for the Rathbones, they were and still are a remarkable family, having been "in full production," so to say, for 200 years—production, that is, of Rathbones of a similar type: the Quakerish, public-spirited, philanthropic, high-minded men and women, which culminated in Eleanor Rathbone,

M.P. (1872–1946); Non-conformist to the core, and Liberal (in the 19th-century sense) to the backbone. Alice, at this time, was no doubt a charming *and* serious young person—just the type to appeal to J.R. She would probably have been staying at Lanehead, with Mrs. Melly.

[September 27, 1877]

Mrs. J. T. ("Kate") Raven

To readers of *Fors Clavigera,* Kate (d. 1937, aged 89), daughter of William Smith, poulterer, was known as the "indoor Stewardess" of Brantwood and as one of the three servants whom Ruskin "wouldn't change for anybody else's servants in the world" (*Works, 28,* 520). She remained at Brantwood until she married the local tailor—John Thomas Raven—in August 1878, when Hollywath Cottage became her home. Thereafter, "tea at Kate's" was a recurrent entry in Ruskin's diaries. By 1883 her daughter Ethel Constance Snowdrop was also there to welcome him. "I remember the Vicar's fury," Miss Gnosspelius comments, "when he saw Snowdrop Raven's headstone inscription already carved in granite with the claim to fame—'Friend of Ruskin.' "

[January 16, 1879]

William Harrison Riley

In 1879 William Harrison Riley (1835–1907—according to his daughter, who inscribed these dates on the back of a photograph acquired by the Yale University Library) was living with his family on Totley Farm, the thirteen acres of impoverished land which the Guild of St. George had bought, in 1877, for a group of Sheffield workingmen who, during spare hours, wished to raise strawberries, currants, and the like.

When he called on Ruskin in 1879, Riley was accompanied by Henry Salt, who was impressed by Riley's "extreme simplicity" and idealism. He now "appeared at Ruskin's door," Salt recalls, "with a big parcel of the moss" which is plentiful in the Coniston district and "gravely presented it as soon as the first salutations were complete. The delightful charm of Ruskin's manner was seen in this little incident; he laughed—for who could have helped laughing?—yet took the gift—and turned the subject—with a graciousness that could leave no hurt" (*Seventy Years among Savages* [New York, 1921], pp. 61–62).

Something of the same naiveté is reflected in a letter which Riley wrote to Walt Whitman some weeks hence, asking Whitman to send a copy of the *Leaves of Grass* and his photograph. "You will know John Ruskin—'Professor Ruskin,'" Riley explained. "He is indeed a Master and a Man eminently just and brave. He is an inspired man, and his utterances are always classical, and mostly divine. A few days ago I sent a few extracts of your poems to him, and though he is ill, he at once answered, as follows:—

"Dear Riley / These are quite glorious things you have sent me. Who *is* Walt (Walter?) Whitman, and is much of him like this! / Ever gratefully yours, / J. Ruskin"

> Please know that Ruskin is esteemed as the greatest critic of scripture, sculpture, and painting that we have any knowledge of, and that he is extremely careful not to use adjectives unsuitably. . . . I never knew him to use the word ["glorious"] before, except as describing some scenery or valorous action. . . . The book and photograph I wish to forward to Ruskin. The money cost shall be remitted—by or for him. . . .
>
> As for *myself*—since I read your book [about 12 years ago] I have been striving to work as a good pupil and companion. You have sent me through poverty and many cruel tribulations, but I have never whined over my work. I joined the "International" and published and edited the only paper it has had in England. I stuck to it, while I had a shot in the locker and never once was tempted to utter a cowardly, sneaking or treacherous word. Out of the strife, through the poverty, and despite the offers of bribe, and attempts to intimidate I came out clean handed and clean hearted—always supported by your great teaching.
>
> My dear Master, *do* write to me, your faithful pupil and lover. My *words* will not prove my love, but could you have seen my *work* since I first read your divine message, you would *know* I loved you, and that you gained one more

loving soldier for your campaign. / William Harrison Riley. (Copy of an unpublished letter, March 5, 1879; Berg Collection, New York Public Library)

The book and photograph for Ruskin were sent without delay, and Riley, acknowledging their arrival, remarked: "Ruskin is a great, good man. He is not only a beautiful writer, but a beautiful worker, and he will always *do* what he thinks he should do, even at the hazard of death or disrepute" (Copy of an unpublished letter to Whitman, April 2, 1879; Berg Collection). Next, hoping that he had helped Whitman, Riley rejoiced: "[Ruskin's] stamp upon any work is regarded as being [as] infallible as the 'Goldsmith's' Hall stamp on British gold ware" (Copy of an unpublished letter to Whitman, April 4, 1879; Berg Collection).

Born in Manchester (his father, according to Riley's Baptismal Certification, a "Fustian-cutter" and "lay-preacher"), Riley had met Whitman during the second of two periods (1866–70) which he had spent in the United States. Returning to England, he had edited liberal periodicals such as the Leeds *Critic* (in 1871) and the London *Herald and Helpmate* (1872–74), an organ of the International Workingmen's Association. In 1876 he moved to Sheffield, where he edited the Sheffield monthly *Socialist* (July–December 1877).

By 1873 he had sought help from Ruskin in connection with some plan for a cooperative organization of workingmen. "I am greatly interested, as always, in your letters, while they much grieve me," Ruskin had responded.

> I see, for one thing, that you are thoroughly honest: and that is the one link which should—the only link which can—primarily, bind men together. I accept now, which I have not hitherto done, the title of your friend. But how far I can or may choose, to help or promote your present plan, is another thing.
>
> You say—"a hundred persons have volunteered".— Do you know that *these* are honest as you are yourself— It is not easy to find such.
>
> You think "cooperation" will do all?
>
> By no means, my friend.

> *Cooperating* rogues are worse than single ones. (Unpublished letter, October 13, 1873; W. H. Montague Collection, New York Public Library)

Subsequently, Ruskin had encouraged Riley to settle in Sheffield as an informal agent of St. George's Guild. "Whatever real power you have to forward the higher objects of the Guild will find the fullest openings in Sheffield—but everything depends upon gentleness and patience" (unpublished letter, February 24 [1879?]; Pierpont Morgan Library). Yet before long, addressing Henry Swan, Ruskin remarked: "I believe Riley is half-mad—he would certainly make me wholly so—if I had more to do with him ¶You may get him employment at 10/ for 6 hours a day—elsewhere if you like. ¶This is seriously meant" (unpublished letter, July 2, 1877; present whereabouts unknown).

Although a confusing account of the workingmen's attempts to manage the farm emerges through scattered articles and letters published in the *Commonweal* of 1889, it seems clear that Ruskin ultimately angered the group by arranging to have Riley and his family live on the premises with authority to direct the enterprise (see M. A. Malory, "St. George's Farm," *Commonweal,* May 25, 1889, pp. 164–65). "I have a letter from Riley, which I like, and am prepared to comply with if you concur with me in thinking it advisable," Ruskin had told Henry Swan when his first attack of insanity was imminent. "I do not think St. George's money wasted in these experiments, (so long as I am able to find men of whom I am sure). Every trial will teach us something. I do not like having to advance money again, but cannot see how the poor fellow can start without it" (unpublished letter, February 7, 1878; present whereabouts unknown). In all, £63.18.0 were paid to Riley in wages and for "sustenance of . . . family (whilst working on St. George's Farm)" during 1878 (*Works, 30,* 115, 117; "St. George's Guild Accounts").

During the early 1880s Riley returned to the United States, no longer honored by Ruskin's faith. Writing to Henry Swan on November 30, 1881, Ruskin parenthetically announced: "of all the blackguards I ever came into collision with in my long life, [Riley] was out and out the worst" (unpublished letter; present whereabouts unknown). Finally, in a Public Letter of 1889: "Mr.

Riley was no friend of *mine.* I *tried* him as an exponent of modern Liberalism, and was as little pleased with the result as the members of *your* league were!" (*Works, 34,* 620; originally published in *Commonweal,* June 15, 1889, p. 189).

[February 22, 1878]

Margaret Robertson (Mrs. W. H. Kendal)

Margaret ("Madge") Robertson (1848–1935), who remained a lifelong friend of Mrs. Severn, had married the actor W. H. Kendal, and when in London, Ruskin enjoyed attending their performance. Rather recently he had seen Ellen Terry in a role which, some years before, he had seen enacted by "much-regarded friend, Mrs. Kendal" (*Works, 26,* 328; from "Living Waves," which he at first had called "A Caution to Snakes," "partly in affectionate remembrance of Madge Robertson's delivery of that phrase, in New Men and Old Acres"). Dame Terry, in this play, "was very delightful," he had noted, "—but a different creature from Madge Robertson: a wonderful study, in what the difference is. Much, I think, in the continual ease of a soul at unity with itself, in a lady, and the abruptness of one broken in two, in those who are less than ladies" (*Diaries,* p. 963; June 28, 1877).

[May 20, 1876] **Egbert Rydings**

In March 1876 Mr. Egbert Rydings (d. 1912, aged 85), one of the original Companions of St. George, had written from his home in Laxey, Isle of Man, to correct the "Master's" addition in a *Fors Clavigera* report of Guild Finances. After finding Ruskin's addition also wrong in the next issue, he asked: "Would it be possible to have these items checked before being printed? I should feel it a pleasure if I could be of use" (*Works, 28,* 611). Soon he was serving as an accountant for the Guild. Now it had been arranged that he should visit Brantwood, staying at the Waterhead Hotel. Nominally, the Guild (effectually, John Ruskin) then loaned him money to revive the home-spinning of yarn in Laxey and to have it woven into cloth at a mill in which the machinery was driven not by steam but by a waterwheel. By 1881 Mr. Rydings was ready to fill orders: he had "on hand a good Stock of Cloth, Tweeds, Home-spun Serges, Flannels, Blankets, Yarns, Stockings, etc." (*Works, 30,* 332). Ruskin, for one, had his grey suits made of Laxey woollens, and he hung among the treasures in the Brantwood drawing room a picture of "St. George's Mill" (see *Works, 30,* Pl. XXXIX, facing p. 331).

[January 17, 1879] HENRY STEPHENS SALT

Henry Stephens Salt (1851–1939) recalls having accompanied W. H. Riley to this luncheon, after which,

> Ruskin . . . showed us his wild strawberry beds, and terraces on the hillside like Swiss roads; also a small beck running through his grounds to the lake, which he said was never dry, and was as precious to him as pure gold. The Lake scenery, he said, almost compensated him for the loss of Switzerland, which he could not hope to see again; his feeling for it was less one of affection than of "Veneration." But the sunsets had been a disappointment to him, for the sky above the Old Man was often sullen and overclouded, and this he attributed to the poisonous influence of the copper mines. (*Seventy Years among Savages,* p. 191)

A disciple of Shelley and Thoreau, Henry Salt was now an Assistant Master at Eton who would win the support of Meredith, Hardy, and G. B. Shaw, among others, through his denunciations of "savages" who ate flesh, practised vivisection, wore furs and feathers, killed animals for sport, flogged schoolboys, mistreated prisoners, waged war, and desecrated "mountains for profit" (*A Group of Unpublished Letters by Henry S. Salt to Joseph Ishill,* with an appreciation by Henry W. Nevinson [Berkeley Heights, N.J., 1942], p. vii and passim).

[June 26, 1883]

FLORA LOUISA SHAW (LADY LUGARD)

Flora Shaw (1852–1929), who married Sir Frederick John, later Lord Lugard, in 1902, had become Ruskin's friend in 1870, when he had lectured at the Royal Military Academy, Woolwich, where her father, General Shaw, was the senior officer. The 18-year-old Flora was then a most lovely debutante who, as her biographer remarks, "called forth all of Ruskin's tenderness." For many years her mother had been an invalid, so that with an older sister, Flora had had to supervise the 11 other children in the family—an entourage portrayed in *Castle Blair* (1878). Exhausted by such responsibilities, as a girl she had developed weakness of the lungs, from which she recovered through a long stay in France; subsequently, as the nurse of her mother (who before her death, in 1870, had to be lifted from her bed), she had permanently hurt her spine. Responding to her courage in bearing anxiety and pain, as well as to "her beauty, her intelligence, and her hunger for learning," Ruskin had lost no time in manifesting his regard. "He directed her reading and saw that she had the books she needed . . . he helped her with lessons for the children, sent her stones for them and geological specimens. Sometimes he invited her to stay at Denmark Hill. . . . He introduced her to Carlyle, taking her to Cheyne Walk," and he even helped her to establish a cooperative store in Woolwich. Needing to make money, in 1874 she had turned to him with the plot of *Castle Blair,* which he had encouraged her to write, rejoicing when it went through eight editions. Thereafter, establishing her name through still other stories, she also served as the head of the Colonial Department of the London *Times*, with special interest in the affairs of South Africa, Australia, Canada, and the Klondike. "To the end of her life she wore a little watch he had given her in the early days of their acquaintance" (Enid Moberly Bell, *Flora Shaw* (*Lady Lugard*), [London, 1947], pp. 20–23 and passim).

[July 5, 1876] ANNIE SOMERSCALES

One of the original Companions of St. George, Miss Annie Somerscales (d. 1928, aged 86)—daughter of Thomas Somerscales, a Master Mariner—taught school in Hull. Her memories of this visit seem to have prompted the letter "from a Companion" published in the December 1876 *Fors Clavigera*: "My dear Master, I have thought so often of the things you said about yourself, in relation to St. George's work; and I feel sure that you are disheartened, and too anxious about it." But since Ruskin had been interested in her "little keel scholars," housed in river boats, she sent him a description of the "water cottages" and the "joyous life" of these "rural sailors" (*Works, 28,* 770–71). Characteristically, Ruskin sent her a box of agates to help her in her teaching (*Works, 26,* 444 n.). In later years she would spend some part of her vacation in a neighborhood which, for her, was enlightened merely by his presence. (See, for example, her letter of April 14, 1888; Letters, XXXVIII. The Frank and Sophie mentioned in this letter are probably the brother and sister with whom she had now made her call.)

[August 26, 1877] ROBERT SOMERVELL

Robert Somervell (1851–1933), of Hazelthwaite, Kendal, was one of the original Companions of St. George. In 1872 he had bought Ruskin's *The Political Economy of Art* for one shilling—"the best spent shilling I can remember" (*Robert Somervell,* ed. by his sons [London, 1935], p. 43). In 1878, aged 27, he entered Cambridge, leaving the family shoe business at Kendal, where he had worked since he was 15. He became a schoolmaster, first at Liverpool College and then, in 1887, at Harrow, where he remained for 33 years, during which he taught Winston Churchill the rudiments of English grammar with an originality and skill to which Churchill pays tribute: "Thus I got into my bones the essential structure of the ordinary British sentence—which is a noble thing" (Sir Winston S. Churchill, *A Roving Commission. My Early Life* [New York, 1940], p. 17). Somervell was now in charge of the legal affairs of the Guild, and was organizing a protest against the proposal to supply Manchester with water from Lake Thirlmere. In 1877 his pamphlet was distributed with *Fors Clavigera* (*Works, 27,* cviii).

[July 14, 1879] AGNES STALKER

Agnes Stalker (b. 1865) was the youngest of the 11 children whose parents were now living in the shepherd's cottage—scarcely larger than an average Park Lane dining room, Ruskin had observed (*Works, 28,* 258)—known as "Lawson Park." This crowded domicile, with its kitchen also serving as its parlor, lay high up on the moor above Brantwood and in April 1883 became the home of the Wilkinsons, with their "Jane Anne" (*Works, 29,* 487–88), the Stalkers by then having lost their mother (Mrs. Chris Stalker, d. July 8, 1881) and moved to How Head Farm.

Agnes was a character who had been well known to readers of *Fors Clavigera* since 1875, when Ruskin had transformed "our little Agnes of the hill-side" into an idyllic Agnes through whose name he could bait, temptingly, his theories about the reforms in education to be instituted "under St. George's rule" (*Works, 28,* 284). From the start, the actual Agnes had been, essentially, but another one of the "duckling[s] astray" who were always likely to arouse his compassion. Her sisters Hannah (b. 1849) and Isabella (b. 1858) were to find employment at Brantwood—Hannah having become the Brantwood cook in 1878 when Kate Smith married Thomas Raven. Into the 1890s the name "Stalker" appears with regularity in the record of Ruskin's personal expenses (his white "bankbooks" from 1885–96 are in the F. J. Sharp Collection). The real Agnes had by then become a creature who could startle tiny tots: "My sister Ursula," Mrs. Gnosspelius writes, "remembers Agnes Stalker as 'someone we [she and her nurse] used to meet on the road, and she was a rather frightening sight, with red hair, and a red face, and looked wild and uncouth.' This would be in the '90s, about 1896–97 perhaps."

[March 29, 1883] James Henry Stead

During the 1870s James Henry Stead (d. 1886) had created a sensation through his song-and-dance act, "The Perfect Cure" (words by Tom Perry, music by Blewitt).

> There he was in his striped clothes, his "lay-down" white collar, his clown's or dunce's hat, his heavy eyebrows, painted moustache and chin tuft, and a red blob on each cheek, singing his little song. When he finished the chorus, he proceeded to leap up and down, holding himself quite erect, with his hands down by his sides. He did not bend his knees, he just jumped, stiff-legged, from his toes. The secret was that he kept on doing it an amazing number of times . . . [In *Household Words* Dickens said] that, on the occasion of his visit, James Henry Stead had leapt up and down no less than sixteen hundred times! (W. MacQueen-Pope, *The Melodies Linger On* [London, 1950], pp. 124–26)

[July 9, 1876] SIR LESLIE STEPHEN

Sir Leslie Stephen (1832–1904) had already made a name for himself as an Alpine climber and a literary critic. His *History of English Thought in the Eighteenth Century* was issued in 1876, and "An Agnostic's Apology" had appeared in the June *Fortnightly*. He was a good friend of Ruskin's trusted Charles Eliot Norton, but otherwise he and Ruskin were as though at opposite poles.

Of late they had twice crossed swords in public. President of the Alpine Club, 1865–68, and editor of the *Alpine Journal,* 1868–71, Stephen was typical of the group whose athletic prowess had "conquered" the Schreckhorn and "vanquished" Monte Rosa, Mont Blanc, and so on. Stephen's Alpine papers had appeared in 1871 as *The Playground of Europe,* the Alps having become, as Ruskin said, "soaped poles" for Englishmen (*Works, 18,* 90). In an Oxford lecture of 1874 he had urbanely pointed out the nonsense of Stephen's having said, in a review of Whymper's *Scrambles among the Alps,* that "if the Alphine Club has done nothing else, it has taught us for the first time really to see the mountains" (*Works, 26,* 102–03), and he had sent Miss Thackeray (in whose London home Stephen was then living) the first two numbers of *Deucalion,* in which this lecture had been published, "thinking they may possibly interest Mr. Stephen also" (*Works, 37,* 725; undated letter [1875?]).

More sharply, in the December *Fors* of 1874, Ruskin had replied to a review of *Fors Clavigera,* published in *Fraser's,* which Stephen had concluded by saying that Ruskin's denunciations of society were due to his having a "sensitive nature" and that therefore "he has certainly more claim on our pity than on our contempt" inasmuch as he "supplies a fresh illustration of the truth . . . that it is among the greatest of all blessings to have a thick skin and a sound digestion" (*Works, 28,* 207 n.). Granting the desirability of these attributes, Ruskin began his reply by describing his delight, at Assisi, as he watched a "little pig in the roundest and conceitedest burst of pig-blossom" (*Works, 28,* 208); he proceeded to equate that little pig with Leslie Stephen and ended with remarks about the son of a clergyman who rejoiced in the stoning of squirrels. (Ordained a minister, Leslie Stephen had become an agnostic with serenity; as he himself said, "I was not discovering that my creed was false, but that I had never really believed it" (*Some Early Impressions,* p. 70). The boy who thoughtlessly stoned squirrels, Ruskin concluded, "had better have been employed in thoughtfully and resolutely stoning St. Stephen—if any St. Stephen is to be found in these days, when men not only can't see heaven opened, but don't so much as care to see it shut" (*Works, 28,* 214).

Ruskin now presented this issue of *Fors* to Mr. Stephen, who in later years would rather naïvely assume that his host "had quite forgotten that he had taken an unfortunate article of mine for a text to illustrate the vulgarity of modern [Alpine] climbers." (In memory, Stephen thus confused Ruskin's presentation of *Fors* with the analogous presentation of *Deucalion.*) At the time, Stephen states, it occurred to him that "some of [Ruskin's] petulant [sic] outbreaks did not imply fierceness or loss of temper, but only the delight of a master of logical fence in administering skilful thrust at the joints of his opponent's armour" (*Some Early Impressions,* pp. 180–82). Unquestionably, Sir Leslie Stephen should have known.

[July 7, 1876] ANNE ISABELLA THACKERAY

Anne Isabella Thackeray (Lady Richmond Thackeray Willoughby Ritchie—1837–1919) and her brother-in-law Leslie Stephen, a friend of Victor Marshall, were staying at Low Bank Ground cottage. Stephen's daughter Laura was with them, his wife Harriet Marian (Anne's beloved sister "Minnie") having died in childbirth in November 1875. Miss Thackeray had met Ruskin (as she noted in her Journal) at a dinner party of 1860, and thereafter she had seen him occasionally at gatherings in London. Now, therefore, with Laura, she announced her presence in the neighborhood: "We didn't mean to go to Mr. Ruskin's, but we found ourselves at his door. Three maids just like *Pilgrim's Progress* maidens said Mr. Ruskin only saw people by appointment; and as I didn't want to go in, I left my address and said it would be very kind of him to come and see me" (Hester R. Fuller and Violet Hammersley, *Thackeray's Daughter. Some Recollections of*

Anne Thackeray Ritchie [Dublin, 1951], p. 144). It was a call which Ruskin returned, "dressed with some ceremony": there "he stood in his tall hat and frock-coat upon the green" (Ritchie, *Records of Tennyson, Ruskin, Browning,* p. 67).

[July 24, 1883] GEORGE THOMSON

George Thomson (d. 1921, aged 79) of Woodhouse Hill, Huddersfield, became a cotrustee (with George Baker) of St. George's Guild, replacing the deceased J. H. Chamberlain. In 1878 he had contributed to the Gift of the *Splügen Pass,* to show "my gratitude and affection for Mr. Ruskin" (from letters and other material related to this Gift; F. J. Sharp Collection). In 1886 he would successfully reorganize his already prosperous woollen mill, in Huddersfield, into a copartnership with the employees: endeavoring "to prove the practicability of many of the truths taught in 'Unto This Last,' " he would explain,

> [he] had pressed into an old-established woollen factory as many truths as it was capable of receiving. On the lines of true co-operation he gave the workers a virtual partnership, and guaranteed the absolute purity of everything made. He was convinced that not only would the character of the worker be improved and his happiness in his work increased, but that also, in spite of opposition he had received from unexpected quarters, he would be able to show that the higher principles of justice to workmen, honesty of work, and refusal of the credit system, as taught by John Ruskin, could be adopted with happy results. (*Igdrasil, 1,* 168)

In 1910, George Baker having died, he became the Master of the Guild.

[January 31, 1883] LUCY TOVEY

For 42 years (1829–71) Lucy was Margaret Ruskin's "parlour-maid"—"whom we took abroad with us sometimes that she might see the places we were always talking of" (*Works, 35,* 518; from *Praeterita*). As thus a member of "Love's Meinie," she is said to have described how Turner, dining at Denmark Hill, "would pull down his coat-sleeves over his wrists to try to hide the dirty, crumpled shirt-cuffs" (ibid., 601 n.), and Ruskin would recall her sorrowful amazement when he sold Turner's *Lucerne* for £1,000 —she having brought the pen for the writing of the check before putting the drawing into the carriage of its new owner (*Works, 13,* 482). With her sister Harriet (his mother's other "parlour-maid" from 1834–71), Lucy had managed his experimental tea shop from 1874–76, when, to his sorrow, Harriet had died.

[July 28, 1877] GEORGE USHER

Mr. Usher was the mason whom Ruskin once embarrassed by holding out a paper as he asked for a receipt. When the country-man at last confessed, " 'Ah mun put ma mark!' . . . Mr. Ruskin rose at once, stretched out both hands to the astonished rustic, with the words: 'I am proud to know you. Now I understand why you are such an entirely good workman' " (Collingwood, *Life, 2,* 531).

[September 16, 1877] AUBREY DE VERE

Ruskin had known Aubrey de Vere (1814–1902) for many years, as a poet, a Catholic convert, and a friend of Coventry Patmore. ". . . he is one of the very, very, *very* few religious men living," Ruskin had written Mrs. Hewitt in 1862. "You may tell him . . . that if I ever get better, *I* mean to be religious again too, but my religion is to be old Greek" (*Works, 38,* 384). As the years passed, Catholic friends never lost their hope that he would join them in their faith. From time to time de Vere would come to Coniston, as a friend of the Victor Marshalls. After Ruskin could no longer meet visitors, de Vere continued to express his affectionate regard, communicating through Mrs. Severn, to whom he wrote in 1891: "I frequently remember the hour I spent with him [probably in 1886] & the deep interest of his conversation, marked as it was with so much pathos & humility. I remember how touchingly he spoke of the merciful intention with which our trials are sent to us, & are adapted to our spiritual needs. ¶Pray remember me most kindly to him, & tell him that he is daily remembered in my prayers, as doubtless he is in those of many who are grateful to him" (letter of March 24, 1891; F. J. Sharp Collection).

[August 17, 1877]

AUGUSTA MARY WAKEFIELD

Miss Wakefield (1853–1915) was one of the four daughters of William Henry Wakefield, the High Sheriff of Westmoreland, who now lived in Kendal. Here, in 1885, she established the competitive music festivals associated with her name. A famous amateur contralto, she dates her friendship with Ruskin and Mrs. Severn from "one particularly bright red-letter day," in 1875, when she first drove the 30 miles between her home and Brantwood (A. M. Wakefield, "Brantwood, Coniston: John Ruskin's Home," *Murray's Magazine, 8* [November 1890], 594). Her book of selections, *Ruskin on Music* (1894), was dedicated to Mrs. Severn—in letters her "dearest Joanie." (Three letters to Mrs. Severn, in which Miss Wakefield arranged to sing at Ruskin's funeral, are in the F. J. Sharp Collection.)

[August 1, 1877] MRS. BERNARD WARD

Emily La Touche (1844–68), familiarly called "Wisie," had married Major the Hon. Bernard Ward, of the Third Light Infantry, in 1865 and had died from dysentery, aboard the Cape Mail Steamer *Saxon,* as she was returning from Mauritius (see *Diaries,* p. 649 [June 1, 1868], where she is unfortunately identified as "Ruskin's dog"), leaving a daughter known as Rose Florence (though christened Florence Rose), born on August 29, 1866, and a son, Ernest Otway, born in 1867.

[August 8, 1877] ALEXANDER WEDDERBURN

After the publication of Xenophon's *Economist* (see entry for June 29, 1876), Alexander Wedderburn (1854–1931) was frequently a guest at Brantwood, helping Ruskin with indexes and other work. He edited, for example, the Traveller's Edition of *The Stones of Venice* (1879–81), *Arrows of the Chace* (1880), *On the Old Road* (1885), *Lectures on Art* (1888), and *Venice Academy Guide* (1891). By 1900 he had undertaken the Library Edition of Ruskin's *Works* with E. T. Cook and was serving, with C. E. Norton, as Ruskin's literary executor.

Index

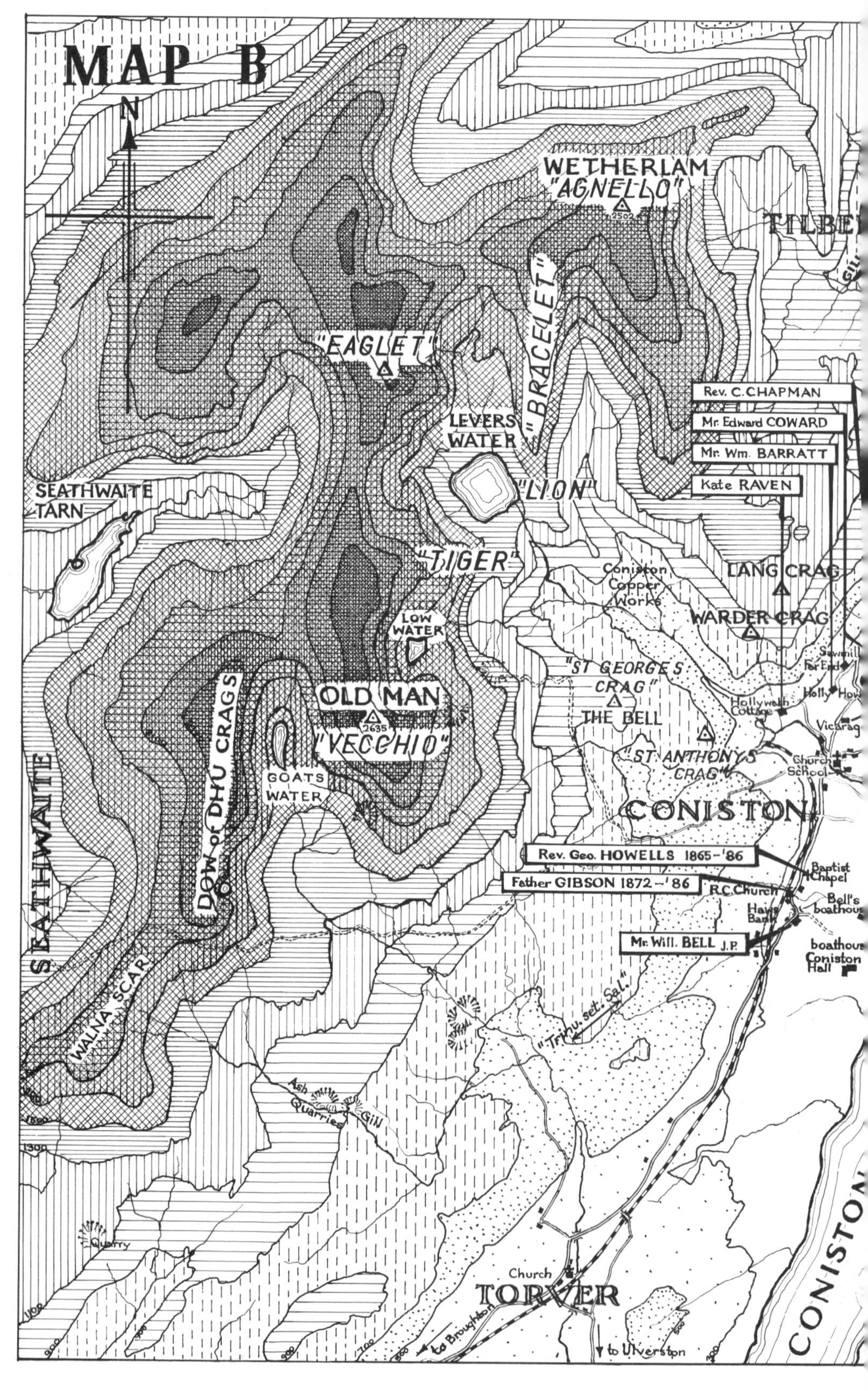

MAP B
N
WETHERLAM
"AGNELLO"
2502
TILBE
"EAGLET"
"BRACELET"
LEVERS WATER
"LION"
SEATHWAITE TARN
"TIGER"
Coniston Copper Works
LANG CRAG
WARDER CRAG
LOW WATER
Rev. C. CHAPMAN
Mr. Edward COWARD
Mr. Wm. BARRATT
Kate RAVEN
"ST GEORGE'S CRAG"
THE BELL
OLD MAN
2635
"VECCHIO"
DOW of DHU CRAGS
GOATS WATER
"ST ANTHONY'S CRAG"
Hollywath Cottage
Holly How
Vicarage
Church
School
CONISTON
Rev. Geo. HOWELLS 1865–'86
Father GIBSON 1872–'86
Baptist Chapel
R.C. Church
Bell's boathouse
Haws Bank
Mr. Will. BELL J.P.
boathouse
Coniston Hall
SEATHWAITE
WALNA SCAR
"Tribu. set. Sal."
Ash Quarries
Gill
Quarry
Church
TORVER
to Broughton
to Ulverston
CONISTON